The Normative Order of the Internet

The Normative Order of the Internet

A Theory of Rule and Regulation Online

MATTHIAS C. KETTEMANN

OXFORD
UNIVERSITY PRESS

OXFORD
UNIVERSITY PRESS

Great Clarendon Street, Oxford, OX2 6DP,
United Kingdom

Oxford University Press is a department of the University of Oxford.
It furthers the University's objective of excellence in research, scholarship,
and education by publishing worldwide. Oxford is a registered trade mark of
Oxford University Press in the UK and in certain other countries

First Edition published in 2020

Published in the United States of America by Oxford University Press
198 Madison Avenue, New York, NY 10016, United States of America

British Library Cataloguing in Publication Data
Data available

Library of Congress Control Number: 2020934581

ISBN 978–0–19–886599–5

The Open Access publication was financially supported by the Leibniz Association's Open Access
Monograph Publishing Fund. It is based on research conducted in the framework of the
DFG-funded Cluster of Excellence "The Formation of Normative Orders," Goethe University Frankfurt am Main.

To my wife and children,
my beloved forces of order and disorder,
and my parents,
who set me on my course from chaos to nomos.

Preface

This study establishes that a normative order of the internet has emerged, which is made up of norms of varied regulatory genesis and legitimacy, but which are all materially and normatively connected to the internet. The challenge of analyzing such an order, its origin, legitimacy, and implications, is substantial in light of the special role of the internet within our lived realities and societies. We used to watch television on our TVs, play music on CD players, listen to radio channels on a radio, go to libraries for printed books, read printed newspapers, and use fixed-line telephones. Today, we use *the* internet to contact friends, to watch video or record it, to seek out information, and to consume entertainment or news. Different media—TV, books, radio, CDs, newspapers—were once regulated by different regimes. Their content is now being delivered, in a trend called *digital convergence*, through Internet Protocol (IP)-based services: through "the internet." This convergence of communicative acts has not yet been mirrored by a clear understanding of the dynamics of the cognate convergence of normativity, of normative rule.

The author set out to normatively frame the implications of this digital convergence. Just as content is now delivered via the internet, norms apply to the internet. They need to be systematized and assessed and understood in their complexity. As digital convergence reduces the number of channels delivering media content and allowing for free expression from many to *one*, any regulation of the internet—nationally, supranationally, internationally, transnationally—has substantial implications for all sectors of society.

People now sell and buy goods online, create non-governmental organizations (NGOs) and vote and run campaigns online, conduct research and scams through the internet, form international NGOs and crime syndicates, conduct peace initiatives and cyberattacks, share videos containing playful cats and hateful speech, create and share memes and viruses, download online courses or upload pirated videos, watch instruction videos on social networking sites or consult bomb-making manuals. All these activities—to a lesser (peace initiatives and cat videos) and greater (cyberattacks and bomb-making manuals) degree—need to be regulated. It is with regard to the multitude of activities and involved actors (individuals, non-state actors, states) and the breadth of the normative vocabulary available (ius cogens, conventions, custom, laws, regulations, standards, soft law, affordances) that the challenge of developing, legitimizing, and implementing a normative order of the internet becomes apparent.

This is a challenge that the author gratefully undertook. The research here conducted builds on previously published studies by the author on the role of individuals, and the legitimizing impact of their participation on international legal aspects of the internet,[1] the influence of internet governance on international customary law (and vice versa),[2] the impact

[1] Matthias C. Kettemann, *The Future of Individuals in International Law. Lessons from International Internet Law* (Utrecht: Eleven, 2013).

[2] Matthias C. Kettemann, "Grotius goes Google: Der Einfluss der Internet Governance auf das Völkergewohnheitsrecht," in Christoph Vedder (ed.), *Völkerrecht 2012. Richterliche Praxis und politische Realität. Tagungsband 37. Österreichischer Völkerrechtstag 2012* (Vienna: Peter Lang, 2013).

of the protection of the internet's integrity as a global interest on international law,[3] the development of international rules for the internet,[4] the emergence of the concept of internet governance,[5] the legality of internet shutdowns and state duties regarding the internet,[6] the protection of freedom of expression online,[7] the protection of cybersecurity through international law,[8] and the role of human rights in the times of multistakeholder approaches to norm creation.[9]

Scholarship and practice can mutually support each other.[10] Throughout the time of this research the author has been involved in the process of developing international legal foundations of the normative order of the internet. As correspondent for the Internet & Jurisdiction Network, thematic lead for a number of research initiatives on human rights on the internet, rapporteur of a number of international conferences on human rights on the internet, former co-chair and steering committee member of the Internet Rights and Principles Coalition, representative of the global academic community in the Executive Multistakeholder Committee of the Global Multistakeholder Meeting on the Future of the Internet, and rapporteur of the Council of Europe Committee of Experts on roles and responsibilities of Internet intermediaries, the author has been deeply involved in the processes of developing norms regarding the internet and its governance. This action-oriented research methodology coupled with a reflective approach is responsive to the challenges of the internet as a relatively new normative field.

This study is based on the author's *Habilitationsschrift* submitted to the Faculty of Law of the University of Frankfurt in November 2018. In June 2019, the Faculty of Law granted the author the *venia legendi* for international law, internet law, and legal theory.

The author was lucky enough to present and discuss some of the ideas that flowed into this study in recent years at institutions such as the universities of Vienna, Linz, Graz, Hamburg, Berlin, and Venice, and at workshops and conferences in London, Paris, Brussels, Lisbon, New York, and Cambridge, MA; and at a number of locations in Frankfurt, including art museums and cinemas. The latter were realized through outreach activities of the Cluster of Excellence "The Formation of Normative Orders" at the University of Frankfurt am Main. The DFG-funded Cluster awarded the author a postdoctoral fellowship for 2014–2018 that allowed him to freely complete this study. For that possibility and the excellent conception

[3] Matthias C. Kettemann, "Das Internet als internationales Schutzgut: Entwicklungsperspektiven des Internetvölkerrechts anlässlich des Arabischen Frühlings,", ZaöRV 72 (2012), 469–82; Matthias C. Kettemann, "The Common Interest in the Protection of the Internet. An International Legal Perspective," in Wolfgang Benedek, Koen De Feyter, Matthias C. Kettemann, and Christina Voigt (eds.), *The Common Interest in International Law* (Antwerp: Intersentia, 2014), 167–84.

[4] Matthias C. Kettemann, *Völkerrecht in Zeiten des Netzes: Perspektiven auf den effektiven Schutz von Grund- und Menschenrechten in der Informationsgesellschaft zwischen Völkerrecht, Europarecht und Staatsrecht* (Bonn: Friedrich-Ebert-Siftung, 2015), http://library.fes.de/pdf-files/akademie/12068.pdf.

[5] Matthias C. Kettemann, "Internet Governance," in Dietmar Jahnel, Alfred Schramm, and Elisabeth Staudegger (eds.), *Informatikrecht*, 3rd edn. (Vienna: Springer, 2012), 48–62.

[6] Matthias C. Kettemann, "Nationale Sicherheit und Informationsfreiheit. Zur Völkerrechtmäßigkeit von Internetabschaltungen," in Kirsten Schmalenbach (ed.), *Aktuelle Herausforderungen des Völkerrechts. Beiträge zum 36. Österreichischen Völkerrechtstag 2011* (Vienna: Peter Lang, 2012), 41–62.

[7] Wolfgang Benedek and Matthias C. Kettemann, *Freedom of Expression on the Internet* (Strasbourg: Council of Europe, 2014).

[8] Matthias C. Kettemann, "Ensuring Cybersecurity through International Law," Revista Española de Derecho internacional (2017), 281–90.

[9] Matthias C. Kettemann, "Menschenrechte im Multistakeholder-Zeitalter: Mehr Demokratie für das Internet," ZFMR 1 (2016), 24–36.

[10] Anne Peters, "Realizing Utopia as a Scholarly Endeavour," EJIL 24 (2013), 533–52 (542–4).

of the Cluster's postdoctoral program the author wishes to extend his thanks to the two coordinators of the Cluster, Prof. Klaus Günther and Prof. Rainer Forst, and to Rebecca Schmidt, the Cluster's head of administration.

The author's biggest gratitude, however, goes to his advisor, Prof. Stefan Kadelbach, LL.M., who is the most excellent of teachers and scholars. While there is a "Doktorvater" (the academic advisor (literally: father) during doctoral studies), in the author's case the highly esteemed Prof. Wolfgang Benedek at the University of Graz, who inspired the author to tackle questions of human rights on the internet early in his career and with whom the author continues to collaborate, the concept of "Habilitationsvater" (advisor for the post-doctoral phase) seems to remain in obscurity. For Stefan Kadelbach, however, the author would definitely feel it apt to introduce the notion into the academic discourse. The author's gratitude further extends to Prof. Dr. Dr. h.c. Thomas Vesting, who was kind enough to write the second evaluation of this study and whose insights into, and reading of, the present study have been important for the author.

At the University of Frankfurt, the author's thanks go further to Professors Georg Hermes, Ute Sacksofsky, and Indra Spiecker gen. Döhmann for enriching discussions. At the Cluster of Excellence "The Formation of Normative Orders" the author is indebted to Professors Christoph Burchard, Rainer Forst, Klaus Günther, and Alexander Peukert. The author's thanks also extend to Professors Anuscheh Farahat, Isabel Feichtner, and Thomas Kleinlein for insights and inputs during the early phases of this work. For input on central theses of the study later in the writing process, the author thanks Julia Pohle, Thorsten Thiel, and the postdoctoral fellows of the Cluster of Excellence "The Formation of Normative Orders."

The last revisions of this study profited from enriching conversations at the Leibniz Institute for Media Research | Hans-Bredow-Institut (HBI), where the author is especially grateful to Wolfgang Schulz, Uwe Hasebrink, Stephan Dreyer, Jan-Hinrik Schmidt, and Kristina Hein. No scholar of the internet and its regulatory framework could wish for a better place at which to study the normative dynamics, regulatory approaches, and technological developments than the HBI, which, under the leadership of Wolfgang Schulz and Uwe Hasebrink, has solidified its position as Germany's foremost interdisciplinary institute studying media, media transformation, and the futures of media—in which the internet will play a key role.

The author could not have successfully completed this study without the love and continued substantial support from his wife, Simone. The love of his two children, Cleo and Philipp, and the love and support of his parents are also essential to him.

Establishing the normative order of the internet as a legal and holistic order feels to the author to be an important exercise of systematizing and of reestablishing epistemic sovereignty, in a certain sense, over seemingly accelerating societal developments connected to the internet and information and communication technologies more broadly. In discussions with representatives from governments from all continents over the last few years, and representatives from many different tech companies, from platforms to Internet Exchange Points to cloud services providers, a sense of wonder, surprise—and less benignly: powerlessness—over the speed of technological progress and the problems inherent in the only reactionary powers of public or private regulation shone through. Technology was perceived by many discussants as an agent, a force (sometimes for the good, sometimes not) that could be harnessed only with difficulty. This study is an attempt to counteract this view by developing a comprehensive legal model for explaining and predicting the origin and application of norms impacting the internet's use and development. In brief, the study will show how the norms that matter online emerge and how they are legitimated.

The author has always appreciated the intellectual vigor of Philip Allott, who, in 2014, held a talk at London's Inner Temple on the dilemma of being an idealist, as a good international lawyer should be in his view.[11] "There has never been a better time to be an international lawyer," Allott said, "International Law is at last emerging as a sophisticated legal system." We international lawyers are the "most privileged of all lawyers. International Law is the law of all laws, the law of the whole human world. International lawyers are front and centre in the drama of making the new international society." He had one important concern though: "The international world suffers from a grotesque *poverty of philosophy*."[12]

The author takes up both ideas—that international law is at the front and center of normatively framing key political and legal challenges of today and that there is too little theory and too much practice—and takes them seriously throughout the following study. The research presented on the subsequent pages thus has two interlinked aims: "making" (that is: providing a normative order for) one important part of "the new international society," namely the society transformed by information and communication technologies mediated through the internet *and* providing a comprehensive theory (or philosophy) of that same order.

The internet is premised upon freely exchanging information. Any research into the internet, especially when publicly funded, should therefore be freely accessible to all. The author is therefore very grateful to the Open Access Monograph Publishing Fund of the Leibniz Association, which enabled the Open Access publication of this book. At the Fund, the author especially thanks Monika Pohlschmidt for her advice.

At Oxford University Press, the author would like to express his thanks to Alex Flach, Imogen Hill, and especially John Smallman for turning this manuscript into a book.

The author is also very thankful for editing and language support by the publisher's team and by Ilse Kettemann (Graz), and formatting and indexing support received from Max Gradulewski, Thorian Schmied, Johanna Friederike Stelling, and Carlotta Siegel (Hamburg), Bernhard Kettemann (Graz), and Birgit David and Polina Kulish (Jena).

In a 2006 article in the Max Planck Yearbook of United Nations Law, Antonio Segura-Serrano, who early on recognized the relevance of international law for the internet, called on international law to "take a normative stance"[13] regarding the internet's future. Some fourteen years later, this study submits that normative progress, and not only in international law, has been substantial: the following study thus shows which normative stance international law, national law, and transnational regulatory arrangements take toward the internet, and how this normative order shapes its (and our) future.

Hamburg and Frankfurt am Main, May 2020
Matthias C. Kettemann

[11] Philip Allott, "The Idealist's Dilemma: Re-Imagining International Society," EJIL: Talk!, June 9, 2014, https://www.ejiltalk.org/the-idealists-dilemma-re-imagining-international-society.
[12] Ibid (emphasis in the original).
[13] Antonio Segura-Serrano, "Internet Regulation and the Role of International Law", Max Planck Yearbook of United Nations Law, Vol. 10 (The Hague: Brill, 2006), 191–272 (271).

Table of Contents

Leading Theses xvii
Judgments xix
Laws xxi
Documents xxiii
List of Tables xxxiii
Abbreviations xxxv

1. Introduction 1
   1.1 *Ubi Societas, Ibi Ius* 1
      1.1.1 *Approaching Online Order* 1
      1.1.2 *Regulating Communicative Spaces as a Historical Constant* 2
      1.1.3 *Distinguishing Cyberspace* 4
      1.1.4 *Norms Without Order?* 5
   1.2 Situating the Research 7
      1.2.1 *Within Interdisciplinary Approaches* 7
      1.2.2 *Within (International) Legal Approaches* 9
      1.2.3 *With Regard to the Concept of "Normative Orders"* 11
   1.3 Hypotheses 14
   1.4 Structure 17

2. Foundations of Online Order 20
   2.1 A Network of Networks 20
      2.1.1 *Foundations* 20
      2.1.2 *Beginnings of the Information Society* 20
      2.1.3 *Internet and "Internet(s)"* 22
   2.2 Criticality of the Internet 24
      2.2.1 *Conditions of its Functionality* 24
      2.2.2 *Internet Integrity* 25
      2.2.3 *The Internet as/and Critical Infrastructure* 26
      2.2.4 *Critical Internet Resources* 27
         2.2.4.1 Concept and Vulnerabilities 27
         2.2.4.2 Addressing System 29
         2.2.4.3 Technical Standards 31
         2.2.4.4 Routing and Interconnections 33
   2.3 Common Interest and the Internet 33
      2.3.1 *Protection of and from the Internet as a Common Interest?* 33
      2.3.2 *Relating Internet Integrity to Human Rights* 36
      2.3.3 *Relating Internet Integrity to Human Development* 37
      2.3.4 *Relating Internet Integrity to International Security* 42
      2.3.5 *Custodial Sovereignty* 43
   2.4 Challenges of Regulating the Internet 45
      2.4.1 *Foundational Myths* 45
      2.4.2 *Evolving Composition of the Normative Medium* 47

2.4.3 *Code and Protocols as Law?* 49
2.4.4 *Algorithmic Decision-Making* 53
2.5 Conclusions 56

3. Law and Governance of the Internet 59
3.1 Foundational Rules 59
3.2 Applicability of International Law 61
3.2.1 *From Disorganized Normativity to the "Ius Necessarium"* 61
3.2.2 *Toward a Consensus* 64
3.2.3 *Old Rules or New Rules?* 66
3.3 International Law of the Internet 68
3.3.1 *Definition* 68
3.3.2 *International Conventions* 69
3.3.2.1 Direct Protection 69
3.3.2.2 Indirect Protection 70
3.3.3 *Custom* 76
3.3.3.1 Direct Protection 76
3.3.3.2 Indirect Protection 79
3.3.4 *General Principles of International Law* 81
3.3.4.1 Origin 81
3.3.4.2 Principle of Sovereign Equality 83
3.3.4.3 Non-Use of (the Threat of) Force 87
3.3.4.4 Non-Intervention in Domestic Affairs 89
3.3.4.5 Duty of Cooperation 90
3.3.4.6 Peaceful Settlement of International Disputes 92
3.3.4.7 Principle of Equal Rights and Self-Determination of Peoples 93
3.3.4.8 Principle of Good Faith 95
3.3.4.9 No Harm Principle (Principle of Good Neighborliness) 95
3.3.4.10 Principle of Prevention and Due Diligence 97
3.3.4.11 Principle of Sustainable Development 101
3.3.5 *Normative Acculturation* 102
3.4 Internet Governance 103
3.4.1 *Introduction* 103
3.4.2 *Concept* 104
3.4.3 *Actors* 105
3.4.4 *Evolution* 107
3.4.4.1 Early Internet Governance Approaches 107
3.4.4.2 First Normative Commitments 110
3.4.5 Internet Governance Forum Process 113
3.4.6 Politicization 116
3.4.7 Taxonomy of Internet Governance 118
3.4.8 Principle Hype 120
3.4.9 Critique 122
3.4.10 *Reform* 124
3.5 Order on the Internet? 127

4. Normative Disorder on the Internet 131
4.1 Dynamics of Disorder 131
4.2 Dimensions of Disorder 132
4.2.1 *Normative Froth* 132

4.2.1.1 *WSIS Principles* 132
4.2.1.2 *New Principles* 136
4.2.1.3 *Degrees of Normativity* 144
4.2.1.4 *Consequences* 147
4.2.2 *Normative Friction* 148
4.2.2.1 *Problem* 148
4.2.2.2 *Intermediaries* 149
4.2.2.3 *Public and Private Spaces* 152
4.2.2.4 *Technical Norm-Setting Cyberwar* 153
4.2.2.5 *Consequences* 154
4.2.3 *Normative Fractures* 155
4.2.3.1 *Problem* 155
4.2.3.2 *International Law and Other Norms* 155
4.2.3.3 *Universality and Subsidiarity* 156
4.2.3.4 *Territoriality and Reterritorialization* 159
4.2.3.5 *Cyberwar* 160
4.2.3.6 *Trust* 161
4.2.3.7 *Regime Deficiencies* 165
4.3 Fragmentation 166
4.3.1 *Forces of Fragmentation* 166
4.3.2 *Technical Fragmentation* 171
4.3.3 *Commercial Fragmentation* 171
4.3.4 *Governmental Fragmentation* 173
4.4 Defragmentation 175
4.4.1 *Technical Predisposition* 175
4.4.2 *Internet Invariants* 175
4.5 Conclusions 177

5. Theorizing Order(s) on the Internet 182
5.1 Introduction 182
5.2 Legal Theory and the Digital Condition 183
5.2.1 *Epistemology of Computer Culture* 183
5.2.2 *Binary Operations Under Uncertainty* 185
5.2.3 *Liquid Law and Networked Regimes* 187
5.2.4 *Dehierarchization and Heterarchy* 189
5.2.5 *Self-Constitutionalizing Regimes* 191
5.2.6 *Internal Politicization of the Lex Digitalis* 194
5.2.7 *Transnational Constellations* 196
5.2.8 *Permeability and Regime Dialog* 199
5.2.9 *Hybrid Legal Spaces* 200
5.2.10 *Exercising Authority Beyond the State* 204
5.2.11 *Normative Ordering and Undernormativity* 207
5.3 Online Order Theories 209
5.3.1 *Internet Constitutionalization* 209
5.3.2 *Interoperability* 213
5.3.3 *Jurisdictional Approaches* 216
5.3.4 *Governance by Microdecisions* 217
5.3.5 *Governance by Infrastructure* 221
5.3.6 *Reconceptualizing Governance* 226

5.4 A Theory of the Normative Order of the Internet 227
5.4.1 *Making Normative Change Visible* 227
5.4.2 *Theoretical Imports* 228
5.5 Envisaging the Normative Turn 231

6. The Normative Order of the Internet 233
6.1 The Normative Turn 233
6.1.1 *A New Regulatory Order for the Internet* 233
6.1.2 *Stopping the Singularity* 235
6.1.3 *Regulatory Remit* 238
6.2 The Nomos of the Internet 240
6.3 Normativity of the Order 242
6.3.1 *Explicit and Implicit Normativity* 242
6.3.2 *Constitutionalization* 242
6.3.3 *Localization* 244
6.4 Legality of the Order 245
6.4.1 *The Normative Order of the Internet as a Legal Order* 245
6.4.2 *Norms of the Order* 247
6.4.3 *Normative Processes* 251
6.5 Principles of the Order 256
6.5.1 *Notions of Principles* 256
6.5.2 *Substantial Principles* 258
6.5.3 *Procedural Principles* 259
6.5.4 *Normative Descriptors of the Order* 261
6.6 Legitimacy of the Order 262
6.6.1 *Conditions of Legitimacy* 262
6.6.2 *Proceduralizing Legitimacy* 264
6.6.3 *Legitimation of the Order* 268
6.7 Narratives of Justification 271
6.8 Facticity of the Order 273
6.8.1 *Facticity and Ordering* 273
6.8.2 *Facticity and Imperfectness* 275
6.9 Conclusions 276

7. The Normative Order of the Internet in National Legal Orders 279
7.1 The Protective Dimension of National Legal Orders 279
7.2 Normative Integration as Legitimation 280
7.3 Constitutional Integration of the Normative Order of the Internet 281
7.3.1 *Multinormativity as Reality* 281
7.3.2 *Permeability* 282
7.3.3 *Openness* 284
7.4 Judicial Integration of the Normative Order of the Internet 286
7.4.1 *Threats to Rights as the Normative Background* 286
7.4.2 *Internet Access as a Precondition for Exercising Fundamental Rights* 287
7.4.3 *Access and Subsistence Minimum* 289
7.4.4 *Fundamental Right to Access as a Human Right to Access* 290
7.5 Systematic Integration of Tertium Norms 291
7.5.1 *Automatic Application* 291
7.5.2 *Post-Consent Application* 291
7.5.3 *Deformalized Application* 293

7.5.4 *Transposition* 295
7.5.5 *Referencing* 296
7.6 Reterritorialization as a Challenge to the Normative Order of the Internet 298
7.7 Conclusions 303

8. Conclusions 305

Bibliography 311
Index 337

Leading Theses

(1) There is a normative order of the internet. This study has established the emergence of a normative order of the internet. This order integrates norms materially and normatively connected to the use and development of the internet at three different levels (regional, national, international), of two types (privately and publicly authored), and of different character (from ius cogens to technical standards).

(2) This order is a legal order. As a legal order, it operates through the form of law and analogously to it. Its actors—states, legal persons, natural persons—fulfil diverse functions as norm entrepreneurs, norm appliers, and norm enforcers. The order's justification narratives control new norms by assessing their technical consistency and their legal-cultural consonance vis-à-vis the order's purposes. Though not without autonomous elements, the normative order of the internet is interlinked through legitimation relationships with national and international legal orders. The study then analyzes the order's genealogy, ontology, legitimacy, finality, and impact.

(3) The order is made up of international law, national law, and transnational regulatory arrangements of variable normativity. Apart from international and national norms, a "third" category of norms exists, a normative tertium, which has only recently emerged as a normative category in its own right. Tertium norms are fundamentally technical standards and soft law norms that emerge in the contested space between technical necessity and socio-legal values. They evidence a variable normativity and transcend binary normative solutions and can thus counteract diffusions of regulatory responsibility in transnational settings.

(4) The order's normativity shapes technicity. The technology-orientation of non-legal normativity, including its focus on code and standards, needs to be reoriented through a value-based normative approach, while the effective internal norm (re)production mechanisms of private standards need to be embraced. It is thus not technicity that shapes normativity. Rather than letting a technical medium define our societal values, it is the values embedded in the normative order of the internet that define the evolution of the internet's underlying technologies through normative framing and regulatory interventions. Value-based normativity, it is hypothesized, must influence standard-setting to ensure the primacy of international legal commitments, and their national legal counterparts, in determining the finality of the normative order of the internet. Rather than accepting arguments out of technical necessity, this study hypothesizes that technical norms are properly placed within the value-oriented common frame of the normative order of the internet.

(5) The internet's forces of normative disorder can be identified and countered. Centrifugal forces contribute to the emergence of normative redundancies ("normative froth"), real conflicts of norms between regulatory layers and geographically bounded normative spheres ("normative friction"), substantial structural problems ("normative fractures"), and political, commercial, and technological fragmentation of the internet. However, technical invariants of the internet exercise

defragmentation forces. These are then normatively reified within the normative order of the internet.

(6) The internet has taken a normative turn. The rules on rule-making that have developed within the normative order of the internet can be used to explain, predict, and legitimize the creation of new order-internal norms through processes of self-learning normativity. These norms are then assessed as to their internal coherence, their consonance with other order norms, and their consistency with the order's finality. The normative order of the internet thus is based on and produces a liquefied system characterized by self-learning normativity. However, normativity that learns from its environment can no longer be described using traditional categories of, and criteria for, subjectivity. Thus a theory of normativity ("of the law") that goes back to Kant needs to be fundamentally rethought: with norm-based self-organization as the principle of life that enables the transcendental constitution of normativity.

(7) The normative order of the internet is a legal and legitimate order which is connected to, and legitimated by, international and national legal processes. The normative order of the internet is a legitimate order of norms. Processes of legitimation of norms take place within the order, but also through national law and the international legal system. Internationally, the norm creation process, which allows for the integration of all actors, legitimizes the normative outcome. Nationally, tertium norms have been progressively recognized within national legal orders through processes of formal and non-formal application, transposition, and referencing.

Judgments

INTERNATIONAL

Arbitral award, *Lake Lanoux Arbitration*, France v. Spain, (1963) XII RIAA 281, (1961) 24 ILR 101, 16th November 1957, Arbitration 95–96

Arbitral award, *Trail Smelter Case*, United States v. Canada, First decision, (1949) III RIAA 1905, (1941) 35 AJIL 684, 16th April 1938, Arbitration 95–96

Human Rights Committee, Mukung v. Cameroon, Comm. No. 458/1991, UN Doc. CCPR/C/51/D/458/1991 of 10 August 1994 223–24

ICJ, *Case Concerning the Frontier Dispute (Burkina Faso/Republic of Mali)* (Merits), ICJ Rep. (1986), 554 80

ICJ, *Case Concerning Delimitation of the Maritime Boundary in the Gulf of Maine Area* (Canada v. United States of America), ICJ Rep. (1984), 246 79

ICJ, *Arrest Warrant Case (Democratic Rep. of the Congo v. Belgium)* (Merits), ICJ Rep. (2002), 3 80

ICJ, *Armed Activities on the Territory of the Congo Cases (Democratic Republic of the Congo v. Uganda)*, ICJ Rep. (2005) 80

ICJ, *North Sea Continental Shelf Cases (Federal Republic of Germany v. Denmark; Federal Republic of Germany v. Netherlands)* (Merits), ICJ Rep. (1969), 3 76

ICJ, *Gabčikovo-Nagymaros Project (Hungary v. Slovakia)* (Merits), ICJ Rep. (1997), 7 101

ICJ, *Military and Paramilitary Activities in and against Nicaragua (Nicaragua v. United States of America)* (Merits), ICJ Rep. (1986), 14 77

ICJ, *Aerial Incident of 10 August 1999 (Pakistan v. India)* (Jurisdiction of the Court) 92–93

ICJ, *Legal Consequences for States of the Continued Presence of South Africa in Namibia (South West Africa) notwithstanding Security Council Resolution 276* (Advisory Opinion), ICJ Rep. (1970), 1971 81–82

ICJ, *Corfu Channel Case (UK v. Albania)*, ICJ Rep. (1949) 4 83–84

ICJ, *Legal Consequences of the Construction of a Wall in the Occupied Palestinian Territory* (Advisory Opinion), ICJ Rep 136, (2004) 94

ICJ, *Legality of the Threat or Use of Nuclear Weapons* (Advisory Opinion), ICJ Rep. (1996), 226 96

PCIJ, *The Factory at Chorzow (Federal Republic of Germany v. Poland)*, judgment on the merits (1928) PCIJ Rep. ser. A, No. 17 81–82

PCIJ, *The Case of the SS Lotus (France v. Turkey)*, judgment, PCIJ Rep. ser. A, No. 10 81–82

PCIJ, *Mavrommatis Palestine Concessions (Greece v. Great Britain)* (Jurisdiction), (1924) PCIJ Rep. ser. B., No. 3 92

PCIJ, *Customs Régime between Germany and Austria* (Protocol of March 19th, 1931), Advisory Opinion, (1931) PCIJ ser. A/B, No. 41; Individual Opinion by M. Anzilotti (55 et seq.) 84

EUROPEAN COURTS

CJEU, C-293/12 and C-594/12, *Digital Rights Ireland and Seitlinger et al.*, judgment of April 8, 2014 74

CJEU, C-131/12, *Google Spain SL, Google Inc. v. Agencia Española de Protección de Datos (AEPD), Mario Costeja González* ("Google Spain"), judgment of May 13, 2014 5

CJEU, C-212/13, *František Ryneš v. Úřad pro ochranu osobních údajů*, judgment of December 11, 2014 74

CJEU, C-230/14, *Weltimmo v. NAIH*, judgement of October 1, 2015 216–17

CJEU, C-362/14, *Schrems v. Data Protection Commissioner*, judgment of October 6, 2015 74

ECtHR, *Klass and Others v. Germany*, judgment of September 6, 1987, application no. 5029/71 75

ECtHR, *Appleby and Others v. United Kingdom* judgement of May 6, 2003, application no.44306/98 152

ECtHR, *Stoll v. Switzerland*, judgment of December 10, 2007, application no. 69698/01 72

ECtHR, *K.U. v. Finland*, judgment of December 2, 2008, application no. 2872/02 46
ECtHR, *Mouvement Raëlien Suisse v. Switzerland*, judgment of January 13, 2011, application no. 16354/06 72
ECtHR, *Shimovolos v. Russia*, judgment of January 28, 2011, application no. 30194/09 75
ECtHR, *Editorial Board of Pravoye Delo and Shtekel v. Ukraine*, judgment of May 5, 2011, application no. 33014/05 46
ECtHR, *Yıldırım v. Turkey*, judgment of December 18, 2012, application no. 3111/10 36
ECtHR, *Bureau of Investigative Journalism and Alice Ross v. the United Kingdom*, judgment of September 11, 2014, application no. 62322/14 178
ECtHR, *Delfi AS v. Estonia*, judgement of June 16, 2015, application no. 64569/09 173–74
ECtHR, *Cengiz and Others v. Turkey*, judgement of December 1, 2015, application nos. 48226/10 and 14027/11 .... 22, 225
ECtHR, *MTE and Index.hu ZRT v. Hungary*, judgment of February 2, 2016, application no. 22947/13 .... 173–74, 225
ECtHR, *Big Brother Watch and Others v. the United Kingdom*, judgement of September 13, 2018, application nos. 58170/13, 62322/14, and 24960/15 178–79
ECtHR (3rd section), *Pihl v. Sweden*, judgement of February 7, 2019), application no. 74742/14 .... 173–74, 225

NATIONAL COURTS

France

French Conseil d'État, *Google Inc.*, n° 399922, decision of July 19, 2017 56
Tribunal de Grande Instance Paris, *Ligue contre le racisme et l'antisémitisme et Union des étudiants juifs de France c. Yahoo! Inc. et Société Yahoo! France (LICRA v. Yahoo!)*, May 22, 2000 154

Germany

Administrative Court of Cologne, *In re Duchy of Sealand, May 3, 1978*, 80 ILR (1978) 683, 685 48–49
BGH, judgment of January 24, 2013, III ZR 98/12 21–22
BVerfG, judgment of November 22, 2001, BVerfGE 104, 151, *NATO-Konzept* 205
BVerfG, order of the Second Senate of October 14, 2004, 2 BvR 1481/04 292
BVerfG, judgment of the First Senate of February 27, 2008, 1 BvR 370/07, BVerfGE 120, 274–350 162
BVerfG, judgment of the First Senate of February 9, 2010, 1 BvL 1/09, *Hartz IV* 289
BVerfG, judgment of February 22, 2011, 1 BvR 699/06, *Fraport* 152
BVerfG, judgment of September 7, 2011, 2 BvR 987/10 205
BVerfG, judgment of the First Senate of July 18, 2012, 1 BvL 10/10, *Asylbewerberleistungsgesetz* ... 71
BVerfG, judgment of March 18, 2014, 2 BvR 1390/12, *European Stability Mechanism* 205
BVerfG, order of the First Senate of July 23, 2014, 1 BvL 10/12 71
Landgericht Berlin, Judgment 16 O 341/15 of January 16, 2018 189–90

United States of America

United States Court of Appeals, Ninth Circuit, 433 F.3d 1199, *Yahoo! Inc. v. LICRA and UEJF*, January 12, 2006 154

Laws

INTERNATIONAL INSTRUMENTS

Agreement on the Conservation of Nature and Natural Resources, July 7, 1985 95–96
African Convention on Human and Peoples' Rights, June 27, 1981 266
American Convention on Human Rights, November 22,1987 266
European Convention on Human Rights, Council of Europe, ETS 9 (1952), March 20, 1952 .... 70, 72, 74, 75, 163, 178–79, 220–21, 266
Charter of the United Nations, 1 UNTS XVI, October 24, 1945 .... 65, 66, 82, 83–84, 88, 90–91, 92–93, 127, 161, 188
Convention Concerning the Protection of the World Cultural and Natural Heritage, UNTS Volume Number 1037 (p. 151), November 16, 1972 34
Convention on Biological Diversity, June 5, 1992, UNTS 1760 (p. 79) 101
Convention on the Law of the Non-Navigational Uses of International Watercourses, May 21, 1997 98
Declaration of the United Nations Conference on the Human Environment ("Stockholm Declaration"), UNTS Volume Number 824 (p. 215), June 16, 1972 95–96
Draft articles on Prevention of Transboundary Harm from Hazardous Activities (2001) 95, 97, 100
International Covenant on Civil and Political Rights, GA Resolution 2200A (XXI), 999 UNTS 171 .... 70–76, 93–94, 223–24
International Covenant on Economic, Social and Cultural Rights, UN Doc. A/RES (1966), UNTS 993 (p.3) 93–94
International Telecommunication Regulations, 2012 .... 69, 122
Rome Statute of the International Criminal Court, July 17, 1998 .... 68–69, 81, 114
Staatsvertrag zwischen Oesterreich, Preußen, Baiern und Sachsen vom 25. Juli 1850 über die Bildung des deutsch-österreichischen Telegraphenvereins, Allgemeines Reichs-Gesetz und Regierungsblatt für das Kaiserthum Österreich, No. CXXVII, September 30, 1850, 266 2–3
United Nations Convention on the Law of the Sea, UNTS vol. 1833 (p. 3), 1834 (p. 3), 1835 (p. 3), December 10, 1982 .... 95–96, 98
United Nations Framework Convention on Climate Change, 1771 UNTS (p. 107), May 9, 1992 .... 62, 116
United Nations Paris Agreement, December 12, 2015 .... 62, 84, 116
Universal Declaration of Human Rights, GA Res. 217A (III), UN Doc A/810, 71 (1948) 65, 71–72, 85–86, 133, 135, 188, 211, 258
U.S.-China Cybersecurity Agreement, October 16, 2015 93

EUROPEAN INSTRUMENTS

Charter of Fundamental Rights of the European Union (CFR) October 2, 2000 75
Directive (EU) 2016/1148 of the European Parliament and of the Council of July 6, 2016 concerning measures for a high common level of security of network and 294–96
Directive (EU) 2008/114/EC of 8 December 2008 on the identification and designation of European critical infrastructures and the assessment of the need to improve their protection, OJ L 345/75, December 23, 2008 26
European Commission, Communication from the Commission to the European Parliament, the Council, the European Economic and Social Committee and the Committee of the Regions, A Digital Agenda for Europe, COM(2010) 245 of August 26, 2010 39
European Commission, Communication from the Commission to the European Parliament, the European Economic and Social Committee and the Committee of the Regions, Internet Policy and Governance. Europe's role in shaping the future of Internet Governance, COM(2014) 72/4 of February 12, 2014 .... 51, 125–26, 143

Regulation (EU) 1025/2012 of the European Parliament and of the Council of October 25, 2012 on European standardisation, OJ L 316/12, November 14, 2012 . . . . . . 295, 296
Regulation (EU) 2016/679 of the European Parliament and of the Council of April 27, 2016 on the protection of natural persons with regard to the processing of personal data and on the free movement of such data, and repealing Directive 95/46/EC (General Data Protection Regulation), OJ L 119/1 of May 4, 2016 . . . . 54–55, 291
Regulation (EU) 2017/1128 of the European Parliament and of the Council of 14 June 2017 on cross-border portability of online content services in the internal market, OJ L 168, June 30, 2017 172

National Legislation

Gesetz über das Bundesamt für Sicherheit in der Informationstechnik (BGBl. I S. 2821 of August 14, 2009) 295–97
Gesetz zur Umsetzung der Richtlinie (EU) 2016/1148 des Europäischen Parlaments und des Rates vom 6. Juli 2016 über Maßnahmen zur Gewährleistung eines hohen gemeinsamen Sicherheitsniveaus von Netz- und Informationssystemen in der Union (BGBl. I, Nr. 40 of June 29, 2017) 294–96
Gesetz zur Verbesserung der Rechtsdurchsetzung in sozialen Netzwerken (Netzwerkdurchsetzungsgesetz – NetzDG) (BGBl. I, No. 61 of September 7, 2017 . . . . 150, 194, 259, 286
Grundgesetz für die Bundesrepublik Deutschland (BGBl. I, No. 1, of May 23, 1949) . . . 159, 205, 245, 282–84, 285–93, 298–99, 300, 303

Documents

Access Now, Keep it on: What is an Internet Shutdown? (2018), https://www.accessnow.org/keepiton 223
Adam Smith Institute, Internet Freedom. A Free Market Digital Manifesto (2013), https://www.adamsmith.org/research/reports/internet-freedom-a-free-market-digital-manifesto 137*t*, 139–42*t*
Affirmation of Commitments by the United States Department of Commerce and the Internet Corporation for Assigned Names and Numbers, September 30, 2009, http://www.icann.org/en/about/agreements/aoc/affir mation-of-commitments-30sep09-en.htm 30, 117–18
APC Internet Rights Charter (2006), http://www.apc.org/en/node/5677 . . . . 137*t*, 139*t*, 141, 142*t*
APC/CoE/UNECE, Code of Good Practice on Information, Participation and Transparency in Internet Governance (2010), http://www.apc.org/en/system/files/COGP_IG_Version_1.1_June2010_EN.pdf 118, 137*t*, 138–42
Articles of Incorporation of Internet Corporation for Assigned Names and Numbers, November 21, 1998, http://www.icann.org/en/about/governance/articles 117
ASEAN Agreement on the Conservation of Nature and Natural Resources, Kuala Lumpur 1985 (not in force), http://www.jus.uio.no/english/services/library/treaties/06/6-01/asean-conservation-nature.xml 95–96
Association for Computing Machinery, Statement on Algorithmic Transparency and Accountability (2017), http://www.acm.org/binaries/content/assets/public-policy/2017_usacm_statement_algorithms.pdf 55
Braden, R., (ed), RFC 1222, Requirements for Internet Hosts—Communication Layers, October 1989, http:// www.ietf.org/rfc/rfc1122.txt 48
Bradner, S. (ed), RFC 2418, Working Group Guidelines, September 1998, http://tools.ietf.org/ html/rfc2418#section-3.3 . . . . 153–54, 260
Carpenter, B., RFC 1958, Architectural Principles of the Internet (1996), http://www.ietf.org/rfc/rfc1958.txt 213
Centre for Internet and Society, India's Statement Proposing UN Committee for Internet-Related Policy, October 26, 2011, http://cis-india.org/internet-governance/blog/indiastatement-un-cirp 123
CGI.br Principles for the Governance and Use of the Internet (2009), http://www.cgi.br/english/regulations/ resolution2009-003.htm 137*t*, 139*t*, 142*t*
Committee on Economic, Social and Cultural Rights, General Comment No. 24 on State obligations under the International Covenant on Economic, Social and Cultural Rights in the context of business activities, UN Doc. E/C.12/GC/24 of 10 August 2017 . . . . 150–51, 155, 250
Community Informatics Research Network (2013), An Internet for the Common Good—Engagement, Empowerment, and Justice for All, http://cirn.wikispaces.com/An+Internet+for+the+Common+Good+-+Engagement%2C+Empowerment%2C+and+Justice+for+All 137*t*, 139–42*t*
Council of Europe, Commissioner for Human Rights, Democratic and Effective Oversight of National Security Services (May 2015), https://book.coe.int/en/commissioner-for-human-rights/6682-pdf-democratic-and-effective-oversight-of-national-security-services.html 76, 163
Council of Europe, Committee of Ministers, Recommendation CM/Rec(2011)7 of the Committee of Ministers to member states on a new notion of media, September 21, 2011 150
Council of Europe, Declaration by the Committee of Ministers on Internet Governance Principles, adopted by the Committee of Ministers on 21 September 2011 at the 1121st meeting of the Ministers' Deputies, https://wcd.coe.int/ViewDoc.jsp?id=1835773 . . . . 57–58, 121–22, 137*t*, 139–42*t*, 144–45

Council of Europe, Internet governance and critical internet resources, 1st Council of Europe Conference of Ministers Responsible for Media and New Communication Services: A New Notion of Media, May 28–29, 2009, Reykjavik, Iceland 35
Council of Europe, MSI-NET: Study on the Human Rights Dimensions of Automated Data Processing Techniques (in Particular Algorithms) and Possible Regulatory Implications, MSI-NET(2016)06rev6 54
Council of Europe, Parliamentary Assembly, Report on Mass surveillance, Rapporteur Mr. Pieter Omtzigt, Doc. 13734 of 18 March 2015 .... 74, 286–87
Council of Europe, Parliamentary Assembly, Resolution 1877 on the protection of freedom of expression and information on the Internet and online media (2012) 36
Council of Europe, Recommendation CM/Rec(2018)2 of the Committee of Ministers to member states on the roles and responsibilities of internet intermediaries, adopted by the Committee of Ministers on 7 March 2018 .... 149, 151, 220–21, 250, 286–87
Council of Europe/APC/UNECE, Code of Good Practice on Information, Participation & Transparency in Internet Governance, June 2010, www.apc.org/en/system/files/COGP_IG_Version_1.1_June2010_EN.pdf 118, 137*t*, 138–39, 142*t*
Council of the European Union, Council conclusions on malicious cyber activities, April 10, 2018, Doc. 7517/18, Annex, http://www.consilium.europa.eu//media/33721/malicious-cyber-activities-en.pdf 293–94
Deutscher Bundestag (Wissenschaftlicher Dienst), Voraussetzungen für die Zuständigkeit US-amerikanischer Gerichte nach dem Alien Torts Claim Act, Schadensersatzklagen der Herero und Nama, AZ WD 2-3000-021/17, March 2, 2017, https://www.bundestag.de/blob/502258/30c9d52ce0e5a6f0a97c3e99b05264f6/wd-2-021-17-pdf-data.pdf............ 291
Economist, Style Guide, Capitals, February 10, 2014, http://www.economist.com/style-guide/capitals 24
ECOSOC, Report of the Working Group on Improvements to the Internet Governance Forum, A67/65-E/2012/48 of 16 March 2012, http://unctad.org/meetings/en/SessionalDocuments/a67d65_en.pdf 123
EU, Digital Agenda for Europe. A Europe 2020 Initiative, http://ec.europa.eu/digital-agenda 39
European Commission for Democracy through Law (Venice Commission), Update of the 2007 Report on the Democratic Oversight of the Security Services and Report on the Democratic Oversight of Signals Intelligence Agencies, adopted by the Venice Commission at its 102nd Plenary Session (March 20–21, 2015), http://www.coe.int/t/dghl/standardsetting/media/Conf-FoE-2015/Venice%20Commission_Study%20No%20719_2013.pdf, Study No. 19/2013, CDL-AD(2015)00 .... 76, 163
European Commission, Digital Single Market: EU Negotiators Agreed to End Unjustified Geoblocking, November 20, 2017, http://europa.eu/rapid/press-release_IP-17-4781_en.htm 172–73
European Commission, European Commission and IT Companies announce Code of Conduct on illegal online hate speech, May 31, 2016, http://europa.eu/rapid/press-release_IP-16-1937_en.htm 150
European Commission, Green Paper on a European Programme for Critical Infrastructure Protection, COM(2005) 576 final, November 17, 2005, 19 26
European Commission, Roaming Charges End in the EU, June 15, 2017, https://ec.europa.eu/digital-single-market/en/news/15-june-roaming-charges-end-eu 172–73
European Parliament resolution of 12 June 2012 on critical information infrastructure protection—achievements and next steps: towards global cyber-security (2011/2284(INI)), http://www.europarl.europa.eu/sides/getDoc.do? type=TA&reference=P7-TA-2012-0237&language=EN 27
European Parliament resolution of 15 June 2010, Internet governance: the next steps, (2009/2229(INI)), http://www.europarl.europa.eu/sides/getDoc.do?pubRef=-//EP//TEXT+TA+P7-TA-2010-0208 +0+DOC+XML+V0//EN 137*t*, 138–42
European Parliament, Report on human rights and technology: the impact of intrusion and surveillance systems on human rights in third countries (2014/2232(INI)), Committee on Foreign Affairs Rapporteur: Marietje Schaake, June 3, 2015 .... 75, 162
Fairness, Accountability, and Transparency in Machine Learning (FATML), Principles for Accountable Algorithms and a Social Impact Statement for Algorithms (2017), http://www.fatml.org/resources/principles-for-accountable-algorithms 55

Federal Ministry for Economic Affairs and Energy, Monitoring Report DIGITAL Economy 2016, https://www.bmwi.de/Redaktion/EN/Publikationen/monitoring-report-digital-economy-2016.pdf. 38

French Government Submission to NetMundial, March 4, 2014, http://content.netmundial.br/contribution/french-government-submission-to-netmundial/154 87

G8, Declaration, Renewed Commitment for Freedom and Democracy, G8 Summit of Deauville, May 26–27, 2011, http://www.g20-g8.com/g8-g20/g8/english/live/news/renewed-commitment-for-freedom-and-democra cy.1314.html 121–22, 137*t*, 139–42*t*

Germany, Federal Foreign Office, Commissioner for International Cyber Policy, German Government Proposal on Global Internet Principles (February 2014), submission to NetMundial, http://content.netmundial.br/contribution/german-government-proposal-on-global-internet-principles/32 . . . . . . 77–78, 285

Global Commission on the Stability of Cyberspace, Call to Protect the Public Core of the Internet, New Delhi, November 2017, https://cyberstability.org/wp-content/uploads/2017/11/call-to-protect-the-public-core-of-the-in ternet.pdf. 57, 129

Global Multistakeholder Meeting on the Future of Internet Governance, April 23–24, 2014, http://www.netmundial.org 87, 285

Global Network Initiative, Accountability, Policy and Learning Framework, February 2015, https://globalnetworkinitiative.org/ content/accountability-policy-and-learning-framework. . . . 198

Global Network Initiative, Principles on Freedom of Expression and Privacy, http://www.globalnetwork initiative.org/principles/index.php. 137*t*, 139–42*t*, 198

Human Rights Committee, General Comment No. 34, Art. 19 ICCPR, UN Doc. CCPR/C/GC/34 of 12 September 2011. . . . . . 71, 72

Human Rights Council, Resolution 20/8, The promotion, protection and enjoyment of human rights on the Internet, UN Doc. A/HRC/RES/20/8 of 16 July 2012, http://ap.ohchr.org/documents/dpage_e.aspx?si=A/HRC/RES/20/8. . . . . . 10–11, 39, 70–71, 137*t*, 139–42*t*, 285

Human Rights Council, Resolution 26/13, The promotion, protection and enjoyment of human rights on the Internet, UN Doc. A/HRC/RES/26/13 of 20 June 2014. 70–71

Human Rights Council, Resolution 28/16, The Right to Privacy in the Digital Age, UN Doc. A/HRC/RES/28/16 of 1 April 2015 73–74

Human Rights Council, Resolution 32/13, The promotion, protection and enjoyment of human rights on the Internet, A/HRC/RES/32/13 of 18 July 2016 . . . . . . 10–11, 58, 70–72, 106, 212, 286–87

IAB, IAB Technical Comment on the Unique DNS Root, RFC 2826, May 2000, http://www.ietf.org/rfc/rfc 2826.txt. 51, 52–53

IAB, RFC 3552, Guidelines for Writing RFC Text on Security Considerations, July 2003, http://tools.ietf.org/html/ rfc355 51–52

IAB, RFC 6973, Privacy Considerations for Internet Protocols, July 2013, http://tools.ietf.org/html/rfc6973. 51–52

IANA, Introducing IANA, http://www.iana.org. 29–30

IANA, Report on Request for Redelegation of the .pn Top-Level Domain, February 11, 2000, http:// archive.icann.org/en/general/pn-report-11feb00.htm 94

IBSA Joint Statement, Open consultations on Enhanced Cooperation, New York, December 14, 2010, http://www.un.int/india/2010/IBSA%20STATEMENT.pdf. 121–22

ICANN CCWG Accountability, Supplemental Final Proposal on Work Stream 1 Recommendations, February 2016, https://www.icann.org/en/system/files/files/ccwg-accountability-supp-proposal-work-stream-1-recs-23feb16-en.pdf 30

ICANN IANA Stewardship Transition Coordination Group (ICG), Proposal to Transition the Stewardship of the IANA Functions from the U.S. Commerce Department's NTIA to the Global Multistakeholder Community, March 2016, https://www.icann.org/en/system/files/files/iana-stewardship-transition-proposal-10mar16-en.pdf. 30

ICANN, Bylaws for Internet Corporation for Assigned Names and Numbers, as amended July 22, 2017, https://www.icann.org/resources/pages/governance/bylaws-en 30

ICANN, Final Implementation Plan for IDN ccTLD Fast Track Process, November 5, 2013, http://www.icann.org/en/resources/idn/fast-track/idn-cctld-implementation-plan-05nov13-en.pdf. 118

ICANN, Internationalized Domain Names, http://www.icann.org/en/resources/idn 118

ICANN, Resolution Thank You to the Global Multistakeholder Community, Res. No. 2016.11.08.19 - 2016.11.08.20, November 8, 2016, https://www.icann.org/resources/board-material/resolutions-2016-11-08-en#2.c. 107
ICANN, Statement of Registrar Accreditation Policy (.com, .net, and .org top-level domains), March 4, 1999, http://www.icann.org/en/resources/registrars/accreditation/policy-statement 31
ICANN, Stewardship of IANA Functions Transitions to Global Internet Community as Contract with U.S. Government Ends, October 1, 2016, https://www.icann.org/news/announcement-2016-10-01-en 61
ICANN, The IANA Functions, December 18, 2015, https://www.icann.org/en/system/files/ files/iana-functions-18dec15-en.pdf 29–30
ICANN/World Economic Forum, Report by the Panel on Global Internet Cooperation and Governance Mechanisms, Towards a Collaborative, Decentralized Internet Governance Ecosystem, May 2014, https://www.icann.org/en/system/files/files/collaborative-decentralized-ig-ecosystem-21may14-en.pdf 254, 268
IEEE, Ethically Aligned Design, December 2016, http://standards.ieee.org/develop/indconn/ec/ead_v1.pdf. 55
IETF, Hypertext Transfer Protocol Version 2 (HTTP/2), RFC 7540 of 15 May 2015, https://tools. ietf.org/html/rfc7540 184
IETF, Public Key Pinning Extension for HTTP, November 26, 2013, https:// datatracker.ietf.org/doc/draft-ietf-websec-key-pinning 50
IETF, Memo: Freedom of Association on the Internet (2018), https://datatracker.ietf.org/doc/draft-tenoever-hrpc-association 32
IETF, Memo: On the Politics of Standards (2018), https://datatracker.ietf.org/doc/draft-tenoever-hrpc-political 32
IGF, Best Practice Forum on Developing Meaningful Multistakeholder Mechanisms (2014) 266–67
IGF, Geneva 2017, Attendance and Programme Statistics, http://www.intgovforum.org/multilingual/con tent/igf-2017-attendance-programme-statistics 114
ILC Draft Articles, Prevention of Transboundary Harm from Hazardous Activities (2001), Official Records of the General Assembly, Fifty-sixth Session, Supplement No. 10 (A/56/10). 95, 97, 100
ILC, Fragmentation of International Law: Difficulties arising from the Diversification and Expansion of International Law, Report of the Study Group of the International Law Commission, April 13, 2006, A/CN.4/L.682 . . . . . . 168, 179–80, 192, 299
International Centre for Dispute Resolution, ICM Registry, LLC v. ICANN, ICDR Case No. 50 117 T 00224 08, Independent Review Panel Declaration (2010), https://www.icann.org/en/news/irp/icm-v-icann 70 116–17
International Code of Conduct for Information Security, Annex to the letter dated 12 September 2011 from the Permanent Representatives of China, the Russian Federation, Tajikistan and Uzbekistan to the United Nations addressed to the Secretary-General, UN Doc. A/66/359 of 14 September 2011 . . . . . . 78, 86
International Covenant on Civil and Political Rights, GA Resolution 2200A (XXI), 21 UN GAOR Supp. (No. 16) at 52, UN Doc. A/6316 (1966), 999 U.N.T.S. 171, entered into force March 23, 1976 70
International Law Association, Accountability of International Organisations (1996-2004), http://www.ila-hq.org/en/committees/index.cfm/cid/9 270–71
International Principles on the Application of Human Rights to Communications Surveillance, Final Version (May 2014), https://necessaryandproportionate.org/text. 137*t*, 139*t*, 142*t*, 163
Internet Crime Report 2012 (2012), http://www.ic3.gov/media/annualreport/2012_IC3Report.pdf 42–43
Internet Governance Forum (IGF) 2014, Best Practice Forum on Developing Meaningful Multistakeholder Mechanisms, http://www.intgovforum.org/cms/documents/best-practice-forums/developing-meaningful-multistakeholder-participation-mechanisms 266–67
Internet Principles Coalition "bestbits" (Jeremy Malcolm), Submission to IGF on themes and formats for the 2014 meeting, http://bestbits.net/igf-2014-submission. 115–16

Internet Research Task Force (IRTF), RFC 8280, Research into Human Rights Protocol Considerations, October 2017, https://tools.ietf.org/html/rfc8280 . . . . 32, 52
Internet Rights and Principles Coalition, 10 Internet Rights and Principles, http://internetrightsand principles.org 121–22, 137*t*, 139*t*, 141, 142*t*
Internet Shutdown Tracker India, Nature of Shutdown, https://www.internetshutdowns.in 224
Internet Society, Internet Invariants: What Really Matters (2012), http://www.internetsociety.org/internet-invariantswhat-really-matters 175
Internet Society, Internet Shutdowns (2018), https://www.internetsociety.org/tag/internet-shutdowns 224
Internet Society, Internet Shutdowns Are Not a Solution to Africa's Challenges (June 2017), https://www.inter netsociety.org/blog/2017/06/internet-shutdowns-are-not-a-solution-to-africas-challenges 26
Internet Society, Perspectives on Internet Content Blocking: An Overview (2017), https://www.internet society.org/resources/doc/2017/internet-content-blocking 26
Internet Usage Statistics, World Internet Users and 2018 Population Stats, December 31, 2017, http://www.Internetworldstats.com/stats.htm 5–6, 286–87
Internet Usage Statistics, World Internet Users and 2019 Population Stats, Internet User Distribution, Mid-Year 2019, http://www.Internetworldstats.com/stats.htm 22
IRP, Charter on Human Rights and Principles for the Internet, http://internetrightsandprinciples.org/site/charter 114, 141
ISO, ISO 3166-1 Decoding Table, http://www.iso.org/iso/home/standards/country_codes/iso-3166-1_decoding_table.htm 108
ITU, International Telecommunication Regulations (IRTs), http://www.itu.int/ITU-T/itr 69, 122
Jason Spingarn-Koff (dir.), "Life 2.0," documentary (100 minutes) (2010), http://life2movie.com 67
Jeremy Malcolm, My proposal to the CSTD Working Group on Enhanced Cooperation (2011), http://igf watch.org/discussion-board/my-proposal-to-the-cstd-working-group-on-enhanced-cooperation#-8xHg3pRM AMtJ2UVoZcsOg 123
Letter dated 12 September 2011 from the Permanent Representatives of China, the Russian Federation, Tajikistan, and Uzbekistan to the United Nations addressed to the Secretary-General, UN Doc. A/66/359 of 14 September 2011, http://blog.internetgovernance.org/pdf/UN-infosec-code.pdf 121–22, 137*t*, 139*t*, 140, 142*t*
McKinsey Global Institute, Internet Matters: The Net's sweeping impact on growth, jobs and prosperity (May 2011), http://www.mckinsey.com/insights/high_tech_telecoms_internet/internet_matters 38
Memorandum of Understanding/Joint Project Agreement between the US Department of Commerce and ICANN, September 29, 2006, http://www.icann.org/en/about/agreements/mou-jpa/jpa-29sep06-en.pdf 116
Ministry of Foreign Affairs of the People's Republic of China, International Code of Conduct for Information Security (February 2014), submission to NetMundial, http://content.netmundial.br/contribution/international-code-of-conduct-for-information-security/67 . . . . 26, 78, 86, 121–22, 267
Ministry of Foreign Affairs of the Russian Federation, Submission to NetMundial, April 23–24, 2014, http:// document.netmundial.br/2-roadmap-for-the-future-evolution-of-the-internet-governance 86–87
Montevideo Statement on the Future of Internet Cooperation, October 7, 2013, http://www.icann.org/en/news/announcements/announcement-07oct13-en.htm 137*t*, 139*t*, 140–41, 142*t*
Necessary and Proportionate, International Principles on the Application of Human Rights to Communications Surveillance (2013), https://en.necessaryandproportionate.org/text 137*t*, 139–42*t*, 163
NetMundial, Global Multistakeholder Meeting on the Future of Internet Governance, Sao Paulo, Brazil, April 23–24, 2014, Content submission by the Federal Government of Mexico, March 2014, http://content.netmundial.br/contribution/content-submission-by-the-federal-government-of-mexico/219 87
NetMundial, Links to internet governance principles (2014), http://content.netmundial.br/internet-governance-principles 136–37

NetMundial, Multistakeholder Statement, Global Multistakeholder Meeting on the Future of Internet Governance, April 23–24, 2014, São Paulo, Brazil, http://netmundial.br/wp-content/uploads/2014/04/NETmundial-Multistakeholder-Document.pdf. 6–7, 126, 251, 258, 286–87
NTIA, Commerce Department Awards Contract for Management of Key Internet Functions to ICANN, July 2, 2012, http://www.ntia.doc.gov/press-release/2012/commerce-department-awards-contract-management-key-internet-functions-icann. 30
NTIA, NTIA Announces Intent to Transition Key Internet Domain Name Functions, March 14, 2014, http:// www.ntia.doc.gov/press-release/2014/ntia-announces-intent-transition-key-internet-domain-name-functions 69, 107
NTIA, NTIA Finds IANA Stewardship Transition Proposal Meets Criteria to Complete Privatization, June 9, 2016, https://www.ntia.doc.gov/press-release/2016/iana-stewardship-transition-proposal-meets-criteria-complete-privatization. 30
NTIA, U.S. Principles on the Internet's Domain Name and Addressing System, June 30, 2005, http://www.ntia.doc.gov/other-publication/2005/us-principles-internets-domain-name-and-addressing-system 110, 116–17
OECD Communiqué on Principles for Internet Policy Making, OECD High Level Meeting: The Internet Economy: Generating Innovation and Growth, June 28–29, 2011, Paris, http://www.oecd.org/dataoecd/ 40/21/48289796.pdf. 121–22, 137*t*, 139–42*t*
OECD, Seoul Declaration on the Future of the Internet Economy, http://www.oecd.org/sti/40839436.pdf, adopted at the OECD Ministerial Meeting on the Future of the Internet Economy, Seoul, Korea, June 17–18, 2008 39
OECD, The Role of Internet Intermediaries in Advancing Public Policy Objectives (2011), http://www.oecd.org/ sti/ieconomy/theroleofinternetintermediariesinadvancingpublicpolicyobjectives.htm 39
Office of the US President, Big Data: A Report on Algorithmic Systems, Opportunity, and Civil Rights, May 2016, https://obamawhitehouse.archives.gov/sites/default/files/microsites/ostp/2016_0504_data_discrimination.pdf 53–54
OHCHR, Compilation of documents or texts adopted and used by various intergovernmental, international, regional and sub-regional organizations aimed at promoting democracy, http://www.ohchr.org/english/law/compilation_democracy/index.htm 266
OpenStand, A Global Community for Open Innovation (2013), http://open-stand.org/principles 137*t*, 139*t*, 142*t*, 154
OSCE, 8th South Caucasus Media Conference, Declaration: Pluralism and Internet governance, Tbilisi, Georgia, October 20–21, 2011, http://www.osce.org/fom/84371 . . . 121–22, 137*t*, 139*t*, 142*t*
People's Republic of China, State Council, The Internet in China, June 8, 2010, http://www.china.org.cn/ government/whitepaper/node_7093508.htm 26, 301–2
Pepper, Robert and John Garrity, ICTs, Income Inequality, and Ensuring Inclusive Growth, World Economic Forum, Global Information Technology Report 2015 (2015), http://reports.weforum.org/global-information-technology-report-2015/1-2-icts-income-inequality-and-ensuring-inclusive-growth 6
President of the United States of America, International Strategy for Cyberspace. Prosperity, Security and Openness in a Networked World, May 2011, http://www.whitehouse.gov/sites/default/files/rss_viewer/international_strategy_for_cyberspace.pdf. 121–22, 137*t*, 139*t*, 142*t*
Ranking Digital Rights, 2017 Corporate Accountability Index, https://rankingdigitalrights.org/index2017 218
Recommendation CM/Rec(2014)6 of the Committee of Ministers to member States on a Guide to human rights for Internet users, Adopted by the Committee of Ministers on 16 April 2014 at the 1197th meeting of the Ministers' Deputies, https://wcd.coe.int/ViewDoc.jsp?id=2184807 48–49
Reflections from APC on the IGF 2013 and recommendations for the IGF 2014, February 19, 2014, http://www.apc.org/en/node/18977 115–16

Report of the Group of Governmental Experts on Developments in the Field of Information and Telecommunications in the Context of International Security, UN Doc. A/68/98 of 24 June 2013 . . . . 6–7, 42, 65
Report of the Office of the United Nations High Commissioner for Human Rights, Navi Pillay, The right to privacy in the digital age, UN Doc. A/HRC/27/37 of 30 June 2014 . . . . 60–61, 70, 74–75
Report of the Special Rapporteur on the promotion and protection of the right to freedom of opinion and expression, David Kaye, A/HRC/29/32 of 5 May 2015, http://www.ohchr.org/EN/HRBodies/HRC/RegularSessions/Session29/Documents/A.HRC.29.32_AEV.doc 74–75, 164, 212
Report of the Special Rapporteur on the promotion and protection of the right to freedom of opinion and expression, Frank La Rue, UN Doc. A/HRC/17/27 of 16 May 2011, http://www2.ohchr.org/english/bodies/hrcounc il/docs/17session/A.HRC.17.27_en.pdf 25, 36, 70–71, 72, 120
Report of the Special Representative of the Secretary-General on the issue of human rights and transnational corporations and other business enterprises, John Ruggie, Guiding Principles on Business and Human Rights: Implementing the United Nations "Protect, Respect and Remedy" Framework, UN Doc. A/HRC/17/31 of 21 March 2011 . . . . 62–63, 71, 151
Report of the Working Group on Internet Governance (2005), http://www.wgig.org/docs/WGIGREPORT.pdf 104-, 111, 119, 248
Report on the Advanced Computer Communication Workshop, Lake Arrowhead, CA, March 30–31, 1987 (July 1988), ftp://ftp.isi.edu/pub/hpcc-papers/arrowhead/report.txt 108
RFC 2418, IETF Working Group Guidelines (1998), https://tools.ietf.org/search/rfc2418 59
RFC 675 (Vinton Cerf, Yogen Dalal, Carl Sunshine), Specification of Internet Transmission Control Program, December 1974, http://tools.ietf.org/html/rfc675 24
RFC 7282, On Consensus and Humming in the IETF (2014), https://tools.ietf.org/html/rfc7282 59
Rio Declaration on Environment and Development (United Nations Environment Programme [UNEP]) UN Doc A/CONF.151/5/Rev.1, UN Doc A/CONF.151/26/Rev.1 Vol.1, Annex 1 95–96
Russia, UAE, China, Saudi Arabia, Algeria, Sudan, and Egypt, Proposal for the Work of the Conference [WCIT-12], ITU Doc. DT-X of 5 December 2012, WCIT12/27(Rev.1)-E, § 3A.2 and 3A.3, http://files.wcitleaks.org/public/Merged%20UAE%20081212.pdf 6–7, 44, 69, 156–57, 301
Saudi Network Information Center, Guideline Rules for Writing Arabic IDNs under the IDN ccTLD (.السعودية) (2010), http://www.nic.sa/en/view/writing_arabic_idn_guideline 171
Special Rapporteur on the promotion and protection of the right to freedom of opinion and expression, Frank La Rue, Promotion and protection of the right to freedom of opinion and expression, UN Doc. A/66/290 of 10 August 2011, http://www.ohchr.org/Documents/Issues/Opinion/A.66.290.pdf 21–22
Speech by Carl Bildt, Foreign Minister of Sweden, Seoul Conference on Cyberspace 2013, http://www.government.se/sb/d/17281/a/226592 . . . . 137*t*, 139*t*, 142*t*
Statement by President Dilma Rousseff, President of Brazil to the UN General Assembly, September 24, 2013, http://gadebate.un.org/sites/default/files/gastatements/68/BR_en.pdf 137*t*, 139*t*, 142*t*
Statement by the Global Commission on Internet Governance, Toward a Social Compact for Digital Privacy and Security, Wednesday, April 15, 2015, https://www.ourinternet.org/publication/toward-a-social-compact-for-digital-privacy-and-security 161
Statista, Internetnutzung in Deutschland (2019), https://de.statista.com/themen/2033/internetnutzung-in-deutschland 22
Stockholm Declaration of the United Nations Conference on the Human Environment (United Nations [UN]) UN Doc A/CONF.48/14/Rev.1, 3, UN Doc A/CONF.48/PC/6 95–96
Telenor/Boston Consulting Group, Towards a Connected World. Socio-economic Impact of Internet in Emerging and Developing Economies (2009) 38
U.S. Department of State, U.S. Government Submission for NetMundial (February 2014), http://content.net mundial.br/contribution/u-s-government-submission-for-netmundial/62 78

UK Attorney General Jeremy Wright, Speech: Cyber and International Law in the 21st Century, May 23, 2018, https://www.gov.uk/government/speeches/cyber-and-international-law-in-the-21st-century 6–7, 129
UN Broadband Commission for Digital Development, The State of Broadband 2013: Universalizing Broadband, September 2013, http://www.broadbandcommission.org/Documents/bb-annualreport2013.pdf, 26 et seq 41
UN General Assembly Resolution 46/62, Developing and strengthening of good-neighbourliness between States, A/RES/46/62 of 9 December 1991 95
UN General Assembly Resolution 55/63 of 4 December 2000 101
UN General Assembly Resolution 56/121 of 19 December 2001 101
UN General Assembly Resolution 56/183, UN Doc. A/RES/56/183 of 21 December 2001 109
UN General Assembly Resolution 57/239 of 20 December 2002 101
UN General Assembly Resolution 58/199 of 23 December 2003 101
UN General Assembly Resolution 64/211, Creation of a global culture of cybersecurity and taking stock of national efforts to protect critical information infrastructures, UN Doc. A/RES/64/211 of 17 March 2010 . . . . 42, 99, 100, 101–2, 106
UN General Assembly Resolution 67/195 of 21 December 2012, Information and communications technologies for development, UN Doc. A/RES/67/195 of 5 February 2013 . . . . 37–38, 41, 115
UN General Assembly Resolution 68/262, Territorial Sovereignty of Ukraine, UN Doc. A/RES/68/262 of 27 March 2014 94
UN Secretary-General, Human Security. Report of the Secretary-General, UN Doc. A/64/701, 8 March 2001 37
UN, Agenda for Democratization, A/51/761 of 20 December 1996. 266
UN, Declaration on Principles of International Law Concerning Friendly Relations and Cooperation among States in Accordance with the Charter of the United Nations, UN Doc A/RES/2625(XXV) of 24 October 1970, Annex 82
UN, General Assembly President Calls for New Culture of International Relations, with Principle of Human Security at Its Core, during Day-long Debate, Press Release, UN Doc. GA/10711 (2008), May 22, 2008, http://www.un.org/News/Press/docs/2008/ga10711.doc.htm. 37
UN/OAS/OSCE/ACHPR, International Mechanisms for Promoting Freedom of Expression, Joint Declaration on Freedom of Expression and the Internet (2011), https://www.osce.org/fom/78309. . . . . 36, 137*t*, 139*t*, 142*t*
UNCTAD, CSTD Working Group on improvements to the IGF, Summary of the 3rd meeting, October 31, 2011, http://unctad.org/ Sections/un_cstd/docs/cstd2011d22_Major_ EN.pdf 123
UNCTAD, Questionnaire of the Working Group on Enhanced Cooperation, http://unctad.org/en/Pages/CSTD/WGEC-Respon ses.aspX 123
UNEP/WCMC, Submarine cables and the oceans: connecting the world, January 2009, https://www.iscpc.org/publications/ICPC-UNEP_Report.pdf. 27–28
UNESCO, Code of Ethics for the Information Society, proposed by the Intergovernmental Council of the Information for All Programme (IFAP), 36 C/49, October 10, 2011, http://goo.gl/nZ0lk. 121–22, 137*t*, 139*t*, 142*t*
UNESCO, Convention Concerning the Protection of the World Cultural and Natural Heritage (1972), http://whc.unesco.org/en/conventiontext 34
UNESCO, International and regional instruments relevant to the areas of access, freedom of expression, privacy and ethics (2018), http://www.unesco.org/new/en/principlesgoverning Internet 132, 143
UNESCO, Report of the Experts' Meeting on Cyberspace Law, Monte Carlo, September 29–30, 1998, http:// unesdoc.unesco.org/images/0011/001163/116300e.pdf. 35
Uniform Domain Name Dispute Resolution Policy, August 26, 1999, https://www.icann.org/resources/pages/ policy-2012-02-25-en 219
United Nations Convention on the Law of the Sea of 10 December 1982 (1833 UNTS 397), http://www.un.org/depts/los//convention_agreements/texts/unclos/UNCLOS-TOC.htm . . . . xxix, 95–96, 98

United Nations, Developments in the Field of Information and Telecommunications in the Context of International Security, Report of the Secretary General, A/70/174 of July 22, 2015, http://www.un.org/ga/search/view_doc.asp?symbol=A/70/174 . . . . 65–66, 67, 78, 83, 90, 92, 96–97, 98–100, 102, 127, 147, 155–56, 160–61, 163–64, 174, 223, 249, 256–57, 272–73, 275, 293, 300, 302
United Nations General Assembly Resolution 55/2, United Nations Millennium Declaration, UN Doc A/RES/55/2 . . . . 82, 92–93
United Nations General Assembly Resolution 60/1, World Summit Outcome, UN Doc A/RES/60/1 82
United Nations General Assembly, Declaration on the Granting of Independence to Colonial Countries and Peoples, UNGA Res 1514 (XV) of 14 December 1960 93–94
United Nations General Assembly, Transforming Our World: The 2030 Agenda for Sustainable Development, UN Doc. A/Res/70/1 of 21 October 2015, https://sustainabledevelopment.un.org/ content/documents/7891TRANSFORMING%20OUR%20WORLD.pdf 40–41, 71, 101–2
US Congress, 109th Congress, 1st Session, H. CON. RES. 268, November 16, 2005, Concurrent Resolution expressing the sense of the Congress regarding oversight of the Internet Corporation for Assigned Names and Numbers, https://www.govtrack.us/congress/bills/ 109/hconres268/text 122
US Department of State, Office of the Spokesman, Internet Freedom Fact Sheet, February 15, 2011, http://www.state.gov/r/pa/prs/ps/2011/02/156623.htm 118
US DOC/NTIA, Management of Internet Names and Addresses, ICANN Statement of Policy ("White Paper"), June 10, 1998, http://www.icann.org/en/about/agreements/whitepaper. 108–9, 301
Vice-President of the European Commission Neelie Kroes, Internet Compact, http://blogs.ec.europa.eu/ neelie-kroes/i-propose-a-compact-for-the-internet/#more-671 . . . . 121–22, 137*t*, 139*t*, 142*t*
Vienna Declaration and Programme of Action, adopted by the World Conference on Human Rights in Vienna on 25 June 1993, http://www.ohchr.org/en/professionalinterest/pages/vienna.aspx 133
W3C, What is HyperText, https://www.w3.org/WhatIs.html. 184
WIPO UDRP Domain Name Decisions (gTLD), Generic Top Level Domains (gTLDs), Numbers up to 2018, http://www.wipo.int/amc/en/domains/decisionsx/index.html 219
WIPO, WIPO Guide to the Uniform Domain Name Dispute Resolution Policy (UDRP) (2018), http://www.wipo. int/amc/en/domains/guide/index.html#a1 219
World Economic Forum, Code of Conduct for Government Leaders (2011), http://www3.weforum.org/docs/WEF_GAC_InformedSocieties_CodeConductGovernmentLeaders_Summary_2012.pdf 121–22, 137*t*, 139*t*, 142*t*
World Economic Forum, The Global Risks Report 2017, January 11, 2017, https://www. weforum.org/agenda/2017/01/technology-risks-amplified-by-global-tensions 6
World Internet Conference (4th WIC, Wuzhen Summit), Report on World Internet Development 2017, http://www.wuzhenwic.org/download/ReportonWorldInternetDevelopment2017overview.pdf 157–58
World Summit on the Information Society (WSIS), Declaration of Principles, WSIS-03/GENEVA/ DOC/4-E, December 12, 2003 . . . 35–36, 65, 105, 109–11, 127, 132–34, 249
World Summit on the Information Society (WSIS), Geneva Plan of Action, WSIS-03/GENEVA/ DOC/5-E, December 12, 2003 . . . . 109–10, 111, 132–33
World Summit on the Information Society (WSIS), Tunis Agenda for The Information Society, WSIS-05/TUNIS/DOC/6(Rev. 1)-E of 18 November 2005 . . . . 44, 105, 109–10, 112, 113, 115, 132–33, 134, 135
World Summit on the Information Society (WSIS), Tunis Commitment, WSIS-05/TUNIS/DOC/7-E, November 18, 2005 . . . . 6, 65, 77, 109–10, 112, 132–33, 286–87
World Wide Web Foundation, Algorithmic Accountability, Applying the Concept to Different Country Contexts, July 2017, http://webfoundation.org/docs/2017/07/Algorithms_Report_ WF.pdf 53–54, 273
Zakon, Robert H., Hobbes' Internet Timeline, http://www.zakon.org/robert/internet/timeline 20–21

List of Tables

2.1. Dichotomies in the Discourse on the Protection of the Internet 25

2.2. Internet Vulnerabilities 28

4.1. Selected Collections of Internet Governance Principles 2005–2013 137

4.2. Selected Internet Principles Ordered According to Leading Paradigm 139

4.3. Selected Internet Principles Ordered According to Author 142

4.4. Selected Internet Governance Issues Represented in the Declarations 144

4.5. Assessment of the Normative Character of the Council of Europe Internet Governance Principles (2011) 145

4.6. Internet Layers 169

4.7. Selected Types of Fragmentation 170

Abbreviations

ADR	Alternative Dispute Resolution
AfrCHR	African Convention on Human and Peoples' Rights
AJIL	American Journal of International Law
AOC	Affirmation of Commitments
AP	Associated Press
API	Application Programming Interface
ARPANet	Advanced Research Projects Agency Network
ASEAN	Association of East Asian Nations
ASN	Autonomous System Number
AVR	Archiv für Völkerrecht
BCG	Boston Consulting Group
BGPs	Border Gateway Protocols
BNS	*Beidou* Navigation Satellite System
BRICS	Brazil, Russia, India, China, and South Africa
BSIG	Gesetz über das Bundesamt für Sicherheit in der Informationstechnik
BVerfG	Bundesverfassungsgericht
ccTLDs	country code TLDs
CERN	European Organization for Nuclear Research
CIRs	critical internet resources
CJEU	Court of Justice of the European Union
CM	Committee of Ministers
CNIL	Commission Nationale de l'Informatique et des Libertés
CoE	Council of Europe
CUP	Cambridge University Press
DARPA	Defense Advanced Research Projects Agency
DNS	Domain Name System
DOC	Department of Commerce
ECHR	European Convention on Human Rights
ECtHR	European Court of Human Rights
ECJ	European Court of Justice
EFF	Electronic Frontier Foundation
EP	European Parliament
EU	European Union
G8	Group of 8
G20	Group of 20
GAC	Governmental Advisory Committee
GDP	Gross Domestic Product
GDPR	General Data Protection Regulation
GG	Grundgesetz
GGE	United Nations Group of Governmental Experts on Developments in the Field of Information and Telecommunications in the Context of International Security
GIC	Global Internet Council
GIGF	Global Internet Governance Forum

GIPC	Global Internet Policy Council
GPS	Global Positioning System
gTLDs	generic TLDs
HStR	Handbuch des Staatsrechts
HTML	HyperText Markup Language
HTTP	Hyper Text Transfer Protocol
IAB	Internet Architecture Board
IANA	Internet Assigned Numbers Authority
IBM	International Business Machines
ICANN	Internet Corporation for Assigned Names and Numbers
ICC	International Criminal Court
ICCPR	International Covenant on Civil and Political Rights
ICESCR	International Covenant on Economic, Social and Cultural Rights
ICJ	International Court of Justice
ICTs	Information and Communication Technologies
IDN	Internationalized Domain Name
IEEE	Institute of Electrical and Electronics Engineers
IETF	Internet Engineering Task Force
IGF	Internet Governance Forum
IIC	International Internet Council
ILC	International Law Commission
IoT	internet of things
IP	Internet Protocol
IPv4	Internet Protocol version 4
IPv6	Internet Protocol version 6
IRP	Internet Rights and Principles
IRTF	Internet Research Task Force
ISOC	Internet Society
ISPs	Internet Service Providers
ITRs	International Telecommunication Regulations
ITU	International Telecommunications Union
IXPs	Internet Exchange Points
JZ	Juristenzeitung
LAN	Local Area Network
MDGs	Millennium Development Goals
MIT	Massachusetts Institute of Technology
MMORPGs	Massively Multiplayer Online Role-Playing Games
NGO	Non-governmental organization
NSA	National Security Agency
NTIA	National Telecommunications and Information Administration
OECD	Organization for Economic Cooperation and Development
OSCE	Organization for Security and Cooperation in Europe
OSI	Open Systems Interconnect
OUP	Oxford University Press
PCIJ	Permanent Court of International Justice
RFC	Request for Comments
RIRs	Regional Internet Registries
SDGs	Sustainable Development Goals
SMEs	Small and Medium Enterprises
TCP/IP	Transfer Control Protocol/Internet Protocol

TLDs	top-level domains
UAs	user agents
UAE	United Arab Emirates
UDHR	Universal Declaration of Human Rights
UDRP	Uniform Dispute Resolution Policy
UK	United Kingdom
UN	United Nations
UNCLOS	United Nations Convention on the Law of the Sea
UNECE	United Nations Economic Commission for Europe
UNESCO	United Nations Educational, Scientific and Cultural Organization
URL	Uniform Resource Locator
USA	United States of America
VoIP	Voice over IP
VPN	virtual private network
VVDStRL	Veröffentlichungen der Vereinigung der Deutschen Staatsrechtslehrer
W3C	World Wide Web Consortium
WCIT	World Conference on International Telecommunications
WEF	World Economic Forum
WGIG	Working Group on Internet Governance
WICANN	World Internet Corporation for Assigned Names and Numbers
WIPO	World Intellectual Property Organization
WSIS	World Summit on the Information Society
WWW	World Wide Web
ZaöRV	Zeitschrift für ausländisches öffentliches Recht und Völkerrecht

1
Introduction

1.1 *Ubi Societas, Ibi Ius*

1.1.1 Approaching Online Order

Law is force of order. It always reacts, usually with a necessary time delay, to technological progress. Only twelve years after Samuel Morse presented the first workable telegraph system in New York in 1838 and six years after completion of the first telegraph line from Washington to Baltimore, central European states agreed on an international framework for telegraphs. It has been much more than twelve years since the technologies underlying the internet's popularity today, such as the "World Wide Web," were invented. No international framework has emerged, even though normative approaches abound. There are norms that are applied to the internet, but the recognition of the existence of an underlying, structuring order is missing. This motivates the present study.

This study will establish the emergence of a normative order of the internet that integrates norms materially and normatively connected to the use and development of the internet nationally, regionally, and internationally. While the establishment of such a normative order of the internet will be an innovative step, concrete legal answers to technological challenges often have a long pedigree.

After showing that regulation of communicative spaces is a historical constant (1.1.2), certain distinguishing features of cyberspace[1] will be discussed (1.1.3) and the need to establish a comprehensive order confirmed (1.1.4). Convincingly establishing the concept of a normative order of the internet is premised upon: first, a clear perspective of current research on orders and ordering; second, and especially, the by now substantial international legal literature on aspects of online (dis)order; and, third, a first exposition of the "normative orders" approach based on the idea that orders are complexes of norms and values through which relationships, exercises of authority, and distributions of basic goods are legitimated (1.2). Then this chapter will turn to the six leading hypotheses of the present study, which frame and underlie the subsequent chapters (1.3). After explaining the methodology used (1.4), the structure of the study itself is presented (1.5) with each of the following chapters following the flow of the argument, namely

- that regulating the internet is challenging in light of its societal role and technical characteristics (chapter 2);

[1] "Cyberspace" is a notion referring to the social sphere that has emerged to describe the loci of mediatized information and communication interchange. Cf. Johann-Christoph Woltag, "Internet," in Rüdiger Wolfrum (ed.), *Max Planck Encyclopedia of Public International Law* (MPEPIL) (Oxford: Oxford University Press, 2008) (September 2010) [online].

The Normative Order of the Internet. Matthias C. Kettemann, Oxford University Press (2020). © Matthias C. Kettemann.
DOI: 10.1093/oso/9780198865995.001.0001

- that international law and internet governance regimes are foundational orders for the internet's regulation (chapter 3);
- that the state of internet regulation is one of normative disorder (chapter 4);
- that theoretical approaches can deliver insights into ordering networked structures (chapter 5);
- that a normative order of the internet exists as a legal and legitimate order with autonomous elements (chapter 6); and
- that this order is integrated into national legal orders with legitimating effects, especially in relation to transnational regulatory arrangements, such as standards (chapter 7).

1.1.2 Regulating Communicative Spaces as a Historical Constant

While the concept of normative order applied to the internet is new, the regulation of communicative spaces appears as a historical constant. Indeed, the regulation of technological progress was one of the dynamizing factors in the evolution of international law and the law of international organizations.[2]

Austria, Prussia, Bavaria, and Saxony signed the 1850 *Treaty on the Creation of the German-Austrian Telegraph Union*[3] "in order to have public and private [communication] traffic profit from the advantages of a telegraph system based on equal principles."[4] The treaty came as an attempt to regulate the free(r) flow of information by telegraphs, a new technology that the conservative regimes in Europe at the time perceived as potentially destabilizing the traditional order and their position in it.

Many of the novel principles introduced in the 1850 Treaty are of great relevance today for the regulation of information and communication technologies (ICTs) and in particular the regulation and governance of the network of interconnected networks we commonly call the *internet*. In Article 4 of the 1850 Treaty, states mutually commit to transmitting "with all possible speed and reliability" telegraphic cables to each other.[5] They agree to a due diligence duty to inform the contracting parties if they need to put a line out of order. The one exception to the duty to transmit cables speedily is contained in Article 19, which allows the head of each telegraph station to decide not to accept and transmit cables if the content violates the law or the transfer seems unsuitable with a view to "the public good and morality."[6] Article 6 of the 1850 Treaty contains a right for

[2] Sabine von Schorlemer, "Telecommunications, International Regulation," in Rüdiger Wolfrum (ed.), *Max Planck Encyclopedia of Public International Law* (MPEPIL) (Oxford: OUP, 2008) (March 2009) [online].

[3] Staatsvertrag zwischen Oesterreich, Preußen, Baiern und Sachsen vom 25. Juli 1850 über die Bildung des deutsch-österreichischen Telegraphenvereins, Allgemeines Reichs-Gesetz und Regierungsblatt für das Kaiserthum Österreich, No. CXXVII of 30 September 1850, 266 et seq.

[4] Ibid., preamble: "[. . .] in der Absicht, dem öffentlichen wie dem Privatverkehre Ihrer respectiven Staaten die Vortheile eines nach gleichmäßigen Grundsätzen geregelten Telegraphensystemes zuzuführen [. . .]" (translation by the author).

[5] Ibid., Art. 4: "mit möglichster Schnelligkeit und Zuverlässigkeit" (translation by the author). The word "telegram" entered common usage only after the Treaty.

[6] Ibid., Art. 19: "[Die Telegraphenbureaus sind] verpflichtet, solche Privatdepeschen von der Annahme oder Weiterbeförderung auszuschließen, deren Inhalt gegen die Gesetze verstößt, oder aus Rücksichten des öffentlichen Wohles und der Sittlichkeit zur Mittheilung für nicht geeignet erachtet wird. [. . .] Die Entschließung liegt

"everyone without exception" to use the telegraphs.[7] They could do so, as per Article 9, daily, including Sundays and holidays, from 7 a.m. to 9 p.m. from April to September and from 8 a.m. to 9 p.m. from October to March.[8] Article 12, in a prefiguration of Twitter's abbreviated style, limits cables to fewer than a hundred words.[9] Data retention *avant la lettre* is also enshrined: "Original concepts [of the cables] and telegraphic renditions of all cables are to be kept for two years."[10] Even reading this from the vantage point of the twenty-first century neither the content of the treaty nor the regulatory goals are surprising.

Though motivated by an anti-liberal impetus (visible especially in the 1850 Treaty's Article 19 with the head of a telegraph station acting as a de facto censor), the nineteenth century distinguished itself, in terms of rapid normative framing of technological development. Similar to international(ized) transport regimes, technology became a vector for the evolution of law-based international cooperation. The normative web woven around ICTs quickly became stronger. The German-Austrian Telegraph Union was complemented by the West European Telegraph Union in 1855, the subsequent foundation of the International Telegraph Union (ITU) in 1865—still an important regulatory player more than 150 years later—, and the adoption of the International Telegraph Treaty in 1875.[11] This normative approach to the telegraph shows how international law—through multilateral treaties and the creation of international organizations—was used from the earliest days of ICTs as an instrument to regulate the use of a new and promising technology in light of international and national public policy concerns.[12]

Many of the themes that the 1850 Treaty regulated reemerged when it came to regulating the telephone and, with even more force, when the advance of ICTs culminated in the widespread use of the internet, its commercialization, and politicization. These include duties of states to each other vis-à-vis the use of the new technology (Article 4), "telegraph neutrality" with public order exceptions (Articles 4 and 19), the right for all to access telegraph services (Article 6), and data retention (Article 14). This time, however, the bottom-up non-statal evolution of the underlying technology and substantial divergences in the regulatory interests discouraged the evolution of an international treaty regime and the foundation of a specialized international organization.

in solchen Fällen dem Vorsteher der Telegraphenstation oder dessen Stellvertreter ob. An welche Behörde die gegen derartige Entscheidungen etwa zu erhebenden Beschwerden zu richten sind, wird von den betreffenden Regierungen bestimmt werden" (translation by the author).

[7] Ibid., Art. 6: "Benützung der Telegraphen […] steht Jedermann ohne Ausnahme zu" (translation by the author).

[8] Ibid., Art. 9.

[9] Ibid., Art. 12: "nicht aus mehr als 100 Worten bestehen" (translation by the author).

[10] Ibid., Art. 14: "Original Concepte der aufgegebenen Depeschen, sowie die telegraphischen Niederschriften sämtlicher Depeschen sind mindestens zwei Jahre lang aufzubewahren" (translation by the author).

[11] Cf. Miloš Vec, *Recht und Normierung in der Industriellen Revolution: neue Strukturen der Normsetzung in Völkerrecht, staatlicher Gesetzgebung und gesellschaftlicher Selbstnormierung* (Frankfurt am Main: Klostermann, 2006), 205–6.

[12] For other examples of technology-responsive regulation, see Gregory N. Mandel, "Legal Evolution in Response to Technological Change," in Roger Brownsword, Eloise Scotford, and Karen Yeung (eds.), *Oxford Handbook of Law, Regulation, and Technology* (Oxford: OUP, 2017), 225–45.

1.1.3 Distinguishing Cyberspace

There is neither a key international treaty document nor a single organization dealing primarily with regulating cyberspace. Yet norms matter on the internet. Cyberspace is not independent of regulation. It is no legal *terra nullius*.[13] An independent "space of sovereignty" does not exist.[14] Indeed, the very concept of "cyberspace" is a politicized fiction and, like other metaphors used to differentiate online and offline experiences and interactions, it is misleading.[15] Online, just as offline, (international) law applies. *Ubi societas, ibi ius* holds true through the long run of human socialization as it does in today's information society. Or as Malcolm N. Shaw put it in the first lines of his introduction into international law: "In the long march of mankind from the cave to the computer a central role has always been played by the idea of law—the idea that order is necessary and chaos inimical to a just and stable existence."[16]

There is a variety of normative gradations between chaos and order. A state of non-normation (*anomia*) may not equal one of chaos (*anarchy*); and not all underregulated societies are necessarily chaotic, especially if they are imagined rather than real. Ovid conceived of his *Golden Age* as one in which people "without coercion, without laws, spontaneously nurtured the good and the true." People lived safely there "without protection,"[17] and, more importantly, without the *need* for protection. The lack of protection through norms thus does not imply *per se* a Hobbesian society. But just as Ovid's vision of a Golden Age turned sour, the increasing level of activities and intricacy of interactions between humans, between humans and things, and between things in today's multidimensional relational spaces have necessitated normative reactions.

Complexity of a relational space is one factor suggesting a need for normativity; the importance of that space within the increasingly globalized processes of production, use, and consumption of public and private goods is another. Indeed, the internet is deeply connected to the provision and enjoyment of public goods and the production and consumption of private ones. In light of these characteristics, especially the internet's universality and global nature, anchoring its protection in the *national* common interest (or a collection thereof) falls short. Public choice analysis shows that (even democratic) governments can be subject to corporate capture;[18] and authoritarian regimes, as monopolizers of legislative normativity, are not accountable to their people. Companies, as actors in the market, are not able to deal effectively with externalities and may overuse common resources or apply norms selectively.

There is "society" on the internet, therefore *ibi ius*. This *ius* is, and must be, more than a collection of discrete national normative orders. Protecting the internet and governing and regulating it with a view to implementing legitimate public policy choices on a national

[13] Stephan Hobe, "Cyberspace—der virtuelle Raum," in Josef Isensee and Paul Kirchhof et al. (eds.), *Handbuch des Staatsrechts, Band XI: Internationale Bezüge*, 3rd edn. (2013), § 231.

[14] Peter Mankowski, *Rechtskultur* (Tübingen: Mohr Siebeck, 2016), 131.

[15] Mark Graham, "Geography/Internet: Ethereal Alternate Dimensions of Cyberspace or Grounded Augmented Realities?" The Geographical Journal 179 (2013) 2, 177–82.

[16] Malcolm N. Shaw, *International Law*, 8th edn. (Oxford: OUP, 2017), 1.

[17] Publius Ovidius (Ovid) Naso, *Metamorphoses* (translated by Anthony S. Kline) (London: Borders, 2004), I, 89–90.

[18] Cf. Terry Moe, "The Positive Theory of Public Bureaucracy," in Dennis C. Mueller (ed.), *Perspectives on Public Choice: A Handbook* (Cambridge: CUP, 1996), 455–80.

level, through integration of the normative order of the internet in national legal orders, lies in the *international* common interest. This presupposes that actors are allocated rights and responsibilities on par with the "needs of the community,"[19] the key standard, according to the International Court of Justice, for assessing progress in the evolution and interpretation of international law.

Even though international law is the most legitimate system to justifiably develop norms relevant for the governance and regulation of the internet, national legal systems also matter. So do transnational regulatory arrangements, such as technical standards and soft law, including rules of internet governance. It is not suggested here that a new normative order needs to be (artificially) *developed* regulating "the internet," similar to international regimes regarding the seabed, Antarctica, or the moon and other celestial objects. Rather, this study argues that the norms which the order is made up of already exist, even if they may not be understood in their impact on the internet and their connection to another.

1.1.4 Norms Without Order?

Cars connected to the internet and sharing routing information, fridges that reorder milk, and networked attacks against companies using robot networks (botnets) challenge the traditional distribution of responsibility between states and non-state actors in safeguarding the common interest. Companies exercise influence over communication and information interchanges online. Courts and, in some cases, states have given them the power (and responsibility) to weigh on a massive scale, algorithmically, freedom of information and privacy rights.[20]

Information and communication technologies, mediated through the internet, have had a substantial impact on global societies, their communicative processes, and the development of individual social mores. The widespread use of the internet has changed specific sectors in most societies more fundamentally and more quickly than any other technology in the past.[21] By the end of 2017, more than half of the world's population, 54.4 percent, were online—some 4.2 billion people.[22] As newly coined or used notions indicate, ICTs have impacted our daily lives on a massive scale: from robots,[23] drones,[24] and (semi-)automated cars (mobility and human–object interaction), cloud computing and big data (data use and storage) to smart grids (energy), from e-government (politics) to mobile banking and bitcoins (finance), from the internet of things (appliances) to Massively Multiplayer Online Role-Playing Games (MMORPGs) (leisure), from cyberwar (security) to online grooming

[19] ICJ, *Reparation for Injuries Suffered in the Service of the United Nations*, Advisory Opinion of April 11, 1949, ICJ Reports (1949), 179.

[20] CJEU, Judgment of the Court (Grand Chamber) of May 13, 2014, Case C-131/12, *Google Spain SL, Google Inc. v. Agencia Española de Protección de Datos (AEPD), Mario Costeja González* ("Google Spain").

[21] Cf. David Reed, Jennifer Haroon, and Patrick Ryan, "Technologies and Policies to Connect the Next 5 Billion," Berkeley Technology Law Journal 29 (2015) 2, 1205–52.

[22] Internet Usage Statistics, World Internet Users and 2018 Population Stats, December 31, 2017, http://www.Internetworldstats.com/stats.htm.

[23] John Jordan, *Robots* (Cambridge, MA/London: MIT Press, 2016).

[24] With implications for all fields of law. For international and constitutional law, see e.g. Robert Frau (ed.), *Drohnen und das Recht. Völker- und verfassungsrechtliche Fragen automatisierter und autonomer Kriegführung* (Tübingen: Mohr, 2014).

and botnets (crime), from fake news and hate speech to microtargeted advertisements, and from social networks to blogs, vlogs, and memes (private-to-private and private-to-public communication).

This massive growth in internet penetration over the last two decades only begins to suggest the implications that ICTs and the underlying infrastructure have on society. The use and development of ICTs need to be studied in tandem in order to ensure a solid foundation for their regulation and governance. These foundations are based, just as early normative approaches to regulating telegraphs, on international law but, unlike their counterpart two centuries ago, extend normatively much beyond treaties and custom. Yet the set of international legal rules relating to internet-based information and communication flows function as the backbone of the normative order of the internet and ensure the internet's security, stability, robustness, resilience, and functionality—thus: its integrity.[25] The protection of the internet's integrity and of states from danger emanating from the use and misuse of the internet lies, as this study will show, in the global (common) interest and the discrete interests of all states and other actors.

Just as technology is important for prosperity,[26] technologies can threaten societal progress. The World Economic Forum's 2017 Global Risks Report names weaponized Artificial Intelligence and digital espionage[27] as key risks. Other opportunities connected to ICTs with hidden risks include robotics, new computing technologies, 3D printing, blockchain and distributed ledger, virtual and augmented realities, and proliferation and ubiquitous presence of linked sensors.[28]

A coordinated international approach to regulating the internet and its key resources—through a treaty regulating or an international organization governing the internet—has not yet materialized, but states have made important commitments bearing upon the regulation of the internet.

In 2005, at the end of the two-phased World Summit on the Information Society (WSIS), states affirmed in the *Tunis Commitment* their goal to build a "people-centred, inclusive and development-oriented Information Society" premised on the "purposes and principles of the Charter of the United Nations, international law and multilateralism, and respecting fully and upholding the Universal Declaration of Human Rights."[29] In "international as in national affairs" relating to internet governance, states "resolve[d] to strengthen respect for the rule of law."[30]

These are indications of (at least) normative preferences, confirmed years later in the reports of a United Nations (UN)-backed expert group, the Group of Governmental Experts on Developments in the Field of Information and Telecommunications in the Context of

[25] In the following, the study will use the notion "integrity" of the internet to refer to its security, stability, robustness, resilience, and functionality.

[26] Robert Pepper and John Garrity, "ICTs, Income Inequality, and Ensuring Inclusive Growth, World Economic Forum," Global Information Technology Report 2015 (2015), http://reports.weforum.org/global-information-technology-report-2015/1-2-icts-income-inequality-and-ensuring-inclusive-growth (with macro- and micro-economic data demonstrating the positive income and growth effects of ICTs on lower-income countries and populations).

[27] World Economic Forum, "The Global Risks Report 2017," January 11, 2017, https://www.weforum.org/agenda/2017/01/technology-risks-amplified-by-global-tensions.

[28] Ibid.

[29] World Summit on the Information Society (WSIS), Tunis Commitment, WSIS-05/TUNIS/DOC/7-E, 18 November 2005, para. 2.

[30] Ibid., para. 3.

International Security (GGE). The group's first report of 2013 underlined that international law, and "in particular the Charter of the United Nations, is applicable and is essential to maintaining peace and stability and promoting an open, secure, peaceful and accessible ICT environment."[31] With important states such as Germany, the US, and China present at the adoption of the report, we find here if not already expressions of opinio iuris then at least clear indicia of common undertakings regarding the importance of international law for the internet and for the ICT environment.[32] These commitments have not (yet) been stabilized by conventional norms;[33] however, customary international law and general principles of international law provide for the protection of and from the internet. The continued absence of a treaty regime complicates the analysis of norms applicable to the internet and its use. Normative preferences for a rule-of-law-based international internet-related governance model[34] are counterindicated by destabilizing state actions including cyberattacks,[35] pervasive state surveillance via the internet,[36] and attempts by states to create national internet segments.[37] The complexity of regulating for these challenges suggests the need for a comprehensive normative order of the internet.

1.2 Situating the Research

1.2.1 Within Interdisciplinary Approaches

In light of the challenge of establishing order on the internet, it is surprising that more than thirty years after the standardization of the internet protocol suites, more than twenty years after the invention of the hypertext system, which enabled the evolution of the internet into the medium we are presented with today, the launch of the World Wide Web, and more than ten years after commitments by states in the WSIS process to a finality of the internet, no theoretically comprehensive and substance-oriented research has been undertaken on the interaction of different regulatory layers on the internet, i.e. international law, national law, and transnational regulatory arrangements. No research, that is, that develops a coherent theory of a law-based normative order of the internet including an approach allowing for the assessment of norms of different character as to their substance, sources, and legitimation.

[31] Report of the Group of Governmental Experts on Developments in the Field of Information and Telecommunications in the Context of International Security, UN Doc. A/68/98 of 24 June 2013, para. 19.

[32] See UK Attorney General Jeremy Wright, Speech: "Cyber and International Law in the 21st Century," May 23, 2018, https://www.gov.uk/government/speeches/cyber-and-international-law-in-the-21st-century (setting out the United Kingdom (UK)'s position on applying international law to cyberspace).

[33] But, as will be shown later, customary international law fills the gap. See chapter 3.

[34] See, e.g., NetMundial Multistakeholder Statement, April 2014, http://netmundial.br/wp-content/uploads/2014/04/NETmundial-Multistakeholder-Document.pdf.

[35] For an overview, see Dan Efrony and Yuval Shany, "A Rule Book on the Shelf? Tallinn Manual 2.0 on Cyber Operations and Subsequent State Practice," Hebrew University of Jerusalem Legal Research Paper No. 18-22, https://papers.ssrn.com/sol3/papers.cfm?abstract_id=3172743.

[36] Marko Milanovic, "Human Rights Treaties and Foreign Surveillance: Privacy in the Digital Age," Harvard International Law Journal 56 (2015) 1, 81–146.

[37] Cf. Russia, UAE, China, Saudi Arabia, Algeria, Sudan, and Egypt, Proposal for the Work of the Conference [WCIT-12], ITU Doc. DT-X of 5 December 2012, WCIT12/27(Rev.1)-E, § 3A.2 and 3A.3, http://files.wcitleaks.org/public/Merged%20UAE%20081212.pdf.

This study will fill the gap by systematically and comprehensively evaluating and normatively framing the (international) legal foundations of norms bearing upon the internet and submitting that a normative order has emerged made up of international law, national law, and transnational regulatory arrangements, encompassing private and public norms, and establishing the primacy of normativity over technicity.

The study can build on important intellectual foundations. Foundational research exists on both the evolution of the internet[38] and the role and impact of the emergence of the information society,[39] a phenomenon as multi-faceted as globalization. The field of "internet studies"[40] includes law, politics, international relations, sociology, and psychology—to name just the non-technical disciplines. The present study uses a normative approach, focusing on normativity and on the normative elements of governing and regulating the internet, but taking into account the substantial literature on the role of power and control in and over the internet,[41] literature on limits of state power on the internet,[42] and the role of institutions that exercise power through managing information.[43] The research also takes inspiration from network and political science approaches[44] in order to better understand the multiple dynamics defining the interactions between actors in complex processes of global politics[45] and global communications governance[46] but will, again, focus on the normative dimension of their relationships. In order to identify myths underlying technological solutionism and *Sachzwang* arguments, the study uses previous research on the relationship of code and law, especially regarding the role of standards[47] and codes in regulating behavior,[48] of code-level interoperability rules,[49] and of the relationship between standards and architectural principles of internet integrity.[50] Previous research has identified the process of code influencing norms as "protocol politics";[51] this study develops the foundations of a normative order within which the limits of protocol politics and their normative basis are delineated.

The importance of internet governance is reflected in the breadth of studies from different methodological angles. Earlier publications have identified the "civilizing" aspect of internet governance.[52] From 2008 onward the focus has lain more on reforming internet

[38] Janet Abbate, *Inventing the Internet* (Cambridge: MIT Press, 2009).

[39] Hassan Robert, *The Information Society* (Cambridge: Polity, 2008).

[40] William H. Dutton, *The Oxford Handbook of Internet Studies* (Oxford: OUP, 2013).

[41] Adam Thierer and Clyde Wayne Crews Jr. (eds.), *Who Rules the Net? Internet Governance and Jurisdiction* (Washington: Cato Institute, 2003); William Drake and Ernest Wilson III, *Governing Global Electronic Networks: International Perspectives on Policy and Power* (Cambridge: MIT Press, 2008).

[42] Jack Goldsmith and Tim Wu, *Who Controls the Internet? Illusions of a Borderless World* (Oxford: OUP, 2008); Tim Wu, *The Master Switch: The Rise and Fall of Information Empires* (New York: Vintage, 2011).

[43] Sandra Braman, *Change of State: Information, Policy, and Power* (Cambridge: MIT Press, 2009).

[44] Mikkel Flyverbom, *The Power of Networks: Organizing the Global Politics of the Internet* (London: Edward Elgar, 2011).

[45] Milton Mueller, *Networks and States: The Global Politics of Internet Governance* (Cambridge: MIT Press, 2010).

[46] Elena Pavan, *Frames and Connections in the Governance of Global Communications* (New York: Lexington Books, 2012).

[47] Laura DeNardis (ed.), *Opening Standards. The Global Politics of Interoperability* (Cambridge: MIT Press, 2011).

[48] Alexander Galloway, *Protocol: How Control Exists after Decentralization* (Cambridge: MIT Press, 2004); Lawrence Lessig, *Code: Version 2.0* (New York: Basic Books, 2007); Shane Greenstein and Victor Stango (eds.), *Standards and Public Policy* (Cambridge: Cambridge University Press, 2007).

[49] John Palfrey and Urs Gasser, *Interop: The Promise and Perils of Highly Interconnected Systems* (New York: Basic Books, 2012).

[50] Barbara van Schewick, *Internet Architecture and Innovation* (Cambridge: MIT Press, 2010).

[51] Laura DeNardis, *Protocol Politics: The Globalization of Internet Governance* (Cambridge: MIT Press, 2009).

[52] Milton Mueller, *Ruling the Root: Internet Governance and the Taming of Cyberspace* (Cambridge: MIT Press, 2002); Daniel J. Paré, *Internet Governance in Transition: Who Is the Master of This Domain?* (London: Rowman

governance[53] and identifying regulatory[54] and institutional[55] shortcomings in terms of legitimacy and effectiveness, both with regard to infrastructure management and institutional design.[56] More recent publications have given new impetus to the study of the role of different actors in internet governance,[57] have diagnosed a "global war for internet governance,"[58] or have discussed legitimacy and the normative integration of multiple actors as aspects of the broader governance debates.[59] Important works have also been written on sectoral issues that influence the use and development of ICTs. To name just three: threats to privacy,[60] the challenges of regulating online speech,[61] and perspectives to solve jurisdictional conflicts.[62]

1.2.2 Within (International) Legal Approaches

In 2006, Antonio Segura-Serrano was already describing international law not only as a "tool for solving regulatory conflicts, but [...] a tool for governance" regarding key aspects of internet regulation, especially privacy, intellectual property, the use of force, and human rights online, such as the right to internet access.[63] He called on international law to "take a normative stance."[64] In 2009, Robert Uerpmann-Wittzack popularized the term "Internetvölkerrecht" ("international internet law")[65] as a descriptive denomination of "all rules of public international law pertaining to the functioning and use of the internet."[66] Other authors have written about "supranational cyberspace law" or a "supranational internet law" developing in tandem with a "customary law of the internet."[67] More

& Littlefield, 2003); Don MacLean, *Internet Governance: A Grand Collaboration* (New York: UN Publications, 2005); Wolfgang Benedek, Veronika Bauer, and Matthias C. Kettemann (eds.), *Internet Governance and the Information Society: Global Perspectives and European Dimensions* (Utrecht: Eleven International Publishing, 2008).

53 William Drake, *Reforming Internet Governance: Perspectives from the Working Group on Internet Governance* (New York: UN Publications, 2008).

54 Rolf H. Weber, *Shaping Internet Governance: Regulatory Challenges* (Vienna/New York: Springer, 2009).

55 John Mathiason, *Internet Governance: The New Frontier of Global Institutions* (London: Routledge, 2008).

56 Lee A. Bygrave and Jon Bing (eds.), *Internet Governance: Infrastructure and Institutions* (Oxford: OUP, 2009).

57 Eric Brousseau, Meryem Marzouki, and Cécile Méadel (eds.), *Governance, Regulation, and Powers on the Internet* (Cambridge: CUP, 2012); Matthias C. Kettemann, *The Future of Individuals in International Law. Lessons from International Internet Law* (Utrecht: Eleven International Publishing, 2013).

58 Laura DeNardis, *The Global War for Internet Governance* (New Haven and London: Yale University Press, 2014).

59 Roxana Radu, Jean-Marie Chenou, and Rolf H. Weber (eds.), *The Evolution of Global Internet Governance. Principles and Policies in the Making* (Zurich: Schulthess, 2014).

60 Lee A. Bygrave, *Data Privacy Law: An International Perspective* (Oxford: OUP, 2014).

61 Emily Laidlaw, *Regulating Speech in Cyberspace. Gatekeepers, Human Rights and Corporate Responsibility* (Cambridge: CUP, 2015).

62 Dan Jerker B. Svantesson, *Solving the Internet Jurisdiction Puzzle* (Oxford: OUP, 2017).

63 Antonio Segura-Serrano, "Internet Regulation and the Role of International Law," in *Max Planck Yearbook of United Nations Law*, Vol. 10 (The Hague: Brill, 2006), 191–272 (192).

64 Ibid., 271.

65 Robert Uerpmann-Wittzack, "Internetvölkerrecht," Archiv des Völkerrechts 47 (2009) 3, 261–83. See, more recently, with the same terminology, Joanna Kulesza, *International Internet Law* (London: Routledge, 2012).

66 Robert Uerpmann-Wittzack, "Principles of International Internet Law," German Law Journal 11 (2010), 1245-63 (1245).

67 Przemysław Paul Polański, *Customary Law of the Internet: in the Search for a Supranational Cyberspace Law* (The Hague: T.M.C. Asser, 2007).

recently, authors have analyzed the reliance of internet-related normative processes on non-traditional norms[68] or criticized their prevalence.[69]

Within traditionalist approaches to internet law it is argued that, as "all online activities have noticeable effects on states' territories [...], current internet problems have to be evaluated relying on traditional concepts and legal structures."[70] Yet "traditional concepts" and "legal structures" do not suffice to explain the norms and normative actors on the internet. While using traditional concepts of (international) law in order to situate the present research and describing how international legal regimes *de lege lata* protect internet integrity and remedy externalities, this study goes further. Where Molly Land develops the "foundation for an 'International Law of the internet' "[71] on principles derived from Article 19 of the International Covenant on Civil and Political Rights, the approach followed here is more comprehensive. Rather than trying to develop a "supranational cyberspace law" on the basis of customary law of the internet, this study has a more ambitious goal in establishing the contours and the content, the genesis and finality of a *normative order of the internet* and assessing how it is implemented in, and legitimized by, the international legal order and national legal orders. An important part of the present research will also lie in assessing the relationship of public and private norms,[72] the authority over public, private, and hybrid spaces online, of co-regulation (also in the form of *regulierte Selbstregulierung*) and state regulation,[73] and the role of hybrid and non-traditional sources of law, such as standards and "Request for Comments."

Ensuring human rights is a key aspect of legitimating normative orders. The dual nature of the internet—as a space to use for the promotion of human rights and a space in which abuses can take place—has been convincingly established.[74] Therefore, achieving public policy goals lying in the international common interest, like the protection of human rights online, figures centrally in the present research. Since at least 2006, the protection of human rights on the internet has been closely studied,[75] with freedom of expression identified as the key "enabling" right.[76] The importance of ensuring human rights on the internet globally has been recognized on the UN level, with states confirming their obligation to respect rights offline just as online.[77] This is an important precedent for procedures to establish

[68] Martha Finnemore and Duncan B. Hollis, "Constructing Norms for Global Cybersecurity," AJIL 110 (2016), 425–79 (477).

[69] Calling on states to develop a treaty-based international law of cybersecurity: Kubo Macak, "From Cyber Norms to Cyber Rules: Re-engaging States as Law-makers," Leiden Journal of International Law 30 (2017) 4, 877–99.

[70] Stefanie Schmahl, "Zwischenstaatliche Kompetenzabgrenzung im Cyberspace," Archiv des Völkerrechts 47 (2009) 3, 284–327.

[71] Molly Land, "Toward an International Law of the Internet," Harvard International Law Journal 54 (2013) 2, 393–458.

[72] Lee A. Bygrave, *Internet Governance by Contract* (Oxford: OUP, 2015).

[73] Christopher T. Marsden, *Net Neutrality: Towards a Co-Regulatory Solution* (London: Bloomsbury, 2010); Christopher T. Marsden, *Internet Co-Regulation* (Cambridge: CUP, 2011); Ian Brown and Christopher T. Marsden, *Regulating Code. Good Governance and Better Regulation in the Information Age* (Cambridge: MIT Press, 2013).

[74] Andrew Murray, "Uses and Abuses of Cyberspace: Coming to Grips with the Present Dangers," in Antonio Cassese (ed.), *Realizing Utopia. The Future of International Law* (Oxford: OUP, 2012), 497–506 (arguing that space and cyberspace are vastly different spheres and international legal regulation of corporeal aspects is limited to objects in actual space).

[75] Rikke F. Jørgensen (ed.), *Human Rights in the Global Information Society* (Cambridge: MIT Press, 2006).

[76] Dragos Cuceranu, *Aspects of Regulating Freedom of Expression on the Internet* (Antwerp: Intersentia, 2012); Wolfgang Benedek and Matthias C. Kettemann, *Freedom of Expression on the Internet* (Strasbourg: Council of Europe, 2014).

[77] See the first Human Rights Council Resolution 20/8, The promotion, protection and enjoyment of human rights on the Internet, UN Doc. A/HRC/RES/20/8 of 5 July 2012 and Human Rights Council Resolution 32/13, The promotion, protection and enjoyment of human rights on the Internet, A/HRC/RES/32/13 of 18 July 2016.

internet-related duties of states based on existing international law. The international monitoring of human rights violations online, through filtering and blocking, gave rise to early analyses of international legal duties of states regarding the internet.[78] Questions of internet access and the bridging of the digital divide have also led to research on the international duties of states regarding infrastructure development.[79]

1.2.3 With Regard to the Concept of "Normative Orders"

From the management of critical internet resources to the uploading of pictures on social networking sites: actions on, and with relevance to the running of, the internet are controlled by norms. International and national rules and public and private norms apply. There are thus rules (or norms)[80] on the internet—but is there also a *rule*, in particular a rule of law? The closest approximation to *a* rule or a coherent and controlling regulatory system of the internet is, this study submits, the concept of a *normative order of the internet*. In light of the importance of the concept for the analytical efforts undertaken here, it must be briefly explained.

The notion of "normative order" suggests an *order* made of *norms*. This misses the point as a normative order is not (or not strictly) an *ordered i.e. layered or hierarchical system* of (only) *explicit norms*. Rather than a hierarchical system, like Kelsen's *Stufenbau*, a normative order, according to Rainer Forst and Klaus Günther, is a "complex of norms and values with which the fundamental structure of a society (or the structure of international, supranational or transnational relationships) is legitimated, in particular the exercise of political authority and the distribution of basic goods."[81]

For the purposes of this study, the normative order of the internet is a complex of norms, values, and practices that relate to the use and development of the internet and with which the activities of, and relationships among, states, private companies, and civil society with regard to the use and development of the internet are legitimated, in particular the exercise of private or public authority and the distribution of basic goods, including internet access and access to internet content. Put more succinctly, *the normative order of the internet is the set of norms and normative expectations that shape the use and development of the internet.*

The concept of normative order is more holistic than that of a "regime," a notion with which International Relations scholars are more familiar. Stephen D. Krasner defined

See, for an introduction, Rebecca MacKinnon, *Consent of the Networked: The Worldwide Struggle for Internet Freedom* (New York: Basic Books, 2012) and Rikke F. Jørgensen, *Framing the Net. The Internet and Human Rights* (Cheltenham: Edward Elgar, 2013).

[78] Ronald Deibert, John Palfrey, Rafal Rohozinski, and Jonathan Zittrain (eds.), *Access Denied: The Practice and Policy of Global Internet Filtering* (Cambridge: MIT Press, 2008); Ronald Deibert, John Palfrey, Rafal Rohozinski, and Jonathan Zittrain (eds.), *Access Controlled: The Shaping of Power, Rights, and Rule in Cyberspace* (Cambridge: MIT Press, 2010); Ronald Deibert, John Palfrey, Rafal Rohozinski, and Jonathan Zittrain (eds.), *Access Contested: Security, Identity, and Resistance in Asian Cyberspace* (Cambridge: MIT Press, 2011).

[79] Nivien Saleh, *Third World Citizens and the Information Technology Revolution* (London: Palgrave Macmillan, 2010); Gaëlle Krikorian and Amy Kapczynski (eds.), *Access to Knowledge in the Age of Intellectual Property* (Cambridge: MIT Press, 2010).

[80] "Norms" is a broader concept and normative theory uses that term over "rules". Cf. Duncan Kennedy, "Form and Substance in Private Law Adjudication," Harvard Law Review 89 (1976), 1685–778.

[81] Rainer Forst and Klaus Günther, "Die Herausbildung normativer Ordnungen. Zur Idee eines interdisziplinären Forschungsprogramms," in Rainer Forst and Klaus Günther (eds.), *Die Herausbildung normativer Ordnungen.*

"regime" as the sum of "implicit or explicit principles, norms, rules and decision-making procedures around which actors' expectations converge in a given area of international relations." The normative order of the internet contains the "internet governance regime" and embraces both explicit norms and implicit norms (normative expectations). The Frankfurt "normative orders" approach offers analytical advantages over a regime-theoretical one, especially by encompassing the importance of narratives (including justification narratives) in establishing, stratifying, and contesting a normative order.

Robert M. Cover developed the notion of nomos (law) and narrative. He argued that we live in a "normative world," in which "law and narrative are inseparably related." Every norm needs to be "located in discourse," to be given "history and destiny, beginning and end, explanation and purpose." The narrative, too, is insistent in its "demand for its prescriptive point, its moral."[82] This location of norms in discourse (by giving it context) and "explanation" (through being imbued with meaning and purpose) is an important characteristic of a normative order and arguably an epistemic advantage over other attempts to stratify norm collections (by describing them, e.g., as a "regime").

The normative orders approach does not only look at norms. Cover, a normative orders designer *avant la lettre*, makes this point in combining nomos and narrative: "[n]o set of legal institutions or prescriptions exists apart from the narratives that locate it and give it meaning."[83] These narratives are important. Each societal order, according to Rainer Forst, is related to a "specific understanding of the purpose, the goals and rules of this order."[84] The purpose, the goals, and rules need to be justified. The orders are thus "orders of justification" (*Rechtfertigungsordnungen*) and the justifications are formulated as narratives ("justification narratives") (*Rechtfertigungsnarrative*).[85] Thus justification narratives are a form of "embodied rationality"[86] and important for normative analysis. This study will show that ensuring internet integrity and protecting states and society from uses and misuses of the internet is the purpose of the normative order of the internet. Further, the order is premised on this justification and through it justifies the norms (and institutions) within it.[87] Though this study will not focus in depth on the narratives of the participants in the normative order of the internet, the fact that they exist matters, because normative orders that are narratively

Interdisziplinäre Perspektiven (Frankfurt/New York: Campus, 2011), 11–30 (15): "Unter 'normativer Ordnung' verstehen wir den Komplex von Normen und Werten, mit denen die Grundstruktur einer Gesellschaft (beziehungsweise die Struktur inter- bzw. supra- oder transnationaler Verhältnisse) legitimiert wird, namentlich die Ausübung politischer Autorität und die Verteilung von elementaren Lebens- und Grundgütern" (translation by the author).

[82] Robert M. Cover, "The Supreme Court, 1982 Term – Foreword. Nomos and Narrative," Harvard Law Review 97 (1983) 4, 1–68 (5).

[83] Ibid., 4 (notes omitted).

[84] Rainer Forst, *Normativität und Macht. Zur Analyse sozialer Rechtfertigungsordnungen* (Frankfurt am Main: Suhrkamp, 2015), 70: "Jede gesellschaftliche Ordnung im Allgemeinen und jedes Subsystem im Besonderen beruht auf einem bestimmten Verständnis des Zwecks, der Ziele und Regeln dieser Ordnung oder des Systems – sie sind somit normative Ordnungen bzw. Teilordnungen als Rechtfertigungsordnungen" (translation by the author).

[85] Ibid., 70, 87. See also Ibid., 96–7.

[86] Ibid., 87: "Rechtfertigungsnarrative betrachten wir als Formen einer verkörperten Rationalität, denn hier verdichten sich Bilder, Partikularerzählungen, Rituale, Fakten sowie Mythen zu wirkmächtigen Gesamterzählungen, die als Ressource der Ordnungssinngebung fungieren."

[87] Cf. ibid., 87: " 'Normative Ordnungen' beruhen auf basalen Rechtfertigungen und dienen entsprechend der Rechtfertigung von sozialen Regeln, Normen und Institutionen; [. . .] Insofern ist eine normative Ordnung als Rechtfertigungsordnung anzusehen: Sie setzt Rechtfertigungen voraus und generiert sie zugleich."

configured exert special force and authority. They are historically meaningful and exert attraction through power of identification,[88] which in turn favors norm adherence.

Importantly, the study will investigate where the power within the normative order of the internet lies. Justifications are related to power: having power means being able to "influence, order, occupy, or close the realm of reasons and justifications for other subjects."[89] The way that this power is distributed and controlled in the normative order of the internet is a key theme of the theoretical approaches presented in chapter 4.

The normative order of the internet (or nomos of the internet following Cover's terminology) is not dependent on any particular state or legal system. Creating legal meaning, the process of "jurisgenesis," takes place "through an essentially cultural medium"[90] in social or collective processes. Similarly, *the normative order of the internet proceduralizes the jurisgenesis related to the use and development of the internet and the services running on it.*

Norms that make up normative orders are not (only or even primarily) Kelsenian *Sollenssätze*[91] but, pursuant to Forst and Günther, "practical reasons to act [containing] the claim of being binding upon the addressee."[92] They are "contextualized culturally, economically, politically, communicatively, and psychologically, sedimented and habituated in practices, contained in conventions as the result of long procedures to find compromises, challenged [...], discussed in processes of interpretation and constant revision [...]."[93] In the context of the normative development of the internet "norms" are normatively relevant commitments, exercising pull on the addressee, that can crystallize into (international) law. Norms in the context of this study are thus not necessarily legally binding but are formulated in a way that influences behavior and, through their consonance with the order's purpose, incentivize adherence.

Actors able to pass legally binding norms may nevertheless use non-binding norms. According to Christoph Möllers, in an in-depth study on norms, setting non-binding norms (he calls them "non-norms") already means accepting their content and showing the recipient a "picture" of expected behavior, thus cognitively closing alternative options.[94] Möllers describes norms as "positively marked possibilities" pointing to a "possible situation" or a "possible event" which "should be realized."[95] This relates single norms to the

[88] Cf. ibid., 87: "In Narrative eingefasst [...] haben normativen Ordnungen eine besondere Bindungskraft und Autorität; sie erhalten historische Bedeutung und zugleich emotionale Identifikationskraft."

[89] Ibid., 96–7: "Macht zu haben bedeutet, den Raum der Gründe und Rechtfertigungen anderer Subjekte – und hier sind die Grade wichtig – beeinflussen, bestimmen, besetzen oder gar abschließen zu können" (translation by the author).

[90] Robert M. Cover, "The Supreme Court, 1982 Term – Foreword. Nomos and Narrative," Harvard Law Review 97 (1983) 4, 1–68 (11).

[91] Hans Kelsen, *Reine Rechtslehre* (1934), 21 (Matthias Jestaedt (ed.), *Reine Rechtslehre.* Studienausgabe der 1. Auflage 1934) (Tübingen: Mohr Siebeck, 2008), 33.

[92] Rainer Forst and Klaus Günther, "Die Herausbildung normativer Ordnungen. Zur Idee eines interdisziplinären Forschungsprogramms," in Rainer Forst and Klaus Günther (eds.), *Die Herausbildung normativer Ordnungen. Interdisziplinäre Perspektiven* (Frankfurt/New York: Campus, 2011), 11–30 (16): "[Normen sind] praktische Gründe für Handlungen, die den Anspruch erheben, verbindlich zu sein, und die ihre Adressaten entsprechend dazu verpflichten, sich diesen Grund als ein Handlungsmotiv zu eigen zu machen" (translation by the author).

[93] Ibid., 16: "[Normen sind] in kulturelle, ökonomische, politische, kommunikative und psychologische Kontexte eingebettet, in Institutionen verkörpert, in Praktiken sedimentiert und habitualisiert, in Konventionen als Ergebnis langwieriger Kompromissbildungsverfahren enthalten, in Konfliktarenen herausgefordert, in Prozessen der Interpretation und Dauerrevision thematisiert und bestritten, in Ritualen und Dramen bekräftigt und stabilisiert" (translation by the author).

[94] Christoph Möllers, *Die Möglichkeit der Normen* (Berlin: Suhrkamp, 2016), 137.

[95] Ibid., 13–14: "Normen sind [...] als positiv markierte Möglichkeiten zu verstehen. Normen verweisen auf einen möglichen Zustand oder ein mögliches Ereignis. [...] Die positive Markierung einer Möglichkeit zeigt an, dass diese sich verwirklichen soll" (translation by the author).

normative order, which defines, through its purpose, embedded in justification narratives, why a certain norm/normative goal should be realized.

The normative order of the internet must be capable of predicting, explaining, or justifying normative challenges for (and normative answers by) different actors for a vast array of challenges: from the right to be forgotten to the exercise of control over Internet Exchange Points, from the development and implementation of cybersecurity strategies to the role of search engines and social media companies vis-à-vis online harassment and hate speech. A successful normative order of the internet must be able to address macro-issues, such as the protection of the internet's critical infrastructure, but must also be detailed enough to contain, contextualize, and justify norms capable of influencing individual decisions regarding the use of the internet and connected technologies.

1.3 Hypotheses

The overall research question that motivates this study is related to a concept this study established for the first time: the normative order of the internet. What is the genealogy, ontology, legitimacy, finality, and impact of the normative order of the internet? Put differently: how did it evolve, what is it made up of, how is it legitimized, what is its finality, and how is it (and its constituent norms) implemented and legitimated within and through the international legal order and in national legal orders?

In developing answers to these queries, the study will test, develop, and confirm six interlinked hypotheses:

(1) The leading hypothesis of this study is that a normative order of the internet has emerged that integrates norms materially and normatively connected to the use and development of the internet at three different levels (national, regional, international), of two types (privately and publicly authored) and of substantially different character (from ius cogens to technical standards). As a legal order it operates through the form of law and analogously to it. Its actors—states, legal persons, natural persons—fulfill diverse functions as norm entrepreneurs, norm appliers, and norm enforcers. The order's justification narratives control new norms by assessing their technical consistency and legal–cultural consonancy with the order's purpose. Though not without autonomous elements, the normative order of the internet is interlinked through legitimation relationships with national and international legal orders. Its genealogy, ontology, legitimacy, finality, and impact are subsequently analyzed.

(2) It is hypothesized that apart from international and national norms a "third" category of norms exists, a normative tertium, which has only recently emerged as a normative category in its own right. Tertium norms are fundamentally technical standards and soft law norms, which emerge in the contested space between technical necessity and socio-legal values. They evidence a variable normativity and transcend binary normative solutions and can thus counteract diffusions of regulatory responsibility in transnational settings.

(3) The study also hypothesizes that the technology-orientation of non-legal normativity, including the focus on code and standards, needs to be reoriented through a value-based normative approach, while embracing the internal norm (re)production mechanisms of private standards. It is thus not technicity that shapes normativity.

Rather than letting a "technical medium [...] define our societal values"[96] it is the values embedded in the normative order of the internet that define the evolution of the internet's underlying technologies through normative framing and regulatory interventions. Value-based normativity, it is hypothesized, must influence standard-setting to ensure the primacy of international legal commitments, and their national legal counterparts, as to the finality of normative ordering on the internet. Rather than accepting arguments out of technical necessity, this study hypothesizes that technical norms are properly placed within the value-oriented common frame of the normative order of the internet.

(4) Centrifugal forces contribute to the emergence of normative redundancies ("normative froth"), real conflicts of norms between regulatory layers and geographically bounded normative spheres ("normative friction"), substantial structural problems ("normative fractures"), and political, commercial, and technological fragmentation of the internet. However, technical invariants of the internet exercise defragmentation forces. These are then normatively reified within the normative order of the internet.

(5) Consequently, it is hypothesized that a normative turn has taken place on the internet allowing norms, which impact its use and development, to self-constitutionalize and—through autonomous normative processes—to develop and legitimize other norms within the order. This approach has considerable explanatory and predictive potential as to the evolution of norms impacting the internet, as norms which do not cohere with other order norms or are in dissonance with key principles of the order will remain unsuccessful attempts at norm entrepreneurship.

(6) It is finally hypothesized that the normative order of the internet is a legitimate order of norms. Processes of legitimation of norms take place within the order, but also through the national law and the international legal system. Internationally, the norm creation process which allows for the integration of all actors legitimizes the normative outcome. Nationally, tertium norms have been progressively recognized within national legal orders through processes of formal and non-formal application, transposition, and referencing.

This study uses a number of different methodological approaches. Aware of the merely epistemic legitimacy of scholars, the author performs normative analysis through evaluation and systematization.[97] Chapters 2 and 3 analytically establish essential concepts and normative dynamics. Analytical parts identify challenges to internet regulation. Descriptive parts provide for a phenomenology of the internet and the technology-related specificities. An empirical and largely positivist analysis of international legal regimes exposes them to rationalized scientific discourse. Chapter 4 will provide space for more normative reflection on the "disordering" of the internet on the basis of critical normativity. Chapter 5 will allow for a comprehensive presentation of the theoretical approaches to ordering the internet's norms, including network theory, systems theory, transnationalism, global constitutionalism, and conflict studies.

[96] Indra Spiecker gen. Döhmann, "Online- und Offline-Nutzung von Daten: Einige Überlegungen zum Umgang mit Informationen im Internetzeitalter," in Michael Bartsch and Robert G. Briner (eds.), *DGRI-Jahrbuch* (Cologne: Verlag Dr. Otto Schmidt), 39–53 (53): "[Das Internet] ist ein rechtsfreier Raum nur solange, wie wir zulassen, dass ein technisches Medium unsere gesellschaftlichen Werte bestimmt" (translation by the author).

[97] As counselled by Anne Peters, "Realizing Utopia as A Scholarly Endeavour," EJIL 24 (2013), 533–52 (552).

It is in chapter 6 where the approach informing all other chapters is centrally employed: the *normative orders* of the Frankfurt School of Critical Norms Studies (or studies of normativity; *Normenforschung, Normativitätsforschung*), developed in a Habermasian tradition by Rainer Forst and Klaus Günther and continued by other researchers within the Cluster of Excellence "The Formation of Normative Orders."[98] The study will empirically assess and describe and normatively reflect on the evolution of the normative order of the internet based on international law, national rules, and private regulation. Informed by critical positivism and following Forst,[99] the study understands normativity as having two dimensions, both of which are necessary to conceptualize normative orders: a descriptive and a critical one. *Descriptive* normativity delineates the normative power of existing justification narratives, while *critical* normativity reflectively analyzes normativity in light of criteria such as generality and reciprocity.[100]

This study seeks to avoid only "identify[ing] the normative world with the professional paraphernalia of social control," as Robert M. Cover warned. A positivistic approach—just or primarily looking at the "rules and principles of justice, the formal institutions of the law and the conventions of a social order"—is methodologically unproductive in a normative field with variable normative geometries such as the internet. The normative order of the internet can only be understood if the narratives behind it are identified and dissected: what applies to normative orders within states applies to the internet: "No set of legal institutions or prescriptions exists apart from the narratives that locate it and give it meaning. For every constitution there is an epic, for each decalogue a scripture."[101]

The normative order of the internet is a theory in the sense that it helps explain, justify, and predict normative phenomena, tie together data points (such as normative developments and behavioral patterns) and, generally, serve as normative orientation in a complex world.[102] The study's analysis is based on a critical analysis of both theory and legal developments, but will go beyond them and take into account what a critical scholar has called the "emancipatory political possibilities [...] within the historically unfolding constellation."[103] Investigating the role of normativity on the internet, this study remains nevertheless cautious: "annoying Westphalian objections" act as an important anchor for overly optimistic approaches to internet regulation.[104] To name just three examples: calls for the independence of cyberspace have given way to an overwhelming consensus regarding the key role of law as an ordering agent in the online world; calls for states to accept their irrelevance in regulating the internet have been silenced by the reality of the continued responsibility of states to secure to everyone within their territories and under their control all human and fundamental rights in exercising the territorial sovereignty; and calls for

[98] Cf., for an introduction, Rainer Forst und Klaus Günther, "Die Herausbildung normativer Ordnungen. Zur Idee eines interdisziplinären Forschungsprogramms," in Rainer Forst and Klaus Günther (eds.), *Die Herausbildung normativer Ordnungen. Interdisziplinäre Perspektiven* (Frankfurt/New York: Campus, 2011), 11–30 (16).

[99] Rainer Forst, *Normativität und Macht. Zur Analyse sozialer Rechtfertigungsordnungen* (Frankfurt am Main: Suhrkamp, 2015), 96–7.

[100] Ibid., 101.

[101] Robert M. Cover, "The Supreme Court, 1982 Term – Foreword. Nomos and Narrative," Harvard Law Review 97 (1983) 4, 1–68 (4) (notes omitted).

[102] Anne Peters, "Realizing Utopia as A Scholarly Endeavour," EJIL 24 (2013), 533–52 (536).

[103] Nancy Fraser, "Transnationalizing the Public Sphere: On the Legitimacy and Efficacy of Public Opinion in a Post-Westphalian World," Theory, Culture & Society 24 (2007) 4, 7–30 (8).

[104] Timothy William Waters, "The Momentous Gravity of the State of Things Now Obtaining: Annoying Westphalian Objections to the Idea of Global Governance," Indiana Journal of Global Studies 16 (2009), 25–58.

complete self-regulation of internet content on privately owned sites by the intermediaries controlling these spaces have given way to (at least) regulated self-regulation by states and international organizations.

Hersch Lauterpacht criticized the tendency of positivists to merely register state practice without relating it to "higher legal principles [or] the conception of international law as a whole."[105] Using a critical positivist approach remedies this problem. In consequence, this study will ensure that observed norms are related to their position in, and justification by (and reciprocal justificatory potential for), the normative order of the internet. This productive tension between positivist and normative analyses allows this study to present a detailed picture of the varied attempts to normatively order the internet.

The research needs to encompass interdisciplinary aspects. ICTs have pervaded most sectors of society so thoroughly that a disciplinary analysis of "the internet" from a uniquely legal perspective is impossible: "digital information exchange diffuses throughout the economy and society."[106] The societal implications of the internet, according to Ian Brown and Christopher T. Marsden, make it impossible to develop "simple magic bullet solutions based on study of one discipline (whether computer science, law, or economics), one industry sector (telecommunication or free software), or one solution (efficiency and human rights)."[107] This holds true to the degree that the challenges of regulating the internet need to be evaluated based on the "dynamism of markets and the even greater dynamism of code."[108] It is only partly true in that there is, as this study posits, a coherent normative order that explains and justifies the functional protection of the internet's integrity (and the protection of states and society from uses and misuses of the internet), the role of actors in normative processes, their justification narratives, and the normative instruments used in regulating and governing the internet: the normative order of the internet.

1.4 Structure

This introductory chapter presents first foundations on normativity on (and of) the internet, situates the research in the global academic discourse, explains the concept of normative orders, and discusses the research questions and hypotheses and the methodology employed.

Chapter 2 opens with a foundational analysis of regulatory approaches to technology. In particular, the chapter's sections sketch the regulation of ICTs through time, the criticality of the internet in its societal context, and the importance of protecting the internet in the common interest. Thereafter, special challenges of internet regulation are examined, including the role of non-state actors (intermediaries) and the flexible use of non-traditional regulatory means, such as code and algorithms.

Chapter 3 analyzes existing international legal rules safeguarding internet integrity and presents the evolution of internet governance as a global regime arrangement for the

105 Hersch Lauterpacht, *The Function of Law in the International Community* (Oxford: Clarendon Press, 1933), 438.

106 Ian Brown and Christopher T. Marsden, *Regulating Code. Good Governance and Better Regulation in the Information Age* (Cambridge: MIT Press, 2013) xi.

107 Ibid., 1.

108 Ibid..

internet. While there exist no international treaties directly protecting the internet (or protecting states and society from its dangers), indirectly protective norms exist both in treaty law and customary international law. Further, the majority of established principles of international law are relevant for the use and development of the internet. By describing existing elements of the internet's order and the normative dynamics that have shaped the evolution of internet-related principles, chapters 2 and 3 together set the scene for the discussion of normative disorder on the internet.

Chapter 4 makes the case that internet regulation today is in normative disarray. Due (inter alia) to normative dissonance and politico-economic preferences of rational actors between normative players and the disconnect between regulatory layers, the internet has partially fragmented. Normative froth, normative friction, and normative fractures are exemplified as elements of disorder. The overall fragmentation of the internet is described in more detail as being caused by technical, political, and legal developments. However, the forces at work are truly *centrifugal* in that they are only "apparent"[109] when experienced from within the system. Observing from the outside, there are actually *centripetal* forces at work, keeping objects within the rotating system. These "centripetal" forces, including not only technical elements of the internet, the "internet invariants," but also shared commitments to internet integrity, are key elements of (the self-constitutionalization of) the normative order of the internet.

Chapter 5 shows the potential of theoretical approaches to solving the normative crisis on the internet. In turn, key theories of order in the broader sense are presented and discussed. Though the majority of these theories were not posited with a view to the internet, the present study draws from their epistemic potential for the regulation of the internet. Theories (and key representatives of that theory) include systems theory (Luhmann/Teubner), constitutionalization/global constitutionalism (Pernice), transnationalism (Viellechner, Calliess), legal pluralism (Seinecke), multi-normativity (Forst), network theory (Vesting), interoperability theory (Palfrey, Gasser, Weber), massive online micro justice (De Werra), conflict studies (Mueller), and infrastructuralization (DeNardis). Further, the study assesses the historically sedimented discourses on internet governance and their influence on ordering the internet as well as more recent attempts to define "cybernorms."

Chapter 6 presents in detail the normative order of the internet based on the notion of a necessary identification of, and turn toward, a nomos of the internet, which is embedded in, and configures, the normative order of the internet. The study shows that this order has many facets, contains national, international, public, and private norms, but has importantly developed its own normative instruments and rules on the relation of actors and the legitimacy of norms. The normative order provides a normative infrastructure in which the internet's nomos, including its means of normative production and justification, are anchored. The study will determine norms belonging to the normative order of the internet to be those that have a *material* (non-trivial) and a *normative* (not merely factual) connection to the internet as a network of networks. These norms will be shown to be *formally* and *materially* legitimated. Formal legitimation will be shown to be achievable through symbolic validation through norm emergence in processes involving multiple actors. Material

[109] Centrifugal force is an "apparent force" (*Scheinkraft*). As part of a (rotating) system you seem to experience centrifugal force pushing you away from the rotating center, while you are actually feeling inward centripetal forces.

legitimation is possible through norms being *determinate* enough for their purpose (thus allowing for non-binding instruments), *coherent* with the core principles of the normative order of the internet, *consonant* with the order's values as expressed in its principles, and *adhering* systematically to the normative order as a whole.

Chapter 7 takes a close look at the norms of the normative order of the internet and studies how they are integrated into national legal orders and especially how non-traditional norms, such as standards and soft law (as a legal "tertium" next to national and international law), are legitimated through national legal processes. The chapter will show that national legal orders have recognized international law and national law. Monism and dualism have emerged to explain how the two dominions relate to each other: the choices ranged from subordination to coordination with varying primacies. Together with global constitutionalists, the study goes beyond this debate. It will argue that this tertium of normativity has been recognized by national orders: normative instruments that are neither "national" law nor "international" law, but part of the normative order of the internet. This enrichment of the legal vocabulary has been called a "change in the composition of the medium of law"[110] by Jürgen Habermas.

The study also demonstrates and justifies the integration into national legal orders of a set of non-binding rules and practices, processes, and normative expectations that are embedded in the normative order of the internet, which influence normative processes impacting the internet (and being impacted by the internet) on a national level.

The study ends with conclusions in chapter 8, in which the study's results will be summarized, namely that, as the following pages will show, a legal and legitimate normative order of the internet has emerged, made up of international and national law and transnational regulatory arrangements.

The regulatory challenges of the internet become clear and the need for a comprehensive order evident when one considers, as the next chapter will suggest we do, how a stable and secure internet is critical and must be ensured in the common interest to reduce dangers to society emanating from its use.

110 Jürgen Habermas, "Im Sog der Technokratie," in Jürgen Habermas, *Im Sog der Technokratie: kleine politische Schriften XII* (Frankfurt: Suhrkamp, 2013), 7.

2
Foundations of Online Order

2.1 A Network of Networks

2.1.1 Foundations

In the following chapter key foundations and first fractures of the internet and its norms will be presented. Section 2.1 discusses the beginning of the information society and clarifies semantic questions. Section 2.2 shows why internet integrity is critical for society and that both the internet's physicality and its intangibles need to be protected. Section 2.3 demonstrates why protecting the internet lies in the global common interest. Section 2.4 shows which (normative) challenges emerge when regulating the internet. The final section 2.5 shows which hypotheses as to the hybridity of the internet and the importance of values-based normativity are already shown to be valid.

2.1.2 Beginnings of the Information Society

The creation of the internet was the key development in the evolution of information society.[1] Just as freedom of expression in all its forms is widely considered the right essential to meaningful internet use,[2] the evolution of the internet has become so determinative of the development of information society that the former notion has largely supplanted the latter in defining our time. We now do not (usually) speak of "information society," but rather of the "internet age." Information and communication technologies, however, predate the internet by far.

Exchanging messages between stations was the premise of telegraphs, with international regulation, as we have seen, going back to the 1850s. But the revolutionary premise of what would later become the internet was that of a global information exchange and communication network. In the *Brief History of the Internet,* some of the key thinkers and engineers behind its evolution pinpoint the 1962 memos of J.C.R. Licklider of the Massachussetts

[1] Especially notable among the large number of publications offering accounts of information society theories are Alistair Duff, *Information Society Studies* (London: Routledge, 2000); Frank Webster, *Theories of the Information Society*, 3rd edn. (London: Routledge, 2006); and Robert Hassan, *The Information Society* (Cambridge: Polity, 2008). For a critical perspective on informationalization, see Christopher May, *The Information Society: A Skeptical View* (Cambridge: Polity, 2002). Fundamental texts still are Manuel Castells's three-part account: Manuel Castells, *The Information Society: Economy, Society and Culture; Vol. 1: The Rise of the Network Society,* 2nd edn. (Oxford: Blackwell, 1996/2000); *Vol. 2: The Power of Identity* (Oxford: Blackwell, 1997); *Vol. 3: End of Millennium*, 2nd edn. (Oxford: Blackwell, 1998/2000).

[2] Cf. Human Rights Council Resolution 20/8, The promotion, protection and enjoyment of human rights on the Internet, July 5, 2012, para. 1: "[The Human Rights Council] [a]ffirms that the same rights that people have offline must also be protected online, *in particular freedom of expression*, which is applicable regardless of frontiers and through any media of one's choice, in accordance with Articles 19 of the Universal Declaration of Human Rights and the International Covenant on Civil and Political Rights" (emphasis added).

The Normative Order of the Internet. Matthias C. Kettemann, Oxford University Press (2020). © Matthias C. Kettemann.
DOI: 10.1093/oso/9780198865995.001.0001

Institute of Technology (MIT) as the first references to the potential of global networking. Licklider called his vision the "Galactic Network."[3] In late 1969, first messages were exchanged via ARPAnet (Advanced Research Projects Agency Network), a network developed through funds of DARPA, the US Defense Advanced Research Projects Agency, that supports research in new technologies. By 1971, emailing technology and by 1973 the Transfer Control Protocol/Internet Protocol (TCP/IP) suite of internet protocols had been developed. It took until 1983, however, for ARPAnet computers to switch to TCP/IP, thus making it part of the newly emerging internet.[4]

The 1980s also saw the "Protocol Wars" take place, a conflict about the best approach to develop a global ICT network. The European competitor OSI (Open Systems Interconnect)[5] and two corporate networks, including one by IBM (International Business Machines), eventually lost because of ARPANnet's higher flexibility. Thus technical fragmentation of the internet, a force of disorder today, was the lived reality for the first two decades of internet-based communication. There were, in fact, *internets*. The year 1984 saw the creation of the Domain Name System (DNS) and 1989 the invention, by Tim Berners-Lee at CERN (the European Organization for Nuclear Research), of WWW, the World Wide Web application, to run on the internet.[6] Following this, from 1991 onward, the first end-user-friendlier web pages were created and the popularization of the internet as a communicative tool outside academia started. From the mid-1990s onward the internet was mainstreamed in that it became relevant beyond the technical and academic sectors and achieved a significant role both as a topic and a medium for business and society. The internet's commercialization ensued which in turn led to a politicization and, responsively, to a still incomplete juridification of the internet.

In decades of internet time, the 1970s appear as the time of the invention of the internet, the 1980s as the time of its operational birth, the 1990s as the time of its increasing commercialization and politicization, the 2000s as the decade of its fruition into the global information and communication network (a role it continues to fulfill), and the 2010s as the emergence of a governance discussion framework in response to the growing role of the internet for human sociality.

The internet today has become, as UN Special Rapporteur on Freedom of Expression, Frank La Rue, put in his 2011 report, a "vital communications medium which individuals can use to exercise their right to freedom of expression, or the right to seek, receive and impart information and ideas of all kinds, regardless of frontiers."[7] Unlike any other medium in history, "the internet allows individuals to communicate instantaneously and inexpensively, and it has had a dramatic impact on the way information and ideas are shared and accessed."[8] It is the most innovative and fastest developing communicative environment in the history of the world and dynamizes human-to-human (e.g. through social networks),

[3] Barry M. Leiner, Vinton G. Cerf, David D. Clark, Robert E. Kahn, Leonard Kleinrock, Daniel C. Lynch, Jon Postel, Larry G. Roberts, and Stephen Wolff, "Brief History of the Internet," Internet Society (2012), http://www.internetsociety.org/brief-history-internet.

[4] Cf. Robert H. Zakon, Hobbes' Internet Timeline 25, http://www.zakon.org/robert/internet/timeline.

[5] See NetAffair (Mariann Unterluggauer), "Background," March 2014, http://www.netaffair.at/background.html.

[6] See Tim Berners-Lee, "Information Management: A Proposal," (1989/1990), http://www.w3.org/History/1989/proposal.html.

[7] Special Rapporteur on the promotion and protection of the right to freedom of opinion and expression, Frank La Rue, Promotion and protection of the right to freedom of opinion and expression, UN Doc. A/66/290 of 10 August 2011, http://www.ohchr.org/Documents/Issues/Opinion/A.66.290.pdf, para. 10.

[8] Ibid.

human-to-object (e.g. through mobile communication devices, such as smartphone), and object-to-object (e.g. smart cars or appliances) interactions.[9] It has developed into, in the words of the European Court of Human Rights (ECtHR) in the 2015 *Cengiz and Others v. Turkey* judgment, "one of the principal means by which individuals exercise their right to freedom to receive and impart information and ideas, providing as it does essential tools for participation in activities and discussions concerning political issues and issues of general interest."[10] Or as the German Federal Court of Justice (BGH) confirmed: the internet is of "central importance" for daily life and non-access "significantly impacts the material foundation of living."[11]

To many, the internet has become a central feature of their lives. The average German internet user is online between 196 and 214 minutes a day, depending on age.[12] Globally, by the end of 2019, more than half of the world's population was online.[13] In developed countries like Iceland and Finland, internet penetration is inching toward 100 percent. There is, however, still a substantial digital divide between North America and Europe (with internet penetration rates of 89.4% and 87.7%, respectively) and Africa and Asia (39.6% and 54.2%, respectively).[14] With just over half (54.2%) of its people connected, Asia amounts to half (50.7%) of the world's internet users. As internet penetration and use in Europe and North America can no longer grow substantially, the majority of new internet users will come from Africa and Asia.

2.1.3 Internet and "Internet(s)"

"The internet is that medium through which your e-mail is delivered and web pages get published," wrote Harvard law professor Lawrence Lessig in a definition of the internet, which resonates with most users, "[i]t's what you use to order books on Amazon […]."[15] Less functionally, the internet can be described as a network of *inter*connected computer *net*works (hence the term *internet*). According to one standard definition, the internet is "[a] global computer network providing a variety of information and communication facilities, consisting of interconnected networks using standardized communication protocols."[16] With a view to its technical DNA,[17] Mueller, Mathiason, and Klein have defined

[9] Cf. Ian Brown and Christopher T. Marsden, *Regulating Code. Good Governance and Better Regulation in the Information Age* (Cambridge: MIT Press, 2013), xi.

[10] ECtHR, *Cengiz and Others v. Turkey*, judgment of December 1, 2015, application nos. 48226/10 and 14027/11, paras. 49 and 52.

[11] BGH, judgment of January 24, 2013 – III ZR 98/12, 22 ("Die Nutzbarkeit des Internets ist ein Wirtschaftsgut, dessen ständige Verfügbarkeit seit längerer Zeit […] auch im privaten Bereich für die eigenwirtschaftliche Lebenshaltung typischerweise von zentraler Bedeutung ist und bei dem sich eine Funktionsstörung als solche auf die materiale Grundlage der Lebenshaltung signifikant auswirkt") (translation by the author).

[12] Statista, Internetnutzung in Deutschland (2019), https://de.statista.com/themen/2033/internetnutzung-in-deutschland.

[13] Internet Usage Statistics, World Internet Users and 2019 Population Stats, Internet User Distribution, Mid-Year 2019, http://www.Internetworldstats.com/stats.htm.

[14] Ibid.

[15] Lawrence Lessig, *Code: Version 2.0* (New York: Basic Books, 2007), 9.

[16] Oxford English Dictionary, s.v. "Internet" (2018), https://en.oxforddictionaries.com/definition/internet.

[17] In German, DNA (deoxyribonucleic acid), the biomolecule carrying the genes, is abbreviated DNS (Desoxyribonukleinsäure). Thus, in German, the internet's "DNS" is actually its "DNS"—the domain name system ensuring unique assignation of numbers and their translation into and from names.

the internet as "the global data communication capability realized by the interconnection of public and private telecommunication networks using [different protocols]."[18] Lessig's definition looks at what we can "do" with the internet, its function, while Mueller et al.'s definition teases out what the internet technically "is," its essence.[19] Both dimensions—the internet as a borderless technological information and communication, empowerment, and consumption facility and the internet as communication capability running on kinetic artifacts—are relevant for a study of the norms to be applied to its governance and its uses.

In the network of interconnected networks, a certain standard protocol (TCP/IP) is used to communicate. The connected networks are private and public. They are linked to each other through different technologies. When we say that we "go on the internet," we usually mean that we send emails, open our browsers to access a page or a search engine on the World Wide Web (WWW), use a hyperlink that connects one website to another, post a status update on a social media site, conduct research in an online repository of academic papers, or play an online game. Mail programs, the WWW, online gaming systems including virtual realities are layered on top of the internet as services of it. The internet enables them, and its running—broadly speaking—is the precondition for their functioning.[20]

Essentially, the internet is hardware-based data-transfer capability running software that ensures *inter*connectivity, that is connectivity between largely privately owned and operated networks. The internet needs physical infrastructure to run, but it does not "consist" (only) of it. However, without the physical infrastructure the internet would not be able to function.[21] The protection *of* the internet is therefore connected to the protection of certain *critical internet resources* (CIRs), but also encompasses protection of its content (information and communication interchange, services, etc.). But the protection *of* the internet also includes protecion *from* the internet, i.e. the dangers of misuses of the internet including dangers for CIRs.

The internet is *not* like the "environment" or the "sea" in that it was created by humans with a distinct purpose in mind. It is not an entity that, if left alone, would thrive according to natural laws. It is made up of a majority of privately owned networks, based on data flows premised upon privately owned cloud-based services offered by private companies, providing applications and social media channels for content consumption and production under private terms and service. All this happens within a frame governed by national law, as states have the sovereign right to regulate for their territory, and international law, applicable to any issues transcending borders. This brief description already hints at the conceptual challenges involved in developing a normative order of the internet.

[18] Milton Mueller, John Mathiason, and Hans Klein, "The Internet and Global Governance: Principles and Norms for a New Regime," Global Governance 13 (2007), 237–54 (245). Protocols include "Internet Protocol (IP), Transmission Control Protocol (TCP), and the other protocols required to implement IP internetworking on a global scale, such as DNS [domain name system] and packet routing protocols" (ibid.). See also John Mathiason, *Internet Governance: The New Frontier of Global Institutions* (London: Routledge, 2008), 11.

[19] Karl Auerbach, "Deconstructing Internet Governance" (2004), http://www.cavebear.com/archive/rw/deconstructing-internet-governance-ITU-Feb26-27-2004.htm uses an even narrower definition: "The internet is the open system that carries IP packets from source IP addresses to destination IP addresses."

[20] Technically, the global Internet would not need to function for services to work. Each company or state could create their own "Internet." Yet calls for "national Internets" or "independent Internets" usually translate into calls for more national oversight or independence of backbone cables managed by the US or US companies or running over US territory.

[21] Cf. Milton Mueller, John Mathiason, and Hans Klein, "The Internet and Global Governance: Principles and Norms for a New Regime," Global Governance 13 (2007), 237–54 (244).

When referring to the internet as the network of networks, the "I" is capitalized more often than not (54%). Though mostly British publications, such as the *Economist*, tend toward the lower-case "i,"[22] most US publications (like *Time, Associated Press* (*AP*), and the *New York Times*[23]) do not.[24] Would capitalizing the "I" in "internet" reflect historic usage (like "States" and "Governments")[25] and assign an ethereal or agent-like function to the "internet"? Rather, capitalizing "Internet" when referring to the global information and communication exchange facility is linguistically correct because it distinguishes between *the Internet* and the internet(s). The *Internet* is made up of many smaller interconnected networks, which are also *internets*. The internet protocol suite was aimed at building a global interconnection out of the various networks, an internetwork, or internet. As an IBM publication points out, "when written with a capital 'I', the 'Internet' refers to the worldwide set of interconnected networks. Therefore, the *Internet* is an *internet*, but the reverse does not apply."[26] In this reading, the *Internet* thus consists of many internets and is an internet itself.[27] Nevertheless, this study will not capitalize *internet* when referring to the global communication facility, as this gives a collection of hardware-based artifacts an ethereal quality and positions it as an actant in its own right.

2.2 Criticality of the Internet

2.2.1 Conditions of its Functionality

Protecting the internet is essential to our way of life. As Laura DeNardis puts it, "[n]o less than economic security, modern social life, culture, political discourse, and national security are at stake in keeping the internet globally operational and secure."[28] This raises the question of what exactly needs to be protected when protecting "the internet."

The internet's functioning is premised on kinetic and non-kinetic resources: cables, data centers, and working internet Exchange Points, and a functioning naming and addressing

[22] Cf. Tony Long, "It's Just the 'internet' Now," August 16, 2004, https://www.wired.com/2004/08/its-just-the-internet-now/´; Economist, *Style Guide* (London: Profile Books, 2005), 46, https://bordeure.files.wordpress.com/2008/11/the-economist-style-guide.pdf.

[23] Philip B. Corbett, "The Latest Style," *New York Times*, October 29, 2013, http://afterdeadline.blogs.nytimes.com/2013/10/29/the-latest-style/?php=true&_type=blogs&_r=0 (summing up updates in the *New York Times Manual of Style and Usage:* "we'll lowercase website and make it one word. [...] But the Internet remains uppercase, in line with the most common current practice in the United. States").

[24] Though this may change in the future, see Katherine Connor Martin, "Should You Capitalize the Word Internet?" Oxford Dictionaries Blog, April 5, 2016, https://blog.oxforddictionaries.com/2016/04/05/should-you-capitalize-internet (predicting that the British English preference for "internet" will prevail, as did the British English preference for "email" over "e-mail").

[25] Language reflects power relations. This author previously made the case for not adhering to the traditional capitalization of states as "States" and governments as "Governments" because it seemed to be as a bow to the traditional assignation of quasi-religious significance to them—just as "He" and "Him" are capitalized in English when referring to God (who is also capitalized): an "international legal order that, figuratively, capitalizes states, and is supported by international legal scholarship that reflects this emphasis and focuses on the protection of states, and the status quo, [...] cannot function as a framework conducive to a holistic assessment of the position of individuals in international law or the interposition of states" (Matthias C. Kettemann, *The Future of Individuals in International Law. Lessons from International Internet Law* (Utrecht: Eleven Publishing, 2013), 8). This applies to the "internet" vs. "Internet" debate as well.

[26] Lydia Parziale, David T. Britt, Chuck Davis, Jason Forrester, Wie Liu, Carolyn Matthews, and Nicolas Rosselot, *TCP/IP Tutorial and Technical Overview*, 8th edn. (IBM: IBM Redbooks, 2006), 4.

[27] Cf. also the RFC 675 (Vinton Cerf, Yogen Dalal, Carl Sunshine), Specification of Internet Transmission Control Program, December 1974, http://tools.ietf.org/html/rfc675.

[28] Laura DeNardis, *The Global War for Internet Governance* (New Haven: Yale University Press, 2014), 17.

system based on technical standards that ensure successful information interchange through routing and interconnections. Given all this, the internet can "work." Protection of and from the internet must therefore necessarily encompass all these elements. However, ensuring basic infrastructure and fundamental non-kinetic elements of the internet is only one aspect of the internet's *functionality*. The functionality of the internet is deeply connected to users' ability to communicate effectively, in realization of their applicable human rights and in fulfillment of their right to human development.[29] Therefore, ensuring a *functioning* (working) internet (that is an internet where data packets are sent and received) is not enough.

This argument runs parallel to the one developed by UN Special Rapporteur on Freedom of Expression, Frank La Rue, in his 2011 report. He distinguished between two dimensions of access: *physical* access to the internet and access to *content* on the internet.[30] Having the infrastructure (cables, computers, routers) necessary to access the internet in place is not enough. The right to internet access, according to the Special Rapporteur, includes access to content "without any restrictions except in a few limited cases permitted under international human rights law."[31] Table 2.1 stratifies the two dimensions of protection:

Table 2.1 Dichotomies in the Discourse on the Protection of the Internet

Comparative Vector	Internet's Physicality	Internet's Intangibles
Internet access as a modus comparandi	infrastructurally premised access to the internet	access to internet content
Infrastructure	physical infrastructure	normative infrastructure
Primary normative sphere	private regulation	public regulation (frame) private regulation (spaces)
Vulnerability	primarily *technical*: physical infrastructure; institution-level outage; Domain Name System; switching-level infrastructure	primarily *institutional*: network management disruptions; application-level blocking; protocol-level blocking; financial and transactional services outages
Possible attack vector	undersea cables, power systems; ISP service termination; cellular service disruption; DNS filtering, registries, and registrars; routing infrastructure, IXPs	Distributed Denial of Service (DDos) attacks, Deep Packet Inspection (DPI) filtering; email, social media sites, Skype; VoIP, HTTP; credit card transactions, payment systems

2.2.2 Internet Integrity

The internet's protection thus encompasses both its physicality and its intangible assets. However, governing and regulating its physicality (e.g. by protecting underwater cables in international

[29] Therefore its protection lies in the common interest, as this study will show at 2.4.

[30] Cf. Report of the Special Rapporteur on the promotion and protection of the right to freedom of opinion and expression, Frank La Rue, UN Doc. A/HRC/17/27 of 16 May 2011, para. 3 (and chapters IV (access to content) and V (availability of infrastructure) of the report).

[31] Ibid., para. 3.

waters) and its intangible assets (e.g. by endangering internet freedom by making internet intermediaries liable for lèse-majesté or hateful comments by angry readers) demands a nuanced approach. At the same time any protection *of* the internet must encompass protection *from* the internet, that is protection of states and society from uses and misuses of the internet.

Most examples of national internet shutdowns show that Internet Service Providers (ISPs) were technically able to cause a blackout (*technical* vulnerability) and that the legal system did not contain enough procedural or substantive safeguards to stop the executive order from being implemented (*institutional* vulnerability).[32]

National internet policies are limited by international legal rules that influence, for instance, under which circumstances content can be censored.[33] This runs counter to the normative narratives of sovereignty-oriented states, who see both the internet's physical infrastructure as far as it can be controlled by states and the internet's content (produced by and consumed from that state) as falling under sovereign regulatory powers.[34] It is at these friction points of internet regulation that the concept of normative order, as detailed below, will offer normative solutions. Protecting the security, stability, robustness, resilience, and functionality of the internet—briefly: its *integrity*—can only be ensured through an approach that includes regulation of technical artifacts *and* a functioning legal system.

2.2.3 The Internet as/and Critical Infrastructure

Even though internet access seems like a given in most of today's developed societies, it is "delicate in many ways, with its unowned character threatened from many quarters."[35] What both the kinetic and the non-kinetic elements of the internet have in common is that they are considered "critical" for our society. The notion of critical infrastructure includes "[s]ensitive elements of a larger ecosystem, encompassing the public and private sectors and society at large."[36] In a directive on the identification and designation of European critical infrastructures the European Union (EU) defined critical infrastructure as

> an asset, system or part thereof located in Member States which is essential for the maintenance of vital societal functions, health, safety, security, economic or social well-being of people, and the disruption or destruction of which would have a significant impact in a Member State as a result of the failure to maintain those functions.[37]

[32] Cf. Matthias C. Kettemann, "Das Internet als internationales Schutzgut: Entwicklungsperspektiven des Internetvölkerrechts anlässlich des Arabischen Frühlings," ZaöRV 72 (2012), 469–82. On shutdowns, see Internet Society, Internet Shutdowns Are Not a Solution to Africa's Challenges (June 2017), https://www.internetsociety.org/blog/2017/06/internet-shutdowns-are-not-a-solution-to-africas-challenges.

[33] Cf. Internet Society, Perspectives on Internet Content Blocking: An Overview (2017), https://www.internetsociety.org/resources/doc/2017/internet-content-blocking.

[34] Cf. Ministry of Foreign Affairs of the People's Republic of China, International Code of Conduct for Information Security, submission to NetMundial, http://content.netmundial.br/contribution/international-code-of-conduct-for-information-security/67. People's Republic of China, State Council, The Internet in China, June 8, 2010, http://www.china.org.cn/government/whitepaper/node_7093508.htm, sect. I.

[35] Jonathan Zittrain, "No, Barack Obama Isn't Handing Control of the Internet over to China," *The New Republic*, March 24, 2014.

[36] Dave Clemente, "Cyber Security and Global Interdependence: What Is Critical?" Chatham House Programme Report (2013), http://www.chathamhouse.org/publications/papers/view/189645.

[37] EU Council Directive 2008/114/EC of 8 December 2008 on the identification and designation of European critical infrastructures and the assessment of the need to improve their protection, OJ L 345/75, 23 December 2008.

Though the internet is not "located" in any single member state, key kinetic elements relevant for the stable running of the internet are. Further, the maintenance of vital state functions—such as energy security—without a stable and secure information and communication infrastructure is very difficult in today's highly technical and interconnected world. The internet can therefore be understood, *first*, as highly critical for other critical infrastructure resources, and, *second*, as technically necessary for the running of ICT systems and thus foundational for critical infrastructures. This duality of the internet's criticality is evident in the EU's definition of critical infrastructural resources as encompassing "ICT systems that are critical infrastructures for themselves or that are essential for the operation of critical infrastructures [...]."[38] The core data centers, internet Exchange Points, and intercontinental cables are included in the notion of critical *information* infrastructure.

Protecting the security, stability, robustness, resilience, and functionality (thus: the integrity) of the internet is also a question of protecting the infrastructure. Both an oversecuritization of infrastructure protection and a lack of sufficient protection can result in insufficient protection and may violate state obligations. In a 2012 resolution by the European Parliament (EP), the need for critical information infrastructure protection was explained by the importance of ICTs "to deploy their full capacity for advancing the economy and society," which can only happen when "users have trust and confidence in their security and resilience, and if existing legislation on matters such as data privacy and intellectual property rights is enforced effectively in the internet environment."[39] This important link between infrastructure protection from a *security* perspective and from a *human rights* perspective[40] lies at the core of the role of the internet as a tool to enhance human development.

We have thus established that protecting the internet is essential for protecting critical infrastructure and critical information infrastructure and that the internet is also, within limits, critical infrastructure. However, clearly not every website, server, or data center is critical information infrastructure. We can differentiate between the critical and non-critical elements of the internet's infrastructure by defining the CIRs.

2.2.4 Critical Internet Resources

2.2.4.1 Concept and Vulnerabilities

What needs to be protected for the internet to function effectively is made visible through the thought experiment of "destroying the internet."[41] Such an attempt would be impossible because of the multiple redundancies built into the infrastructure. Nevertheless, if one were to entertain the notion, the following three steps would be necessary: cutting the transcontinental internet

[38] European Commission, Green Paper on a European Programme for Critical Infrastructure Protection, COM(2005) 576 final, 17 November 2005, 19.

[39] European Parliament resolution of 12 June 2012 on critical information infrastructure protection—achievements and next steps: towards global cyber-security (2011/2284(INI)), http://www.europarl.europa.eu/sides/getDoc.do?type=TA&reference=P7-TA-2012-0237&language=EN, para. A.

[40] Following the human security approach, security and human rights "approaches" should actually be the same perspective: Cf. Shahrbanou Tadjbakhsh, "In Defense of the Broad View of Human Security," in Mary Martin and Taylor Owen (eds.), *Routledge Handbook on Human Security* (London: Routledge, 2013), 43–56; and Gerd Oberleitner, "Human Security: Idea, Policy and Law," in ibid., 219–30.

[41] Sam Biddle, "How to Destroy the Internet," *Gizmodo*, May 23, 2012, http://gizmodo.com/5912383/how-to-destroy-the-internet.

cables, disabling the root servers, and destroying the data centers containing the physical data. The cables, the actual root servers, and the data centers are aspects of the internet's physicality and need to be physically protected. The larger ones are doubtless CIRs. Natural events, foraging, pipeline building, or fishing regularly damages overland and underwater cables. A 2006 earthquake in southern Taiwan led to underwater slides that broke nine fiber optic cables, which led to substantial connectivitiy problems in the proximity of the event. Usually, however, a multitude of cables ensuring connection redundancies allows rerouting.[42]

The most effective "kill-switch" for the internet thus lies less in its technical infrastructure alone than in a combination of control over physical infrastructure, such as servers, and institutional-legal authority.[43] In a study of the "dark side" of internet governance, Laura DeNardis identifies eight levels of control of the internet where interruption, unintentional or not, can take place.[44] These can be stratified according to four key aspects internet integrity is meant to ensure: the internet's basic functionality; access through a working addressing and routing system; communication and information through applications based on protocols ("use"); and transactions or transactionary functionality (see Table 2.2).

As demonstrated before, for the internet to function properly, non-kinetic internet resources need to be protected as well. CIRs are more than key cables, root servers, and data centers. They include names and numbers (numerical addresses)[45] and the addressing

Table 2.2 Internet Vulnerabilities

Goal	Control Question	Vulnerability	Attack Vector
Functionality	Does the internet work?	physical infrastructure	undersea cables, power systems
		institution-level outage	ISP service termination, cellular service disruption
Access	Can I access specific sites?	Domain Name System	DNS filtering, registries and registrars
		switching-level infrastructure	routing infrastructure, IXPs
Use	Is my content transmitted?	network management disruptions	DDos attacks, DPI filtering
		application-level blocking	email, social media sites, Skype
		protocol-level blocking	VoIP, HTTP
Transactions	Can I pay for services?	financial and transactional services outages	credit card transactions, payment systems

Based on Figure 9.1 "Inter Control Points Susceptible to Intentional or Unintentional Disruptions" (DeNardis (2014), 209).

[42] UNEP/WCMC, Submarine cables and the oceans: connecting the world, January 2009, http://www.iscpc.org/publications/ICPC-UNEP_Report.pdf, 42.
[43] Cf. Laura DeNardis, *The Global War for Internet Governance* (New Haven: Yale University Press, 2014), 211.
[44] Ibid., 209.
[45] Laura DeNardis, "Internet Points of Control as Global Governance," CIGI Internet Governance Paper No. 2 (2013), http://www.cigionline.org/publications/2013/8/internet-points-of-control-global-governance, 3.

system that ensures they are properly resolved (i.e. decoded) to facilitate human use and interaction. Thus 199.59.148.10 becomes twitter.com, and vice-versa.

Other studies entertain broader notions of CIRs, including e.g. "policies supporting trust" and "affordable end-point access devices."[46] These notions, however important for a development-oriented conception of the internet, are too vague to enter the protective sphere of CIRs in the sense used in this study. Nevertheless, there are two further aspects of the internet that need protection and coordination: technical standards and the routing system and the administration of interconnections. Together with the management of the addressing system, they are non-kinetic CIRs. It is with regard to them that key governance decisions are made, and they have to be part of any meaningful conception of a normative order of the internet. The control over these decisions, and the resources themselves, is at the center of the debate over the governance and regulation of the internet. Their analysis will also serve as an introduction into the key technical actors of internet governance.

2.2.4.2 Addressing System

The two elements of the addressing system on the internet are the names and numbers making up Internet Protocol (IP) addresses and the Domain Name System, which translates the names (for the use of humans) to binary addresses (used by computers) and back. The IPv4 (Internet Protocol version 4) standard assigns 32 bits—0s and 1s—to a binary address which, when written in decimal form, becomes four groups of numbers, such as 199.59.148.10. The newer IPv6 (Internet Protocol version 6) substantially increases the number of available addresses by increasing the bits assigned per address from 32 to 128. Users do not have to enter the decimal form of the binary address, but—because the DNS translates between humans and computer—can use the alphanumeric equivalent of the address, such as ejil.org.

Just as having two houses with identical numbers on the same street address would lead to confusion with the postal services, the internet is premised upon unique identifiers. Each IP address is linked to one addressee (a computer or a handheld device, for example, but also, in the internet of things, a freezer or a pair of smart glasses).[47] Allocating IP addresses (actually IP address blocks) needs to be coordinated to ensure that no number is assigned twice. IP address blocks have to be distributed to regional registrars who further distribute the numbers to ISPs. Further, the management of Autonomous System Numbers (ASNs) that are necessary for other networks to become network operators have to be coordinated, as do top-level domains (TLDs), both country code (ccTLDs, such as .at or .de) and generic (gTLDs, such as .com or .org) ones. It is necessary, DeNardis writes, to have "a definitive record of how to resolve names into numbers for each TLD and for the root zone file containing the master, most centralized list that dictates how each TLD maps to binary addresses."[48]

This task is performed by ICANN, the Internet Corporation for Assigned Names and Numbers, a not-for-profit entity incorporated under Californian law, and its entities and affiliates. The key coordination, administration, and allocation tasks regarding protocols,

[46] Center for Democracy and Technology (CDT), "What Does 'Governance' Mean? What are 'Critical Internet Resources'?" November 2007, https://www.cdt.org/files/pdfs/20071114Internet%20gov.pdf.
[47] Samuel Greengard, *The Internet of Things* (Cambridge, MA/London: MIT Press, 2015).
[48] Laura DeNardis, *The Global War for Internet Governance* (New Haven: Yale University Press, 2014), 17.

DNS root zone management, and internet numbering resources are ICANN's so-called "IANA (Internet Assigned Numbers Authority)" functions.[49] These include management of the DNS Root Zone (and assigning ccTLDs and gTLDs), the coordination of the global internet protocol and autonomous server number spaces, including allocations made to Regional Internet Registries (RIRs), and acting as a repository for protocol names and numbers used in internet protocols.[50]

Public Technical Identifiers,[51] an ICANN affiliate established to provide the IANA functions on behalf of ICANN, assumed responsibility for the operational aspects of coordinating the internet's unique identifiers in October 2016. ICANN used to be the *operator* of the IANA functions "on behalf of the United States Government, through a [procurement] contract"[52] with the National Telecommunications and Information Administration (NTIA) of the United States Department of Commerce (DOC).[53] The last zero-cost contract was terminated by NTIA, which asked ICANN to develop a system to replace NTIA's stewardship role and enhance ICANN accountability toward the "global multistakeholder community,"[54] a vague term that has been only imperfectly clarified through later practice. ICANN submitted two proposals regarding its technical performance of the IANA functions[55] and enhancements of its accountability.[56] The intricate accountability mechanisms are enshrined in ICANN's bylaws.[57] ICANN's chief mission (also with regard to IANA functions) is to "coordinate the development and implementation of policies [...] developed through a bottom-up consensus-based multistakeholder process and designed to ensure the stable and secure operation of the internet's unique names systems."[58] Note the continued commitment to "multistakeholderism," which is characteristic of the internet governance discourse field. Unfortunately, often these commitments are not realized by a truly effective "consensus-based multistakeholder process" as a tool to develop policies because power imbalances within norm-making processes and standardization organizations continue to undermine commitments to the inclusion of all relevant actors.

The transition of the responsibility of all functions related to the internet's unique identifier system to ICANN was a big step. The IANA functions include running the DNS root, which

[49] Cf. IANA, Introducing IANA, http://www.iana.org.

[50] Ibid. See further, ICANN, The IANA Functions, December 18, 2015, https://www.icann.org/en/system/files/files/iana-functions-18dec15-en.pdf.

[51] Public Technical Identifiers, http://pti.icann.org.

[52] Affirmation of Commitments by the United States Department of Commerce and the Internet Corporation for Assigned Names and Numbers, September 30, 2009, http://www.icann.org/en/about/agreements/aoc/affirmation-of-commitments-30sep09-en.htm.

[53] NTIA, Commerce Department Awards Contract for Management of Key Internet Functions to ICANN, July 2, 2012, http://www.ntia.doc.gov/press-release/2012/commerce-department-awards-contract-management-key-internet-functions-icann.

[54] NTIA, NTIA Finds IANA Stewardship Transition Proposal Meets Criteria to Complete Privatization June 9, 2016, https://www.ntia.doc.gov/press-release/2016/iana-stewardship-transition-proposal-meets-criteria-complete-privatization.

[55] ICANN IANA Stewardship Transition Coordination Group (ICG), Proposal to Transition the Stewardship of the IANA Functions from the U.S. Commerce Department's NTIA to the Global Multistakeholder Community, March 2016, https://www.icann.org/en/system/files/files/iana-stewardship-transition-proposal-10mar16-en.pdf.

[56] ICANN CCWG Accountability, Supplemental Final Proposal on Work Stream 1 Recommendations, February 2016, https://www.icann.org/en/system/files/files/ccwg-accountability-supp-proposal-work-stream-1-recs-23feb16-en.pdf.

[57] ICANN, Bylaws for Internet Corporation for Assigned Names and Numbers, as amended July 22, 2017, https://www.icann.org/resources/pages/governance/bylaws-en.

[58] Ibid., section 1.1 (i).

encompasses the root zone file and the root name servers.[59] The authoritative root servers (where the root zone file is first uploaded) distribute the information on to thirteen root name servers who copy the file. Before the transition in 2016, any change in the authoritative root zone had to be authorized by the US government. Other root servers then cache the authoritative root to reduce dependence. The number of root servers is limited to thirteen, but two of them are distributed using "anycast" and have multiple "instances" amounting to hundreds of copies of the root which ensure quicker access for users worldwide.[60]

Though formally allowing the US to exercise geo-strategic power over the internet, the US control of the DNS was theoretical. The US could (have) order(ed) ICANN to delete a ccTLD in the master zone file. However, there were a number of technical ways for a concerned country to limit the impact of such a step. Internationally, it would have ruined the US reputation as a responsible steward of the DNS and would have further been ineffective as other root servers, especially those located outside of the US, would either not have copied the altered master root or reverted to cached versions.[61]

The US-centrality of key internet resource management is only somewhat alleviated by ICANN's accountability to the "global multistakeholder community" and its formal commitment to "multistakeholder" decision-making. In practice, however, the inclusion of all relevant actors in decision-making processes is complicated by high levels of entry due to the technicality of discussions, lack of epistemic authority by non-ICANN-related norm entrepreneurs, and simple economic reasons. More effective than mere commitments to vague notions such as "multistakeholderism" is the allocation by ICANN of local address management to the RIRs.[62] The RIRs distribute their tasks (and their address spaces) to local and national internet registries that assign IP addresses to ISPs who then assign them to their customers. The contractual and non-contractual framework underlying the DNS and ICANN's relationship with other registries is highly complex—both with regard to the types of normative mechanisms and the quantity of mechanisms used.[63] ICANN also accredits registrars to manage TLDs. These can sell domain names further on, either directly to consumers or to registries.[64]

2.2.4.3 Technical Standards

The internet's universality is premised upon universal standards and protocols that ensure frictionless use of software on hardware. They are, as DeNardis notes, "written specifications

[59] Mueller, Milton, *Ruling the Root: Internet Governance and the Taming of Cyberspace* (Cambridge: MIT Press, 2002), 47. Historically, the key coordination functions regarding the address space were performed by DARPA and the University of Southern California (and originally by one person, Jon Postel), but in 1999 the coordination was handed to ICANN by the NTIA.

[60] These servers are run by private and public entities: Verisign, Inc. (two), University of Southern California, Cogent Communications, University of Maryland, NASA, Internet Systems Consortium, Defense Information Agency, US Army Research lab, Netnod, RIPE NCC, ICANN, and the WIDE Project. Cf. Root Servers, http://www.root-servers.org.

[61] Froomkin, Michael, "Almost Free: An Analysis of ICANN's 'Affirmation of Commitments,'" Journal of Telecommunications and High Technology Law 9 (2011), 187–233 (219).

[62] AFRINIC (Africa, portions of the Indian Ocean), APNIC (parts of Asia and Oceania), ARIN (Canada, US, Caribbean, and North Atlantic Islands), LACNIC (Latin America, parts of the Caribbean), and RIPE NCC (Europe, Middle East, Central Asia).

[63] Cf. Emily M. Weitzenboeck, "Hybrid net: the regulatory framework of ICANN and the DNS," International Journal of Law and Information Technology 22 (2014) 1, 49–73 (62) (arguing for the applicability of Ost and van de Kerchove's mesh (or network) theory of regulation).

[64] ICANN, Statement of Registrar Accreditation Policy (.com, .net, and .org top-level domains), http://www.icann.org/en/resources/registrars/accreditation/policy-statement.

dictating how to develop software and hardware to be compatible with any other type of software and hardware that also adheres to these specifications."[65] Some of the best known and most often used standards are HTTP, the HyperText Transfer Protocol, and VoIP, Voice over IP. The introduction of the TCP/IP suite was central to the evolution of the internet. A key element of standards is that they ensure interoperability.[66] Without interoperability, devices from different manufacturers or devices running different operating systems or applications would not be able to communicate. Much of the internet's economic ecosystem is premised upon interconnectedness and interoperability.[67] Defining standards ensuring interoperability thus has substantial implications for the way information is transmitted and communication takes place.

The standards are interesting normatively because they are authored and implemented not by states or their national standardization bodies but by international, private, non-profit standard-setting technical entities, such as the Internet Engineering Task Force (IETF). Today, the IETF is part—actually an "organized activity"[68]—of ISOC, the Internet Society, founded in 1992.[69] As discussed in more detail below,[70] the IETF is an influential body as it proposes, accepts by consensus, and applies standards, including in recent years a number of them with relevance to public policy issues, including Request for Comments (RFC) 8280 on Research into Human Rights Protocol Considerations.[71] Before IETF proposals crystallize into standards, they often begin as "memos." Two current memos, *Freedom of Association on the Internet*[72] and *On the Politics of Standards*,[73] as well an intensive discussion on how to transcend the nomenclature of controlling/controlled components in software engineering ("master/slave") show that the IETF understands itself as beyond a technicity-oriented normative focus. The master/slave terminology was only recently removed from the popular programming language Python and some years earlier by programming languages Drupal and Django.[74]

The World Wide Web Consortium (W3C) is responsible for establishing standards for the Web. Founded by WWW inventor and programmer of the HTML (HyperText Markup Language), Tim Berners-Lee, the W3C adopts by consensus, in a process in which all actors can participate, Web standards (called recommendations) related to web design and applications (e.g. rendering of web pages, internationalizing them, and making them more

[65] Laura DeNardis, *The Global War for Internet Governance* (New Haven: Yale University Press, 2014), 8.

[66] Cf. John Palfrey and Urs Gasser, *Interop: The Promise and Perils of Highly Interconnected Systems* (New York: Basic Books, 2012). They argue that at the institutional level of interoperability, legal systems must engage effectively (6). International private law, then, could be considered as an interoperability standard (for legal systems).

[67] Law can be responsible for creating beneficial forms of interoperability, creating fair market rules through interoperability, and constraining unwanted interoperability effects, such as a race to the bottom in privacy and security standards (cf. Palfrey and Gasser (2012), 88).

[68] Cf. Internet Engineering Task Force, http://www.ietf.org.

[69] ISOC oversees the Internet Architecture Board (IAB) that directs both the IETF and the Internet Research Task Force (IRTF). The Internet Engineering Steering Group (IESG) is responsible for managing IETF activities and the Internet standards process technically. ISOC has 65,000 personal members, 100 chapters and 145 organization members. Cf. Internet Society, Our Members, http://www.internetsociety.org/who-we-are/our-members.

[70] See 2.4.4.

[71] Internet Research Task Force (IRTF), RFC 8280, Research into Human Rights Protocol Considerations, https://tools.ietf.org/html/rfc8280.

[72] IETF, Memo: Freedom of Association on the Internet (2018), https://datatracker.ietf.org/doc/draft-tenoever-hrpc-association.

[73] IETF, Memo: On the Politics of Standards (2018), https://datatracker.ietf.org/doc/draft-tenoever-hrpc-political.

[74] Daniel Oberhaus, "'Master/Slave' Terminology Was Removed from Python Programming Language," *Motherboard*, September 13, 2018, https://motherboard.vice.com/en_us/article/8x7akv/masterslave-terminology-was-removed-from-python-programming-language.

accessible to people with different abilities), web of devices-applications (including usage of Web technology in cars and consumer goods), web architecture, and semantic web (web of data).[75] A further standard-setter with relevance for internet traffic is IEEE, the Institute of Electrical and Electronics Engineers, which is responsible for setting certain ethernet Local Area Network (LAN) standards and Wi-Fi specifications.

2.2.4.4 Routing and Interconnections

Further critical kinetic elements of the internet are the autonomous systems or collections of routers. Each system is identified by a unique number (its ASN), which ensures that traffic reaches its destination. It is between routers (or rather collections of routers, and then routers) that packets of information are transmitted. It is ICANN's responsibility to ensure that the ASNs are properly registered for an autonomous system to be identified. There are, however, no formal agreements between the managers of autonomous systems and ICANN. Interconnection is based largely on trust between operators of networks. Physically, networks connect at large shared Internet Exchange Points (IXPs). The costs of managing the IXPs are not settled but rather depend on market forces and the relevance of companies and ISPs within specific regions. Sometimes this "peering" is settlement-free, sometimes there are paid (transit) arrangements.[76] Within autonomous systems, so-called Interior Gateway Protocols regulate routing. Between systems, Border Gateway Protocols (BGPs) fulfill this function.

2.3 Common Interest and the Internet

2.3.1 Protection of and from the Internet as a Common Interest?

We have already established what aspects of the internet need to be protected (2.2). We now need to discuss whether protecting these kinetic and non-kinetic resources, including the normative infrastructure, lie in the common interest. If they do, then there is a strong prima facie case to be made for the necessity of a coherent normative order. First, we will look at how safeguarding an entity, good, or commons becomes a "common interest' in international law and what consequences follow from such designation.

There is no closed list of global common interests. Due to the state-orientation of traditional international law, the development of international legal protection regimes of the common interest has progressed only slowly[77] between, what Bardo Fassbender argued were, the two normative poles of *Staatsräson* and *Gemeinschaftsbindung*.[78] Under the conditions of today's connected world and the facticity of globalized communication and trade flows, however, pursuing common interests is *Staatsräson*. States that withdraw from the

[75] W3C, W3C standards, https://www.w3.org/standards.

[76] Cf. Laura DeNardis, *The Global War for Internet Governance* (New Haven: Yale University Press, 2014), 12.

[77] Matthias C. Kettemann, "The Common Interest in the Protection of the Internet: An International Legal Perspective," in Wolfgang Benedek, Koen De Feyter, Matthias C. Kettemann, and Christina Voigt (eds.), *The Common Interest in International Law* (Antwerp: Intersentia, 2014), 167–84, from which this section draws.

[78] Bardo Fassbender, "Zwischen Staatsräson und Gemeinschaftsbindung. Zur Gemeinwohlorientierung des Völkerrechts der Gegenwart," in Herfried Münkler and Karsten Fischer (eds.), *Gemeinwohl und Gemeinsinn im Recht: Konkretisierung und Realisierung öffentlicher Interessen* (Berlin: Akademie Verlag, 2002), 231–74.

international arena by putting up figurative and actual walls reduce their impact as actors in the international community. As a growing number of regulatory challenges migrates to the realm of international law, they thereby disenfranchise their citizens and violate their rights to—varying Thomas M. Franck—(global) democratic governance.[79] The transformation of the pursuance of common interest goals by international law from a choice based on narrowly interpreted notions of national interest to an obligation owed both to citizens and to the international community as a whole has evolved gradually, with the League of Nations, and more decisively with the foundation of the UN and the treaty regimes developed under its aegis, but has gathered substantial momentum in the second half of the last century. The protection of common interest values has become essential to international law, from peace, human rights, human dignity, and equality of men and women to justice and social and economic progress.[80] It is no coincidence that the preamble of the United Nations Charter forbids the use of force "save in the common interest."[81]

A growing number of references to "common interest," "common responsibilities," "common heritage of mankind," or "common concerns of humanity" have been made both in international legal instruments and in legal literature on internet law over the years. Already in 2006, Artura Seguro-Serrano argued for the installation of a system of "common management" of the "common heritage of mankind" he saw embodied in the communicative potential of the internet and the technology undergirding it and called for the creation of a "centralized, democratically structured international regime [. . .] in order to achieve a legitimate representation" in the process of managing these common resources.[82] The heritage, concerns, and interests described as being "of mankind" or "of humanity" or "common" are not of states alone. The pursuit of these common interests lies in the collective national interests. As put previously, *Gemeinwohlorientierung ist Staatsraison*. Article 6(1) of the UNESCO (United Nations Educational, Scientific, and Cultural Organization) Convention Concerning the Protection of the World Cultural and Natural Heritage, for instance, refers to "the duty of the international community as a whole" to cooperate in safeguarding cultural and natural heritage.[83] But protection takes place not only through treaties but also through ius cogens, customary law, and general principles of international law.

International legal norms of different character and obligatory nature are connected through a common "Gemeinwohlorientierung,"[84] a normatively relevant orientation toward the common good.[85] Fassbender enumerates four categories: ius cogens, erga omnes duties, international crimes, and "constitutional law" of the international community. Today, it is more common to approach "areas" of international law with prominent

[79] Cf. Thomas M. Franck, "The Emerging Right to Democratic Governance," AJIL 86 (1992), 46.

[80] Cf. on the fundamental change from coexistence to cooperation, Wolfgang Friedmann, *The Changing Structure of International Law* (New York: Columbia University Press, 1974).

[81] UN Charter, preamble: "We the Peoples of the United Nations Determined [...] to ensure, by the acceptance of principles and the institution of methods, that armed force shall not be used, save in the common interest, [. . .]."

[82] See already Antonio Segura-Serrano, "Internet Regulation and the Role of International Law," in *Max Planck Yearbook of United Nations Law*, Vol. 10 (The Hague: Brill, 2006), 257–8.

[83] UNESCO, Convention Concerning the Protection of the World Cultural and Natural Heritage (1972), http://whc.unesco.org/en/conventiontext.

[84] Bardo Fassbender, "Zwischen Staatsräson und Gemeinschaftsbindung. Zur Gemeinwohlorientierung des Völkerrechts der Gegenwart," in Herfried Münkler and Karsten Fischer (eds.), *Gemeinwohl und Gemeinsinn im Recht: Konkretisierung und Realisierung öffentlicher Interessen* (Berlin: Akademie Verlag, 2002), 231–74 (242 ff).

[85] For an ethical analysis of the common good, see Donna Dickenson, "The Common Good," in Roger Brownsword, Eloise Scotford, and Karen Yeung (eds.), *Oxford Handbook of Law, Regulation, and Technology* (Oxford: OUP, 2017), 135–52.

common interests. These include the law of the sea (protecting the international seabed), cultural heritage (protection of monuments), development law (sustainable development), climate change law (protecting biological diversity, reducing emission of greenhouse gases, and counteracting man-made influence on climate change), human rights law (safeguarding human dignity), international criminal law (ending impunity for genocide), and non-proliferation law (stopping nuclear proliferation).[86]

Following Fassbender, international law has arrived at a point in its development where pursuing the common interest is the only reasonable answer to its *Sinnfrage*[87] (as opposed to its *Existenzfrage* as a normative order, which is no longer of particular interest[88]). Apart from some voices among the postmodernist authors critical of the transformative power of concepts such as international law, there is no *Gegenentwurf* against an international law oriented toward pursuing common interests.[89] But the pursuit of the common interest is still disorganized and the identification of issues as lying in the common interest, especially in emerging areas of law, is challenging.

In 1998, experts working on behalf of UNESCO posed the question of whether the "United Nations General Assembly [could] affirm the principle of regarding cyberspace as 'the common heritage of humanity' "[90] and thus safeguard it. But only designating cyberspace (or, rather, the internet) as such is not enough. Safeguarding the internet means ensuring that the internet is stable, secure, and functional—that its integrity is ensured. This is premised upon the protection of CIRs, including the kinetic and non-kinetic (and normative) infrastructures, "in the same way that other critical common resources are protected."[91]

The definition of a global common interest is a process driven by international actors. In that process, we have to be aware of the danger of interest capture, namely that a particular group of actors with specific interest wishes to establish their particular interest as a global interest. Though defining the integrity of a network (of interconnected networks) as a common interest would be a first, the case for the protection of and from the internet as a common interest is convincing in light of its functions and role in today's economy and social reality.

The internet's security, stability, robustness, resilience, and functionality—its integrity—are essential to national and international economies, financial systems, transnational communications infrastructure, national defense, national and international energy networks

[86] Cf. the contributions to Wolfgang Benedek, Koen De Feyter, Matthias C. Kettemann, and Christina Voigt (eds.), *The Common Interest in International Law* (Antwerp: Intersentia, 2014).

[87] Bardo Fassbender, "Zwischen Staatsräson und Gemeinschaftsbindung. Zur Gemeinwohlorientierung des Völkerrechts der Gegenwart," in Herfried Münkler and Karsten Fischer (eds.), *Gemeinwohl und Gemeinsinn im Recht: Konkretisierung und Realisierung öffentlicher Interessen* (Berlin: Akademie Verlag, 2002), 231–74 (231).

[88] With few exceptions: Cf. Jack L. Goldsmith and Eric A. Posner, *The Limits of International Law* (New York: OUP, 2005), 188–9. But see Anne van Aaken, "To Do Away with International Law? Some Limits to 'The Limits of International Law'," EJIL (2006), 289–308.

[89] Bardo Fassbender, "Zwischen Staatsräson und Gemeinschaftsbindung. Zur Gemeinwohlorientierung des Völkerrechts der Gegenwart," in Herfried Münkler and Karsten Fischer (eds.), *Gemeinwohl und Gemeinsinn im Recht: Konkretisierung und Realisierung öffentlicher Interessen* (Berlin: Akademie Verlag, 2002), 231–74 (239).

[90] UNESCO, Report of the Experts' Meeting on Cyberspace Law, Monte Carlo, 29–30 September 1998, http://unesdoc.unesco.org/images/0011/001163/116300e.pdf, para. 9.

[91] Council of Europe, Internet governance and critical internet resources, 1st Council of Europe Conference of Ministers Responsible for Media and New Communication Services: A New Notion of Media, May 28–29, 2009, Reykjavik, Iceland, 23.

and electricity grids, commerce, and, of course chiefly, the full realization of all human beings of their human rights.[92]

2.3.2 Relating Internet Integrity to Human Rights

The internet's integrity is important for human rights, human security, and human development. Let us address these claims in turn. The UN Special Rapporteur for freedom of expression, Frank La Rue, in his 2011 report on the impact of the internet on freedom of expression, described the internet as a "catalyst for individuals to exercise their right to freedom of opinion and expression."[93] Freedom of expression on the internet, being intrinsically linked to information, is a key human right of the *information* society. It includes freedom of opinion, of information, of the press and the media, of international communication, of artistic expression, of cultural expression, and of science.[94] But it also facilitates the realization of other human rights, notwithstanding the multiple challenges of human rights protection under conditions of connectedness, internet blackouts, or failures that seriously challenge the realization of human rights. There are important corollary rights that are premised upon exercising free speech on the internet. These include the freedom of assembly and association online, the right to (digital) education, and the right of access to digital knowledge.[95] From all these rights we can also derive a dual right to internet access which is crucial for human rights protection:[96] access to internet content (threatened, inter alia, by filtering) and access to the internet per se (threatened, inter alia, by underdeployment of ICTs).

The importance of access to internet content has been echoed by courts and international organizations.[97] Ensuring universal access, as the Special Rapporteur, La Rue, concluded in his report, "should be a priority for all States."[98] Similarly, the four rapporteurs on freedom of expression made it clear in a joint declaration in 2011 that "giving effect to the right to freedom of expression imposes an obligation on States to promote universal access to the internet."[99] The internet introduces new threat vectors to human rights, but greatly enhances the potential of people to realize their human rights. It is similarly a facilitator for human security.

[92] WSIS, Geneva Declaration of Principles, WSIS-03/GENEVA/ DOC/4-E, 12 December 2003, para. 1.

[93] Report of the Special Rapporteur on the promotion and protection of the right to freedom of opinion and expression, Frank La Rue, UN Doc. A/HRC/17/27 of 16 May 2011, paras. 22, 23.

[94] Wolfgang Benedek, Koen De Feyter, Matthias C. Kettemann, and Christina Voigt (eds.), *The Common Interest in International Law* (Antwerp: Intersentia, 2014), 26–36.

[95] Ibid., 39. See also Mary Rundle and Malcolm Birding, "Filtering and the International System: A Question of Commitment," in Ronald Deibert, John Palfrey, Rafal Rohozinski, and Jonathan Zittrain (eds.), *Access Denied. The Practice and Policy of Global Internet Filtering* (Cambridge, Mass./London: The MIT Press, 2008), 73–102.

[96] Cf. Matthias C. Kettemann, "Das Internet als internationales Schutzgut: Entwicklungsperspektiven des Internetvölkerrechts anlässlich des Arabischen Frühlings," ZaöRV 72 (2012), 469–82, 475 (arguing for a right to access which translates into an institutional protection of the internet).

[97] ECtHR, *Yıldırım v. Turkey* (18 December 2012), application No. 3111/10, and Council of Europe, Parliamentary Assembly, Resolution 1877 on the protection of freedom of expression and information on the Internet and online media (2012).

[98] Special Rapporteur on the promotion and protection of the right to freedom of opinion and expression, Frank La Rue, Promotion and protection of the right to freedom of opinion and expression, UN Doc. A/66/290 of 10 August 2011, http://www.ohchr.org/Documents/Issues/Opinion/A.66.290.pdf, para. 85.

[99] International mechanisms for promoting freedom of expression (1 June 2011), Joint Declaration on Freedom of Expression and the Internet, http://www.osce.org/form/78309.

The concept of human security (connected to but different from the concept of human rights[100]) de-emphasizes state-centricity and reconsiders traditional conceptualizations of states as the (only) providers and referents of security. The United Nations[101] (and the EU[102]) have committed to the concept, which the 2010 Secretary-General's report on human security describes as providing for "people-centred, comprehensive, context-specific and preventive responses" that "focus attention on current and emerging threats."[103] Human security approaches favor bottom-up responses to threats and are targeted at protecting and empowering people and communities.[104] The stability, security, and functionality of the internet is essential for certain aspects of human security. In light of the informationalization of critical infrastructure and the character of the internet as critical information infrastructure in its own right, serious threats to the security, stability, and the functionality of the internet can endanger human security. The concept is also interesting in another light: human security approaches treat state failure[105] and state fragility[106] as serious threats to human security just as securitization by states. Similarly, a lack of regulation or regulatory failure can endanger the internet's integrity just as much as state overreach (such as in the "War against Terror"[107]) and the nationalization of CIRs.

2.3.3 Relating Internet Integrity to Human Development

A similar case can be made with regard to human development (which is interlinked with both the protection of human rights and human security[108]). The General Assembly, in a 2012 resolution on ICTs and development,[109] acknowledged the "positive trends in the global connectivity and affordability of information and communications technologies, in particular the steady increase in internet access to one third of the world's population" and reaffirmed the need to harness the potential of ICTs to promote achieving the Millennium

[100] See Gerd Oberleitner, "Human Security: Idea, Policy and Law," in Mary Martin and Taylor Owen (eds.), *Routledge Handbook on Human Security* (London: Routledge, 2013), 324–5: "Human rights provide the strongest legal underpinning of human security and can give content, structure and clarity to a concept which suffers from analytical uncertainties but the relationship between the political concept of human security and the legal regime of human rights remains precarious and the two are by no means synonymous" (notes omitted).

[101] UN, General Assembly President Calls for New Culture of International Relations, with Principle of Human Security at Its Core, during Day-long Debate, Press Release, UN Doc. GA/10711 (2008) of 22 May 2008, http://www.un.org/News/Press/docs/2008/ga10711.doc.htm.

[102] See Wolfgang Benedek, "Mainstreaming Human Security in United Nations and European Union Peace and Crisis Management Operations: Policies and Practice," in Wolfgang Benedek, Matthias C. Kettemann, and Markus Möstl (eds.), *Mainstreaming Human Security in Peace Operations and Crisis Management. Policies, Problems, Potential* (Routledge: London, 2010), 13–31.

[103] UN Secretary-General, Human Security. Report of the Secretary-General, UN Doc. A/64/701 of 8 March 2001, para. 69.

[104] Barbara Tigerstrom, *Human Security and International Law - Problems and Prospects* (Oxford: Hart, 2007).

[105] Tobias Debiel, *UN-Friedensoperationen in Afrika. Weltinnenpolitik und die Realität von Bürgerkriegen* (Bonn: J.H.W. Dietz Nachf., 2003).

[106] Monty Marshall, Benjamin Cole, Global Report 2009: Conflict, Governance, and State Fragility (2009), http://www.humansecuritygateway.com/documents/CSP_GlobalReport2009_ConflictGovernanceStateFragility.pdf.

[107] Wolfgang Benedek, "Human Security and Prevention of Terrorism," in Wolfgang Benedek and A. Yotopoulos-Marangopoulos (eds.), *Anti-terrorist Measures and Human Rights* (Leiden: Brill, 2004), 171–83 (on violations of human security through anti-terrorism policies and law).

[108] Shahrbanou Tadjbakhsh and Anuradha M. Chenoy, *Human Security. Concepts and Implications* (London: Routledge, 2007) 98–122 (on human security and development).

[109] UN General Assembly, Resolution 67/195 of 21 December 2012, Information and communications technologies for development, UN Doc. A/RES/67/195 of 5 February 2013.

Development Goals (MDGs) "through sustained, inclusive and equitable economic growth and sustainable development."[110]

It is difficult to prove empirically a measurable positive impact of the internet or of ICTs on human development because numerous other factors influence causality. Merely finding correlations between heuristical stand-ins, such as internet penetration and development measured by numbers taken from the Human Development Index, does not fully satisfy. It may well be impossible to scientifically establish a causal relationship between the increased use of ICTs and the elimination of absolute poverty because of the complexity of the use of technology and its impact, because of the lack of useful data, and because levels of absolute poverty are worryingly resistant.[111] A 2009 study for the World Bank by the Boston Consulting Group (BCG) on behalf of Telenor exemplifies these problems. The study concentrates on Gross Domestic Product (GDP) growth arguing that a "10 percentage point increase in internet penetration is *correlated* with a 1% increase in the annual rate of new business formation."[112] Similarly, a World Bank reports concludes that a 10 percent increase in broadband penetration *correlates* with a 1.38 percent increase in GDP growth.[113]

Economic growth does not equal human development, but it is a useful heuristic. The internet has had a demonstrably positive impact on economic growth.[114] Already in 2010, the internet economy amounted to $ 2.3 trillion or 4.1 percent of GDP across the G-20 countries and was expected to rise to $ 4.2 trillion or 5.3 percent of GDP by 2016.[115] A McKinsey report on internet economies of the G-8 and Brazil, China, India, South Korea, and Sweden finds that, as a sector, internet-related consumption and expenditure surpasses both agriculture and energy. By 2011, on average, the internet made a contribution of 3.4 percent to the GDP[116] and up to 8 percent in countries with higher ICT use.[117] By 2017 its contribution to the US economy in real terms was around 10 percent (5% as share of GDP in official statistics),[118] though the impact of the internet economy on other economies makes it difficult to establish indisputable figures.[119]

[110] Ibid., para. 1.

[111] Cf. Tim Unwin, *ICT4D: Information and Communication Technologies for Development* (Cambridge: CUP, 2009). Cf. also Tim Unwin, "The Internet and Development: A Critical Perspective," in William H. Dutton (ed.), *The Oxford Handbook of Internet Studies* (Oxford: OUP, 2013), 531–54 (533) (criticizing that most ICT-related studies are based on the "dominant hegemonic model of development").

[112] Telenor/Boston Consulting Group, Towards a Connected World. Socio-economic Impact of Internet in Emerging and Developing Economies (2009), https://www.telenor.com/wp-content/uploads/2012/03/Towards-a-Connected-World-1MB.pdf, 7 (my emphasis).

[113] Christine Zhen-Wei Qiang, Carlo M. Rossotto, and Kaoru Kimura, "Economic Impacts of Broadband," in World Bank, *Information and Communications for Development 2009: Extending Reach and Increasing Impact* (2009), http://siteresources.worldbank.org/EXTIC4D/Resources/IC4D_Broadband_35_50.pdf, ch 3, 25–50.

[114] Cf. for an overview of studies confirming the positive impact of the internet and the internet economy on economic growth, Value of the Web, http://www.valueoftheweb.com.

[115] International Digital Economy Alliance, "The Trillion Dollar Question: How Trade Agreements Can Maximise the Economic Potential of Data in the Networked Economy and Support the Internet as the World"s Trading Platform" (2013), http://www.internet-economy.org.

[116] McKinsey Global Institute, "Internet Matters: The Net"s Sweeping Impact on Growth, Jobs and Prosperity" (May 2011), http://www.mckinsey.com/insights/high_tech_telecoms_internet/internet_matters.

[117] Boston Consulting Group, "The Internet Economy in the G-20: The $4.2 Trillion Growth Opportunity" (March 2012), https://www.bcgperspectives.com/content/articles/media_entertainment_strategic_planning_4_2_trillion_opportunity_internet_economy_g20.

[118] James Manyika, McKinsey Global Institute Research, "Digital Economy: Trends, Opportunities and Challenges" (2016), https://www.ntia.doc.gov/files/ntia/publications/james_manyika_digital_economy_deba_may_16_v4.pdf. For Germany, see Federal Ministry for Economic Affairs and Energy, Monitoring Report DIGITAL Economy 2016, https://www.bmwi.de/Redaktion/EN/Publikationen/monitoring-report-digital-economy-2016.pdf (€ 223 billion revenue generated by the ICT sector; € 111 billion revenue generated by the Internet economy in 2016).

[119] Christopher Hooton, "Refreshing Our Understanding of the Internet Economy," Internet Association (2017), https://internetassociation.org/reports/refreshing-understanding-internet-economy-ia-report.

Cloud computing, made possible through broadband connections and decreasing data storage costs,[120] has had, according to another study focusing on the EU, "a significant impact for the European Union with the creation of a few hundred thousand new SMEs [small and medium enterprises] and a significant contribution to growth."[121] The Organization for Economic Cooperation and Development (OECD), an organization dedicated to furthering economic progress, has successfully linked reaching economy-related public policy objectives to engaging with internet intermediaries.[122] Economic growth is a public policy objective; but so is development which is—it is worth repeating—more than economic growth.

The 2008 Seoul Declaration on the Future of the Internet Economy underlined that expanding the "internet Economy" will lead to "sustainable economic growth and prosperity." The internet "will bolster the free flow of information, freedom of expression, and protection of individual liberties, as critical components of a democratic society and cultural diversity."[123] Similarly, the EU Digital Agenda's objective is to "maximize the social and economic potential of ICT, most notably the internet, a vital medium of economic and societal activity: for doing business, working, playing, communicating and expressing ourselves freely."[124]

Development is more than the elimination of absolute poverty: it is also the reduction of relative poverty and, as Amartya Sen demonstrated, the freedom of people to realize their capabilities.[125] But even with a critical perception of the concrete impact of ICTs for development, we can accept, with the United Nations and its Human Rights Council, that the potential of the internet for development is great.[126] Human Rights Council Resolution 20/8 (2012) recognized the globality and openness of the internet as a "driving force in accelerating progress towards development in its various forms."[127] The Human Rights Council also confirmed the connection between development, human rights, and the internet by committing itself to further studying how the internet can be an "important tool for development and for exercising human rights."[128]

The Resolution's reference to the internet's positive impact on development in its "various forms" is prefigured in the BCG/Telenor study that points to the social benefits of increased internet penetration for education, better income, enhanced healthcare, and

[120] Nayan B. Ruparelia, *Cloud Computing* (Cambridge, MA/London: MIT Press, 2016).

[121] Federico Etro, "The Economic Impact of Cloud Computing on Business Creation, Employment and Output in Europe. An application of the Endogenous Market Structures Approach to a GPT innovation," Review of Business and Economics 2 (2009), 180–208.

[122] OECD, The Role of Internet Intermediaries in Advancing Public Policy Objectives (2011), http://www.oecd.org/sti/ieconomy/theroleofinternetintermediariesinadvancingpublicpolicyobjectives.htm.

[123] OECD, Seoul Declaration on the Future of the Internet Economy, http://www.oecd.org/sti/40839436.pdf, adopted at the OECD Ministerial Meeting on the Future of the Internet Economy, Seoul, Korea, 17–18 June 2008, 4.

[124] EU, Digital Agenda for Europe. A Europe 2020 Initiative, http://ec.europa.eu/digital-agenda. See also Communication from the Commission to the European Parliament, the Council, the European Economic and Social Committee and the Committee of the Regions, A Digital Agenda for Europe, COM(2010) 245 of 26 August 2010, 1.

[125] Amartya Sen, *Development as Freedom* (Oxford: OUP, 1999).

[126] Cf. Tim Unwin, "The Internet and Development: A Critical Perspective," in William H. Dutton (ed.), *The Oxford Handbook of Internet Studies* (Oxford: OUP, 2013), 549.

[127] Human Rights Council, Resolution 20/8, The promotion, protection and enjoyment of human rights on the Internet, UN Doc. A/HRC/RES/20/8 of 16 July 2012, para. 2, https://documents-dds-ny.un.org/doc/RESOLUTION/GEN/G12/153/25/PDF/G1215325.pdf?OpenElement.

[128] Ibid., para. 4.

increased lifestyle opportunities, especially in rural areas.[129] These benefits, though real, are usually presented anecdotally. Taken together, however, they leave little doubt as to the potential of ICTs for economic growth and human development. The example of many African states shows how big (government) data and open data approaches are used by local start-ups in cooperation with communities to monitor delivery of health services.[130] The internet and internet-based applications can be effective tools to visualize money flows and increase accountability of public officials, which in turn has positive effects on development. In fact, Judith Randel of Development Initiatives, an organization working toward poverty eradication, argues that "the effective use of information [is] key to the debate on resource allocation and ultimately poverty eradication."[131] Similarly, a comprehensive study by the think tank Dalberg finds positive anecdotal and systemic impacts of the internet in African areas as different as agriculture, health, education, SMEs, and financial inclusion.[132]

This approach unites human rights-based and human development-oriented internet policy development in that the right to access the internet (and through it receive and impart ideas) is a key, enabling the right to realize the potential of human rights online and ensure human development.[133] This approach has emerged as a common theme in development policy. The UN 2030 Agenda for Sustainable Development[134] identified the building of resilient infrastructure, the promotion of inclusive and sustainable industrialization, and the fostering of innovation as key goals of sustainable development.[135] In Target 9.c of the Sustainable Development Goals (SDGs) states commit to "[s]ignificantly increase[ing] access to information and communications technology and striv[ing] to provide universal and affordable access to the internet in least developed countries by 2020." There exists thus a commitment by UN member states to strive for universal internet access by 2020. Even if this commitment is difficult to realize, the importance of the commitment, which evidences these states' opinion vis-à-vis the internet, is hard to overstate. Committing to universal

[129] Telenor/BCG (2009), 8. Interestingly, the report defines benefits that the internet can bring as "needs" and "wants": needs include productivity gains from household businesses and agriculture, cost savings from online shopping, and time savings. "Wants" relate to "perceived benefits of Internet use": "1) Information search, 2) entertainment, 3) social networking, and 4) 'sophistication', by which is meant the ability to keep up with global trends" (ibid., 86–7). This is obviously far from the traditional approach to development.

[130] Cf. Loren Treisman, "Power to the People: How Open Data is Improving Health Service Delivery," *The Guardian*, December 2, 2013, http://www.theguardian.com/global-development-professionals-network/2013/dec/02/open-data-healthcare-accountability-africa.

[131] Judith Randel, "Why Access to Information Needs to Be Central to the Debate on Poverty," *The Guardian*, February 18, 2013, http://www.theguardian.com/global-development-professionals-network/2013/jan/18/mdgs-poverty-eradication-information-access.

[132] Dalberg, "Impact of the Internet in Africa: Establishing Conditions for Success and Catalysing Inclusive Growth in Ghana, Kenya, Nigeria and Senegal" (April 2013), https://docplayer.net/945127-Dalberg-impact-of-the-internet-in-africa-establishing-conditions-for-success-and-catalysing-inclusive-growth-in-ghana-kenya-nigeria-and-senegal.html. The study argues that positive results are premised upon investment in "core infrastructure as well as usage conditions in order to maximise the Internet's impact" (ibid.).

[133] Cf. a statement by ninety-five civil society groups from seventy-seven countries: Statement: Post-2015: Access to Information and Independent Media Essential to Development, February 3, 2014, http://www.article19.org/resources.php/resource/37435/en/post-2015:-access-to-information-and-independent-media-essential-to-development. Cf. Thomas Hughes, "UN: Don't Overlook Access to Information in Goal on Governance," *The Guardian*, February 11, 2014, http://www.theguardian.com/global-development-professionals-network/2014/feb/11/un-information-sdg-accountability-development.

[134] United Nations General Assembly, Transforming Our World: The 2030 Agenda for Sustainable Development, UN Doc. A/Res/70/1 of 21 October 2015, https://sustainabledevelopment.un.org/content/documents/7891TRANSFORMING%20OUR%20WORLD.pdf.

[135] Ibid., Goal 9.

access means, by implication, that internet integrity as a precondition for meaningful access needs to be ensured and is therefore in the common interest.

This commitment closes the circle to the BCG report, which evidentiates the positive impact of the internet for private businesses. The High Level Panel established by United Nations Secretary-General Ban Ki-moon also called for a "data revolution for sustainable development, with a new international initiative to improve the quality of statistics and information available to citizens." ICTs were considered crucial for development as empowering tools: "new technology, crowd sourcing, and improved connectivity to empower people with information on the progress towards the [development] targets."[136] Disaggregated data to ensure that the "neediest [...] are receiving essential services" is necessary—and the "revolution in information technology over the last decade provides [us with] an opportunity to strengthen data and statistics for accountability and decision-making purposes."[137]

This is not to deny that digital inequalities are persistent and the different dimensions of the digital divide, even within developed societies, are difficult to bridge.[138] The General Assembly resolution on ICTs and development expresses concerns at the digital divide, at the gender divide within the digital divide, and that the development promise of ICTs remains unfulfilled for the majority of the poor.[139] Targeted policies are required to ameliorate this situation, but the finding does not detract from the validity of identifying the internet's protection as lying in the common interest because of its potential for human rights protection and development.

ICTs and their facility to organize data and draw societal benefits from data are thus accepted tools in pursuance of the UN's development goals. The Broadband Commission for Digital Development, established by the ITU and UNESCO in 2010, confirmed that without the internet the MDGs of 2015 could not have been achieved nor progress effectively monitored.[140] The internet does not equal ICTs, but ICTs run on the internet. Therefore, the use of ICTs is premised upon the protection of and from the internet—which is in the common interest. ICTs are a "growth driver and transformative technology for the global economy,"[141] and for human information and communication—and as such for the realization of human rights, human security, and human development. Harnessing ICTs in order to ensure human rights, human security, and human development (and, as a means toward these ends, economic growth) is premised upon the integrity of the internet. If ensuring these goals lies in the common interest—as it indubitably does—, the latter needs to be protected in the common interest.

[136] Ibid., 7.

[137] Ibid., 23.

[138] Cf. Eszter Hargittai and Yuli Patrick Hsieh, "Digital Inequality," in William H. Dutton (ed.), *The Oxford Handbook of Internet Studies* (Oxford: OUP, 2013), 129–50.

[139] UN General Assembly, Resolution 67/195 of 21 December 2012, Information and communications technologies for development, UN Doc. A/RES/67/195 of 5 February 2013, paras. 3–5.

[140] Cf. UN Broadband Commission for Digital Development, The State of Broadband 2013: Universalizing Broadband, September 2013, http://www.broadbandcommission.org/Documents/bb-annualreport2013.pdf, 26 et seq. (citing examples such as improved exam results through computers-to-schools projects, closing gender gaps through ICT programs targeted at women, mobile apps assisting parents in developing countries assess immunization, height, weight, and child development milestones, ultrasound tests through telemedicine, web-based hubs for healthcare workers, and reduction of Greenhouse gases emissions through smart ICT use (30)).

[141] Ian Brown and Christopher T. Marsden, *Regulating Code. Good Governance and Better Regulation in the Information Age* (Cambridge: MIT Press, 2013), 196.

2.3.4 Relating Internet Integrity to International Security

Protecting the internet's integrity and (global) society from the dangers emanating from or mediated through the internet is essential for ensuring international security and the effective fight against cybercrime. Political and legal approaches to preventing cyberwar[142] and cybercrime[143] have attracted considerable attention internationally. This study has shown that the internet is critical infrastructure in itself and also functionally essential for other critical infrastructure. The General Assembly, in Resolution 64/211 of 21 December 2009, promoted the creation of a global culture of cybersecurity[144] and expressed concerns in light of growing threats to the reliable functioning of the internet (technically: "of critical information infrastructures and to the integrity of the information carried over those"). These affect "domestic, national and international welfare." The Resolution affirms that states are obliged to deal systematically with these threats and coordinate both with national actors and internationally with the goal of facilitating the achievement of cybersecurity.[145]

The 2013 GGEs report underlined that applying norms derived from "existing international law relevant to the use of ICTs by States is an essential measure to reduce risks to international peace, security and stability." The Charter of the United Nations is applicable to the whole gamut of socioeconomic activity on the internet and in that "essential to maintaining peace and stability and promoting an open, secure, peaceful and accessible ICT environment."[146] Applying international law to the internet lies in the common interest and safeguarding the internet as such also lies in the common interest because a stable, secure, and functional internet is essential for international security.

Protecting internet integrity and protecting kinetic artifacts and the offline world by reducing the potential for criminal misuses of computers and networks is important in the international fight against cybercrime and cyberterrorism. Common criminals continue to misuse the internet both for online variants of common scams and for internet-specific (technology-based) attacks. The size of monetary loss is small compared to the scale of the internet economy,[147] but the problem is nevertheless serious.[148] Black markets both for buying cybercrime tools (such as complete botnets for as little as 50 USD) and for selling on the proceeds of cybercrime activities (such as credit card information) are increasingly

[142] Cf. just Katharina Ziolkowski, *Peacetime Regime for State Activities in Cyberspace. International Law, International Relations and Diplomacy* (Tallinn: NATO CCD COE Publications, 2013), http://ccdcoe.org/427.html; and Michael N. Schmitt (ed.), *The Tallinn Manual on the International Law Applicable to Cyber Warfare* (Cambridge: CUP, 2013), http://issuu.com/nato_ccd_coe/docs/tallinnmanual?e=5903855/1802381.

[143] Cf., on the taxonomy of cybercrime, David S. Wall, *Cybercrime* (Cambridge: CUP, 2007); and Jonathan Clough, *Principles of Cybercrime* (Cambridge: CUP, 2010) (arguing that broad consensus on fighting cybercrime has led to the successful Council of Europe Cybercrime Convention, 22).

[144] General Assembly, Resolution 64/211 of 21 December 2009, Creation of a global culture of cybersecurity and taking stock of national efforts to protect critical information infrastructures, UN Doc. A/RES/64/211 of 17 March 2010.

[145] Cybersecurity is discussed in more detail below, at 4.3. Customary duties regarding cybersecurity, including the principle of prevention, are discussed below, in 3.3.

[146] Report of the Group of Governmental Experts on Developments in the Field of Information and Telecommunications in the Context of International Security, UN Doc. A/68/98 of 24 June 2013, para. 19.

[147] According to its latest available report, the US-based Internet Crime Complaint Center has received, in 2012, just under 300,000 consumer complaints with an adjusted dollar loss of US$ 530 million, an increase of 8.3% since 2011 (cf. Internet Crime Complaint Center (I3C), Internet Crime Report 2012 (2012), http://www.ic3.gov/media/annualreport/2012_IC3Report.pdf).

[148] Cf. Robert Moore, *Cybercrime: Investigating High-Technology Computer Crime* (Oxford: Elsevier, 2011) (arguing that cybercrimes have been steadily increasing in recent years and now amount to "a very serious problem," 5).

sophisticated, resilient, and international.[149] This threat requires international cooperation. At the same time, most criminal misuses of the internet are not direct threats to the internet's integrity, as criminal networks rely on the internet to conduct their activities. However, attacks, especially if conducted for purposes not linked to monetary gain—such as terrorism or political destabilization—can amount to substantial threats to the internet's functionality and threaten offline values, institutions, and society.

The internet has been used for the coordination of terrorist attacks and the promotion of terrorist ideology.[150] However, the internet is only one factor or mode in radicalization processes and not a key method. Its relative significance remains unclear.[151] But at the same time the technologicalization and informationalization of many key infrastructure provision functions and of many industry control systems open up new vulnerabilities within states that can threaten, if an attack is substantial, international peace and security. Similarly, the increased use of mobile devices, cloud computing, and the use of social networks increases the vulnerability of citizens to acts of cybercrime.[152]

Different levels of internet security awareness and capabilities globally matter to all states because of the interconnectedness of ICTs and the networked nature of the internet. "These vulnerabilities are amplified," the UN's Group of Governmental Experts complained in 2013, "by disparities in national law, regulations and practices related to the use of ICTs."[153] Only international cooperation in the protection of and from the internet can help meet these challenges. The role of the internet's integrity in ensuring international security and the threats posed by international cybercrime and cyberterrorism are further reasons for considering that the protection of the integrity of the internet lies in the common interest.

2.3.5 Custodial Sovereignty

The normative ordering of the internet necessitates a review of traditional notions of sovereignty.[154] But the consequences of identifying an issue as lying in the common interest of all states remain the same with regard to the public core of the internet as with regard to other common interest goods: that the state exercising primary jurisdiction is limited in its sovereignty. Its acts may not affect negatively the pursuance of the common interest. Other states have a right to monitor this respect and offer assistance. They also have duties regarding the international community with a view to safeguarding common interests which are normatively framed, inter alia, as the *no harm* and the *sic utere tuo* principles.

While protection of the integrity of the internet lies in the common interest, there is no intrinsic value in the internet. Its protection is functional. To the extent that a state controls CIRs, it has to exercise this jurisdiction in a manner that ensures the common interest.

[149] Lillian Ablon, Martin C. Libicki, and Andrea A. Golay, "Markets for Cybercrime Tools and Stolen Data. Hackers' Bazaar," RAND National Security Research Division (March 2014), http://www.rand.org/pubs/research_reports/RR610.html.

[150] GGE Report (2013), para. 7.

[151] Ines von Behr, Anais Reding, Charlie Edwards, and Luke Gribbon, "Radicalisation in the Digital Era. the Use of the Internet in 15 Cases of Terrorism and Extremism," RAND Europe (2013), http://www.rand.org/pubs/research_reports/RR453.html, 48.

[152] Cf. GGE Report (2013)., para. 9.

[153] Ibid., para. 10.

[154] Rolf H. Weber, "New Sovereignty Concepts in the Age of Internet?" Journal of Internet Law 14 (2010), 12–20.

To the extent that national politics, e.g. new laws, could affect the internet negatively, a state must refrain from their implementation. This will often be a question of weighing probabilities while respecting the precautionary principle.[155] The limit of a state's equal sovereignty is rechartered in light of its erga omnes obligations regarding the protection of and from the internet as a common interest.

Even when the US still exercised ultimate authority over the internet's key addressing resources, including its root servers, it could be argued that the US government only had "custodial sovereignty" regarding the delegated IANA functions.[156] This approach combines a common global responsibility of all states for the internet with differentiated responsibilities of the custodial state to protect and all other states to support the state in its custodial role (and, if needed, take measures to ensure that the custodial state does not fail the international community).[157]

In delegating and supervising the delegated exercise of the root zone management authority, the US had to act as a custodian of the global common interest in the internet's integrity. This implies that the US had to enter into consultations with other states with regard to the management of CIRs and make sure that the management is transparent and accountable, ideally to all actors of the international community. States also have to ensure that they implement the protection of and from the internet as a common interest within their territory (through national legislation) and that all actors, including private actors, contribute to the protection.

Though sovereignty-oriented states have suggested exercising exclusive sovereignty over a "national internet segment,"[158] the character of the internet as protected by international law as a common interest limits their sovereignty. Even criminal legislation, often perceived as a hallmark of state sovereignty, has been influenced (if not actively shaped) by international cooperation to combat cybercrime, though it remains at the core of national sovereignty. The 2005 Tunis Agenda, though valuable in its description of the normative goals of information society, supports a more traditional view in equating "policy authority for internet-related public policy issues" to a "sovereign right of States."[159] This needs to be qualified in light of a common interest approach to protecting the internet in that the states' policy authority is no longer an exclusively sovereign right but, as part and parcel of their sovereignty, to be exercised in the common interest, when common interest issues are at stake. Sovereignty has to be understood in light of changing circumstances and the importance of the pursuance of the common interest of protecting the integrity of the internet.

[155] On its applications both in international law and in national jurisdictions, see Joakim Zander, *The Application of the Precautionary Principle in Practice. Comparative Dimensions* (Cambridge: CUP, 2010) (internationally, at 3; EU law at 76; UK at 215; and the US at 267). More critically, see Cass R. Sunstein, *Laws of Fear. Beyond the Precautionary Principle* (Cambridge: CUP, 2005) (arguing for alternatives to the precautionary principle (especially its unreflective use) because it may paralyze policymakers, 31).

[156] On the concept of custodial sovereignty, see Werner Scholtz, "Custodial Sovereignty: Reconciling Sovereignty and Global Environmental Challenges amongst the Vestiges of Colonialism," Netherlands International Law Review 3 (2008), 323–41. With the transitioning of the NTIA's IANA-related functions completed by 2015, this assessment is still of historical value.

[157] Cf. Werner Scholtz, "Collective (Environmental) Security: The Yeast for the Refinement of International Law," in Ole Kristian Fauchald, David Hunter, and Wang Xi (eds.), *Yearbook of International Environmental Law*, Vol. 19 (Oxford: OUP, 2008), 135–62 (148).

[158] Cf. Russia, UAE, China, Saudi Arabia, Algeria, Sudan, and Egypt, Proposal for the Work of the Conference [WCIT-12], ITU Doc. DT-X of 5 December 2012, WCIT12/27(Rev.1)-E, § 3A.2 and 3A.3, http://files.wcitleaks.org/public/Merged%20UAE%20081212.pdf.

[159] World Summit on the Information Society (WSIS), Tunis Agenda for The Information Society, WSIS-05/TUNIS/DOC/6(Rev. 1)-E of 18 November 2005.

In order to ensure that all states exercise their sovereignty in a way that reflects the global common interest in the internet, all other states have monitoring and assistance rights and duties.[160] This also applied to the exercise, by the United States, of its custodial sovereignty regarding root zone management and IANA functions before the transition to the internet's technical organizations, as well as to states that host important Internet Exchange Points, like Germany with the DE-CIX in Frankfurt/Main. Monitoring includes a right to oversee and criticize implementation, and suggest improvements, and may amount—in extreme cases—in rights to take, collectively, action against a state if the failure to protect common interests leads or amounts to a situation under Chapter VII of the Charter of the United Nations (a threat to, or a breach of, the peace), similar to the concept of humanitarian intervention. Assistance by the international community includes, if needed, financial, technical, and organizational support, but also further ex ante obligations such as an extraterritorial duty not to cause harm in its preventive and due diligence dimensions. The principles of good neighborliness and *sic utere tuo* have especially strong implications when states regulate common interest resources.[161]

This section has established that protecting the integrity of the internet lies in the global common interest. Therefore, international law obliges states to protect the integrity of the internet. Yet there exist a number of challenges of regulating the internet that lie in its special character.

2.4 Challenges of Regulating the Internet

2.4.1 Foundational Myths

This study has established that regulating the internet in the common interest is essential to safeguarding the values of the international community. Previously, this chapter has identified how standards and contracts, and non-binding norms, safeguard the internet's criticality for societal progress. This study has earlier hypothesized that a normative order has emerged, made up of international law, national law, and transnational regulatory arrangements. The last category has been shown to exist. But what about "international law of the internet"? Can the internet be ruled by (international) law? The affirmative answer seems obvious, but it is historically contingent. In the early phase of the internet's development neither national laws nor international law were perceived as necessary to structure the address space or solve transnational technological conflicts as to its use and evolution. The development of standards took place in private academic settings. The first larger (and internationally relevant) legal questions emerged when the internet was commercialized and politicized in the 1990s. Pioneers of technological development discounted any normative legitimacy for states regarding the rule of the internet and questioned traditional democratic means of conferring legitimacy to rule through democratic processes. In 1992, David Clark of the IETF explained the philosophy of engineers in the following words: "We

160 Cf. Wolfgang Benedek, Koen De Feyter, Matthias C. Kettemann, and Christina Voigt, "Introduction," in Wolfgang Benedek, Koen De Feyter, Matthias C. Kettemann, and Christina Voigt (eds.), *The Common Interest in International Law* (Antwerp: Intersentia, 2014), 1–8.

161 These rules and their legal status and effect will be discussed in more detail in section 3.3.4.

reject kings, presidents and voting. We belive in rough consensus and running code."[162] In 1996, former Grateful Dead lyricist and later founder of the Electronic Frontier Foundation (EFF), John Perry Barlow, argued in Davos that "governments of the industrial world" had "no moral right to rule us [citizens of cyberspace] nor do [they] possess any methods of enforcement we have true reason to fear."[163]

The internet challenges the law and traditional notions of normativity. The defenders of utopian models, such as Barlow, attacked the law as a legitimate normative tool.[164] But "cyberspace" or "the internet" does not exist as an "independent area of sovereignty."[165] States have a *moral right* (and even a *legal duty*), based on their obligations both toward their citizens and toward the global community of states, to develop the normative order of the internet and to apply and enforce norms on the internet.[166]

Though discounting the role of traditional norms, neither Barlow nor Clark argued for a completely unregulated societal space. They realized that this would be inimical to progress in science as in economy and human sociality. What they saw as the real alternative to the application of national laws—thus enforcing a hetero-normative order on the internet—was self-regulation by engineers through standards. Though the normative difference between standards and laws is one of gradation, not of principle, the complexification of the internet, its international dimension, the hurdles to participation in standard-setting processes, and the progressive exercise of public authority by non-traditional and non-state actors necessitate critical thinking about their legitimation.[167] Providing legitimation for the exercise of authority is a key component of law, and, in international settings, of international law. The homogeneity of users of the 1970s and 1980s—academics and engineers—is gone, the commercialization and politicization of the internet has delegitimized utopian approaches: "user-generated law is a utopia."[168]

Historically, the internet was not "ruled" by any single normative order. But this is not necessary for establishing that it *can* be ruled by laws and norms from different sources systematized within the normative order of the internet. When David Clark rejected "kings, presidents and voting," he implied that democratic legitimacy (*voting*) was not something he sought for standard-setting authorities (neither did he seek charismatic or traditional legitimacy, through *kings* or *presidents*). Denying ex ante the importance of democratic legitimacy is problematic. As Malcolm N. Shaw put it, "[p]rogress, with its inexplicable leaps and bounds, has always been based upon the group as men and women combine to pursue commonly accepted goals [. . .]."[169] This common pursuit is

[162] David Clark, in a 1992 talk describing the Internet Engineering Task Force (IETF). Cf. David D. Clark, "A Cloudy Crystal Ball, Visions of the Future," plenary presentation, 24th meeting of the Internet Engineering Task Force, Cambridge, MA, 13–17 July 1992, http:/ietf20.isoc.org/videos/future_ietf_92.pdf.

[163] John Perry Barlow, "A Declaration of the Independence of Cyberspace," Davos, February 8, 1996, https://projects.eff.org/~barlow/Declaration-Final.html.

[164] Cf. Peter Mankowski, *Rechtskultur* (Tübingen: Mohr Siebeck, 2016), 192.

[165] Ibid., 131.

[166] Just see ECtHR, *K.U. v. Finland* (2 December 2008), application No. 2872/02 (confirming that states have obligations to protect children online); *Editorial Board of Pravoye Delo and Shtekel v. Ukraine* (5 May 2011), application No. 33014/05 (states must create a regulatory framework to ensure effective protection of freedom of expression on the internet for journalists).

[167] Myriam Senn, *Non-State Regulatory Regimes. Understanding Institutional Transformation* (Heidelberg: Springer, 2011).

[168] Peter Mankowski, *Rechtskultur* (Tübingen: Mohr Siebeck, 2016), 131 (translation by the author).

[169] Malcolm N. Shaw, *International Law*, 6th edn. (Oxford: OUP, 2008), 1.

explained and justified by the concomitant evolution of (international) legal norms and their influence on the rule of the internet.

2.4.2 Evolving Composition of the Normative Medium

In their introduction to a collection of essays on *Law without the State* (Recht ohne Staat), Stefan Kadelbach and Klaus Günther describe the "*lex digitalis*, the law of the internet" as "perhaps the biggest challenge for the representatives of a state-oriented notion of law."[170] Though they admit that states have technical difficulties to police events happening "on the internet" but outside their jurisdiction, they diagnose a lack of "meta norms" enabling the emergence of *lex digitalis* as a self-regulated order: "private law of the internet seems to be currently rather a virtual project if [it] develops any rules at all."[171] As this study will show in chapter 6, these meta-norms have developed and can be substantiated to the point where they shape the normative order of the internet.

As this study will submit in chapter 5, the notion of normative order of the internet is useful to overcome the state- vs. self-regulation debate that Kadelbach and Günther correctly identify as non-productive. As indicated in the previous section on intermediaries, companies' terms of service as private law fulfill an important normative function within the normative order of the internet. There is not, however, an independent private law of the internet. Rather, it is one of the challenges of regulating the internet that it is made up of public and private norms (contract being often preferred over less flexible statutes[172]), authored and executed by governments and companies alike.

Jürgen Habermas identified this trend as a "change in the composition of the medium of law."[173] Indeed, as this section and the following demonstrate, what is considered "law" within a society has been greatly impacted by the development of the internet with its norms and standards. Legal orders are not closed in the sense that only norms exist which have been (democratically) legitimated by those subjected to the norm.[174] The classical state-oriented law paradigm is challenged by globalization and deterritorialization through the use of ICTs.[175] This does not, of course, mean that states fade away: "The virtual space does not mean [. . .] the end of the sovereign constitutional state."[176] States

[170] Stefan Kadelbach und Klaus Günther, "Recht ohne Staat?" in Stefan Kadelbach und Klaus Günther (eds.), *Recht ohne Staat? Zur Normativität nichtstaatlicher Normsetzung* (Frankfurt/New York: Campus, 2011), 9–47 (23): "Die vielleicht größte Herausforderung für die Vertreter eines staatszentrierten Rechtsbegriffes ist die lex digitalis, das Recht des Internet" (translation by the author).

[171] Ibid., 35: "Allerdings scheint auch ein von wem auch immer initiiertes privates Recht des Internet derzeit ein eher virtuelles Projekt zu sein – soweit es überhaupt Regelungen treffen kann" (translation by the author).

[172] Lee A. Bygrave, *Internet Governance by Contract* (Oxford: OUP, 2015).

[173] Jürgen Habermas, "Im Sog der Technokratie," in Jürgen Habermas, *Im Sog der Technokratie: kleine politische Schriften XII* (Frankfurt: Suhrkamp, 2013), 7: "Heute zeigen sich auch auf internationaler Ebene Anzeichen für eine Rationalisierung der staatlichen Herrschaftsausübung, welche einer Veränderung in der Komposition des Rechtsmediums entspricht" (translation by the author).

[174] Klaus Günther, "Normativer Rechtspluralismus—Eine Kritik," Normative Orders Working Paper 03/2014, http://publikationen.ub.uni-frankfurt.de/files/34664/Guenther_Normativer+Rechtspluralismus.pdf, 1.

[175] Lars Viellechner, *Transnationalisierung des Rechts* (Weilerswist: Velbrück, 2013), 99. On ICANN's domain regime, see ibid., 127 et seq.

[176] Stephan Hobe, "Cyberspace—der virtuelle Raum," in Josef Isensee, Paul Kirchhof et al. (eds.), *Handbuch des Staatsrechts, Band XI: Internationale Bezüge*, 3rd edn., § 271, no. 44 ("Der virtuelle Raum bedeutet [. . .] nicht das Ende des souveränen Verfassungsstaates") (translation by the author).

continue to exercise an essential role in protecting their citizens from threats emanating from new technologies and from social change that these technological advances engender. This task is made difficult because of the multilayer, multiplayer normative architecture and norm production machinery on the internet. The norms on which internet regulation and internet governance are based emanate from state constitutions, public law, supranational (EU) law, international law, private law-based contracts and terms of service, standards, code, and hybrid sources, such as internet principles and cybernorms.[177] It is difficult to ensure coherent protection of fundamental freedoms in this mosaic of rules ("Regelungsmosaik"[178]).

The real issue with the evolving composition of the normative medium is thus not that the internet is a space without applicable national norms, as the foundational myths of the internet would have us believe (recall Barlow's axiom that states had "no authority where we [denizens of cyberspace] gather"[179]). Rather, the internet is a space with too many norms by too many normative actors and varying normative geometries. Depending on which aspect of the use and development we focus on, we will find regulation leaning more toward self-regulation through e.g. informal agreement, toward private law and contract, and toward public law.

The public core of the internet (the fundamental parts of infrastructure and the key standards necessary for the internet to run) have always been ruled (and managed) effectively. Without rules in the broadest sense (in their emanation as technical specifications), without some norms on cooperation and sharing information, information and communication exchange would not have been possible at all. The fact that the more technical "rules of the road" for the early internet were published in RFCs and developed bottom-up in meetings of engineers does not detract from the fact that some (mainly technical) norms have been considered highly legitimate by the norm subjects. But engineers have also formulated behavior-oriented norms such as Jon Postel's "Be liberal in what you accept, and conservative in what you send."[180] Furthermore, the activity of engineers and companies has taken place within a framework of national and international norms that have bearing upon everything they do. These norms emerging in the force field of technology and law may be hybridized and to a large degree privatized but remain within the confines set by national and international law.

That norms rule the internet is not an issue of much controversy today. Jack L. Goldsmith, even doubtful as to the normative pull of international law,[181] still agrees that law governs activities in cyberspace.[182] "Persistent" objections are usually based on misunderstandings of the dynamic character of "norms." Andrew Murray, for instance, argues that "legal documents" cannot rule cyberspace but rather a "web of terms and conditions of service and

[177] Matthias C. Kettemann, "Internet Governance," in Dietmar Jahnel, Peter Mader, and Elisabeth Staudegger (eds.), *IT-Recht*, 3rd edn. (Vienna: Verlag Österreich, 2013), 43–63.

[178] Wolfgang Hoffmann-Riem, "Freiheitsschutz in den globalen Kommunikationsinfrastrukturen," JZ 69 (2014) 2, 53–63 (63).

[179] John Perry Barlow, "A Declaration of the Independence of Cyberspace," Davos, February 8, 1996, https://projects.eff.org/~barlow/Declaration-Final.html.

[180] R. Braden (ed.), RFC 1222, Requirements for Internet Hosts—Communication Layers, October 1989, http://www.ietf.org/rfc/rfc1122.txt, 1.2.2.

[181] Cf. Jack L. Goldsmith and Eric A. Posner, *The Limits of International Law* (New York: OUP, 2005), 188–9.

[182] Cf. Jack L. Goldsmith, "Regulation of the Internet: Three Persistent Fallacies," Chicago-Kent Law Review 73 (1998), 1119.

[...] Lessigian code-based solutions."[183] Murray misunderstands the diffused normativity in the regulation of online behavior. There is indeed no *single* international "legal document" that regulates cyberspace, but there are many international and national norms that shape the behavior of actors online. Terms and conditions of service are influenced by national and international law, laying down standards for behavior of corporate actors and protecting individual internet users.[184] There can be no action by natural or legal persons outside sovereign jurisdictions.[185]

Internet companies' terms of service are normative in nature and embedded in an infra- and suprastructure of norms (including laws and treaties) that together form the normative order of the internet.[186] Murray is right in arguing that the "transborder nature of internet activity has presented a significant challenge to traditional legal institutions in enforcing jurisdiction over online activities."[187] But the fact that challenges to enforcing national jurisdiction exist means that more international cooperation and coordination, through international law, are necessary (and have partly been achieved[188])—and not that regulation itself is impossible.

National law is important to normatively frame the development and applications of norms and processes bearing upon the evolution of the internet on a local level. Some argue that the role of national laws in mediating conflicting values has been supplanted by "technologies of internet governance" that have become the "new global spaces" for these norm and values conflicts.[189] Technologies are not spaces, but technologies enable human behavior in these spaces, and states need to respect, protect, and fulfill their human rights obligations through law. Even in times of shifting media of law, states need to regulate with a view to certain values that are extrinsic to technology and must be imported through a controlling normative order.

2.4.3 Code and Protocols as Law?

On a normative micro-scale, code has been said to supplant law in cyberspace.[190] But code, though important for the development of programs and defining in many ways the direction into which information society is heading, is not law. Code-based regulation is either

183 Andrew Murray, "Uses and Abuses of Cyberspace: Coming to Grips with the Present Dangers," in Antonio Cassese (ed.), *Realizing Utopia. The Future of International Law* (Oxford: OUP, 2012), 497–506 (497).

184 Cf. Recommendation CM/Rec(2014)6 of the Committee of Ministers to member States on a Guide to human rights for Internet users, Adopted by the Committee of Ministers on 16 April 2014 at the 1197th meeting of the Ministers' Deputies, https://wcd.coe.int/ViewDoc.jsp?id=2184807.

185 Apart from special cases of acts taken, for instance in international waters or outer space. But even these actions are regulated under the relevant regimes, providing for the protection of these areas of common concern for mankind. Once these acts have implications in sovereign jurisdictions, they can directly be regulated by them. Cf. Administrative Court of Cologne, In re *Duchy of Sealand*, May 3, 1978, 80 ILR (1978) 683, 685, http://www.uniset.ca/naty/80ILR683.htm.

186 On the role of intermediaries as information gatekeepers, see below, 2.4.3.

187 Andrew Murray, "Uses and Abuses of Cyberspace: Coming to Grips with the Present Dangers," in Antonio Cassese (ed.), *Realizing Utopia. The Future of International Law* (Oxford: OUP, 2012), 497–506 (502).

188 Cf. just the Council of Europe Cybercrime Convention of 2001, which Murray also sees as a successful example (ibid., 499).

189 Laura DeNardis, *Protocol Politics: The Globalization of Internet Governance* (Cambridge: MIT Press, 2009), 14.

190 See already Lawrence Lessig, "The Code Is the Law," The Industry Standard, August 9, 1999, http://www.lessig.org/content/standard/0,1902,4165,00.html. For a more recent take by the same author, see Lawrence Lessig, *Code: Version 2.0* (New York: Basic Books, 2007).

hailed as a tool to ensure human development and fulfillment[191] or as a false trend reflecting techno-centrism.[192] If norms are the language of rules (and rulers) in a democracy, then code is the language of rules (and rulers?) in a technocracy. Yet technocratic knowledge, though an important vector of power in developing code, does not justify, by itself, a normative impact of code—nor does the epistemic authority of the code creator. Put succinctly: legitimacy cannot be coded. Arguing that code, and not law, rules is premised upon a sense of technological solutionism and fueled by *Sachzwang* arguments. These are not intrinsically opposed to normative (ethical) ordering but need to be harmonized. We also need to be aware of the tendency to overdetermine the possible impact of coding and design decisions.[193]

If code is law,[194] then it has to be explained and justified by certain values. However, the technocratic argument usually implies that law, and the legal order, is unnecessary for (in the sense that it is not normatively influential in) the process of developing new protocols. This view is wrong. Code *is* law in that it is normative. Code is *not* law in that it eliminates law as a normative measure. As a normative instrument, code therefore has to be treated as law and similarly legitimated—and it is.

Let us consider, for example, the RFC for a new Public Key Pinning Extension for HTTP, which allows "web host operators to instruct user agents (UAs) to remember ('pin') the hosts' cryptographic identities for a given period of time" in order to "reduce the incidence of man-in-the-middle attacks due to compromised Certification Authorities."[195] International law is relevant for such a standard on many levels: it provides an argumentative and normative framework for competing values such as privacy and security. The very fact that an organization such as IETF develops these standards essential for the use and development of the internet also has to be explained and justified within the argumentative ambit of international law.

At the example of the limited success of the robots.txt exclusion command, Greg Elmer shows that some protocols (or rather the adoption or non-adoption of some protocols) can be political decisions in the sense that they engage issues of public policy.[196] Elmer calls protocols therefore "distinct political artifacts, tools [...] that political actors use to supplement their more traditional communication strategies."[197] But precisely by showing that decisions about adopting or non-adopting protocols take place within a specific matrix of non-technical norms, normative arrangements, and normative expectations, he confirms my approach. International and national law stratify the order in which decisions on protocols are made. If, in the early phase of the internet, these decisions were seemingly taken by technical actors without reference to other normative systems, then this—doubtful

[191] Robin Mansell, *Imagining the Internet. Communication, Innovation, and Governance* (Oxford: OUP, 2012).

[192] Evgeny Morozov, *To Save Everything, Click Here. Technology, Solutionism and the Urge to Fix Problems That Don't Exist* (London: Allen Lane, 2013), 203–4.

[193] Cf. Alison Powell, "Arguments-by-technology: How Technical Activism Contributes to Internet Governance," in Ian Brown (ed.), *Research Handbook on Governance of the Internet* (Cheltenham: Edward Elgar, 2013), 198–217 (199).

[194] Lawrence Lessig, *Code: Version 2.0* (New York: Basic Books, 2007); Shane Greenstein and Victor Stango (eds.), *Standards and Public Policy* (Cambridge: CUP, 2007).

[195] IETF, Public Key Pinning Extension for HTTP: "draft-ietf-websec-key-pinning-09," November 26, 2013, https://datatracker.ietf.org/doc/draft-ietf-websec-key-pinning.

[196] Greg Elmer, "Exclusionary Rules? The Politics of Protocols," in Andrew Chadwick and Philip N. Howard (eds.), *Routledge Handbook of Internet Politics* (London: Routledge, 2009), 376–82.

[197] Ibid., 376.

a statement as it is, since even these technical actors have values which they derive from a value system that will, in most cases, echo the principles and purposes of international law—only illustrates that the governance of the internet has progressed to a point where protocol decisions engage public policy issues.

The argument ex technical "necessity" usually has no traction. In RFC 2826, the internet Architecture Board underlined that the existence of a globally unique, hierarchical public name space deriving from a globally unique root is inherent in the design of the DNS. Having a single globally unique root was therefore "a technical requirement, not a policy choice."[198] Alternatives, according to RFC 2826, do not exist; there is "no getting away from the unique root of the public DNS." Does this mean that international law does not apply to the questions of managing the root server? Does defining an arrangement as a "technical requirement" absolve it from being explained and justified in light of values enshrined in the international normative order? Every specification or arrangement that engages an issue of public policy needs to be explained and justified (or at the least be explainable and justifiable) according to universal values, as enshrined by international law. As the European Commission put it in its 2014 Communication, technical specifications must "more systematically take into account public policy concerns." This is already important as a matter of principle, but particularly when "legal rights of individuals, especially their human rights, are clearly impacted."[199]

At the same time, legislators (and more generally, actors establishing normative instruments for the internet) need to be aware of standards in their function as safeguards of key features of a technology or an application. "Lawmakers should understand," Richard S. Whitt argues, "and, where appropriate, defer to the substance and processes imbued in the internet's functional design." But this does not amount to a call for a technical "veto" over lawmakers, but rather a cautious suggestion to choose among the variety of legal instruments the one most likely to "preserve the integrity of [the internet's] overall design."[200]

Ten years after RFC 3552 on security in coding,[201] RFC 6973 of 2013 laid down "privacy considerations for internet Protocols"[202] that designers "should consider in addition to regular security analysis."[203] Clearly, issues of communication security (confidentiality, data integrity, peer entity authentication) and system security engage questions of public policy. Protocol designers, working for example on HTML extensions, are asked to describe "the privacy properties specific to the extensions and any particular uses of the extensions that are expected and foreseen at design time."[204] Pursuant to the RFC, they have to keep in mind the principles of data minimization, user participation (including user control and preferences expression), and security (protection against surveillance, mitigation of stored data compromise).[205] Two further general principles are laid down for designers to consider: trade-offs and default settings. Protocol designers are asked to ensure

[198] IAB, IAB Technical Comment on the Unique DNS Root, RFC 2826, May 2000, http://www.ietf.org/rfc/rfc2826.txt.

[199] European Commission, Communication COM(2014) 72 final, para. 9.

[200] Richard S. Whitt, "A Deference to Protocol: Fashioning a Three-Dimensional Public Policy Framework for the Internet Age," Cardozo Arts & Entertainment Law Journal 31 (2013), 689–768 (695–6).

[201] IAB, RFC 3552, Guidelines for Writing RFC Text on Security Considerations, July 2003, http://tools.ietf.org/html/rfc355.

[202] IAB, RFC 6973, Privacy Considerations for Internet Protocols, July 2013, http://tools.ietf.org/html/rfc6973.

[203] Ibid., para. 9.

[204] Ibid.

[205] Ibid., para. 7.

that the protocol does not make illegitimate trade-offs between competing design goals, such as "privacy and usability, privacy and efficiency [and] privacy and implementability." Importantly, designers should make sure that the default mode or option "minimize[s] the amount, identifiability, and persistence of the data and identifiers exposed by the protocol [and] maximize the opportunity for user participation."[206] If designers choose not to use a pro-privacy default option, they are instructed to provide a rationale, thereby making privacy-friendly coding the default option.

More recently, RFC 8280 on Research into Human Rights Protocol Considerations[207] provided a detailed model for considering human rights for protocol developers, providing "questions that engineers should ask themselves when developing or improving protocols if they want to understand their impact on human rights." These range from issues of connectivity, privacy, "content agnosticism," and security to censorship resistance, accessibility, and transparency.[208]

These RFCs make clear that protocols have "politics" and that the decisions that protocol developers make are similar to those that legislators make. "Design choices in code can be as normative as law," Brown and Marsden write. But the next step is not abdicating normative responsibility to code-makers, but rather ensuring that the code reflects value judgments and the finality of the normative order of the internet: actors with a stake in the normative outcome of processes within the normative order of the internet need to make decisions regarding the values embedded by all normative instruments, including code.[209] Arguments for trade-offs need to be nuanced and informed (e.g. privacy and protection of national security). Default settings (opt-ins, opt-outs) can massively influence user behavior.[210] This confirms that the politics of protocols needs an overarching policy that is explained and justified by overarching values as enshrined by law and, as protocols transcend territorial boundaries, measured against the international legal order and its values, including the pursuance of global common interests.[211]

It is true that many technical necessities will constrain the way the internet is managed. We need one central repository of internet names and addresses, one DNS. But how the DNS is managed, and by whom, is not a decision to which technology dictates the answer. Code is agnostic when it comes to key questions of online regulation, such as who should be allowed to manage the critical resources of the internet that have to be safeguarded in the global common interest and based on what authority should management decisions be taken and to what end management reform implemented. Accepting that there can be only one authoritative root server as a technical requirement takes nothing away from the debate over who manages this server and how decisions on root server management are reached. That the importance of the stability of the DNS calls for "extremely conservative and cautious management of the public root zone"[212] is an argument, based on technical necessity,

[206] Ibid., para. 7.4.

[207] Internet Research Task Force (IRTF), RFC 8280, Research into Human Rights Protocol Considerations, https://tools.ietf.org/html/rfc8280.

[208] Ibid., paras. 42–61.

[209] Ian Brown and Christopher T. Marsden, *Regulating Code. Good Governance and Better Regulation in the Information Age* (Cambridge: MIT Press, 2013), 30.

[210] Richard H. Thaler and Cass R. Sustein, *Nudge. Improving Decisions about Health, Wealth, and Happiness* (New Haven: Yale University Press, 2008).

[211] Ian Brown and Christopher T. Marsden, *Regulating Code. Good Governance and Better Regulation in the Information Age* (Cambridge: MIT Press, 2013), 31.

[212] Cf. IAB, IAB Technical Comment on the Unique DNS Root, RFC 2826, May 2000, http://www.ietf.org/rfc/rfc2826.txt.

that might caution against, say, installing a General Assembly-like institution for managing the root server and voting on changes by majority vote. This, however, is already a question that concerns "*how*" (and not "*if*") law regulates the use and development of the internet.

We have thus established that the internet *can* be ruled by national and international law and that code is law in the sense that it is normative and therefore has to submit to (some of) the same tests of legitimacy as other norms with reference to certain values that are enshrined in (international) law. Code is also law in that it is man-made and can be based on biased assumptions. Code is also *not* law in that it does not supplant law. Rather, the relationship between code and law is more complex and law can encourage the use of code (in programs and algorithms) to overcome code that is not consonant with international legal values.

2.4.4 Algorithmic Decision-Making

For norm theorist Christoph Möllers, algorithms and normativity are mutually exclusive: "a society, whose behaviour is programmed, has no place for norms."[213] This study contends differently. Just as norms and code, norms and algorithms are intricately interlinked. Algorithms, in Tarleton Gillespie's definition, are "encoded procedures for transforming input data into a desired output, based on specified calculations. The procedures name both a problem and the steps by which it should be solved."[214] They are usually coded "steps undertaken in order to solve a particular problem or accomplish a defined outcome."[215] Using this broad definition, the normative choices in designing and applying algorithms become obvious. Algorithms perform important functions on the internet and are present in all applications and services. Their functions include prioritization (rank association according to pre-defined criteria—e.g. search engines such as Google, social media timelines as used by Facebook and Twitter), classification (grouping information based on source data features—e.g. reputation systems like eBay, Uber, Airbnb, news scoring sites such as Reddit, Digg), association (determining relationships via semantics and connotation, e.g. predictive policing), and filtering (spam filters such as Norton, recommender systems used by Spotify and Netflix, and news aggregation services as present in the Facebook News Feed).[216]

Big data and algorithms can be used to positively impact bias and discrimination in lending, employment, higher education, and criminal justice, but can also perpetuate discriminatory practices[217] and amplify structural discrimination, including through predictive

[213] Christoph Möllers, *Die Möglichkeit der Normen* (Berlin: Suhrkamp, 2016), 455: "Ein Algorithmus schließt Normativität aus. Eine Gemeinschaft, deren Verhalten programmiert wird, hat keinen Raum für Normen." (translation by the author).

[214] Tarleton Gillespie, "The Relevance of Algorithms," in Tarleton Gillespie et al. (eds.), *Media Technologies: Essays on Communication, Materiality, and Society* (Cambridge, MA: MIT Press, 2014), 167–94 (167).

[215] Nicholas Diakopoulos, "Algorithmic Accountability," Digital Journalism 3 (2015) 3, 398–415 (400).

[216] World Wide Web Foundation, Algorithmic Accountability, Applying the concept to different country contexts, July 2017, http://webfoundation.org/docs/2017/07/Algorithms_Report_WF.pdf, 7.

[217] Office of the US President, Big Data: A Report on Algorithmic Systems, Opportunity, and Civil Rights, May 2016, https://obamawhitehouse.archives.gov/sites/default/files/microsites/ostp/2016_0504_data_discrimination.pdf. See also, The Guardian, "AI Programs Exhibit Racial and Gender Biases, Research Reveals," April 13, 2017, https://www.theguardian.com/technology/2017/apr/13/ai-programs-exhibit-racist-and-sexist-biases-research-reveals.

policing.[218] Algorithmic discrimination can be caused by biased input data, poorly defined rules that allow discrimination, lack of contextual awareness, and socio-algorithmic feedback loops reinforcing existing biases that are then again fed into algorithms.[219] Algorithm-based calculation and estimates can also produce a false sense of security. Real-time data based on algorithmic calculations predicted a win for Hillary Clinton in the 2016 US elections.[220]

More generally, the design and use of algorithms can interfere with human rights.[221] The rights to fair trial and due process can be impacted by biased use of algorithms in court proceedings, including through the use of reoffending "risk scores" in probation vs. jail decisions. Privacy and data protection rights are impacted through the collection, processing, and use of vast amounts of data in online tracking algorithms.[222] Freedom of expression, which includes the right to receive information, is interfered with when predictive algorithms shape the content users see in light of prior interests or, more harmful, biased economic incentives of third actors,[223] even though the fear of "filter bubbles," that is selective publics with ever more extreme views among in-group members, seems to be empirically overblown.[224] Algorithms are also used by internet platforms to scan for problematic content, which can lead to overblocking, and to select and recommend news, which impacts the way broadcasters can reach and engage with their audiences.[225]

The right to an effective remedy can also be infringed if intermediaries using algorithms in removal contestation proceedings program an anti-reversal bias into them. Social rights are impacted when the delivery of services is premised upon algorithmic decisions which may, again, be biased and result in social sorting and denial of access to certain services. The right to free and fair elections can be impacted by algorithms that use disinformation tactics to shape content users see or that are employed in "fake news" or "disinformation" campaigns,[226] including through "social bots" that act as influencers.[227]

In light of the growing critique of "black box" algorithms, some approaches to hold authors and operators of algorithms accountable have emerged. The EU's new General Data

[218] Kristian Lum and William Isaac, "To Predict and Serve?" Significance 13 (2016) 5, 14–19, http://onlinelibrary.wiley.com/doi/10.1111/j.1740-9713.2016.00960.x/full.

[219] World Wide Web Foundation, Algorithmic Accountability, Applying the concept to different country contexts, July 2017, 9.

[220] Michael Reilly, "Prediction Models Gone Wild: Why Election Forecasts and Polls Were So Wrong," *Technology Review*, November 9, 2016, https://www.technologyreview.com/s/602829/prediction-models-gone-wild-why-election-forecasts-and-polls-were-so-wrong.

[221] Council of Europe, MSI-NET: Study on the Human Rights Dimensions of Automated Data Processing Techniques (in Particular Algorithms) and Possible Regulatory Implications, MSI-NET (2016)06rev6.

[222] Chris Jay Hoofnagle, "Behavioural Advertising: The Offer You Cannot Refuse," Harvard Law & Policy Review 6 (2012), 273–96.

[223] Report of the UN Special Rapporteur on the promotion and protection of the right to freedom of opinion and expression, David Kaye, UN Doc. A/HRC/32/38 of 11 May 2016, para. 21 ("search engine algorithms dictate what users see and in what priority, and they may be manipulated to restrict or prioritize content").

[224] Jan-Hinrik Schmidt, "Filterblasen und Algorithmenmacht. Wie sich Menschen im Internet informieren," in C. Gorr and M. C. Bauer (eds.), *Gehirne unter Spannung: Kognition, Emotion und Identität im digitalen Zeitalter* (Berlin/Heidelberg: Springer, 2018), 35–51.

[225] Cf. Jan-Hinrik Schmidt, Jannick Sørensen, Stephan Dreyer, and Uwe Hasebrink, *Algorithmische Empfehlungen. Funktionsweise, Bedeutung und Besonderheiten für öffentlich-rechtliche Rundfunkanstalten* (Hamburg: Verlag Hans-Bredow-Institut, 2018), Hans-Bredow-Institut Working Papers No. 45, https://www.hans-bredow-institut.de/uploads/media/default/cms/media/w188msk_45AlgorithmischeEmpfehlungen.pdf.

[226] Andrew Griffin, "How Facebook Is Manipulating You to Vote," *The Independent*, http://www.independent.co.uk/life-style/gadgets-and-tech/news/uk-elections-2016-how-facebook-is-manipulating-you-to-vote-a7015196.html.

[227] The Guardian, "The Great British Brexit Robbery: How Our Democracy Was Hijacked," *The Guardian*, May 7, 2017, https://www.theguardian.com/technology/2017/may/07/the-great-british-brexit-robbery-hijacked-democracy.

Protection Regulation (GDPR)[228] establishes standards for data collection through algorithms, including a limited right to information or "explanation." Article 13(2)(f) EU GDPR forces controllers to provide data subjects, in cases where personal data is collected from them, with information about the existence of automated decision-making and, at least in cases of profiling in the sense of Article 9, "meaningful information about the logic involved, as well as the significance and the envisaged consequences of such processing." Article 9 prohibits processing of certain personal data (revealing inter alia racial or ethnic origin, political opinions, religious or philosophical beliefs) unless the data subject has given consent (Article 9(2)(a)) or the processing is necessary for reasons of substantial public interest. While this does not amount to a full right to explanation of the logic behind algorithms (which is often very difficult to present in an understandable way), it does amount to a right to be sufficiently informed to be able to give informed consent to data processing.

In 2016 and 2017 the notion of algorithmic accountability slowly gathered momentum. Engineering and computer associations understood the challenge and committed to "algorithmic transparency"[229] or "ethically aligned design," underlining the need for accountability that can help "[prove] why a system acts in certain ways to address legal issues of culpability, and to avoid confusion or fear within the general public."[230] The most extensive normative approach, the *Principles for Accountable Algorithms* (2017),[231] considers accountability through five principles: responsibility (redress mechanisms for adverse effects must be provided), explainability (concerned parties must be able to understand how algorithms reach a decision), accuracy (errors need to be logged and planned for), auditability (third parties must be able to study and monitor the algorithm), and fairness (discriminatory or unjust impacts must be avoided).[232]

Algorithms are not "actants," but technological artifacts. Undesired normative consequences cannot (yet) be attributed to them, but only to the natural or legal persons that are responsible for their development and use.[233] At the same time, algorithms clearly play an important role as (quasi-)normative instruments within the normative order of the internet. Ensuring that algorithm use is consonant with the values the order expresses is among the more difficult challenges of internet regulation. Regulating code and algorithms are key elements of normative order approaches to the internet.

[228] Regulation (EU) 2016/679 of the European Parliament and of the Council of 27 April 2016 on the protection of natural persons with regard to the processing of personal data and on the free movement of such data, and repealing Directive 95/46/EC (General Data Protection Regulation), OJ L 119/1 of 4 May 2016.

[229] Cf. Association for Computing Machinery, Statement on Algorithmic Transparency and Accountability (2017), http://www.acm.org/binaries/content/assets/public-policy/2017_usacm_statement_algorithms.pdf.

[230] IEEE, Ethically Aligned Design, December 2016, http://standards.ieee.org/develop/indconn/ec/ead_v1.pdf.

[231] Fairness, Accountability, and Transparency in Machine Learning (FATML), Principles for Accountable Algorithms (2017), http://www.fatml.org/resources/principles-for-accountable-algorithms.

[232] This merits extensive quotation, ibid.: "Responsibility. Make available externally visible avenues of redress for adverse individual or societal effects of an algorithmic decision system, and designate an internal role for the person who is responsible for the timely remedy of such issues; Explainability. Ensure that algorithmic decisions as well as any data driving those decisions can be explained to end-users and other stakeholders in non-technical terms; Accuracy. Identify, log, and articulate sources of error and uncertainty throughout the algorithm and its data sources so that expected and worst case implications can be understood and inform mitigation procedures; Auditability. Enable interested third parties to probe, understand, and review the behavior of the algorithm through disclosure of information that enables monitoring, checking, or criticism, including through provision of detailed documentation, technically suitable APIs, and permissive terms of use; Fairness. Ensure that algorithmic decisions do not create discriminatory or unjust impacts when comparing across different demographics (e.g. race, sex, etc)."

[233] Ibid.

2.5 Conclusions

The internet has become a vital medium of communication that mediates much of our lived experience and through which individuals exercise their human rights, especially through the enabling right to freedom of expression, including the right to seek, receive, and impart information and ideas of all kind, regardless of frontiers. At the same time, "the internet" is merely a hardware-based data-transfer capability running software based on protocols that ensure interconnectivity. In order to *use* the internet, both its public core and its "content"—the sites and services that make it attractive—have to be protected as must be the enabling normative system(s) that ensure(s) its functioning.

The internet's public core and the servers necessary for it to function are both indispensable for critical infrastructure (e.g. power grids) to work and, in themselves, critical (information) infrastructure. Safeguarding the internet's integrity (its security, stability, robustness, resilience, and functionality) has become an essential goal of any normative order that includes internet regulation, including national, European, and international law. Any protection must extend to the internet's hardware: cables, data centers, root servers, internet Exchange Points, and a working naming and addressing system. These are critical internet resources.

Protecting the internet in both its dimensions—kinetic and non-kinetic, including a protective normative framework—lies in the common interest of all states. The goals pursued by states within the framework of creating a people-centered, development-oriented information society, in which international law is fully applicable, of promoting development, and of respecting, protecting, and enforcing human rights are clearly common interest goals. They cannot be reached without immunizing both the public core of the internet and the *Möglichkeitsraum* (realm of possibilities) of the internet against illegitimate state intervention. This implies that states exercising jurisdiction over a "piece" of the internet (be it specific sites, servers, services, or users) are limited in their sovereignty by the prohibition of affecting negatively the pursuance of the common interest.

Before discussing, in the next chapter, how international law and internet governance normatively frame the internet, this chapter has identified key challenges of regulating the internet. Having deconstructed the foundational myth that the internet is a space free of laws, this chapter has shown that states have a duty to protect their citizens with regard to the internet (and regarding their online activities). Companies, too, have a corporate social responsibility to respect human rights within their sphere of influence, which—on the internet—is growing rapidly as the majority of relevant communicative acts takes place in private spaces. The special role of intermediaries is another challenge for regulating the internet. As the majority of online spaces lies in private hands, it is private law that prima facie frames many norm conflicts online. When states react belatedly through laws or judgments, these may lead to overblocking or legal conflicts between competing jurisdictions.[234]

The normative actors on the internet have influenced the composition of the medium of law and moved it toward a more flexible geometry of normativity, including non-binding

[234] See the evolution of the "right to be forgotten": Years of uncertainty followed the CJEU judgment in *Google Spain and Google* (2014). They culminated in a July 19, 2017 referral decision by the French Conseil d'État, of its case *Google Inc.*, n° 399922, to the CJEU to clarify the geographical reach of its 2014 ruling (delisting globally or only within the EU). The right to erasure ("right to be forgotten") can now be found in Article 17 GDPR.

norms and principles, standards and codes, which have been influential in the development of the internet. This normative architecture and norm production machinery is characteristic of the internet, as is the reliance on code and algorithms as quasi-normative tools.

In light of the hypotheses put forward in the introduction, this chapter has demonstrated the conceptual genealogy of norms on the internet and analyzed the categories of norms relevant for the establishment of the normative order. This chapter has further shown how non-state actors, such as technical standard-setters, develop norms through non-traditionally legitimated norm-making processes. Technical norms, standards, contracts—and European and international legal rules (here: establishing and implementing common interest regulation)—form a hybrid order. Importantly, the non-traditional normative instruments form part of a third category of norms, the normative tertium. In light of the lack of a general treaty regulating the normative order of the internet, this normative disarray makes evident the need for structural principles of the order. Their foundations will be developed in the next chapter.

Already at this stage of the study, the hypothesis that through norms we can apply values to standards and code and "renormativize" them stands as correct. Just as has happened with industrial norms in the last century, codes and standards are shown to be part of the normative order of the internet and not technical artifacts.

The key critical internet resources—internet routing, the Domain Name System, certificates and trust, and communications cables—have also been called the "public core of the internet" and deserve special protection.[235] The hypothesis that value-based normativity must influence technical standard-setting to ensure, inter alia, the protection of the common interest is shown to be valid. Far from being a space where only ad hoc norms develop, essential elements of the internet's architecture are based on stable normative arrangements.

These include, as this chapter has shown, the stable system of unique identifiers, secure information interchange through routing, cable connections, working Internet Exchange Points, and common standards. The regulatory order of the internet oriented toward ensuring its integrity is therefore a CIR, but at the same time protects other CIRs, including kinetic ones. Many of the internet's information interchanges are based on "gentlemen's agreements," trust or mutual interest and reliance, or private contracts. Only a few root servers are run by governmental institutions. The normative order of the internet has to encompass all these elements of the normative infrastructure: the normative instruments with varying degrees of normativity and different actors.

The normative infrastructure of the internet protects the internet directly and indirectly. To illustrate this approach, consider Principle No. 5 of the Declaration by the Committee of Ministers (CM) on internet governance principles,[236] on the universality of the internet, which provides that "internet-related policies should recognize the global nature of the internet and the objective of universal access [and] should not adversely affect the unimpeded

[235] In late 2017, the Global Commission on the Stability of Cyberspace proposed a norm to specifically protect the core and establish a principle of non-interference with the public core: "Without prejudice to their rights and obligations, state and non-state actors should not conduct or knowingly allow activity that intentionally and substantially damages the general availability or integrity of the public core of the Internet, and therefore the stability of cyberspace." (Global Commission on the Stability of Cyberspace, Call to Protect the Public Core of the Internet, New Delhi, November 2017, https://cyberstability.org/wp-content/uploads/2017/11/call-to-protect-the-public-core-of-the-internet.pdf).

[236] Council of Europe, Declaration by the Committee of Ministers on Internet governance principles, adopted by the Committee of Ministers on 21 September 2011 at the 1121st meeting of the Ministers' Deputies, https://wcd.coe.int/ViewDoc.jsp?id=1835773.

flow of transboundary internet traffic." This rule, if established that it has crystallized into a rule of international customary law, protects the internet directly in that it secures the unimpeded transfer of data packages, which is key to its functioning.

By contrast, para. 1 of the Human Rights Council Resolution on the promotion, protection, and enjoyment of human rights on the internet (2016) affirms that "the same rights that people have offline must also be protected online, in particular freedom of expression, which is applicable regardless of frontiers and through any media of one's choice [...]."[237] The primary normative objects here are the rights which are applicable online just as offline. But, indirectly, the internet's intangible dimension of offering a space for the exercise of these rights is protected as well. The internet's integrity is a structural condition of the exercise of human rights,[238] which are both challenged by technology[239] and realized through it.

Refuting technicity as a normative argument, this chapter confirms the hypothesis that the technocratic preference for code over law (implying that value-based norms are unnecessary for the process of developing new code and protocols and other normative instruments) is wrong. Code *is* law in that it is normative, but not law in the sense of it supplanting norms. Code and protocols are man-made artifacts and as building blocks of programs (and algorithms) they influence how people use the internet and how it develops. Simply put, protocols "have politics" and must be assessed and treated like other norms.

Algorithms (coded steps undertaken in a certain order to solve a problem according to preprogrammed rules) have emerged as important objects of normative scrutiny. Their design and use can interfere with human rights. Used by all internet companies and in most ICTs, in everything from smart home heating systems to predictive policing and regulating hate speech on social media, they can have substantial discriminatory effects and externalities. This study has identified two normative approaches to ensure more accountability of algorithms. First, at least one legal document, the EU General Data Protection Regulation, forces data controllers to provide subjects with an "explanation" of the logic of the algorithm using the data. Second, notions of algorithmic transparency and ethically aligned design have cumulated in the publication of the Principles for Accountable Algorithms, which formulated demands regarding the responsibility, explainability, accuracy, fairness, and auditability of algorithms.

Having shown that the internet's order of norm is a hybrid made of national, European, and international law, code, and technical standards, and that it is value-based normative choices that, in contrast to foundational myths of the internet, influence the normative development of the internet, the need for first structuring principles of the order becomes evident. Let us thus turn now from the new normative instruments of algorithms to the more traditional one of international law[240] and the newer but well-established norms of internet governance, two key foundational orders of the internet.

[237] Human Rights Council, Resolution 32/13, The promotion, protection and enjoyment of human rights on the Internet, UN Doc. A/HRC/RES/32/13 of 18 July 2016.

[238] For this argument, see in more detail 2.3.2.

[239] Cf. Giovanni Sartor, "Human Rights and Information Technologies," in Roger Brownsword, Eloise Scotford, and Karen Yeung (eds.), *Oxford Handbook of Law, Regulation, and Technology* (Oxford: OUP, 2017), 424–50.

[240] Though their name goes back to the eighth century Persian mathematician Al-Khwārizmī, who was latinized to *Algoritmi*. The first international treaty apparently also stems from that region: the 4500 BC political treaty between the city-states of Ebla and Abarsal (now Syria) (see Malcolm N. Shaw, *International Law*, 8th edn. (Oxford: OUP, 2017), 10, note 50) and the 2100 BC border agreement between the rulers of two city-states in Mesopotamia (see Arthur Nussbaum, *A Concise History of the Law of Nations* (New York: Macmillan, 1947), 8.

3

Law and Governance of the Internet

3.1 Foundational Rules

As technologies progress, the need for normation—either through social norms, through self-regulation, through co-regulation, or through state regulation—emerges. In light of the internet's and its technological predecessors' genesis as a project of, first, the US Department of Defense and, then, academia and the technical community,[1] this regulatory need was answered first by decentralized, non-binding normative approaches that were nevertheless very effective because of the small circle of specialized norm producers who were largely identical with the norm recipients.

From 1969 onwards, suggestions for standards, rules, and procedures, called "Requests for comments," were sent out by members of standard-setting bodies such as the IETF.[2] They were phrased as suggestions (requesting a comment), but through the authority of their authors and their acceptance through "rough consensus" procedures they developed quasi-obligatory power.[3] "Rough consensus" was based on the "dominant view" of the concerned group, deduced not from volume or persistence but on the basis of a "more general sense of agreement."[4]

It was not until 1994, when the US National Science Foundation decided to contract out the management of the domain name system to a private party, that a comprehensive policy debate on the regulation of the internet arose. States and international organizations became progressively involved as normative actors. In 1996, as a reaction to this trend, John Perry Barlow published his Declaration of the Independence of Cyberspace and called upon the "Governments of the Industrial World, you weary giants of flesh and steel[,]" to leave cyberspace "alone." "You are not welcome among us," he wrote, "[y]ou have no sovereignty where we gather."[5] This was empirically untrue already in 1996; it is even more so today. As argued above, states need to exercise their sovereignty over situations emerging in cyberspace and have consistently done so, albeit with varying degrees of situational and technological awareness, legal sense, and political sensibility.

John Perry Barlow not only questioned the sovereignty of states to regulate where the "digital natives" gathered,[6] but generally discounted the right of states to regulate what lay

[1] On the history of the Internet, see Wolfgang Kleinwächter, "Multi-Stakeholder Internet Governance: The Role of Governments," in Wolfgang Benedek, Veronika Bauer, and Matthias C. Kettemann (eds.), *Internet Governance and the Information Society. Global Perspectives and European Dimensions* (Utrecht: Eleven, 2008), 9–29.

[2] See the RFC (Request for Comments) series, http://www.rfc-editor.org. On the nature of the "Requests for comments," see Heinz Schulte, *RFCs und Internetstandards im Überblick* (Kissing: Interest-Verlag, 2004).

[3] Cf. RFC 2418—IETF Working Group Guidelines (1998), https://tools.ietf.org/search/rfc2418, delineating the "Working Group Guidelines" and providing for the principle of "rough consensus" as a decision-making paradigm in actor.

[4] RFC 7282—On Consensus and Humming in the IETF (2014), https://tools.ietf.org/html/rfc7282.

[5] John Perry Barlow, "A Declaration of the Independence of Cyberspace," Davos, February 8, 1996, http://www.actlab.utexas.edu/~captain/cyber.decl.indep.html.

[6] For an early use of the term "digital native," see Marc Prensky, "Digital Natives, Digital Immigrants," *On The Horizon* 9 (October 2001), 5; a more comprehensive study is provided in John Palfrey and Urs Gasser, *Born*

The Normative Order of the Internet. Matthias C. Kettemann, Oxford University Press (2020). © Matthias C. Kettemann.
DOI: 10.1093/oso/9780198865995.001.0001

beyond their "borders." This critique of the effectiveness of state regulation in times of globalization is not original. As Gerd Winter notes, in today's polity the state is hampered by borders in exercising its sovereignty effectively over issues that happen beyond them but impact its citizens. States have called upon the "sorcerer's apprentice" of the global economy but have given up their control ("Meisterschaft") over him. They are only needed to "assuage the social costs and to pacify social frustration."[7]

This study makes the case that it is rather international law that is the legal framework regulating what lies beyond the borders of any one state, including the frame and foundations for decisions related to internet-related public policy issues. It is, further, international law that manages the global common interest in the internet's functionality and, through its norms (including e.g. a right to universal access for all), promotes both technological progress collectively and self-actualization individually (which also works against social frustration). However, as already shown in the previous chapter, the normative order of the internet contains national legal rules, international legal rules, and transnational normative arrangements. While the code and standards discussed in the previous chapter form part of the normative "tertium" (that is norms that do not belong clearly to either the international or the national legal order), this section analyzes the applicable rules of international law and the norms of internet governance, as they relate to the internet and the protection of states and societies from the dangers emanating from its use and development. The hypothesis tested in this chapter is that international legal rules exist that can form a foundational part of the normative order of the internet and that no new "international law of the internet" needs to be created.

The internet was never ruled anarchically, that is through spontaneous non-centrally enforced ordering,[8] though some elements of anarchy persist, including the focus on voluntariness, community-consent, and a quick, partly non-planned emergence of rules. As Jeremy Malcolm analyzes, anarchistic ordering of the internet would be "consistent" with both the internet's principles on a technical level and "consonant" with "many of them on a cultural level."[9] But technical consistency and cultural consonancy (or consonancy with the culture of (non-)regulation formally, and materially with the (non-)regulatory purpose) are not enough to suppose that an anarchistic system-structure for the internet would be preferable. The spontaneous emergence of anarchistic structures and their fluidity make it difficult to provide for participation of as many actor groups as possible which are necessary for ensuring legitimacy. Effectiveness of rules further cannot be guaranteed in light of the voluntary nature of actor involvement in anarchistic structures and the spontaneous emergence (or non-emergence) of norms.[10]

The purpose of regulating the internet (by international law) remains clear: the internet's functionality is essential to areas as diverse as the international economy, the transnational

Digital: Understanding the First Generation of Digital Natives (New York: Basic Books, 2008), http://borndigitalbook.com.

[7] Gerd Winter, "Transnationale informelle Regulierung: Gestalt, Effekte und Rechtstaatlichkeit," in Gralf-Peter Calliess (ed.), *Transnationales Recht. Stand und Perspektiven* (Tübingen: Mohr Siebeck, 2014), 95–112 (96–7).

[8] Though some elements of spontaneous ordering are present in certain internet subcultures. Cf., for an overview of the anarchic elements of Internet Governance, Jeremy Malcolm, *Multi-Stakeholder Governance and the Internet Governance Forum* (Perth: Terminus Press, 2008), 191 et seq.

[9] Ibid., 191.

[10] Cf. Ibid. 194–5.

communications infrastructure, national defense, and human rights protection. But states alone cannot effectively regulate the internet as it transcends their territorial sovereignty and many of its key resources are not controlled by states. Overreaching regulatory endeavors by states and state-sponsored cyber-espionage, such as China's in 2015–2016,[11] or information (or influence) operations, such as Russia's in 2016–2017,[12] can endanger the stability and functionality of the internet (on a factual level and on a trust level[13]) as a whole. Therefore, before endeavoring to develop a normative order of the internet, the international law of the internet and the regulatory approaches through internet governance need to be examined.

After clarifying the applicability of international law to the internet (3.2), the rules relating to the internet will be explored in section 3.3. The "softer" regulatory approach of internet governance, including its practice of involving all actors in order to legitimize normative outcomes ("multistakeholderism"), will be examined in section 3.4. Their interaction and mutual reinforcement will be the topic of section 3.5. Their common and individual shortfalls lead to regulatory lacunae and normative fractures. Their identification and exposition will begin this study's analysis of forces of disorder, which will be the main topic of the next chapter (4) on the normative disorder on the internet. But first, this chapter focuses on the traditional orders on the internet, international law, and internet governance.

3.2 Applicability of International Law

3.2.1 From Disorganized Normativity to the "Ius Necessarium"

International law plays an important role in this study and as a foundational body of rules within the normative order of the internet. The military–academic history of the internet and the private sector-led development of key architectural elements (through government-financed projects and on government grants) have contributed to a state of disorganized normativity. Private actors exercise substantial normative influence both on the macro-level (by coordinating critical internet resources, for a long time on behalf of a single state steward (the United States of America (USA)), now on behalf of the "global multistakeholder community," that is all relevant actors[14]) and on the micro-level (by setting the terms of services of the private spaces where the overwhelming majority of internet users are active and with regard to the services they use).

[11] Even though US President Obama and Chinese President Xi Jinping signed a Cybersecurity Agreement in 2015 after the US Department of Justice indicted five Chinese Army officers for economic espionage (see Gary Brown and Christopher D. Yung, "Evaluating the US-China Cybersecurity Agreement," *The Diplomat*, January 19, 2017, https://thediplomat.com/2017/01/evaluating-the-us-china-cybersecurity-agreement-part-1-the-us-approach-to-cyberspace).

[12] Scott Shane, "The Fake Americans Russia Created to Influence the Election," *New York Times*, September 7, 2017, https://www.nytimes.com/2017/09/07/us/politics/russia-facebook-twitter-election.html (describing a "cyberarmy of counterfeit Facebook and Twitter accounts, a legion of Russian-controlled impostors" and arguing that Russia turned Facebook and Twitter into "engines of deception and propaganda").

[13] Report of the Office of the United Nations High Commissioner for Human Rights, Navi Pillay, The right to privacy in the digital age, UN Doc. A/HRC/27/37 of 30 June 2014.

[14] ICANN, Stewardship of IANA Functions Transitions to Global Internet Community as Contract with U.S. Government Ends, October 1, 2016, https://www.icann.org/news/announcement-2016-10-01-en (announcing that this date marked "the transition of the coordination and management of the Internet's unique identifiers to the private-sector" within a multistakeholder model of Internet governance validated by the community).

Over the years a body of norms and corollary normative expectations has emerged that constitutes one of few international orders regulating the administration and development of an issue of common interest without a comprehensive, systematic, and planned international legal foundation in the form of a treaty. The normative approach to the internet thus varies greatly from approaches of regulating and safeguarding other issues of common interest, sometimes metaphorically compared to the internet such as the air, the sea(bed), or polar regions[15] or even more technical ones such as disarmament, nuclear non-proliferation, postal services, international rivers, or telecommunication services—all of which are based on one or many international treaties with (mostly) Secretariats and (often) decision-making bodies.

Regulating the internet may be complex with intersecting responsibilities in different policy arenas lying with different actors on multiple normative levels, from ensuring the internet's addressing space to safeguarding free expression online, from realizing the development-orientation of the information society to regulating platforms and search engines, from limiting the power of algorithms to fighting cybercrime.[16] But the real difference, it is submitted, to other regimes lies in the intensity, depth, and breadth of transformations that the internet has brought with it for all areas of human sociality. Simply put, traditional regimes such as the law of non-proliferation or the law of outer space may ask one big question (How to safeguard the world from nuclear destruction? How to ensure that space is not used as a military staging post?), but the regulation of the internet leads to many smaller questions that impact the daily lives of humans, companies, and states more intensively.

While, for example, the international climate regime relies on a key treaty, the United Nations Paris Agreement (2015), which drew from the normative success of the United Nations Framework Convention on Climate Change (1992), the internet has no such central normative framework, nor is it likely to have one in the foreseeable future. This study, however, shows that a normative framework for the regulation and governance of the internet already exists, which limits state interventions,[17] delineates rights and obligations of companies, and ensures a position for internet users. International law provides the foil against which the normative tensions between global and regional normative endeavors, binding rules and soft law arrangements, self-regulated and state-regulated spaces, and public and private normative orders can be resolved.

International law protects the security, stability, robustness, resilience, and functionality of the internet—its integrity—as a matter of common interest.[18] International law helps determine under which conditions rules crystallize into international legal duties and which remain soft law (and international legal research then needs to identify whether these

[15] International environmental law is also often cited as an example of a regime where international legal rules took time to develop. Cf. Andreas Zimmermann, "International Law and 'Cyber Space'," ESIL Reflections 3 (2014) 1, http://www.esil-sedi.eu/node/481,4.

[16] On cybercrime and security, see David S. Wall, "Crime, Security, and Information Communication Technologies: The Changing Cybersecurity Threat Landscape and Its Implications for Regulation and Policing," in Roger Brownsword, Eloise Scotford, and Karen Yeung (eds.), *Oxford Handbook of Law, Regulation, and Technology* (Oxford: OUP, 2017), 1075–96.

[17] Cf. Anne Peters, "Realizing Utopia as A Scholarly Endeavour," EJIL 24 (2013), 533–52 (551) (identifying a similar problem with regard to international law as a whole: "Because of the openness of international norms [...] states will tend to assert rules which are in their favour [...] or they will do what they want". Purely positive analysis cannot help. Peters therefore counsels a normative approach, similar to the one employed here.

[18] See 2.3.

conditions are met). International law empowers individuals by ensuring that they can exercise their human rights online and obliges them not to violate international rules prohibiting, for example, online calls to genocide. International law allocates duties to states (e.g. regarding the internet's stability), but it also empowers them vis-à-vis internet companies by demonstrating their key role in safeguarding the rights of their citizens. International law finally obliges companies to respect international legal rules, especially in the field of human rights, through a long normative tradition of turning corporate social responsibility into duties to respect human rights,[19] including rights to data protection and privacy in outside jurisdictions.

Early reports by international organizations already addressed the fact that the internet (or "cyberspace") challenged traditional concepts of ensuring rights. An experts' study for UNESCO found in 1998 that "[c]yberspace calls into question frontiers, which it bypasses, and the state laws, which it challenges."[20] It is true that the internet challenges national laws, but so do other forces such as globalization without invalidating them. In addition, it is international law that has developed for this purpose: to provide globally equitable solutions for normative challenges beyond frontiers and in cases where national laws, alone and in their interaction, may be difficult to apply.

If a brief tangent is permitted: The question of *why* international law should regulate affairs between nations (or, in a more modern version, international actors) is one of the more interesting posed by international legal philosophy because of the many possible answers.[21] According to *Jellinek* the reason is to be found in the "objectiven Principe"[22] that the nature of living conditions demands legal normation based on a common "Rechtsanschauung." Put differently: international law exists because it is necessary, a "ius necessarium."[23] This necessity of international relations to be regulated applies to the internet as well: its actors need an international law-based normative order that stabilizes normative expectations and allows for a critique of developments in light of the values enshrined by international law.

Already Immanuel Kant saw world peace as dependent on the juridification of international relations. He, however, saw international law's function as complementing, rather than evolving into, cosmopolitan law.[24] Taking the last step was left to Jürgen Habermas.[25] Though we are not actually in a "global war for internet governance"[26] and even if the controversies between the US and Russia on internet regulation—starting at ITU's World

[19] Cf. Report of the Special Representative of the Secretary-General on the issue of human rights and transnational corporations and other business enterprises, John Ruggie, Guiding Principles on Business and Human Rights: Implementing the United Nations "Protect, Respect and Remedy" Framework, UN Doc. A/HRC/17/31 of 21 March 2011.

[20] UNESCO, Report of the Experts' Meeting on Cyberspace Law, Monte Carlo, September 29–30, 1998, http://unesdoc.unesco.org/images/0011/001163/116300e.pdf, para. 10. UNESCO, confident about its role in international affairs, had its experts ask whether the UN General Assembly should "approve the establishment of an international legal framework or system for cyberspace under the aegis of UNESCO" (ibid., 9). The UN General Assembly did not.

[21] For some of them, see the contributions in Samantha Besson and John Tasioulas, *The Philosophy of International Law* (Oxford: OUP, 2010).

[22] Georg Jellinek, *Die rechtliche Natur der Staatsverträge. Ein Beitrag zur Juristischen Construction des Völkerrechts* (Vienna: Alfred Hölder, 1880), 43.

[23] Georg Dahm, Jost Delbrück, and Rüdiger Wolfrum, *Völkerrecht*, Vol. I/3 (Berlin: De Gruyter, 2002), 41, 43.

[24] See Amanda Perreau-Suassine, "Immanuel Kant on International Law," in Samantha Besson and John Tasioulas, *The Philosophy of International Law* (Oxford: OUP, 2010), 53–75 (72).

[25] Jürgen Habermas, "Hat die Konstitutionalisierung des Völkerrechts noch eine Chance?," in Jürgen Habermas, *Der gespaltene Westen. Kleine politische Schriften X* (Frankfurt: Suhrkamp, 2004), 142.

[26] Cf. Laura DeNardis, *The Global War for Internet Governance* (New Haven: Yale University Press, 2014).

Conference on International Telecommunications (WCIT) Summit in 2012 and continuing into the influence over information operations in the US elections in 2016—have not started a new Cold War about the internet, there are substantial conflicts of interests that need to be resolved and regulatory challenges for actors at different levels of the international spectrum that need to be met.

States are not able to regulate through national law a *global* socio-technological facility as the internet. There are four main reasons for this: *first*, the internet has become a critical infrastructural resource and critical for other critical infrastructural resources (as has been shown *supra*, in 2.2); *second*, the internet, and its regulation and governance (and constitutionalization), has itself become an issue of global common interest and the protection of its integrity is necessary for safeguarding other global common interests (as has been demonstrated, *supra*, in 2.3); *third*, the "embedded politics of technical architecture"[27] do not allow for ex post qualification in light of 192 (and more) national legal systems—one normative system needs to establish the values to be enshrined in architecture or criticize existing architecture in light of these values; *fourth*, the privatization of internet management functions and the delegation of aspects of state tasks such as law enforcement to internationally active private sector entities have put states in a position where only coordinated international actions according to internationally accepted principles can set necessary limits.

To recapitulate: essential internet points of control—addresses, root servers, IXPs, but also standards—are coordinated and managed by private entities that are not accountable through traditional democratic processes with a prima facie innate legitimacy-conferral function in the Habermasian sense.[28] At the same time, protecting the security, stability, robustness, resilience, and functionality (thus: the integrity) of the internet lies in the global common interest. If a good or entity or facility is thus marked, international law is not only a possible but rather a *necessary* normative regulator.

3.2.2 Toward a Consensus

International law is thus the only normative order that can deal systemically with the variety of actors relevant for the internet's use and development. Only international law can coherently deal with companies and NGOs (non-governmental organizations), states, individuals, and international organizations on a local, regional, and global level—and although the actors differ and the normative geometries are varied, what these situations have in common is an international (transborder) setting. Internet "controllers," in a wide sense, such as ICANN and key Internet Exchange Points, social networks, and search engines, exercise (limited) (semi- or quasi-)public authority under conditions of internationality and relative normative instability, especially when private regimes and public law collide. We must determine the frame (especially for states) underlying the rule of these actors through international law. As national democratic normative processes are determined and

[27] Ibid., 2.

[28] Jürgen Habermas, *Faktizität und Geltung. Beiträge zur Diskurstheorie des Rechts und des demokratischen Rechtsstaats* (Frankfurt: Suhrkamp, 1992/1998), 369, 492. Cf. among many others, Jeffrey Flynn, "Communicative Power in Habermas's Theory of Democracy," European Journal of Political Theory (2004), 433–54.

overshadowed by technologist decision-making, international law is the only normative order that can, as a legitimate order, qualify rules on, and rules of, the internet and provide states with foundational principles for normative and factual action impacting the internet.

Already during the first phase of the United Nations World Summit on the Information Society (WSIS) in 2003, states expressed their

> common desire and commitment to build a people-centred, inclusive and development-oriented Information Society, [...] enabling individuals, communities and peoples to achieve their full potential in promoting their sustainable development and improving their quality of life, *premised on the purposes and principles of the Charter of the United Nations and respecting fully and upholding the Universal Declaration of Human Rights.*[29]

The commitment in principle by states to development (MDGs), human rights (Universal Declaration of Human Rights (UDHR)), and international law (the principles and purposes of the UN Charter) in the process of developing and using the internet has a long pedigree.[30] But no single body of norms can be easily identified as being, by itself, able to lay the normative foundations. Yet international law has the best claim to being a foundational order. The 2013 Report of the Group of Governmental Experts on Developments in the Field of Information and Telecommunications in the Context of International Security (GGE) built on the Geneva and Tunis documents by confirming that applying norms derived from "existing international law relevant to the use of ICTs by States is an essential measure to reduce risks to international peace, security and stability." International law, and "in particular the Charter of the United Nations, is applicable and is essential to maintaining peace and stability and promoting an open, secure, peaceful and accessible ICT environment."[31]

Leading studies of the GGE 2013 report agreed.[32] The GGE 2013 is an important report because until that date some states, including powerful states with a strong and developed internet with local companies offering alternative services to Silicon Valley's, had previously been reluctant to formally acknowledge the premise of "offline international law" being applicable to online forums. With the agreement in the 2013 report that, *first*, international law, and in particular the UN Charter, is applicable, *second*, it is essential for world peace, and *third*, international law is important for human development (via an enabling internet), a global consensus was reached,[33] even though some states, such as China, adopted a very sovereignty-oriented interpretation.[34] Building on this consensus, the 2015[35] report of the

[29] WSIS, Declaration of Principles, WSIS-03/GENEVA/DOC/4-E, 12 December 2003, para. 1 (emphasis added).

[30] WSIS, Tunis Commitment, WSIS-05/TUNIS/DOC/7-E, 18 November 2005, para. 2.

[31] Report of the Group of Governmental Experts on Developments in the Field of Information and Telecommunications in the Context of International Security, UN Doc. A/68/98 of 24 June 2013, para. 19.

[32] See Michael N. Schmitt and Liis Vihul, "The Nature of International Law Cyber Norms," Tallinn Paper No. 5 (NATO CCD COE), 2014, 16; Katharina Ziolkowski, "General Principles of International Law as Applicable in Cyberspace," in Katharina Ziolkowski (ed.), *Peacetime Regime for State Activities in Cyberspace. International Law, International Relations and Diplomacy* (Tallinn: NATO CCD COE Publications, 2013), 135–84 (151–2).

[33] Michael N. Schmitt and Liis Vihul, "The Nature of International Law Cyber Norms" (2015), https://ccdcoe.org/uploads/2018/10/Tallinn-Paper-No-5-Schmitt-and-Vihul.pdf, 12.

[34] Cf. Adam Segal, "Chinese Cyber Diplomacy in a New Era of Uncertainty," Hoover Institution, Aegis Paper Series No. 1703, June 2, 2017, https://www.hoover.org/research/chinese-cyber-diplomacy-new-era-uncertainty.

[35] United Nations, Developments in the Field of Information and Telecommunications in the Context of International Security, Report of the Secretary General, A/70/174 of July 22, 2015, http://www.un.org/ga/search/view_doc.asp?symbol=A/70/174 (hereinafter: "GGE report (2015)").

GGE again confirmed that international law, the UN Charter, and international legal principles apply to the internet,[36] stating inter alia that the international community aspired to regulate the internet in a peaceful manner "for the common good of mankind":[37] "[t]he adherence by States to international law, in particular their Charter obligations, is an essential framework for their actions in their use of ICTs and to promote an open, secure, stable, accessible and peaceful ICT environment."[38]

The appearance of a global consensus on the subject is only somewhat tampered by the failure of the GGE to conclude with a third consensus report in 2017. This breakdown was caused mainly by certain states (including China and Russia) arguing that explicitly applying the UN Charter's provisions regarding use of force to cyberspace before technical means of attribution delivered more reliable results would lead to the militarization of cyberspace. Other states wanted to include references to the application of countermeasures even in situations falling below the "use of force" threshold.[39] Both groups consciously ignored previous firm commitments in the WSIS documents, and the 2013 and 2015 GGE reports, which all included references to the applicability on the internet of the UN Charter, in fact "in particular the UN Charter." It should be noted, however, that already in the run-up to the 2015 report China, Russia, Pakistan, Malaysia, and Belarus had opposed language favored by the US to include an *explicit* reference to Article 51 with its authorization of self-defense against armed attacks.[40] Nevertheless, the 2013 and 2015 reports (which contain the same basic commitments to the applicability and relevance of international law for the internet) and the apparent consensus, in the 2017 draft, to "stabilizing measures, including voluntary, non-binding norms of responsible State behavior in cyberspace and confidence-building measures"[41] are a sound basis for future normative developments and a good indication of state normative preferences, if not yet clearly their opinio iuris.

3.2.3 Old Rules or New Rules?

Andreas Zimmermann, in a brief study of international law and "cyber space" (his quotation marks), argues that, as "with other novel areas of international law which have developed in the last decennials [...] only time will tell whether the international community of States will be able and willing to over time come up with specific and adequate rules of

[36] Ibid., para. 26.

[37] Ibid., para. 28 (c).

[38] Ibid., para. 25.

[39] Cf. Adam Segal, "The Development of Cyber Norms at the United Nations Ends in Deadlock. Now What?" Council on Foreign Relations, June 29, 2017, https://www.cfr.org/blog/development-cyber-norms-united-nations-ends-deadlock-now-what; Arun M. Sukumar, "The UN GGE Failed. Is International Law in Cyberspace Doomed As Well?," *Lawfare*, July 4, 2017, https://lawfareblog.com/un-gge-failed-international-law-cyberspace-doomed-well; and Ann Väljataga, "Back to Square One? The Fifth UN GGE Fails to Submit a Conclusive Report at the UN General Assembly," NATO CCDCOE Incyder database, https://ccdcoe.org/incyder-articles/back-to-square-one-the-fifth-un-gge-fails-to-submit-a-conclusive-report-at-the-un-general-assembly.

[40] Eneken Tikk and Mika Kerttunen, "The Alleged Demise of the UN GGE: An Autopsy and Eulogy," Cyber Policy Institute (2017), http://cpi.ee/wp-content/uploads/2017/12/2017-Tikk-Kerttunen-Demise-of-the-UN-GGE-2017-12-17-ET.pdf.

[41] Michele G. Markoff, Deputy Coordinator for Cyber Issues, US State Department, "Explanation of Position at the Conclusion of the 2016-2017 UN Group of Governmental Experts (GGE) on Developments in the Field of Information and Telecommunications in the Context of International Security," June 23, 2017, https://www.state.gov/s/cyberissues/releasesandremarks/272175.htm.

international law applicable to 'cyber space.'"[42] As the following sections show, there have been few new rule-making endeavors. Even in their absence, international lawyers have the "fallback position" of relying on existing (therefore not internet-specific), general (thus rather vague) rules of international law. But this is not a problem that is particular to the internet. As Zimmermann notes, "we have previously seen the very same development in other areas, international environmental law again being a particularly relevant example at hand before specific treaty regimes were established."[43] This is possible, though unlikely, given the current international normative climate regarding the internet.

The internet exhibits several of these unique features (including its impact on our daily lives, the asynchronicity of information flows and threats, non-temporality, and network effects), to which general rules of international law may not be normatively convincing answers. Yet already GGE underlined in both reports that, taking into account "the complexity and unique attributes of ICTs,"[44] additional international legal norms may need to be developed. Further specificities include the central role of private actors in managing both critical resources and communicative spaces (platforms) and the invocation of processes of normative deliberation that involve all relevant actors in their respective roles. The role and responsibilities of actors in international law, and international law more generally, are influenced by the development of the world in which it exists: "[T]he development of international law," the International Court of Justice (ICJ) wrote in *Reparation for Injuries*, "has been influenced by the requirements of international life."[45] Today's international life is a "life 2.0,"[46] as the often-used indication of a superior version of an original idea, concept, or program[47] (version 2.0 follows version 1.x) would make us believe.

But we do not need an "international law 2.0." The emergence of the internet and the pervasiveness of ICTs in today's societies have not *fundamentally* changed or challenged international law. Recall the WSIS documents referring to the importance of international law and the commitments by both GGE reports in 2013 and 2015. Applying existing and developing new rules in light of changing technological realities, economic developments, and social mores speaks to the essence of a dynamic international legal order: its ability to be normatively responsive with a view to a certain finality. Treaties continue to regulate state behavior, but now with regard to the internet. General principles of international law still apply, online as offline. Foundational tenets of international law, such as sovereign equality and territorial sovereignty, are still applicable, but they are challenged by phenomena such as cloud computing, anonymity online, and the difficulties of enforcing laws tied to corporeal phenomena in cyberspace. States have always exercised sovereignty over their territories, with small restrictions. They now do so with regard to the internet's physical artifacts within their territory, such as servers with cloud computing services, and apply their laws to human action on the internet—be it active or passive use from the area within each state's jurisdiction and control.

[42] Andreas Zimmermann, "International Law and 'Cyber Space,'" ESIL Reflections 3 (2014) 1, http://www.esil-sedi.eu/node/481, 4, 6.

[43] Ibid.

[44] GGE (2015), 11.

[45] ICJ, *Reparation for Injuries Suffered in the Service of the United Nations* (Advisory Opinion of April 11, 1949), ICJ Reports (1949), 174.

[46] Cf. Jason Spingarn-Koff (dir.), "Life 2.0," documentary (100 minutes) (2010), http://life2movie.com.

[47] Oxford Living Dictionaries, s.v. "2.0," https://en.oxforddictionaries.com/definition/2.0.

The internet's physicality is often underestimated. It is tied to geography and state borders, thus falling more clearly under states' jurisdiction to *prescribe* and even more clearly under their respective jurisdictions to *enforce*. Yet physical resources, such as cables, data centers, and Internet Exchange Points, are necessary for global connectivity. States can and do censor the internet, oblige internet intermediaries to delete information, divulge customer data, or simply proceed to shut down the internet. The European Commission identified this "tension between an international internet and national jurisdictions" and called for more "thorough reflection on how existing rules apply on the internet."[48] Reflection and detection of lacunae is necessary—but the rules apply.

3.3 International Law of the Internet

3.3.1 Definition

The German equivalent of international law of the internet—*Internetvölkerrecht* or *Völkerrecht des Netzes*[49]—has been defined as "the common denominator for all rules of public international law pertaining to the functioning and use of the internet."[50] This study will adapt this definition in the following way: international law of the internet encompasses all (existing and emerging) rules of international law that regulate the evolution and use of the internet. Including a rule is an epistemic exercise in evaluative systematization.[51] Rules can belong to different international legal regimes; and general principles of international law are relevant for all regimes, including an international law of the internet. The concept is thus narrower than internet governance, though it is determinative for it and influences its legitimacy, and much narrower than the concept of the normative order of the internet, though being foundational for it.

Any study must begin with those rules of international law applicable to all subject areas. These are the rules enumerated as sources of international law in Article 38 (1) of the Statute of the International Court of Justice: (a) international conventions, (b) international custom, (c) general principles of law recognized by civilized nations, and—as a subsidiary means of establishing the law—(d) judicial decisions and the teachings of the most highly qualified publicists of the various nations. Already the practice of the ICJ with regard to

[48] European Commission, Communication from the Commission to the European Parliament, the European Economic and Social Committee and the Committee of the Region, Internet Policy and Governance. Europe's role in shaping the future of Internet Governance, COM(2014) 72 final of 12 February 2014, 10.

[49] Cf. for recent use, Ingolf Pernice, "Die Verfassung der Internetgesellschaft: Zur Rolle von Staat und Verfassung im Zuge der digitalen Revolution," in Alexander Blankenagel (ed.), *Den Verfassungsstaat nachdenken. Eine Geburtstagsgabe* (Berlin: Duncker & Humblot, 2014) 171–208, (HIIG Discussion Paper Series No. 2017-03, https://ssrn.com/abstract=2964926) and Ingolf Pernice, "Vom Völkerrecht des Netzes zur Verfassung des Internets: Privacy und Digitale Sicherheit im Zeichen eines schrittweisen Paradigmenwechsels (International Law of the Net and the Constitution of the Internet: Privacy and Cybersecurity in the Light of a Progressive Change of Paradigm)," HIIG Discussion Paper Series No. 2017-02 (2017), https://ssrn.com/abstract=2959257.

[50] See Robert Uerpmann-Wittzack, "Principles of International Internet Law," German Law Journal 11 (2010), 1245–63, http://www.germanlawjournal.com/index.php?pageID=11&artID=1293, 1245. Further, see Robert Uerpmann-Wittzack, "Internetvölkerrecht," Archiv des Völkerrechts 47 (2009) 3, 261–83. See Joanna Kulesza, *International Internet Law* (London: Routledge, 2012).

[51] Cf. Matthias C. Kettemann, *Völkerrecht in Zeiten des Netzes: Perspektiven auf den effektiven Schutz von Grund- und Menschenrechten in der Informationsgesellschaft zwischen Völkerrecht, Europarecht und Staatsrecht* (Bonn/Berlin: Friedrich-Ebert-Stiftung, 2015).

general principles of law is inconsistent and difficult to systemize.[52] To add another layer of complexity, there exists another source of international legal obligations: general principles *of international law*. These sources will now be looked at in turn.

3.3.2 International Conventions

3.3.2.1 Direct Protection

There are currently no international non-regime-specific conventions enshrining the protection of and from the internet and its key resources or establishing institutions for the management of the dangers for the international community from the development and use of the internet. Attempts to instigate the development of a Cybersecurity Treaty or of an "Internet United Nations" have been unsuccessful.[53] Attempts to broaden the remit of ITU's International Telecommunication Regulations (ITRs) in 2012[54] to include technological aspects necessary for running the internet met with substantial resistance and led to a stalemate at ITU's 2012 WCIT-12 Summit in Tunis.

Sovereignty-oriented states, including Algeria, China, Egypt, Russia, Saudi Arabia, Sudan, and the United Arab Emirates (UAE) had called for state-based mechanisms to manage key internet resources, such as the DNS via the reformed ITRs, and wanted to enshrine national oversight over certain internet segments. They suggested including language in the reformed ITRs to the effect of giving states "equal rights to manage the internet, including in regard to the allotment, assignment and reclamation of internet numbering, naming, addressing and identification resources and to support for the operation and development of basic internet infrastructure," including "the sovereign right [. . .] to regulate the national internet segment."[55]

In its announcement regarding the transition of US stewardship of changes in the root zone file and its management, the US government confirmed that it would "not accept a proposal that replaces the NTIA role with a government-led or an inter-governmental organization solution."[56] This, coupled with a commitment to the transition of IANA functions to the "global multistakeholder community" excludes a convention-based mechanism with state parties agreeing on the administration of IANA functions through a treaty-organ. By 2016, the transition had been successfully made and neither a treaty-based global alternative administration of the internet's public core nor the creation of a dedicated organization like a World Intellectual Property Organization (WIPO) for the internet is realistically on the normative horizon.

[52] Rüdiger Wolfrum, "General International Law (Principles, Rules and Standards)," in Rüdiger Wolfrum (ed.), *Max Planck Encyclopedia of Public International Law (MPEPIL)* (Oxford: OUP, 2008) (December 2010) [online], para. 20.

[53] Calling on states to develop a treaty-based international law of cybersecurity: Kubo Macak, "From Cyber Norms to Cyber Rules: Re-engaging States as Law-makers," Leiden Journal of International Law (2017), 877–99.

[54] ITU, International Telecommunication Regulations, http://www.itu.int/ITU-T/itr.

[55] Russia, UAE, China, Saudi Arabia, Algeria, Sudan, and Egypt, Proposal for the Work of the Conference [WCIT-12], ITU Doc. DT-X of 5 December 2012, WCIT12/27(Rev.1)-E, § 3A.2 and 3A.3, http://files.wcitleaks.org/public/Merged%20UAE%20081212.pdf.

[56] NTIA, NTIA Announces Intent to Transition Key Internet Domain Name Functions, March 14, 2014, http://www.ntia.doc.gov/press-release/2014/ntia-announces-intent-transition-key-internet-domain-name-functions.

3.3.2.2 Indirect Protection

The internet is offered indirect protection through sectoral treaties, including chiefly international human rights conventions. This protection also extends to protection *from* (mis)uses of the internet. Globally, the International Covenant on Civil and Political Rights (ICCPR)[57] has been identified as a key instrument for indirect protection of and from the internet, by protecting the enabling function of the internet, as a precondition for exercising rights contained therein, including especially its rights to privacy (Article 17 ICCPR) and free expression (Article 19 ICCPR).[58] Within Europe, the European Convention on Human Rights (ECHR) and its guarantee of freedom of expression (Article 10 ECHR), as interpreted by the ECtHR, plays a special role. Both indirect approaches to protecting the integrity of the internet as necessary for the exercise of human rights (indirectly) rely upon internet access. They also protect from misuses of the internet, by excluding internet-based pervasive communications surveillance (privacy) and setting clear limits for online speech.

According to the Governmental Group of Experts for the second edition of the Tallinn Manual, this leading analysis of the applicability of international law to cyberspace confirms that states must not only respect human rights, but also *protect* them, on the internet and from the internet.[59] Apart from conventional human rights protection, individuals enjoy customary international human rights protection "with respect to their cyber-related activities."[60] States need to respect, protect, and implement these rights. This implies protecting the public core of the internet and protecting the rights of persons under their jurisdiction or control (and also the states' own critical internet resources and information and communication structures necessary for exercising all necessary state functions under the conditions of the information society) from the dangers emanating from the internet.

Without access to the internet (through relevant infrastructure, including devices) or access to internet content people cannot realize their human rights online.[61] Since 2012, the Human Rights Council, in its biannual resolution on promoting, protecting, and enjoying human rights on the internet, has called upon states to "to promote and facilitate access to the internet."[62] In its first resolution it relied, inter alia, on a key 2011 report by the then-UN Special Rapporteur for freedom of expression, Frank La Rue, who established internet access as a condition to exercise freedoms connected to information and communication: "the internet has become a key means by which individuals can exercise their

[57] International Covenant on Civil and Political Rights, GA Resolution 2200A (XXI), 21 UN GAOR Supp. (No. 16) at 52, UN Doc. A/6316 (1966), 999 U.N.T.S. 171, entered into force March 23, 1976.

[58] Report of the Office of the United Nations High Commissioner for Human Rights, Navi Pillay, The right to privacy in the digital age, UN Doc. A/HRC/27/37 of 30 June 2014.

[59] Arguing that states have largely ignored the rules contained in the Tallinn Manual: Dan Efrony and Yuval Shany, "A Rule Book on the Shelf? Tallinn Manual 2.0 on Cyber Operations and Subsequent State Practice," Hebrew University of Jerusalem Legal Research Paper No. 18-22, https://papers.ssrn.com/sol3/papers.cfm?abstract_id=3172743.

[60] Michael N. Schmitt (ed.), *Tallinn Manual 2.0 on the International Law Applicable to Cyber Operations* (Cambridge: CUP, 2017), 181.

[61] Cf. Matthias C. Kettemann, *Völkerrecht in Zeiten des Netzes: Perspektiven auf den effektiven Schutz von Grund- und Menschenrechten in der Informationsgesellschaft zwischen Völkerrecht, Europarecht und Staatsrecht* (Bonn/Berlin: Friedrich-Ebert-Stiftung, 2015), 30 et seq.

[62] Human Rights Council, Resolution 20/8, The promotion, protection and enjoyment of human rights on the Internet, UN Doc. A/HRC/20/8 of 16 July 2012; Human Rights Council, Resolution 26/13, The promotion, protection and enjoyment of human rights on the Internet, UN Doc. A/HRC/RES/26/13 of 20 June 2014; Human Rights Council, Resolution 32/13, The promotion, protection and enjoyment of human rights on the Internet, UN Doc. A/HRC/RES/32/13 of 18 July 2016.

right to freedom of opinion and expression."[63] Freedom of expression is also an "enabler" of other rights online, including economic, social, and cultural rights, like the right to education (using the internet to gain knowledge) or civil and political rights, such as freedom of assembly.[64]

Both dimensions of access—*through* infrastructure and *to* content—are protected by international law. International law also, by protecting access, protects the technological premises of access, namely the public core of the internet and its integrity. States have started to implement the duty to provide internet access either by explicitly guaranteeing a right to access (under certain conditions) or by having a right to access, at least "in theory" through dogmatic construction.[65] Explicit codification is not a precondition for the existence of a right. The international legal duties provide the framework within which states must guarantee access; within that framework they are free.[66]

Realizing the right to internet access in practice is also important for human development. In the *2030 Agenda for Sustainable Development*, the world's states have committed to ensuring universal and affordable internet access in developing countries by 2020.[67] In view of this, states must also act as part of their obligation under the right to development. The Human Rights Committee confirms this approach by writing, in its General Comment No. 34 to Art. 19, that "[s]tates parties should take all necessary steps to foster the independence of these new media and to ensure access of individuals thereto."[68]

Dominant technology companies have a graduated human rights responsibility in terms of the right of access as a prerequisite for the exercise of other human rights, which is explicated in the *Guiding Principles on Business and Human Rights: Implementing the United Nations "Protect, Respect and Remedy" Framework*.[69] In particular, they must not undermine access to the internet through entrepreneurial activity or contribute to it through their products.

Another avenue of indirect protection is freedom of expression. In its biannual resolution on human rights on the internet in 2012, 2014, and 2016, the Human Rights Council affirmed, with references to Articles 19 of the UDHR and the ICCPR, the special role of freedom of expression online: "the same rights that people have offline must also be

[63] Report of the Special Rapporteur on the promotion and protection of the right to freedom of opinion and expression, Frank La Rue, UN Doc. A/HRC/17/27 of 16 May 2011, http://www2.ohchr.org/english/bodies/hrcouncil/docs/17session/A.HRC.17.27_en.pdf, 20.

[64] Mary Rundle and Malcolm Birdling, "Filtering and the International System: A Question of Commitment," in Ronald Deibert et al. (eds.), *Access Denied: The Practice and Policy of Global Internet Filtering* (Cambridge, MA: MIT Press, 2008), 73–102.

[65] Cf. ECtHR, *Yıldırım v. Turkey*, judgment of December 18, 2012, application no. 3111/10, para. 31: "in theory" such a right exists in more than ten Council of Europe member states.

[66] BVerfG, 1 BvL 10/10; 1 BvL 2/11 (July 18, 2012), rec. 94; BVerfG, 1 BvL 10/12 (July 23, 2014), rec. 74: "Dem Gesetzgeber steht ein Gestaltungsspielraum zu [...]; [dabei] ist er auch durch völkerrechtliche Verpflichtungen gebunden" (translation by the author).

[67] United Nations General Assembly, Transforming Our World. The 2030 Agenda for Sustainable Development, UN Doc. A/RES/70/1 of 21 October 2015, goal 9.c.: "Significantly increase access to information and communications technology and strive to provide universal and affordable access to the Internet in least developed countries by 2020."

[68] Human Rights Committee, General Comment No. 34, Art. 19 ICCPR, UN Doc. CCPR/C/GC/34 of 12 September 2011, para. 15.

[69] Report of the Special Representative of the Secretary-General on the issue of human rights and transnational corporations and other business enterprises, John Ruggie, Guiding Principles on Business and Human Rights: Implementing the United Nations "Protect, Respect and Remedy" Framework, UN Doc. A/HRC/17/31 of 21 March 2011, Annex.

protected online, *in particular freedom of expression*, which is applicable regardless of frontiers and through any media of one's choice [...]."[70]

Article 19 (2) of the ICCPR guarantees that "[e]veryone shall have the right to freedom of expression; this right shall include freedom to seek, receive and impart information and ideas of all kinds, regardless of frontiers, either orally, in writing or in print, in the form of art, or through any other media of his choice." Similarly, Article 10 (1) of the ECHR enshrines to everyone "the right to freedom of expression. This right shall include the freedom to hold opinions and to receive and impart information and ideas without interference by public authority and regardless of frontiers." States are obliged to protect freedom of expression both as a free-standing right and as an essential "enabler" of other rights through the internet. As former UN Special Rapporteur for Freedom of Expression, Frank La Rue, wrote, "by acting as a catalyst for individuals to exercise their right to freedom of opinion and expression, the internet also facilitates the realisation of a range of other human rights."[71]

Article 19 (2) of the ICCPR guarantees interconnection technologies with its reference to the protection of expression by "any [...] media of [one's] choice." If the internet does not function, most "media" will cease to work as well.[72] This point is well made also by the Human Rights Committee, which, in the most recent General Comment on Article 19 ICCPR, recalls the technological premises of the internet's communication function: "[a]ny restrictions on the operation of websites, blogs or any other internet-based, electronic or other such information dissemination system, including systems to support such communication, such as internet service providers or search engines, are only permissible to the extent that they are compatible with paragraph 3."[73] Interfering with ISPs thus amounts to interfering with the right to privacy.

The jurisprudence of the European Court of Human Rights helps understand how freedom of expression, as enshrined in the ECHR, can be considered to indirectly protect the integrity of the internet. According to established case law, freedom of expression can be considered "one of the essential foundations for a democratic society and one of the basic conditions for its progress and for each individual's self-fulfillment."[74] The Strasbourg Court interprets the Convention "in the light of present-day conditions,"[75] taking into account the specific nature of the internet, as a "modern means of imparting information,"[76] in particular because of the greater impact, accessibility, durability, and asynchronicity of information on the internet.[77]

70 Human Rights Council, Resolution 32/13, The promotion, protection and enjoyment of human rights on the Internet, UN Doc. A/HRC/RES/32/13 of 18 July 2016, para. 1 (emphasis added).

71 Report of the Special Rapporteur on the promotion and protection of the right to freedom of opinion and expression, UN Doc. A/HRC/17/27 of 16 May 2011, paras. 22 and 23. But the Internet also brings about new challenges to these same human rights.

72 Molly K. Land, "Toward an International Law of the Internet," Harvard International Law Journal, 54 (2013), 393–458.

73 Cf. Human Rights Committee, General Comment No. 34, Art. 19 ICCPR, UN Doc. CCPR/C/GC/34 of 12 September 2011, para. 43.

74 E.g. ECtHR, *Stoll v. Switzerland*, judgment of December 10, 2007, application no. 69698/01, para. 104 with further references.

75 Ibid., para. 101.

76 ECtHR, *Mouvement Raëlien Suisse v. Switzerland*, judgment of January 13, 2011, application no. 16354/06, para. 54 as endorsed by the Great Chamber judgment in para. 40.

77 Nina Vajic and Panayotis Voyatzis, "The Internet and Freedom of Expression: A 'Brave New World' and the European Court of Human Rights' Evolving Case Law," in Josep Casadevall et al. (eds.), *Freedom of Expression. Essays in Honour of Nicolas Bratza* (Osterwijk: Wolf, 2012), 391–420 (395 and 399).

In the first of a series of cases against Turkey's blocking of internet platforms, *Yıldırım v. Turkey* (2012), the Court confirmed that publishing information online constitutes a means of exercising freedom of expression,[78] and that the public had a right, under Article 10, to receive it.[79] In particular, the court held that state measures stopping access to specific sites engaged the responsibility of the state under Article 10.[80] In the 2015 *Cengiz and Others v. Turkey* judgment, the Court went further and clearly committed to the importance of the internet as a forum for freedom of expression (which, again, presupposes its integrity). The Court's reasoning for rejecting a Turkish ban of YouTube on the application of three academics underlined the importance of the internet: "[T]he internet has now become one of the principal means by which individuals exercise their right to freedom to receive and impart information and ideas, providing as it does essential tools for participation in activities and discussions concerning political issues and issues of general interest." The internet as a whole has thus become an important means to exercise freedom of expression. Specific sites, especially "[u]ser-generated expressive activity on the internet[,] provides an unprecedented platform for the exercise of freedom of expression." This also applies to consuming news and disseminating information: "in the light of [the internet's] accessibility and its capacity to store and communicate vast amounts of information, [it] plays an important role in enhancing the public's access to news and facilitating the dissemination of information in general"[81]

The internet as a "principal means" (*Yıldırım*) to exercise freedom of expression and the latter right as an "essential foundation for a democratic society and one of the basic conditions for its progress" (*Stoll*) are closely connected, and through the explicit protection of freedom of expression in international law, the internet's integrity is indirectly protected.

Another normative avenue is the right to privacy.[82] After the Snowden revelations of global mass surveillance by the so-called Five Eyes states,[83] the Civil Covenant's right to privacy has been a starting point for scholars making the case for a stronger protection of "global communication structures" (rather *infra*structures)[84] and a higher level of "digital security" (cybersecurity) through progressive constitutionalization (and thus increased protection) of the internet's core (principles and architecture) ("Internetverfassung").[85] This is consonant with German foreign policy: the global right to privacy in light of internet (mass) surveillance became an important aspect of (cyber)diplomacy culminating in a 2016

[78] ECtHR, *Yıldırım v. Turkey*, judgment of December 18, 2012, application no. 3111/10, para. 49.

[79] Ibid., para. 50.

[80] Ibid., para. 53, with reference to *Vereinigung demokratischer Soldaten Österreichs et Gubi v. Austria*, judgment of December 19, 1994, para. 27.

[81] ECtHR, *Cengiz and Others v. Turkey*, judgment of December 1, 2015, applications nos. 48226/10 and 14027/11, paras. 49 and 52.

[82] Cf. Matthias C. Kettemann, *Völkerrecht in Zeiten des Netzes: Perspektiven auf den effektiven Schutz von Grund- und Menschenrechten in der Informationsgesellschaft zwischen Völkerrecht, Europarecht und Staatsrecht* (Bonn/Berlin: Friedrich-Ebert-Stiftung, 2015), 32–40.

[83] Among many, see Marko Milanovic, "Human Rights Treaties and Foreign Surveillance: Privacy in the Digital Age," Harvard International Law Journal 56 (2015) 1, 81–146, http://www.harvardilj.org/wp-content/uploads/561Milanovic.pdf.

[84] Andreas Fischer-Lescano, "Der Kampf um die Internetverfassung. Rechtsfragen des Schutzes globaler Kommunikationsstrukturen vor Überwachungsmaßnahmen," JZ 69 (2014), 20, 965–74.

[85] Ingolf Pernice, "Vom Völkerrecht des Netzes zur Verfassung des Internets: Privacy und Digitale Sicherheit im Zeichen eines schrittweisen Paradigmenwechsels (International Law of the Net and the Constitution of the Internet: Privacy and Cybersecurity in the Light of a Progressive Change of Paradigm)," HIIG Discussion Paper Series No. 2017-02 (2017), https://ssrn.com/abstract=2959257.

Human Rights Council resolution on privacy confirming that "the same rights that people have offline must also be protected online, including the right to privacy."[86]

The right to privacy is protected by Article 17 of the ICCPR and Article 8 of the ECHR. Article 8 ECHR protects an individual's privacy, which is necessary in order to develop the personality freely. It has both a defensive and proactive dimension. Not only do states have to refrain from interfering illegitimately with privacy, they also need to ensure that other social actors (and other states) do not violate the privacy of individuals.[87] The assessment of mass surveillance by the National Security Agency (NSA) is less concerned with the interpretation of Article 17 (at most the question of its extraterritorial effect, which is rejected by the USA—in contrast to the majority opinion[88]) than with its practical relevance.[89] Not that the international law of the internet is (necessarily) incomplete. Rather, the acts of the US and the other "Five Eyes" states as well as European states that have cooperated closely with them are illegal, jeopardizing the right to privacy in the internet age and the nature of the internet as a space of trust.[90]

Data transfer regimes by companies have also been viewed critically. The Court of Justice of the European Union (CJEU), in the *Schrems* case of October 6, 2015,[91] invalidated the European Commission's "Safe Harbour" decision and criticized the Commission for not ensuring that the US provide an equal level of fundamental rights protection.[92] Together with *Digital Rights Ireland*,[93] *Google Spain and Google* (the "right to be forgotten" ruling),[94] and *Ryneš* (private parties are bound by privacy rights as well),[95] the Court has developed within two years comprehensive multidimensional (and only slightly expansive) jurisprudence on privacy and data protection with substantial extraterritorial effects.

The protection of privacy is essential for the use and development of the internet as a "gateway" for freedom of expression.[96] Only those who feel secure can seek and receive information, form an opinion, and share it with others. Both rights are therefore closely intertwined and affirm each other. In this view, encryption technology and anonymity also play a critical role in the realization of human rights online.[97] It is not the law that is incomplete.

[86] Human Rights Council, Resolution 28/16, The Right to Privacy in the Digital Age, UN Doc. A/HRC/RES/28/16 of 1 April 2015, para. 3. See also General Assembly, Resolution 68/167, The Right to Privacy in the Digital Age, UN Doc. A/RES/68/167 of 21 January 2014.

[87] Just see Helmut Philipp Aust, Opinion of the Expert Witness Testimony, June 5, 2014, 1st Investigation Committee of the 18th German Bundestag, https://www.bundestag.de/blob/282870/fc52462f2ffd254849b-ce19d25f72fa2/mat_a_sv-4-1_aust-pdf-data.pdf.

[88] See the US reply to the recommendations during the Universal Periodic Review, Addendum of the United States of America to the Report of the Working Group on its Universal Periodic Review (September 16, 2015), https://geneva.usmission.gov/2015/09/01/addendum-of-the-united-states-of-america-to-the-report-of-the-working-group-on-its-universal-periodic-review: Recommendations leading to a higher level of protection of privacy are supported insofar as "they recommend respect for ICCPR Article 17, which applies to individuals within a state's territory and subject to its jurisdiction." An extraterritorial application is expressly prohibited.

[89] Similarly, Marko Milanovic, "Human Rights Treaties and Foreign Surveillance: Privacy in the Digital Age," Harvard International Law Journal 56 (2015) 1, 81–146.

[90] Cf. Council of Europe, Parliamentary Assembly, Report on Mass surveillance, Rapporteur Mr. Pieter Omtzigt, Doc. 13734 of 18 March 2015, http://www.coe.int/t/dghl/standardsetting/media/Conf-FoE-2015/Report%20on%20Mass%20Surveillance%20of%20Mr%20Pieter%20Omtzigt.pdf.

[91] CJEU, C-362/14, *Schrems v. Data Protection Commissioner*, judgment of October 6, 2015.

[92] Ibid., rec. 97–8.

[93] CJEU, C-293/12 and C-594/12, *Digital Rights Ireland and Seitlinger et al.*, judgment of April 8, 2014.

[94] CJEU, C-131/12, *Google Spain and Google*, judgment of May 13, 2014.

[95] CJEU, C-212/13, *František Ryneš v. Uřad pro ochranu osobních údajů*, judgment of December 11, 2014.

[96] Report of the Special Rapporteur on the promotion and protection of the right to freedom of opinion and expression, David Kaye, A/HRC/29/32 of 22 May 2015.

[97] Ibid., rec. 17.

As the United Nations High Commissioner for Human Rights clearly states in a report on the right to privacy on the internet, state practice is the problem: "*International human rights law provides a clear and universal framework for the promotion and protection of the right to privacy*, including in the context of domestic and extraterritorial surveillance, the interception of digital communications and the collection of personal data. Nevertheless, many states have ignored international law: "Practices in many States have [. . .] revealed a lack of adequate national legislation and/or enforcement, weak procedural safeguards, and ineffective oversight, all of which have contributed to a lack of accountability for arbitrary or unlawful interference in the right to privacy."[98]

The Snowden revelations have "chilling effects" on the use of the internet.[99] The social costs of mass surveillance are far higher than their returns. The weakening of encryption standards or the coded opening of backdoors for government agencies, especially, can have negative consequences for national security. The European Parliament's *Schaake* report, adopted in September 2015, underlines the importance of privacy encryption technologies, including the right to encryption and the introduction of end-to-end encryption standards for all communications.[100]

Democratic societies have long been threatened by espionage and terrorism. As early as 1978, the ECtHR held in *Klass and others v. Germany* that the "existence of some legislation granting powers of secret surveillance over the mail, post and telecommunications is, under exceptional conditions, necessary in a democratic society in the interests of national security and/or for the prevention of disorder or crime."[101]

However, this does not mean that states can ignore human rights or are completely free in the choice of the means and the intensity of surveillance. They need to be aware that such laws contain the danger "[of] undermining or even destroying democracy on the ground of defending it. States cannot do what they want in the name of the struggle against espionage and terrorism."[102] The ECtHR in *Shimovolos v. Russia* underlined the need for "detailed rules on the application of secret measures of surveillance, especially as the technology available for use is continually becoming more sophisticated."[103]

In order to strengthen the protection of privacy on the internet, states must review and align their national laws and policies with their human rights obligations under the ECHR and ICCPR (and relevant European law and, in particular, the Charter of Fundamental Rights (CFR)), as interpreted by the ECtHR (regarding the ECHR), Human Rights Committee (regarding the ICCPR), and CJEU (regarding the CFR). Normative measures to remedy gaps must be developed in the context of easily accessible, open, societal discussion processes.[104]

[98] Report of the Office of the United Nations High Commissioner for Human Rights, Navi Pillay, The right to privacy in the digital age, UN Doc. A/HRC/27/37 of 30 June 2014, para. 47 (emphasis added).

[99] See EU, Report on human rights and technology: the impact of intrusion and surveillance systems on human rights in third countries (2014/2232(INI)), Committee on Foreign Affairs Rapporteur: Marietje Schaake, June 3, 2015, rec. 3: "the active complicity of certain EU Member States in the NSA's mass surveillance of citizens and spying on political leaders, as revealed by Edward Snowden, has caused serious damage to the credibility of the EU's human rights policy and has undermined global trust in the benefits of ICTs."

[100] Ibid., rec. 61–2.

[101] ECtHR, *Klass and others v. Germany*, no. 5029/71, judgment of September 6, 1978, rec. 48.

[102] Ibid., rec. 49.

[103] ECtHR, *Shimovolos v. Russia*, no. 30194/09, judgment of November 28, 2011, rec. 68.

[104] Any law that enables data collection must be measured against recognized human rights criteria (such as specificity and purpose). The conditions under which collected data may be searched by means of selectors must

The ECtHR has shown, in important judgments, which obligations states have with regard to the protection of privacy. Particularly relevant are *Weber and Saravia v. Germany*, *Klass and Others v. Germany* (judicial control of surveillance measures), *Bucur and Toma v. Romania* (protection of whistleblowers), *Iordachi and others v. Moldova* (narrow definition of "national security" for the legitimization of interventions), and *El-Masri v. the former Yugoslav Republic of Macedonia* (extraterritorial effect of the ECHR, importance of democratic control of intelligence services).

Democratic control of security and intelligence services is important for the protection of human rights and the rule of law. The Council of Europe Commissioner for Human Rights recommends that a national dialog on ways to ensure legal control be established.[105] Similar suggestions are made by the Venice Commission of the Council of Europe.[106] A lack of trust in a protected private sphere on the internet, as a principal means to exercise freedom of expression, undermines the central participatory rights in the information society and especially freedom of expression which, let us recall, is an essential foundation for a democratic society. The right to privacy creates the freedom to exercise other rights and thus indirectly protects the internet's integrity as well.

The internet as a "principal means" (*Yıldırım*) to exercise freedom of expression and the latter right as an "essential foundation for a democratic society and one of the basic conditions for its progress" (*Stoll*) are closely connected and, through the explicit protection of freedom of expression in international law, the internet's integrity is indirectly protected. After this analysis of direct and indirect treaty-based approaches to protecting the internet's integrity, let us turn to the role of custom.

3.3.3 Custom

3.3.3.1 Direct Protection

In order to establish the existence of a customary rule, traditional international law requires the presence of two elements: settled practice based on the belief that there is rule requiring it.[107] This two-element approach is expressed, for example, in the ICJ's 1969 judgment in the *North Sea Continental Shelf Cases* (Merits), where the Court found that "two conditions must be fulfilled. Not only must the acts concerned amount to a settled practice, but they must also be such, or be carried out in such a way, as to be evidence of a belief that this practice is rendered obligatory by the existence of a rule of law requiring it."[108]

be discussed publicly. Selectors must be published to ensure non-discriminatory application. The use of selectors to be assigned to identifiable persons must pass even higher protective barriers.

[105] Council of Europe Commissioner for Human Rights, Democratic and effective oversight of national security services (May 2015), para. 18.

[106] European Commission for Democracy through Law (Venice Commission), Update of the 2007 Report on the Democratic Oversight of the Security Services and Report on the Democratic Oversight of Signals Intelligence Agencies, adopted by the Venice Commission at its 102nd Plenary Session (March 20–21, 2015), http://www.coe.int/t/dghl/standardsetting/media/Conf-FoE-2015/Venice%20Commission_Study%20No%20719_2013.pdf,StudyNo.19/2013,CDL-AD(2015)006.

[107] Just see Malcolm N. Shaw, *International Law*, 8th edn. (Oxford: OUP, 2017), 53 et seq.

[108] ICJ, *North Sea Continental Shelf Cases (Federal Republic of Germany v. Denmark; Federal Republic of Germany v. Netherlands)* (Merits), ICJ Rep. (1969), 3, para. 77.

There is thus an objective and a subjective element to establishing a rule of custom: the "belief" in the obligatory nature of carrying out (or not) a certain act is "implicit in the very notion of the opinio juris sive necessitatis. The States concerned must therefore feel that they are conforming to what amounts to a legal obligation." Finding that states act in a certain way, even repeatedly, does not suffice: "frequency or even habitual character of the acts is not in itself enough."[109] Almost twenty years later, in *Military and Paramilitary Activities in and against Nicaragua Case (Nicaragua v. United States of America)* (Merits), the ICJ reiterated the finding emphasizing that "for a new customary rule to be formed, not only must the acts concerned "amount to a settled practice" [as per the *North Sea Continental Shelf Cases*], but they must be accompanied by the *opinio juris sive necessitatis.*"[110]

Let us suppose a customary law rule exists that protects the internet's integrity and protects states from misuses of the internet. It could be formulated in the following way: the (integrity of the) internet must be protected. Risks emanating from the internet must be managed according to international law. The second-order responsibility rule could be termed thus: state actions violating the integrity of the internet are contrary to international law and thus engage state responsibility, as does the lack of internet-related "risk management." Is there sufficient uniform (and sufficiently uniform) practice evidencing opinio iuris for such a customary first order norm? The answer can only be negative. Though there is a wealth of relevant state practice on the protection of and from the internet, it is too diffuse and not of a level of consistency or normativity that we could deduce relevant opinio iuris from it.

Internationally, we have seen important commitments to a development-oriented, people-centered information society premised upon human rights and international law. But as the designation "commitment" suggests, this was not an exercise in codification or progressive development of international law. Rather, states assembled during WSIS developed a common understanding of what information society should look like: based on the "purposes and principles of the Charter of the United Nations, international law and multilateralism, and respecting fully and upholding the Universal Declaration of Human Rights."[111] We can conclude that states agreed to pursue policies regarding the development of information society that would be based on the principles and purposes of the UN and on international law, as has also been confirmed by the reports of the Group of Governmental Experts in 2013 and 2015. Yet no direct independent customary protection of and from the internet can be deduced from (or interpreted into) these commitments. Further, the vagueness of national policy commitments and the lack of an irreducible normative rule protecting the internet is a substantial challenge when analyzing state practice regarding the internet.

This conclusion is only reinforced when parsing state submissions to the 2014 "NetMundial" meeting, which is considered an important normative turning point of the process of internet governance. A number of states submitted proposals under the rubrics "roadmaps" and "principles." The "German Government Proposal on Global

[109] Ibid.

[110] ICJ, *Military and Paramilitary Activities in and against Nicaragua Case (Nicaragua v. United States of America)* (Merits), ICJ Rep. (1986), 14, para. 207.

[111] WSIS, Tunis Commitment, WSIS-05/TUNIS/DOC/7-E, 18 November 2005, para. 2.

internet Principles (2014),"[112] for example, included, as Principle 1, a commitment to a "global, open and free nature of the internet as a single commons" that has to be ensured. It is described as "a driving force for progress towards development in its various forms including economic growth, encouraging innovation and allowing for creativity." Clearly, this can only be counted as a general policy statement. The submission's title alone—a proposal on principles—is strongly indicative of its normative content amounting to being prima facie non-binding. Yet just as international legal scholarship has progressively distanced itself from the binding/non-binding binarity,[113] the commitments are still relevant to assess national policy preferences (if not already their opinio iuris).

Similarly, the US government submission notes that normative efforts in the past have included certain "goals for internet governance and policymaking" including reliance on, and integration of, multiple actors in normative processes rooted in "democratic values," human rights protection, universal and non-discriminatory access to the internet, and the "promotion of the stability, security, interoperability, and functionality of the network."[114] We see here the expression of policy preferences and goals, but not the proposition of rules. China resubmitted the International Code of Conduct for Information Security[115] it had proposed, together with Russia, Tajikistan, and Uzbekistan, at the UN in 2011.[116] But adherence to the code is "voluntary,"[117] which precludes its qualification as being, in the Chinese and Russian opinion, a document codifying customary rules. In addition, the content of the code rather than offering protection for the functionality of the internet is targeted at ensuring state sovereignty.[118]

The development of principles suffers from serious normative shortcomings, including their lack of precision and lack of normative clarity. Committing to principles is an example of state practice and, in the absence of discernible opinio iuris, cannot count as custom. Opinio can be inferred from practice, but such practice must reach a certain level of consistency and must be based on, or refer to, a certain rule (or rules).

The GGE report of 2015 included a number of "[v]oluntary, non-binding norms of responsible State behaviour" with the function to reduce risks, reflect expectations of the international community, and set standards, thus allowing each state to assess another's activities and intentions. The norms are not meant to "limit or prohibit action that is otherwise consistent with international law," and they thus do not set out to change international law.[119] However, these soft law norms can crystallize into customary law through use and the formation of a relevant opinio iuris.[120]

[112] Germany, Federal Foreign Office, Commissioner for International Cyber Policy, German Government Proposal on Global Internet Principles (February 2014), submission to NetMundial, http://content.netmundial.br/contribution/german-government-proposal-on-global-internet-principles/32.

[113] Cf. Jean d'Aspremont, "Bindingness," in Jean d'Aspremont and Sahib Singh (eds.), *Concepts for International Law. Contributions to Disciplinary Thought* (Cheltenham: Edward Elgar, 2018), 67–82.

[114] US Department of State, U.S. Government Submission for NetMundial (February 2014), http://content.netmundial.br/contribution/u-s-government-submission-for-netmundial/62.

[115] Ministry of Foreign Affairs of the People's Republic of China, International Code of Conduct for Information Security (February 2014), submission to NetMundial, http://content.netmundial.br/contribution/international-code-of-conduct-for-information-security/67.

[116] International Code of Conduct for Information Security, Annex to the letter dated 12 September 2011 from the Permanent Representatives of China, the Russian Federation, Tajikistan, and Uzbekistan to the United Nations addressed to the Secretary-General, UN Doc. A/66/359 of 14 September 2011.

[117] Ibid.

[118] Ibid., littera (a), (c), (e).

[119] GGE report (2015), para. 10.

[120] For further consideration of the norms, see below, at 3.5.

Summing up, there are not yet any identifiable customary rules extending to the protection of and from the internet's integrity. Developing principles and discussing the goals of information society, including the internet's integrity, in international settings can lead to the codification and progressive development of international law in this subject area. If an international treaty on the protection of and from the internet is concluded, it may then codify custom that has substantially crystallized. But this is well into the future. In the clear absence of customary rules laying formally down the protection of the (and from the) internet, we can only conclude that customary law cannot serve as a direct source of protection of the internet's functionality and from (criminal or state-sponsored or tolerated) misuses. There are, however, a number of customary rules indirectly protecting (us from) the internet.

3.3.3.2 Indirect Protection

It is difficult to establish the extent to which customary rules indirectly protect the internet and protect society from misuses of the internet, by obliging states to exercise, inter alia, due diligence in preparing for threats and developing and discussing, together with other states, as necessary, strategies to counter them. This is because any customary rule protecting state infrastructure can be considered to indirectly protect the internet, as it is part of a state's critical information infrastructure (and a critical information resource in itself). Yet such a statement would be too broad to be of much more than epistemic value. It would therefore make sense to briefly discuss those rules of custom that offer discernible (and not just theoretical) protection of and from the internet. However, the rules of customary law that are of interest here can also be framed as general principles of international law (often with a broader content). It would be artificial to formulate substantially similar norms (with an indirect protective dimension for the internet's integrity) first as customary norms and then, again, as general principles.

In presenting the general principles of international law that bear upon the protection of the internet's integrity and the protection of societies from misuses of the internet often caused by violations of integrity-related guarantees, this chapter will include brief discussions on the principles' character—as ius cogens norms, custom, or "just" principles. Before taking this step, however, the question of why the lack of identifiable custom protecting the internet is neither surprising nor a fundamental challenge to establishing international law as an order containing rules protecting the internet's integrity and protecting societies from (mis)uses of the internet merits consideration.

The lack of direct custom and the small number of identifiable customary norms protecting the internet should not surprise. Customary law takes time to evolve (though it need not *per se*). As the ICJ formulated in *Gulf of Maine*, it is "unrewarding" in a new field "to look to general international law to provide a readymade set of rules that can be used for solving any [...] problems that arise."[121] In that case the court looked specifically at norms regarding delimitation problems in the "new and still unconsolidated field [...] involving the quite recent extension of the claims of States to areas which were until yesterday zones of the high seas."[122]

[121] ICJ, *Case Concerning Delimitation of the Maritime Boundary in the Gulf of Maine Area* (Judgment), ICJ Rep. (1984), 246, para. 111.

[122] Ibid.

What was true for maritime delimitation problems applies to the internet. The protection of the internet (and the protection *from* negative uses of the internet, which always needs to be read into any norms *protecting* the internet) is a "new and still unconsolidated field" of international law and the search for a "readymade set of [customary] rules" is in vain. In *Gulf of Maine*, the ICJ counsels were seeking "a better formulation of the fundamental norm [. . .] whose existence in the legal convictions not only of the Parties to the present dispute, but of all States, is apparent from an examination of the realities of international legal relations." Unlike the delimitation of adjacent continental shelves at issue in *Gulf of Maine*, there is no single preexisting "fundamental norm" applicable to state behavior regarding the internet that can be formulated "more complete[ly] and more precise[ly]."[123]

How to proceed if no such fundamental norm can be found and if state practice does not allow for the deduction of customary rules? In *Gulf of Maine*, the ICJ introduced an important distinction. It argued that customary international law

> comprises a *limited set of norms for ensuring the co-existence and vital co-operation* of the members of the international community, together with a set of customary rules whose presence in the opinio juris of States can be tested by induction based on the analysis of a sufficiently extensive and convincing practice, and not by deduction from preconceived ideas.[124]

The court thus draws a distinction within customary international law between "a limited set of norms for ensuring the co-existence and vital co-operation of the members of the international community" (category 1 rules) and "customary rules whose presence in the opinio juris of States can be tested by induction based on the analysis of a sufficiently extensive and convincing practice, and not by deduction from preconceived ideas" (category 2 rules). To establish the existence of a category 2 rule, we need to inductively establish the opinio iuris of states through extensive and convincing practice. For category 1 rules, e contrario, this is not necessary. Establishing this "limited set of norms ensuring co-existence and vital cooperation" is thus not based on opinio iuris and practice but rather, again e contrario, by "deduction from preconceived ideas." The lack of opinio iuris and practice cannot be used as an argument against the existence of category 1 rules. Further, states cannot choose *not* to be bound by them (though they can, of course, choose not to follow them, thus violating international law).

Category 1 rules can be characterized as *customary law rules* "with a twist": the twist being that their existence can be stated (or deducted from ideas and values) and no test of opinio iuris needs to be made.[125] This, it is submitted, assimilates category 1 rules to principles (as the normative variance of "preconceived ideas") or, rather, makes them the binding, normatively more stringent, and concrete form of principles.[126]

[123] Ibid., para. 112.
[124] Ibid., para 111 (emphasis added).
[125] In this sense, Tullio Treves, "Customary International Law," in Rüdiger Wolfrum (ed.), *Max Planck Encyclopedia of Public International Law (MPEPIL)* (Oxford: OUP, 2008) (2006) [online], paras. 19–22 (citing ICJ jurisprudence) *Case concerning the Frontier Dispute (Burkina Faso/Republic of Mali)* (Merits) ICJ Rep. (1986), 554; *Armed Activities on the Territory of the Congo Cases (Democratic Republic of the Congo v. Uganda)*, ICJ Rep. (2005); *Arrest Warrant Case (Democratic Republic of the Congo v. Belgium)* (Merits), ICJ Rep. (2002), 3.
[126] See, on this, Anja Mihr, "Cyber Justice: Cyber Governance through Human Rights and Rule of Law in the Internet," US–China Law Review 13 (2016) 314.

When the ICJ referred to the fundamental norm regarding the delimitation of adjacent continental shelves in *Gulf of Maine*, it made an important point. Just establishing that neither treaty nor customary law gives answers to a legal question (such as, in our case, if the internet's integrity is protected) does not give rise to an epistemic *non liquet*. In such a situation, we can take recourse to general principles of international law, which do not only help pull international law together in light of normative centrifugal forces leading to fragmentation, but also serve as normative guidelines for the progressive development of international law. They can also help, in this instance, to delimitate state behavior regarding the internet and to provide protection for the internet's integrity. Let us also recall that, to the extent that general principles are the normative versions of the "preconceived ideas" from which "norms [essential for] the co-existence and vital co-operation of the members of the international community" can be deduced, states neither need to "opt into" them nor can they "opt out" of them.[127] Let us turn, therefore, to general principles of international law and their relevance for the protection of and from the internet.

3.3.4 General Principles of International Law

3.3.4.1 Origin

The existence of general principles of international law has been confirmed by judgments of international courts, state practice, and international treaties. A modern treaty provision referring to principles is, for example, Article 21 (1) of the Rome Statute of the International Criminal Court ("ICC Statute"). According to this provision, the Court shall apply

> […] (b) where appropriate, applicable treaties and the principles and rules of international law, including the established principles of the international law of armed conflict; (c) Failing that, general principles of law derived by the Court from national laws of legal systems of the world.

Littera (b) and (c) offer compelling evidence of a distinction drawn, by the now 138 signatories and 123 state parties,[128] between the "principles and rules of international law" (the general principles of international law) and the "general principles of law" derived from national laws.

Similarly, both the Permanent Court of International Justice (PCIJ) and the ICJ have confirmed the existence of general principles of international law in their jurisprudence. To give just a few examples, in the *SS Lotus* case, the PCIJ referred to "general principles of international law,"[129] including sovereignty "on which this [international] law is based,"[130] and in the *Factory at Chorzow* case clearly saw general principles to be sources of legal obligations: "To this obligation, in virtue of the general principles of international law, must

[127] Katharina Ziolkowski, "General Principles of International Law as Applicable in Cyberspace," in Katharina Ziolkowski (ed.), *Peacetime Regime for State Activities in Cyberspace. International Law, International Relations and Diplomacy* (Tallinn: NATO CCD COE Publications, 2013), 135–84 (151–2).
[128] Cf. UNTS, Rome Statute of the International Criminal Court, Rome, 17 July 1998, UNTS vol. 2187, 3, https://treaties.un.org/Pages/ViewDetails.aspx?src=TREATY&mtdsg_no=XVIII-10&chapter=18&lang=en, status as of January 24, 2018.
[129] PCIJ, *The Case of the SS Lotus (France v. Turkey)*, judgment, PCIJ Rep. Series A, No 10, para. 189.
[130] Ibid., para. 157.

be added that of compensating loss sustained as the result of the seizure."[131] The ICJ also referred in a number of cases to "general principles of international law" (regulating termination of a treaty relationship on account of breach)[132] and described the prohibition of the use of force as a "fundamental or cardinal principle of [international] law."[133]

General principles of international law often develop from particular treaty regimes, including notably the peace and security-related principles contained in Article 2 of the UN Charter.[134] When principles from non-universal regimes are enshrined in documents by universal bodies, such as General Assembly resolutions, an important step toward their generalization is taken. This holds particularly for principles that were already expressed in universal documents in the first place, such as the Article 2 UN Charter principles. These have been reaffirmed in the 1970 Friendly Relations Declaration,[135] which was adopted by the General Assembly without a vote[136] and codifies "basic principles of international law."[137] These include the non-use of (the threat of) force, the peaceful settlement of international disputes, the non-intervention in domestic affairs, the duty of cooperation, the principle of equal rights and self-determination of peoples, the sovereign equality of states, and the principle of good faith. These principles were confirmed in regional contexts—such as in the 1975 Helsinki Declaration of the CSCE[138]—and on a universal level in the UN Millennium Declaration[139] and the 2005 World Summit Outcome document.[140]

The normativity of principles diverges. They can be peremptory norms of international law (such as the non-use of force principle) or form, in a normatively more stringent form, customary law (such as the non-intervention principle). A principle can be semantically equal to a customary law rule without losing its status as a principle. Other principles, though not as such legally binding, have legally binding content and exercise normative pull beyond the binding core. This holds especially true for principles stemming from international environmental law: the principle of good neighborliness, the principle of prevention, the principle of sustainable development, and the precautionary principle.[141] For the first

[131] PCIJ, *The Factory At Chorzow (Claim for Indemnity)*, judgment on the merits (1928) PCIJ Rep. Series A, No 17, para. 126.

[132] ICJ, *Legal Consequences for States of the Continued Presence of South Africa in Namibia (South West Africa) notwithstanding Security Council Resolution 276 (1970)* (Advisory Opinion), ICJ Rep. (1971), 6, Para. 94.

[133] ICJ, *Military and Paramilitary Activities in und against Nicaragua (Nicaragua v. United States of America)* (Merits, Judgment), ICJ Rep. (1986), 14, para. 190.

[134] Cf. Rüdiger Wolfrum, "Cooperation, International Law of," in Rüdiger Wolfrum (ed.), *Max Planck Encyclopedia of Public International Law* (MPEPIL) (Oxford: OUP, 2008) (December 2010) [online], paras. 41 et seq.

[135] Declaration on Principles of International Law Concerning Friendly Relations and Cooperation among States in Accordance with the Charter of the United Nations, UN Doc A/RES/2625(XXV) of 24 October 1970, Annex. See Gaetano Arangio-Ruiz, "The Normative Role of the General Assembly of the United Nations and the Declaration of Principles of Friendly Relations," RdC 137 (1972), 419–742.

[136] Helen Keller, "Friendly Relations Declaration," in Rüdiger Wolfrum (ed.), *Max Planck Encyclopedia of Public International Law* (MPEPIL) (Oxford: OUP, 2008) (June 2009) [online], para. 2. See also ibid., para. 31 (for later references to the Declaration) and para. 33 (for ICJ case law referencing it).

[137] UN General Assembly, Res. 2625 (XXV) (24 October 1970) (Friendly Relations Declaration), General Part, No. 3.

[138] Final Act of the Conference on Security and Cooperation in Europe (Commission on Security and Cooperation in Europe (historical) [CSCE]), Questions relating to Security in Europe, 1(a) Declaration on Principles Guiding Relations between Participating States.

[139] United Nations General Assembly Resolution 55/2, United Nations Millennium Declaration, UN Doc A/RES/55/2.

[140] United Nations General Assembly Resolution 60/1, World Summit Outcome, UN Doc A/RES/60/1.

[141] On normative precaution in technology governance, see Andres Stirling, "Precaution in the Governance of Technology," in Roger Brownsword, Eloise Scotford, and Karen Yeung (eds.), *Oxford Handbook of Law, Regulation, and Technology* (Oxford: OUP, 2017), 645–69.

three, Wolfrum argues that they have metamorphosized from regime-centric principles to general principles:[142] the principle of sustainable development has developed, according to him, from a principle dedicated to managing only renewable resources, "but now it is being used to govern non-renewable resources, too."[143]

Insofar as this development has taken place, principles can bridge fragmentation trends and act as normative unifiers. They can take in (that is: scholars and courts can interpret them in the light of) new normative developments and are, "due to their abstractness,"[144] important mechanisms to ensure the progressive development of international law. The GGE, in its 2015 report, identified the commitment by States to certain key principles of the Charter and other international law as centrally important. These principles are

- sovereign equality;
- the settlement of international disputes by peaceful means in such a manner that international peace and security and justice are not endangered;
- refraining in their international relations from the threat or use of force against the territorial integrity or political independence of any State [. . .];
- respect for human rights and fundamental freedoms; and
- non-intervention in the internal affairs of other States.[145]

Some of these principles, such as respect for human rights, have been discussed in this study. The other principles will now be looked at in turn.

3.3.4.2 Principle of Sovereign Equality

Article 2 (1) of the UN Charter confirms that all states enjoy sovereign equality, thus confirming that states are both sovereign and, in that sovereignty, legally equal to all other states. Sovereignty is both a norm of international law and a source of international legal norms, has customary value, and is of peremptory character. Sovereignty is a "pivotal principle" of modern international law.[146] The respect of states for each other's territorial sovereignty is, per the ICJ in the *Corfu Channel Case*, "an essential foundation of international relations."[147] Having a normative and empirical dimension,[148] sovereignty denotes both "supreme authority" and "ultimate power" within and over a territory. Or, as was formulated in the *Island of Palmas* arbitral award, "[s]overeignty [. . .] signifies independence. Independence in regard to a portion of the globe is the right to exercise therein, to the exclusion of any other State, the functions of a State."[149] This approach also applies to "cyberspace" in the sense of the cyberspatial realm of activity of natural and legal persons tied to a territory, to a portion of the globe.[150] An internet user sitting at a desk in Germany and

142 Cf. Wolfrum (2010), para. 51.
143 Ibid., para. 62.
144 Ibid., para. 60.
145 GGE report (2015), 26 (bullet points added).
146 Samantha Besson, "Sovereignty," in Rüdiger Wolfrum (ed.), *Max Planck Encyclopedia of Public International Law (MPEPIL)* (Oxford: OUP, 2008) (2011), para. 1.
147 ICJ, *Corfu Channel Case (UK v. Albania)*, ICJ Rep. 4 (1949), 35.
148 Cf. Samantha Besson, "Sovereignty," in Rüdiger Wolfrum (ed.), *Max Planck Encyclopedia of Public International Law (MPEPIL)* (Oxford: OUP, 2008) (2011), para. 56.
149 Reports of International Arbitral Awards, April 4, 1928, *Island of Palmas*, arbitral award (Max Huber), at 838.
150 Michael N. Schmitt (ed.), *Tallinn Manual on the International Law Applicable to Cyber Warfare* (Cambridge: CUP, 2013), 11 (as Rule 1).

commenting in German as a user of a US social network site on a video by a US citizen, stored on a US server, is still "in" Germany though his activities decidedly have an international dimension. In this case, the US and Germany, based on their sovereignty, can plausibly exercise jurisdiction. They are sovereign and equal in their basic claim to do so.

Sovereignty knows restrictions, as already Judge Anzilotti held in his dissent in *Customs Regime*.[151] States only lose their independence if they cease to "exercise within [their] own territory the summa potestas or sovereignty." Accepting restrictions on their sovereignty, Anzilotti states, does not "affect [a state's] independence, provided that the State does not thereby deprive itself of its organic powers." It is only natural in an increasingly interdependent international order that states enter into relations with each other and submit to obligations. But withdrawing from the international system and cutting a state off the increasingly thickly woven fabric of international obligations may lead to the unwelcome status of a rogue state.[152] Rather than ensuring "more" sovereignty (with sovereignty understood as power flowing from membership and thus *Mitspracherecht* in the global community of states), this process would diminish it.[153] To graduated degrees, any withdrawal from international obligations and systems, such as Brexit or President Trump's non-submission to the Paris Agreement, only prima facie increases sovereignty (understood traditionally as doing what pleases). Not submitting to international regimes has substantial costs in terms of sovereignty reduction[154] in times of the international law of cooperation, not coordination.[155]

Sovereignty today protects chiefly the *domaine réservé* as is confirmed by the principles of non-intervention of Article 2 (7) and the non-use of force rule of Article 2 (4) of the UN Charter. However, the concept of what a domain reserve is has substantially altered over the years. The progressive pursuance of common interest issues in international settings through common organizations, the even stronger supranational regionalization, and the underlying economic and financial interdependencies have reduced the importance of sovereignty as a defensive concept. States still benefit from sovereignty, but only if and insofar as they exercise their sovereign rights with a view to the progressively codified purposes of the international order.

Already in 1992, former UN Secretary-General Boutros Boutros-Ghali wrote in his Agenda for Peace that "[t]he time of absolute and exclusive sovereignty [...] has passed [and that] its theory was never matched by reality."[156] Sovereignty never meant that states

[151] PCIJ, *Customs Régime between Germany and Austria* (Protocol of March 19th, 1931), (Advisory Opinion), PCIJ (1931), ser. A/B, No. 41; Individual Opinion by M. Anzilotti (55 et seq.), para. 160–1.

[152] Petra Minnerop, *Paria-Staaten im Völkerrecht* (Heidelberg: Springer, 2004) (criticizing the notion of "pariah state" as a stigmatizing instrument of hegemony, at 447).

[153] Luigi Corrias, "Guises of Sovereignty: 'Rogue States' and Democratic States in the International Legal Order," in Wolfgang Wagner, Werner Wouter, and Michal Onderco (eds.), *Deviance in International Relations* (London: Palgrave Macmillan, 2014), 38–57.

[154] Yong-Xiang Zhanga, Qing-Chen Chaoa, Qiu-Hong Zheng, and Lei Huang, "The Withdrawal of the U.S. from the Paris Agreement and Its Impact on Global Climate Change Governance," Advances in Climate Change Research 8 (2017) 4, 213–19.

[155] Just see Benedict Kingsbury and Megan Donaldson, "From Bilateralism to Publicness in International Law," in Ulrich Fastenrath et al. (eds.), *From Bilateralism to Community Interests: Essays in Honour of Judge Bruno Simma* (Oxford: OUP, 2011), 79–89.

[156] Boutros Boutros-Ghali, "An Agenda for Peace. Preventive Diplomacy, Peacemaking and Peace-Keeping. Report of the Secretary-General Pursuant to the Statement Adopted by the Summit Meeting of the Security Council on 31 January 1992," in Adam Roberts and Benedict Kingsbury (eds.), *United Nations, Divided World. The UN's Role in International Relations* (Oxford: OUP, 1993), 468–98.

were free to deal with their citizens as they chose.[157] Sovereignty is progressively disaggregated and new concepts of sovereignty imply obligations (such as the responsibility to protect) rather than defensive rights.[158] In light of the regulatory challenges, states have chosen, with graduations, to transfer some sovereignty in the form of public authority or even normative power with direct effect to supranational organizations, international organizations, or private norm-setters.[159] This transfer of sovereignty fragments on the international level presupposes the emergence of adequate normative structures.[160]

Upon the urging of sovereignty-oriented states, the GGE, in its 2015 report, highlighted twice the importance of sovereignty for information and communication technologies. The group identified "as of central importance the commitments of States" to sovereign equality, as the first principles of the Charter and other international law to be singled out (para. 26). Again, in paragraph 28 (b), the group confirmed that when using ICTs, states must observe, "among other principles of international law, State sovereignty [and] sovereign equality [. . .]."

It can be correctly observed that territorial sovereignty in the sense of jurisdiction *ratione loci* and *personae* is challenged by the ubiquity of the internet and the technological realities of how data packages are routed through networks and the cloud. Yet as far as the internet has kinetic resources, these still fall under the jurisdiction of a sovereign state exercising territorial sovereignty. With regard to cyber infrastructure, persons, and cyber activities within its territory, states enjoy "internal sovereignty" subject only to "international legal obligations."[161] This applies to the physical layer, the logical layer (a state may demand cryptographic protocols, electronic signatures, and encryption), and the social layer (regulating activities of those on its territory).[162] However, to the degree that we accept that protecting the internet's integrity lies in the global common interest, states can no longer exercise their jurisdiction without considering their duties vis-à-vis the international community (viz. "subject to international legal obligations").[163]

According to Wolff Heintschel von Heinegg, this right (of controlling access to and egress from a state's territory) "seems to also apply to all forms of communication."[164] This approach ignores the realities of how data is routed through networks. Once a state is connected to the global internet backbone, data may be routed through a variety of ways and it cannot be safely said whether or not a specific transmission will travel through a territory or not. Heintschel von Heinegg argues that just because kinetic resources form part of the

[157] Cf. Wolfgang Benedek and Matthias C. Kettemann, "Menschliche Sicherheit und Menschenrechte," in Claudia Ulbert and Sascha Werthes (eds.), *Menschliche Sicherheit. Globale Herausforderungen und regionale Perspektiven* (Vienna/Baden-Baden: Nomos, 2008), 94–109.

[158] Cf. Abram Chayes and Antonia H. Chayes, *The New Sovereignty: Compliance with International Regulatory Agreements* (Cambridge, MA: Harvard University Press, 1995), 4, 26.

[159] For this process, see Armin von Bogdandy, Philipp Dann, and Matthias Goldmann, "Völkerrecht als öffentliches Recht: Konturen eines rechtlichen Rahmens für Global Governance," Der Staat 49 (2010), 23 (30 et seq.).

[160] Cf. Thomas Kleinlein, *Konstitutionalisierung im Völkerrecht* (Heidelberg: Springer, 2012); Jan Klabbers, Anne Peters, and Geir Ulfstein, *The Constitutionalization of International Law* (Oxford: OUP, 2009); Benedict Kingsbury, Nico Krisch, and Richard Stewart, "The Emergence of Global Administrative Law," Law and Contemporary Problems 2 (2005), 15–62.

[161] Michael N. Schmitt (ed.), *Tallinn Manual 2.0 on the International Law Applicable to Cyber Operations* (Cambridge: CUP, 2017), 13 (Rule 2).

[162] Ibid., 14.

[163] International law can also be approached via a layered approach, see Joseph H. H. Weiler, "The Geology of International Law – Governance, Democracy, and Legitimacy," ZaöRV 64 (2004), 547–62.

[164] Ibid., 8.

global internet, territorial sovereignty over resources lying with a state's jurisdiction must be largely discounted.[165] Yet accepting that states exercise territorial sovereignty over kinetic resources does not contradict the acceptance of certain obligations with regard to the way they can exercise this sovereignty. Article 19 UDHR assures everyone the right to freedom of opinion and expression including the freedom to "seek, receive and impart information and ideas through any media and *regardless of frontiers*" (emphasis added). Giving states a right to control data flows would run counter to this human rights-based commitment.

The sovereignty principle thus protects kinetic infrastructure located within a state from activities attributable to other states that would amount to exercises of state jurisdiction. But not every impact on kinetic infrastructure by another state amounts to violations of sovereignty.[166] Just as with the non-intervention principle, the sovereignty principle precludes other states from launching, for example, information operations within other countries. Yet the principle of territorial sovereignty is rather used by sovereignty-oriented states to assume more oversight (and control) over national dimensions of internet infrastructure (e.g. Russia's and China's calls to control over a "national internet segment"). The principle of sovereign equality, as it is used in this interpretation, rather threatens the internet's integrity than protect it. A case in point is the *International Code of Conduct for Information Security*[167] proposed by China together with Russia, Tajikistan, and Uzbekistan at the UN in 2011[168] and resubmitted to the 2014 NetMundial meeting. It envisages tighter control of the state vis-à-vis kinetic and non-kinetic internet resources "within" a state's territory, including websites targeting nationals of that state, data stored in that state, and data flows running through that state.[169]

Similarly, the Russian submission to NetMundial highlighted that in certain areas "States have the exclusive authority and responsibility." The Ministry of Foreign Affairs of the Russian Federation identified the "absence of international legal norms developed under the aegis of the UN, establishing common and obligatory rules of internet governance for the governments and other interested parties to implement" as one of the internet's "[k]ey problems." As a solution, the Russian Ministry of Foreign Affairs suggested that "states must preserve their sovereign right to regulate their telecommunications." States "have to be able to regulate their national internet segments" and must have an "equal right to govern" the internet, including "allocation, assignment and withdrawing numbering [resources,] names, addressing and identification of the internet, operation support and development of primary internet infrastructure."[170] This is clear evidence of a call for more national control

[165] Wolff Heintschel von Heinegg, "Legal Implications of Territorial Sovereignty in Cyberspace," in Christian Czosseck, Rain Ottis, and Katharina Ziolkowski (eds.), *Proceedings of the 4th International Conference on Cyber Conflict* (Tallinn: NATO CCD COE Publications, 2012), 7 (14).

[166] Wolff Heintschel von Heinegg, "Legal Implications of Territorial Sovereignty in Cyberspace," in Christian Czosseck, Rain Ottis, and Katharina Ziolkowski (eds.), *Proceedings of the 4th International Conference on Cyber Conflict* (Tallinn: NATO CCD COE Publications, 2012), 7, 12 (note 24) (arguing that there are "good reasons to maintain that damage below the threshold of severity must be tolerated and does not violate the territorial sovereignty [. . .]").

[167] Ministry of Foreign Affairs of the People's Republic of China, International Code of Conduct for Information Security (February 2014), submission to NetMundial, http://content.netmundial.br/contribution/international-code-of-conduct-for-information-security/67.

[168] International code of conduct for information security, Annex to the letter dated 12 September 2011 from the Permanent Representatives of China, the Russian Federation, Tajikistan, and Uzbekistan to the United Nations addressed to the Secretary-General, UN Doc. A/66/359 of 14 September 2011.

[169] Ibid., lit. (a), (c), (e).

[170] Ministry of Foreign Affairs of the Russian Federation, Submission to NetMundial, April 23–24, 2014, http://document.netmundial.br/2-roadmap-for-the-future-evolution-of-the-internet-governance.

over international management functions regarding key internet naming and numbering resources.

Other states, such as India, submitted notably different arguments to NetMundial, which evidence a more nuanced conception of sovereignty vis-à-vis the internet. India argued that the "internet is a shared resource and a global commons available to public" and that only "[p]olicy authority for internet-related public policy issues is the sovereign right of states."[171] Mexico did not speak of sovereignty, but pointed to the "special role of governments in areas such as national security and critical infrastructure stability," which implied that they "should be active participants in [the] multi[-]stakeholder process."[172] The French government distinguished between a commitment to multistakeholder approaches regarding internet governance and those normative arenas where states play a role through domestic legislation. "In areas such as cybersecurity, intellectual property, privacy, consumer protection, child protection or taxation, [...] governments clearly dominate the process, although not to the exclusion of other stakeholders."[173] This evidences a nuanced understanding of sovereignty that can be termed *cooperative* or *shared sovereignty*.

How differently traditionally important states such as France approach the development of international legal arrangements bearing upon the internet can be seen from the French government's suggestion to rely, in the formulation of internet-related policy, on the "basic principle of subsidiarity [...] whereby any internet governance issue ought to be handled by the smallest body capable of addressing that issue effectively."[174] This is a far cry from the Russian statement that governments must "preserve their sovereign right to regulate their telecommunications."

Understanding sovereignty as a right to control exclusively both the architecture and the content of the "national internet segment" can endanger the integrity of the internet. Having sovereign uncoordinated decision-making over almost 200 national internet "segments" is likely to lead to substantial technological problems in light of the necessity of centrally managing key naming and addressing resources, and ensuring human rights-based standards globally. "National internets," as pursued by states such as China, through massive filtering programs currently work because they are not completely divorced from the global internet. If control over naming and addressing resources were nationalized, the stability of the internet's core architecture would not be enhanced.

3.3.4.3 Non-Use of (the Threat of) Force

Article 2 (4) of the UN Charter prohibits the threat or use of force in international relations: "All Members shall refrain in their international relations from the threat or use of force against the territorial integrity or political independence of any State, or in any other manner inconsistent with the Purposes of the United Nations." The prohibition of the use of

[171] Global Stakeholder Meeting on the Future of Internet Governance, Sao Paulo, Brazil, April 23–24, 2014, Government of India's initial submission, http://content.netmundial.br/contribution/government-of-india-s-initial-submission-to-global-multistakeholder-meeting-on-the-future-of-internet-governance-sau-paulo-brazil-april-23-24-2014/138, paras. 1 and 5.

[172] NetMundial, Global Stakeholder Meeting on the Future of Internet Governance, Sao Paulo, Brazil, April 23–24, 2014, Content submission by the Federal Government of Mexico, March 2014, http://content.netmundial.br/contribution/content-submission-by-the-federal-government-of-mexico/219, Principle 11.

[173] Global Stakeholder Meeting on the Future of Internet Governance, Sao Paulo, Brazil, April 23–24, 2014, French Government Submission to NetMundial, http://content.netmundial.br/contribution/french-government-submission-to-netmundial/154, para. 3.

[174] Ibid., para. 4.

force is a customary law rule, a peremptory norm of international law, and, as the ICJ ruled in the *Nicaragua* case, a "fundamental or cardinal principle of [international] law."[175] (The prohibition of the threat itself seems not to have reached ius cogens status.[176]) Both the use of force and the threat itself are illegal; the threat being illegal if the "use of force contemplated would be illegal."[177] Employing force goes substantially beyond bringing economic or political pressure to bear on another state—which might violate the non-intervention principle, but would not amount to a violation of the non-use of force rule. For Oliver Dörr, force in the context of Article 2 (4) of the UN Charter can only include "armed or military force."[178] Yet not only the direct employment of armed force is prohibited. As the ICJ confirmed in *Nicaragua*[179] *and Armed Activities on the Territory of the Congo (Democratic Republic of the Congo v. Uganda),*[180] supporting private actors that then commit violence in the territory of another state can violate the non-use of force rule.

Applied to the internet, any "cyber operation constituting a threat or use of force against the territorial integrity or political independence of any State, or that is in any other manner inconsistent with the purposes of the United Nations, is unlawful."[181] The application of the non-use of force rule to cyber attacks has been controversially debated, with most scholars agreeing on an effects-based approach, thus admitting that certain cyber attacks can amount to an armed attack if they surpass a certain threshold of intensity and cause substantial kinetic damage.[182] Rule 69 (Definition of the use of force) of the Tallinn Manual 2.0 defines a cyber operation as a use of force "when its scale and effects are comparable to non-cyber operations rising to the level of a use of force."[183] A cyberattack can be unlawful even if it does not rise to the level of use of force. It could then be qualified as an illicit intervention. The Tallinn Manual 2.0 suggests a number of criteria to measure whether an action amounts to use of force, including: severity, immediacy, directness, invasiveness, measurability of effects, military character, state involvement, and presumptive legality.[184]

On the other hand, not all uses of force may amount to an "armed attack," triggering the right to self-defense.[185] What interests here is not primarily whether the non-use of force rule applies to internet-mediated attacks (it does, even though the GGE report in 2017

[175] ICJ, *Military and Paramilitary Activities in und against Nicaragua (Nicaragua v. United States of America)* (Judgment), ICJ Rep. (1986), 14, para. 190.

[176] Michael Wood, "Use of Force, Prohibition of Threat," in Rüdiger Wolfrum (ed.), *Max Planck Encyclopedia of Public International Law (MPEPIL)* (Oxford: OUP, 2008) (2013) [online], para. 12.

[177] ICJ, *Military and Paramilitary Activities in and against Nicaragua Case (Nicaragua v. United States of America)* (Merits), ICJ Rep. (1986), para. 47.

[178] Oliver Dörr, "Use of Force, Prohibition of," in Rüdiger Wolfrum (ed.), *Max Planck Encyclopedia of Public International Law (MPEPIL)* (Oxford: OUP, 2008) (2011) [online], para. 11.

[179] IICJ, *Military and Paramilitary Activities in and against Nicaragua Case (Nicaragua v. United States of America)* (Merits), ICJ Rep. (1986), para. 228.

[180] ICJ, *Armed Activities on the Territory of the Congo (Democratic Republic of the Congo v. Uganda)*, paras. 163–5.

[181] Michael N. Schmitt (ed.), *Tallinn Manual 2.0 on the International Law Applicable to Cyber Operations* (Cambridge: CUP, 2017), 329 (Rule 68).

[182] Already Michael N. Schmitt, "Computer Network Attack and the Use of Force in International Law: Thoughts on a Normative Framework," Columbia Journal of Transnational Law 37 (1999) 3, 885, 913; Torsten Stein and Thilo Marauhn, "Völkerrechtliche Aspekte von Informationsoperationen," ZaöRV 60 (2000), 6.

[183] Michael N. Schmitt (ed.), *Tallinn Manual 2.0 on the International Law Applicable to Cyber Operations* (Cambridge: CUP, 2017), 330 (Rule 69).

[184] Ibid., 336–7.

[185] ICJ, *Military and Paramilitary Activities in and against Nicaragua Case (Nicaragua v. United States of America)* (Merits), ICJ Rep. (1986), para. 191. See further Sven Hendrik Schulze, *Cyber-"War" – Testfall der Staatenverantwortlichkeit* (Tübingen: Mohr Siebeck, 2015).

failed to reach a consensus on the question of "how" exactly it should be applied[186]), but rather whether the rule offers protection for the internet and from internet-based attacks. This is clearly the case. The prohibition of (the threat of) force protects national physical elements of the internet's functionality just as it does other aspects of critical (information) infrastructure and enjoins states from using the internet to conduct an operation in violation of the principle.

3.3.4.4 Non-Intervention in Domestic Affairs

The customary law rule regarding non-intervention in internal affairs reflects the customary expression of the non-intervention principle.[187] As by the 1970 Friendly Relations Declaration, no state may intervene "directly or indirectly, for any reason whatever, in the internal or external affairs of any other State." Both "armed intervention and all other forms of interference or attempted threats against the personality of the State or against its political, economic and cultural elements, are in violation of international law." This implies each state's "inalienable right to choose its political, economic, social and cultural systems, without interference in any form by another State." As the ICJ found in the *Nicaragua* case, non-intervention only protects a state with regard to "matters in which each State is permitted, by the principle of State sovereignty, to decide freely. One of these is the choice of a political, economic, social and cultural system, and the formulation of foreign policy."[188]

Non-intervention therefore only extends to the *domain réservé* of a state, which is quickly diminishing in times of increased international cooperation and progressive codification of international law. As soon as a normative field is "internationalized" through state commitments to the international community, calling that state to order and reminding it of its duties is no longer interference or intervention, but rather the international legal right (and often duty) of other states. With regard to certain issues of international law, namely the management of common areas and the regulation of issues of common interest of the international community, states cannot argue that criticism of domestic policies violates the non-intervention principle as they are not free under international law to set their own policies in these arenas. The non-intervention rule protects internet integrity by way of its content. The 2015–2017 information operations of Russia against the US in the run-up to the US presidential elections and thereafter[189] can be judged in light of the non-intervention principle as being "interferences" against the "political, economic and cultural elements" of the US, as per the Friendly Relations Declaration.

The Tallinn Manual 2.0 confirms, in Rule 66, the prohibition of interventions by cyber means: "A State may not intervene, including by cyber means, in the internal or external affairs of another State."[190] This also includes intervention by non-cyber means in internal

[186] Cf. Adam Segal, "The Development of Cyber Norms at the United Nations Ends in Deadlock. Now What?," *Council on Foreign Relations*, June 29, 2017, https://www.cfr.org/blog/development-cyber-norms-united-nations-ends-deadlock-now-what.

[187] Philip Kunig, "Prohibition of Intervention," in Rüdiger Wolfrum (ed.), *Max Planck Encyclopedia of Public International Law (MPEPIL)* (Oxford: OUP, 2008) (2008) [online], para. 2.

[188] ICJ, *Military and Paramilitary Activities in and against Nicaragua Case (Nicaragua v. United States of America)* (Merits), ICJ Rep. (1986), para. 205.

[189] See Keir Giles, "Countering Russian Information Operations in the Age of Social Media," *Council on Foreign Relations*, November 21, 2017, https://www.cfr.org/report/countering-russian-information-operations-age-social-media.

[190] Michael N. Schmitt (ed.), *Tallinn Manual 2.0 on the International Law Applicable to Cyber Operations* (Cambridge: CUP, 2017), 312 (Rule 66).

affairs pertaining to the internet, such as exerting pressure to compel a state to adopt certain internet-related legislation. The domain reserve of states includes the political and social system and their organization. Thus any coercive action by cyber means to alter the social or governmental structure is prohibited. Interventions need not be oriented toward State infrastructure (e.g. government website) but must be "designed to undermine the State's authority over the *domain réservé*."[191] Cyber interventions need not produce kinetic effects to be coercive; it is the goal of the attack (coercion) that counts. Interferences below the coercion threshold (including persuasion, criticism, public diplomacy, and propaganda such as online ads or social media postings) are not coercive in nature and therefore not prohibited under the non-intervention principle.

The GGE 2015 report, in its section on "norms, rules and principles for the responsible behaviour of States," recalls that states should not knowingly allow their territory to be used for internationally wrongful acts (thus including possible interventions), that states should not conduct or knowingly support ICT activity contrary to its obligations under international law (including interventions), and that states should take appropriate measures against interventions by other states by protecting their critical infrastructure from ICT threats with a view to creating a global culture of cybersecurity.[192] As a particular intervention-related norm, the GGE report introduces the norm that states should not conduct or knowingly support activity to harm "the information systems of the authorized emergency response teams" of other states or use their own teams to engage in "malicious international activity."[193]

3.3.4.5 Duty of Cooperation

In the above-cited 1984 *Gulf of Maine* case, the ICJ distinguished a "limited set of norms for ensuring the co-existence and vital co-operation of the members of the international community" from other customary rules *whose existence* in the opinio iuris could be inductively inferred from practice. The ICJ thus considers among the most important rules of international law those ensuring "vital co-operation." Can we deduce from this that a general duty of "vital co-operation" between states exists, distinguishable from a duty to cooperate that would need to be deduced from opinio iuris and practice? Can cooperation with a view to ensuring the integrity of the internet be established as a "vital" duty or does it concern non-vital issues of cooperation?

There is no intrinsic value in "cooperating" as cooperation, as Rüdiger Wolfrum reminds us, can also be "co-operation to start a war of aggression."[194] But used in the context of a normatively deeper international order—thus in the sense of the international law of co-operation between all actors as contrasted with an international order merely focused on the coexistence of states—cooperation must be understood as international legal persons striving together to increase "the social welfare of the world community" with a "distributive effect."[195] Article 1 (1) and (3) of the UN Charter already commits the organization and its members to effective cooperation, with the latter provision declaring it a purpose of the

191 Ibid., 315.
192 GGE report (2015), para. 13(c), (f), and (g).
193 Ibid., para. 13(k).
194 Rüdiger Wolfrum, "Cooperation, International Law of," in Rüdiger Wolfrum (ed.), *Max Planck Encyclopedia of Public International Law (MPEPIL)* (Oxford: OUP, 2008) (2010) [online], para. 2.
195 Ibid.

organization: "[to] achieve international co-operation in solving international problems of an economic, social, cultural, or humanitarian character [...]." Article 11 (1) of the UN Charter allows the General Assembly to consider "the general principles of co-operation in the maintenance of international peace and security." Chapter IX of the Charter is specifically dedicated to "international economic and social cooperation," with Article 56 containing a pledge by all members "to take joint and separate action in co-operation with the Organization for the achievement of the purposes of Article 55," including "creation of conditions of stability and well-being," development, and human rights. There is not, however, a formal *general* legal obligation to cooperate.

Following Wolfrum, the recognition of such an obligation would have three consequences for international law: it would have to be normatively reoriented toward promoting certain communal values (to be achieved through cooperation) (e.g. through the "humanization" of international law[196]); the management of "common international spaces" would be a "common concern for all States;"[197] and the significance of international organizations would increase.[198] All three elements are visible in international law. This principle has cognizable normative content with relevance for the internet (and for the protection of states from dangers emanating from the internet) in three constellations: cooperation within thematically specific fields, namely science and technology; cooperation within (regional) political arrangements; and cooperation with regard to managing common spaces[199] and issues in the global interest.

First, a duty of cooperation in the fields of science and technology has been submitted as Principle 4 of the Friendly Relations Declaration, in which states committed to cooperate in the fields of science and technology. Second, regionally, the obligation to cooperate has been confirmed in regional political arrangements, such as the 1975 Helsinki Final Act of the Conference for Security and Co-operation in Europe,[200] which confirms that "participating States will develop their co-operation with one another and with all States in all fields [with the goal of] improve[ing] the well-being of peoples and contribut[ing] to the fulfilment of their aspirations." Third, as Wolfrum notes, "recent international agreements for the use of common spaces and concerning issues in the interest of the international community" are evidence of a normatively stronger cooperation principle.[201] Cooperation regarding innovative technologies, in regional arrangements, and with regard to shared spaces and global interest issues is based on the conviction that certain common goals cannot be achieved through uncoordinated action of individual states, but are premised upon cooperation.[202]

Two reasons thus exist for accepting international obligations regarding the protection of and from the internet. States are normatively constrained in the way they manage national kinetic and non-kinetic infrastructure and develop and apply the normative framework, nationally, regionally, and internationally, related to the integrity of the internet.

[196] Cf. Theodor Meron, *Humanization of International Law* (Amsterdam: Brill, 2014).

[197] Wolfgang Benedek, Koen De Feyter, Matthias C. Kettemann, and Christina Voigtde, "Introduction," in Wolfgang Benedek et al. (eds.), *The Common Interest in International Law* (Antwerp: Intersentia, 2014), 10.

[198] See Wolfrum (2010), paras. 10–12.

[199] Articles II and III of the Antarctic Treaty; Articles III, IX-XI Outer Space Treaty; Part XI of UNCLOS.

[200] Final Act of the Conference for Security and Co-operation in Europe (adopted August 1, 1975).

[201] Wolfrum (2010), para. 25.

[202] Cf. Jost Delbrück, "The International Obligation to Cooperate: An Empty Shell or a Hard Law Principle of International Law? – A Critical Look at a Much Debated Paradigm of Modern International Law," in Holger P. Hestermeyer et al. (eds.), *Coexistence, Cooperation and Solidarity, Liber Amicorum Rüdiger Wolfrum* (2 vols.) (Amsterdam: Brill, 2011), vol. 1, 1–16.

These are, first, the heightened cooperation obligations regarding the areas of science and technology—the internet, being a network of networks that grew out of scientific cooperation, is based on technology and furthers both science and technology—and, second, the cooperation obligations in relation to the management of common spaces and regarding issues of international common interest. There is thus an obligation to cooperate with regard to safeguarding the integrity of the internet.

Similarly, the GGE report of 2015 highlighted the importance of cooperation. It recommended setting confidence-building measures to strengthen international peace and security, which would increase interstate cooperation, transparency, predictability, and stability.[203] In particular, states should seek to "facilitate cross-border cooperation to address critical infrastructure vulnerabilities" and transcend national borders by, for example, introducing confidence-building measures to strengthen cooperation on a bilateral, subregional, regional, and multilateral basis.[204] The report dedicates a whole section to "international cooperation and assistance in ICT security and capacity-building" and, in paragraph 19, recalls that "international cooperation and assistance can play an essential role in enabling States to secure ICTs and ensure their peaceful use." In light of the development of the internet, and dangers to society posed by it, international law can be considered to have evolved to a point where the principle of cooperation includes a duty to cross-border cooperation to address critical infrastructure vulnerabilities transcending national borders.

3.3.4.6 Peaceful Settlement of International Disputes

As defined by the PCIJ in the *Mavrommatis Palestine Concessions* case, a dispute is a "disagreement on a point of law or fact, a conflict of legal views or of interests between two persons"[205] or other international legal entities. It needs to be international in character or at least have not only incidental international implications to fall within the ambit of international law. The rule of peaceful settlement of international disputes limits the sovereignty of the involved parties by committing them to settle their disagreement without recourse to force. Insofar it refines the prohibition of the (threat or) use of force in international relations. Settling disputes by peaceful means is one of the principles of the United Nations. According to Article 2 (3), all members commit to settling their "international disputes by peaceful means in such a manner that international peace and security, and justice, are not endangered." Chapter VI of the UN Charter is specifically entitled "pacific settlement of disputes" and formalizes, in Article 33 (1), the duty of the parties to any dispute likely to endanger the maintenance of international peace and security to "first of all, seek a solution by negotiation, enquiry, mediation, conciliation, arbitration, judicial settlement, resort to regional agencies or arrangements, or other peaceful means of their own choice." Once disputes rise to a certain level—endangering international peace and security—they can give rise to situations of individual self-defense (Article 52 of the UN Charter) or collective self-defense pursuant to chapter VII.

Outside of extreme situations, the peaceful settlement of international disputes "has become the general rule."[206] The ICJ recognized it as a "principle of customary International

[203] GGE report (2015), 16.

[204] Ibid., para. 16(d).

[205] PCIJ, *Mavrommatis Palestine Concessions (Greece v. Great Britain)* (Jurisdiction), (1924) PCIJ Rep. ser. B., No. 3, para. 19.

[206] Cf. Alain Pellet, "Peaceful Settlement of International Disputes," in Rüdiger Wolfrum (ed.), *Max Planck Encyclopedia of Public International Law (MPEPIL)* (Oxford: OUP, 2008) (2010) [online], para. 1.

law"[207] and it has been considered a peremptory norm of international law.[208] The concrete obligation is to enter into settlements, in good faith,[209] not to achieve specific results—however, the status quo of a "frozen" conflict must not endanger international peace and security, which brings chapter VII of the UN Charter to bear upon it. The duty to settle disputes peacefully has been reiterated by the international community in the 1970 Friendly Relations Declaration[210] and the 2000 United Nations Millennium Declaration.[211]

The younger an international legal regime is, the fewer institutionalized means to solve conflicts peacefully exist. The progressive institutionalization of dispute settlement mechanisms can therefore be roughly equated with normative progress within a regime. This holds true for the internet as well. In light of the recent evolution of first governance structures regarding the internet, the importance for some states of exerting control over "national internet segments" and the fluidity of the management of certain key internet resources, disputes are more likely than in certain traditional international regimes. Coupled with an absence of formal settlement procedures, the obligation to settle international disputes peacefully, though it applies, is difficult to implement.

There is no direct protection of internet integrity through the obligation to peaceful settlement of disputes. Insofar as the normative development of the protection of the internet's functionality gives rise to international disputes, however, the obligation to peacefully settle these indirectly protects the internet and other critical infrastructure. It also safeguards us from threats emanating from disputes over the use and development of the internet. Though there have not yet been any formal international developments regarding the pacific settlement rule (such as the installation of an international arbiter), some disputes between states have already been normatively solved through international law. After the indictment by the US Department of Justice of five Chinese Army officers for economic espionage, then-US President Obama and Chinese President Xi Jinping signed a Cybersecurity Agreement in 2015. Though the dispute does not seem to have been "settled,"[212] the use of an international legal instrument is encouraging.

3.3.4.7 Principle of Equal Rights and Self-Determination of Peoples

Art 1 (2) of the UN Charter declares developing "friendly relations among nations based on respect for the principle of equal rights and self-determination of peoples" as one of the purposes of the organization. Article 55 also refers to the principle, as does implicitly Article 73 UN Charter. The 1960 Declaration on the Granting of Independence to Colonial Countries and Peoples of the General Assembly[213] confirmed it and the 1970 Friendly Relations Declaration[214] found a nuanced formulation in its Principle 5: "all peoples have the right

[207] ICJ, *Military and Paramilitary Activities in and against Nicaragua Case (Nicaragua v. United States of America)* (Merits), ICJ Rep. (1986), para. 290.

[208] Cf. Alain Pellet, "Peaceful Settlement of International Disputes," in Rüdiger Wolfrum (ed.), *Max Planck Encyclopedia of Public International Law (MPEPIL)* (Oxford: OUP, 2008) (2010) [online], para 5.

[209] ICJ, *Aerial Incident of 10 August 1999 (Pakistan v. India)* (Jurisdiction of the Court), para. 53.

[210] UN General Assembly, Res. 2625 (XXV) (24 October 1970) (Friendly Relations Declaration).

[211] UN General Assembly, Res. 55/2, United Nations Millennium Declaration (8 September 2000), paras. 4 and 9.

[212] Gary Brown and Christopher D. Yung, "Evaluating the US-China Cybersecurity Agreement," *The Diplomat*, January 19, 2017, https://thediplomat.com/2017/01/evaluating-the-us-china-cybersecurity-agreement-part-1-the-us-approach-to-cyberspace.

[213] United Nations General Assembly, Declaration on the Granting of Independence to Colonial Countries and Peoples, UNGA Res 1514 (XV) of 14 December 1960.

[214] UN General Assembly, Res. 2625 (XXV) (24 October 1970) (Friendly Relations Declaration).

freely to determine, without external interference, their political status and to pursue their economic, social and cultural development, and every State has the duty to respect this right in accordance with the provisions of the Charter." Further, Common Article 1 of the International Covenant on Economic, Social and Cultural Rights (ICESCR) and the ICCPR confirms the "right [of all peoples] of self-determination" and prescribes that all peoples may, "for their own ends, freely dispose of their natural wealth and resources without prejudice to any obligations arising out of international economic co-operation, based upon the principle of mutual benefit, and international law."

Though the ICJ has by now accepted that self-determination is a right,[215] the extent and content of self-determination remains much discussed. Daniel Thürer and Thomas Burri argue that, rather than querying into the concrete normative content of the right, it is better to understand self-determination as a flexible principle underlying "the whole international order" and informing the "development of international law" more broadly.[216] Both the Kosovo case[217] and the Russian intervention in Crimea and the subsequent referendum[218] have shown that the international debate on self-determination is highly politicized.

The right to self-determination is not directly linked to the internet, though the internet can be used as a tool in the fight for self-determination and against it. One can therefore make the claim that the development potential lying in the management of local internet resources according to national political preferences can be considered as part of the "natural wealth and resources" of a country that the country can "for their own ends [...] freely dispose of" (as per Article 1 (2) ICCPR and ICESCR). The claim is tenuous and yet there have been cases where internet-related resources were linked to questions of self-determination in the limited sense of self-determinate disposal of the management duties regarding them.

The case of delegation, dereliction of managerial duties, and subsequent redelegation of Pitcairn Island's .pn TLD took five years to resolve. After "[a]ll residents of Pitcairn Island, other than the administrative contact and his wife," who had received .pn management rights, signed a petition requesting redelegation, which was endorsed by both the Pitcairn Island Council (the local government) and the UK government (administering the territory's affairs), IANA proceeded to redelegate the TLD.[219] Yet the line to be drawn from cases such as this to a more general protection of the national dimension of the internet's integrity remains thin.

[215] ICJ, *Legal Consequences of the Construction of a Wall in the Occupied Palestinian Territory* (Advisory Opinion), para. 118; *East Timor (Portugal v. Australia)*, paras. 31 and 37.

[216] Daniel Thürer and Thomas Burri, "Self-Determination," in Rüdiger Wolfrum (ed.), *Max Planck Encyclopedia of Public International Law (MPEPIL)* (Oxford: OUP, 2008) (2008) [online], para. 26.

[217] Independent International Commission on Kosovo, *The Kosovo Report: Conflict, International Response, Lessons Learned* (Oxford: OUP, 2000).

[218] But see the clear General Assembly Resolution 68/262, Territorial Sovereignty of Ukraine, UN Doc. A/RES/68/262 of 27 March 2014: "[...] [n]oting that the referendum held in the Autonomous Republic of Crimea and the city of Sevastopol on 16 March 2014 was not authorized by Ukraine, (1) Affirms its commitment to the sovereignty, political independence, unity and territorial integrity of Ukraine within its internationally recognized borders; (2) Calls upon all States to desist and refrain from actions aimed at the partial or total disruption of the national unity and territorial integrity of Ukraine, including any attempts to modify Ukraine's borders through the threat or use of force or other unlawful means [...]."

[219] IANA, Report on Request for Redelegation of the .pn Top-Level Domain, February 11, 2000, http://archive.icann.org/en/general/pn-report-11feb00.htm.

3.3.4.8 Principle of Good Faith

Article 2 (2) of the UN Charter obliges member states to fulfill "in good faith the obligations assumed by them in accordance with the present Charter." Similarly, the Friendly Relations Declaration underlines that states have the duty to fulfill "in good faith the obligations assumed by it in accordance with the Charter of the United Nations, [...] under the generally recognized principles and rules of international law [and] under international agreements valid under the generally recognized principles and rules of international law." Good faith is a key principle applicable to the relationship between nations and is important for treaty interpretation.[220] Beyond pointing to preexisting international legal commitments, which are to be exercised in good faith, the principle does not have an internet-specific content.

3.3.4.9 No Harm Principle (Principle of Good Neighborliness)

This no harm principle has roots in the UN Charter, with Article 74 (in the context of non-self-governing territories) referring to the "general principle of good-neighbourliness, due account being taken of the interests and well-being of the rest of the world, in social, economic, and commercial matters." Further, the ICJ in the 1949 *Corfu Channel Case* referred to the "general and well-recognized principle [], namely: [...] every State's obligation not to allow knowingly its territory to be used for acts contrary to the rights of other States."[221] Sometimes expressed in the maxim *sic utere tuo ut alienum non laedas*, the no harm principle limits how a state can use its territory: not in a way that its neighbors are harmed. The duty not to cause transboundary (especially environmental) harm is connected to the equal sovereignty of states. Yet neighboring states, just as neighbors generally, must "tolerate certain interferences—a duty that is coextensive with the neighbouring State's right to use its territory."[222]

In light of the interdependence of states and the relative unimportance of actual neighborliness with regard to the technological realities of ICTs, the concept of what a neighboring state is must be interpreted broadly in the sense of an effects-based approach.[223] The no harm principle applies to states with regard to any state they can, in effect, harm. This is in line with Article 2 (c) of the International Law Commission (ILC) Draft Articles on the Prevention of Transboundary Harm from Hazardous Activities (2001) that defines "transboundary harm" as harm caused by one state to another "whether or not the States concerned share a common border."[224]

The no harm principle has normative roots in the *Trail Smelter*[225] and *Lac Lanoux*[226] arbitration proceedings. The normative content of the no-harm-rule has been formulated, in

[220] Cf. Markus Kotzur, "Good Faith (Bona fide)," in Rüdiger Wolfrum (ed.), *Max Planck Encyclopedia of Public International Law (MPEPIL)* (Oxford: OUP, 2008) (2009) [online].

[221] ICJ, *Corfu Channel Case (UK v. Albania)*, ICJ Rep. 4 (1949), 22.

[222] Jutta Brunnée, "Sic utere tuo ut alienum non laedas," in Rüdiger Wolfrum (ed.), *Max Planck Encyclopedia of Public International Law (MPEPIL)* (Oxford: OUP, 2008) (2010), para. 4.

[223] Cf. UN GA Resolution 46/62, Developing and strengthening of good-neighbourliness between States, A/RES/46/62 of 9 December 1991, para. 2 (states should act as good neighbors "whether or not they are contiguous") and para. 3 (states need to act as good neighbors "when taking decisions that could affect [other states]").

[224] ILC Draft Articles, Prevention of Transboundary Harm from Hazardous Activities (2001), Official Records of the General Assembly, Fifty-sixth Session, Supplement No. 10 (A/56/10).

[225] *Trail Smelter Case*, United States v. Canada, First decision, (1949) III RIAA 1905, (1941) 35 AJIL 684, 16th April 1938, Arbitration.

[226] *Lake Lanoux Arbitration*, France v. Spain, (1963) XII RIAA 281, (1961) 24 ILR 101, 16th November 1957, Arbitration.

Principle 21 of the Stockholm Declaration of 1972[227] and Principle 2 of the Rio Declaration of 1992,[228] as such: states have a duty "to ensure that activities within their jurisdiction or control do not cause damage to the environment of other States or of areas beyond the limits of national jurisdiction." The duty not to cause transboundary harm has crystallized into a rule of customary law on the basis of substantial practice,[229] including international conventions evidencing the rule, such as Article 194 (2) of the 1982 United Nations Convention on the Law of the Sea of 10 December 1982 (UNCLOS)[230] and, regionally, Article 20 (1) of the ASEAN (Association of East Asian Nations) Agreement on the Conservation of Nature and Natural Resources of 1985.[231]

In 1996, the ICJ confirmed the duty of states not to cause transboundary environmental harm in the *Legality of the Threat or Use of Nuclear Weapons Advisory Opinion*.[232] The Court recognized that "the environment is under daily threat," it was no "abstraction but represents the living space, the quality of life and the very health of human beings, including generations unborn." Therefore, it found, the "existence of the general obligation of States to ensure that activities within their jurisdiction and control respect the environment of other States or of areas beyond national control is now part of the corpus of international law relating to the environment." The no harm principle thus applies not only to states but also, at least in the environmental context, to areas beyond national control but whose protection is in the common interest. Meeting both of these criteria, the Court's arguments in the *Nuclear Weapons Advisory Opinion* can therefore be extended to the internet, as can the no harm principle.

No state may allow its territory to be used in a way that violates the rights of other states. This is echoed by the GGE in its 2015 report, which recalled, among the norms and standards, that "[s]tates should not knowingly allow their territory to be used for internationally wrongful acts" and that they "should also respond to appropriate requests to mitigate malicious ICT activity aimed at the critical infrastructure of another State emanating from their territory, taking into account due regard for sovereignty."[233] The territory of a state, such as servers located territorially in a state, can be used to commandeer and steer bot networks used in cybercrime activities or even cyberattacks with or without terrorist purposes. If a state has the duty not to allow knowingly its territory to be used for acts contrary to the rights of other states, then it must take preventive measures to stop such use. Recognizing

[227] Stockholm Declaration of the United Nations Conference on the Human Environment (United Nations [UN]) UN Doc A/CONF.48/14/Rev.1, 3, UN Doc A/CONF.48/PC/6, Principle 21.

[228] Rio Declaration on Environment and Development (United Nations Environment Programme [UNEP]) UN Doc A/CONF.151/5/Rev.1, UN Doc A/CONF.151/26/Rev.1 Vol.1, Annex 1, Principle 2.

[229] Cf. Jutta Brunnée, "Sic utere tuo ut alienum non laedas," in Rüdiger Wolfrum (ed.), *Max Planck Encyclopedia of Public International Law (MPEPIL)* (Oxford: OUP, 2008) (2010), paras. 1–12.

[230] United Nations Convention on the Law of the Sea of 10 December 1982, http://www.un.org/depts/los//convention_agreements/texts/unclos/UNCLOS-TOC.htm, Article 194 (2): "States shall take all measures necessary to ensure that activities under their jurisdiction or control are so conducted as not to cause damage by pollution to other States and their environment, and that pollution arising from incidents or activities under their jurisdiction or control does not spread beyond the areas where they exercise sovereign rights [. . .]."

[231] ASEAN Agreement on the Conservation of Nature and Natural Resources, Kuala Lumpur 1985 (not in force), http://www.jus.uio.no/english/services/library/treaties/06/6-01/asean-conservation-nature.xml, Article 20 (1): "Contracting Parties have in accordance with generally accepted principles of international law the responsibility of ensuring that activities under their jurisdiction or control do not cause damage to the environment or the natural resources under the jurisdiction of other Contracting Parties or of areas beyond the limits of national jurisdiction."

[232] ICJ, *Legality of the Threat or Use of Nuclear Weapons* (Advisory Opinion), ICJ Rep. (1996), 226, para. 29.

[233] GGE report (2015), para. 13 (c) and (h).

this, states have a positive obligation to provide for a secure cyber infrastructure that ensures that no cyberattacks stemming from their territory can cause damage to other states.[234] This also indirectly protects the integrity of the internet insofar as preventive measures against criminal exploits of security gaps in national cyber-infrastructure installations can be used to conduct denial-of-service attacks that can endanger the internet's stability.

3.3.4.10 Principle of Prevention and Due Diligence

Scholars differ as to whether the preventive principle has a due diligence dimension or whether "States' *due diligence* obligations" are broadened "even towards the environment of the global commons" through the no harm principle.[235] Similarly, the normative relationships between the good neighborliness principle, the no harm principle, the *sic utere tuo* maxim, and the principles of prevention and due diligence are difficult to pin down.[236] For Jutta Brunnée, it is the concept of good neighborliness "that gives rise to related procedural duties, such as those of notification and consultation in relation to transboundary harm."[237]

Arguably, the no harm principle encompasses the *sic utere tuo* maxim and contains a preventive dimension that is concretized by due diligence obligations.[238] That the no harm principle has a preventive dimension can already be read into the ICJ's arguments in the *Tehran Hostage Case*, where the Court concluded that Iranian authorities had been required to take "appropriate steps" to prevent violations of international law.[239] Similarly, Article 3 of the ILC Draft Articles on the Prevention of Transboundary Harm from Hazardous Activities (2001)[240] obliges states to take "all appropriate measures to prevent significant transboundary harm or at any event to minimize the risk thereof." These preventive obligations are substantial and include risk assessment (Article 7), notification and information including transmitting "available technical [. . .] information" (Article 8), consultation on preventive measures (Article 9), exchange of information during hazardous activity (Article 12), information to the public (Article 13), contingency plans for responding to emergencies (Article 16), and notification of an emergency (Article 17). Prevention thus presupposes positive activities. The normative substance of the principle of prevention is substantiated by and translated into due diligence obligations.

As Timo Koivurova writes, "due diligence has developed mostly in the field of transboundary physical harm, but there are also other branches of international law [. . .] that contain similar primary norms, norms requiring States to take diligent steps to achieve a

234 This duty will be explored right below under the principle of prevention and due diligence.

235 Timo Koivurova, "Due Diligence," in Rüdiger Wolfrum (ed.), *Max Planck Encyclopedia of Public International Law (MPEPIL)* (Oxford: OUP, 2008) (2010) [online], para. 3.

236 For environment-related diligence obligations reflected in international law, see Rosemary Rayfuse, "Public International Law and the Regulation of Emerging Technologies," in Roger Brownsword, Eloise Scotford, and Karen Yeung (eds.), *Oxford Handbook of Law, Regulation, and Technology* (Oxford: OUP, 2017), 500–21 (on geoengineering and ocean fertilization).

237 Jutta Brunnée, "Sic utere tuo ut alienum non laedas," in Rüdiger Wolfrum (ed.), *Max Planck Encyclopedia of Public International Law (MPEPIL)* (Oxford: OUP, 2008) (2010), para. 4.

238 On the notion of cyber diligence, see Karine Bannelier and Theodore Christakis, "Cyber-Attacks – Prevention-Reactions: The Role of States and Private Actors," *Les Cahiers de la Revue Défense Nationale*, Paris (2017), https://papers.ssrn.com/sol3/papers.cfm?abstract_id=2941988.

239 ICJ, *United States Diplomatic and Consular Staff in Tehran* (Judgment of May 24, 1980), ICJ Rep. (1980), 3, para. 68.

240 ILC Draft Articles, *Prevention of Transboundary Harm from Hazardous Activities* (2001), Official Records of the General Assembly, Fifty-sixth Session, Supplement No. 10 (A/56/10).

certain result."[241] Due diligence duties have also become relevant in the fight against terrorism and its financing.[242] Interestingly, the concept of due diligence first evolved in relation to the responsibility of a state for private actors requiring them to take "preventive measures [. . . .] in its sphere of exclusive control when international law was breached by private persons."[243]

Today, however, due diligence is not connected to activities of private actors. In international law the notion "due diligence" is usually replaced by "all appropriate" or "all necessary measures." Article 7 (1) of the Convention on the Law of the Non-Navigational Uses of International Watercourses[244] contains, for instance, a duty for watercourse states "in utilizing an international watercourse in their territories [to] take *all appropriate measures* to prevent the causing of significant harm to other watercourse States." In an earlier version the rapporteur, Mr. Robert Rosenstock, had still proposed a wording using *due diligence*: "Watercourse States shall exercise *due diligence* to utilize an international watercourse in such a way as not to cause significant harm to other watercourse States [. . .]."[245] Similarly, Article 194 (2) of UNCLOS[246] obliges states to take "*all measures necessary* to ensure that activities under their jurisdiction or control are so conducted as not to cause damage by pollution to other States and their environment."

Neither the principle of prevention nor due diligence obligations directly protects the internet. However, the principle of prevention and internet-related due diligence obligations can have a substantial indirect impact on the internet's integrity. The indirect impact of the no harm principle protects the internet's integrity by forcing states to suppress illegal cybercrime activities on its territory and any actions that threaten the integrity of the internet. This duty has a clear preventive character. States have "an affirmative duty to prevent cyberattacks from their territory against other states," which encompasses further preventive duties, including "passing stringent criminal laws, conducting vigorous investigations, prosecuting attackers, and, during the investigation and prosecution, cooperating with the victim-states of cyberattacks that originated from within their borders."[247] Similar duties exist with regard to terrorism and its financing.[248] What engages the state duty to prevent attacks, apart from the abstract preventive duties, is knowledge of such activity—but *presumptive* knowledge suffices.[249]

The Tallinn Manual 2.0 contains rule 6 on due diligence, which obliges states to "exercise due diligence in not allowing its territory or cyber infrastructure under its governmental

[241] Timo Koivurova, "Due Diligence," in Rüdiger Wolfrum (ed.), *Max Planck Encyclopedia of Public International Law (MPEPIL)* (Oxford: OUP, 2008) (2010) [online], para. 45.

[242] Cf. Vincent-Joel Proulx, "Babysitting Terrorists: Should States Be Strictly Liable for Failing to Prevent Transborder Attacks?," Berkeley Journal International Law 23 (2005), 615, 629.

[243] Timo Koivurova, "Due Diligence," in Rüdiger Wolfrum (ed.), *Max Planck Encyclopedia of Public International Law (MPEPIL)* (Oxford: OUP, 2008) (2010) [online], para. 2.

[244] Convention on the Law of the Non-Navigational Uses of International Watercourses, New York, May 21, 1997 (emphasis added).

[245] First report on the law of the non-navigational uses of international watercourses, by Mr. Robert Rosenstock, Special Rapporteur, UN Doc. A/CN.4/451, Extract from the Yearbook of the International Law Commission 1993, p. 185 (emphasis added).

[246] United Nations Convention on the Law of the Sea of 1982 (1833 UNTS 397) (emphasis added).

[247] Matthew J. Sklerov, "Solving the Dilemma of State Responses to Cyberattacks: A Justification for the use of Active Defenses Against States Who Neglect Their Duty to Prevent," Military Law Review 201 (2009), 1–85 (62).

[248] Cf. Vincent-Joel Proulx, "Babysitting Terrorists: Should States Be Strictly Liable for Failing to Prevent Transborder Attacks?" Berkeley Journal International Law 23 (2005).

[249] Cf. Heintschel von Heinegg (2013), 16.

control, to be used for cyber operations that affect the rights of, and produce serious adverse consequences for, other States."[250] The reference in the GGE 2013 and 2015 reports (states "should" engage in due diligence)[251] was overly cautious and does not reflect lex lata.[252] The due diligence duty also extends extraterritorially in cases of military occupation or when governmental cyber infrastructure is located abroad.[253] Rule 7 of the Tallinn Manual 2.0 prescribes how states should comply with the due diligence principle: they need to take "all measures feasible in the circumstances" to end the cyber operation (coming from their territory) that affects other states' rights or has serious adverse consequences for them.[254] This does not imply a duty to prevent the operation, which would be an unreasonable interpretation of due diligence and, most likely, violate human rights commitments, as it would necessitate substantial filtering.[255]

Due diligence approaches refine the obligations of states especially in the areas of cybercrime, cybersecurity, and capacity-building. The GGE in its 2015 report also devotes substantial space to due diligence obligations in the wider sense. Though there is no internationally agreed catalog of due diligence obligations indirectly protecting the integrity of the internet, central ones, based on the consensus report and prior commitments mainly in the UN framework, may be said to include:

- that governments and other actors enhance the security of ICT systems and develop cybersecurity strategies that include, as a priority, the protection of critical information infrastructures;[256]
- that states acknowledge the challenge of attribution in case of ICT incidents before envisaging consequences;[257]
- that states consider how best to set up information interchanges regarding the prosecution of terrorist and criminal uses of ICTs;[258]
- that states support other states when their critical infrastructure is subject to malicious ICT acts and mitigate malicious ICT activity emanating from their territory;[259]
- that states, in cooperation with the private sector, ensure that the integrity of the supply chain is intact so that end users can have confidence in the security of ICT products;[260] and
- that states should support responsible reporting of ICT vulnerabilities.[261]

[250] Michael N. Schmitt (ed.), *Tallinn Manual 2.0 on the International Law Applicable to Cyber Operations* (Cambridge: CUP, 2017), 30.

[251] GGE report 2013, para. 23; GGE report 2015, 13 (c) ("States should not knowingly allow their territory to be used for internationally wrongful acts using ICTs"). But see ibid., para. 28(e) ("States *must not* use proxies to commit internationally wrongful acts using ICTs, and should seek to ensure that their territory is not used by non-State actors to commit such acts") (emphasis added).

[252] Michael N. Schmitt (ed.), *Tallinn Manual 2.0 on the International Law Applicable to Cyber Operations* (Cambridge: CUP, 2017), 31.

[253] Ibid., 33.

[254] Ibid., 43.

[255] Ibid., 45.

[256] GGE report (2015), para. 13 (i). See further UN General Assembly Resolution 64/221, Creation of a global culture of cybersecurity and taking stock of national efforts to protect critical information infrastructures, UN Doc. A/RES/64/211 of 17 March 2010 (with references, in PPs 1 and 2, to previous resolutions on cybersecurity).

[257] GGE report (2015), para. 13 (b).

[258] Ibid., para. 13 (d).

[259] Ibid., para. 13 (h).

[260] Ibid., para. 13 (i).

[261] Ibid., para. 13 (j).

Less normatively settled than due diligence obligations are voluntary confidence-building measures that, though not yet part of due diligence obligations of states, normatively set the frame for emerging duties[262] and contribute to international peace and security by increasing cooperation, transparency, predictability, and stability.[263] They include:

- identifying points of contact for serious ICT incidents;
- developing mechanisms for interstate confidence-building;
- encouraging transparency by e.g. sharing national views on national and transnational threats and best practices;
- publishing national views of categories of infrastructure considered critical;
- facilitating cross-border cooperation to address critical infrastructure vulnerabilities, including developing a repository of national laws, and mechanisms for consultations on protection of ICT-enabled critical infrastructure and on addressing ICT-related requests;[264]
- strengthening cooperative mechanisms between agencies responsible for ICT security incidents and malicious ICT use;
- establishing national computer emergency response/cybersecurity incident response teams.[265]

Though going beyond existing due diligence obligations, we see the normative trajectory, especially when comparing these to the ILC Draft Articles on the Prevention of Transboundary Harm from Hazardous Activities (2001), which contain similar provisions—on transmitting "available technical [. . .] information" (Article 9), on consultation on preventive measures (Article 13), on contingency plans for responding to emergencies (Article 16), and on the notification of an emergency (Article 17), to name but a few.

Beyond existing due diligence obligations, we also find capacity-building measures, which further elucidate the normative trajectory of the preventive principle coupled with the duties flowing from the principle of sustainable development. Recognizing that some states may lack the capacity to protect their ICT networks, states agreed in the GGE report to provide assistance to build ICT security capacities as "essential for international security, by improving the capacity of States for cooperation and collective action."[266] Building on General Assembly Resolution 64/211, "Creation of a global culture of cybersecurity and taking stock of national efforts to protect critical information infrastructures,"[267] states are encouraged to, inter alia, assist in providing access to technologies essential for ICT security and facilitate cross-border cooperation to address critical infrastructure vulnerabilities transcending national borders.[268]

[262] Cf. Katharina Ziolkowski, "Confidence Building Measures for Cyberspace," in Katharina Ziolkowski (ed.), *Peacetime Regime for State Activities in Cyberspace. International Law, International Relations and Diplomacy* (Tallinn: NATO CCD COE Publications, 2013), 533–64.

[263] GGE report (2015), para. 16.

[264] Ibid.

[265] Ibid., para. 17.

[266] Ibid., para. 19.

[267] UN General Assembly Resolution 64/211, Creation of a global culture of cybersecurity and taking stock of national efforts to protect critical information infrastructures, UN Doc. A/RES/64/211 of 17 March 2010.

[268] GGE report (2015), para 21, 23. States are also encouraged to develop partnerships with competent international organizations, including the United Nations and its agencies, the private sector, academia, and civil society organizations, in order to more effectively react to ICT incidents.

Due diligence obligations, coupled with further reaching good practices and with a view to increasing the protection of critical national information infrastructures, became a topic of the global community as early as the 2000s with two General Assembly resolutions on international and national efforts to combat criminal misuses of information technologies,[269] and, following a broader approach to infrastructure protection, two Resolutions, in 2002–2003, on creating a global culture of cybersecurity.[270]

The follow-up 2010 General Assembly Resolution 64/211 on the global culture of cybersecurity expressly notes the importance of critical information infrastructures and the integrity of the information they carry, the importance of supporting national efforts by international collaboration, the "increasing contribution made by networked information technologies to many of the essential functions of daily life, commerce and the provision of goods and services, research, innovation and entrepreneurship, and [..] the free flow of information." The Resolution also includes a "voluntary self-assessment tool for national efforts to protect critical information infrastructures." Though *voluntary*, it is part of the increasingly densely woven fabric of international legal norms and normative expectations regarding the internet and can help clarify which obligations states have under the due diligence principle.

3.3.4.11 Principle of Sustainable Development

Though at least one notable author has stated that there can be "little doubt that the concept of 'sustainable development' has entered into the corpus of international customary law,"[271] it is a general principle of international law and arguably more than just a "crucial political precept."[272] Conventions, such as the UN Convention on Biological Diversity,[273] enshrine it and even the ICJ, in the case of the *Gabčikovo-Nagymaros Project* of 1997,[274] referred to the "concept of sustainable development," which expressed the need to "reconcile economic development with protection of the environment." Judge Weeramantry, in his separate opinion, referred to sustainable development as a "principle with normative value" and an "integral part of modern international law […] clearly of the utmost importance, both in this case and more generally." The principle helps, according to Judge Weeramantry, to hold the balance even between environmental and developmental considerations and rests "on a basis of worldwide acceptance."[275] The concrete normative content of the principle, however, is difficult to establish.

The principle of sustainable development does not protect the internet directly. Yet the internet is essential for achieving the goals outlined in the UN's *2030 Agenda for Sustainable Development*.[276] The document identifies the building of resilient infrastructure, the

[269] UN General Assembly Resolutions 55/63 of 4 December 2000 and 56/121 of 19 December 2001 on combating the criminal misuse of information technologies.

[270] UN General Assembly Resolution 57/239 of 20 December 2002 on the creation of a global culture of cybersecurity and Resolution 58/199 of 23 December 2003 on the creation of a global culture of cybersecurity and the protection of critical information infrastructures.

[271] Philippe Sands and Jacqueline Peel, *Principles of International Environmental Law*, 3rd edn. (Cambridge: CUP, 2012), 208.

[272] Cf. Ulrich Beyerlin, "Sustainable Development," in Rüdiger Wolfrum (ed.), *Max Planck Encyclopedia of Public International Law (MPEPIL)* (Oxford: OUP, 2008) (2009) [online], para. 1.

[273] UN Convention on Biological Diversity, 1760 UNTS 79.

[274] ICJ, *Gabčikovo-Nagymaros Project (Hungary v. Slovakia)* (Merits), ICJ Rep. (1997), 7, para. 140.

[275] Ibid., Separate Opinion of Vice-President Weeramantry, ibid., 88, 89, 94.

[276] United Nations General Assembly, Transforming Our World: The 2030 Agenda for Sustainable Development, UN Doc. A/Res/70/1 of 21 October 2015..

promotion of inclusive and sustainable industrialization, and the fostering of innovation as essential for sustainable development[277] and includes a commitment, in Target 9.c, to "[s]ignificantly increase access to information and communications technology and strive to provide universal and affordable access to the internet in least developed countries by 2020." This study has also earlier identified the clear links between the internet and development, as do UN documents on a regular basis. The 2010 General Assembly Resolution on the global culture of cybersecurity, for example, reaffirms "the need to harness the potential of information and communications technologies to promote the achievement of the internationally agreed development goals."[278] In this reading, the principle of sustainable development does not serve to protect the internet. Rather, information and communication technologies, and their development, "serve" to reach development goals, and their development-oriented use is essential for sustainable development.

3.3.5 Normative Acculturation

In the previous section we have seen how the integrity of the internet is protected and threats emanating from the internet and from its misuse are curtailed by international treaties, custom, and general principles of international law. The analysis has shown that there are currently no international universal conventions that protect the internet and its resources. Similarly, in light of the difficulties of establishing custom, it is no surprise that there has not yet emerged a customary rule directly protecting the integrity of the internet. Indirect protection can be found in existing customary law norms that protect territorial sovereignty and national critical infrastructure. These also protect the internet's integrity. National kinetic resources of the internet, such as Internet Exchange Points, form part of such infrastructure. But this protection is too indirect to be of much more than epistemic value.

This is not surprising as the extent and meaning of general principles of international law only crystallize over time and, being "general" principles, their normative content is not tailored to any specific situation. However, a substantial number of general principles protect the internet indirectly or directly. At this point the different categories of norms in the wider context of due diligence should be noted: norms, standards, principles for responsible state behavior, as per the GGE report (2015), such as the important principle of due diligence, and confidence-building and capacity-building measures. This normative "acculturation" is an important phenomenon, which will also be of interest when discussing the normative order of the internet (chapter 6).

The international law of the internet is a foundational order, containing key international standards for state behavior with regard to the internet. Some standards limit what states can do online, such as ius cogens norms forbidding interventions. Some empower states, but the majority of norms will have to be qualified as formally non-binding, yet as important parts of an increasingly intricate and normatively graduated ordering structure or normative order—and they can only be properly understood and evaluated, contested, and

[277] Ibid., Goal 9.

[278] UN General Assembly Resolution 64/221, Creation of a global culture of cybersecurity and taking stock of national efforts to protect critical information infrastructures, UN Doc. A/RES/64/211 of 17 March 2010, preamble.

revised in that context. Together, the principles provide for more nuanced protection of the internet's integrity and from dangers emanating from (mis)uses of the internet than states may think. They also provide a frame in which internet governance approaches take place, the "practice" of regulating the internet.

3.4 Internet Governance

3.4.1 Introduction

Internet governance is a complex process. Scholars speak of an "internet governmentality paradox"[279] and an "internet governance oxymoron."[280] Yet internet governance is neither paradox nor oxymoron, though paradoxa and oxymora are present in the regulation of the internet and its actors. Internet governance, as governance generally, is complex and consists of multiple layers and normative actors. In 2004, Karl Auerbach suggested that there were actually five different aspects of "the internet" that needed to be governed separately—that were thus issues of internet governance. These were

> First, a system of IP address allocation [...]. Second, a system of inter-carrier/inter-ISP traffic exchange [...]. Third, a system to allocate protocol numbers and other similar identifiers [...]. Fourth, the responsible and accountable operation of the upper layers of the DNS hierarchy including oversight, on behalf of the community of internet users, of a suite of Domain Name System (DNS) root servers. Fifth, the management of the DNS root zone file. [...][281]

Most of these tasks are today within the remit of ICANN. If internet governance was really only governance of the internet's critical resources, then it would be much less controversial and difficult to normatively frame than it is. However, this narrow notion of internet governance does not reflect the governance challenges to which the internet exposes societies. It is true that the IP address allocation needs a regulatory frame and that the DNS root zone file needs to be managed in a way that is, if not democratically legitimate in the absence of global legitimacy-conferring decision-making procedures and oversight institutions, then at least accountable to the global multistakeholder community—as is the current setup.[282] Yet internet governance has become a much broader notion.

Visualizations of the ecosystem of internet governance have often relied on layered approaches including a social layer, a content layer, a logical-technical layer, and an infrastructure layer.[283] Others have preferred to speak of five "baskets" of internet governance issues: infrastructure and standardization, legal, economic, development, and

[279] M.I. Franklin, *Digital Dilemmas: Power, Resistance, and the Internet* (Oxford: Oxford University Press, 2013), 141.
[280] Laura DeNardis, *The Global War for Internet Governance* (New Haven: Yale University Press, 2014), 1.
[281] Karl Auerbach, "Deconstructing Internet Governance" (2004), http://www.cavebear.com/archive/rw/deconstructing-internet-governance-ITU-Feb26-27-2004.htm.
[282] See 2.2.4.2.
[283] Cf. Vint Cerf, Patrick Ryan, and Max Senges, "Internet Governance is our Shared Responsibility," I/S: A Journal of Law and Policy for the Information Society, 10 (2014) 1.

sociocultural.[284] Both approaches have in common the wish to stratify vertically or horizontally the issues internet governance debates engage.[285]

In the context of this study, internet governance is important as a second foundational order of the internet, one that translates into practice the norms and normative expectations of the first order, international law. Delineating the two is difficult at the edges. A pro-capacity-building norm is, as a normative predecessor of a due diligence norm, part of international law. At the same time, capacity-building is a key factor within the social and infrastructure layers (or the sociocultural and development basket) of internet governance. It is not so much the clear delineation of legal and governance-related norms and practices that interest here, but rather governance *as* the practice of the participants in the normative order of the internet.

3.4.2 Concept

Internet governance is the steering and shaping, the coordinating and integrating of rules and normative expectations regarding the development of the internet. It has been defined by the UN-backed Working Group on internet governance as

> the development and application by Governments, the private sector and civil society, in their respective roles, of shared principles, norms, rules, decision-making procedures, and programmes that shape the evolution and use of the internet.[286]

It becomes apparent that both on the level of actors—"governments, the private sector and civil society, in their respective roles"—and on the level of normative forms—"principles, norms, rules, decision-making procedures, and programmes"—internet governance is a multilayered process. It has been described as the internet's "multi-layer multi-player mechanism of coordination and collaboration."[287] Briefly put, internet governance refers both to the evolution and implementation of ICTs necessary to keep the internet functional and to the decision-making on, contestation of, and implementation of substantive policies (and norms) around these technologies.[288]

Internet governance impacts the arrangements of technical architecture, which is, however, largely undisputed.[289] It governs internet control points as sites of global conflict, with states progressively trying to re-nationalize oversight over "national internet segments" and thus contributing to fragmentation.[290] A key problem lies in the (lack of) internet governance (decision-making) infrastructure, which is informal and ad hoc and offers no

[284] Jovan Kurbalija, An Introduction to Internet Governance, 7th edn. (Geneva: DiploFoundation, 2016).

[285] Yochai Benkler, "From Consumers to Users: Shifting the Deeper Structures of Regulation Towards Sustainable Commons and User Access," Federal Communications Law Journal 52 (2000), 561, http://www.yale.edu/lawweb/jbalkin/telecom/benklerfromconsumerstousers.pdf.

[286] Report of the Working Group on Internet Governance (2005), http://www.wgig.org/docs/WGIGREPORT.pdf.

[287] Rolf H. Weber, *Realizing a New Global Cyberspace Framework* (Zurich: Schulthess, 2016), 147.

[288] Ibid., 6, 10.

[289] See 2.2.

[290] See 4.3.

democratic proceduralization and legitimacy-conferral systems. Finally, the privatization of the internet in the sense that private spaces fulfill a central role as loci for discourse on issues of public interest has led to conflicts between states, companies, and users on the normative control over the internet and to normative disorder.[291]

3.4.3 Actors

Internet governance relies on the integration of all relevant actors in a process termed multistakeholderism. Examples of this (but often without explicitly referring to the notion) are present in many regimes, ranging from sustainable development[292] and international peacebuilding[293] to fighting transnational terrorism and organized crime,[294] from setting standards for accounting (International Accounting Standards Board) and securities (IOSCO) to corporate social responsibility (UN Global Compact) and fighting health-related crises (Global Fund to Fight AIDS, Tuberculosis and Malaria, Global Alliance for Vaccines and Immunization). Within the internet governance regime, however, the approach is applied most consistently.[295]

Taken together, the focus on the constituent actors in internet governance thus necessitates normative cooperation from five actors with diverging roles: (1) *states*, who enjoy "[p]olicy authority for internet-related public policy issues" as a sovereign right; (2) the *private sector*, enjoying an "important role in the development of the internet, both in the technical and economic fields;" (3) *civil society*, playing "an important role on internet matters, especially at community level;" (4) *intergovernmental organizations*, having a "facilitating role in the coordination of internet-related public policy issues;" and (5) *international organizations*, filling an important function "in the development of internet-related technical standards and relevant policies."[296] As intergovernmental organizations and international organizations are constituted by states (though with an independent international legal personality), this study can use a simplified and three-part model of involved actors that includes states, the private sector, and civil society.

Integrating, as a matter of principle, all actors has, by now, become an accepted feature of internet governance,[297] even though the practice of integrating multiple actors is beset

[291] See 4.2.2.

[292] Karin Bäckstrand, "Multi-Stakeholder Partnerships for Sustainable Development: Rethinking Legitimacy, Accountability and Effectiveness," European Environment 16 (2006) 5, 290–306.

[293] Cf. Wolfgang Benedek, "Multi-Stakeholderism in the Development of International Law," in Ulrich Fastenrath, Rudolf Geiger, Daniel-Erasmus Khan, Andreas Paulus, Sabine von Schorlemer, and Christoph Vedder (eds.), *From Bilateralism to Community Interest. Essays in Honour of Bruno Simma* (Oxford: OUP, 2011), 201–10.

[294] Cf. Wolfgang Benedek, "The Human Security Approach to Terrorism and Organized Crime in Post-Conflict Situations," in Wolfgang Benedek, Christopher Daase, Vojin Dimitrijevic, and Petrus van Duyne (eds.), *Transnational Terrorism, Organized Crime and Peace Building* (London: Palgrave, 2010), 3–16.

[295] See Matthias C. Kettemann, *The Future of Individuals in International Law. Lessons from International Internet Law* (Utrecht: Eleven Publishing, 2013), 111 et seq.

[296] WSIS, Tunis Agenda for The Information Society, WSIS-05/TUNIS/DOC/6(Rev. 1)-E of 18 November 2005, para. 35. See also WSIS, Declaration of Principles, WSIS-03/GENEVA/DOC/4-E, 12 December 2003, para. 49. The academic and technical communities are not usually counted as separate actors, but rather as members of one of the existing groups, often civil society (see Tunis Agenda (2015), para. 36).

[297] Just see Jeanette Hoffmann, "Multi-Stakeholderism in Internet Governance: Putting a Fiction into Practice," Journal of Cyber Policy 1 (2016) 1, 29–49.

by problems of capture of actors[298] and has structural limits.[299] Apart from very few unsuccessful normative outliers favoring "multi*lateral*" approaches,[300] normative commitments on internet governance continue to reiterate their support of a multi*stakeholde*r model, namely one involving all relevant actors in their respective roles. However, just as with ICANN's commitment to accountability toward the "global stakeholder community," commitments to "multistakeholderism" often seem to replace meaningful commitments to the actual integration of all actors in their relevant roles. Calls for multistakeholderism are often combined with the impetus of artificially creating a form of global democracy. In this light, integrating all actors must always fall short of the goal of "multistakeholderists." Problematic as the concept is, international organizations, including within the UN system, have consistently committed to the concept in the context of internet regulation.

The most recent 2018 Human Rights Council resolution on human rights on the internet, just like the previous ones of 2012, 2014 and 2016, stressed the importance of a comprehensive human rights-based approach to expanding access to an open and accessible internet, "nurtured by multi-stakeholder participation." It further considered "the key importance" of engagement by states "with all relevant stakeholders, including civil society, private sector, the technical community and academia, in promoting and protecting human rights and fundamental freedoms online."[301] Indeed, states have the dual obligation to respect international human rights and to protect the human rights of individuals from abuse by third parties.[302]

The General Assembly, in its resolutions on the global culture of cybersecurity, highlighted that each actor has a responsibility "in a manner appropriate to their roles" and that the "multistakeholder model" of internet governance, realized in this case in the annual Internet Governance Forum, is essential "[to discuss] public policy issues related to key elements of internet governance in order to foster sustainability, robustness, security, stability and development of the internet."[303]

Even though ICANN's attempts to engage with issues outside of its technical remit, such as the promotion of democracy, have been criticized,[304] ICANN is the first private entity borne out of a non-formal, non-statal, decentralized, and non-international (or

[298] Magnus Boström and Kristina Tamm Hallström, "Global Multi-Stakeholder Standard Setters: How Fragile Are They?," Journal of Global Ethics 9 (2013) 1, 93–110.

[299] Jochen von Bernstorff, "The Structural Limitations of Network Governance: ICANN as a Case in Point," in Christian Jörges, Inger-Johanne Sand, and Gunther Teubner (eds.), *Transnational Governance and Constitutionalism* (Oxford: Hart, 2004), 257–81.

[300] Such as the 2014 "International code of conduct for information security," suggested by China, Kazakhstan, Kyrgyzstan, the Russian Federation, Tajikistan, and Uzbekistan. See Letter dated 9 January 2015 from the Permanent Representatives of China, Kazakhstan, Kyrgyzstan, the Russian Federation, Tajikistan and Uzbekistan to the United Nations addressed to the Secretary-General, UN Doc. A/69/723 of 13 January 2015, Annex, para. 2 (8): "All States must play the same role in, and carry equal responsibility for, international governance of the Internet, its security, continuity and stability of operation, and its development in a way which promotes the establishment of *multilateral*, transparent and democratic international Internet governance mechanisms which ensure an equitable distribution of resources, facilitate access for all and ensure the stable and secure functioning of the Internet" (emphasis added).

[301] Human Rights Council, Resolution 38/7, The promotion, protection and enjoyment of human rights on the Internet, UN Doc. A/HRC/RES/38/7 of 17 July 2018, preamble. The resolution was notably adopted without a vote and was co-sponsored by more than 60 states. No state formally disassociated itself from the language in the resolution at adoption.

[302] Michael N. Schmitt (ed.), *Tallinn Manual on the International Law Applicable to Cyber Warfare* (Cambridge: CUP, 2013), 196 (Rule 36).

[303] UN General Assembly Resolution 64/211, Creation of a global culture of cybersecurity and taking stock of national efforts to protect critical information infrastructures, UN Doc. A/RES/64/211 of 17 March 2010, preamble.

[304] Cf. John Palfrey, "The End of the Experiment: How ICANN"s Foray into Global Internet Democracy Failed," Harvard Journal of Law & Technology 17 (2004) 2, 409–73.

international law-based) process to manage resources in the global common interest. ICANN has committed itself to including all relevant actors at all possible normative steps of any process, even though the practice suffers from functional deficits and problems of capture of the employed processes by powerful actors, states, companies, or individuals of high standing within the community exercising epistemic authority.

It is a serious error on the part of ICANN to simply commit to "multistakeholderism" and support the participation, through funds and programs, of selected members of the "multistakeholder community," especially from less developed regions. Reiterations of the notion and good-will gestures do not equal fairness in outcome. During the transition to ICANN of the NTIA's role with regard to the coordination of the internet's domain name system, the NTIA demanded, inter alia, that the new model must enjoy broad community support and "[s]upport and enhance the multistakeholder model" without defining either "community support" or the "multistakeholder model."[305] Though ICANN's proposal remained unclear on the model of actor participation employed, the identification of the global "community," or the level of its support, the IANA Stewardship Transition Proposal was accepted. Thus the "global multistakeholder community" is legally established as an actor within the accountability architecture for the management of the internet's public core, including its naming and addressing system.[306]

3.4.4 Evolution

3.4.4.1 Early Internet Governance Approaches

Already in the 1970s and 1980s, the US Federal Communication Commission supported the emergence of a free market in information services, through dismantling the AT&T monopoly and distinguishing traditional telecommunications and value-added telecommunication services, such as the transmission of data through networks (the technology at the basis of what is now the internet). It was this combination of "a competitive telecommunication infrastructure with the separation and deregulation of value-added information services"[307] that was important for the internet to develop. Indeed, these two policies together created an "ideal platform for the unrestricted spread of the global internet."[308] Therefore, the history of the internet is also a history of state (de)regulation and thus of active normative state involvement.

This normative involvement continued. As the usage practices of the internet complexified and the technology was progressively commercialized and politicized, states started to apply existing laws to internet-related cases (e.g. private law to online contracts) and, where necessary, created new laws (e.g. cybercrime statutes since nulla poena sine lege excluded analogies in criminal law). Yet the emergence of an internet governance framework took longer.

[305] NTIA, NTIA Announces Intent to Transition Key Internet Domain Name Functions, March 14, 2014, http://www.ntia.doc.gov/press-release/2014/ntia-announces-intent-transition-key-internet-domain-name-functions.

[306] ICANN, Resolution Thank You to the Global Multistakeholder Community, Res. No. 2016.11.08.19-2016.11.08.20, November 8, 2016, https://www.icann.org/resources/board-material/resolutions-2016-11-08-en#2.c.

[307] Milton Mueller, *Networks and States: The Global Politics of Internet Governance* (Cambridge: MIT Press, 2010), 56 (emphasis in the original).

[308] Ibid.

Unlike many suppose, the internet's critical resources have always been regulated.[309] The internet's technological predecessors, such as ARPAnet, relied on the non-legal but no less effective instruments of informal coordination based on rough consensus among academics[310] as well as other early users. Decisions on top-level domains were made by individuals who used technical expertise to formulate what they saw as common sense approaches. When internet pioneer Jon Postel sought to find combinations of letters to denote states, he adopted the International Organization for Standardization's ISO-3166 standard of country codes.[311] This solution seems sensible, but was taken by a single person whose legitimacy, as a scientist, was merely epistemic but not democratic, though it seems that Jon Postel tried hard to increase legitimacy by having different (mainly technical, business, and academic) stakeholders, who were also primarily epistemically legitimate, confirm their agreement.[312] The decision itself can be described as rationally legitimate, since it makes sense. But if such a decision was to be taken in the same way today, the relevant actors—states, civil society, and the private sector—would strongly disagree for the reason of not having been consulted. This normative expectation is based on two decades of internet governance[313] and intensive global debates on the evolution of a legitimate global policy framework.[314] Early approaches to regulating the internet's key resources therefore worked well because the technical community committed to ensuring the key architectural principles of the internet was small enough to take largely consensual decisions efficiently and shared a common regulatory culture. The US government played a "largely hands-off role"[315] and the internet had not yet become a global and national public policy issue.

It was the critique of the privatization of the management of the DNS and its conferral to Networks Solutions, Inc. that substantially dynamized internet governance and led to calls for the transformation of the processes of managing CIRs by "internationalizing and diversifying the structures of political control and accountability."[316] In 1998, as a result of this "DNS war," the US committed to transitioning IANA functional management to a private

[309] Malte Ziewitz and Ian Brown, "A Prehistory of Internet Governance," in Ian Brown (ed.), *Research Handbook on Governance of the Internet* (Cheltenham: Edward Elgar, 2013), 3–26 (32).

[310] Cf. Milton Mueller, *Ruling the Root: Internet Governance and the Taming of Cyberspace* (Cambridge: MIT Press, 2002).

[311] See ISO, ISO 3166-1 Decoding Table, http://www.iso.org/iso/home/standards/country_codes/iso-3166-1_decoding_table.htm.

[312] It seems that, at the 1987 Advanced Computer Communication Workshop at Lake Arrowhead, Jon Postel received a written confirmation from participants from different actors that they would accept his naming and numbering decisions. These included Cisco, AT&T, Bellcore, Xerox-PARC (business), University of Delaware, Stanford, University of Michigan, USC-ISI (academia), and government representatives. Cf. for a list of those present, the Report on the Advanced Computer Communication Workshop, Lake Arrowhead, CA, March 30–1, 1987 (July 1988), http://www.postel.org/files/arrowhead-after.txt. The document itself is present in Postel's archive. As Bill Manning of USC-ISI, Postel's institute, writes, "[a]t one of the dinner meetings, the compact was scribbled on the paper which covered the tables. Folks signed it and it was torn off. Jon had it framed and it hung in his office until he died." (Email by Bill Manning to the author, February 21, 2014, http://1net-mail.1net.org/pipermail/discuss/2014-February/002063.html).

[313] It is interesting to note that the syllable "cyber-" to denote ICT-related phenomena (as in "cyberspace") shares etymological roots with governance. The sources of both can be traced to the ancient Greek κυβερνητικός (relating to the helmsman; related to steering).

[314] Cf. Milton Mueller, John Mathiason, and Hans Klein, "The Internet and Global Governance: Principles and Norms for a New Regime," Global Governance 13 (2007), 237–54.

[315] William H. Dutton and Malcolm Peltu, "The New Politics of the Internet: Multi-Stakeholder Policy-Making and the Internet Technocracy," in Andrew Chadwick, and Philip N. Howard (eds.), *Routledge Handbook of Internet Politics* (London: Routledge, 2009), 384–99 (391–2).

[316] Ibid., 384.

sector entity.[317] Thus, the Internet Corporation of Assigned Names and Numbers (ICANN) was created to take over key coordination and management tasks for the internet: the coordination of the internet domain names and of the address assignments, including the management of the root servers.[318]

The move to create ICANN (and task it with the IANA functions) effectively stopped efforts by the ITU and WIPO for a domain name administration system. The ICANN Statement of Policy by the US Department of Commerce expressly stated that "neither national governments acting as sovereigns nor intergovernmental organizations acting as representatives of governments should participate in management of internet names and addresses."[319] To alleviate concerns by other states for a continued monopolization of the management of the internet's key resources, US authorities agreed to set up a Governmental Advisory Committee (GAC) within ICANN through which states could provide non-binding advice to the ICANN Board. Over 130 governments and more than thirty international organizations are represented in the GAC.

Soon after ICANN's creation, ITU officials started to promote a broader debate on governance issues in the information society.[320] In 2001, after preparation in ITU conferences, the UN General Assembly, "[recognizing] the pivotal role of the United Nations system in promoting development, in particular with respect to access to and transfer of technology [...] through partnerships with all relevant stakeholders,"[321] embraced the organization of the two-tiered World Summit on the Information Society in 2003 (Geneva) and 2005 (Tunis).

Under the patronage of the UN Secretary-General and with the ITU taking the lead, the WSIS meetings—including an extensive preparatory phase—allowed states to voice their criticism of ICANN, based mainly on the conviction that they should exercise more control over internet-related policy matters, insofar as "national aspects" of the internet, such as ccTLDs, national namespaces, and allocation of IP addresses to companies and registrars within the country were concerned. The US and private sector interests defended the status quo. The preparatory phase of WSIS also saw the emergence of coordinated civil society activism and mobilization.

At WSIS, no concrete agreement on governance reform was reached, but the 11,000 participants, including fifty heads of state or their representatives, 100 ministers from 175 countries (in Geneva) and 19,000 participants, including fifty heads of state or their representatives and 200 ministers from 174 countries (in Tunis),[322] adopted four key documents that contain fundamental commitments regarding the purpose of internet

[317] US DOC/NTIA, Management of Internet Names and Addresses, ICANN Statement of Policy ("White Paper"), June 10, 1998, http://www.icann.org/en/about/agreements/whitepaper: "The U.S. Government is committed to a transition that will allow the private sector to take leadership for DNS management." The Statement of Policy also argued that "[b]ecause of the significant U.S.-based DNS expertise and in order to preserve stability, it makes sense to headquarter the new corporation in the United States." (Ibid.)

[318] Cf. Milton Mueller, John Mathiason, and Hans Klein, "The Internet and Global Governance: Principles and Norms for a New Regime," Global Governance 13 (2007), 237–54, 238–40.

[319] US DOC/NTIA, Management of Internet Names and Addresses, ICANN Statement of Policy ("White Paper"), June 10, 1998, http://www.icann.org/en/about/agreements/whitepaper.

[320] Cf. Milton Mueller, *Networks and States: The Global Politics of Internet Governance* (Cambridge: MIT Press, 2010), 58.

[321] UN General Assembly Resolution 56/183, UN Doc. A/RES/56/183 of 21 December 2001, PP 2.

[322] Milton Mueller, *Networks and States: The Global Politics of Internet Governance* (Cambridge: MIT Press, 2010), 58.

governance: building a people-centered, development-oriented information society, based on international law and the UN Charter.[323]

3.4.4.2 First Normative Commitments

Before WSIS, no real debate had taken place regarding the role of states in internet governance beyond general criticism of the US dominance. Yet as heterogeneous civil society and private sector emerged and partially consolidated (a process facilitated by the internet and ICTs[324]), they challenged not only, and not primarily, the role of the US regarding key internet resources, but the role of states in regulating behavior online within their jurisdiction. Dutton and Peltu argued, "[p]eople do not seek to govern the internet or the information society as such, but aim to achieve more immediate and focused objectives."[325] While this may be empirically true, the broader *governance* questions of the internet are connected to *governments'* regulatory approaches online. Establishing the normative parameters of governance *on* the internet means—to a certain degree—establishing them for the governance *of* the internet.

Coming to WSIS, the US set out to defend its view that it was the only one who should hold a controlling role regarding the internet's critical resources. This oversight position vis-à-vis ICANN was at that time enshrined through three instruments: the IANA contract with ICANN, the Memorandum of Understanding/Joint Project Agreement between the DOC and ICANN, and the contract between the DOC and Verisign, Inc. regarding the managing of the root zone. During the WSIS process the US was adamant that it would "maintain its historic role in authorizing changes or modifications to the authoritative root zone file." This commitment to the "effective and efficient operation of the DNS" was made in the 2005 *U.S. Principles on the internet's Domain Name and Addressing System.*[326] But in these Principles, the US for the first time acknowledged that other governments had "legitimate concerns" in terms of both public policy and sovereignty with regard to its management of their ccTLD.[327]

This position is reflected in the Geneva outcome documents. In the *Geneva Declaration of Principles*, states agree that the "international *management* of the internet" (emphasis added; viz. not its *governance*) should be "multilateral, transparent and democratic, with the full involvement of governments, the private sector, civil society and international organizations."[328] The *full involvement* of all actors makes the distinction between *multilateral* and *multistakeholder* one without immediately obvious difference. But the Declaration still envisaged a special role for states: "Policy authority for internet-related public policy

[323] WSIS, Declaration of Principles, WSIS-03/GENEVA/DOC/4-E, 12 December 2003; WSIS, Geneva Plan of Action, WSIS-03/GENEVA/DOC/5-E, 12 December 2003; WSIS, Tunis Agenda for the Information Society, WSIS-05/TUNIS/DOC/6(Rev. 1)-E, 18 November 2005; WSIS, Tunis Commitment, WSIS-05/TUNIS/DOC/7-E, 18 November 2005.

[324] Derrick L. Cogburn, "Enabling Effective Multistakeholder Participation in Global Internet Governance Through Accessible Cyberinfrastructure," in Andrew Chadwick, and Philip N. Howard (eds.), *Routledge Handbook of Internet Politics* (London: Routledge, 2009), 401–13 (402).

[325] William H. Dutton and Malcolm Peltu, "The New Politics of the Internet: Multi-Stakeholder Policy-Making and the Internet Technocracy," in Andrew Chadwick and Philip N. Howard (eds.), *Routledge Handbook of Internet Politics* (London: Routledge, 2009), 384–99 (394).

[326] NTIA, U.S. Principles on the Internet's Domain Name and Addressing System, June 30, 2005, http://www.ntia.doc.gov/other-publication/2005/us-principles-internets-domain-name-and-addressing-system.

[327] Ibid.

[328] WSIS, Declaration of Principles, WSIS-03/GENEVA/DOC/4-E, 12 December 2003, para. 48.

issues is the sovereign right of States. They have rights and responsibilities for international internet-related public policy issues."[329] The reference to the "multilateral" management of the internet and the reference to the "full involvement" of governments and other actors are critiques of the special role of the US. But the role of non-state actors and their potential influence on public policy questions of internet governance remained unclear.

To remedy this, the *Geneva Plan of Action*, the second document of the WSIS' first phase, called for the creation of a Working Group on Internet Governance (WGIG), which was tasked with delineating public policy issues relevant to internet governance, developing an understanding of the roles and responsibilities of different actors, and defining the concept of internet governance.[330] It was WGIG that drafted the most widely accepted definition of internet governance as

> the development and application by Governments, the private sector and civil society, in their respective roles, of shared principles, norms, rules, decision-making procedures, and programmes that shape the evolution and use of the internet.[331]

WGIG also identified five—controversial—public policy areas relevant to internet governance (critical internet resources, spam/network security, cybercrime, intellectual property rights/trade, and development) and assessed the adequacy of existing governance arrangements. It painted a dismal picture. There was no appropriate "global internet governance mechanism" to resolve the lack of a formal relationship between the root server operators and the uneven distribution of interconnection costs for ISPs in developing countries; there was a "lack of multilateral mechanisms" ensuring network stability and security of internet infrastructure services and applications; there were no "efficient tools and mechanisms" states could use to prevent and prosecute cybercrime; there was no unified, coordinated approach to fighting spam and not even a consensus on how to define spam; and there were "significant barriers" to multistakeholder participation in governance mechanisms because of a lack of "transparency, openness and participatory processes." WGIG also raised human rights concerns: for reasons of security or fighting crime, measures were being taken that led to violations of the right to freedom of expression. In light of the NSA scandal and the discovery of the "Five Eyes" surveillance architecture, the 2005 warning that there was a "lack of national legislation and enforceable global standards for privacy and data-protection rights over the internet"[332] sounds clairvoyant.

Regarding the key public policy question—whether any one state should control the internet—WGIG clearly came out against US oversight: "No single Government should have a pre-eminent role in relation to international internet governance." Governance of the internet should be "multilateral, transparent and democratic, with the full involvement of Governments, the private sector, civil society and international organizations […] within their respective roles."[333]

[329] Ibid., para. 49 a).
[330] Cf. WSIS, Geneva Plan of Action, WSIS-03/GENEVA/DOC/5-E, 12 December 2003, para. 13. b).
[331] Report of the Working Group on Internet Governance (2005), http://www.wgig.org/docs/WGIGREPORT.pdf, para. 10.
[332] Cf. ibid., paras. 15–27.
[333] Ibid., para. 48.

WGIG also developed four models for alternative internet governance institutions that were to be present in the background of many of the following debates. These included the creation of an International Internet Council (IIC) to take over ICANN's IANA competencies, the enhancement of the role of the GAC, the creation of a Global Internet Council (GIC) taking over the supervisory function of the DOC and that of the GAC, and the creation of a Global Internet Policy Council (GIPC), a World Internet Corporation for Assigned Names and Numbers (WICANN), and a Global Internet Governance Forum (GIGF).[334]

Most of the Tunis phase of WSIS was impacted both by the US Principles asserting sovereignty over the root zone file and the WGIG report with its determination that "[n]o single government" should be preeminent in the fulfillment of the internet governance function. Though political tensions were high in Tunis, states managed to adopt two documents. The *Tunis Commitment* and the *Tunis Agenda for the Information Society* affirm much of the principles elaborated in Geneva. The *Tunis Agenda* describes internet governance as an "essential element for a people-centred, inclusive, development-oriented and non-discriminatory Information Society."[335] Though the US managed to include language confirming "existing arrangements for internet governance," which were effective in making the internet the "highly robust, dynamic and geographically diverse medium that it is today,"[336] the *Agenda* rejects a US-led model: "all governments should have an equal role and responsibility for international internet governance and for ensuring the stability, security and continuity of the internet."[337]

The four WSIS outcome documents contain foundational principles for internet governance. Key among them is the affirmation of states, as per the *Tunis Commitment*, of their goal of a "people-centred, inclusive and development-oriented Information Society."[338] This society should be premised on the "purposes and principles of the Charter of the United Nations, international law and multilateralism, and respecting fully and upholding the Universal Declaration of Human Rights"[339]—and especially freedom of expression and the free flow of information, ideas, and knowledge as "essential for the Information Society."[340] States affirmed the importance for individuals "to achieve their full potential and to attain the internationally agreed development goals and objectives, including the Millennium Development Goals."[341] The Commitment also confirms the "universality, indivisibility, interdependence and interrelation of all human rights and fundamental freedoms, including the right to development, as enshrined in the Vienna Declaration" and underlines the interdependence of democracy, sustainable development, respect for human rights and fundamental freedoms, and good governance at all levels. In "international as in national affairs" relating to internet governance, states "resolve[d] to strengthen respect for the rule of law."[342]

334 Cf. ibid., para. 52–71.

335 WSIS, Tunis Agenda for The Information Society, WSIS-05/TUNIS/DOC/6(Rev. 1)-E of 18 November 2005, para. 31.

336 Ibid., para. 51.

337 Ibid., para. 68.

338 World Summit on the Information Society (WSIS), Tunis Commitment, WSIS-05/TUNIS/DOC/7-E, 18 November 2005, para. 2.

339 Ibid.

340 Ibid., para. 4.

341 Ibid., para 2.

342 Ibid., para. 3.

Toward the end of the WSIS process, it became clear to the involved actors that Geneva and Tunis were only the starting points of the debate. Since no agreement could be reached on the creation of a new international organization with responsibilities for internet governance or international oversight over ICANN (none of the models proposed by WGIG garnered substantial support), states agreed to keep the communicative channels open by asking the UN Secretary-General to create an "Internet Governance Forum" (IGF) as an "open and inclusive process." The IGF was mandated, inter alia, to "[d]iscuss public policy issues related to key elements of internet governance in order to foster the sustainability, robustness, security, stability and development of the internet," to "[i]dentify emerging issues, [...] and, where appropriate, make recommendations," and to "promote and assess, on an ongoing basis, the embodiment of WSIS principles in internet governance processes."[343] The key elements here are that the IGF is constituted as an ongoing process, rather than a single event, that it should ensure that internet governance processes reflect the principles agreed in WSIS, and that it has rights to make recommendations, a role it has not fulfilled.

3.4.5 Internet Governance Forum Process

The Internet Governance Forum, convened by the Secretary-General of the United Nations, is a unique annual meeting involving all interested actors. It now includes a broad array of intersessional activities, such as thematic Dynamic Coalitions, and a platform for discussion on public policy issues regarding the internet, its use, and development.[344] These activities cultivate norm adherence through acculturation: norms that are developed by the actors in these open processes have great adherence pull, through self-identification as the norm-giver and subsequent norm propagation.

Since 2006, annual IGFs haven taken place in all regions of the world. As by their mandate, they do not possess any decision-making power. They are forums involving all actors, but little more effective at (or formally legitimated for) the creation of new rules than a standard non-normative conference.[345] They differ, however, from traditional international (diplomatic) conferences in that they allow and encourage multistakeholder access. Without solving the foundational problem of including all relevant actors—namely its inability to reflect the "full complexity of the actors and their interplay of objectives and motives that shape choices about the internet"[346]—IGFs still enable the participation by all on a formally equal footing. Especially to non-state actors, accustomed to being shut out of important deliberations in international conferences, the advances of the IGF setup were perceived as "a major conceptual innovation."[347] This perception as a new means of international

[343] WSIS, Tunis Agenda for The Information Society, WSIS-05/TUNIS/DOC/6(Rev. 1)-E of 18 November 2005, para. 72.

[344] Dmitry Epstein, "The Making of Institutions of Information Governance: The Case of the Internet Governance Forum," Journal of Information Technology 28 (2013), 2, 137–49.

[345] Cf. on the history of the IGFs, Jeremy Malcolm, *Multi-Stakeholder Governance and the Internet Governance Forum* (Perth: Terminus Press, 2008), 353–94.

[346] William H. Dutton and Malcolm Peltu, "The New Politics of the Internet: Multi-Stakeholder Policy-Making and the Internet Technocracy," in Andrew Chadwick and Philip N. Howard (eds.), *Routledge Handbook of Internet Politics* (London: Routledge, 2009), 384–99, 394.

[347] See Bertrand de la Chapelle, "The Internet Governance Forum: How a United Nations Summit Produced a New Governance Paradigm for the Internet Age," in OSCE/The Representative on Freedom of the Media, *Governing the Internet. Freedom and Regulation in the OSCE Region* (Vienna: OSCE RFoM, 2007), 25.

diplomacy overshadowed critique targeted at the limited normative progress and the failure to follow through on all aspects of the mandate, including giving recommendations.

However, including non-state actors in international deliberations is not a new phenomenon. NGOs have had substantial input in international normative processes in the past, notably during the issue shaping of international criminal law leading up to the creation of the International Criminal Court (ICC),[348] the elaboration of the ICC Statute itself, and the running of the ICC.[349] What was novel in the IGF was its premise: discussions on the governance of an issue in the international common interest should be conducted on an equal footing by all actors' groups. In that, it also had a crucial stabilizing function regarding the normative expectation of how norms with relevance for internet governance are developed—to the extent that other actors, such as standardization organizations or engineering task forces, have started to adopt processes to similarly legitimize the norms they develop.[350]

Formally, IGFs show how issues of common interest can be discussed in multistakeholder settings. They enshrine discursive practices and allow for the consolidation and reaffirmation of civil society policy networks. They allow for the airing of new ideas and are, as far as states are involved, an important example of public multilateral diplomacy. The added value of the IGFs are its agenda-setting function, the consolidation of critical issues, its annual return which ensures that internet governance issues are put on the table regularly, the link the meetings provide to WSIS and the WSIS principles, and its function as a place to consolidate international networks of civil society actors. These include the so-called *Dynamic Coalitions*, which coalesce around a certain topic and continue to work outside IGF sessions. One example is the Internet Rights and Principles (IRP) Coalition, which has produced two normative documents on principles and rights for the internet.[351]

The creation of the IGF has thus led to an institutionalization of the dialog on internet governance with subject-area IGFs (such as the Youth IGF), regional IGFs (African IGF, Arab IGF, European IGF (EuroDIG)), and national IGFs (from Australia and Kenya to Russia and the UK). The numbers of participants vary from IGF to IGF, but have been between 1,000 (Athens 2006), 1,500 (Bali 2013), and 2,000 (Geneva 2017). IGFs also allow for remote participation, thus enabling the participation by non-present actors (1,700 in Geneva 2017).[352]

There are, however, obvious disadvantages to using the IGF. States who wish to be seen to adhere to the concept of integrating multiple actors while not actually supporting any solutions coming out of "multistakeholder-led" processes might want to support *governance decoys* "deliberately designed to pre-empt governance."[353] Again, the mere commitment to

[348] Cf. Michael J. Struett, *The Politics of Constructing the International Criminal Court: NGOs, Discourse, and Agency* (Basingstoke: Palgrave Macmillan, 2008), 83–107 (arguing, inter alia, that NGOs have already "shaped the terms of the ICC debate" between 1995 and 1998).

[349] Benjamin N. Schiff, *Building the International Criminal Court* (Cambridge: CUP, 2008) (calling the relationship between the ICC and NGOs "symbiotic" and describing them as "crucial to the Court's creation [and] vital to its operations" (144)).

[350] Cf. Jeremy Malcolm, *Multi-Stakeholder Governance and the Internet Governance Forum* (Perth: Terminus Press, 2008), 514.

[351] Cf. IRP, Charter on Human Rights and Principles for the Internet, http://internetrightsandprinciples.org/site/charter.

[352] IGF, Geneva 2017, Attendance and Programme Statistics, http://www.intgovforum.org/multilingual/content/igf-2017-attendance-programme-statistics.

[353] Radoslav S. Dimitrov, "Hostage to Norms: States, Institutions and Global Forest Politics," Global Environmental Politics 5 (2005) 1–24, (4).

formal multistakeholderism (through similar speaking times for state and civil society representatives, for example) seems to be a stand-in for more nuanced integration on an equal footing of different actors.

Dimitrov, who developed the concept of *governance decoys* with a view to the UN forest regime, saw a "conceptual disconnection between institutions and governance" and the United Nations Forum on Forests (UNFF) as the "institutional excuse of government for not having an international forest policy."[354] Can a similar case be made against the IGF? The IGF is not a decoy for states to avoid being criticized for not having an internet governance policy. Rather, it evidences the fact that states have *no coherent* internet policy and that all actors still cannot agree on key internet governance principles. The very things that make the IGF a unique forum of public diplomacy make norm-development hard. It can (and by its mandate should) develop not binding norms but rather recommendations (which it has not successfully done). It cannot create international law. It cannot exemplify custom (though certain acts of participating states might be so construed).

Dimitrov argues that the UNFF is "singular" in that it was "deliberately designed not to deliver any policy output at all, and that *all* participating states wanted this."[355] This opens up an important distinction. The IGF was not created to *not* deliver any *policy* output, but rather *not* to be a decision-making forum. Identification of "emerging issues," the making of recommendations, and the promotion of the "embodiment of WSIS principles in internet governance processes," as WSIS outcome documents charged the IGF with doing,[356] are clearly policy-oriented tasks. They are simply not normative in the classic understanding of international conferences adopting international norms. As Gunter Pleuger has shown though, developing norms is not a necessity for international deliberations to have normative impact.[357]

If a comparison to an entity clearly relevant for the development of international law was sought, IGFs could be linked to regime-specific preparatory forums (think tanks) of the International Law Commission with the task of identifying, aggregating, and articulating issues of internet governance. Thus, IGFs are rather a *practice* within the emerging normative order of the internet, where expectations of participants are reinforced through discursive practices, networks essential for governance are created and strengthened, and thematic coalitions coalesce. This does not mean IGFs are unimportant—either factually or normatively. The General Assembly, in a 2012 resolution on ICTs for development, underscored the importance it attached to IGFs by stressing that all developing countries, in particular the least developed countries, needed to participate "in all Internet Governance Forum meetings" and needed support to that end.[358]

Ever since the first IGF, there have been suggestions regarding its reform. Key recommendations include a more carefully tailored thematic approach on key policy questions and mutual reinforcement of discussions between the global and regional IGFs; the ability

354 Ibid., 18.

355 Ibid., 20.

356 WSIS, Tunis Agenda for The Information Society, WSIS-05/TUNIS/DOC/6(Rev. 1)-E of 18 November 2005, para. 72.

357 Cf. Gunter Pleuger, "Die normativen Wirkungen multilateralen Verhaltens," in Andreas Fahrmeier (ed.), *Rechtfertigungsnarrative. Zur Begründung normativer Ordnungen durch Erzählen* (Frankfurt/New York: Campus 2013), 89–99.

358 The UN General Assembly, Resolution 67/195 of 21 December 2012, Information and communications technologies for development, UN Doc. A/RES/67/195 of 5 February 2013, para. 19.

to deliberate online and the increased capacity to sustain work programs between meetings; a more substantial management structure; more funding for a bureau of the IGF; and generally a more stable funding mechanism.[359] Yet in the absence of a change in mandate, the IGFs "practice" remains outside of traditional international law-making processes. We also see, however, that in aggregate the selection of topics and the articulation of concerns can have a normative dimension as they stabilize normative expectation and may give rise to normative processes outside the conference setting.

Internet governance is still a young international field. In order to increase the normativity of governance arrangements and mechanisms and to translate normative practices into international law, internet governance may go the way of climate governance. Early climate diplomacy depended less on states and more on civil society and academia,[360] and states only later emerged, by necessity, as key players within the debate on the UN Framework Convention on Climate Change and the later Paris Agreement.

3.4.6 Politicization

In the year after the end of the WSIS process and the first IGF, 2006, the US Department of Commerce (DOC) reacted to international critique of the unilateral oversight of the DNS by reassessing its links to ICANN. ICANN and the DOC adopted a new Memorandum of Understanding that gave more independence to ICANN, but still allowed the US government to retain ultimate control.[361] The DOC's underlying policy objective of "transitioning the technical coordination of the DNS to the private sector in a manner that promotes stability and security, competition, bottom-up coordination, and representation"[362] was tested a year later in the .xxx case.

The question behind the .xxx case was whether ICANN should admit a new TLD (.xxx), sponsored by a private company, ICM Registry, in face of DOC and GAC expressions of discomfort, motivated by concerns for morality (the TLD was supposed to cater to the adult entertainment industry). After first allowing the new TLD, the ICANN Board reconsidered.[363] De facto vetoing a new TLD, whose admittance was within ICANN's "core technical mission," put into question whether the US "oversight" was really only targeted at ensuring the stability of the underlying DNS of the internet.[364] The arbitration confirming the violation lasted until 2010. In the declaration, the panel held that the policy change was "not consistent with the application of neutral, objective and fair documented policy"[365]

359 IRP Coaliton "bestbits" (Jeremy Malcolm), Submission to IGF on themes and formats for the 2014 meeting, http://bestbits.net/igf-2014-submission. Cf. also Reflections from APC on the IGF 2013 and recommendations for the IGF 2014, February 19, 2014, http://www.apc.org/en/node/18977.

360 Cf. Lorraine Elliott, "Climate Diplomacy," in Andrew F. Cooper, Jorge Heine, and Ramesh Tahkur (eds.), *The Oxford Handbook on Modern Diplomacy* (Oxford: OUP, 2013), 840–55 (842).

361 Memorandum of Understanding/Joint Project Agreement between the US Department of Commerce and ICANN, September 29, 2006, http://www.icann.org/en/about/agreements/mou-jpa/jpa-29sep06-en.pdf.

362 Ibid., 1.

363 Cf. Milton Mueller, *Networks and States: The Global Politics of Internet Governance* (Cambridge: MIT Press, 2010), 71–3.

364 Cf. NTIA, U.S. Principles on the Internet's Domain Name and Addressing System, June 30, 2005, http://www.ntia.doc.gov/other-publication/2005/us-principles-internets-domain-name-and-addressing-system.

365 International Centre for Dispute Resolution, *ICM Registry, LLC v. ICANN*, ICDR Case No. 50 117 T 00224 08, Independent Review Panel Declaration (2010), https://www.icann.org/en/news/irp/icm-v-icann, 70.

and could be traced back to ICANN's receipt of two letters by the Assistant Secretary for Communications and Information of the US Department of Commerce and the Chairman of the GAC.[366]

The panel[367] held 2–1 that ICANN was "charged with acting consistently with relevant principles of international law, including the general principles of law recognized as a source of international law,"[368] and specifically the principle of good faith. This finding relied on Article 4 of ICANN's Articles of Incorporation, which obliges ICANN to carry out its activities "in conformity with the relevant principles of international law and applicable international conventions and local law."[369] ICM Registries relied on the reference to international legal principles to introduce the notion of "good faith" which ICANN was supposed to have violated (as the panel confirmed).[370] ICANN's denial to admit .xxx to the domain space showed that the argument of ICANN being merely a technical actor, implementing technical standards without a view to moral questions, was insincere and that governments (especially the US) were willing and able (though not through binding action) to enforce their offline values (objection to pornography) to online surroundings.

The case also shows how governance and international legal questions are intertwined when it comes to regulating the internet and its key resources and that ICANN, as well as its critics, use international legal arguments to frame the responsibilities of the organization. The previously confirmed hypothesis that the normative order of the internet encompasses international legal rules, national legal rules, and transnational normative arrangements is again given substance by cases such as this that show how norms of different "affiliation," pedigree, and bindingness are applied in concert and without clearly defined hierarchical relationships.

In reaction to criticism of its handling of the .xxx case, the US continued to implement its policy of privatizing ICANN's IANA functions. In 2009, ICANN and the Department of Commerce concluded the *Affirmation of Commitments* (AOC) that supplanted the Joint Project Agreement, one of the three ties between the DOC and ICANN.[371] With the IANA contract still in place at that time,[372] the Affirmation of Commitments nominally increased ICANN's independence by including a (rather weak) accountability framework.[373] In the

[366] Ibid., 14.

[367] Consisting of former president of the International Court of Justice, Stephen M. Schwebel, as Chair, the former president of the London Court of International Arbitration and the World Bank Administrative Tribunal, Jan Paulsson, and Dickran M. Tevrizian, a US federal judge for the Central District of California.

[368] International Centre for Dispute Resolution, *ICM Registry, LLC v. ICANN*, ICDR Case No. 50 117 T 00224 08, Independent Review Panel Declaration (2010), https://www.icann.org/en/news/irp/icm-v-icann, 64.

[369] Articles of Incorporation of Internet Corporation for Assigned Names and Numbers, November 21, 1998, http://www.icann.org/en/about/governance/articles, Art. 4.

[370] International Centre for Dispute Resolution, *ICM Registry, LLC v. ICANN*, ICDR Case No. 50 117 T 00224 08, Independent Review Panel Declaration (2010), https://www.icann.org/en/news/irp/icm-v-icann, 54: ICANN disagreed, arguing that it was not bound, as a private party, to international law in a dispute between private entities located in one country. The issue was not decided by the panel, which argued that good faith as a principle was present in all—international and national—legal orders.

[371] Affirmation of Commitments by the United States Department of Commerce and the Internet Corporation for Assigned Names and Numbers, September 30, 2009, https://www.icann.org/resources/pages/affirmation-of-commitments-2009-09-30-en.

[372] Cf. A. Michael Froomkin, "Almost Free: An Analysis of ICANN"s "Affirmation of Commitments"", Journal of Telecommunications and High Technology Law 9 (2011), 187–233.

[373] Cf. Milton Mueller, *Networks and States: The Global Politics of Internet Governance* (Cambridge: MIT Press, 2010), 249–50. But see, for a more positive take, Mawaki Chango, "Accountability in Private Global Governance: ICANN and Civil Society," in Jan Aart Scholte (ed.), *Building Global Democracy?: Civil Society and Accountable Global Governance* (Cambridge: CUP, 2011), 267–88 (270–1).

AOC, the NTIA also committed to "a multi-stakeholder, private-sector-led, bottom-up policy development model for DNS technical coordination."[374]

From 2010 onwards, responsibility for internet governance seemed to move from technical entities to foreign policy makers. China and Russian authorities argued, in 2010 and 2011, for a stronger "internationalization" (read: nationalization) of the internet,[375] and then-US Secretary of State Hillary Clinton started a foreign policy initiative tailored around the concept of "internet freedom," an open and secure internet based on human rights and dignity.[376]

Further, in 2010, ICANN introduced the first internationalized domain names in Arabic and Chinese, thus opening the ccTLDs for top-level domains in non-Latin-based local scripts.[377] In light of this first successful attempt at internationalizing the names and numbering system, and the stronger infusion of internet governance in foreign policy, the Council of Europe (CoE), the Association of Progressive Communications (APC), and the United Nations Economic Commission for Europe (UNECE) published, in 2010, a Code of Good Practice on Information, Participation and Transparency in Internet Governance[378] that called for sharing information and increasing transparency in internet governance processes. It was less a compilation of internet governance principles and more a meta-compilation of how to reach these principles, but also a prefiguration of the year 2011, which would be determinative for the future of internet governance.

3.4.7 Taxonomy of Internet Governance

The commitments to integrating all actors in normative processes notwithstanding, there is considerable uncertainty about what exactly this entails in practice. There is no single accepted model of including all actors in governance-related processes on the internet; it is therefore a misnomer to speak of "*the* multistakeholder model for internet governance."[379] Commitments to such a model are more evidence of a common intellectual heritage of the speakers or of a shared impetus to create an artificial semblance

[374] AOC (2009), para. 4. DOC also confirmed the relevance of (global) public interest: "[a] private coordinating process, the outcomes of which reflect the *public interest*, is best able to flexibly meet the changing needs of the Internet and of Internet users" (emphasis added).

[375] Cf. People's Republic of China, State Council, The Internet in China, June 8, 2010, http://www.china.org.cn/government/whitepaper/node_7093508.htm, sect. I: "China holds that the role of the UN should be given full scope in international Internet administration. China supports the establishment of an authoritative and just international Internet administration organization under the UN system through democratic procedures on a worldwide scale."

[376] Cf. US Department of State, Office of the Spokesman, Internet Freedom Fact Sheet, February 15, 2011, http://www.state.gov/r/pa/prs/ps/2011/02/156623.htm.

[377] ICANN, Internationalized Domain Names, http://www.icann.org/en/resources/idn. See, further, the implementation plan for IDNs: ICANN, Final Implementation Plan for IDN ccTLD Fast Track Process, November 5, 2013, http://www.icann.org/en/resources/idn/fast-track/idn-cctld-implementation-plan-05nov13-en.pdf.

[378] Council of Europe/APC/UNECE, Code of Good Practice on Information, Participation & Transparency in Internet Governance, https://www.apc.org/en/system/files/COGP_IG_Version_1.1_June2010_EN.pdf.

[379] Mark Raymond and Laura DeNardis, "Multi-stakeholderism: Anatomy of an Inchoate Global Institution," Centre for International Governance Innovation Paper Series No. 41, September 2016, https://www.cigionline.org/sites/default/files/gcig_no.41web.pdf (also as Mark Raymond and Laura DeNardis, "Multistakeholderism: Anatomy of an Inchoate Global Institution," International Theory 7 (2015) 3, 572–616 (9)).

of global democracy in small formats. Various tasks within the internet's regulatory field are fulfilled by different actors within normative structures by adopting normative instruments of varied bindingness. Similar to the distributed architecture of the internet (with root servers around the world to ensure stability and reduce lag), the governance tasks are also distributed between normative layers (local-national-regional-supranational-international) and actors, actor groups, and institutions. The functional areas of internet governance can be used to disaggregate the responsibilities to be distributed among internet governance actors: control of critical internet resources, setting internet standards, access and interconnection coordination, cybersecurity governance, information intermediation, and enforcement of intellectual property rights, to give just a few examples.[380]

One level of granularity higher, the variety of tasks within the functional areas illustrates both the difference between governance-oriented and international law-based approaches. International law has little to say (beyond providing a general distribution of responsibilities) about, for example, app mediation (including the rules on monetization within app stores), but a lot about assessing governmental requests for content removal (consider issues of sovereignty, extraterritoriality, fundamental rights). Internet governance, as a concept, appears more holistic because it encompasses the whole gamut of internet regulation(s). This makes governance-oriented analysis of normative dynamics useful but may lead to normative *overcrowding* in the sense that a non-manageable plethora of standards and principles is developed with governance processes that are not tied to existing or crystallizing international legal duties. In this sense, international law is a normative anchor for developments in internet governance processes. All these normatively relevant processes and outcomes form part of the hybrid normative order of the internet.

The normative instruments used in internet governance are defined as "shared principles, norms, rules, decision-making procedures, and programs that shape the evolution and use of the internet."[381] *Shared principles* have evolved into an important normative instrument in internet governance. They are well suited to unite the diverging normative trajectories of enabling economic progress, providing for security and ensuring human rights. From 2011 onwards, different states and groups of states, international and intergovernmental organizations, and non-state actors published declarations of principles (or "compact" or "strategy").[382] Though non-binding, these principles have orientative value, can be considered "rational reconstructions" of legal discourse,[383] and exert normative influence on actors. Due to their variety, they are also an element of normative disorder between layers.[384]

[380] Cf. ibid., 10–11.

[381] Report of the Working Group on Internet Governance (2005), http://www.wgig.org/docs/WGIGREPORT.pdf.

[382] For an overview, see Rolf H. Weber, *Principles for Governing the Internet a Comparative Analysis* (Paris: UNESCO, 2015), http://unesdoc.unesco.org/images/0023/002344/234435e.pdf and the declarations of principles quoted in notes 765 to 775 therein.

[383] Matthias Goldmann, "Principles in International Law as Rational Reconstructions. A Taxonomy," November 13, 2013, https://ssrn.com/abstract=2442027.

[384] See 4.2.2.

Norms and rules are largely synonymous, but this study will focus on "norms."[385] Some instruments—procedures and programs—do not prescribe (actual) behavior of social actors within the normative order. Others, such as principles, are the "production of conceptual abstractions."[386] However, all these instruments are nevertheless normative in that they guide the normative orientation of the internet's order (principles), influence the evolution of norms (procedures), or shape user behavior (programs). Programs are written in code and contain algorithms.[387] Algorithms, especially, can be unpacked in order to discover their normative content. A key hypothesis of this study is that the normative order as presented here is based on an inclusive concept of normativity that extends to all instruments of governance alike and does not exclude "technical" artifacts, such as lines of code or algorithms.[388] They all form part of the internet's normative order.

3.4.8 Principle Hype

The year 2011 saw the emergence of three related phenomena that foreshadowed much of the internet governance debate today: *first,* the debate on state duties toward the internet intensified. On January 28, 2011, on instruction by the Mubarrak regime, Egyptian ISPs withdrew the Border Gateway Protocols (BGPs), thus effectively shutting the country off the internet.[389] A similar internet shutdown occurred before the intervention in March 2011 in Libya.[390]

Second, the discussion on the role of human rights online intensified. The UN Special Rapporteur on Freedom of Expression, Frank La Rue, published his influential report on the overwhelming importance of freedom of expression online, as an essential "enabler" of the exercise of other rights through the internet: "by acting as a catalyst for individuals to exercise their right to freedom of opinion and expression, the internet also facilitates the realization of a range of other human rights."[391]

Third and most importantly, 2011 proved to be the year of the "internet principle hype."[392] It was an interesting example of international institutional psychology, normative peer pressure, and norm diffusion that different actors felt, at the same time, that internet governance merited more than a general commitment to principles, as had been achieved in WSIS, but a more detailed principled approach. Developing principles for internet governance is a normative endeavor that tells a lot about the norm producers and their intentions, especially in a critical and comparative perspective. By publishing principles, different actors publicize

[385] See 1.2.3.

[386] Matthias Goldmann, "Principles in International Law as Rational Reconstructions. A Taxonomy," November 13, 2013, https://ssrn.com/abstract=2442027.

[387] Jeremy Malcolm, *Multi-Stakeholder Governance and the Internet Governance Forum* (Perth: Terminus Press, 2008), 138.

[388] See 2.4.3.

[389] Cf. James Cowie, "Egypt Leaves the Internet," January 28, 2011, http://www.renesys.com/blog/2011/01/egypt-leaves-the-internet.shtml.

[390] Cf. Matthias C. Kettemann, "Das Internet als internationales Schutzgut: Entwicklungsperspektiven des Internetvölkerrechts anlässlich des Arabischen Frühlings," ZaöRV 72 (2012), 469–82 (470).

[391] Report of the Special Rapporteur on the promotion and protection of the right to freedom of opinion and expression, Frank La Rue, UN Doc. A/HRC/17/27 of 26 April 2011.

[392] Wolfgang Kleinwächter, "Internet Principle Hype: How Softlaw is Used to Regulate the Internet", dotnxt, http://news.dot-nxt.com/2011/07/27/internet-principle-hype-anon.

their normative expectations and assert not only which rules could apply but also which should apply. In that, the principles—their divergences and convergences—inform us about actors' views on certain rules of the internet, some of which can develop or have developed into binding international law.

To name but a few:[393] US President Barack Obama proposed an *International Strategy for Cyberspace*;[394] Brazil, India, and South Africa—on behalf of the Group of 77—proposed to launch a new intergovernmental working group on internet governance;[395] and China, Russia and two Asian nations proposed an *International Code of Conduct for Information Security*[396] (which China still considered important enough to submit to the 2014 NetMundial meeting in Brazil[397]). International organizations developed governance concepts as well. UNESCO published a *Code of Ethics for the Information Society*,[398] the Organization for Security and Cooperation in Europe (OSCE) adopted *a Declaration on Pluralism and Internet Governance*,[399] and OECD developed a *Communiqué on Principles for Internet Policy Making*.[400] The Council of Europe's Committee of Ministers adopted a well-received *Declaration on Internet Governance Principles*.[401] The Vice-President of the European Commission, Neelie Kroes, presented an *Internet Compact*[402] and non-state actors, such as the Internet Rights and Principles Coalition, published collections of human rights online—in the Coalition's case, the *Charter for Internet Rights and Principles*.[403] The political importance of developing principles for internet governance also trickled up (in an interesting reversal of more traditional trickle-down diplomacy) to traditional meetings between powerful states. The G8 (Group of 8) Summit of Deauville adopted a *Renewed Commitment for Freedom and Democracy*[404] with implications for the internet and the

[393] For a more complete overview, see Rolf H. Weber, *Realizing a New Global Cyberspace Framework* (Zurich: Schulthess, 2016), 147.

[394] US President Barack Obama proposed 10 principles in his strategy paper in May 2011, see President of the United States of America, International Strategy for Cyberspace. Prosperity, Security and Openness in a Networked World, May 2011, http://www.whitehouse.gov/sites/default/files/rss_viewer/international_strateby_for_cyberspace.pdf, 10.

[395] India, Brazil, and South Africa—on behalf of the Group of 77—proposed to launch a new "intergovernmental working group [to] be established under the UN Commission on Science and Technology for Development," IBSA Joint Statement, Open consultations on Enhanced Cooperation, New York, December 14, 2010, http://www.un.int/india/2010/IBSA%20STATEMENT.pdf.

[396] Letter dated 12 September 2011 from the Permanent Representatives of China, the Russian Federation, Tajikistan and Uzbekistan to the United Nations addressed to the Secretary-General, UN Doc. A/66/359 of 14 September 2011, http://blog.internetgovernance.org/pdf/UN-infosec-code.pdf.

[397] Ministry of Foreign Affairs of the People's Republic of China, International Code of Conduct for Information Security, submission to NetMundial, http://content.netmundial.br/contribution/international-code-of-conduct-for-information-security/67.

[398] UNESCO, Code of Ethics for the Information Society, proposed by the Intergovernmental Council of the Information for All Programme (IFAP), 36 C/49, October 10, 2011, http://goo.gl/nZ0lk.

[399] OSCE, 8th South Caucasus Media Conference, Declaration: Pluralism and Internet governance, Tbilisi, Georgia, October 20–21, 2011, http://www.osce.org/fom/84371.

[400] OECD Communiqué on Principles for Internet Policy Making, OECD High Level Meeting: The Internet Economy: Generating Innovation and Growth, June 28–29, 2011, Paris, http://www.oecd.org/dataoecd/40/21/48289796.pdf.

[401] Council of Europe, Declaration by the Committee of Ministers on Internet governance principles, adopted on September 21, 2011, http://goo.gl/RxDWs.

[402] Vice-President of the European Commission Neelie Kroes, Internet Compact, http://blogs.ec.europa.eu/neelie-kroes/i-propose-a-compact-for-the-internet/#more-671.

[403] Cf. Internet Rights and Principles Coalition, 10 Internet Rights and Principles, http://internetrightsandprinciples.org.

[404] G8 Declaration, Renewed Commitment for Freedom and Democracy, G8 Summit of Deauville, May 26–27, 2011, http://www.g20-g8.com/g8-g20/g8/english/live/news/renewed-commitment-for-freedom-and-democracy.1314.html.

World Economic Forum (WEF) adopted a *Code of Conduct for Government Leaders*[405] that bears upon internet policymaking. Most collections of principles gravitate to certain topics. These include access and openness, freedom of expression, privacy, ethics more generally, participation by all relevant actors, gender equality, sustainable development and cultural diversity, science, and education—with diverging emphasis according to normative preferences.[406]

Attempts to reorient normative processes toward international organizations by the ITU, which was in the process of passing new International Telecommunication Regulations[407] to be adopted in 2012 in Dubai at the World Conference on International Telecommunications (WCIT-12), met with strong resistance.[408] In the negotiation process, a number of sovereignty-oriented states, such as Russia and China, but also India, Brazil, and South Africa, tried to reassert national control over some aspects of internet governance, namely the "national internet segment," by extending the reach of ITU norms to other aspects of ICT management. They suggested including into the purview of the ITRs parts of what has been described in this study as the internet's public core. This attempted nationalization by way of a multilateral "internationalization" in ITU was met with the strong opposition of almost half of ITU's member states, which led to a stalemate at the Summit.[409]

The progressive mainstreaming of the concept of globalization of internet governance is also illustrated by two resolutions, seven years apart, by the US Congress and the House of Representatives, respectively, regarding the US approach to internet policy. Shortly before the Tunis phase of WSIS, in the 2005 resolution *Expressing the sense of the Congress regarding oversight of the internet Corporation for Assigned Names and Numbers*,[410] the US legislature cautioned that "internet governance discussions in the World Summit should focus on the real threats to the internet's growth and stability, and not recommend changes to the current regime of domain name and addressing system management and coordination on political grounds unrelated to any technical need." According to paragraph 2, changes to the root zone server and the oversight system were unnecessary: "the authoritative root zone server should remain physically located in the United States and the Secretary of Commerce should maintain oversight of ICANN." The resolution was adopted unanimously.

3.4.9 Critique

Presenting existing issues raised in internet governance reform processes is important for this study because the reform process identifies normative dissonances between the values the actors have committed themselves to, including international law, human rights, and

[405] World Economic Forum, Code of Conduct for Government Leaders (2011), http://www3.weforum.org/docs/WEF_GAC_InformedSocieties_CodeConductGovernmentLeaders_Summary_2012.pdf.

[406] Cf. Rolf H. Weber, *Realizing a New Global Cyberspace Framework* (Zurich: Schulthess, 2016), 147, 23–74.

[407] ITU, International Telecommunication Regulations (ITRs), http://www.itu.int/ITU-T/itr.

[408] David P. Fidler, "Internet Governance and International Law: The Controversy Concerning Revision of the International Telecommunication Regulations," ASIL Insights 17 (2013) 6, https://www.asil.org/insights/volume/17/issue/6/internet-governance-and-international-law-controversy-concerning-revision.

[409] Cf. Patrick S. Ryan, "The ITU and the Internet's Titanic Moment," Stanford Technology Law Review 8 (2012).

[410] 109th Congress, 1st Session, H. CON. RES. 268, 16 November 2005, Concurrent Resolution expressing the sense of the Congress regarding oversight of the Internet Corporation for Assigned Names and Numbers, https://www.govtrack.us/congress/bills/109/hconres268/text.

development, as per the WSIS outcome documents, and the status quo. But the standards and architecture of internet governance were seen very critically by actors. Summarizing their criticism of internet governance, the following main points of critique emerge:

- *first*, the continued oversight by the US over critical internet resources (before the IANA transition in 2016);
- *second*, the failure to harness the internet's potential for development based on a conviction that the current setup entrenches the interests of the North and marginalizes the Global South and that the promise of WSIS remains unfulfilled;
- *third*, the lack of legitimate processes for developing internet governance. The IGF is seen as having underperformed, and commitments to the normatively flexible notion of "multistakeholderism" are used as a fig leaf for stasis and for the lack of a coherent vision of normative progress on the internet and in the many institutions and commissions working in parallel on its development;
- *fourth*, the power of the private sector (internet content provider and internet service providers) without clear lines of legitimacy and accountability; and
- *fifth*, the renationalization/resovereignization of the internet characterized by a nationalization of oversight over global public policy issues of the internet, state-led initiatives on sectorial issues, such as cybersecurity, cybercrime, and cyber-warfare, that are insufficiently reflective of other actors, and the recurring argument of sovereignty over the "national internet segment."[411]

There have been a number of suggestions on the best means to ensure inclusive, transparent, accountable, and effective internet governance processes that operationalize existing commitments, are stable enough to ensure the internet's functionality, and are flexible enough to deal with upcoming challenges. These include:

- the creation of a UN Committee of fifty members with a mandate over public policy issues of the internet and oversight of the technical bodies;[412]
- a Multistakeholder Internet Policy Council under the auspices of or attached to the IGF, made up of equal numbers of representatives from all actor groups to discuss issues forwarded to it by IGF plenaries and to agree by rough consensus mechanisms on non-binding recommendations;[413]

[411] Cf. ECOSOC, Report of the Working Group on Improvements to the Internet Governance Forum, A67/65-E/2012/48 of 16 March 2012, http://unctad.org/meetings/en/SessionalDocuments/a67d65_en.pdf; UNCTAD, CSTD Working Group on improvements to the IGF, Summary of the 3rd meeting, October 31, 2011, http://unctad.org/Sections/un_cstd/docs/cstd2011d22_Major_EN.pdf; UNCTAD, Questionnaire of the Working Group on Enhanced Cooperation, http://unctad.org/en/Pages/CSTD/WGEC-Responses.aspx. For non-governmental stakeholders, see bestbits (Jeremy Malcolm), Internet Governance: proposals for reform, with contributions from Access, Article 19, CDT, CTS/FGV, GPD, Internet Democracy Project (2014); IT for Change India, A Development Agenda in Internet Governance Outlining Global Public Policy Issues and Exploring New Institutional Options, April 2012, http://www.itforchange.net/sites/default/files/ITfC/%20%20Dev%20agenda%20in%20IG%20200412.pdf; Avri Doria, "The IETF as a model for the IGF," http://www.intgovforum.org/contributions/IETF-as-model.pdf.

[412] Centre for Internet and Society, India's Statement Proposing UN Committee for Internet-Related Policy, October 26, 2011, http://cis-india.org/internet-governance/blog/india-statement-un-cirp.

[413] Jeremy Malcolm, My proposal to the CSTD Working Group on Enhanced Cooperation (2011), http://igfwatch.org/discussion-board/my-proposal-to-the-cstd-working-group-on-enhanced-cooperation#-8xHg3pRMAMtJ2UVoZcsOg.

- a coordinating body under the CSTD to identify issues and appropriate institutions to deal with them in a distributed multistakeholder process;[414]
- self-forming multistakeholder issue processes to suggest non-binding solutions to specific questions of public policy on the internet.

None of these approaches has come close to being used. Even applying permissive criteria of inclusivity, transparency, accountability, and effectiveness, all models have serious shortcomings. A single body with overall control of the internet would be very powerful and its decisions highly controversial. Only firm international legal foundations would allow for such a body to function effectively, but this would not guarantee its legitimacy. The other suggestions, while more inclusive, suffer from serious doubts as to their effectiveness. Non-binding resolutions and soft law are important normative instruments,[415] but certain public policy questions can—under current international law—be very difficult to resolve outside of traditional regimes dominated by states as the (continued) repositories of legitimate international policy approaches through democratic processes.

3.4.10 Reform

Other reform proposals focus directly on key institutions of the current internet infrastructure. The IGF could take up the role of observatory with a reporting duty to the international community; a space for adopting messages to all actors; or a watchdog for actors with critical issues through an international internet policy review similar to the Human Rights Council's Universal Periodic Review process, in which all states undergo a peer-based human rights assessment at regular intervals.[416] But implementing any of these suggestions would demand a substantial revision of the role of the IGF. Instituting a UPR-like process would necessitate an international agreement. The majority of states are, at the present stage of international legal development, unable or unwilling to submit to a formalized policy review at the hand of (also) non-state actors.

What unites the models is the importance of achieving a greater sense of clarity as to who discusses internet-related public policy questions. The centralization of issue-unspecific decision-making power is highly problematic from both a policy and a pragmatic perspective. However, leaving decision-making structures on public policy issues uninstitutionalized risks nationalization through sovereignty-oriented states. The key challenge thus seems to lie in establishing whether there can be one model of governance of the internet with an entity including all relevant actors with clearer responsibilities for public policy questions and ad hoc issue-specific working groups.

[414] Anja Kovacs, "A Third Way? Proposal for a Decentralised, Multistakeholder Global Internet Governance Involving All Stakeholders" (2011) http://internetdemocracy.in.

[415] Rolf H. Weber, "Overcoming the Hard Law/Soft Law Dichotomy in Times of (Financial) Crises," Journal of Governance and Regulation 1 (2012), 8–14.

[416] Cf. Wolfgang Kleinwächter, "Towards an Improvement of the IGF. Eight Proposals for an Enhanced Role of the IGF," March 14, 2011, http://www.unctad.info/upload/CSTD-IGF/Contributions/M1/Wolfgang_Kleinwachter.pdf.

In order to remedy critique of its lack of accountability to any institution but the US government, ICANN, in early 2014, published reports by two panels on its future outlining vectors for reform. The first panel, dedicated to parsing and improving ICANN's role within the internet ecosystem, concluded that reliance on all actors should be "elaborated and reinforced."[417] All actors, including ICANN, had "a *shared or entangled responsibility for the stewardship* of the common internet infrastructure."[418] Therefore, ICANN was to *globalize, but not internationalize*: "Countries are stakeholders, to be sure, but the structure of ICANN and its associated or related institutions are now and should become increasingly global or regional in scope."[419] The root zone management should be consolidated and simplified and agreement should be reached on an accountability mechanism, which is "broadly accepted as being in the global public interest."[420] Generally, the report underlines the importance of increasing accountability and enmeshing ICANN in a "web of affirmations of commitments," tailored to its responsibilities.[421]

The second strategy panel, on "multistakeholder innovation," highlighted the importance of making ICANN more effective (transparent, smart, cost-effective) and legitimate: "[a]nyone must [...] have easy and equitable access to participate in the process of shaping the policies and standards of the internet that ICANN helps facilitate."[422] One avenue proposed to increase ICANN legitimacy is including subsidiarity approaches and leaving issues that can be administered at a less-centralized level to other entities, those "best equipped and most competent" to handle them. The reports of both panels pointed the way to the adoption, in 2016, of the IANA transition, which allowed ICANN to change its bylaws in a way that represents more accountability to the global actor community. The transition has alleviated all concerns regarding the US dominance over the internet's public core and has immunized ICANN against critique in this regard.

In February 2014, the European Commission presented a Communication on Europe's role in shaping the future of internet governance[423] to guide EU institutions through the internet governance debates. As the surveillance revelations had raised doubts as to the "stewardship of the US,"[424] the Commission suggested creating a clear timeline for the globalization of ICANN and the IANA functions, strengthening the IGF, creating a set of

[417] Vinton G. Cerf et al., "ICANN's Role in the Internet Governance Ecosystem," Report of the ICANN Strategy Panel, February 20, 2014, http://www.icann.org/en/about/planning/strategic-engagement/governance-ecosystem/report-20feb14-en.pdf, 4 (emphasis added).

[418] Ibid., 5 (emphasis added).

[419] Ibid., 8–10.

[420] Suggestion on /1net listserv by George Sadowsky, January 22, 2014 "[discuss] Problem definition 1, version 5", http://1net-mail.1net.org/pipermail/discuss/2014-January/001400.html, as cited in Vint Cerf, Patrick Ryan, and Max Senges, "Internet Governance is our Shared Responsibility," I/S: A Journal of Law and Policy for the Information Society 10 (2014) 1, 53.

[421] Cerf, Ryan, and Senges (2014), 23–5.

[422] GovLab/ICANN Strategy Panel on Multistakeholder Innovation, The Quest for a 21st Century ICANN. A Blueprint, January 30, 2014, http://www.icann.org/en/about/planning/strategic-engagement/multistakeholder-innovation/quest-blueprint-30jan14-en.pdf, 3.

[423] European Commission, Communication from the Commission to the European Parliament, the European Economic and Social Committee and the Committee of the Regions, Internet Policy and Governance. Europe's role in shaping the future of Internet Governance, COM(2014) 72/4, http://ec.europa.eu/information_society/newsroom/cf/dae/document.cfm?doc_id=4453.

[424] Ibid.

principles of internet governance, and globalizing decision-making on the coordination of domain names and IP addresses "to safeguard the stability, security and resilience of the internet."[425] The Communication by the Commission firmly commits it to transparent, inclusive, and accountable multistakeholder processes[426] and a

> genuine multistakeholder model where the necessary inter-governmental discussions are anchored in a multistakeholder context in the full understanding that the internet is built and maintained by a variety of stakeholders, as well as governments; where decisions are taken on the basis of principles of good governance, including transparency, accountability, and inclusiveness of all relevant stakeholders [. . .] with a globalized [ICANN] and [IANA].[427]

Both calls for reform and the proliferation of principles led to the most normative basis for the global internet governance ecosystem today, the *NETmundial Multistakeholder Statement,* agreed upon at the conclusion of the Global Multistakeholder Meeting on the Future of Internet Governance (2014).[428] The document first identifies a set of common principles and values contributing to an "inclusive, multistakeholder, effective, legitimate, and evolving internet governance framework and recognized that the internet is a global resource which should be managed in the public interest."[429]

These principles include: human rights and shared values, including freedom of expression, privacy, and accessibility; the protection of intermediaries through liability limitations; a commitment to culture and linguistic diversity; the protection of a unified and unfragmented space (the internet should remain the "globally coherent, interconnected, stable, unfragmented, scalable and accessible network-of-networks"); security, stability, and resilience of the internet; open and distributed architecture; an enabling environment for innovation and creativity; and Internet Governance Process principles that define how internet governance should be practiced, namely through democratic multistakeholder processes ensuring the meaningful and accountable participation of all actors, processes that are open, participative, consensus-driven, transparent and accountable, inclusive, and equitable. Institutions and processes connected with the internet should be inclusive and open to all. Technically, internet governance should be carried out through a distributed, decentralized, and multistakeholder ecosystem using collaborative approaches and open standards (these should be promoted, informed by expertise and "rough consensus").

These principles influence the normative orientation of current internet governance debates by providing a foil against which reform proposals can be measured. They also show how governance norms transcend the binarity of legal vs. illegal and provide for a more nuanced normative approach. Principles and commitments, though not immediately implementable, are nonetheless normatively interesting as they contain implicit

[425] Ibid., 2.
[426] Ibid., 5.
[427] Ibid., 2.
[428] NetMundial Multistakeholder Statement, Global Multistakeholder Meeting on the Future of Internet Governance, April 24, 2014, http://netmundial.br/wp-content/uploads/2014/04/NETmundial-Multistakeholder-Document.pdf.
[429] Ibid.

assumptions about the character of the internet, which, in turn, allows drawing conclusions as to the finality of the online order in light of the view of the norm entrepreneur.

3.5 Order on the Internet?

States are not able to regulate through national law alone the network of networks as a multilayered socio-technological facility. The internet has become a critical infrastructural resource and essential for other critical infrastructural resources; its regulation and governance (and constitutionalization) has become an issue of global common interest, and the protection of its integrity is necessary for safeguarding other global common interests. As hypothesized, the normative order of the internet encompasses international legal rules, national legal rules, and transnational normative arrangements.

International law thus plays a key role in the regulation of the internet as one of its foundational orders. The hypothesis of a hybrid order is thus correct, as is the hypothesis that no new and independent international law of the internet needs to be developed. As this study has shown, early regulatory approaches to the internet were already committed to an international law-based order of the internet: a "people-centred, inclusive and development-oriented Information Society [...] premised on the purposes and principles of the Charter of the United Nations and respecting fully and upholding the Universal Declaration of Human Rights."[430] The purposes and principles of the UN Charter are foundational elements of the international legal order, some of them having ius cogens character. The 2015 GGE report also confirmed that international law, including the UN Charter and international legal principles, apply fully to the internet.[431] Indeed, the international community aspires to regulate the internet in a peaceful manner "for the common good of mankind."[432]

The additional hypothesis that there is no need for the creation of a new international law of the internet is also proven correct through the previous substance-oriented analysis of international legal rules applicable to the internet. International law is the ius necessarium of the internet. It is only international law that can successfully protect global common interests: the integrity of the internet's public core lies in the global common interest as does the mitigation of dangers stemming from misuses of the internet.

As this chapter has also shown, there are no international conventions pertaining to the internet, but its foundations are protected indirectly through the enabling dimension of human rights treaties. As the International Group of Experts for the Tallinn Manual 2.0 confirmed, states must not only respect human rights but also *protect* them. Individuals enjoy "customary international human rights protection with respect to their cyber-related activities." States need to ensure the respect for these rights.[433] Of particular importance are the right to privacy, freedom of expression, and the overarching right to internet access.

430 WSIS, Declaration of Principles, WSIS-03/GENEVA/DOC/4-E, 12 December 2003, para. 1.
431 GGE report (2015), para. 26.
432 Ibid., para. 28 (c).
433 Michael N. Schmitt (ed.), *Tallinn Manual 2.0 on the International Law Applicable to Cyber Operations* (Cambridge: CUP, 2017), 181.

This chapter has also analyzed the protection of the internet (and our protection from the internet) by customary international law. There are no customary rules that directly protect internet integrity, but important general principles of international law offer indirect protection for (and from) the internet. This is not surprising as the international law of the internet is still a relatively new field and, as the ICJ noted in *Gulf of Maine*, it may be unrewarding to look for a "readymade set of rules" in newly emerged regulatory arenas.[434]

However, general principles of international law offer substantial protection of the internet and from its (mis)uses. Not all of these principles have already reached the status of custom, though some are even considered ius cogens. In aggregate, they provide substantial protection for the internet's integrity and, conversely, protect states (and individuals) from attacks by cyber means. General principles can guide codification and progressive development of international law; the ones this study has analyzed include Non-Use of (the Threat of) Force, Peaceful Settlement of International Disputes, Non-Intervention in Domestic Affairs, Duty of Cooperation, Principle of Equal Rights and Self-Determination of Peoples, Principle of Sovereign Equality, No Harm Principle (Principle of Good Neighborliness), Principle of Good Faith, Principle of Prevention and Due Diligence, and the Principle of Sustainable Development.

This chapter has also served as an introduction into the notion of internet governance, its actors, its instruments (including a taxonomy of internet governance), its history (including the internet governance process), and more recent developments, namely its politicization and the normative trend of establishing principles. Internet governance—the development and application by states, the private sector, and civil society, in their respective roles, of norms and procedures shaping the evolution and use of the internet—is the second foundational order of the internet. The norms developed within the normative processes of internet governance are part of the category of transnational regulatory arrangements, which form—as has been hypothesized—an element of the normative order of the internet, which is thus substantialized as a hybrid order.

Internet governance has a much broader ambit than international law in that it focuses less on norms and more on responsibilities of actors for different aspects of the governance of the internet. Internet governance tends to normatively frame, in a non-binary (legal/illegal) logic, with varying, flexible normativity, the "softer" topics of internet regulation such as accountability in contrast to traditional (international) legal approaches focusing on, for example, international cooperation to fight cybercrime. Principles such as due diligence and initiatives for internet-related capacity-building blur the differences and consequently have foundations in both orders. This also makes the deep connection between law and governance of the internet clear and further confirms that both—international law and governance-related norms forming part of the normative tertium—are intrinsic parts of the normative order of the internet. While specific international legal principles, such as non-intervention, sovereignty, and due diligence, are particularly important, governance-related good practices are still part of the normative order of the internet.

Internet governance processes suffer from vague language, repeated normative mantras ("multistakeholderism"), and intellectual paucity, as principles developed within internet governance processes tend to draw from only a few sources (such as the outcome documents of the WSIS process and the 2014 NetMundial meeting). They nevertheless matter

[434] Ibid.

because they produce norms and legitimize procedures in which these norms are developed. Norms developed in internet governance processes are part of the hybrid normative order of the internet. Many of the norms of internet governance fall under the category of the normative "tertium" as unique to the international normative order of the internet and belonging neither to national nor to international law. As transnational regulatory arrangements they need to be legitimated through either their genesis or the results they produce. As this study will show below, these processes of integration of tertium norms in national legal orders are complex but, designed along the lines of previous integrations of technical standards, such as DIN norms (the standards of German industry, or *Deutsche Industrienormen*), are functional and legitimate.

Just as elaborating and accepting internet governance mechanisms are important examples of state practice, new legal instruments, including court decisions, can strongly influence governance decisions and processes. A case in point is the Global Commission on the Stability of Cyberspace, a commission charged with refining internet governance to ensure a stable internet. The Commission, in late 2017, proposed a norm to specifically protect the public core of the internet and establish a principle of non-interference with it: "Without prejudice to their rights and obligations, state and non-state actors should not conduct or knowingly allow activity that intentionally and substantially damages the general availability or integrity of the public core of the internet, and therefore the stability of cyberspace."[435] This is obviously a more precise formulation of the non-interference principle, oriented toward the public core of the internet, whose protection lies in the common interest. As states are enjoined, by customary international law, from damaging infrastructure essential for ensuring internet integrity (because its protection lies in the common interest), the norm does not include a new duty but rather puts an existing one into sharper focus and thus promotes norm-conforming behavior.

Summing up, we see that states have sovereignty over their territories and all layers of the internet within them. International law applies fully to their activities.[436] Internet governance includes them as important actors within a matrix of other actors in the development and application of norms, standards, and processes regarding the internet. They can coordinate via traditional international treaties but are limited by stronger legitimacy demands of international internet-related norms than in establishing non-internet-related regimes.[437] Technical organizations continue to play an essential role in the managing of the internet's architecture and its core resources and their cooperation—largely informal or at most regulated by private law—will not change in the foreseeable future.

The practical relevance of internet governance norms for the order of the internet lies, finally, also in the observation that on the internet the question of legality/illegality is often a false dichotomy. While international law traditionally focused on the binarity legal/illegal, governance norms allow for the conceptualization and critique of regimes of responsibility.

[435] Global Commission on the Stability of Cyberspace, Call to Protect the Public Core of the Internet, New Delhi, November 2017, https://cyberstability.org/wp-content/uploads/2017/11/call-to-protect-the-public-core-of-the-internet.pdf.

[436] States, individually, begin to express their opinio iuris on this, after having contributed to similar endeavours internationally, such as in the framework of the GGE. Just see UK Attorney General Jeremy Wright, Speech: Cyber and International Law in the 21st Century, May 23, 2018, https://www.gov.uk/government/speeches/cyber-and-international-law-in-the-21st-century (setting out the UK's position on applying international law to cyberspace).

[437] Cf. Kettemann (2013), 138–41.

In light of the dynamic nature of the internet, this variable normativity is a key characteristic of normative evolution.

Yet in light of the multitude of political and legal questions the internet faces, even combining the two regimes of "law" and "governance" leaves substantial regulatory holes and normative fractures.[438] Though law and governance of the internet are enmeshed, these fractures readily appear in a critical view of the internet's order. This study calls this trend the "normative disorder on the internet." In the following chapter, forces of normative disorder will be identified, examples analyzed, and the state of disorder on the internet assessed.

[438] This study understands a "fracture," as opposed to regulatory holes/lacunae, to be present in a case of legal uncertainty because of conflicts of laws or regulatory orders or cases of strong contestation of a norm.

4
Normative Disorder on the Internet

4.1 Dynamics of Disorder

As has been both hypothesized and established, the activities of actors on the internet are regulated by national law, international law, and transnational normative arrangements. However, as with any system of laws (and governance), conflicts emerge. Within states, governed by the rule of law, they are usually solved by courts as "managers" of legal conflicts. If they "solve" a conflict in violation of social mores, a backlash may follow,[1] after which governments may become involved to pacify the conflict by way of legislation.[2] Societies based on the rule of law usually accept court decisions as stabilizing forces pulling together societies toward constitutional values. Such fundamental, stabilizing institutions are missing on the internet. "Institutions" (rather: norm producers) that do exist are non-formalized and may act primarily in their own self-interest, such as companies. When judges do apply the law, it may solve a particular conflict but create others or lead to uncertainty. Judgments from different jurisdictions may also conflict. These normative stressors, in aggregate, lead to a state of normative disorder.

In a first step, section 4.2 will establish the forces and factors responsible for normative disorder online. It will differentiate between four normative dimensions of disorder: froth (4.2.1), friction (4.2.2), fractures (4.2.3), and fragmentation (4.3). Normative *froth* is the explosion of norms pertaining to the internet (or subfields relevant for the internet's functionality). These norms may have no clear hierarchy, be of diverging normative character, and be authored by different norm-makers (with very different intents). They are like the froth (bubbles) on top of a bath: difficult to firmly grasp (define) and obfuscating the water below (in this simile: the deeper issues of internet regulation). Normative *frictions* are conflicts of (private and public) norms or judgments. These may happen, for example, when different legal systems or systems of social ordering collide, when courts from different jurisdictions apply diverging rules to factually similar cases, or when equally applicable national laws collide. When normative frictions multiply, normative *fractures* may appear. *Fractures* are the faultlines within the international law of the internet and internet governance processes. Their existence points to a larger issue with the coherence of the order, a fundamental conflict that influences substantially how the internet is used and developed.

The importance of this section lies in the subsequent analysis of these factors of disorder within fragmentation processes. This study posits that, because of disordering forces, a

[1] On societal backlash faced with judicial approaches to solving social conflicts in the fields of desegregation and sexual equality: Michael J. Klarman, *Brown v. Board of Education and the Civil Rights Movement* (Oxford: OUP, 2007) and Michael J. Klarman, *From the Closet to the Altar: Courts, Backlash and the Struggle for Same-Sex Marriage* (Oxford: OUP, 2012).

[2] Matthias C. Kettemann, "How to Implement Controversial Court Decisions: International Constitutional Lessons from Brown v. Board of Education for the Austrian Cases on Topographical Signs in Carinthia," Vienna Online Journal on International Constitutional Law 4 (2010) 4, 590–623.

The Normative Order of the Internet. Matthias C. Kettemann, Oxford University Press (2020). © Matthias C. Kettemann.
DOI: 10.1093/oso/9780198865995.001.0001

certain fragmentation of the internet and its order in technical, political, and legal terms is under way. This fragmentation cuts across both the internet's normative layers and its actors. In aggregate, the dimensions of fragmentation discussed amount to a serious threat to the coherence of the rules pertaining to the online order.

If existing dynamics of disorder are not normatively countered by countervailing coherence-promoting forces, fragmentation takes place. Fragmentation is corrosive to the common purpose of the normative order. It questions the conception of the internet as a universal network and unfragmented space. Safeguarding the universal character of the internet motivates approaches to "defragment" the internet. These find a firm technical footing in the technical invariants of the internet. (4.4)

This chapter will thus test the dual hypothesis that centrifugal forces contribute to the emergence of normative redundancies, real conflicts of norms, substantial structural problems, and the political, commercial, and technological fragmentation of the internet; but further, that technical invariants exercise a technical defragmentation pull which the law (through the normative turn discussed in the following chapter) reifies.

4.2 Dimensions of Disorder

4.2.1 Normative Froth

One dimension of disorder on the internet is the multiplication of non-hierarchical norms or normative expectations pertaining to a specific regulatory aim. This study calls this normative *froth*.

The key example of normative froth is the publication by various organizations, institutions, states, and non-state actors of internet (governance) principles, mainly between 2011 and 2013.[3] Analyzing them shows how normative froth is an important factor of normative disorder online.

4.2.1.1 WSIS Principles

Principles have been an influential normative tool in internet regulation since the four WSIS outcome documents.[4] The outcome documents merit scrutiny because they are still today important state commitments regarding the goals of the information society and internet governance as the process of realizing them. They are still routinely cited by actors and are conceptually comparable, in their importance for the field of internet governance, to the role of the Universal Declaration of Human Rights of 1948 for the field of human rights. In both historic constellations, states wanted to ensure certain standards that had been endangered or broken previously. The scale, of course, was vastly different: the success of the UDHR can be explained against the foil of the outrages upon human dignity of World

[3] More than sixty are collected here: UNESCO, International and regional instruments relevant to the areas of access, freedom of expression, privacy and ethics (2018), https://en.unesco.org/international_and_regional_instruments.

[4] WSIS, Declaration of Principles, WSIS-03/GENEVA/DOC/4-E, 12 December 2003; WSIS, Geneva Plan of Action, WSIS-03/GENEVA/DOC/5-E, 12 December 2003; WSIS, Tunis Agenda for the Information Society, WSIS-05/TUNIS/DOC/6(Rev. 1)-E, 18 November 2005; WSIS, Tunis Commitment, WSIS-05/TUNIS/DOC/7-E, 18 November 2005.

War II. WSIS can be understood as an international response to the previous unilateral privatization by the US of address space and root server management through the foundation of ICANN.

In the Geneva Declaration of Principles, states affirmed a common vision for information society. It should be "people-centred, inclusive and development-oriented." The process toward this information society would be "premised on the purposes and principles of the Charter of the United Nations and respecting fully and upholding the Universal Declaration of Human Rights."[5] The development-orientation of the process of building an information society (a process of which internet governance is an important part) was reiterated in paragraph 2. States reaffirm "the universality, indivisibility, interdependence and interrelation of all human rights and fundamental freedoms, including the right to development, as enshrined in the Vienna Declaration [and Programme of Action of the World Conference on Human Rights 1993[6]]." States also reaffirm that democracy, sustainable development, human rights, and good governance "at all levels" are interdependent and mutually reinforcing. Human rights inform rule of law, and states resolve to "strengthen respect for the rule of law in international as in national affairs."[7]

In the 2005 Tunis Commitment[8] states reaffirmed their desire and commitment to build a "people-centred, inclusive and development-oriented Information Society" that is premised upon the UN Charter, international law, and multilateralism, upholding the UDHR. The goal was for people "to achieve their full potential and to attain the internationally agreed development goals and objectives, including the Millennium Development Goals."[9]

Moving away from commitments to development and human rights, para. 6 of the Geneva Declaration confirms that states "rededicate [themselves] to upholding the principle of the sovereign equality of all States." The exact role of governments and other actors is described in paragraph 20: In the process toward "[b]uilding a people-centred Information Society" all actors have "an important role and responsibility," which extends from the "development of the Information Society" to, "as appropriate, [. . .] decision-making processes." States describe the internet as a "global facility available to the public." Its regulation therefore constitutes "a core issue of the Information Society agenda."[10] This process should be "multilateral, transparent and democratic, with the full involvement of governments, the private sector, civil society and international organizations." The goals of internet management should be "equitable distribution of resources, [. . .] access for all and [. . .] a stable and secure functioning of the internet, taking into account multilingualism."[11]

The first clear distribution of governance tasks between actors, which would be confirmed in essence during the Tunis Phase of WSIS, was laid down in paragraph 49 of the Geneva Declaration. The paragraph does not refer to "governance," but rather to internet "management," and describes it as encompassing "technical and public policy issues." In it, "all stakeholders and relevant intergovernmental and international organizations" should be involved. Between the actors—states, private sector, civil society—and organizations

[5] WSIS, Declaration of Principles, WSIS-03/GENEVA/DOC/4-E, 12 December 2003, para. 1.

[6] Vienna Declaration and Programme of Action, adopted by the World Conference on Human Rights in Vienna on June 25, 1993, http://www.ohchr.org/en/professionalinterest/pages/vienna.aspx.

[7] WSIS, Declaration of Principles, WSIS-03/GENEVA/DOC/4-E, 12 December 2003, para. 3.

[8] WSIS, Tunis Commitment, WSIS-05/TUNIS/DOC/7-E, 18 November 2005, para. 2.

[9] Ibid., para. 3.

[10] WSIS, Geneva Declaration of Principles, WSIS-03/GENEVA/DOC/4-E, 12 December 2003, para. 48.

[11] Ibid.

through which states act as well responsibility for different tasks is clearly distributed. This was highly controversial and still is. The Geneva Declaration is state-centric in its approach and lays down that

a) Policy authority for internet-related public policy issues is the sovereign right of States. They have rights and responsibilities for international internet-related public policy issues;
b) The private sector has had and should continue to have an important role in the development of the internet, both in the technical and economic fields;
c) Civil society has also played an important role on internet matters, especially at community level, and should continue to play such a role;
d) Intergovernmental organizations have had and should continue to have a facilitating role in the coordination of internet-related public policy issues;
e) International organizations have also had and should continue to have an important role in the development of internet-related technical standards and relevant policies.[12]

The Tunis Agenda reaffirmed the principles enunciated in Geneva and described the internet as a "global facility available to the public." Therefore "its governance should constitute a core issue of the Information Society agenda." Such "international management" of the internet should be "multilateral, transparent and democratic, with the full involvement of governments, the private sector, civil society and international organizations."[13] We note how, within one paragraph, the Agenda switches from internet "governance" to "international management." Usually "management" in the WSIS documents refers to technical aspects, not policy-oriented ones. In paragraph 31, states recognize the importance of "internet governance": "carried out according to the Geneva principles, [internet governance] is an essential element for a people-centred, inclusive, development-oriented and non-discriminatory Information Society." States committed themselves, again, to the "stability and security of the internet as a global facility and to ensuring the requisite legitimacy of its governance, based on the full participation of all actors, from both developed and developing countries, within their respective roles and responsibilities."[14] Para. 35 of the Tunis Agenda reiterates para. 49 of the Geneva Declaration, relating to the role of actors in "internet management."

During governance processes, no state should play a domineering role: "all governments should have an equal role and responsibility for international internet governance and for ensuring the stability, security and continuity of the internet." In formulating public policy, they have to consult with all actors.[15] The goal of cooperation in such a process should be to develop "globally-applicable principles on public policy issues associated with the coordination and management of critical internet resources."[16]

The first two principles visible in WSIS are the *meta-principles* that new principles on public policy issues associated with managing critical internet resources are necessary and

[12] Ibid., para. 49.
[13] WSIS, Tunis Agenda for the Information Society, WSIS-05/TUNIS/DOC/6(Rev. 1)-E, 18 November 2005, para. 29.
[14] Ibid., para. 31.
[15] Ibid., para. 68.
[16] Ibid., para. 70.

that they need to be globally applicable (let us call them *reform principle* and *globality principle*). The other WSIS principles can be classified into three broad categories: structural, procedural, and substantive principles.

The following structural (i.e. fundamental) principles can be deduced: the internet is a global facility available to the public (*universality principle*) and existing arrangements for internet governance have worked effectively (*status quo principle*). The internet itself is, ideally, highly robust, dynamic, and geographically diverse (*robustness principle*) and the security and stability of the internet must be maintained (*"don't mess with a running system" principle*, a variation of the status quo principle). It can further be argued that the clear commitment to the purposes and principles of the UN Charter and international law and the UDHR also allow for the inclusion of an *international law principle* and a *human rights principle* at the structural level.

Among the procedural principles, we find that all governments should have an equal role and responsibility for international internet governance and for ensuring the stability, security, and continuity of the internet and that, in formulating policy, they must consult with all actors (*equality principle, sovereignty principle*, and *multistakeholder principle*). Further, the goal of legitimacy of internet governance can only be reached if there is "full participation of all stakeholders, from both developed and developing countries, within their respective roles and responsibilities" (*differentiated responsibility principle*). Management (and this is true for governance as well) must be "multilateral, transparent and democratic" (*transparency and democratic legitimacy principle*) "with the full involvement of governments, the private sector, civil society and international organizations within their respective roles" (with policy authority for internet-related public policy issues remaining a right of states) (*public policy priority principle*).

Among the substantive principles we find important values of the international community: that the information society must be people-centered, inclusive, and non-discriminatory (*inclusiveness principle*); that it must allow people to share information to achieve their full potential and to attain the internationally agreed development goals and objectives, including the MDGs (*human development principle*); that it must be premised upon purposes and principles of the UN Charter and international law and the UDHR (*international law principle* and *human rights principle*); that it must be democratic and illustrative of good governance and the rule of law nationally and internationally (*rule of law and good governance principle*); and that it promotes an enabling environment for innovation, competition, and investment (*market principle*).

The internet itself as a global facility needs to be stable, safe, and secure. A further important value confirmed by WSIS is the commitment by states to the inclusion of other actors in the processes leading toward norms relevant for the use and development of the internet. In this reading, the legitimacy of norms related to the internet can only be assured when there is meaningful participation of all actors in transparent, democratic, inclusive processes. Yet the WSIS principles are state-centered in their assignment of roles. They are sovereignty-oriented and characterized by the commitment by states present at WSIS to the primacy of states in the development of internet-related (governance) norms and follow the traditional international law approach to give states responsibility for the development of norms relevant for the use of the internet. Yet the broad majority of states supports the development of internet-related public policy by governments with all relevant actors.[17]

[17] Ibid., para. 68.

The WSIS principles are a reflection of a period in the evolution of internet governance when an attempt was made to combine the sovereignty justification paradigm and the justification paradigm regarding the inclusion of all relevant actors: the intergovernmental and the multi-actor model of normativity on the internet. It is because of this dialectic that we see diverging commitments: to reform and to stasis; to human rights and human development but with a public policy reservation for states; to policy authority for states while technical and operational responsibilities remain with the private sector actors and are artificially separated from public policy questions; to multistakeholderism, but also only to a weak statement of the "important role [civil society] has played."

4.2.1.2 New Principles

It is this dialectic of competing narratives and paradigms that is reflected in the internet governance principles developed between 2011 and 2015 that could draw legitimacy from competing parts of WSIS outcome documents. In all, the WSIS commitments were a conservative starting point for the normative development of native internet governance principles. Some of the WSIS principles are demonstrably at odds with each other; the roles of non-state actors are described in little detail.[18] Yet this does not detract from their value as important waypoints in the process of normative stratification of the internet. Over the years, they have substantially influenced the evolution of other internet governance principles.

This process of developing new internet governance principles was largely duplicative, a key element of normative *froth*-making. The principles themselves overlap to a large degree, as much as 80 percent with regard to topics connected to internet freedom, for example.[19] This can be seen as a confirmation of common commitments and a positive element in the identification of principles that seem in consonance with the community's normative expectations. But the collections of principles, and this is also determinative of *froth*, evidence dinstinctly diverging approaches that are reflective of the relevant normative bias of the author, i.e. the "vision" of the internet the author(s) adhere(s) to or the narrative or paradigm of internet governance they seek to promote. After presenting a selection of them[20] in Table 4.2,[21] the study will stratify the principles to illustrate the problems associated with this normative froth. Structuring the principles is essential to visualizing the demands by actors on the normative frame of the internet. Ordering them allows us to see commonalities and trends. At a first stage, they can be arranged according to the paradigms they exemplify (including a "human rights paradigm" that exemplifies less a general governance approach and more an

[18] This has led to calls to abolish "stakeholder 'roles'" and allow for the participation of all individuals on an "equal status" (cf. Milton L. Mueller, "The need to abolish stakeholder 'roles'," Submission to NetMundial (2014), http://content.netmundial.br/contribution/the-need-to-abolish-stakeholder-roles/80). This, of course, is in conflict with the traditional allocation of roles and responsibilities to international actors.

[19] Jeonghyun Baak and Carolina Rossini, *Issue Comparison of Major Declarations on Internet Freedom* (2013), http://bestbits.net/issue-comparison-of-major-declarations-on-internet-freedom.

[20] For a fuller picture with more than fifty sets of principles (including declarations and conference outcomes containing principles), see Rolf H. Weber, *Principles for governing the Internet. A comparative analysis* (Paris: UNESCO Publishing, 2015), http://unesdoc.unesco.org/images/0023/002344/234435e.pdf.

[21] During the preparation of the 2014 NetMundial Summit in Brazil, which tasked itself with developing further internet governance principles, stakeholders self-identified key declarations on Internet governance principles. I have adapted this list which does not contain all declarations, but the most important ones. This is, naturally, also a normative selection. Cf. NetMundial, Links to internet governance principles (2014), http://content.netmundial.br/internet-governance-principles.

advocacy focus) (Table 4.2) and according to their authors (Table 4.3). In a second step, the principles themselves will be analyzed according to their normative orientation: structural, procedural, or substantive (Table 4.4).

The following principles vary greatly in their normative approach, their authors (from Presidents to international organizations, from civil society actors to clubs of powerful states), and their form (from speeches to declarations to "paradigms"). What they have in common, however, is that their creators wished to influence the normative development of the internet, its governance, and regulation. They thus tell us a lot about the normative expectations of different actors, and their overlap, as we will soon see, is as telling as are the differences.

Table 4.1 shows that within a short time frame the number of published internet governance principle declarations has grown substantially. Rather than evidencing a common

Table 4.1 Selected Collections of Internet Governance Principles 2005–2013

- US Principles on the Internet's Domain Name and Addressing System (2005)[a]
- APC Internet Rights Charter (2006)[b]
- CGI.br Principles for the Governance and Use of the Internet (2009)[c]
- European Parliament resolution, Internet governance: the next steps (2010)[d]
- APC/CoE/UNECE, Code of Good Practice on Information, Participation and Transparency in Internet Governance (2010)[e]
- OECD, Communiqué on Principles for Internet Policy Making (2011)[f]
- European Commission, Internet Compact (2011)[g]
- UNESCO, Code of Ethics for the Information Society (2011)[h]
- OSCE, Declaration on Pluralism and Internet Governance (2011)[i]
- Internet Rights and Principles Coalition, Charter of Internet Rights and Principles (2011) and 10 Internet Rights and Principles (2012)[j]
- G8 (Deauville Summit), Renewed Commitment for Freedom and Democracy (2011)[k]
- Council of Europe, Committee of Ministers, Declaration on Internet Governance Principles (2011)[l]
- China/Russia et al., International Code of Conduct for Information Security (2011)[m]
- WEF, Code of Conduct for Government Leaders (2011)[n]
- US International Strategy for Cyberspace (2011)[o]
- UN/OAS/OSCE/ACHPR, International Mechanisms for Promoting Freedom of Expression, Joint Declaration on Freedom of Expression and the Internet (2011)[p]
- Human Rights Council, Resolution 20/8, The promotion, protection and enjoyment of human rights on the Internet (2012)[q]
- OpenStand Principles (2013)[r]
- IETF/IAB/W3C/ICANN et al., Montevideo Statement on the Future of Internet Cooperation (2013)[s]
- Global Network Initiative, Principles on Freedom of Expression and Privacy (2013)[t]
- Adam Smith Institute, Internet Freedom. A Free Market Digital Manifesto (2013)[u]
- Brazilian President Rousseff's Principles, Address to the General Assembly (2013)[v]
- Swedish Foreign Minister Carl Bildt's Principles, Speech at the Seoul Conference on Cyberspace (2013)[w]
- International Principles on the Application of Human Rights to Communications Surveillance (2013)[x]
- Community Informatics, An Internet for the Common Good—Engagement, Empowerment, and Justice for All (2013)[y]

[a] NTIA, U.S. Principles on the Internet's Domain Name and Addressing System, June 30, 2005, http://www.ntia.doc.gov/other-publication/2005/us-principles-internets-domain-name-and-addressing-system.
[b] APC Internet Rights Charter (2006), http://www.apc.org/en/node/5677.
[c] CGI.br Principles for the Governance and Use of the Internet (2009), http://www.cgi.br/english/regulations/resolution2009-003.htm.
[d] European Parliament resolution of 15 June 2010, Internet governance: the next steps, (2009/2229(INI)), https://eur-lex.europa.eu/legal-content/EN/TXT/?uri=CELEX%3A52010IP0208.

Table 4.1 *Continued*

[e] APC/CoE/UNECE, Code of Good Practice on Information, Participation and Transparency in Internet Governance (2010), http://www.apc.org/en/system/files/COGP_IG_Version_1.1_June2010_EN.pdf.
[f] OECD Communiqué on Principles for Internet Policy Making, OECD High Level Meeting: The Internet Economy: Generating Innovation and Growth, June 28–29, 2011, Paris, http://www.oecd.org/dataoecd/40/21/48289796.pdf.
[g] Vice-President of the European Commission Neelie Kroes, Internet Compact, http://blogs.ec.europa.eu/neelie-kroes/i-propose-a-compact-for-the-internet/#more-671.
[h] UNESCO, Code of Ethics for the Information Society, proposed by the Intergovernmental Council of the Information for All Programme (IFAP), 36 C/49, October 10, 2011, http://goo.gl/nZ0lk
[I] OSCE, 8th South Caucasus Media Conference, Declaration: Pluralism and Internet governance, Tbilisi, Georgia, October 20–21, 2011, http://www.osce.org/fom/84371.
[j] Cf. Internet Rights and Principles Coalition, 10 Internet Rights and Principles, http://internetrightsandprinciples.org.
[k] G8, Declaration, Renewed Commitment for Freedom and Democracy, G8 Summit of Deauville, May 26–27, 2011, http://www.g20-g8.com/g8-g20/g8/english/live/news/renewed-commitment-for-freedom-and-democracy.1314.html.
[l] Council of Europe, Declaration by the Committee of Ministers on Internet Governance Principles, adopted on 21 September 2011 at the 1121st meeting of the Ministers' Deputies, https://wcd.coe.int/ViewDoc.jsp?id=1835773.
[m] Letter dated 12 September 2011 from the Permanent Representatives of China, the Russian Federation, Tajikistan, and Uzbekistan to the United Nations addressed to the Secretary-General, UN Doc. A/66/359 of 14 September 2011, https://documents-dds-ny.un.org/doc/UNDOC/GEN/N11/496/56/PDF/N1149656.pdf?OpenElement.
[n] World Economic Forum, Code of Conduct for Government Leaders (2011), http://www3.weforum.org/docs/WEF_GAC_InformedSocieties_CodeConductGovernmentLeaders_Summary_2012.pdf.
[o] US President Barack Obama proposed ten principles in his strategy paper in May 2011, see President of the United States of America, International Strategy for Cyberspace. Prosperity, Security and Openness in a Networked World, May 2011, http://www.whitehouse.gov/sites/default/files/rss_viewer/international_strategy_for_cyberspace.pdf, 10.
[p] UN/OAS/OSCE/ACHPR, International Mechanisms for Promoting Freedom of Expression, Joint Declaration on Freedom of Expression and the Internet (2011), https://www.osce.org/fom/78309.
[q] Human Rights Council, Resolution 20/8, The promotion, protection and enjoyment of human rights on the Internet, UN Doc. A/HRC/RES/20/8 of 5 July 2012, http://ap.ohchr.org/documents/dpage_e.aspx?si=A/HRC/RES/20/8. The resolution is identical, in terms of "principles" discussed here, to the resolutions of 2014 and 2016.
[r] OpenStand, A Global Community for Open Innovation, http://open-stand.org/principles.
[s] Montevideo Statement on the Future of Internet Cooperation, October 7, 2013, http://www.icann.org/en/news/announcements/announcement-07oct13-en.htm.
[t] Global Network Initiative, Principles on Freedom of Expression and Privacy, http://www.globalnetworkinitiative.org/principles/index.php.
[u] Adam Smith Institute, Internet Freedom. A Free Market Digital Manifesto (2013), http://www.adamsmith.org/research/reports/internet-freedom-a-free-market-digital-manifesto.
[v] Statement by President Dilma Rousseff, President of Brazil to the UN General Assembly, September 24, 2013, http://gadebate.un.org/sites/default/files/gastatements/68/BR_en.pdf.
[w] Speech by Carl Bildt, Foreign Minister of Sweden, Seoul Conference on Cyberspace 2013, http://www.government.se/sb/d/17281/a/226592.
[x] Necessary and Proportionate, International Principles on the Application of Human Rights to Communications Surveillance (2013), https://en.necessaryandproportionate.org/text.
[y] Community Informatics Research Network (2013), An Internet for the Common Good—Engagement, Empowerment, and Justice for All, http://cirn.wikispaces.com/An+Internet+for+the+Common+Good+-+Engagement%2C+Empowerment%2C+and+Justice+for+All.

commitment or reifying shared normative expectations, their normative divergence leads to disorder. Early documents, such as the *U.S. Principles on the Internet's Domain and Addressing System* of 2005, did not contain new proposals but rather sought to legitimize the status quo. Later declarations, however, often focused on specific issues connected to the principles' authors, such as human rights.

An early example of meta-principles, that is principles targeted at establishing the normative frame within which to develop further internet governance principles (e.g. through describing the processes wherein they can be developed), is illustrated by the APC and two international organizations, Council of Europe and UNECE, in their common adoption of the *Code of Good Practice on Information, Participation and Transparency in Internet*

Governance. Also in Europe, the European Parliament expressed, in its 2010 resolution, that internet governance should be exercised "in the common interest."[22] Exactly how this common interest can be defined was the issue underlying the "principle hype" of 2011 when some ten declarations were adopted. They are called "compact," "code," "declaration," "commitment," "code of conduct," and "strategy" and show a broad variety of normative preferences. It is interesting to see how the normative imperative to adopt a statement vis-à-vis the future of internet governance developed a momentum independent of the real changes that were envisaged at the time in forums as different as UNESCO, OSCE, OECD, the European Commission, G8, US, China, and Russia—a clear case of normative international peer pressure, another key element of *froth*, unexplainable norm growth unrelated to a regulatory need growing with the same speed.

The documents have different preconceptions of what governance questions of the internet are, which public policy questions need to be addressed, and what role the different actors should play. They lack—another characteristic of normative *froth*—a common focus. A first attempt at stratification can be made by assigning the documents to the justification narrative/paradigm that they reflect and follow (Table 4.2), even though it must be cautioned that some can be considered to be reflective of more than one paradigm.

Table 4.2 Selected Internet Principles Ordered According to Leading Paradigm

Sovereignty Paradigm	Regulation-Through-Code/Standards Paradigm	Multistakeholder Paradigm	Human Rights-Based Approach
China/Russia et al., International Code of Conduct for Information Security (2011)	OpenStand Principles (2013)	CGI.br Principles for the Governance and Use of the Internet (2009)	APC Internet Rights Charter (2006)
Qualified sovereignty paradigm WEF, Code of Conduct for Government Leaders (2011)	IETF/IAB/W3C/ICANN et al., Montevideo Statement on the Future of Internet Cooperation (2013)	APC/CoE/UNECE, Code of Good Practice on Information, Participation and Transparency in Internet Governance (2010)	Charter of Internet Rights and Principles (2011) and 10 Internet Rights and Principles (2012)
US Principles on the Internet's Domain Name and Addressing System (2005)	Global Network Initiative, Principles on Freedom of Expression and Privacy (2013)	Council of Europe, Committee of Ministers, Declaration on Internet Governance Principles (2011)	UNESCO, Code of Ethics for the Information Society (2011)
OECD, Communiqué on Principles for Internet Policy Making (2011)	Adam Smith Institute, Internet Freedom. A Free Market Digital Manifesto (2013)	European Parliament resolution (2010)	UN/OAS/OSCE/ACHPR, Joint Declaration on Freedom of Expression and the Internet (2011)

[22] European Parliament resolution of 15 June 2010, Internet governance: the next steps, (2009/2229(INI)), http://www.europarl.europa.eu/sides/getDoc.do?pubRef=-//EP//TEXT+TA+P7-TA-2010-0208+0+DOC+XML+V0//EN.

Table 4.2 *Continued*

Sovereignty Paradigm	Regulation-Through-Code/Standards Paradigm	Multistakeholder Paradigm	Human Rights-Based Approach
European Commission (Neelie Kroes), Internet Compact (2011)			Human Rights Council, Resolution 20/8, The promotion, protection and enjoyment of human rights on the Internet (2012)
G8 (Deauville Summit), Renewed Commitment for Freedom and Democracy (2011)		Rousseff Principles (2013)	International Principles on the Application of Human Rights to Communications Surveillance (2013)
US, International Strategy for Cyberspace (2011)		Carl Bildt's Principles (2013)	Community Informatics, An Internet for the Common Good—Engagement, Empowerment, and Justice for All (2013)
OSCE, Declaration on Pluralism and Internet Governance (2011)			

As has previously been discussed, only very few states demand control over the national internet segment and follow the "sovereignty paradigm" in their internet governance policies. The *International Code for Information Security*, proposed by China, Russia, Tajikistan, and Uzbekistan, is not so much a governance proposal for the internet as a template for non-governance, because under the sovereignty paradigm states see no need for international internet approaches. They underline national control over important aspects of the internet's infrastructure and call for cooperation between states in "curbing the dissemination of information that incites terrorism, secessionism or extremism or that undermines other countries' political, economic and social stability, as well as their spiritual and cultural environment."[23] The majority of states and international organizations, however, adhere to the qualified sovereignty paradigm, accepting that some aspects of the internet need to be controlled by states, but that important oversight functions should not be administered by states individually.

The declarations adhering to the regulation-through-code/standards paradigm differ conceptually from those following (qualified) sovereignty paradigms in that they focus on the normative importance of code and standards, such as the *OpenStand Principles*. Developed by the internet's leading technical organizations, the standards-based approach focuses on ensuring cooperation between standards organizations, with each respecting the autonomy, integrity, processes, and intellectual property rights of the other organizations,

[23] Letter dated 12 September 2011 from the Permanent Representatives of China, the Russian Federation, Tajikistan, and Uzbekistan to the United Nations addressed to the Secretary-General, UN Doc. A/66/359 of 14 September 2011, http://blog.internetgovernance.org/pdf/UN-infosec-code.pdf.

as fundamental for the integrity of the internet. Alternative declarations focus on the forces of the internet "market," such as the *Free Market Digital Manifesto*. The *Montevideo Statement on the Future of Internet Cooperation* is different in that the authors specifically wished to delineate the issues facing the "future of the Internet" and presented themselves as "the leaders of organizations responsible for coordination of the Internet's technical infrastructure globally"[24]—and therefore responsible for the "grand design."

The most strongly represented paradigm is the multistakeholder paradigm. This is because it has been, at least since WSIS, the most accepted approach to developing norms regarding the use and development of the internet. It is also easy to refer to it without committing to substantial rules. A classic example of such a collection of principles is the Council of Europe Committee of Ministers' Declaration on Internet Governance Principles (2011).[25] The document includes commitments to human rights and the rule of law, multistakeholder governance arrangements, and the equal and full participation of all actors. The declaration also discusses the responsibilities of states and the empowerment of internet users and contains a commitment to the universality of the internet and its integrity (security, stability, robustness, and resilience). It also contains commitments to basic technical foundations of the way the internet is run: decentralized management, architectural principles (open standards, interoperability, end-to-end nature), and the open network. The declaration thus combines technical, architectural, legal, and aspirational elements—which form an interesting normative mesh but are difficult to parse, in their individual impact. The normativity of the declaration, as of others, suffers from the lack of clarity regarding the character of the principles expressed.

Finally, a number of principle declarations follow a human rights-based approach. They argue that ensuring internet governance must be premised upon human rights (e.g. *APC Internet Rights Charter*) or include general governance principles in a document focused principally on human rights (e.g. the *IRP Charter of Internet Rights and Principles*). The IRP Charter[26] is the most comprehensive document on internet-related human rights and principles to date. A condensed version highlights eight rights and rights-related principles (universality of human rights; right to access; network neutrality; internet as a space of human rights; freedom of expression; rights to life, liberty, and security online; right to privacy online; cultural and linguistic diversity) and two general principles: open standards ensuring interoperability and inclusion; and rights-based, transparent, multilateral operation and governance of the internet, "based on principles of openness, inclusive participation and accountability as prescribed by law."[27] The human rights-based approach has some merit because human rights are an important vehicle for governance issues. Where human rights are violated (e.g. through pervasive internet surveillance), the assumption is strong that governance reform is needed, and normative changes have to be implemented.

Let us now consider the authors of the declarations (Table 4.3), who can be categorized according to the three traditional actor groups—states, civil society, private sector (and technical organizations)—and (for purposes of clarity in this table) international organizations as a distinct formation of coordinated state action.

[24] Montevideo Statement on the Future of Internet Cooperation, October 7, 2013, http://www.icann.org/en/news/announcements/announcement-07oct13-en.htm 1.

[25] Council of Europe, Declaration by the Committee of Ministers on Internet Governance Principles, adopted on 21 September 2011 at the 1121st meeting of the Ministers' Deputies, https://wcd.coe.int/ViewDoc.jsp?id=1835773.

[26] IRP, Charter on Human Rights and Principles for the Internet, http://internetrightsandprinciples.org/site/charter.

[27] Ibid., Principle No. 10.

Table 4.3 Selected Internet Principles Ordered According to Author

States	International Organizations	Technical Organizations and Private Sector	Civil Society
US Principles on the Internet's Domain Name and Addressing System (2005)	UNESCO, Code of Ethics for the Information Society	OpenStand Principles (2013)	APC Internet Rights Charter (2006)
China/Russia et al., International Code of Conduct for Information Security (2011)	APC/CoE/UNECE, Code of Good Practice on Information, Participation and Transparency in Internet Governance (2010)	IETF/IAB/W3C/ICANN et al., Montevideo Statement on the Future of Internet Cooperation (2013)	CGI.br Principles for the Governance and Use of the Internet (2009)
US International Strategy for Cyberspace (2011)	Council of Europe, Committee of Ministers, Declaration on Internet Governance Principles (2011)	Global Network Initiative, Principles on Freedom of Expression and Privacy	Charter of Internet Rights and Principles (2011) and 10 Internet Rights and Principles (2012)
WEF, Code of Conduct for Government Leaders (2011)	European Parliament resolution (2010)	Adam Smith Institute, Internet Freedom. A Free Market Digital Manifesto (2013)	Community Informatics, An Internet for the Common Good—Engagement, Empowerment, and Justice for All (2013)
G8 (Deauville Summit), Renewed Commitment for Freedom and Democracy (2011)	European Commission (Neelie Kroes), Internet Compact (2011)		International Principles on the Application of Human Rights to Communications Surveillance (2013)
Carl Bildt's Principles (2013)	UN/OAS/OSCE/ACHPR, Joint Declaration on Freedom of Expression and the Internet (2011)		
Rousseff Principles (2013)	OSCE, Declaration on Pluralism and Internet Governance (2011)		
	OECD, Communiqué on Principles for Internet Policy Making (2011)		
	Human Rights Council, Resolution 20/8, The promotion, protection and enjoyment of human rights on the Internet (2012)		

Civil society and international organizations have developed most principles while states and the technical standard-setters lag behind.[28] This can be readily explained. Developing new principles suggests that existing arrangements are dissatisfactory. In existing arrangements standard-setting technical bodies are solely (with some US oversight that has now transitioned to the ethereal "global multistakeholder community") responsible for both the day-to-day management of the internet and for managing its key resources. They—until recently—had no reason to change the status quo. It was only after the surveillance revelations that a document such as the Montevideo Statement was published, in which technical organizations called for a globalization of ICANN and IANA functions with very similar language to the European Commission in its 2014 Communication.

States were reluctant to get involved through principles, as they are normative vehicles that lend themselves to diverse interpretations. Until 2013, only the US on the one side and China and Russia on the other side had developed clear policy visions. The US wanted to develop legitimacy narratives for retaining the status quo. China and Russia wished to exercise sovereign control over "their" parts of the internet. Only after the Snowden revelations did states such as Brazil, Sweden, and Germany unilaterally suggest governance reform. Yet states also act through international organizations and it is in that form that they have most often publicized their approaches to principles. Organizations that were most active include the Council of Europe, the EU, OSCE, and the UN (through UNESCO and the Human Rights Council (HRC)). There is a noticeable predominance of organizations with a European membership and organizations with a focus on human rights. Indeed, the *human "rightsization"* (*Vermenschenrechtlichung*) of the internet governance discourse can be traced back to the primacy of human rights in the principles discussions. This is not without its problems when attempting to frame the debate in larger governance questions.

Let us now look at the principles themselves. In a study of eighteen declarations, including those presented in the tables above, two researchers have identified twenty-two "issues" discussed in the principles.[29] When adapted and incorporated in the three groups of principles identified earlier—relating to structure (the basic architecture), procedure (how to adapt the structure), and substance (which values should influence the normative evolution)—the following picture showing the normative principle froth emerges (see Table 4.4).

Basic commitments to structural principles figure in many of the declarations that are not dedicated exclusively to human rights and most prominently in the ones of technical entities. These declarations also underline the importance of architecture-based principles of the internet: network stability, neutrality and integrity, and technical standards. Among the process-related commitments, we often find references to the importance of participation and norm-development and application by all relevant actors and the different roles of actors. Later declarations, and especially those from civil society, tend to ignore the WSIS concept of diverging "roles" because of its focus on states. Even more seldom

[28] This is confirmed by the more extensive list contained in Rolf H. Weber, "Legal Interoperability as a Tool for Combatting Fragmentation," Global Commission on Internet Governance Paper Series No. 4 (2014), https://www.cigionline.org/sites/default/files/gcig_paper_no4.pdf and UNESCO, International and regional instruments relevant to the areas of access, freedom of expression, privacy and ethics (2018), http://www.unesco.org/new/en/principlesgoverningInternet.

[29] Jeonghyun Baak and Carolina Rossini, *Issue Comparison of Major Declarations on Internet Freedom* (2013), http://bestbits.net/issue-comparison-of-major-declarations-on-internet-freedom.

Table 4.4 Selected Internet Governance Issues Represented in the Declarations

Related to Structure	Related to Process	Related to Substance
Commitment to UN Charter and international human rights law	Participation and multistakeholder governance	Access
Network stability	Role of companies, governments, and civil society	Diversity
Network neutrality	Transparency	Human development and economic progress
Open standards and interoperability		Substantive human rights (generally, and specifically, freedom of expression and privacy)
		Procedural human rights (due process, legal remedies)
		Protection of vulnerable groups (children, minorities)
		User empowerment
		Rule of law

do we find more precise prefiguration of what the process to reform internet governance should look like. Substance-related principles, by contrast, figure prominently in all declarations. They often contain both a commitment to human rights protection and then go on to discuss the relevance of selected human rights. Among the rights, the right to access (sometimes also seen as a foundational right), privacy, and freedom of expression are often highlighted. This echoes the clear language of the WSIS outcome documents but does not carry the normative debate further.

It is also difficult to establish whether common ground exists between many declarations as actors use different language for similar concepts, a further characteristic of normative froth. When civil society declarations speak of human development, private sector declarations talk about economic progress. Private sector-led initiatives often refer to "user empowerment," but "user"-led (that is civil society-led) principle collections do not, the one exception being the Declaration by the Committee of Ministers on internet governance principles, which understands user empowerment in terms of human rights and participation rights in global governance discussions. This suggests a preference on the part of companies to self-identify as the agent (who empowers the user) and reflects a certain bias but is not substantially different from a commitment to access to the internet as an enabler of human rights (and thus a legal-institutional "empowerer" as well).

4.2.1.3 Degrees of Normativity

As expected, the type of author (or institutional sponsor) demonstrably influences the content and form of the principles. Private sector-led initiatives tend to focus on human rights and often disregard the importance of structural and procedural principles. Standard-setting bodies give short shrift to substantial, e.g. human rights-related, principles. International organizations prefer broad statements and highlight the importance of states, but often lack substance and are reluctant to provide templates for internet governance reform. Yet the main issue to take with principles is a more fundamental one. They contribute, through the variety, to normative disorder on the internet and, individually, suffer from normative deficits related to the varying levels of normativity.[30]

An overview of the Council of Europe Declaration on Internet Governance Principles[31] illustrates the different levels of normativity that principles, even those from an established international organization, can take (Table 4.5).

Table 4.5 Assessment of the Normative Character of the Council of Europe Internet Governance Principles (2011)

Principle	Character
1. Human rights, democracy and the rule of law	
Internet governance arrangements must ensure the protection of all fundamental rights and freedoms [. . .]	Restatement of international law
[States] must also ensure full respect for democracy and the rule of law and should promote sustainable development. [. . .]	Restatement of international law, but with a policy dimension
They should be aware of developments leading to the enhancement of, as well as threats to, fundamental rights and freedoms, and fully participate in efforts aimed at recognizing newly emerging rights.	Policy statement
2. Multi-stakeholder governance	
The development and implementation of internet governance arrangements should ensure, in an open, transparent and accountable manner, the full participation of governments, the private sector, civil society, the technical community and users, taking into account their specific roles and responsibilities. [. . .]	Policy statement
3. Responsibilities of states	
States have rights and responsibilities with regard to international internet-related public policy issues. [/] In the exercise of their sovereignty rights, states should, subject to international law, refrain from any action that would directly or indirectly harm persons or entities outside of their territorial jurisdiction.	Restatement of international law
Furthermore, any national decision or action amounting to a restriction of fundamental rights should comply with international obligations. [. . .]	Restatement of international law
4. Empowerment of internet users	
Users should be fully empowered to exercise their fundamental rights and freedoms, [. . .] in particular in governance mechanisms and in the development of Internet-related public policy, in full confidence and freedom.	Policy statement

Continued

[30] For the evolution of normativity, see Matthias Lutz-Bachmann, "The Concept of the Normativity of Law: 'Ius gentium' in the Writings of Francisco Suárez and Thomas Aquinas," in Thilo Marauhn and Heinhard Steiger (eds.), *Universality and Continuity in International Law* (The Hague: Eleven, 2011), 235–47.

[31] Council of Europe, Declaration by the Committee of Ministers on Internet Governance Principles, adopted on 21 September 2011 at the 1121st meeting of the Ministers' Deputies, https://wcd.coe.int/ViewDoc.jsp?id=1835773.

Table 4.5 *Continued*

Principle	Character
5. Universality of the internet	
Internet-related policies should recognize the global nature of the internet and the objective of universal access.	Policy statement
They should not adversely affect the unimpeded flow of transboundary internet traffic.	Emerging International legal principle
6. Integrity of the internet	
The security, stability, robustness and resilience of the internet as well as its ability to evolve should be the key objectives of internet governance. [. . .]	Policy statement
7. Decentralised management	
The decentralised nature of the responsibility for the day-to-day management of the internet should be preserved.	Architectural principle
The bodies responsible for the technical and management aspects of the internet, as well as the private sector, should retain their leading role in technical and operational matters. [. . .]	Architectural principle and policy statement
8. Architectural principles	
The open standards and the interoperability of the internet as well as its end-to-end nature should be preserved. [. . .]	Architectural principle
There should be no unreasonable barriers to entry for new users or legitimate uses of the internet. [. . .]	Policy statement
9. Open network	
Users should have the greatest possible access to internet-based content, applications and services of their choice [..].	Architectural principle
Traffic management measures which have an impact on the enjoyment of fundamental rights and freedoms [. . .] must meet the requirements of international law on the protection of freedom of expression and access to information, and the right to respect for private life	Restatement of international law
10. Cultural and linguistic diversity	
Preserving cultural and linguistic diversity and fostering the development of local content, regardless of language or script, should be key objectives of internet-related policy and international co-operation, as well as in the development of new technologies.	Policy statement based on international human rights law

We see a variation of restatements of international law and certain "architectural" principles of the internet and a number of policy statements, often based on international human rights law. Even clear-sounding restatements of international law—that "internet governance arrangements must ensure the protection of all fundamental rights and freedoms"—are clouded by references to ensuring "full respect for democracy and the rule of law" and the "promot[ion] of sustainable development." From the principles alone, one cannot establish what exactly the Council of Europe means by establishing internet governance arrangements that ensure the full respect for democracy. It leaves open what democracy may mean in the context of internet governance arrangements that are—at least as far as the management of critical internet resources is concerned—not developed in (national) democratic or international (accountable) processes.

Even the latest compilation of principles, the NetMundial Principles,[32] did not manage to achieve a substantial normative pull. Participants agreed on a "set of common principles and important values that contribute for an inclusive, multistakeholder, effective, legitimate, and evolving internet governance framework." They included human rights and shared values, the protection of intermediaries, the protection of culture and linguistic diversity, the stability of the internet as a unified and unfragmented space (globally coherent, interconnected, stable, unfragmented, scalable, and accessible), the security, stability, and resilience of the internet, open and distributed architecture, an enabling environment for sustainable innovation and creativity, open standards, and Internet Governance Process Principles (democratic multistakeholder processes, open, participative, consensus driven governance, transparent decision-making, checks-and-balances, inclusive institutions, distributed, decentralized ecosystem of governance, collaborative and cooperative approaches, meaningful participation, access and low barriers, future-oriented and technology-neutral policies for internet access).

Parsing the principles, we see again a normative amalgamation of exhortative statements ("internet should continue to be an [...] unfragmented [...] network-of-networks"), sweeping statements of law ("internet governance must respect, protect and promote cultural and linguistic diversity in all its forms") and muddled ones ("Governments have [...] accountability for the protection of human rights"), and explanatory statements ("[e]nterprise and investment in infrastructure are essential components of an enabling environment").[33] Given this, it is unsurprising that the "NetMundial Process," an attempt to use its principles as a key normative commitment to internet governance, has not succeeded.

Internet governance principles, and even UN-led studies on how international law applies to the ICT environment,[34] suffer from the amalgamation of architectural principles, policy statements, hortatory statements, and restatements of (possible) legal rules and from serious defects in terms of clarity by including, in a single document, notions such as norms, rules, non-binding norms, common understandings, shared expectations, or principles for state behavior. Within this normative multitude, normative froth emerges. But in their aggregate, principles and the other normative sources stabilize expectations. They do so especially when they overlap. In the areas where they do, the stabilization of the normative expectation is strongest. When a principle is an outlier, its normative pull is especially weak. Principles that are reiterated over time in different declarations grow in strength and are stabilized.

4.2.1.4 Consequences

The reliance on principles is detrimental to the development of international norms bearing upon the internet and ensuring its integrity. There is, put simply, too little law in internet governance and too little normativity in the principles. There is a dissonance between the perceived importance of formulating new principles and their actual impact: the normativity

[32] Based on the NetMundial, Multistakeholder StatementNetMundial, Global Multistakeholder Meeting on the Future of Internet Governance, April 23–24, 2014, São Paulo, Brazil, http://netmundial.br/netmundial-multistakeholder-statement.

[33] Ibid.

[34] United Nations, Developments in the Field of Information and Telecommunications in the Context of International Security, Report of the Secretary General, A/70/174 of July 22, 2015, http://www.un.org/ga/search/view_doc.asp?symbol=A/70/174 (hereinafter: "GGE report (2015)"). On its normative vagueness, see 4.2.3.2.

of the factual (the architectural set-up and the relations between non-state actors including, for the internet's public core, the global accountability regime with mainly non-state and technical actors and, for much of the other resources, national legal systems) is greater than the facticity of the (semi)normative, i.e. the principles. They are created and promoted as representing new "principled" approaches to internet governance, but their normative impact is very limited. The value added of each further declaration of internet governance principles, which evidence a certain normative path dependency, declines, if they do not reiterate and let crystallize the same principles. Summing up, there are four key problems with the principles as tools for the normative development of internet governance.

First, there is a lack of a coherent vision and agreed finality for internet governance. The principles reflect competing visions of "institutional trajectories"[35] for internet governance. As Mark Raymond and Gordon Smith argue, only sovereignty-oriented states have developed a strategic vision of internet governance based on national oversight.[36] Other actors have failed to develop and present strategic counter-visions beyond the usual commitments to a human rights-based, development-oriented information society. *Second*, even with regard to shared goals, different actors will use different language, thus clouding the issue. *Third*, since internet governance principles are not situated within a Kelsenian system of norms, it is difficult to determine which principles are more powerful than others. Discourse analysis may help, but also has its limits. The *pouvoir constituant* cannot become *pouvoir constitué* without a (semblance of a) constitutional process. The principles themselves define different *pouvoirs constituants* and express diverging opinions on the legitimate architecture of the process of ruling the internet. The reputation of the authoring entity plays an important role in establishing the "compliance pull" of a principle, but so does the adherence of the principle to the perceived international order of the internet and the coherence to other governance norms. *Fourth*, principles contribute to stabilizing normative expectations and reify legitimacy narratives by actor groups but have no distinct legal content. They are often amalgams of technical preferences, policy statements, or restatements of law (as interpreted by the authoring entity). They can thus mostly not be measured against standards of international law.

Taken together, the internet governance principles have led to the emergence of normative froth, which this study identifies as an element of disorder of the internet, because it obfuscates the real legal issues. Most of the different principles are not, however, in active conflict with another. Yet these conflicts exist and persist and give rise to normative friction.

4.2.2 Normative Friction

4.2.2.1 Problem

Normative friction is understood here to mean conflicts between norms or their application that are more serious than the mere uncoordinated, non-hierarchical coexistence of

[35] Michèle Rioux, "Competing Institutional Trajectories for Global Regulation—Internet in a Fragmented World," in Roxana Radu, Jean-Marie Chenou, and Rolf H. Weber (eds.), *The Evolution of Global Internet Governance. Principles and Policies in the Making* (Zurich: Schulthess, 2014), 37–56.

[36] Cf. Mark Raymond and Gordon Smith, "Reimaging the Internet: The Need for a High-level Strategic Vision for Internet Governance, 2015–2020," CIGI Internet Governance Paper Series No. 1 (2013), http://www.cigionline.org/sites/default/files/no1_4.pdf, 16.

duplicative norms (froth) and less serious than substantial, identifiable rifts within the online order (fractures). Normative friction can happen, for example, when national courts diverge in their rulings on matters that are substantially similar across borders or when the laws of states diverge so that applying one state's laws to online settings leads to conflicts with another state's laws. Examples of normative friction, an element of the normative disorder of the internet, also emerge in the implementation by intermediaries of their terms of service and community guidelines, regulating their private corporate discourse sphere when countering countervailing public interests, such as protection against hate speech, enforced through laws and courts. Among the many examples, a selected few will serve to illustrate the problem of friction.

4.2.2.2 Intermediaries

Internet intermediaries play an important role on the internet. They connect users to the internet, process information and data, host user-generated content, enable searches, index content, facilitate the sale of goods, and enable payments and other transactions.[37] This study identifies the regulation of intermediaries, their self-regulation and the regulatory conflicts that emerge between these two normative approaches as examples of normative friction: there are not too many rules, but the existing rules sometimes contradict each other and lead to legal uncertainty.[38]

Intermediaries affect issues of social interest. They provide the communicative spaces necessary for the articulation and aggregation of opinions essential for democratic processes. Discussions take place under the terms of service of the intermediary. This "internet governance by contract"[39] is an important source of friction as terms of service tend not to be essential normative tools to regulate behavior in the offline world, which takes place—to a large degree—either in public spaces (e.g. demonstrations) or in spaces owned/controlled by ourselves (e.g. our homes and offices), in which we can self-moderate our communication (by deciding what to speak about, not by having an intermediary decide that discussing certain, especially controversial, topics leads to an account or post deletion or suspension).

Social interactions and information and communication flows essential for the creation of a public sphere take place in privately owned and governed spaces where, prima facie, the terms of service of intermediaries apply. Often the interests between customer/user and company/intermediary diverge. Then conflicts arise that are repeatedly expressed in legal disputes. Frictions can also emerge between the terms of service themselves and national legislation, in particular since globally active intermediaries are subjected to almost two hundred different legal orders. These can contain prohibitions on holocaust denial (Austria, Germany, France), on criticizing Atatürk (Turkey), on criticizing the ruling monarch (Thailand)—which then need to be measured against the global human rights canon. A recurrent theme is the question of whether restrictions on the right to freedom of

[37] Cf. Council of Europe, Recommendation CM/Rec(2018)2 of the Committee of Ministers to member states on the roles and responsibilities of internet intermediaries (2018) ("Recommendation on Internet intermediaries"), preambular para. 6.

[38] This section draws from Matthias C. Kettemann, "Hassrede und Katzenbilder: Wie können im globalen Netz nationale Gesetze respektiert werden?" in Lorena Jaume-Palasí, Julia Pohle, and Matthias Spielkamp (eds.), *Digitalpolitik. Eine Einführung* (Berlin: Wikimedia, 2017).

[39] Lee A. Bygrave, *Internet Governance by Contract* (Oxford: OUP, 2015).

expression are allowed or even required—for example, when it comes to content prohibited under international law.

Frictions also emerge when intermediaries are subjected to traditional media regimes ill-suited to their function in (information) society. The question of where exactly the line between media companies (which are usually responsible for content) and intermediaries (which enjoy, as a general rule, a liability exception) should be drawn is difficult to answer. Rather, a graduated approach, taking into account concrete functions of intermediaries within the intermediary's field of activities, should be used.[40]

States have a duty, flowing from sovereignty, to ensure to everyone within their jurisdiction or control all human rights. This applies to states' relationships with intermediaries as well. It is a continuing source of normative friction that states fail to protect persons under their jurisdiction or control from intermediaries, and that they then find antisocial behavior is present online that may even threaten democratic processes or constitutionally protected human rights, subsequently call for tighter self-regulation or, failing that, for regulated self-regulation or supranational international regulation, and, as a last step, pass intrusive national laws. These steps have been evident, for instance, in government approaches to regulating hate speech, such as in Germany, including attempts at intermediary self-regulation through the EU's Code of Conduct on illegal online hate speech[41] and, eventually, the Network Enforcement Act,[42] against which serious constitutional law-based arguments can be brought to bear.[43]

Pursuant to the UN Guiding Principles on Business and Human Rights, intermediaries have an independent obligation to respect human rights, a "corporate responsibility to protect" that is independent of the state's duty to safeguard human rights. States, as per the most

[40] On the graduated approach, see already Council of Europe, Committee of Ministers, Recommendation CM/Rec(2011)7 of the Committee of Ministers to member states on a new notion of media, September 21, 2011 (recommending that "all actors—whether new or traditional—who operate within the media ecosystem should be offered a policy framework which guarantees an appropriate level of protection and provides a clear indication of their duties and responsibilities in line with Council of Europe standards." Any policy response should be "*graduated and differentiated* according to the part that media services play in content production and dissemination processes" (emphasis added). To these ends, the document recommends that member states "have regard to [the media actors'] specific functions in the media process and their potential impact and significance in ensuring or enhancing good governance in democratic society."

[41] European Commission, European Commission and IT Companies announce Code of Conduct on illegal online hate speech, May 31, 2016, http://europa.eu/rapid/press-release_IP-16-1937_en.htm (including the following "public commitments" with "[the] IT Companies, taking the lead on countering the spread of illegal hate speech online":

- The IT Companies to have in place clear and effective processes to review notifications regarding illegal hate speech on their services so they can remove or disable access to such content. The IT companies to have in place Rules or Community Guidelines clarifying that they prohibit the promotion of incitement to violence and hateful conduct. [. . .]
- Upon receipt of a valid removal notification, the IT Companies to review such requests against their rules and community guidelines and where necessary national laws transposing the Framework Decision 2008/913/JHA, with dedicated teams reviewing requests.
- The IT Companies to review the majority of valid notifications for removal of illegal hate speech in less than 24 hours and remove or disable access to such content, if necessary.

[42] Gesetz zur Verbesserung der Rechtsdurchsetzung in sozialen Netzwerken (Netzwerkdurchsetzungsgesetz – NetzDG), Federal Gazette 2017 Part I No. 61, September 7, 2017.

[43] Wolfgang Schulz, "Regulating Intermediaries to Protect Privacy Online – the Case of the German NetzDG," HIIG Discussion Paper Series 2018-01, https://www.hiig.de/publication/regulating-intermediaries-to-protect-privacy-online-the-case-of-the-german-netzdg. See further the references contained in Alexander Peukert, "Gewährleistung der Meinungs- und Informationsfreiheit in sozialen Netzwerken. Vorschlag der Ergänzung des NetzDG um sog. Put-Back-Verfahren," MMR (2018), 572, note 2.

recent General Comment of the Committee on Economic, Social and Cultural Rights on state obligations in the context of business activities (2017), have "to respect, to protect and to fulfill"[44] human rights. The obligation to protect includes a "positive duty to adopt a legal framework requiring business entities to exercise human rights due diligence in order to identify, prevent and mitigate the risks of violations of Covenant rights."[45]

This is echoed in the 2018 Council of Europe Recommendation on roles and responsibilities of internet intermediaries, which confirms that

> Member States have the obligation to refrain from violating the right to freedom of expression and other human rights in the digital environment. They also have a positive obligation to protect human rights and to create a safe and enabling environment for everyone to participate in public debate [...]. This positive obligation to ensure the exercise and enjoyment of rights and freedoms includes, due to the horizontal effects of human rights, the protection of individuals from actions of private parties by ensuring compliance with relevant legislative and regulatory frameworks.[46]

States are thus obliged to provide a legal framework that ensures meaningful protection of all from the actions of private parties. In order to understand the impact of the activities of companies on human rights, transparency is necessary. Therefore human rights obligations of companies under the Ruggie Framework are often implemented through transparency reports, increased control of subcontractors along the supply chain, and Human Rights Impact Assessments.[47] While committing to human rights-based principles would seem like a strategy to avoid friction (in light of their presumed global reach), the terms of service of intermediaries and national laws are increasingly in conflict. The role of intermediaries will be discussed in more detail below;[48] to name just one example here: the territorial application of national judgments protecting national interpretations of human rights commitments is challenging.

Google has been engaged in proceedings in France against the French data protection authority CNIL (Commission Nationale de l'Informatique et des Libertés) and its claims that the right to be forgotten (established by the CJEU in its *Google Spain case* as a limited right to be delisted from a search engine's results when the information meets certain criteria of e.g. irrelevance[49]) should be implemented globally with regard to French delisting requests.[50] By 2017, some 800,000 URLs (Uniform Resource Locators) had been removed. The French data protection authority CNIL, however, ordered Google to remove URLs

[44] Committee on Economic, Social and Cultural Rights, General Comment No. 24 on State obligations under the International Covenant on Economic, Social and Cultural Rights in the context of business activities, UN Doc. E/C.12/GC/24 of 10 August 2017, para. 10.

[45] Ibid., para. 16.

[46] Council of Europe, Recommendation CM/Rec(2018)2 of the Committee of Ministers to member states on the roles and responsibilities of internet intermediaries (2018) ("Recommendation on Internet intermediaries"), PP 6.

[47] Report of the Special Representative of the Secretary-General on the issue of human rights and transnational corporations and other business enterprises, John Ruggie, Guiding Principles on Business and Human Rights: Implementing the United Nations "Protect, Respect and Remedy" Framework, UN Doc. A/HRC/17/31 of 21 March 2011.

[48] See 7.5.2.

[49] CJEU, C-131/12, *Google Spain und Google*, judgment of May 13, 2014.

[50] Peter Fleischer, "Reflecting on the Right to be Forgotten," December 9, 2016, https://blog.google/topics/google-europe/reflecting-right-be-forgotten.

globally, for users from Australia (google.com.au) to Zambia (google.co.zm). Applying this regional ruling globally would be very problematic because of potential reciprocal expectations from non-democratic countries regarding content they wish to suppress (e.g. democratic reform). This is a clear example of normative friction, where national laws and terms of service are in conflict. In 2017, the French Conseil d'État, France's highest court, asked the CJEU for a ruling.[51] Thus it becomes apparent that national rulings that force national norms on companies' operations outside the territory of that state are a source of normative friction.

4.2.2.3 Public and Private Spaces

Another large source of normative friction is the application to private spaces of the rules (and normative expectations) developed for and formed in public spaces. A criterion for the difference between private and public spaces, in light of the role of intermediaries that is of interest here, can be found in the decision of the ECtHR, in the case of *Appleby and Others v. United Kingdom*.[52] In this case, political activists had complained that the operator of a shopping mall prevented them from distributing leaflets and collecting signatures in the mall. The judges rejected the claims of the activists, reasoning that they could advertise their concerns outside or communicate via local media. Conversely, it follows from this reasoning: if a discourse important for the community outside of privately constituted spaces can actually no longer take place successfully, a normative intervention into the privately governed area (be it a shopping mall or a communication platform operated by an internet intermediary) seems not only legitimate but necessary.

Are malls less "public" than airports? This was the question the judges of the German Federal Constitutional Court were faced with in the *Fraport* decision.[53] The case concerned the question of whether gathering signatures, conducting opinion polls, and organizing demonstrations in Frankfurt Airport could be banned by the airport's (private) operating company. A central concept in the ruling is that of the "public forum," which is characterized by the fact that it allows for the pursuance of "a variety of different activities and concerns and thus creates a versatile and open communication." From such a public forum, according to the Karlsruhe judges, the "political debate in the form of collective expression of opinion through meetings cannot be kept out."[54] This is a source of friction between the normative approaches by different actors. The question whether the internet has evolved into a privately run, semi-public forum like the mall in *Appleby* or a public "institution," as an essential transport facility run privately, like the airport in the *Fraport* decision, will be discussed in the context of the presentation of the normative order.[55]

[51] See referral of the case to the CJEU, French Conseil d'État, Google Inc., n° 399922, decision of July 19, 2017, with the following questions "Le 'droit au déréférencement' [. . .] doit-il être interprété en ce sens que l'exploitant d'un moteur de recherche est tenu, lorsqu'il fait droit à une demande de déréférencement, d'opérer ce déréférencement sur l'ensemble des noms de domaine de son moteur de telle sorte que les liens litigieux n'apparaissent plus quel que soit le lieu à partir duquel la recherche lancée sur le nom du demandeur est effectuée, y compris hors du champ d'application territorial de la directive du 24 octobre 1995?" and, should the first questions be answered in the negative, should *Google Spain* be interpreted to mean rather that search engine operators need to delete links in all EU member states or only in the home state of the applicant; and finally, whether geolocation and IP address filtering should be used to suppress search results in the home state of the applicant or all EU member states.

[52] ECtHR, *Appleby and Others v. United Kingdom* (May 6, 2003), application no. 44306/98.

[53] BVerfG, judgement of February 22, 2011, 1 BvR 699/06, *Fraport*.

[54] Ibid.

[55] See chapter 6.

4.2.2.4 Technical Norm-Setting Cyberwar

Apart from the power asymmetry and the informal or inter partes instruments used between technical actors, the normative processes in standard-setting bodies give rise to issues of accountability and transparency; this causes normative friction. Participation in technocratic gatherings demands arcane specialized knowledge which is usually produced and reproduced in elite institutions; lack thereof is a very effective entry barrier. IETF develops important standards, protocols, and architecture to solve operational and technical problems of the internet, but its legitimacy does not come from elections or democratic processes. It describes itself as a "loosely self-organized group of people who contribute to the engineering and evolution of internet technologies."[56] That self-organized "collection[s] of happenings"[57] develop and implement essential standards on the management of critical internet resources is one of the characteristics of the internet and its order, set at the intersection of technology and normativity. When standards and laws, traditionally legitimated through national democratic processes, collide, friction arises. This is especially problematic when laws are "overruled" by standards. These situations can lead to legitimacy paradoxa: what if a (not democratically legitimated) standard offers a higher level of privacy protection than a (democratically legitimated) national or regional norm?

Progressively, standards organizations have developed simulacra of legitimacy conferral by proceduralizing legitimacy and discourse settings that appear to follow a technologist interpretation of the Habermasian approach: broad membership, active support for members from non-Western countries to participate in meetings, efforts to "educate" new members, same formal rights to participate for everyone.

Technical standards proposed by IETF are published in a series called *Request for Comments* (RFCs), which are publicly available and were first published in 1969.[58] The normative impact of RFCs is based on community acceptance and premised upon the authority of the sender and the technical logic of the proposal. The influential RFC 2418 laid down that "[w]orking groups make decisions through a 'rough consensus' process." For an IETF consensus to be established not all participants have to agree.[59] In general, we read in RFC 2418, "the dominant view of the working group shall prevail," with "dominance" to be determined on a "general sense of agreement."[60] This approach is difficult to reconcile with traditional international legal concepts of consent (of states and internationally relevant actors) but is common in international diplomacy. Rough consensus is similar to "adoption without a vote," a practice often used in UN meetings when a resolution is broadly accepted but would probably not be unanimous. After reaching a rough consensus, the suggested new standard is published as a "proposed standard" in a six-month *pilot phase*. After positive impact has been proven twice, the standard can then become a "draft standard" and be recommended for global use. Then the internet community uses the standard (or not) as

[56] Paul Hoffman (ed.), *The Tao of IETF: A Novice's Guide to the Internet Engineering Task Force* (2012), https://www.ietf.org/tao.html.

[57] Ibid.

[58] IETF, Request for Comments (RFC), http://www.ietf.org/rfc.html.

[59] Cf. Gralf-Peter Calliess and Peer Zumbansen, *Rough Consensus and Running Code. A Theory of Transnational Private Law* (Oxford/Portland, OR: Hart, 2012), 135 (pointing to three dimensions of a rough consensus: a social dimension (near unanimity), a substantial dimension (shared opinion regarding the common core), and a temporal dimension (interim character of the standard with potential for improvement at a later stage).

[60] Cf. the influential RFC 2418: S. Bradner (ed.), *RFC 2418, Working Group Guidelines*, September 1998, http://tools.ietf.org/html/rfc2418#section-3.3, 3.3.

it enters its *recognition phase*. Only after use has become widespread, the standard will become *binding*.[61]

Technical standard-setters have realized that both the standards they develop and the process in which they are developed need to meet certain minimum criteria of openness and accountability. An example of such a commitment to certain principles in the development of standards is the *OpenStand* initiative by influential internet technical organizations.[62] The five principles described as fundamental for a "modern paradigm" for standards are: cooperation between standards organizations with each one respecting "the autonomy, integrity, processes, and intellectual property rules of the others"; adherence to five key principles in the process of standards developments (due process, broad consensus, transparency, balance, openness); collective empowerment (by striving for standards that are chosen and defined "based on technical merit, as judged by the contributed expertise of each participant," that ensure "interoperability, scalability, stability, and resiliency," enhance competition and innovation, and "contribute to the creation of global communities, benefiting humanity"); availability; and voluntary adoption ("success is determined by the market").[63] The values and policy choices expressed in the *OpenStand* paradigm are not arbitrary. Rather, they can be traced back to international legal commitments regarding the fundamental values and finality of the information society and are an attempt to reduce friction.

4.2.2.5 Consequences

From the effective fight against hate speech to the application of private or public norms in online settings, from standards to privacy protection across jurisdictions and between actors, legal conflicts and normative frictions persist. This is not a new trend,[64] as is evidenced by a number of well-known lawsuits involving online speech, from *LICRA v. Yahoo!*,[65] to the Twitter user Paul Chambers, whose joke (that he would "blow the airport sky high!!" if the weather-related closure did not end) resulted in a conviction of making statements of a menacing character, with the High Court of the United Kingdom finally overturning the judgment,[66] to French cases forcing social media companies to identify authors of anti-Semitic messages[67] or organizers of neo-Nazi groups.

Normative frictions emerge especially when otherwise legitimate rules produce disproportionate interferences. Blacklists of sites are a case in point, such as the one used by the UK Internet Watch Foundation (IWF), with its hotline against illegal content. In December 2008, for instance, IWF blacklisted the image of a child on the 1976 album by the German

[61] Gralf-Peter Calliess and Peer Zumbansen, *Rough Consensus and Running Code. A Theory of Transnational Private Law* (Oxford/Portland, OR: Hart, 2012), 135–6.

[62] Open Stand, A Global Community for Open Innovation (2013), http://open-stand.org/principles.

[63] Ibid.

[64] See Wolfgang Benedek and Matthias C. Kettemann, *Freedom of Expression on the Internet* (Strasbourg: Council of Europe, 2014), 118–23.

[65] Tribunal de Grande Instance Paris, *Ligue contre le racisme et l'antisémitisme et Union des étudiants juifs de France c. Yahoo! Inc. et Société Yahoo! France* (*LICRA v. Yahoo!*), May 22, 2000. See also the US "follow-up": United States Court of Appeals, Ninth Circuit, 433 F.3d 1199, *Yahoo! Inc. v. LICRA and UEJF*, January 12, 2006 (Sup. Ct. denied certiorari).

[66] Owen Bowcott, "Twitter Joke Trial: Paul Chambers Wins High Court Appeal Against Conviction," *The Guardian*, July 27, 2012, www.guardian.co.uk/law/2012/jul/27/twitter-joke-trial-high-court.

[67] Cyrus Farivar, "Twitter Must Identify Racist, Anti-Semitic Posters, French Court Says," *CNN*, http://edition.cnn.com/2013/01/24/tech/social-media/twitter-racist-posts-france/index.html.

band Scorpions. As a result of the inclusion of the address on the blacklist, the majority of UK internet users were no longer able to access the content and were no longer able to edit Wikipedia pages.[68] If "unremedied" by normative interventions or changes in the sociopolitical sphere, normative frictions can widen into normative fractures.

4.2.3 Normative Fractures

4.2.3.1 Problem

Unlike normative froth and normative frictions, normative fractures are evidence of larger structural problems that the law and governance regimes of the internet are confronted with. Among the fractures present in the normative order of the internet, we find those between international law and non-international legal norms (such as non-binding internet standards), between universal and particular (sovereignty-oriented) normative approaches by states, and between the necessity to trust the internet and political developments, including massive online surveillance practices that destabilize trust.

4.2.3.2 International Law and Other Norms

Among the key fractures are those between the traditional legal and the non-legal "dominion." In Louis Henkin's famous words: "almost all nations observe almost all principles of international law and almost all of their obligations almost all of the time."[69] But how do states react to standards that do not amount to principles of international law or international legal rules which do not oblige them to act in a certain way? Can we diagnose a fracture between international law and the other norms influential for internet law and governance?

States are obliged to ensure that they and the internet companies active on their territory respect human rights. They also have extraterritorial obligations, which extend to economic, social, and cultural rights.[70] It is impossible to conceptualize these without recourse to international law. Not only *should* the normative order of the internet be founded on the principles of international law, indeed it *has* to be if the goal of the international community regarding the future development of the information society should be met. International law is the only internationally agreed normative system providing vectors for the evolution of the legitimate normative order.

But there is a fracture between legal rules of international law and other bodies of norms that influence the use and evolution of the internet. DeNardis reminds us that internet governance is enacted also through "technical design decisions, private corporate policies, global institutions and national laws and policies."[71] Even within international law, there is little clarity as to which "norms" are actually binding on states and which are soft law norms that may nevertheless be both orientative and influential.[72] The approach of the GGE

[68] BBC, "Scorpions Censored," August 12, 2008, www.bbc.co.uk/6music/news/20081208_scorpians.shtml.

[69] Louis Henkin, *How Nations Behave*, 2nd edn. (New York: Columbia University Press, 1979), 47.

[70] See the Committee on Economic, Social and Cultural Rights, General Comment No. 24 on State obligations under the International Covenant on Economic, Social and Cultural Rights in the context of business activities, UN Doc. E/C.12/GC/24 of 10 August 2017.

[71] Laura DeNardis, *The Global War for Internet Governance*, 2nd edn. (New Haven: Yale University Press, 2014), 23.

[72] See, for an early approach to soft law, Christine M. Chinkin, "The Challenge of Soft Law: Development and Change in International Law," International and Comparative Law Quarterly 38 (1989) 4, 850–66.

report 2015 is similarly muddled. In just one paragraph the consensus report refers to the challenges of determining how "norms, rules and principles can apply to State conduct of ICT-related activities," the objective of identifying further "voluntary, non-binding norms for responsible State behaviour" and "strengthen[ing] common understandings to increase stability and security in the global ICT environment."[73] The report does not clearly distinguish between norms, rules, principles, non-binding norms, common understandings, and "existing international norms and commitments."[74]

The report does offer a definition of its notion of norms as "reflect[ing] the expectations of the international community, set[ting] standards for responsible State behaviour and allow[ing] the international community to assess the activities and intentions of States,"[75] but this does not square with the tentatively worded "recommendations for consideration by States for voluntary, non-binding norms, rules or principles of responsible behaviour of States." Either a norm reflects existing expectations, or it should help them crystallize. Confidence-building measures, though voluntary, can be considered to be (partially) encompassed by due diligence obligations of states. Further, the report includes existing norms of international law ("international law [being] an essential framework for [state] actions in their use of ICTs and to promote an open, secure, stable accessible and peaceful ICT environment"[76]) by referring to "principles of the Charter and other international law" and naming six of them

- state sovereignty;[77]
- sovereign equality;
- settlement of international disputes by peaceful means;
- non-intervention in the internal affairs of other States;
- prohibition of the threat or use of force; and
- respect for human rights and fundamental freedoms.[78]

4.2.3.3 Universality and Subsidiarity

Over time a fracture has emerged in the international regulation of the internet between states supporting the current model of including, at least in principle, all relevant actors in normative processes on the internet and pursuing, at least by and large, common interests, including internet integrity, and those states aiming for the internationalization of more sovereignty-oriented internet politics.[79]

Sovereignty-oriented states, such as Algeria, China, Egypt, Russia, Saudi Arabia, Sudan, and UAE, have argued, for instance during ITU's WCIT-12 conference, for state-focused mechanisms to manage key internet resources, such as the DNS—thus establishing "control over the internet" through the ITU.[80] In a leaked submission to the ITU conference

[73] GGE report (2015), para. 9.
[74] Ibid., para. 11.
[75] Ibid., para. 10.
[76] Ibid., para. 25.
[77] Ibid., para. 27.
[78] Ibid., para. 26.
[79] Matthias C. Kettemann, *Völkerrecht in Zeiten des Netzes: Perspektiven auf den effektiven Schutz von Grund- und Menschenrechten in der Informationsgesellschaft zwischen Völkerrecht, Europarecht und Staatsrecht* (Bonn: Friedrich-Ebert-Siftung, 2015), http://library.fes.de/pdf-files/akademie/12068.pdf, 53 et seq.
[80] Russia, UAE, China, Saudi Arabia, Algeria, Sudan, and Egypt, Proposal for the Work of the Conference [WCIT-12], ITU Doc. DT-X of 5 December 2012, WCIT12/27(Rev.1)-E, § 3A.2 and 3A.3, http://files.wcitleaks.org/public/Merged%20UAE%20081212.pdf.

(which ultimately failed to come to an agreement), these states suggested including paragraphs in the reformed treaty that would allow ITU member states "equal rights to manage the internet, including in regard to the allotment, assignment and reclamation of internet numbering, naming, addressing and identification resources and to support for the operation and development of basic internet infrastructure" [and] "the sovereign right to establish and implement public policy, including international policy, on matters of internet governance, and to regulate the national internet segment, as well as the activities within their territory of operating agencies providing internet access or carrying internet traffic."[81] Though it is difficult to understand the content of a "sovereign right to implement [. . .] international policy [. . .] on matters of internet governance" in light of the non-exclusive sovereignty inherent in the very notion of *international* policy, it was the notion of a "national internet segment" that attracted most criticism.

In a white paper outlining the Chinese approach[82] to the internet, the People's Republic of China's State Council argued that "the role of the UN should be given full scope in international internet administration." An "authoritative and just international internet administration organization" should be installed under UN auspices. Through it, all countries should be able to participate "in the administration of the fundamental international resources of the internet, and a multilateral and transparent allocation system should be established on the basis of the current management mode."[83] Section III of the white paper also says, apparently without irony, that "Chinese citizens fully enjoy freedom of speech on the internet."[84] This claim is inaccurate in light of international human rights standards,[85] but serves to illustrate the dissonance between the self-declared accordance with international internet principles of national internet policies, especially the ones oriented toward ensuring or based on sovereignty, and the tenets of the normative order of the internet, including integrity of the internet and its universality.

As sovereignty-oriented states such as Russia and China progressively feel that the current universal approach to internet regulation is not reflective of their values and interests, they have started building alternate institutions and developing alternative normative vehicles, while formally referring to multistakeholderism. These initiatives include political alignment among BRICS countries (Brazil, Russia, India, China, and South Africa) on internet policy[86] and the organization by China of the annual (Wuzhen) "World Internet Conferences."

At the Wuzhen Conference in 2016, President Xi noted that China would "work with the international community for the common welfare for all people [and] uphold the concept of cyberspace sovereignty and to make the global cyberspace governance system fairer

[81] Ibid.

[82] For an analysis of Chinese internet governance approaches, see Gianluigi Negro, "Chinese Internet Governance—Some Domestic and Foreign Issues," in Roxana Radu, Jean-Marie Chenou, and Rolf H. Weber (eds.), *The Evolution of Global Internet Governance. Principles and Policies in the Making* (Zurich: Schulthess, 2014), 141–56.

[83] People's Republic of China, State Council, The Internet in China, June 8, 2010, http://www.china.org.cn/government/whitepaper/node_7093508.htm, sect. I.

[84] Ibid., sect. 3.

[85] Cf. Rebecca MacKinnon, *Consent of the Networked. The Worldwide Struggle for Internet Freedom* (New York: Basic Books, 2012), 133–9 (recounting Yahoo's complicity in human rights violations in China).

[86] Cf. Tim Stevens, "BRICS Vision for International Information Security" (2015), http://thesigers.com/analysis/2015/7/3/brics-set-out-vision-for-international-information-security.

and more reasonable."[87] *Reasonable* changes in cyberspace governance coupled with a reference to sovereignty tend to lead normative developments away from universality.[88] This assessment rests, inter alia, on the foundations of the Chinese organizer's "Report on World Internet Development 2017," in which Chinese authorities reiterated their conviction that "[n]o cyberspace hegemony is allowed, neither is single domination or only a few countries' decision." (sic)[89] It should be noted though that hegemonic tendencies, which are not present in the internet governance system to the extent that China seems to claim (though they are with regard to certain aspects of cybersecurity), do not even constitute, per se, a violation of international law.[90]

Further anti-universal initiatives from among BRICS countries include important communications-related aspects of China's "Belt & Road" initiative. China has launched satellites allowing its *Beidou* Navigation Satellite System (BNS)[91] to establish itself as a rival to the US' Global Positioning System (GPS), Russia's Globalnaya Navigatsionnaya Sputnikovaya Sistema (GLONASS), and Europe's Global Navigation Satellite System (GALILEO) with stations in countries in Asia and beyond and internet-related services provided through Chinese-run satellites.[92]

A final example is Russia's building of an alternate root for itself and its allies.[93] Such a root would serve, according to the Russian Federation's Security Council, as "independent internet infrastructure for BRICS nations, which would continue to work in the event of global internet malfunctions." In effect, as the Security Council put it, "параллельный и нтернет,"[94] a parallel internet. According to the minutes of the Security Council meeting, "Western countries," in particular the "US and some European countries," were "run[ning] the internet" and thus had the "opportunity to organize cyber attacks and conduct information wars [. . .] threatening the security of Russia."[95]

Threats to internet universality can also come from the application of the subsidiarity principle, which has been successfully established in regional integration law and can be applied with gradation also in international law. In principle, it should be the case that

[87] Xinhua, "President Xi Stresses Int'l Cooperation in Cyberspace Governance," November 17, 2016, http://www.wuzhenwic.org/2016-11/17/c_61495.htm.

[88] But seeing limited convergences between European and Chinese approaches to the rule of law in cyberspace: Zhixiong Huang and Kubo Mačák, "Towards the International Rule of Law in Cyberspace: Contrasting Chinese and Western Approaches," Chinese Journal of International Law 16 (2017), 271, https://ssrn.com/abstract=2979896.

[89] World Internet Conference (4th WIC, Wuzhen Summit), Report on World Internet Development 2017, http://www.wuzhenwic.org/download/ReportonWorldInternetDevelopment2017overview.pdf.

[90] Nico Krisch, "International Law in Times of Hegemony: Unequal Power and the Shaping of the International Legal Order," EJIL (2005), 369–408.

[91] Tristan Kenderdine, "Coordinating China's Satellite Constellations. a New Era in the Space Race Begins," Asia & the Pacific Policy Society, APPS Policy Forum, July 20, 2017, https://www.policyforum.net/coordinating-chinas-satellite-constellations.

[92] Saadia M. Pekkanen, "China's Ambitions Fly High: 'One Belt, One Road' To Extend Into Space," *Forbes.com*, May 26, 2017, https://www.forbes.com/sites/saadiampekkanen/2017/05/26/chinas-ambitions-fly-high-one-belt-one-road-to-extend-into-space/#48bfb10d4c0c.

[93] As cited by Eli Noam, "Russia Orders Alternate Root Internet System," *Net Policy News*, December 15, 2017, http://netpolicynews.com/index.php/component/content/article/89-r/941-russia-orders-alternate-internet-system.

[94] Afisha Daily, "Альтернативный интернет из России: что это такое и чем он нам грозит," November 30, 2017, https://daily.afisha.ru/technology/7543-alternativnyy-internet-iz-rossii-chto-eto-takoe-i-chem-on-nam-grozit.

[95] Ibid.: "В протоколе заседания Совета безопасности [. . .] говорится, что у «западных стран» появилась возможности устраивать кибератаки и вести информационные войны. Это угрожает безопасности России. На заседании решили, что интернетом сегодня управляют США и некоторые европ ейские страны."

regulation is carried out at the level of the people closest to the citizen, unless there are good reasons (global need for harmonization, necessity of universal technical solutions) that global rules are preferable. The disadvantage of subsidiary standardization, of course, lies in the promotion of different normative approaches that can only be reconciled with effort. This contradicts the global, interoperational nature of information and communication technologies that are just crossing borders. Therefore, and to avoid substantial fractures, a strong responsive component must always be implemented in orders incorporating the subsidiarity principle.[96]

4.2.3.4 Territoriality and Reterritorialization

Fractures have appeared in the internet's order in relation to those actors favoring territory-based solutions and those relying on a normative approach *sans* géographie. (Re)territorialization (the attempt to tie the internet, its servers, data flows, or users to a specific country) is a fracturing force in the online order.

Critics of state-focused approaches to law and governance of the internet question the effectiveness of central regulation in comparison to decentralized, naturally developing private legal regimes.[97] But states can regulate the internet with great effect.[98] A study on the effect of the German *Grundgesetz* on the internet diagnoses few deficits in the legal and constitutional framework, as long as the facts are "purely national."[99] The constitutional system of values was "incorporated into the social-ethical principles of German society" so that rule of law and peaceful relations between individuals (*Rechtsfrieden*), both offline and online, are assured. As soon as cases, however, go beyond the borders of one state (in this case: Germany), fundamental rights positions become more difficult to ensure. In these cases (and they have become an important part in times of international communication flows) the individual "cannot rely on the state's guarantee of their fundamental rights."[100]

This is problematic because internet users cannot always distinguish between national constellations of facts and those transcending borders due to the ubiquity of the internet. How can users know which servers and which clouds[101] their data is stored on and retrieved from? How could they understand and predict how the data packets of an email find their way to the recipient? It is precisely the decentralization of the internet and the end user-to-end user conception that makes it difficult to geographically pinpoint actions and attribution of responsibilities to private and public actors.[102]

[96] Cf. Lars Viellechner, *Transnationalisierung des Rechts* (Weilerswist: Velbrück, 2013), 265 et seq.

[97] Gerd Winter, "Transnationale informelle Regulierung: Gestalt, Effekte und Rechtsstaatlichkeit," in Gralf-Peter Calliess (ed.), *Transnationales Recht. Stand und Perspektiven* (Tübingen: Mohr Siebeck, 2014), 95–112, (96).

[98] Cf. Kettemann (2015), 53 et seq.

[99] Utz Schliesky, Christian Hoffmann, Anika D. Luch, Sönke E. Schulz, and Kim Corinna Borchers, *Schutzpflichten und Drittwirkung im Internet. Das Grundgesetz im digitalen Zeitalter* (Baden-Baden: Nomos, 2014), 146.

[100] Ibid., 147.

[101] Notably, cloud-based storage solutions are not, as the notion of "cloud" would seem to indicate, without territorial anchor. Data has to be stored physically on servers in buildings.

[102] See David Bethlehem, "The End of Geography: The Changing Nature of the International System and the Challenge to International Law," EJIL 25 (2014) 1, 9–24. But see the critique of David S. Koller and Carl Landauer: David S. Koller, "The End of Geography: The Changing Nature of the International System and the Challenge to International Law: A Reply to Daniel Bethlehem" EJIL 25 (2014) 1, 25–9 and Carl Landauer, "The Ever-Ending Geography of International Law: The Changing Nature of the International System and the Challenge to International Law: A Reply to Daniel Bethlehem," EJIL 25 (2014) 1, 31–4.

Of course, this does not mean that territoriality becomes irrelevant as an international legal principle with regard to jurisdiction to prescribe and enforce on the internet.[103] Recall the commitment by the Group of Governmental Experts in its 2015 report to sovereignty: "State sovereignty and international norms and principles that flow from sovereignty apply to the conduct by States of ICT-related activities and to their jurisdiction over ICT infrastructure within their territory."[104] States continue to have jurisdiction over those parts of the internet, physical and non-kinetic, that are located within their territory. Only the options for action by the state (and thus also its obligations) are restricted.[105] Schliesky et al. correctly state that the "control capacity" of nation states is limited in times of globalization. They issue the apt warning that whoever benefits from "globalization, from the increasing interconnectedness of services based on ubiquity and independence from space and time constraints, must realize in return that they cannot claim protection of the state in the same way as in purely national situations."[106]

However, the fact that the nation-state cannot effectively safeguard all fundamental rights positions does not yet immunize the legal systems relevant to the internet against criticism. Though the fractures persist, there are concrete avenues of redress, including clarifying the reach of the obligation of states to ensure human rights (which encompasses third-party effects of fundamental rights) (via, e.g., the legal framework of the law on terms of service (here: §§ 307 et seq. of the German Civil Code (BGB))).

Can the territorialization fracture be overcome? The case can be made that some territorialization is a positive development. Local storage can lead to a higher level of protection of citizen data and is certainly needed in the area of public authority activities. However, duplicating commercial non-native services is not effective (at least not at a public expense) and would not be appropriate in view of the ubiquity of the internet.

4.2.3.5 Cyberwar

An important fracture in the international order of the internet lies in the approach to cyberwar. During the 2017 GGE discussions, states started to build on commitments from the 2013 and 2015 reports, especially with reference to the applicability of international law to the internet, the importance of the Charter, and key international legal principles, such as territorial sovereignty, non-intervention, and due diligence.[107] Recall that the 2015 report stated that the international community aspired to regulate the internet in a peaceful manner "for the common good of mankind":[108] "[t]he adherence by States to international law, in particular their Charter obligations, is an essential framework for their actions

[103] Just see Christian Walter, "Cyber Security als Herausforderung für das Völkerrecht," JZ 14/2015, 685–93 (691ff).

[104] GGE report (2015), para. 27.

[105] See the decision BVerfG, 16.12.1980 - 2 BvR 419/80, *Hess*, BVerfGE 55, 349 et seq. The German Federal Constitutional Court argues that involving other countries in factual constellations can lead to problems with ensuring fundamental rights, because "foreign policy and international law" might set limits to the process.

[106] Utz Schliesky, Christian Hoffmann, Anika D. Luch, Sönke E. Schulz, and Kim Corinna Borchers, *Schutzpflichten und Drittwirkung im Internet. Das Grundgesetz im digitalen Zeitalter* (Baden-Baden: Nomos, 2014), 181. "[W]er die Vorteile der Globalisierung, der zunehmenden Vernetzung, der auf Ubiquität sowie Raum- und Zeitunabhängigkeit basierenden Dienste nutzt, muss sich im Gegenzug vergegenwärtigen, dass er nicht in gleicher Weise Schutz des Staates beanspruchen kann wie in rein nationalen Sachverhalten" (translation by the author).

[107] GGE report (2015).

[108] Ibid., para. 28 (c).

in their use of ICTs and to promote an open, secure, stable, accessible and peaceful ICT environment."[109]

However, when it came to discussing the applicability of the UN Charter to the internet, in particular Chapter VII with its references to "use of force" (allowing for Chapter VII situation findings by the Security Council) and "armed attack" (triggering self-defense), states disagreed. Sovereignty-oriented states that were also criticized in the past for having condoned or even organized cyberattacks against foreign targets argued that applying the UN Charter's provisions regarding use of force to cyberspace before technical means of attribution delivered more reliable results would lead to the militarization of cyberspace.[110] This approach seems to be a backtracking exercise in light of international commitments, both in the WSIS documents and in the 2013 and 2015 GGE reports, which all included references to the applicability on the internet of the UN Charter, in fact "in particular the UN Charter." Though it should be noted that, already in the run-up to the 2015 report, China, Russia, Pakistan, Malaysia, and Belarus had opposed language favored by the US to include an *explicit* reference to Article 51 with its authorization of self-defense against armed attacks, the norm was contained implicitly in any case by reference to the UN Charter.[111]

4.2.3.6 Trust

An important fracture has opened in the realm of trust in internet integrity. States need to seriously address the issue of what action they can take quickly to restore confidence in the integrity of the internet, which has been substantially endangered through the revelations of pervasive data collection schemes by the Five Eyes states and their massive surveillance systems (*Snowden* revelations). In its proposal for a new social contract, the Global Commission on Internet Governance, a study group on the future of internet regulation, focused its efforts on linking privacy and security. States needed to act: to better safeguard privacy; to subject every surveillance to a strict necessity and proportionality test; to guarantee transparency in monitoring measures and legal remedies; to protect online data and to sensitize consumers; to raise confidence in big data solutions; to strengthen private communications; not to introduce backdoors to private data; to highlight good practices in the field of cybersecurity; and to work together against dangers emanating from cyberspace.[112]

In the aftermath of the Snowden revelations, the United Nations HRC expressed "serious concern" in its recent resolution on the right to privacy in the digital age because of the "negative impact that surveillance and/or interception of communications, including extraterritorial surveillance and/or interception of communications, as well as the collection of

[109] Ibid., para. 25.

[110] Cf. Adam Segal, "The Development of Cyber Norms at the United Nations Ends in Deadlock. Now What?" *Council on Foreign Relations*, June 29, 2017, https://www.cfr.org/blog/development-cyber-norms-united-nations-ends-deadlock-now-what; Arun M. Sukumar, "The UN GGE Failed. Is International Law in Cyberspace Doomed As Well?," *Lawfare*, July 4, 2017, https://lawfareblog.com/un-gge-failed-international-law-cyberspace-doomed-well; and Ann Väljataga, "Back to Square One? The Fifth UN GGE Fails to Submit a Conclusive Report at the UN General Assembly," NATO CCDCOE Incyder database, https://ccdcoe.org/back-square-one-fifth-un-gge-submit-conclusive-report-un-general-assembly.html.

[111] Eneken Tikk and Mika Kerttunen, "The Alleged Demise of the UN GGE: An Autopsy and Eulogy," Cyber Policy Institute (2017), http://cpi.ee/wp-content/uploads/2017/12/2017-Tikk-Kerttunen-Demise-of-the-UN-GGE-2017-12-17-ET.pdf.

[112] Statement by the Global Commission on Internet Governance, Toward a Social Compact for Digital Privacy and Security, Wednesday, April 15, 2015, https://www.ourinternet.org/publication/toward-a-social-compact-for-digital-privacy-and-security.

personal data, in particular when carried out on a mass scale, may have on the exercise and enjoyment of human rights."[113] The internet as such needs to be protected and we need protection from dangers through misuse of the internet.

The necessary protection must be oriented toward the structure of the system. This is a point that had already been made in 2008 by the German *Bundesverfassungsgericht* (BVerfG),[114] which developed a new fundamental right to fill the protective gap left by fundamental rights regarding the integrity of information systems. The Court found that the "general right of personality" manifested itself also as a "fundamental right to the guarantee of the integrity and confidentiality of information technology systems." Interferences with this right may be justified for preventive purposes or for criminal prosecution but must be based on law that is constitutional and proportionate. Therefore any secret infiltration of an information technology system needs to meet strict criteria, including indications of concrete danger for a legal value of paramount importance, such as the body, life, and freedom of the person or goods of the general public that, when threatened, impact the foundations or the existence of the state or the foundations of human existence.[115] The Court did not, however, develop this right further in its jurisprudence.

The Snowden revelations have "chilling effects" on the use of the internet and our understanding of the internet as a technology to bring about positive social change toward an information society based on human rights.[116] The social costs of mass surveillance are far higher than their returns. The weakening of encryption standards or the coded opening of backdoors for government agencies, especially, can have negative consequences for national security. The European Parliament's Schaake report, adopted in September 2015, underlines the importance of privacy encryption technologies, including the right to encryption and the introduction of end-to-end encryption standards for all communications.[117]

Democratic societies have long been threatened by espionage and terrorism.[118] Already in 1978, the ECtHR ruled in *Klass and others v. Germany* that the "existence of some legislation granting powers of secret surveillance over the mail, post and telecommunications is, under exceptional conditions, necessary in a democratic society in the interests of national security and/or for the prevention of disorder or crime."[119] However, this does not mean that states could ignore human rights or be completely free in the choice of their means and the intensity of surveillance: aware that such laws contain the danger "[of] undermining or even destroying democracy on the ground of defending it 'states could not do what they wanted' in the name of the struggle against espionage and terrorism."[120] In *Shimovolos v. Russia*, the Court underscored the necessity of "detailed rules on the application of secret

[113] Human Rights Council, Resolution 28/16, The Right to Privacy in the Digital Age, A/HRC/RES/28/16 of 1 April 2015.

[114] BVerfG, judgment of the First Senate of February 27, 2008, 1 BvR 370/07, BVerfGE 120, 274–350 ("Das allgemeine Persönlichkeitsrecht (Art. 2 Abs. 1 i.V.m. Art. 1 Abs. 1 GG) umfasst das Grundrecht auf Gewährleistung der Vertraulichkeit und Integrität informationstechnischer Systeme.")

[115] Ibid.

[116] European Parliament, Report on human rights and technology: the impact of intrusion and surveillance systems on human rights in third countries (2014/2232(INI)), Committee on Foreign Affairs Rapporteur: Marietje Schaake, June 3, 2015, para. 3.

[117] Ibid., paras. 61–2.

[118] Tom Sorell and John Guelke, "Liberal Democratic Regulation and Technological Advance," in Roger Brownsword, Eloise Scotford, and Karen Yeung (eds.), *Oxford Handbook of Law, Regulation, and Technology* (Oxford: OUP, 2017), 90–112.

[119] ECtHR, *Klass and Others v. Germany*, no. 5029/71 of September 6, 1978, para. 48.

[120] Ibid., para. 49.

measures of surveillance, especially as the technology available for use is continually becoming more sophisticated."[121]

In order to strengthen the protection of privacy on the internet, states must align their national laws and policies with their human rights obligations under the ECHR and ICCPR (and relevant European primary law and, in particular, the Charter of Fundamental Rights), as interpreted by the ECtHR, Human Rights Committee, and European Court of Justice (ECJ), respectively. Normative measures to remedy gaps must be developed in the context of easily accessible, open, societal discussion processes. Any law that enables data collection must be measured against recognized human rights criteria (such as specificity and purpose). The conditions under which collected data may be searched by means of selectors must be discussed publicly. Selectors must be published to ensure non-discriminatory application. The use of selectors that can be assigned to specific persons must pass even higher protective barriers.

Democratic control of security and intelligence services is important for the protection of human rights and the rule of law. The Council of Europe Commissioner for Human Rights recommends that a national dialog be held on ways to ensure the control of law.[122] Similar demands are formulated by the Venice Commission of the Council of Europe.[123] To sum up, the protection of the right to privacy is central to the further development of a development-oriented and human-centered information society. A lack of trust in a protected private sphere undermines the central participatory rights in the information society with the freedom of communication. The right to privacy creates the freedom to exercise all other rights. The historic struggle for a state-free sphere of the private sphere, which has historically been central to the development of human rights, must be placed at the center of efforts to protect human rights on the internet in order to extend the right to an "entrepreneurial" sphere.

In more detail, the principles that should be applied to a human rights-sensitive surveillance of internet communication have been laid out in the International Principles on the Application of Human Rights to Communications Surveillance (May 2014).[124] These in turn show what normative potential non-state actors could have as standard aggregators and standards promoters.

The central regulatory objective of international law must be to guarantee the integrity of the internet as a resource in the global public interest and to protect global society from dangers emanating from the (mis)use of the internet. In the words of the 2015 GGE report, "[a]n open, secure, stable, accessible and peaceful ICT environment is essential for all [..] to reduce risks to international peace and security. [. . .] ICTs provide immense opportunities

[121] ECtHR, *Shimovolos v. Russia*, judgment of January 28, 2011, application no. 30194/09, para. 68.

[122] Council of Europe, Commissioner for Human Rights, Democratic and Effective Oversight of National Security Services (May 2015), https://book.coe.int/en/commissioner-for-human-rights/6682-pdf-democratic-and-effective-oversight-of-national-security-services.html, para. 18.

[123] European Commission for Democracy through Law (Venice Commission), Update of the 2007 Report on the Democratic Oversight of the Security Services and Report on the Democratic Oversight of Signals Intelligence Agencies, adopted by the Venice Commission at its 102nd Plenary Session (March 20–21, 2015), http://www.coe.int/t/dghl/standardsetting/media/Conf-FoE-2015/Venice%20Commission_Study%20No%20719_2013.pdf, Study No. 719/2013, CDL-AD(2015)006.

[124] International Principles on the Application of Human Rights to Communications Surveillance, Final Version (May 2014), https://necessaryandproportionate.org/text.

for social and economic development and continue to grow in importance for the international community."[125]

Many aspects of societal life are globally networked in the sense that their premises or conditions, under which situations are justified, contested, changed, and justified again, are influenced by international law. Therefore, even in primarily national cases, effective protection of fundamental rights is supported by appropriate protection through international law.[126] However, this does not mean that new rules have to be passed. Proposals such as those of Joseph Cannataci, the newly appointed Special Rapporteur on the right to privacy (a new "Geneva Convention" on the protection of data and the prevention of massive internet communications surveillance)[127] and that of German Chancellor Angela Merkel (calling for a "Global Privacy Agreement Modeled on the Kyoto Protocol for climate protection") may be useful but are not viable.[128] There are already sufficient standards that limit the surveillance power of states, but these need to be better implemented.

Discussions about a fundamental right to encryption, which have been given an impetus in view of the German pioneering position by the fundamental right to IT security,[129] must be accelerated and led internationally. A right to encryption is an outflow of the right to privacy.[130] In view of the systemic monitoring of internet communication, a fundamental right both to encryption and to the choice of the encryption method is important: as a kind of "right of digital self-defense."[131] The knowledge of being able to communicate in a protected manner can increase the interest in participation in the internet's normative processes. States must—in the negative effect of the right to encryption—not try to incorporate "back doors" in encryption technologies or dissuade citizens from their use. Special access to states should not be allowed without compelling reasons: "It is a seemingly universal position among technologists that there is no special access that can be made available only to government authorities […]. In the contemporary technological environment, intentionally compromising encryption, even for arguably legitimate purposes, weakens everyone's security online."[132]

The protection of encryption technology and its increased use are important safeguards for privacy and with it the precondition for exercising freedom of expression. Both are thus important foundations for the realization of democratic participation perspectives.

[125] GGE report 2015, paras. 2–3.

[126] See Wolfgang Hoffmann-Riem, "Freiheitsschutz in den globalen Kommunikationsinfrastrukturen," JZ 69 (2014) 2, 53–63, (62).

[127] Adam Alexander, "Digital Surveillance 'Worse Than Orwell', Says New UN Privacy Chief," *The Guardian*, August 24, 2015, http://www.theguardian.com/world/2015/aug/24/we-need-geneva-convention-for-the-internet-says-new-un-privacy-chief ("British surveillance oversight [is] 'a joke'; […] the situation is worse than anything George Orwell could have foreseen").

[128] FAZ, "Spähaffäre: Merkel regt globales Datenschutz-Abkommen an," July 20, 2015 http://www.faz.net/aktuell/politik/spaehaffaere-merkel-regt-globales-datenschutz-abkommen-an-12288963.html.

[129] Julia Gerhards, *(Grund-)Recht auf Verschlüsselung?* (Frankfurt am Main: Nomos, 2010).

[130] Report of the Special Rapporteur on the promotion and protection of the right to freedom of opinion and expression, David Kaye, A/HRC/29/32 of 22 May 2015, http://www.ohchr.org/EN, passim and especially para. 5: "Encryption and anonymity, separately or together, create a zone of privacy to protect opinion and belief."

[131] Andreas Fischer-Lescano, "Der Kampf um die Internetverfassung. Rechtsfragen des Schutzes globaler Kommunikationsstrukturen vor Überwachungsmaßnahmen," JZ 20 (2014), 965–74 (974).

[132] Report of the Special Rapporteur on the promotion and protection of the right to freedom of opinion and expression, David Kaye, A/HRC/29/32 of 22 May 2015, http://www.ohchr.org/EN, para. 8.

4.2.3.7 Regime Deficiencies

Another fracture in the broader sense can be diagnosed when it comes to regime deficiencies. Every legal system is in flux and constantly adapt to new circumstances. For example, changing conceptions of social morality create incremental pressure for norms to evolve. The formation of social will and the legal order are therefore communicating vessels with a delaying factor.[133] The decisive question is therefore in which way the regime is deficient and what the comparative vector is: a possible alternative regime or an ideal legal system?

In the case of the online order, the only meaningful answer can be: deficient in comparison to a legal system designed to meet the objectives of the international community for the information society. Legislative deficits therefore exist in regulation and implementation when the normative order of the internet does not reach these goals legitimately and effectively. Simply put, a normative order that contains fractures is deficient.

The concept of the unity of the legal system in the sense of the exclusive validity of laws legitimized by the people (and no norms beyond that) is a fiction.[134] The legality (but perhaps not the rule of law[135]) paradigm created with the modern constitutional state is challenged by globalization and the relativization of territoriality by information and communication technologies.[136] That does not mean that the state ceases to matter: "Virtual space does not mean [...] the end of the sovereign constitutional state."[137] The state—through the legislature, the executive, and above all the judiciary—must remember its central functions and protect its citizens, without violating their rights, in an increasingly challenging "regulatory mosaic."[138] Another complicating factor is the emergence on the internet of spontaneous, decentralized, private legal regimes in which neither traditional nor charismatic and not even regularly rationally legitimated actors and institutions exercise international public authority.[139] In view of the large number of actors involved and the decreasing relevance of borders on the internet, it is also a challenge to identify the "appropriate" normative level—global, regional, national—for standardizing certain internet-related issues. In fact, not one level is regularly affected, and all three levels could legitimately be subject to a standardization interest. This is illustrated by the example of the local storage requirement for user data.[140]

[133] When courts are too quick for changing social mores, social unrest can be the result. Cf. Matthias C. Kettemann, "How to Implement Controversial Court Decisions: International Constitutional Lessons from Brown v. Board of Education for the Austrian Cases on Topographical Signs in Carinthia," Vienna Online Journal on International Constitutional Law 4 (2010) 4, 590–623.

[134] Klaus Günther, "Normativer Rechtspluralismus—Eine Kritik," Normative Orders Working Paper 3/2014 (2014), http://publikationen.ub.uni-frankfurt.de/files/34664/Guenther_Normativer+Rechtspluralismus.pdf, 1.

[135] Cf. Armin von Bogdandy, "Prinzipien von Staat, supranationalen und internationalen Organisationen," § 232 (275–304), in Josef Isensee, Paul Kirchhof, et al. (eds.), *Handbuch des Staatsrechts, Band XI: Internationale Bezüge*, 3rd edn. (2013) (also published as Armin von Bogdandy, "Prinzipielles zur Pluralität normativer Ordnungen. Zu den Anforderungen an die Ausübung öffentlicher Gewalt," Normative Orders Working Paper 1/2013), 12.

[136] Lars Viellechner, *Transnationalisierung des Rechts* (Weilerswist: Velbrück, 2013), 99.

[137] Hobe, Stephan, "Cyberspace—der virtuelle Raum," in Josef Isensee, Paul Kirchhof, et al. (eds.), *Handbuch des Staatsrechts, Band XI: Internationale Bezüge*, 3rd edn. (2013), § 271, Rn. 44.

[138] Wolfgang Hoffmann-Riem, "Freiheitsschutz in den globalen Kommunikationsinfrastrukturen," 69 JZ 2/2014, 53–63 (63).

[139] Matthias Goldmann, *Internationale öffentliche Gewalt. Handlungsformen internationalen Institutionen im Zeitalter der Globalisierung* (Heidelberg: Springer, 2015).

[140] There are similar duties in other jurisdictions. Australian law limits the export of health-related data; South Korea demands that geographical data be stored locally. Vietnam forces companies to have a local backup copy of its data. See, critically, Anupam Chander and Uyen P. Le, "Breaking the Web: Data Localization vs. the Global Internet," UC Davis Legal Studies Research Paper Series No. 378 (April 2014), 1: "Data localization requirements threaten the major new advances in information technology—not only cloud computing, but also the promise of big data and the Internet of Things."

On September 1, 2015, a new Russian law came into force, which includes a data localization rule: data related to Russian citizens must be stored on servers in Russia. The Russian Data Protection Agency, *Roskomnadzor*, needs to be informed where the data is physically located.[141] Here, state law seems to supplant international legal protection of free internet communication and the freedom of the internet as a global communication infrastructure.[142]

At the European level, in the *Schrems* case, the CJEU stated that the level of data protection in other states must be "reasonable" (i.e. "equal in substance" to the Union if a transfer of European users' data were to be allowed). Equivalence is subsequently substantiated by the CJEU with reference to European data protection law (emphasizing at the same time that the level of protection need not be *identical*).[143] In doing so, the CJEU continued its expansive data protection jurisprudence, setting uniform ("adequate") protection standards for "European" data, whether in Europe or as an export. If this ensures a comprehensive, multidimensional protection of fundamental rights, however, it is urgent to fill the gap with rules. The data protection principles and the high standard of protection used by the CJEU cannot be directly applied to national situations (see Art. 51 (1) GRC). Furthermore, there is no basis in European law for the assessment of member states' data access regulations, such as the German "Article 10 Law," regarding their respective conformity with fundamental rights.

This is a contradiction that needs to be resolved if the EU wants to remain credible as an advocate of high data protection standards. Together with the consequences of the verdict at that time for the negotiations on international treaties touching upon the protection of data in international trade, this example shows the connectedness of legal systems and the dangers of allowing fractures to persist. If fractures are strong enough, they can, alone or in aggregate, develop forces leading to fragmentation.

4.3 Fragmentation

4.3.1 Forces of Fragmentation

Given the different character of norms present in the regulation of the internet, both legal norms and governance-related norms, the lack of a hierarchical normative structure specific to the internet leads to a situation of normative flux.[144] The relationship between norms on the internet needs to be judged according to criteria that are not immediately obvious, as they are in Kelsenian-style national systems of hierarchically ordered norms. Apart from certain key norms, such as the principle of sovereignty, the position of most more-detailed norms within the normative order of the internet (which this study will present in detail in

[141] Michael Malloy and Pavel Arievich, "Russia's Data Localization Requirement Will Take Effect September 1," Data Protection, Privacy and Security Alert (US), July 8, 2015, https://www.dlapiper.com/en/us/insights/publiccations/2015/07/russia-data-localization-requirement.

[142] Critically, Daniel Joyce, "Internet Freedom and Human Rights," EJIL 26 (2015) 2, 493–514. See also on data localization as an aspect of governmental fragmentation, 4.3.

[143] CJEU, C-362/14, *Schrems v. Data Protection Commissioner*, judgment of October 6, 2015.

[144] Kevin Werbach, "The Centripetal Network: How the Internet Holds Itself Together, and the Forces Tearing It Apart," University of California, Davis Law Review (2008) 42, 343–412 (seeing multidimensional "balkanization" trends).

chapter 6) has to be negotiated and is tied to the narrative(s) that inhabits the nomos (as the "norm-total" of the internet) and depends inter alia on the consistency of the norm with other norms of the order and the consonancy of the norm with the purpose of the order.

This is a key difference between the norms pertaining to the internet and general norms of international law (or of national law). Both are, whether in a naturalist or a positivist analysis, firmly placed within a hierarchical system of admittedly various complexities.[145] Hierarchies have advantages. They decomplexify relations between norms and actors. They enable the foreseeable production of norms within the system and their contestation. Norms can be overruled (or at least delegitimized) by contrary higher norms. Within the normative order of the internet, however, production and contestation take place in a more flexible and much less predictable way. Already this allows the preliminary conclusion that the online order is more likely to fragment than national legal systems.

In the previous section, this study presented selected examples of normative froth, friction, and fractures. This section discusses the question whether or not fragmentation of the online order has taken place or is taking place and what evidence is marshaled for such fragmentation in the interconnected economic, technical, and legal dimensions. If fragmentation is perceived within the online order, arguments for the establishment of a normative order of the internet are imbued with greater urgency, given the common interests at stake in the protection of and from the internet.

Just as societal cohesion is impacted by technological advancements, technology-related regulation itself is prone to fragmentation.[146] In a study of regulatory approaches in the time of the Industrial Revolution, Miloš Vec identified a "fragmentation of the normative" that was caused by two main factors: that experts did not yet know enough about the technology to be regulated and the impetus not to normatively frame too early (and thus limit) technical-scientific developments.[147] Both factors are present in the normative instruments pertaining to the protection of the internet and relevant for the protection of the international community and its members from the internet. However, the internet today is much more regulated than technology in the industrial revolution[148] and fragmentation has to be discussed on a technological, political, and legal-diplomatic level.

Fragmentation is present in many societal sectors relevant under a public law perspective.[149] Indra Spiecker gen. Döhmann identifies digitalization (alongside globalization) as a key driver of (societal and legal) fragmentation.[150] She points to the changing role of internet intermediaries as agents of fragmentation based on distinction inferable from the

[145] See Martti Koskenniemi, "Hierarchy in International Law: A Sketch," EJIL 8 (1997), 571–2.

[146] On the role of technology in societal processes of order and regulation, see Christian Katzenbach, *Die Regeln digitaler Kommunikation: Governance zwischen Norm, Diskurs und Technik* (Berlin: Springer VS, 2017), 236–53.

[147] Cf. Miloš Vec, *Recht und Normierung in der Industriellen Revolution: neue Strukturen der Normsetzung in Völkerrecht, staatlicher Gesetzgebung und gesellschaftlicher Selbstnormierung* (Frankfurt am Main: Klostermann, 2006), 206.

[148] But see instructively on nuanced regulated self-regulation in the late eighteenth and early nineteenth century, Peter Collin, *Privat-staatliche Regelungsstrukturen im Frühen Industrie- und Sozialstaat* (Berlin/Boston: De Gruyter, 2016) (showing, for example, how "verbandsinterne technische Standards" developed "Bindungswirkung" through "staatliche Aufwertungsakte," 114).

[149] Cf. the contributions by Indra Spiecker gen. Döhmann, Stefan Magen, Andreas Kley, Stephan Kirste, Stefan Griller, Uwe Kischel, Olivier Jouanjan, and Franz Reimer on *Fragmentierungen* (fragmentations) in public international and national public law, constitutional and administrative law, in VVDStRL 77 (2018).

[150] Indra Spiecker gen. Döhmann, "Kontexte der Demokratie: Parteien—Medien—Sozialstrukturen," VVDStRL 77 (2018), 9–56 (36).

data collected to the detriment of a mediated public sphere with a common discourse base.[151]

Fragmentation is also an important conceptual concern for the international legal order, as it contradicts the premise of international law's universality.[152] The 2006 International Law Commission's (ILC) report on fragmentation of international law already pointed to the "deepening complexity of late modern societies, tolerance and encouragement of conflicting traditions and social objectives within national societies, and the needs of technical specialization" that have, in aggregate, "undermined [...] the homogeneity of the nation-State" with the law of late modern states today, emerging from "several quasi-autonomous normative sources, both internal and external." This has destabilized the coherence of national law based on the constitution, but has been mostly counterbalanced by the "contextual responsiveness and functionality of the emerging (moderate) pluralism."[153] Within international law, however, no single central "constitutional" order ensuring responsiveness and implementing pluralism exists: "*no homogenous, hierarchical meta-system is realistically available to do away with such problems.*"[154] With demands of coherence and universality, on the one hand, and pluralism, on the other, pulling international law in different directions, the consideration of regime collisions and of collision regimes (regimes dealing with the collision of regimes, including conflict-of-laws regimes) becomes increasingly important.

Fragmentation is thus not a surprising development in complexifying normative orders (especially) without a strong constitutional center, such as international law, and even more so the online order. It can take different characters: actual or potential, intentional or unintended, deep and structural or superficial, and positive, negative, or neutral with a view to universality.[155] While the internet's technical premise is interconnection through shared protocols, recent times have seen the (re)emergence of proprietary systems, especially in connection with the internet of things (IoT) and in relation to the mobile internet where apps that are often platform-specific mediate the online experience.[156]

In aggregate, there are substantial challenges to the universality of the internet that have affected the development of the internet measurably.[157] Together with normative froth, frictions, and fractures identified earlier, important normative forces are pulling the internet into diverging directions. But is fragmentation fatal to the theories of online order, presented in chapter 5, and the prospect, explained in more detail in chapter 6, of a coherent normative order of the internet that is based, inter alia, on its universality and integrity?

[151] Ibid.

[152] Alfred Verdross and Bruno Simma, *Universelles Völkerrecht. Theorie und Praxis* (reprint of the 3rd edn.) (Berlin: Duncker & Humblot, 1984/2010).

[153] ILC, Fragmentation of International Law: Difficulties arising from the Diversification and Expansion of International Law, Report of the Study Group of the International Law Commission, 13 April 2006, A/CN.4/L.682, para. 493.

[154] Ibid. (emphasis in the original).

[155] Cf. William J. Drake, Vinton G. Cerf, and Wolfgang Kleinwächter, "Internet Fragmentation: An Overview," World Economic Forum, Future of the Internet Initiative White Paper, January 2016, 4.

[156] Ibid., 3.

[157] Sarah Box, "Openness and Fragmentation: Toward Measuring the Economic Effects," GCIG Papers Series No. 36 (2016), http://www.cigionline.org/publications/internet-openness-and-fragmentation-toward-measuringeconomic-effects.

While this is not the case, fragmentation tendencies teach us a lot about existing challenges to the normative status quo.

Before considering the dimensions of fragmentation, let us assess universality-oriented forces within the "layers" of the internet (see table 4.6). Depending on the technological focus, there are usually four of them, ranging from the physical infrastructure and logical resources (including IP addresses) (with a third transport layer sometimes included, sometimes differentiated from the logical resources) to application(s) and content/transactions (data). A legal layer (national law, international law) can be added specifically, but is sometimes integrated into other layers.

On the physical layer, the conclusion is easy that the internet is not yet universal, as half the world's population still has no internet access. Even those users that have access have different online experiences, given diverging bandwidth strength and "last mile" connection technology (in extremis: modem vs. fiber). Further, not more than half of the world's countries have major Internet Exchange Points (IXPs), which serve as interconnectors of the networks and ensure quick data traffic throughput.[158]

On the network/logical resources layer we find that the transition to newer, longer domain names (necessary for the growing need for IP addresses in the internet of things) has not yet been completely implemented. Currently, the address space is non-uniform as addresses based on IPv4 (shorter addresses) coexist with the 128 bits long IPv6 addresses (of which 2^{128} are possible). Even given this non-uniformity on both the physical layer and the network layer, fragmentation tendencies do not seem to be strongly present. Yet at the application and content layers (or application, content, and transaction layers), fragmentation can be observed. These fragmentation tendencies can be mapped onto three connected dominions of internet regulation: technological fragmentation, commercial fragmentation, and politics/law-driven fragmentation.[159] Selected types or classes of fragmentation can be seen in table 4.7.

Table 4.6 Internet Layers

DeNardis (2016)[a]	Drake/Cerf/Kleinwächter (2016)[b]
1. Physical Infrastructure Layer	1. Physical/Link Layer
2. Logical Resources Layer	2. Network/IP Layer
integrated in (2)	3. Transport Layer
3. Application and Content Layer	4. Application Layer
integrated in (3)	5. Content and Transactions Layer
4. Legal Layer	*integrated passim, especially in (5)*

[a] Laura DeNardis, "One Internet: An Evidentiary Basis for Policy Making on Internet Universality and Fragmentation," CIGI/Chatham House, Global Commission on Internet Governance Paper Series No. 38 (2016), 4.

[b] William J. Drake, Vinton G. Cerf, and Wolfgang Kleinwächter, "Internet Fragmentation: An Overview," *World Economic Forum*, Future of the Internet Initiative White Paper, January 2016, 14.

[158] Cf. Laura DeNardis, "One Internet: An Evidentiary Basis for Policy Making on Internet Universality and Fragmentation," CIGI/Chatham House, Global Commission on Internet Governance Paper Series No. 38 (2016), 4 et seq.

[159] William J. Drake, Vinton G. Cerf, and Wolfgang Kleinwächter, "Internet Fragmentation: An Overview," World Economic Forum, Future of the Internet Initiative White Paper, January 2016, 14–16 and 20 et seq.

Table 4.7 Selected Types of Fragmentation[a]

Fragmentation	Character
Network address translation failures	Technical
IPv4 and IPv6 incompatibility and the dual-stack requirement	Technical
Routing corruption	Technical
Firewall protections	Technical
Virtual private network isolation and blocking	Technical
The Onion Router (TOR) server network and the "dark web"	Technical
Technical errors with the Internationalized Domain Name System	Technical
Blocking of new gTLDs	Technical
Private name servers and the split-horizon DNS	Technical
Segmented Wi-Fi services in private/public spaces	Technical
Significant alternate DNS roots	Technical
Certificate authorities producing false certificates	Technical
Potential changes in interconnection agreements	Commercial
Proprietary technical standards impeding interoperability in the IoT	Commercial
Discriminatory departures from network neutrality	Commercial
Walled gardens	Commercial
Geo-blocking of content	Commercial
Content blocks for the purpose of IP protection	Commercial
Filtering and blocking websites/services	Governmental
Attacks on information resources offering undesired contents	Governmental
Digital protectionism	Governmental
Centralizing and terminating international interconnection	Governmental
Attacks on national networks and key assets	Governmental
Local data processing and/or retention requirements	Governmental
Architectural or routing changes to keep data flows within a territory	Governmental
Prohibitions on the transborder movement of certain categories of data	Governmental
Strategies for "national internet segments" or "cybersovereignty"	Governmental
International frameworks intended to legitimize restrictive practices	Governmental

[a] Adapted from Laura DeNardis, "One Internet: An Evidentiary Basis for Policy Making on Internet Universality and Fragmentation," CIGI/Chatham House, Global Commission on Internet Governance Paper Series No. 38 (2016), 4–6.

4.3.2 Technical Fragmentation

Technical fragmentation relates to impediments to the full interoperability of the underlying internet infrastructure.[160] Apart from the fragmentation produced by the migration from the IPv4 to the IPv6 address space, as just discussed, a possible source of technical fragmentation is the corruption of global routing data by the border routers of each autonomous system (network). Firewalls can be used to "fragment" the internet, but do so in a positive way, as they shield, for instance, children from certain content. They can, however, be misused by states and repurposed as censorship tools. Virtual private networks (VPNs), The Onion Router (TOR) server network, and "dark web" users are consciously decoupling from the global internet, thus supporting its fragmentation.

If Internationalized Domain Names (IDNs), such as domain names in Cyrillic[161] or Arabic[162] script, are not implemented correctly, technical fragmentation may occur.[163] Similarly, the prevalence of new gTLDs, including controversial ones such as .xxx,[164] may incentivize technical blocking and thus fragmentation. Coerced DNS lookups, usually used by Wi-Fi networks in airports, hotels, and public spaces, are also a form of fragmentation as the DNS lookup (the query to resolve, e.g., www.spiegel.de) is redirected to the log-in site. A more serious threat to internet universality lies in the (remote) possibility of a significant alternate DNS root.[165]

4.3.3 Commercial Fragmentation

Commercial fragmentation refers to business practices constraining or preventing internet universality. Companies, for instance, have incentives to organize markets and spaces in a way that favor their business practices, thus contributing to fragmented online spaces. They have further incentives to "lock in" customers to their commercial software, based on the belief that their software will become the "de facto standard."[166] This trend seems particularly prevalent in the relatively newly emerged internet of things, which still has few globally accepted interoperability standards, thus motivating companies to use siloed approaches.

Unlike services such as the World Wide Web, a number of mobile applications allow users to interact (and extract their data) only via APIs, application programming interfaces, that are based on proprietary software, thus allowing interconnections and universal

160 Cf. Ibid., 4.

161 With the Cyrillic country code TLD ".рф" only accepting Cyricllic subdomain applications. Cf. Stéphane Van Gelder, "The Rise of Cyrillic Domain Names," *CircleID*, June 3, 2013, http://www.circleid.com/posts/20130603_the_rise_of_cyrillic_domain_names.

162 Cf., for instance, Saudi Network Information Center, Guideline Rules for Writing Arabic IDNs under the IDN ccTLD (.2010) (السعودية), http://www.nic.sa/en/view/writing_arabic_idn_guideline.

163 Considering the multitude of IDNs, this is not trivial. Currently, the following internationalized ccTLD exist: .中国 and .中國 (Zhōngguó, China), .مصر (maṣr, Egypt), .한국 (hangūk,̕ South Korea), .香港 (Hongkong), .ايران (īrān, Iran), .الاردن (al-urdunn, Jordan), .فلسطين (filasṭīn, Palestine), .рф (RF, Russia), .السعودية (as-saʿūdīya, Saudi Arabia), .台灣 and .台湾 (Taiwan), .تونس (tūnis, Tunisia), .امارات (imārāt, UAE).

164 See 3.4.6.

165 This section is based onWilliam J. Drake, Vinton G. Cerf, and Wolfgang Kleinwächter, "Internet Fragmentation: An Overview," World Economic Forum, Future of the Internet Initiative White Paper, January 2016, 20 et seq.

166 Patrik Fältström, "Market-Driven Challenges to Open Internet Standards," GCIG Papers Series No. 33 (2016), http://www.cigionline.org/publications/marketdriven-challenges-open-internet-standards, 7.

sharing only under the conditions of the companies' terms of service. Today, a lot of data is tied to certain platforms or operating systems and needs "curation and mediation" by the platform in order to be communicated, if at all, outside and shared. Sometimes the reasons are based on security, such as with certain financial applications,[167] but the majority of non-interoperability decisions are based on market strategy.[168]

Companies have also introduced products and followed strategies that run counter to the idea of universal access by creating "digital enclosures." When entering emerging markets, some internet companies, including Facebook, have used an approach called "zero-rating," which allows free (or very cheap) access to a fraction of the internet, namely through the service of the company offering "free" access. Users cannot enter the internet proper through a browser, but can only navigate within an application or service, such as Facebook, and use the "parts" of the internet included by the company within its service.

Similarly, companies attempt to bind customers ever closer to their services by attractivizing staying within their "walled gardens,"[169] where it is not the open web that is used as a platform to convey content but rather semi-closed or closed platforms (or apps) running on de facto non-negotiable terms of service. The higher the investment of a person in the creation and curation of their "digital persona" (with friends, chat histories, pictures), the more difficult will it be (in terms of individual psychology) to leave the platform (as there are, currently, few portability rights for data/content running on proprietary software, unlike cross-border streaming services[170]). But having a "growing share of digital life retreat behind companies' walled gardens"[171], within algorithmically constructed "filter bubbles,"[172] runs counter to the internet's role as, recalling the ECtHR in *Cengiz*, "one of the principal means by which individuals exercise their right to freedom to receive and impart information and ideas."[173]

Selected companies have also practically engaged in, and supported as matter of policy, non-neutral treatment of internet content, in violation of the principle of network neutrality. If they depart in discriminatory ways from the principle or attempt to disadvantage users seeking to access services from other internet service providers, companies can de facto fragment the internet in the form of the mediated user experience.[174]

Further commercial fragmentation is caused by the use of geo-targeting—allowing companies to make increasingly detailed choices about what to offer users based on geographical location—and geo-blocking of content. Geo-blocking requirements may be imposed

[167] James Kaplan and Kayvaun Rowshankish, "Addressing the Impact of Data Location Regulation in Financial Services," GCIG Paper Series No. 14 (2015), http://www.ourinternet.org/publication/addressing-the-impact-ofdata-location-regulation-in-financial-services.

[168] Cf. Laura DeNardis, "One Internet: An Evidentiary Basis for Policy Making on Internet Universality and Fragmentation," CIGI/Chatham House, Global Commission on Internet Governance Paper Series No. 38 (2016), 5.

[169] Ibid., 2.

[170] Regulation (EU) 2017/1128 of the European Parliament and of the Council of 14 June 2017 on cross-border portability of online content services in the internal market, OJ L 168, 30 June 2017, 1–11.

[171] William J. Drake, Vinton G. Cerf, and Wolfgang Kleinwächter, "Internet Fragmentation: An Overview," World Economic Forum, Future of the Internet Initiative White Paper, January 2016, 56.

[172] Eli Pariser, *The Filter Bubble: How the New Personalized Web Is Changing What We Read and How We Think* (New York: Penguin, 2012).

[173] ECtHR, *Cengiz and Others v. Turkey*, judgment of December 1, 2015, application nos. 48226/10 and 14027/11, paras. 49 and 52.

[174] William J. Drake, Vinton G. Cerf, and Wolfgang Kleinwächter, "Internet Fragmentation: An Overview," World Economic Forum, Future of the Internet Initiative White Paper, January 2016, 53.

by companies because of national legislation or global (especially intellectual property-related) rights management issues. But it can also be unjustified, as the EU Commission found in adopting legislative instruments to end geo-blocking by 2018 for all sales of goods without physical delivery, sale of electronically supplied services, and sale of services provided in a specific physical location,[175] thus reducing internet fragmentation within the EU's Digital Single Market. Similarly, the end of roaming charges within the EU[176] and the cross-border portability of online content services in the internal market are regulatory steps to counter commercial fragmentation.

4.3.4 Governmental Fragmentation

Political-legal, or governmental, fragmentation refers to policies, laws, and judgments that impact the internet's universality or borderless nature by preventing "certain uses of the internet to create, distribute, or access information resources."[177] Factors of fragmentation in politico-legal terms include filtering and blocking websites, social networks, or other resources offering undesired content. While states that interfere with freedom of expression (provided that these interferences are based on law) follow a legitimate aim and are proportionate to the aim pursued, overbroad blocking orders, such as Turkey's blocking of internet platforms in *Yıldırım v. Turkey* (2012)[178] and *Cengiz and Others v. Turkey* (2015), clearly show the limits of states' abilities to fragment the global internet by creating a national "criticism-free" zone. As a "principal means by which individuals exercise their right to freedom to receive and impart information and ideas, providing as it does essential tools for participation in activities and discussions concerning political issues and issues of general interest,"[179] the internet and its universal information and communication interchange function are protected through states' duties to respect, protect, and fulfill human rights (obligations).

Further fragmentation can occur by judgments leading to specific internet sub-regimes within regional/national jurisdictions (in casu Europe: e.g. the *Delfi*, *MTE* and *Pihl* cases by the ECtHR, establishing a regime of targeted monitoring duties for certain intermediaries;[180] the CJEU's *Google Spain* case regarding the right to be forgotten;[181] and the international data traffic regime declared illegal by the CJEU in its *Schrems* case[182]). The prevalence of regimes may lead, some have feared, to a legal fracturing of the internet.[183]

[175] Cf. European Commission, Digital Single Market: EU Negotiators Agreed to End Unjustified Geoblocking, November 20, 2017, http://europa.eu/rapid/press-release_IP-17-4781_en.htm.

[176] European Commission, Roaming Charges End in the EU, June 15, 2017, https://ec.europa.eu/digital-single-market/en/news/15-june-roaming-charges-end-eu.

[177] Cf. William J. Drake, Vinton G. Cerf, and Wolfgang Kleinwächter, "Internet Fragmentation: An Overview," World Economic Forum, Future of the Internet Initiative White Paper, January 2016, 4.

[178] ECtHR, *Yıldırım v. Turkey*, judgment of December 18, 2012, application no. 3111/10, para. 49.

[179] ECtHR, *Cengiz and Others v. Turkey*, judgment of December 1, 2015, application nos. 48226/10 and 14027/11, paras. 49 and 52.

[180] ECtHR, *Delfi AS v. Estonia* (June 16, 2015), application no. 64569/09; ECtHR, *MTE and Index.hu ZRT v. Hungary* (February 2, 2016), application no. 22947/13; ECtHR (3rd section), *Pihl v. Sweden* (February 7, 2017), application no. 74742/14.

[181] CJEU, C-131/12, *Google Spain and Google*, judgment of May 13, 2014.

[182] CJEU, case C-362/14, *Schrems v. Data Protection Commissioner*, judgment of October 6, 2015.

[183] See, e.g., Michael Chertoff and Paul Rosenzweig, "A Primer on Globally Harmonizing Internet Jurisdiction and Regulations," GCIG Paper Series No. 10 (2015), http://www.ourinternet.org/publication/a-primer-on-globally-armonizinginternet-jurisdiction-and-regulations.

The cross-border data flows characteristic of the internet and the bordered nature of states, and thus the limited nature of their jurisdiction, are in conflict.

A further example of governmental fragmentation (connected though to commercial interests) is digital protectionism limiting the access of one state's users to the platform by another state.[184] Cyber operations might also lead to fragmentation. These include forbidden attacks on national networks and the termination of international interconnections by channeling them through an increasingly small number of thus more easily controlled gateways. The internet shutdown in Libya was so easy for the Ghaddafi regime to accomplish because one gateway managed all international traffic.[185]

Applying national laws to data flows can lead to fragmentation.[186] This can happen through routing changes to keep data flows artificially within a jurisdiction, by including geographic limitations for data, such as national data storage requirements, or the prohibition of transborder channeling of certain sensitive categories of data.[187] Indeed, increasing attempts to localize data and establish state control over "national internet segments" have led a number of authors to identify political fragmentation as a serious concern for the internet.[188] States attempt to impose national rules on the internet and subjugate activities perceived as relevant for their interest to their national jurisdictions, a process that has been called "alignment."[189] There is a tension between the internet's universality and the attempted alignment by (some) states of (some of) their laws and jurisdiction pertaining to the internet within their borders. Arguably, alignment-motivated fragmentation (that is chiefly political fragmentation) is an attractive proposition for all states. Based on its duty to safeguard fundamental rights for persons within its territory or under its control, applying laws to the internet "within the territory" seems both an international right based on territorial sovereignty and a constitutional duty of the state. However, as "irresistible" as alignment may seem, resovereignization is "impossible for states fully to achieve" because of the "inherent clash between alignment and the economic efficiencies and capabilities of digital technology."[190]

Further fragmentation can be caused by attempts to construct "national internet segments" or reterritorialize the internet. States should not misread the Group of Governmental Experts 2015 commitment to the importance of state sovereignty in applying laws and exercising jurisdiction because the group also included references to "international norms and principles that flow from sovereignty," which need to apply to the conduct by states of ICT-related activities and to their jurisdiction over ICT infrastructure within their territory.[191]

[184] Cf. William J. Drake, Vinton G. Cerf, and Wolfgang Kleinwächter, "Internet Fragmentation: An Overview," World Economic Forum, Future of the Internet Initiative White Paper, January 2016, 36.

[185] Matthias C. Kettemann, "Das Internet als internationales Schutzgut: Entwicklungsperspektiven des Internetvölkerrechts anlässlich des Arabischen Frühlings," ZaöRV 72 (2012), 469–82 (470).

[186] Cf. Christopher Kuner, "Data Nationalism and its Discontents," Emory Law Journal 64 (2015), 2089–98, http://law.emory.edu/elj/_documents/volumes/64/online/kuner.pdf.

[187] William J. Drake, Vinton G. Cerf, and Wolfgang Kleinwächter, "Internet Fragmentation: An Overview," World Economic Forum, Future of the Internet Initiative White Paper, January 2016, 38.

[188] See references in Milton Mueller, *Will the Internet Fragment? Sovereignty, Globalization and Cyberspace* (Malden, MA: Polity Press, 2017), 1.

[189] Ibid., 71.

[190] Ibid., 104.

[191] GGE report (2015), para. 27.

4.4 Defragmentation

4.4.1 Technical Predisposition

Defragmentation is originally a term from computer science referring to the organization of the contents of storage devices within the smallest possible number of neighboring storage spaces.[192] Within the present context "defragmentation" means countervailing forces to the policies and practices of fragmentations described in the previous section. The tension between these forces and alignments is normative in that norms are produced by different norm-makers and of different normative character to allay these tensions. These normative processes are not perfect, as we have seen in sections 4.1 and 4.2. Examples of normative froth, normative frictions, and normative fractures persist. Alignment itself, if unchecked, can lead to fragmentation of the online order. But the fragmentation of the internet is not an insurmountable problem in theory or practice.[193]

There are intrinsic defragmentation forces within the internet. Though some forms of fragmentation are present on the internet today, its technical characteristics are powerful forces against fragmentation, once it reaches a certain level. Simply put, the added value of information and communication flows over the internet is lost once the networks fragment. It is in this vein that the Internet Society has defined certain characteristics of the internet as its "invariant properties" or "invariants."[194]

4.4.2 Internet Invariants

These "internet invariants" include the internet's *global reach and integrity* in that any endpoint of the internet can address any other endpoint as long as global addressing services are guaranteed. The internet is a *general purpose network* that does not, on principle, discriminate against any specific kind of content. It supports *permissionless innovation* by anyone and is *accessible* to anyone, both actively (by e.g. adding a server) and passively. It is based on *interoperability* through open standards for technologies *and mutual agreement* between network operators, inspired by a "spirit of collaboration." The internet is not defined by any specific technology (the generalized functionality of technology should be kept *unrestricted*) and there are no *permanent favorites*.[195]

Analyzing previously described fragmentation trends in light of these invariants, we see that they offer an important buffer. Again, if these invariant properties of the internet are degraded, the advantages for governments (through alignment) and companies (through "walled gardens" or corporate internet ecosystems) greatly diminish. Thus the internet can be considered to have embedded self-protective qualities, a normative autoimmune reaction. That these qualities do not work the other way, safeguarding government, businesses,

[192] Tim Fisher, "What is Fragmentation and Defragmentation," *Lifewire*, April 6, 2017, https://www.lifewire.com/what-is-fragmentation-defragmentation-2625884.

[193] Just see Bruno Simma, "Universality of International Law from the Practice of a Practitioner," EJIL 20 (2009) 2, 265–97 (concluding that, fragmentation and regime proliferation trends notwithstanding, "the universality of international law in all its variations is in relatively good shape," 297). For a US perspective, see Jonathan I. Charney, "Universal International Law," AJIL 87 (1993) 4, 529–51.

[194] Internet Society, "Internet Invariants: What Really Matters" (2012), http://www.internetsociety.org/internet-invariantswhat-really-matters.

[195] Ibid.

and civil society from dangers emanating from the internet, makes the need for a normative order of the internet essential. Such an order must conceptualize and legitimize regulatory powers pertaining to the network of networks.

Returning to the invariants: attempts by companies to entrench themselves as "favorites" by siloing users through proprietary technology and by restricting its generalized functionality exist but have limits once the disadvantages of "zero-rated" internet access is realized through access alternatives in developing states and the disadvantages of non-migration of data out of closed applications become evident. With regard to governmental fragmentation, an alignment (in the sense described above of the attempt to align internet-based information and communication flows with national jurisdiction) functions (without social costs) up to the point of harming the *global reach* invariant. The Chinese Firewall, for instance, is an example of a technological fragmentation that violates, to a certain degree, the *global reach* invariant (Chinese users simply cannot reach certain international newspaper websites.)[196] However, Chinese authorities seem to realize that they need to ensure a "buffer" so that the internet inside China remains vibrant for its citizens,[197] and ensures a certain level of global reach.[198] Even China cannot "eviscerate the value of the internet by building walls around their pieces of the internet (and fight a never-ending, expensive battle to keep those walls from being eroded or circumvented)."[199] This illustrates the anti-fragmentation forces that necessarily inhere in fragmentation policies.

Forced normative defragmentation does not lend itself to positive results. As the experience with developing new ITRs within the ITU during WCIT-12[200] and the backlash against harmonizing treaties such as the Anti-Couterfeiting Trade Agreement[201] have shown, legal harmonization is often based on an international minimum consensus which is more illiberal than the chaotic status quo: "legal harmonization [tends] toward repressive information policies."[202] Rather, issue-based governance networks[203] and legal interoperability,[204]

[196] Cf. Marcin Przychodniak, "China's Internet Policy," Polish Institute of International Affairs (PISM) Bulletin 75 (2017) 1015, http://www.pism.pl/publications/bulletin/no-75-1015.

[197] Christian Fuchs, "Baidu, Weibo and Renren: The Global Political Economy of Social Media in China," Asian Journal of Communication 26 (2016) 1, 14–41.

[198] Jan Fell, "Chinese Internet Law: What the West Doesn't See. Yes, China's Internet Policy Quashes Dissent—But it Also Fosters Innovation," *The Diplomat*, October 18, 2017, https://thediplomat.com/2017/10/chinese-internet-law-what-the-west-doesnt-see (arguing that "[t]hanks to China's innovation security, defended by the Great Firewall, the government provides a protected environment for domestic innovators and start-ups." Fell defines the Chinese approach to "innovation security" (創新安全 [literally: innovative and safe]) as the "protection of an environment in which society is able to make the required intellectual efforts to achieve substantial innovation and in parallel a national economy that is able to sustain commercial applications of such innovation from erosion and destruction by internal and external hostile forces.")

[199] Milton Mueller, *Will the Internet Fragment? Sovereignty, Globalization and Cyberspace* (Malden, MA: Polity Press, 2017), 104.

[200] David P. Fidler, "Internet Governance and International Law: The Controversy Concerning Revision of the International Telecommunication Regulations," ASIL Insights 17 (2013) 6, https://www.asil.org/insights/volume/17/issue/6/internet-governance-and-international-law-controversy-concerning-revision.

[201] Matthias C. Kettemann, "Das Internet als internationales Schutzgut: Entwicklungsperspektiven des Internetvölkerrechts anlässlich des Arabischen Frühlings," ZaöRV 72 (2012), 138–40 (describing the failure of the Anti-Couterfeiting Trade Agreement as a consequence of changing legitimacy demands on international lawmaking in the context of an information society).

[202] Laura DeNardis, "One Internet: An Evidentiary Basis for Policy Making on Internet Universality and Fragmentation," CIGI/Chatham House, Global Commission on Internet Governance Paper Series No. 38 (2016), 6.

[203] Bertrand de la Chapelle and Paul Fehlinger, "Jurisdiction on the Internet: From Legal Arms Race to Transnational Cooperation," CIGI Paper Series No. 28, April 2016, http://www.ourinternet.org/publication/jurisdiction-onthe-internet.

[204] See 5.3.2. See also Rolf H. Weber, "Legal Interoperability as a Tool for Combatting Fragmentation," Global Commission on Internet Governance Paper Series No. 4 (2014), https://www.cigionline.org/sites/default/files/gcig_paper_no4.pdf, 5.

based on a clearer understanding of the law of conflict-of-laws, are usable tools to combat fragmentation.

4.5 Conclusions

This chapter was dedicated to identifying the countervailing forces to the project of establishing a normative *order* of the internet. Every legal system (and even non-legal systems) has certain chaotic tendencies in the sense that order is (usually) artificial and chaos the state of nature. While forces of disorder within traditional legal systems are tamed by formal institutions (national law) or decentralized control (international law), no norm-producing and -enforcing institutions exist for the global internet. This is a threat to the project of ordering the internet, which is premised upon commitments to a common normative goal. Three dimensions of disorder (froth, friction, fractures) and an overarching force of disorder (fragmentation) have been identified and discussed in this chapter.

Normative froth can be identified when a number of different norms are applicable to similar situations without clear indications that one norm is preferred. A classic example of normative froth on the internet is the internet principle hype. While early collections of principles contained clear commitments to central regulatory goals, such as information society premised upon international law, different groups of actors started to develop new principles that, rather than seeking to increase through reiteration the normative pull of existing principles, provided for variation on the normative content motivated by particular sectoral interests. In only eighteen declarations, twenty-two issues were normatively framed, but without references to previously agreed language or sensitivity to the liquidification of commitments by their variation.

Normative frictions are more serious norm conflicts that go beyond the non-hierarchical coexistence of duplicative norms (froth), but do not yet cause, even in aggregate, a rift within the online order (fractures). Examples of normative friction abound as national courts often diverge in their judgments on factually similar issues, which leads to jurisdictional conflicts—as the aftermath of the foundational *LICRA v. Yahoo!*[205] case amply demonstrates. Issues of normative friction emerge especially when comparing and applying the normative responses by national legal orders to the challenge of regulating intermediaries. Frictions can stem from direct legal conflicts (with one judicial body ordering a different outcome than the next) or from substantial conflicts between the preferences of states and companies or individuals and companies. One example discussed in the chapter is the treatment of intermediary liability, another one the frictions regarding the rules applicable to public and private spaces in online settings. A further example would be the demands by authorities to gain access to the sensitive information of customers in the framework of fighting crime with the friction lying in the company's primordial interest in keeping that information secure. Summing up, frictions emerge especially when otherwise legitimate rules produce disproportionate interferences.

205 Tribunal de Grande Instance Paris, *Ligue contre le racisme et l'antisémitisme et Union des étudiants juifs de France c. Yahoo! Inc. et Société Yahoo! France* (*LICRA v. Yahoo!*), May 22, 2000. See also the US "follow-up": United States Court of Appeals, Ninth Circuit, 433 F.3d 1199, *Yahoo! Inc. v. LICRA and UEJF*, January 12, 2006 (Sup. Ct. denied certiorari).

Normative fractures, as presented here, evidence a larger problem of rule on the internet. They refer to substantial conflicts that can lead to disorder. Among the examples discussed in this chapter we find fractures resulting from the application of international law-based rules and non-international law rules, including soft law standards. Even the GGE, which set out to *clarify* the application of international law on the internet during two cycles of analysis, fails to distinguish, in its 2015 report, between norms, rules, principles, understandings, and existing commitments.

A further fracture has emerged between universal and particular (sovereignty-oriented, anti-universal) normative approaches by states. Sovereignty-oriented states, such as Algeria, China, Egypt, Russia, Saudi Arabia, Sudan, and UAE, argue for more governmental control of the internet, nationalize telecommunications providers, provide for data localization laws, and apply strong penalties to online dissent (or filter dissenting speech). This approach is often coupled with general references to the normative tropes of internet governance, including "multistakeholderism." This shows, again, the malleability of the concept to the point where it can no longer be used to denote the effective and legitimacy-conferring integration of all relevant actors in their respective roles. Often coupled to sovereignty-oriented normative approaches to the internet are territory-based solutions, including data localization rules or profit nationalization decrees for globally active internet companies.

A substantial fracture has also emerged regarding the treatment of cyberwar in the normative order of the internet. While references to the UN Charter being a foundational document have been present in the normative ordering of the internet for a long time, the concrete references, in Chapter VII, to the "use of force" (allowing for Chapter VII situation findings by the Security Council) and "armed attack" (triggering self-defense) have been contested. Sovereignty-oriented states, including those accused in the past of having committed offensive cyberattacks, argue against applying the Charter before attribution techniques become more reliable.[206]

Finally, a fracture has appeared when it comes to trust in internet integrity because of massive online surveillance practices that destabilize trust relationships. While surveillance, even secret surveillance, is necessary in a democratic society under specific circumstances, the practices of many states, including chiefly the "Five Eyes" and Germany, have been in violation of international rules. The ECtHR has shown in important judgments which obligations states have with regard to the protection of privacy. These include *Weber and Saravia v. Germany, Klass and Others v. Germany* (judges must review surveillance measures), *Bucur and Toma v. Romania* (whistleblowers are to be protected), *Iordachi and others v. Moldova* (when legitimizing an interference, "national security" must be interpreted narrowly) and *El-Masri v. the former Yugoslav Republic of Macedonia* (the ECHR can have extraterritorial impact; necessity to control security services).

More recently, in *Big Brother Watch and Others v. the United Kingdom* (2018), the Court inter alia declared illegal parts of the former British law allowing for online surveillance,[207]

[206] Cf. Adam Segal, "The Development of Cyber Norms at the United Nations Ends in Deadlock. Now What?" *Council on Foreign Relations*, June 29, 2017, https://www.cfr.org/blog/development-cyber-norms-united-nations-ends-deadlock-now-what; Arun M. Sukumar, "The UN GGE Failed. Is International Law in Cyberspace Doomed As Well?" *Lawfare*, July 4, 2017, https://lawfareblog.com/un-gge-failed-international-law-cyberspace-doomed-well; and Ann Väljataga, "Back to Square One? The Fifth UN GGE Fails to Submit a Conclusive Report at the UN General Assembly," NATO CCDCOE Incyder database, https://ccdcoe.org/back-square-one-fifth-un-gge-submit-conclusive-report-un-general-assembly.html.

[207] ECtHR, *Big Brother Watch and Others v. the United Kingdom*, judgment of September 13, 2018, application nos. 58170/13, 62322/14, and 24960/15.

in particular the bulk interception regime (which violated Article 8 ECHR because of insufficient oversight structures) and the regime for obtaining communications data from communications service providers.

Finally, section 4.3 discussed the challenge that fragmentation poses to the international order of the internet. Arguing that just as societal cohesion is impacted by technological advancements, technology-related regulation itself can fragment. Indra Spiecker gen. Döhmann, for instance, identifies digitalization (alongside globalization) as a key driver of fragmentation. This section identified three key arenas of fragmentation: technical, commercial, and legal.

Technical fragmentation impedes the full interoperability of the underlying internet infrastructure. Commercial fragmentation is caused by business practices constraining or preventing internet universality, such as "enclosures" by companies that try to "lock in" their customers by making data extraction very difficult and using single profiles across platforms. Political-legal, or governmental, fragmentation includes policies, laws, and judgments that impact the internet's universality or borderless nature by inhibiting free internet use through, e.g., filters. But even cases that increase human rights protection can lead to fragmentation by introducing specific internet sub-regimes within regional/national jurisdictions (such as through the *Delfi*, *MTE*, and *Pihl* cases, by the ECtHR establishing a regime of targeted monitoring duties for certain intermediaries).[208]

This chapter's leading hypothesis is tested and validated: though centrifugal forces contribute to the emergence of normative redundancies, conflicts of norms, and structural fractures as well as fragmentation, countervailing technical forces (the internet invariants) exist. They are the foundation of a technical defragmentation pull which the law—through the normative turn—realizes through norms.

On a different normative level, the ILC's *Fragmentation Report* came to a similar conclusion, arguing that "increasing attention will have to be given to the collision of norms and regimes and the rules, methods and techniques for dealing with such collisions."[209] In particular, the report counseled paying more attention to the role of the Vienna Convention on the Laws of Treaties as a basis for an "International law of conflicts" and "attention to the notion and operations of 'regimes.'"[210]

Interoperability theory[211] and jurisdiction-based conflict-of-laws approaches[212] provide some answers for the online order of how a law of conflicts for the internet may look. But it is the notion and operation of regimes that is most interesting here. The report identifies three kinds of regimes, including "special sets of rules and principles on the administration of a determined problem" and "special branches of international law with their own principles, institutions and teleology."[213] The internet is probably too multifaceted to

[208] ECtHR, *Delfi AS v. Estonia* (June 16, 2015), application No. 64569/09; ECtHR, *MTE and Index.hu ZRT v. Hungary* (February 2, 2016), application No. 22947/13; ECtHR (3rd section), *Pihl v. Sweden* (February 7, 2017), application No. 74742/14.

[209] ILC, Fragmentation of International Law: Difficulties arising from the Diversification and Expansion of International Law, Report of the Study Group of the International Law Commission, 13 April 2006, A/CN.4/L.682, 249 (emphasis removed).

[210] Ibid.

[211] See 5.3.3.

[212] See 5.3.4.

[213] ILC, Fragmentation of International Law: Difficulties arising from the Diversification and Expansion of International Law, Report of the Study Group of the International Law Commission, 13 April 2006, A/CN.4/L.682, 252.

be considered amenable to being administered as a "determined problem." Rather, it could be considered a regime in the sense of a special branch of (not only) international law. As shown above, the online order has its own principles and purpose (teleology); it does not yet have proper institutions beyond informal networks, non-governmental structures, and ad hoc structures with a formal presence by different actors. But it could be argued that institutions are supplanted by the unique structure of normative development and decentralized enforcement, depending on the relevant norm; and that norms within the normative exercise compliance-pull even without institutions.

The *Fragmentation Report* argues that a regime may function outside of treaties "in more broadly 'cultural' ways."[214] Regimes may also have non-governmental participants and "represent non-governmental interests in a fashion that might influence their interpretation and operation." The modus operandi may be different from treaty regimes: "[o]ften regimes operate on the basis of administrative coordination and 'mutual supportiveness,' the point of which is to seek regime-optimal outcomes."[215] Much of what Rapporteur Martti Koskenniemi asks the Commission to consider can be read as a programmatic statement as to the next steps into the elaboration, by this study, of a normative order the internet,[216] in particular

- The manner of the autonomous operation of regimes [including] formation and operation of internal regime-hierarchies, the principles of interpretation applicable to regime-instruments, the specific types of rules or institutions needed to enable the coherent operation of regimes […];
- The role of general (public) international law in regimes, including in the solution of interpretative conflicts and providing for responsibility for any violation of regime-rules. The relations of public and private law, including soft law and other non-binding instruments in such regimes […];
- […] Any study of regime-rules should take into account such contrast in the normative power of particular regime-rules;
- The conditions and consequences of regime failure […];
- The whole complex of inter-regime relations […];
- The settlement of disputes within regimes [and] settlement of disputes across regimes. […][217]

While the normative order of the internet is more than merely a regime of international law in the sense of the ILC *Fragmentation Report*, it still needs a firm theoretical foundation. In Koskenniemi's terms, deconstructing hierarchies is a device to better understand international law: "It [reveals] hidden priorities and principles of political value."[218] Similarly, constructing quasi-hierarchies, where they do not formally exist, allows us, as an exercise in critical reconstruction,[219] to develop theories about the normative order

[214] Ibid.
[215] Ibid.
[216] See chapter 6.
[217] ILC, Fragmentation of International Law: Difficulties arising from the Diversification and Expansion of International Law, Report of the Study Group of the International Law Commission, 13 April 2006, A/CN.4/L.682, 253.
[218] Martti Koskenniemi, "Hierarchy in International Law: A Sketch," EJIL 8 (1997), 571–2 (582).
[219] Cf. Caroline Fehl, "Navigating Norm Complexity. A Shared Research Agenda for Diverse Constructivist Perspectives," August 2018, PRIF Working Paper No. 41 (Frankfurt: HSFK, 2018).

with a view to finding its priorities and principles and discovering how they influence the order.

Just as the "reversal of hierarchies is a liberating experience,"[220] the establishment of flexible hierarchies of norms (or orders of norms, normative orders) can be a stabilizing one and thus also a liberating experience—freeing actors from normative uncertainty. This reconstruction of a normative order necessitates an understanding of transnational theories of order and, in particular, a firm foundation in theoretical attempts to undergird an online order. This exercise will be conducted in the subsequent chapter 5.

220 Ibid., with references to it being "just possibly the only way in which law can be an art of the just," as suggested by Jacques Derrida. Of course, Derrida is in line with Thomas S. Kuhn. Hierarchies are very much like ruling paradigms; Koskenniemi's "flux" is Kuhn's "paradigm change," though it will be difficult to argue that law has become just at any one point, with both hierarchies in flux and paradigms being overthrown by scientific revolutions.

5
Theorizing Order(s) on the Internet

5.1 Introduction

This study develops the foundations of normative order of the internet. Such a normative order is complex, as it must be able to integrate norms at at least three different levels (national, regional, international), of two types (privately and publicly authored), of substantially different character (from ius cogens to soft law), and provide standards to measure norms as to their technical consistency and legal-cultural consonancy with the order's purpose. Such a normative order must therefore rest on firm theoretical foundations, especially when its ontology is dynamic. The underlying theoretical foundations can only be established analytically and reflectively relative to (1) existing theoretical approaches (theories and concepts) to (international) ordering and authority in transnational constellations and (2) theories of law, or concepts within these theories, for the information or network(ed) society. This is attempted in the present chapter. While fully acknowledging that the selected theoretical approaches are only a selection of theories on order, important elements of the more influential approaches relevant for the establishment of the normative order of the internet, as understood in this research, are discussed and contextualized in the following.

This study will take a novel approach in that it will not discuss general theories of order and identify their argumentative hold on the approach followed here. Rather, the following section (5.2) will identify selected imports from different theories going, by and large, from the more general theory to the more specific one. The approaches discussed first include general theories such as systems theory and poststructuralism, but also (in a presentation reflective more of the equality of the power of ideas than a theory's position in the market of theories) more targeted concepts within larger theories, seeking to explain aspects of public (dis)order, such as international public authority and principles theory, transnationalism, legal hybridity, and multinormativity. These sectoral orders are of interest here, in particular as they relate to the normative order of the internet and can inform, in aggregate, the process of refining the theoretical frame of the theory of the normative order of the internet.[1]

Section 5.3 will focus on theories of online order and concepts related to phenomena of online order. Most of the theories are not conceptualized as holistic theories of order online. Some theorists only look at specific phenomena within, what this study terms, the normative order of the internet or use a phenomenological perspective attempting to explain, justify, or contest aspects of online order(ing): cases in point are *infrastructuralization theory*'s

[1] It should also be stated at the outset that the choice, exposition, and analysis of the theories below is highly selective. Space only permits a narrow treatment of those aspects of the theories that can be considered particularly useful in the context of this research. This study will therefore engage theories and their authors only on a narrow scope with a conscious focus on epistemological considerations.

The Normative Order of the Internet. Matthias C. Kettemann, Oxford University Press (2020). © Matthias C. Kettemann.
DOI: 10.1093/oso/9780198865995.001.0001

focus on the internet's tangible technological core and kinetic interconnection resources or *interoperability theory*'s focus on the importance of interoperability of programs and devices, for instance. The notion of "theory" is used rather loosely here and does not imply affiliation to a theoretical school or a theoretical supra- or infrastructure.

No single comprehensive theory of online order exists to date. This is why section 5.4 pulls together key elements, insights, and considerations of the theories discussed in previous sections in an attempt to provide a theoretical foundation for the normative order of the internet presented in chapter 6. This ensures a comprehensive exposition and analysis of the theoretical underpinnings of the normative order of the internet. This is necessary because the internet is neither a space without laws nor is it (or should it be) a space without legal theory. Section 5.5 contains conclusions.

5.2 Legal Theory and the Digital Condition

5.2.1 Epistemology of Computer Culture

Legal theory has adapted to the epistemology of computer culture and provides a meaningful horizontal hypertext for the normative order of the internet.

Already in the late 1980s, Karl-Heinz Ladeur could argue that the use of computers—even then—had fragmented the foundations of traditional positive systems of law: new narrative frames of modernity and of modern law were necessary.[2] Similarly, Thomas Vesting identifies a shift in culture to one "dominated by the computer [...] in particular through the new hypertext structure of the internet," which renders the "uniform form of systematic book-centred knowledge, the normative framework narratives of modernity, natural and social philosophy and the legal-positivist system [...] progressively anachronistic."[3] Vesting understands culture as having an "orientative function for the way individuals live their lives and for the reproduction of institutions and rules"[4] (without supposing the consistency and systematicity of all cultural phenomena). The rise of a "universal network of digital media"[5] enables and determines our understanding of legal culture as *network culture*, implying new narratives, new narrativized orders (of knowledge, including judicial knowledge production, dissemination and consumption[6]) and a new networked, "relational" individual at its center.

[2] Karl-Heinz Ladeur, "Computerkultur und Evolution der Methodendiskussion in der Rechtswissenschaft," ARSP 74 (1988), 218ff, 222.

[3] Thomas Vesting, *Die Medien des Rechts. Computernetzwerke* (Weilerswist: Velbrück, 2015), 83–4 (notes omitted): "Die Einheitsform des systematischen Buchwissens, auf der sowohl die normative 'Rahmenerzählung' der Moderne, die Natur- und Sozialphilosophie, als auch das rechtspositivistische System beruhten, wird in einer vom Computer dominierten Kultur [...]—insbesondere durch die neuartige Hypertextstruktur des Internets—zunehmend anachronistisch" (translation by the author).

[4] Vesting, *Die Medien des Rechts. Computernetzwerke* (2015), 130: "Ordnet man der Kultur [...] orientierungsleistende Funktionen für die Lebensführung des Einzelnen und die Reproduktion von Institutionen und Regeln zu, so ist damit keineswegs die Behauptung der Konsistenz und Systematizität aller kulturellen Phänomene verbunden" (translation by the author).

[5] Vesting, *Die Medien des Rechts. Computernetzwerke* (2015), 7: "[Es ist] der Aufstieg eines weltweiten Verbundes aus digitalen Medien, der den Verständnishorizont der Rechtskultur als Netzwerkkultur ermöglicht und bestimmt" (translation by the author).

[6] Thomas Vesting, *Rechtstheorie*, 2nd edn. (Munich: Beck, 2015), 180.

A newly networked order may seem to need a new legal theory. Legal philosophers have reacted to the technical-normative instantiation variously described as *computer culture* (Vesting[7]) or *computerization* (Ladeur[8]), including and characterized by the emergence of *lex digitalis* (Fischer-Lescano/Teubner[9]) in order to remain normatively relevant as an *Ordnungsidee* ("idea of order"[10]). Legal theory has to adapt itself to the epistemology of computer culture, including its cognitive dimension as a self-learning and evolving system without clear central authority,[11] the broadening of the normative vocabulary, and the involved actors. This has consequences.

Already Luhmann noted that incorporating cognitive mechanisms into the normative structure of law seems to further the "development of a world society"[12] based on multiple foundations. "[R]eality is no longer structurally tied to one foundation," Vesting argues, identifying the rise of "computer culture" as the transitional point to a new "post-ontological, post-metaphysical and post-modern epistemological situation."[13] Reality-producing instruments, including knowledge production mechanisms, are networked, making knowledge out of existing knowledge,[14] norms out of norms.

It is in this process of dynamic normativity that legal theory has to intervene by providing a "horizontal hypertext."[15] The notion of "hypertext" is more apt than Vesting's brief reference to it may lead readers to believe.[16] Hypertext—in the context of the internet—is "text which is not constrained to be linear."[17] It can combine natural (linear) language text with interactive or dynamic displays and contain links to other texts. Theory as hypertext thus flows in and out of practice (the linear text in this simile), influences practice, and allows for its confirmation and contestation. Hypertext on the internet, just as legal theory, is difficult to describe meaningfully in abstract, just as theories are best observed in operation. Writing in 1987, Jeffrey Conklin explained that "[j]ust as a description of electronic spreadsheets will not get across the real elegance of that tool, [describing hypertext] can only hint at [its] potentials. In fact, one must work in current hypertext environments [. . .] for the collection of features to coalesce into a useful tool."[18]

[7] Vesting, *Die Medien des Rechts. Computernetzwerke* (2015).

[8] Karl-Heinz Ladeur, *Die Textualität des Rechts. Zur poststrukturalistischen Kritik des Rechts* (Weilerswist: Velbrück, 2016), 308.

[9] Andreas Fischer-Lescano and Gunther Teubner, *Regime-Kollisionen. Zur Fragmentierung des globalen Rechts* (Frankfurt am Main: Suhrkamp, 2006), 44.

[10] Vesting, *Die Medien des Rechts. Computernetzwerke* (2015), 83–4.

[11] Ibid.

[12] Niklas Luhmann, *Rechtssoziologie*, 4th edn. (Wiesbaden: Verlag für Sozialwissenschaften, 2008), 340f: "Dieser Einbau kognitiver Mechanismen in die an sich normative Struktur des Rechts scheint der Entwicklung einer Weltgesellschaft zu entsprechen" (translation by author).

[13] Vesting, *Die Medien des Rechts. Computernetzwerke* (2015), 84: "Die neue Computerkultur leitet den Übergang in eine neuartige postontologische, post-metphysische und postmoderne epistemologische Situation ein, in der man sich die Wirklichkeit nicht mehr als eine fest in einem einzigen Fundament verankerte Struktur denken kann" (notes omitted, translation by the author).

[14] Ibid.

[15] Ibid., 181.

[16] When considering hypertext, one should not forget that the most commonly used data transfer protocol on the application layer of the internet is the Hypertext Transfer Protocol (HTTP). Cf., for the current standardized version HTTP/2, IETF, Hypertext Transfer Protocol Version 2 (HTTP/2), RFC 7540 of 15 May 2015, https://tools.ietf.org/html/rfc7540. The more secure version is the HTTPS. Compared to HTTP/1.1, HTTP/2 provides for optimized transport for HTTP semantics, including better flow control, prioritization, and server push (ibid.).

[17] W3C, What is HyperText, https://www.w3.org/WhatIs.html.

[18] See already Jeffrey Conklin, "Hypertext: An Introduction and Survey," *Computer* 20 (1987), 17–41 (17–18), http://www.ics.uci.edu/~andre/informatics223s2009/conklin.pdf.

This is, as this study submits, important for two reasons: first, theory's chief import is being a "useful tool" to shape practice, in the present case to explain and justify the emergence of the normative order of the internet and its integration into national normative orders; second, this chapter is based on the approach that, once described and analyzed, features from different theories will coalesce "into a useful tool." For these processes, theories, and concepts that have been tested in the purgatories of academic discourses are essential: "As societal change quickens, legal theory has to provide legal practice with a varied pool of ideas, including possible alternative developments."[19] These need to be sufficiently detailed to be practically and dogmatically relevant and useful. This is exactly what the present chapter attempts to provide: filling the "pool of ideas" by describing a number of connected theories and developing paths for practice to follow.

5.2.2 Binary Operations Under Uncertainty

The legal system (like the internet) is based on binary operators, is multi-layered, and operates under conditions of uncertainty and contingency. As the network of interconnected networks and the network of interconnected laws are similar, similar normative interventions can be made at the level of modulating the operators, the logics of interactions, and the practices of the respective "operating" system.

Niklas Luhmann and, later, Gunther Teubner saw law as a functionally differentiated subsystem of society. For Luhmann, law's productivity lies in generalizations allowing the coordination of an increasingly complex sociality or societal reality. Law's function to him was the contrafactual stabilization of expectations in a world of contingency, where alternative possibilities are rampant.[20] Later, Christoph Möllers would term a similar approach the *possibility* of norms and develop a normative practice transcending morality and causality: to him norms are significants and evaluators of a certain future in that they allow us to distance ourselves from these possible futures: in the practice of norms we can disassociate ourselves from the practice of norms.[21]

To Luhmann, the legal system is made up of "communications," which are special because they (unlike other communications) are based on the binarity of legality/illegality. This binarity is encoded: "society's law realizes itself through reference to code—and not via a (however hypothetical or categorical, sensible or factual) rule of origin."[22] This binarity allows Luhmann to identify a positive value—law/*Recht*—and a negative value—illegality/*Unrecht*. If a societal communication, by framing itself in the positive/negative *Recht*/*Unrecht* code, demands recognition as legal, it becomes part of the legal system, which is thus operatively closed or autopoietic.[23] Operative closure (autopoiesis) means that legal systems are made up of, and only use, legal communications with encoded binarity to communicate, thus relying on their own network of operations/operators to establish

[19] Vesting, *Rechtstheorie* (2015), 181.
[20] Niklas Luhmann, *Kontingenz und Recht* (Frankfurt: Suhrkamp, 2013).
[21] Christoph Möllers, *Die Möglichkeit der Normen* (Berlin: Suhrkamp, 2016), 442.
[22] Niklas Luhmann, *Das Recht der Gesellschaft* (Frankfurt am Main: Suhrkamp, 1993), 55.
[23] Gunther Teubner, *Recht als autopoietisches System* (Suhrkamp: Frankfurt am Main, 1989), chapter 3.

operations/to operate. The legal order (and society through it) reproduces itself.[24] As such, autopoiesis, as a concept, is not far away from automated blockchain-based applications, based on communal ledgers, where each new entry is based on and changes the whole blockchain.[25] Blockchain applications, including the challenging distributed ledger currencies, like BitCoin, are from a systems theoretical view as autopoietic as Luhmann's legal system—with many of the similar advantages (cohesiveness of a grand design; independence from other theories/systems) and problems (technical oversophistication;[26] practical overhype[27]) as a consequence.

The strong conceptual similarities of systems theory and computer programming are notable and encompass semantics. Building on this realization, Thomas Vesting assimilates Luhmann's (and Teubner's) autopoietic system to the emergence of "computer culture" and its epistemological conditions. Among the key similarities he finds are the operation, by Luhmann's legal system just as by computers, through a binary code (*Recht/Unrecht* vs. 0s and 1s) and the system set-up: the networked nature of the legal system and the internet itself. The inclusion of known unknowns (*Nicht-Wissen*) and the operation under uncertainty and in recognition of the contingency or regime operators/operations have constitutive functions with Luhmann and with regard to the technical (and normative) dimensions of internet system administration. Legal positivism, by contrast, favors the untenable hypothesis of a knowable order without lacunae.[28] Similarities notwithstanding, it can be doubted with Vesting whether Luhmann's approach is actually tailored to the challenges of the internet and whether systems theory can offer substantial intellectual import for online order, especially with a view to systems theory's silence on the functional logic of networks.

Luhmann's approach to law as an autopoietic system is prima facie open to the changed epistemological conditions of "computer culture,"[29] even if it is not—as much of systems theory—nuanced enough in its treatment of the functional logic of computers and networks as media of historic change of societies, including heterarchical conceptions of order in networks. Especially Luhmann's treatment of the discursive network within and of the legal systems as an invariant property—the autopoiesis—is problematic in light of the dynamic flexibility and changing environment characteristic of network society.[30] As Vesting puts it, the categories of the autopoietic system only apply in specific temporal linearity: a "specific media *environment*."[31]

[24] Gralf-Peter Calliess, "Systemtheorie," in Sonja Buckel, Ralph Christensen, and Andreas Fischer-Lescano (eds.), *Neue Theorien des Rechts*, 2nd edn. (Stuttgart: Lucius&Lucius, 2009), 53–71 (55).

[25] Cf. Julie Maupin, "Mapping the Global Legal Landscape of Blockchain and Other Distributed Ledger Technologies," CIGI Paper No. 149, October 13, 2017, https://www.cigionline.org/publications/mapping-global-legal-landscape-blockchain-and-other-distributed-ledger-technologies.

[26] Gideon Greenspan, "Avoiding the Pointless Blockchain Project," *MultiChain* (2015), http://www.multichain.com/blog/2015/11/avoiding-pointless-blockchain-project (showing use-by-use that blockchains are usually unnecessary and offering as alternatives "regular file storage, [. . .] a centralized database, [. . .] master-slave database replication [and] multiple databases to which users can subscribe").

[27] Karl Wüst and Arthur Gervais, "Do You Need a Blockchain," International Association for Cryptologic Research, Working Paper 375 (2017), https://eprint.iacr.org/2017/375.pdf.

[28] Vesting, *Rechtstheorie* (2015), 84, note 137.

[29] Niklas Luhmann, "Die Codierung des Rechtssystems," Rechtstheorie 17 (1986), 171 et seq. (176).

[30] Cf. the critique by Vesting, *Rechtstheorie* (2015), 86–8.

[31] Ibid., 89: "alle Kategorien der Rechtstheorie [entfalten] ihre volle Gültigkeit nur in einer bestimmten historischen Epoche und nur in einem bestimmten medialen *environment*" (translation by the author).

5.2.3 Liquid Law and Networked Regimes

Computerization leads to new "liquid" forms of law and necessitates new networked regimes with effective regime-internal self-reflection and self-optimization processes.

Karl-Heinz Ladeur has developed fundamental rights approaches based on non-subject-related constitutional theories. This is helpful as a theoretical offer, as it enables us—for a while—to ignore the challenges of conceptualizing *demoi* on the multiple normative layers (national, regional, international) and within the transnational functional sections of the internet (such as the internet of things) relevant for the legitimation of online ordering. Describing the postmodern condition as characterized by uncertainty, necessitating a forward-looking law,[32] Ladeur asserts that the knowledge structure of law is in flux. To him, a dynamic network of information exchange must take the place of general laws.[33] He diagnoses that the break or fracture in the evolution of the law caused by computers has to be reconstructed with the help of a logic of intra- and interorganisatorial networks.[34] Arguing that technical systems are only partially controlled by explicit rules, Ladeur finds it difficult to normatively accept the loose connection between functions of regulation and regulatory means in structuralism:[35] technology's materialist logic is not characterized by a strategic-instrumental functionality, but by "operative regimes" with their embedded intelligibility schemes.[36]

Computers and computer networks demand legal forms reactive to social change. Programs encode and encourage learning by monitoring. This leads Ladeur to identify the emergence of a "liquid law."[37] For Ladeur this means that conflicts are no longer solved—as in positivist hard law-based regimes—by courts and judges and by references to knowable law, but rather by "procedural forms that allow problem description and solving in a liquefied [read: more dynamic] context."[38] Ladeur's example is the "completely unstructured cooperation between [...] programmers."[39] The cooperation is not quite as unstructured as he may believe in light of the demands of project management in highly competitive fields. Literature on computer programming project management abounds.[40] Indeed, the normative order of the internet is, as this study shows passim, less liquefied than Ladeur suggests. For Ladeur, liquefied contexts demand informal norms. As formal (positivist, hard) norms

[32] Karl-Heinz Ladeur, *Cyber Courts: Private Rechtsprechung in den neuen Medien*, Kursbuch 177 (Hamburg: Murmann, 2014).

[33] Matthias Kronenberger, "Theorien der radikalen Fragmentierung," in Sonja Buckel, Ralph Christensen, and Andreas Fischer-Lescano (eds.), *Neue Theorien des Rechts*, 2nd edn. (Stuttgart: Lucius&Lucius, 2009), 229–52 (244–5).

[34] Karl-Heinz Ladeur, *Der Staat gegen die Gesellschaft* (Tübingen: Mohr, 2006), 296.

[35] Karl-Heinz Ladeur, *Die Textualität des Rechts. Zur poststrukturalistischen Kritik des Rechts* (Weilerswist: Velbrück, 2016), 188.

[36] Ibid., citing Gilbert Simondon, "About Technical Mentality," Revue philosophique de la France et de l'étranger 131 (2006), 343.

[37] Karl-Heinz Ladeur, *Die Textualität des Rechts. Zur poststrukturalistischen Kritik des Rechts* (Weilerswist: Velbrück, 2016), 306.

[38] Ibid.

[39] Ibid.

[40] Just see Andrew Stellman and Jennifer Greene, *Applied Software Project Management* (Boston, MA: O'Reilly, 2005) and Adolfo Villafiorita, *Introduction to Software Project Management* (Boca Raton, FL: CRCPress, 2016).

can no longer regulate (most) behavior, new norms are generated and applied in processes of "pragmatic governance."[41]

This pragmatic approach can realize itself in a debate of normative expectations.[42] But pragmatic approaches often suffer from an absence of orientation, or normative "red lines." Variously reiterated commitments by states and other relevant actors on the internet to a human rights-based, development-oriented information society, based on the UDHR and upholding fully international law and the principles and purposes of the UN Charter, seem to allow some doubts as to how pragmatic (read in Ladeur's sense here as "non-principled") norms regulating the internet really are. The growing breadth and depth of norms within its normative order, as will be shown in the next chapter, have led to a solidification and stabilization of Ladeur's liquefied contexts.

In Ladeur's internet, the law as a stable order is supplanted by an aggregate of operations that contextualize the formation of orders. Can we speak, Ladeur asks, of an emerging "Recht der Dinge," a law of (the connected) things? In the internet of things such a notion makes much sense. Indeed, a law of the things already exists—it is the law applicable to these things. It is not, as Ladeur seems to imply, an independent system of law where the connected things (like smart fridges, home management systems, and smart cars) start adjudicating conflicts among themselves, but smart things take decisions (albeit based on human-made code and algorithms with some encoded self-learning capabilities) on a daily basis.

Ladeur's concept further differentiates: *Computerisierung*/Computerization[43] has shattered law's traditional approach to power over and through definitions such as *rules*, *exceptions*, and *public/private* sphere. Therefore, new "control projects of the law" appear necessary. Ladeur calls for "new network-ready reflective procedures and regimes," which are "functionally equivalent to powers of reflection embedded in [traditional, positivist] legal systems."[44] These new rules are characterized by new forms of hybridization between public and private spheres, collective and individual legal reforms.

Ladeur's *new* law for the computerized age is further different in that norms and normative concepts are not created ex ante but rather in real time next to (or with little reflection after) operations. This reading of hybrid fluidity of the normative condition is premised upon a system in which purpose and means are no longer hierarchically ordered but connected on a more intricate level.[45] These newly emerging orders oscillate between information technology-based operations (influencing the emergence of norms/"coding") and social coding (influencing "operations") on the internet.[46]

[41] Karl-Heinz Ladeur, *Die Textualität des Rechts. Zur poststrukturalistischen Kritik des Rechts* (Weilerswist: Velbrück, 2016), 307.

[42] Christian Katzenbach, *Die Regeln digitaler Kommunikation: Governance zwischen Norm, Diskurs und Technik* (Berlin: Springer VS, 2017), 280–91.

[43] Karl-Heinz Ladeur, *Die Textualität des Rechts. Zur poststrukturalistischen Kritik des Rechts* (Weilerswist: Velbrück, 2016), 308.

[44] Ibid., 309.

[45] Ibid.

[46] Ibid., 310.

5.2.4 Dehierarchization and Heterarchy

Network culture has destabilized the normative hierarchy in legal orders. This has led to a dehierarchization of norms and to the progressive recognition of a heterarchy of sources of law. Transitioning towards a Weltrecht *(as idea, not fact), theory helps divorce normative ordering from national boundaries.*

Systems theory explains, without justifying, the transition of law from a hierarchical-deductive problem horizon to a heterarchic process of case-by-case normative solutionism. On the internet, the law is in flux and traditional inductive and deductive reasoning takes a step behind the demands of "dynamic, recursive and horizontal internetworking of [normative] operations" as a justification of the law.[47] Indeed, justifications (for norms and normative orders) are productive, as Rudolf Wiethölter reminds us: any *Rechtfertigung* is also a "Recht-Fertigung,"[48] a making (*Fertigung*) of the law (*Recht*). By justifying (the application of) a norm, the legal community "makes" it. In Wiethölter's reading, each application is thus—at least partly—an act of creation.

This creation takes place in a disordered setting since in information society sources of law are no longer contained in the *Stufenbau* of Kelsen's ideal order. Rather, the study of the sources of law needs to consider new kinds of normative operations on the internet. As Vesting writes, "the law of computer culture shatters the concept of norm hierarchy. [...] This is why the state-centred hierarchy of legal sources needs to be either substantially modified or even given up completely."[49]

In particular, decentralized and privatized norm production, including that of codes, principles, and terms of service, is necessary for solving regulatory challenges in multilayered normative settings.[50] National law sets limits to private ordering. Courts may declare some private norms, such as terms of service, to be in violation of national or regional law, thus contributing to legal certainty and demonstrating the stability of the national legal form.[51] The result of the approach is nevertheless interesting: the historically grounded state monopoly on legislation is challenged in a legislative contest and the state-centered hierarchization of sources of law supplanted by a heterarchy of sources. The singularity of the authority of the state is progressively enlarged by the "fluid, nameless authority of dispersed horizontal movements." Instead of a *Grundnorm*, we experience (when it comes to norms online) *Normen ohne Grund (und Ende)*, which through finding them are "founded" as norms. This is, in a different setting, what Stanley Cavell describes as "finding as founding,"

47 Vesting, *Rechtstheorie* (2015), 80.

48 Rudolf Wiethölter, "Recht-Fertigungen eines Gesellschaftsrechts," in Christian Joerges and Gunther Teubner (eds.), *Rechtsverfassungsrecht. Recht-Fertigung zwischen Privatrechtsdogmatik und Gesellschaftstheorie* (Baden-Baden: Nomos, 2003), 13 et seq.

49 Vesting, *Rechtstheorie* (2015), 111–12.

50 Ibid.

51 Just compare the previously discussed cases of *Google Spain* (CJEU, case C-131/12, *Google Spain SL, Google Inc. v. Agencia Española de Protección de Datos (AEPD), Mario Costeja González*, judgment (Grand Chamber) of May 13, 2014), *Digital Rights Ireland* (CJEU, C-293/12 and C-594/12, judgment of April 8, 2014), and *Schrems* (CJEU, case C-362/14, *Schrems v. Data Protection Commissioner*, judgment of October 6, 2015) or the more recent invalidation of certain terms and conditions within Facebook's terms of service ("AGBs") by a Berlin court: Landgericht Berlin, Judgement 16 O 341/15 of January 16, 2018, https://www.vzbv.de/sites/default/files/downloads/2018/02/12/facebook_lg_berlin.pdf.

of reasons, reasons for norms, and norms.[52] For Vesting, the role of code in digital communication amounts to a takeover of computer technology of the "old world" of consciously conceptualized *Sollen*.[53]

While it is true that the pervasive use of computing technology and the internet have substantially changed society,[54] technology has not "taken over." It is a concept, not a person, and has agency only in the metaphorical sense or when someone wishes to personalize arguments for technical solutionism. It is never true that *technology* demands a certain solution. It is always some other normative actor, pursuing limited self-interests, who uses technological solutionism as a crude tool to reach that goal.

What is true, however, is that computers[55] have become a "meta-medium"[56] with which we operate in a world of connected objects, the internet of things. This, according to Vesting's media theory, is a fundamental fracture in the history of our culture evolution because symbolic forms of culture are now made dependent on "digital machines."[57] This has introduced a new third societal layer within modern society: after the society of individuals and the society of organizations, we are now experiencing the emergence of the society of networks.

This society of networks (or in Castells' terminology, *the Network Society*[58]) is based on a three-layer model of regulation, which is responsive to new and disparate legal phenomena. There is continuity in this change: "Just as the community right of the welfare state changed the cultural frame of the state centered on individual rights, the group right of the welfare state is now placed within an enlarged cultural frame: the law of the network culture."[59] Legal theory has to put front and center the "networked, non-hierarchical, dynamic reproduction of systems." These dynamic approaches to ordering are connected to computer culture's influence on the legal order, namely dynamization, fluctuance, and a softening and widening of the border from a *Trennlinie* to a *Kontaktzone,* from a clear line (legality/illegality; norm/not norm; public/private) to an area of enmeshed normative productivity (e.g. norms of a public character set by private actors, enforced by them, and then tested in public forums, such as terms of service that may ultimately fail before national courts).[60]

This applies, according to Vesting, to national and international law: a functional, fragmented law of the world is progressively "decomposing international law" and setting it

[52] Stanley Cavell, "This New Yet Unapproachable America. Lectures after Emerson after Wittgenstein," *Carpenter Lectures, II. Finding as Founding* (Chicago: University of Chicago Press, 1989/2013).

[53] Vesting, *Rechtstheorie* (2015), 146.

[54] From the perspective of the theory of media this dehierarchization/heterarchy of sources is an echo of the transition from the book, containing text, read in a linear fashion, to the medium of the internet, based on non-linear hypertext and creating norms in decentralized networks (Ibid., 2015), 113).

[55] Or rather: the connected circuits within computers, as computers have just been the internet age's most characteristic technical artifact. Given the rise in internet use via mobile technology, especially in countries with fast growing internet penetration rates, the next generation of users may not associate the internet with the computer to the same degree and other devices or a new form of interaction with artificial intelligence might become the "meta-medium" used.

[56] Vesting, *Rechtstheorie* (2015), 152.

[57] Ibid.

[58] Manuel Castells, *The Information Society: Economy, Society and Culture; Vol. 1: The Rise of the Network Society*, 2nd edn. (Oxford: Blackwell, 1996/2000); *Vol. 2: The Power of Identity* (Oxford: Blackwell, 1997); *Vol. 3: End of Millennium*, 2nd edn. (Oxford: Blackwell, 1998/2000).

[59] Vesting, *Rechtstheorie* (2015), 153.

[60] Ibid., 179: "[...] muss auch die Rechtstheorie die netzwerkförmige, nicht-hierarchische, dynamische Reproduktion von Systemen in den Vordergrund rücken. [...]" (translation by the author).

aside for "new networked, heterarchic patterns of orders."[61] Of course, one could make the opposite case. Functional, regime-specific norms with import on the internet's regulation are, rather than decomposing international law, adding to it; they are not setting it and its mechanisms aside, but rather developing existing normative mechanisms or creating new ones that are more answerable to the challenges of channeling effective ICT governance globally and are making transnationally exercised public authority accountable.

As Luhmann noted, politics and law are key "risk carriers of social evolution" that tie the development of "contingent expectations structures" (one of his ways of describing "law") to consolidated political systems. In his reading, only by giving up the state-bound capacity of legal-political standardization can a transition to a system of world society be achieved.[62]

Teubner takes things a step further by providing the argumentative ground for the crystallization of a *Weltrecht*, the world's law. Using the autopoietic model, such *Weltrecht* can be considered to be made up of all communications that are based on the legality/illegality code.[63] But this is of little epistemic value and offers no prescriptive insights. It is more interesting to note that Teubner's *Weltrecht* is made up of different legal systems that are traditionally segmented primarily by borders (national legal systems) or regions (regional systems of integration). However, national legal systems are not "closed" off. National rules allowing for the application of non-national law (*Geltungsbrücken*, "bridges/avenues of applicability") ensure transfers between orders within the *Weltrecht*.[64]

According to systems theorists, the concept of *Weltrecht* helps overcome the "legal-philosophical stateism" that blocks progressive conflict resolution models on a global scale. Law and politics remain inextricably state-bound, while economic processes and, it should be added for the purposes of this study, global information and communication flows argue against a differentiation on the basis of national boundaries.[65] If states cannot fulfill the global need for law and order on a macro level, private ordering and self-organization will fill the normative vacuum. Simply put: if there is no "constitution" on the *Weltrecht* level—and there are only a few principles[66] and fewer processes,—regimes will self-constitutionalize.

5.2.5 Self-Constitutionalizing Regimes

Fragmentation and decentralized norm production have led to the development of self-constitutionalizing sub-legal orders, civil sectors or regimes, including and especially with regard to the internet with humans positioned at the center of the Digitalverfassung *as the regime's* Eigenverfassung.

[61] Ibid., 87: "So wird das staatszentrierte Völkerrecht herkömmlicher Prägung seit einiger Zeit durch ein funktional ausgerichtetes, 'fragmentiertes Weltrecht' unterlaufen, das die Hierarchie des Völkerrechts dekomponiert und durch neue netzwerkartige, heterarchische Ordnungsmuster ablöst" (notes omitted; translation by the author).

[62] Niklas Luhmann, *Rechtssoziologie*, 4th edn. (Wiesbaden: Verlag für Sozialwissenschaften, 2008), 338 (emphasis omitted).

[63] Gralf-Peter Calliess, "Systemtheorie," in Sonja Buckel, Ralph Christensen, and Andreas Fischer-Lescano (eds.), *Neue Theorien des Rechts*, 2nd edn. (Stuttgart: Lucius&Lucius, 2009), 64.

[64] Ibid., 65.

[65] Gunther Teubner, *Verfassungsfragmente. Gesellschaftlicher Konstitutionalismus in der Globalisierung* (Frankfurt am Main: Suhrkamp, 2012), 87.

[66] See 5.2.7 and 5.2.8.

Fragmentation is a less serious problem for (international) law[67] and for the internet[68] than is often claimed.[69] As Anne Peters has shown at the example of international law, substantial parts of the alarmist fragmentation discourse developed from the assumption, more misguided than accurate, that international law (and, it can be added, law more generally) would have to be completely coherently structured if it was to be effective and legitimate.[70]

But effectivity and legitimacy of a regime are not properties intrinsically tied to regime coherence. It is true that norms that cohere with the normative goal of a system are usually more effective and legitimate and through their coherence stabilize the system, but norms can develop outside of coherence relationships and still be effective and legitimate, given that other "character traits" act in compensation of the failure of coherence, such as legal-cultural consonance or a very high level of norm effectivity.

Especially as societies develop and technologies demand more detailed regulation, regime disintegration through normative centrifugal forces may take place. Central principles (of international law), however, exercise a normative pull toward the center, even in times of ordered disorder. Here, a phenomenon reemerges that the ILC *Fragmentation Report* has also identified: regime development. That special fields within international law should emerge is not surprising. It is an "adequate response to the complexification of global society."[71] The normative tools we need to ensure coherence across the system and integration within it are present in international law. Peters also identifies the demise of hierarchy in (international) law but argues that traditional mechanisms of ordering, in which she includes hierarchy, "have been largely *replaced* by new mechanisms of stabilization."[72]

Teubner is stricter when it comes to coherence. He identifies as a problem the move away of norm-making processes from traditional national centers toward the transnational periphery, where different entities engage in the self-production of rules that are sometimes detailed enough to serve as a regime unto itself: "lex mercatoria, lex sportiva, lex electronica."[73] Calliess similarly names *lex mercatoria* as an example of a private regime, developing a non-state legal order with global legitimacy (demands) without a (state) mediated coupling of economics and law.[74] The newly emerging co-regulatory regimes contribute to global legal pluralism[75] and have led to

[67] Anne Peters, "The Refinement of International Law: From Fragmentation to Regime Interaction and Politicization," ICON 15 (2017) 3, 671–704 (702).

[68] Milton Mueller, *Will the Internet Fragment? Sovereignty, Globalization and Cyberspace* (Malden, MA: Polity Press, 2017).

[69] See 4.3 and 4.4, where this point is made. See also ILC, Fragmentation of International Law: Difficulties arising from the Diversification and Expansion of International Law, Report of the Study Group of the International Law Commission, 13 April 2006, A/CN.4/L.682, para. 493.

[70] Anne Peters, "The Refinement of International Law: From Fragmentation to Regime Interaction and Politicization," ICON 15 (2017) 3, 671–704 (702).

[71] Ibid.

[72] Ibid.

[73] Gunther Teubner, *Verfassungsfragmente. Gesellschaftlicher Konstitutionalismus in der Globalisierung* (Frankfurt am Main: Suhrkamp, 2012), 87. See, in a similar vein: Vesting, *Rechtstheorie* (2015), 143.

[74] Gralf-Peter Calliess, "Systemtheorie," in Sonja Buckel, Ralph Christensen, and Andreas Fischer-Lescano (eds.), *Neue Theorien des Rechts*, 2nd edn. (Stuttgart: Lucius&Lucius, 2009), 53–71 (67).

[75] Gunther Teubner, "Globale Bukowina. Zur Emergenz eines transnationalen Rechtspluralismus," Rechtshistorisches Journal 15 (1996) 255 ff.

regime collisions and to a certain level of fragmentation of global law.[76] Calliess applies the concept of legal institutions to functionally differentiated, specialized cross-border regimes constructed by multiple actors.[77] They can be considered regimes of law/legal regimes (Rechtsregime) when they contribute to legal certainty in the world legal system.

Teubner has termed these regimes "autonomous constitutions of civil sectors of society": *Eigenverfassungen der [gesellschaftlichen] Zivilsektoren*.[78] This begs the two questions: first, how—in general—these auto-constitutionalist approaches can be legitimized, especially within developed societies; and second, how this applies to the digital sphere. Vesting, parsing Teubner, concludes that the problem of a "necessary digital constitution [Digitalverfassung] remains unsolved."[79] Certain societal values and goals must remain protected and must be channeled, in their performative energy, through norms, by the *pouvoir constituant*, to influence the behavior of those (same selves) in the *pouvoir constitué* of the digital. Fundamental and human rights come into play as background to the constitutional self-control of the order online as "norms of collision for evaluating contrary logics of acting,"[80] usually put in wrong dichotomies such as sovereignty vs. internet universality or state control over internet speech vs. internet freedom.

Similarly, Teubner measures autonomous standards that emerge from within regimes and the dangers they might have for other sectors of society, not against the "political constitution" (of states) but against the *Eigenverfassung*.[81] These standards can be accepted as law (having *Rechtsnormqualität*) if their production is tied (procedurally) to regime-specific human rights standards, which are sensitive to the challenges of information and communication technologies.[82] This translates into a systems theoretical explanation of why internet standards, contained e.g. in IETF's Request for Comments series,[83] are legitimate as instruments of normative ordering. The processes of norm production are open and based on the inclusion of all relevant actors in their respective roles. However, the question remains whether a procedural tie-in to human rights is enough.[84] The importance of standards within the normative order of the internet, or in Teubner's terminology within the *Eigenverfassung* of the internet, makes it imperative that the standards themselves, and not only the procedures in which they are established, are based on, and pursue, accepted purposes of the normative order/*Eigenverfassung* that are framed in terms of human rights.

[76] Andreas Fischer-Lescano and Gunther Teubner, *Regime-Kollisionen. Zur Fragmentierung des globalen Rechts* (Frankfurt am Main: Suhrkamp, 2006), 24, 28 et seq.

[77] Gralf-Peter Calliess, "Systemtheorie," in Sonja Buckel, Ralph Christensen, and Andreas Fischer-Lescano (eds.), *Neue Theorien des Rechts*, 2nd edn. (Stuttgart: Lucius&Lucius, 2009), 53–71 (59).

[78] Gunther Teubner, "Globale Zivilverfassungen: Alternativen zur staatszentrierten Verfassungstheorie," ZaöRV 63 (2003), 1–28 (1, 16).

[79] Vesting, *Rechtstheorie* (2015), 144.

[80] Ibid.

[81] Gunther Teubner, "Globale Zivilverfassungen: Alternativen zur staatszentrierten Verfassungstheorie," ZaöRV 63 (2003), 1–28 (22).

[82] Vesting, *Rechtstheorie* (2015), 144.

[83] See 2.4.2.

[84] On the importance of processes, see Thomas Vesting, "Instituierte und konstituierte Normativität. Prozeduralisierung und multi-normative Systeme," in Tatjana Sheplyakova (ed.), *Prozeduralisierung des Rechts* (Tübingen: Mohr, 2018), 101–122.

5.2.6 Internal Politicization of the *Lex Digitalis*

Transnational regimes, such as the lex digitalis, *need to be politicized internally (i.e. rendered normatively more granular) as global constitutional fragments.*

Global society is increasingly functionally differentiated.[85] We can observe temporal inconsistencies in the political, economic, social, cultural, and legal processes, collectively described as globalization: "functionally differentiated systems such as law and politics remain stubbornly national, the economy and other societal systems refuse an internal differentiation on the basis of territorial borders."[86] Put differently: politics and law are still to a large degree tied to the state, while the economy is global. With regard to the politics and law of the internet, this holds true to a certain degree only.

It is correct that certain processes within internet regulation take place exclusively or primarily within national political and legal systems (such as the German Network Enforcement Act). There are, however, two caveats: First, even issues of primarily national concern have an international dimension, especially in countries with an international, law-friendly constitution, such as Germany—from international legal norms relating to the role and responsibilities of actors to the position of the national normative intervention vis-à-vis the normative order of the internet. Second, the majority of norm-making that impacts the internet and that seeks to safeguard states and global society from the internet transcends bordered discourses.

Andreas Fischer-Lescano and Gunther Teubner identified the emergence of autonomous private regimes as characteristic of modern international ordering.[87] Cautioning that not any order of norms by transnational entities is already a *legal order*, they demand the presence of a second order set of rules, institutionalizing processes for legal—first order—decisions.[88] For Fischer-Lescano and Teubner, the "lex digitalis of the internet" is among the most prominent autonomous legal regimes. Their prime example of second order rules is the secondary normation for contesting acts of ICANN by internet users through the rules regarding the *Uniform Dispute Resolution Policy* (UDRP) rules. Today, this normative element is only a fragment, albeit an admittedly well entrenched one, of the internet's order. More often used second order rules, albeit within the field of private regulatory arrangements, are those enshrining legal recourses to content moderation decisions by intermediaries providing online discussion and interaction spaces, such as social networking services.

Global regimes were first identified as being "functional [and] focused on solving *specific* international problems."[89] Yet at least the regime of online order has stabilized

[85] Gunther Teubner, *Verfassungsfragmente. Gesellschaftlicher Konstitutionalismus in der Globalisierung* (Frankfurt: Suhrkamp, 2012), 258.

[86] Gralf-Peter Calliess, "Systemtheorie," in Sonja Buckel, Ralph Christensen, and Andreas Fischer-Lescano (eds.), *Neue Theorien des Rechts*, 2nd edn. (Stuttgart: Lucius&Lucius, 2009), 53–71 (67).

[87] Andreas Fischer-Lescano and Gunther Teubner, *Regime-Kollisionen. Zur Fragmentierung des globalen Rechts* (Frankfurt am Main: Suhrkamp, 2006), 41.

[88] Ibid., 43.

[89] Gralf-Peter Calliess, "Systemtheorie," in Sonja Buckel, Ralph Christensen, and Andreas Fischer-Lescano (eds.), *Neue Theorien des Rechts*, 2nd edn. (Stuttgart: Lucius&Lucius, 2009), 53–71 (69): "[globale Regimes], die sich nicht unter territorialen, sondern unter funktionalen Gesichtspunkten auf die Lösung spezifischer grenzüberschreitender Problemlagen spezialisieren" (emphasis added; translation by the author).

normatively since then, from a collection of norms aiming at solving specific conflicts and modulating behavior for regime-internal purposes, albeit on a transnational plane,[90] to a *Rechtsregime*, a legal regime that contributes—beyond conflict resolution and steering behavior—to the creation and safeguarding of legal certainty in the international community, as a "partial system of the system of global law"[91] with a self-constitutionalizing dimension.

If we accept this claim, constitutionalists then demand that the partial order needs to be politicized internally (to self-constitute). The democratizing potential of segmented orders can be realized through a dualism of "formally organized rationality and informal spontaneity."[92] In this reading, the normative order of the internet—the "constitution of the internet" (*Verfassung des Internets*)—would need to provide rules for both a stable normative setting and procedures for developing spontaneous rules. Each order needs then to establish the normative preconditions for its "internal politicization": the inclusive processes in which actors of the order dispute the societal role of the order and possible dangers for natural, social, and human environments.[93] This discursive process functions as an "auto-constitutionalization of global orders without a state,"[94] or as the creation of "global orders beyond law."[95] It allows partial (sectoral, issue-specific) subsystems or regimes to develop their "constitutional" norms, stabilizing auto-constitutionalization processes. There is no guarantee for optimal outcomes: power constellations within "global fragments" can influence these processes. "Corporate capture" or, in Fischer-Lescano's and Teubner's wording, "totalization dispositions"[96] need to be countered through opposing forces, ensuring civil society participation in norm-making processes and individuals' access to decentralized and centralized adjudicating institutions.

Transnational regimes can be considered as "carriers of constitutionalization processes": they are "constitutionable social orders."[97] This conclusion is premised upon a redefinition of constitutionality: "constitutions" and "states" need to be decoupled as well as "constitutionalization" and "institutionalized political processes" and "constitutionalization" and "power." These processes can then lead to the transfer of sovereignty fragments to intermediary powers on the internet, which are at the center of social regimes that they then constitute. They thus paradoxically constitute their autonomy through self-referential processes[98] that are influenced by the embossing forces (*Prägekräfte*) of instituted (present) and constituted (created) normativity.[99]

[90] Ibid.
[91] Ibid.
[92] Ibid., 168 (translation by the author).
[93] Gunther Teubner, *Verfassungsfragmente. Gesellschaftlicher Konstitutionalismus in der Globalisierung* (Frankfurt am Main: Suhrkamp, 2012), 258.
[94] Ibid., 87.
[95] Thomas Dietz, *Global Order Beyond Law. How Information and Communication Technologies Facilitate Relational Contracting in International Trade* (London: Bloomsbury, 2014) (showing empirically that neither national laws nor international enforcement are used to execute many contracts. With international commercial arbitration also limited, complex decentralized and informal governance structures have emerged bottom-up as tools of enforcement).
[96] Andreas Fischer-Lescano and Gunther Teubner, *Regime-Kollisionen. Zur Fragmentierung des globalen Rechts* (Frankfurt am Main: Suhrkamp, 2006), 41.
[97] Ibid., 96 et seq.
[98] Ibid., 108.
[99] This is an important duality this study will return to, 6.3.

5.2.7 Transnational Constellations

Even though the online order as lex digitalis *has diversified to include non-highly coherent communities, its normative mixture of national legal orders, international regimes and transnational regulatory arrangements makes it a characteristic regime in which actors/institutions exercise transnational legal authority to varying degrees.*

The exercise of legal authority is traditionally bordered and centralized, after a century-long process of monopolization of power, with the constitutionally legitimated institutions of modern states. But in recent decades, globalization-related processes have diversified the pool of actors exercising authority, diversified their nature, and influenced the way authority is exercised internationally or transnationally. As theory after the fact, transnationalist approaches to (international) law emerged, attempting to conceptualize the *transnational legal authority*. This authority can be understood as "being largely coterminous with community expectations regarding the legitimate exercise of power transnationally,"[100] thus the administration of international legitimate rule that encompasses law but is not limited to it.

In these times of the pervasive use of information and communication technologies, the "paradigm of nation-state law" (*staatliches Rechtsparadigma*)[101] experiences limitations. While fact patterns and data flows transcend borders, states are (usually) estopped from transcending borders in exercising their jurisdiction. Gerd Winter has used the image of Goethe's sorcerer's apprentice. States have called the *Zauberlehrling* of globalization and entered the transnational constellation but have lost control. States are still necessary, Winter argues, to "pay the social costs and pacify social frustration," but they are endowed neither with the necessary financial support nor the personnel. This is a rather skeptical view (and premises a lot on the narrow foundation that it was indeed states who have "invoked" globalization[102] and that globalization is a recent process,[103] two contentions that are problematic[104]).

International law, the second order of norms coming to mind when fact patterns cross borders, may be applicable, but, as Winter writes, it is slow when measured against the substantial "need for norms": cultural divergence and the sovereign equality make finding common normative solutions difficult.[105] This frees up the normative space for a third

[100] Günther Handl, "Extra-territoriality and Transnational Legal Authority," in Günther Handl, Joachim Zekoll, and Peer Zumbansen (eds.), *Beyond Territoriality. Transnational Legal Authority in an Age of Globalization* (Leiden/Boston: Martinus Nijhoff, 2012), 3–12 (8).

[101] Lars Viellechner, *Transnationalisierung des Rechts* (Weilerswist: Velbrück, 2013), 99.

[102] But see Dilip K. Das, "Globalisation: Past and Present," Economic Affairs 30 (2010) 1, 66–70; Jerry Bentley, "Globalizing History and Historicizing Globalization," Globalizations 1 (2004) 1, 68–81.

[103] David Northrup, "Globalization and the Great Convergence: Rethinking World History in the Long Term," Journal of World History 16 (2005) 3, 249–67.

[104] The Silk Road in Asia of the first century AD is one immediately identifiable but by no means essential avenue of "globalization" (Peter Frankopan, *The Silk Roads: A New History of the World* (London: Bloomsbury, 2016)). For the importance of integrating markets, see already Adam Smith, *An Inquiry into the Nature and Causes of the Wealth of Nations* (1775). Cf. Economist, "When did globalization start?" September 23, 2013, https://www.economist.com/blogs/freeexchange/2013/09/economic-history-1 (arguing that market integration is "almost as old as humanity").

[105] Gerd Winter, "Transnationale informelle Regulierung: Gestalt, Effekte und Rechtsstaatlichkeit," in Gralf-Peter Calliess (ed.), *Transnationales Recht. Stand und Perspektiven* (Tübingen: Mohr Siebeck, 2014), 95–112 (96–7).

category of norms, transnational norms in the narrower sense: informal regulation by transnational actors or applicable to transnational settings which might be, in aggregate, highly suitable to ensure a fair distribution of rights and goods.

The primary attachment of rights to territories thus changes in light of the growing number of moving parts (and people, and (even connected) things) in times of globalization. Illustrating this with the example of human rights, Stefan Kadelbach finds that these are no longer "exclusively attached to territories, but to actors as well, so that they cross state borders with international organisations, transnational enterprises, or development agencies."[106] Similarly, on the internet, actors, data, their "attached" human rights, the cross-border nature of communications, and the difficulties of localizing internet traffic at any given point in time (and place) are in steady (and not always productive) conflict with the state obligation to respect, protect, and implement human rights.

Applying this to the internet, we see that internet intermediaries, standard-setting bodies, and international organizations exert what Gerald Spindler terms "external [and real] pressure on virtual spaces." Acting within a national (and it should be added: international) normative frame, these actors develop *private* transnational norms.[107] Spindler contrasts these transnationalization dynamics with a perceived "renationalization of the law on the internet": attempts and reactions of national legal orders to "re-localize fact patterns."[108] For him, statal renationalization by law seems so powerful that it would be "hubris" to talk of a "lex informatica in analogy to a lex mercatoria."[109] By contrast, this study submits that *lex informatica*, as the sum of norms of what this study terms the "normative order of the internet," is substantially more diverse than *lex mercatoria*. It is not hubris or talk ex nihilo to posit the existence of an online order. Rather, it is analytically correct, empirically founded,[110] and prescriptively necessary.[111]

Spindler argued that examples such as ICANN[112] showed that private norm-creation on the internet primarily worked within "small highly coherent communities with similar values and ideals," in which enforcement is guaranteed by social control.[113] In non-homogeneous normative communities, the externalities (costs) of enforcement would be too high. This claim, if true, would make a strong case against the normative order of the internet. However, it is submitted here, and will be explained in more detail in the next chapter, that the coherence is also present in the normative macro-order of the internet, that commitment to values and ideals exist, and that enforcement, where decentralized enforcement is necessary to realize a norm's content, has fewer costs than imagined. Many norms

[106] Stefan Kadelbach, "The Territoriality and Migration of Fundamental Rights," in Günther Handl, Joachim Zekoll, and Peer Zumbansen (eds.), *Beyond Territoriality. Transnational Legal Authority in an Age of Globalization* (Leiden/Boston: Martinus Nijhoff, 2012), 295–326 (323).

[107] Gerald Spindler, "Transnationalisierung und Renationalisierung des Rechts im Internet," in Gralf-Peter Calliess (ed.), *Transnationales Recht* (Tübingen: Mohr Siebeck, 2014), 219.

[108] Ibid., 221.

[109] And let us keep in mind that the *Zauberlehrling's* messages are to avoid hubris and listen to one's teacher/master.

[110] See chapters 2 to 4.

[111] See chapters 6 and 7.

[112] ICANN is indeed a special case in point for a largely autonomous transnational regime. See Lars Viellechner, *Transnationalisierung des Rechts* (Weilerswist: Velbrück, 2013), 99, who made an important contribution to the more recent literature on transnationalization of law, with unparalleled clarity regarding the domain name management by ICANN as an effective and legitimate case of normative transnationalism online (127 et seq).

[113] Ibid., 221.

of the normative online order do not need to be "enforced." Rather, they shape behavior and invoke *suo quoque* justificatory narratives from the "space of reasons."

Transnationalism can be approached via private[114] and via public law.[115] Descriptively, transnational law in the broader sense is a hybrid, containing rules from national legal orders, public international law regimes, and transnational sets of rules (Viellechner calls them *Regelungsarrangements*).[116]

Transnational law in a narrower sense is only the third category of norms relevant in transnational constellations: regulatory arrangements that are neither primarily affiliated with national legislators or part of international law.[117] For Calliess, transnational law is characteristically created through the normative powers of global civil society, "founded on general principles of law and their concretization through societal practice." Transnational norms are applied, interpreted, revised "primarily" by private actors. Calliess and Zumbansen see providers of alternative dispute resolution mechanisms in this role,[118] but they are only few good examples, such as ICANN's dispute resolution policy regarding domain names. Rather, ICT companies are in the position of primary norm-producers and appliers within the transnational order online. It thus makes sense that (limited) codification of transnational norms (of the internet) takes place through collections of principles,[119] standardized terms of service,[120] and codes of conduct by private actors.[121]

Transnationalism sharpens the evaluative focus regarding the quality of norms and their origin on the internet: they can be norms of self-regulation,[122] norms of state regulation,[123] norms of international regulation,[124] and norms of hybrid regulatory forms. Especially the latter norms are a regulatory arrangement that is characterized by its transnationality.[125] Together, transnationalized law is developed in processes of responsive legal pluralism, which allows combining contrarian but valid objectives—such as state sovereignty and internet universality—without "falling prey to radical particularity."[126]

[114] Gralf-Peter Calliess and Peer Zumbansen, *Rough Consensus and Running Code. A Theory of Transnational Private Law* (Oxford and Portland, OR: Hart, 2012).

[115] Lars Viellechner, *Transnationalisierung des Rechts* (Weilerswist: Velbrück, 2013), 301.

[116] Ibid.

[117] Though arguably, international law encompasses soft law and most norms within transnational regulatory arrangements fall within this category and are thus part of international law in this reading. However, this study presents, in this section, the transnational approach to norm differentiation, which in its three-part structure has some advantages of clarity.

[118] Gralf-Peter Calliess and Peer Zumbansen, *Rough Consensus and Running Code. A Theory of Transnational Private Law* (Oxford/Portland, OR: Hart, 2012).

[119] As we have seen in 3.4.8.

[120] See Lee A. Bygrave, *Internet Governance by Contract* (Oxford: OUP, 2015).

[121] See, for example, Global Network Initiative, Principles on Freedom of Expression and Privacy, http://www.globalnetworkinitiative.org/principles/index.php and the Accountability, Policy and Learning Framework, February 2015, https://globalnetworkinitiative.org/wp-content/uploads/2019/03/Acct-Policy-Learning-Framework.pdf.

[122] David R. Johnson and David G. Post, "Law and Borders," Stanford Law Review 48 (1996), 1367 (1367) (developing a theory of a newly bordered "cyberspace," a "distinct Cyberspace that needs and can create its own laws and legal institutions").

[123] Just see, already: Franz C. Mayer, "Europe and the Internet," EJIL (2000), 149.

[124] Franz C. Mayer, "Das Internet, das Völkerrecht und die Internationalisierung des Rechts," ZfRSoz (2002), 93 (arguing that the internet is the "natural object of international law, if not its ideal object: a global phenomenon, transcending borders [...], a phenomenon, that a state can hardly regulate by itself").

[125] Lars Viellechner, *Transnationalisierung des Rechts* (Weilerswist: Velbrück, 2013), 147.

[126] Ibid., 301.

The normativity of transnationalism and its constituant order is of importance. In transnational settings, just as within states, law and law-like norms can reign in what Gerd Winter described in his study on transnational private regulation as the "subcutaneous power" of private actors.[127] Within states the duty of state authorities to apply existing laws (or develop new ones) to private actors is well established as part of their duty to protect (and implement) the rights of all persons under states' jurisdiction or control. On the international level, this duty is only emerging.

5.2.8 Permeability and Regime Dialog

Transnational theory provides us with normative concepts of how to integrate different regimes, including the horizontal application of human rights, dialogical normativity, a Vernetzung, *and dual constitutionalization.*

Transnational theorists provide the system with important tools to keep the different regulatory fields open for each other and to enable processes of norm transfer and re-transfer. We can call this phenomenon "transnational dialogical normativity." Behind this dialogical normativity lie transnationalism's coherence-promoting powers. The three constituent parts of transnational law *sensu lato* (national law, international law, transnational sets of rules/regulatory arrangements) are, to functionally differentiated degrees, interdependent, interrelated, and mutually reinforcing—and continuously engaged in processes of integration at variable speeds and geometries.

One avenue of normative interchange is the use of the transnational dimension of fundamental rights as a rule of collision for conflicts between national law(s) and transnational norms: in this reading fundamental rights in a horizontal application would function as foundation and limit for transnational regulatory arrangements.[128]

A second approach, formulated by Luhmann *avant la lettre* of transnationalism, seems to be the inclusion of cognitive mechanisms within the normative structure of transnational arrangements,[129] so that these can self-adapt as autonomous systems and solve conflicts between the three constituant orders of transnational law.

A promising third approach is refining the three normative fields of transnational law (national, international, transnational regulation *strictu sensu*) to make them responsive to and for each other's norms and narratives, and normative processes, through rules of collision.[130] For Viellechner, responsivity means a combination of complementarity and subsidiarity,[131] a *Vernetzung* of national legal orders, international regimes, and transnational regulatory arrangements through a new "law of collision as horizontal constitutional law."[132] Even if the characterization of responsivity as part of a global "constitutional law" is not shared, the law of collision regulating interaction of the three normative sources is an essential element of the normative order of the internet.

[127] Gerd Winter, "Transnationale informelle Regulierung: Gestalt, Effekte und Rechtstaatlichkeit," in Gralf-Peter Calliess (ed.), *Transnationales Recht* (Tübingen: Mohr Siebeck, 2014), 95–112(108).

[128] Ibid., 217–18, 293.

[129] Niklas Luhmann, *Rechtssoziologie*, 4th edn. (Wiesbaden: Verlag für Sozialwissenschaften, 2008), 340 et seq.

[130] Lars Viellechner, *Transnationalisierung des Rechts* (Weilerswist: Velbrück, 2013), 117.

[131] Ibid., 269.

[132] Ibid., 265.

The permeability of the three orders is one based on implied reciprocity which presupposes that each order can conceive of and processes its limits and has meta-rules for performing these operations and for normative self-reflection.[133] A regime's ability to self-reflect (premised upon a collection of meta-rules allowing its participants to reflect on the regime's limits and purpose) is tied to the power of regimes to center on their own identity and develop interdependency relationships with other orders/systems. Teubner and Willke see this self-reflection as a "higher form of self-reference [...] oriented intentionally on [the regime's] own identity."[134]

Once regimes are considered to reach these levels of normative intricacies, the last step is their dual constitutionalization.[135] Building on Teubner and Fischer-Lescano's work on regimes, regime collisions, and constitutional fragments, Viellechner identifies the dimensions of *Eigenkonstitutionalisierung* and *Fremdkonstitutionalisierung*: auto- and hetero-constitutionalization. These processes will be discussed in more depth in the next chapter, as they can be usefully applied to the normative order of the internet. Let it be said here simply that auto-constitutionalization necessitates meta-rules, allowing for a system's self-reflection, and that hetero-constitutionalization allows for important legitimacy transfers: by interacting with them, national constitutions provide legitimacy for transnational regulatory arrangements, but also recognize them as law.[136]

Transnational law has developed into an accepted field of law. It has been stratified and sedimented to the point that interlegal dialog between national law, international law, and transnational regulatory arrangements can ask after the validity of national approaches and the force of law accorded to national legal phenomena in cross-border settings. Positing a norm as imbued with national legal *Rechtskraft* is not the end of processes of legal communication, as before, but the first step toward what Fischer-Lescano, in opposition to Agamben, argues is "the very condition of transnational contestability [*Appellabilität*]."[137]

5.2.9 Hybrid Legal Spaces

The normative order of the internet can reestablish normative unity in light of norm conflicts in hybrid legal spaces, characterized by legal pluralism and multinormativity—normative phenomena, which have dealt a serious blow to monist and dualist conceptions of law.

Transnational law is connected to multinormativity and legal pluralism as one possible normative response.[138] Multinormativity refers to "the coexistence of different modi of

[133] Lars Viellechner, *Transnationalisierung des Rechts* (Weilerswist: Velbrück, 2013), 268–9. Niklas Luhmann, "Selbstreflexion des Rechtssystems," Rechtstheorie 10 (1979), 159 et seq.

[134] Gunther Teubner and Helmut Willke, "Kontext und Autonomie," Zeitschrift für Rechtssoziologie 5 (1984), 4 (14).

[135] Lars Viellechner, *Transnationalisierung des Rechts* (Weilerswist: Velbrück, 2013), 287.

[136] Ibid.

[137] Andreas Fischer-Lescano, *Rechtskraft* (Berlin: August Verlag, 2013), 30. On the Weberian origin of *Appellabilität*, see Agathe Bienfait, Die "Verantwortungsgesellschaft 'als "Konfliktgesellschaft:' Max Webers Beitrag jenseits von Fatalismus und Moralismus," in Ludger Heidbrink and Alfred Hirsch (eds.), *Verantwortung in der Zivilgesellschaft. Zur Konjunktur eines widersprüchlichen Prinzips* (Frankfurt/New York: Campus, 2006), 165–87 (172).

[138] Michael Grünberger, "Transnationales Recht als responsiver Rechtspluralismus," Der Staat 55 (2016), 117–33.

normativity within the same social space and the connected questions of classification, legitimation and collision."[139] It also includes forms of normativity, which are not traditional sources of law, and offers conceptual advantages over "legal pluralism"/*Rechtspluralismus* by avoiding the reference to "legal"/*Recht* (thus excluding "non-legal" norms) and to "pluralism," which implies a deviancy from non-pluralism.[140] But both notions will be used in the following. Multinormativity is present also in "mononormatively conceived legal orders," especially in sub-sectors of society.[141] Each plurality of legal orders, each multinormativity, also equates to a plurality of other normative orders."[142]

The unity of law within a state is a fiction, though it has not always been recognized as such: "Just a generation ago," Michael Stolleis writes, "the world of law [...] seemed relatively clear [*übersichtlich*]," at least to a "beginner" [emerging lawyer-scholar].[143] Historically, the coexistence (and concurrence and collision) of lawmakers and legal orders was more the rule than the exception.[144] It was rather the anti-feudalist liberalism and state/nation-building of the nineteenth century, together with nationalisms of the early twentieth century and the later democratization, that shattered class-, wealth-, job-, and gender-based traditional societal structures, flattened the social order[145] and broke open the circles of law/*Rechtskreise,* formally conceived of as unchanging, unchangeable, and divinely ordained. Recall, for instance, the right of universities to police their students, including by using university prisons,[146] to the exclusion of other (e.g. city and ecclesiastic) authorities. Progressively, however, legal plurality has been recognized as fact. Especially in social fields "connected through modern communication technologies [...] non-statal, autonomous norm-setting processes" can be seen, including "internet, sports and science."[147]

Especially in these fields, norms emerge within "self-regulating systems" that Stolleis sees organized by "global companies, communication networks and market-regulating associations." The other "players" are then subjected to these specific rules. Writing already in 2008, Stolleis foresees the problems: "It starts with the fine-print terms and conditions and ends with global regulations of monopolists, to which the individual has to submit, when they wish to receive the service or information offered."[148] Eventually, individuals are confronted with "non-statal norm collections," especially when following the "order 'Click here.'"[149] This description holds true today.

[139] Thomas Duve, "Was ist 'Multinormativität?'—Einführende Bemerkungen," Rechtsgeschichte—Legal History 25 (2017), 88–101(90).

[140] Ibid., 92.

[141] Ibid., 98.

[142] Klaus Günther, "Normativer Rechtspluralismus—Eine Kritik," Normative Orders Working Paper 03/2014, http://publikationen.ub.uni-frankfurt.de/files/34664/Guenther_Normativer+Rechtspluralismus.pdf, 3.

[143] Cf. Michael Stolleis, "Vormodernes und postmodernes Recht?" Quaderni Fiorentini 37 (2008), 543–51.

[144] At least until the French Revolution, the parallelity of legal worlds (*Rechtswelten*) was "part of the everyday experience, just as everyday inequality" (ibid., 547).

[145] In theory, of course, in practice inequality persists: see just, Thomas Piketty, *Le capital au XXI siècle* (Paris: Éditions du Seuil, 2013).

[146] See Hans Günther Bickert and Norbert Nail, *Marburger Karzer-Buch: Kleine Kulturgeschichte des* Universitätsgefängnisses (Marburg: Jonas Verlag, 2013).

[147] Klaus Günther, "Normativer Rechtspluralismus—Eine Kritik," Normative Orders Working Paper 03/2014, http://publikationen.ub.uni-frankfurt.de/files/34664/Guenther_Normativer+Rechtspluralismus.pdf, 3.

[148] Michael Stolleis, "Vormodernes und postmodernes Recht?" Quaderni Fiorentini 37 (2008), 543–51 (544) (translation by the author).

[149] Ibid.

In light of the coexisting and colliding legal and quasi-legal norms, norm givers, and norm appliers, Schiff Berman diagnosed the emergence of a "hybrid legal space."[150] Similarly, Gerald Spindler identified the external pressure on "virtual spaces, platforms and organizations" as a driving force behind the emergence of "complementary, private, autonomous, transnational norm-making processes and nationally produced legal frameworks which, together, can be characterized as hybrid regulation."[151]

It is clear that the world's hybrid legal space cannot be reconceptualized in a monist fashion. Universalist approaches are unrealistic in light of progressive diversification and complex normative dynamics within the global society.[152] Global legal monist approaches are neither possible nor normatively preferential outside of institutionalizations of ius cogens norms, e.g. through treaty regimes against genocide (international criminal law), apart from key universal human rights commitments, and (and this is where it gets interesting for the purpose of the present study) with regard to the regulation of regimes protecting global common interests, such as the integrity of the internet (and the protection of the international community from the internet and its uses and applications.)

A theory of *normative* legal pluralism queries less whether the state of legal pluralism is an empirically correct description of the normative status quo, but rather whether it is *normatively preferential* over a return to models of norm-creation oriented toward equivalents of legal monism. Legal pluralism may indeed be normatively preferable over non-pluralist approaches within functional systems, as autonomous normative processes may be more responsive to their internal rationalities (and thus more responsive and legitimate) than "global law."[153] (This is the logic behind the normative preference for subsidiarity in most legal systems.) The diverse functional systems could then progressively auto-constitutionalize. This connects Günther to Fischer-Lescano's and Teubner's *Verfassungsfragmente* and regime collisions (if plural orders collide).[154] A further normative advantage would be an increased level of accountability of actors within pluralist sub-regimes.[155]

However, smaller pluralist orders are also more likely to be captured by special interests. Within any normative order the justification of norms is a matter of power.[156] This power is connected to resources, including information and communication technology. "Who[ever] with the help of [ICTs] can successfully disseminate normative reasons or successfully immunize against criticism," as Günther writes, can also determine the aggregation and articulation of opinions in political processes and thus has "greater opportunities to enforce [their] normative order over others and to immunize against criticism,

[150] Paul Schiff Berman, *Global Legal Pluralism: A Jurisprudence of Law Beyond Borders* (Cambridge: CUP, 2012). First developed in Paul Schiff Berman, "Global Legal Pluralism," Southern California Law Review 80 (2007), 1155.

[151] Gerald Spindler, "Transnationalisierung und Renationalisierung des Rechts im Internet," in Gralf-Peter Calliess (ed.), *Transnationales Recht* (Tübingen: Mohr Siebeck, 2014), 193–223 (219).

[152] Klaus Günther, "Normativer Rechtspluralismus—Eine Kritik," Normative Orders Working Paper 03/2014, http://publikationen.ub.uni-frankfurt.de/files/34664/Guenther_Normativer+Rechtspluralismus.pdf, 6.

[153] Ibid., 7.

[154] Cf. Andreas Fischer-Lescano and Gunther Teubner, *Regime-Kollisionen. Zur Fragmentierung des globalen Rechts* (Frankfurt am Main: Suhrkamp, 2006), 24; Gunther Teubner, *Verfassungsfragmente. Gesellschaftlicher Konstitutionalismus in der Globalisierung* (Frankfurt am Main: Suhrkamp, 2012), 87.

[155] Nico Krisch, *Beyond Constitutionalism. The Pluralist Structure of Postnational Law* (Oxford: OUP, 2012), 58 et seq., 225 et seq.

[156] Rainer Forst und Klaus Günther, "Die Herausbildung normativer Ordnungen. Zur Idee eines interdisziplinären Forschungsprogramms," in Rainer Forst und Klaus Günther (eds.), *Die Herausbildung normativer Ordnungen. Interdisziplinäre Perspektiven* (Frankfurt/New York: Campus, 2011), 11–30 (16).

dissidence, and resistance, at least for extended periods of time."[157] Once the internal pressure within the immunized system becomes too high, the normative order is in crisis—and might be overthrown. A revolution is thus an exchange in normative orders through means not foreseen in that order.

Schiff Berman shows that the capture of normative orders by special interests, especially the epistemic monopolization of the "space of reasons," can be overcome by configuring the "internal management" processes of multi-normative spaces within the hybrid global legal space,[158] to conceive of themselves as a "shared social space," wherein everyone can take part in a "common set of discursive forms"[159] to discuss the justifications for the order and its norms—a variation on both Forst (regarding justifications) and Habermas (regarding almost ideal discursive processes). Schiff Berman's second condition would be the acceptance by all of certain principles and values necessary for finding functional solutions—another Habermasian contention – thus turning the shared social into a shared *symbolic* space.

Accepting multinormativity as a given, and as normatively preferable over monism in the global legal sphere, we need to ask how the global plurality of legal and quasi-legal orders can be made compatible with each other. One answer is clearly the reliance on fundamental norms of international law and international legal principles as providing the frame. Teubner calls these "common reference points for all regimes to counterfactually imply a necessary abstract sense horizon,"[160] whereas Günther refers to "common good-related formulations relative to the system."[161] More practically, Günther's suggestion for compatibilitization relates to the technicians of compatibility, including global legal experts, and those active in the communication of legal processes to the public to participate in the "cosmopolitan pluralist jurisprudence" by demanding publicly "reasons and justifications."[162]

The system of law to manage multinormativity thus seems to be the *Recht des Rechtspluralismus*[163] (the law of legal pluralism) as an "implicit meta-law of global actors," containing rules on mutual recognition between normative orders. This meta-law is not new: already Rudolf Wiethölter's model of institutionalism with a theory of collisions of interests (*Kollisionstheoretische Institutionalismus*)[164] argues for the development of a "meta-system law" to avoid one interest, within collisions of interests, turning paramount, leading to "*Guts*"-*Abwägung* instead of "*Güter*"-*Abwägung*, that

[157] Klaus Günther, "Normativer Rechtspluralismus—Eine Kritik," Normative Orders Working Paper 03/2014 (2014), 8: "Wer über größere und stärkere ökonomische Ressourcen oder Gewaltmittel verfügt, wer mit Hilfe moderner Informationstechnologien normative Gründe strategisch erfolgreich verbreiten oder gegen Kritik erfolgreich immunisieren, die politische Agenda bestimmen und den politischen Prozess mit je eigenen Themen und Gründen erfolgreich beeinflussen kann, wer ganze Bevölkerungsgruppen in Abhängigkeit bringen oder Eliten zu Klienten machen kann, hat größere Chancen, seine normative Ordnung gegenüber anderen durchzusetzen und gegen Kritik, Dissidenz und Widerstand zumindest über längere Zeiträume zu immunisieren" (translation by the author).

[158] Paul Schiff Berman, *Global Legal Pluralism: A Jurisprudence of Law Beyond Borders* (Cambridge: CUP, 2012), 152ff.

[159] Ibid., 145–50 (145).

[160] Gunther Teubner, *Verfassungsfragmente. Gesellschaftlicher Konstitutionalismus in der Globalisierung* (Frankfurt am Main: Suhrkamp, 2012), 241.

[161] Klaus Günther, "Normativer Rechtspluralismus—Eine Kritik," Normative Orders Working Paper 03/2014, http://publikationen.ub.uni-frankfurt.de/files/34664/Guenther_Normativer+Rechtspluralismus.pdf, 17.

[162] Ibid., 14.

[163] Ralf Seinecke, *Das Recht des Rechtspluralismus* (Tübingen: Mohr Siebeck, 2015).

[164] Andreas Fischer-Lescano and Gunther Teubner, "Prozedurale Rechtstheorie: Wiethölter," in Sonja Buckel, Ralph Christensen, and Andreas Fischer-Lescano (eds.), *Neue Theorien des Rechts*, 2nd edn. (Stuttgart: Lucius&Lucius, 2009), 75–89 (77).

is the balancing of *an interest* instead of the balancing of *interests*.[165] Such a meta-law that is based on safeguarding international common interest through multi-normative ordering must be sensitive to interest capture and can unite legal traditions by responsive pluralistic approaches.[166]

5.2.10 Exercising Authority Beyond the State

In a growing number of international administrations, international public authority (IPA) is exercised by non-traditionally legitimated regimes. By applying fundamental principles present across a plurality of national and international normative orders, we can assess the legitimacy of exercise of IPA through actors/institutions within the regime. This can be usefully translated to cases of exercise of international (public) authority within the normative order of the internet.

Changes in the concept of sovereignty[167] and an internationalization of constitutional and administrative challenges in transnational constellations and, subsequently, the internationalization of constitutional[168] and administrative[169] law and the development of transnational constitutional law[170] have moved research into the administration of issues of common interest and into the intersection of a plurality of normative orders.

Administration is power.[171] The key question behind global administration is thus the exercise of authority on a transnational level. Traditionally, public authority (*öffentliche Gewalt*) was exercised by state powers within their bordered regimes. Following von Bogdandy's work on international public authority,[172] this authority can be understood as the "legally founded ability to legally or factually influence other actors in their freedom or use thereof."[173] Such authority can take the form of legally binding acts (e.g. supranational

[165] Rudolf Wiethölter, "Begriffs- und Interessenjurisprudenz—falsche Fronten im IPR und Wirtschaftsverfassungsrecht. Bemerkungen zur selbstgerechten Kollisionsnorm," in Alexander Lüderitz and Jochen Schröder (eds.), *Internationales Privatrecht und Rechtsvergleichung im Ausgang des 20. Jahrhunderts. Bewahrung oder Wende? Festschrift für Gerhard Kegel* (Frankfurt am Main: Suhrkamp, 1977), 213, 232. See also Claus Becker, *Von Namen und Nummern. Kollisionen unverträglicher Rechtsmassen im Internet* (Baden-Baden: Nomos 2005), 13 (using Wiethölter's approach to reconstruct collisions of law in the Internet domain market).

[166] Lars Viellechner, *Transnationalisierung des Rechts* (Weilerswist: Velbrück, 2013), 302.

[167] See 2.3.5 (on conceptions of custodial sovereignty for internet resources) and 3.3.4.2 (on the principle of sovereign equality on the internet).

[168] Thomas Kleinlein, *Konstitutionalisierung im Völkerrecht. Konstruktion und Elemente einer idealistischen Völkerrechtslehre* (Heidelberg: Springer, 2012) (arguing that hierarchization, objectivization, and comprehensive models of rendering accountable any exercise of authority together with human rights obligations of international organizations have led to a "constitutionalization" in international law). Earlier approaches are contained in Jan Klabbers, Anne Peters, and Geir Ulfstein, *The Constitutionalization of International Law* (Oxford: OUP, 2009).

[169] Introducing the concept: Benedict Kingsbury, Nico Krisch, and Richard Stewart, "The Emergence of Global Administrative Law," Law and Contemporary Problems 2 (2005), 15.

[170] Stefan Kadelbach and Thomas Kleinlein, "Überstaatliches Verfassungsrecht," AVR (2006), 235. For a more function-oriented analysis, see Anne Peters, "Compensatory Constitutionalism: The Function and Potential of Fundamental International Norms and Structures," Leiden Journal of International Law (2006), 579.

[171] Norton E. Long, "Power and Administration," Public Administration Review 9 (1949) 4, 257–64 (arguing that "[t]he lifeblood of administration is power" and that there is "no more forlorn spectacle [. . .] than an agency [. . .] deprived of power. An object of contempt to its enemies and of despair to its friends").

[172] Just see Armin von Bogdandy, Philipp Dann, and Matthias Goldmann, "Völkerrecht als öffentliches Recht: Konturen eines rechtlichen Rahmens für Global Governance," Der Staat 49 (2010), 23.

[173] Armin von Bogdandy, "Prinzipien von Staat, supranationalen und internationalen Organisationen," § 232 (275–304), in Josef Isensee, Paul Kirchhof, et al. (eds.), *Handbuch des Staatsrechts, Band XI: Internationale Bezüge,*

legislation within the EU, sanction regimes of the UN Security Council), but can also be reified through non-binding acts. Decisions of international courts have been influential in shaping the international community, and courts and quasi-court adjudicatory systems have established themselves as administrators of some global common interest.[174]

International actors can also exercise authority through non-binding acts, when such acts "exercise pressure on other subjects which they can resist only with difficulties,"[175] e.g. by publishing non-binding but influential standards whose acceptance is in the interest of states, however such interest may be measured (financial or reputational). Even standards without deontic quality, such as statistical data within state reports under the educational assessment system known as PISA, can functionally fulfill the definition of exercise of public authority, as they influence state policy and through it the freedom spheres of individuals like binding acts.[176]

The Basic Law expressly foresees the possibility to transfer sovereign powers to the EU (Article 23 (1)) and to international organizations (Article 24 (1)). Such transfers are the basis for the (at least formally legitimated instances of the) exercise of international public authority. Article 23, especially, is clear as to why these transfers are allowed: with a view to "establishing a united Europe," Germany shall participate in the EU's development "that is committed to democratic, social and federal principles, to the rule of law, and to the principle of subsidiarity, and that guarantees a level of protection of basic rights essentially comparable to that afforded by this Basic Law." Transfer of powers to international public authorities thus does not mean that a state gives up its principles or *Hoheitsrechte*.[177] Rather, these principles need to be reconceptualized for the transnational constellations.

Under conditions of legal plurality and the plurality of normative orders, the exercise of legitimate public authority transnationally becomes intricate. As Armin von Bogdandy

3rd edn. (2013) (also published as Armin von Bogdandy, "Prinzipielles zur Pluralität normativer Ordnungen. Zu den Anforderungen an die Ausübung öffentlicher Gewalt," Normative Orders Working Paper 1/2013), 12.

[174] Armin von Bogdandy and Ingo Venzke, *In wessen Namen? Internationale Gerichte in Zeiten globalen Regierens* (Frankfurt am Main: Suhrkamp, 2014) (showing that international courts have long transcended their dispute settlement function and are now exercising international public authority which needs to (and can be) legitimated democratically).

[175] Armin von Bogdandy, "Prinzipielles zur Pluralität normativer Ordnungen. Zu den Anforderungen an die Ausübung öffentlicher Gewalt," Normative Orders Working Paper 1/2013, 14–15.

[176] Matthias Goldmann, *Internationale öffentliche Gewalt. Handlungsformen internationaler Institutionen im Zeitalter der Globalisierung* (Heidelberg: Springer, 2015).

[177] Just see BVerfG, judgment of November 22, 2001, BVerfGE 104, 151, *NATO-Konzept* (no development of a system of collective security that transcends legislative permission pursuant to Article 24 (2) Basic Law) and BVerfG, judgment of September 7, 2011, 2 BvR 987/10 (recalling that citizens are protected from their decision-making power in a democracy by broad transfers of responsibilities of the Bundestag to supranational institutions: "Art. 38 GG schützt die wahlberechtigten Bürger vor einem Substanzverlust ihrer verfassungsstaatlich gefügten Herrschaftsgewalt durch weitreichende oder gar umfassende Übertragungen von Aufgaben und Befugnissen des Bundestages, vor allem auf supranationale Einrichtungen." In particular, Article 38 (1) of the Fundamental Law protects from situations where "die Kompetenzen des gegenwärtigen oder künftigen Bundestages auf eine Art und Weise ausgehöhlt werden, die eine parlamentarische Repräsentation des Volkswillens, gerichtet auf die Verwirklichung des politischen Willens der Bürger, rechtlich oder praktisch unmöglich macht." See also BVerfG, judgment of March 18, 2014, 2 BvR 1390/12, *European Stability Mechanism*:

> the right to vote, which is protected by Art. 38 sec. 1 GG, guarantees the self-determination of the citizens and guarantees free and equal participation in the exercise of public power in Germany. Its guarantees include the principles of the requirement of democracy [...]. Art. 79 sec. 3 GG protects these principles as the identity of the Constitution even against interference by the constitution-amending legislature. In view of this, the legislature must take sufficient measures to be able to permanently meet its responsibility with respect to integration (*Integrationsverantwortung*). In particular, it may not relinquish its right to decide on the budget, not even in a system of intergovernmental governance (2 (a)).

writes, national, international, and supranational institutions are not organs of *one common* legal community, but because of the influence of EU law and the internationalization of (German) law, "national, supranational and international organs exercising authority [*Hoheitsträger*] are connected so closely that the legitimation of effective public authority within Germany can only be established in a holistic context."[178]

This holistic context is framed by common fundamental principles, namely human rights protection, rule of law, and democracy. They frame dogmatic discussions and discourses on legitimacy, transcending the three legal bodies and, as von Bogdandy argues, explain why institutions of one legal order resist acts of another—when the acts violate the principles.[179] Three principles (human rights protection, rule of law, and democracy) within the three orders (constitutional law, EU law, and international law) can be considered to form a minimum global consensus on legitimate exercise of public authority and apply to institutions and to the interacting legal orders.[180]

The theory and practices of the increasingly diverse administrations of international affairs have stabilized as *Global Administrative Law* approaches.[181] In these approaches we see social ordering on the trans-state level,[182] which becomes increasingly detailed in light of complexifying transnational social spheres, with the private sector and civil society very active as participants in normative processes. However, with Teubner we have to agree that the "constitutional" elements of sectoral administrative ordering relate more to the demands formulated by the internal, explicit or implicit, "constitutions" of regulatory actors (companies, civil society) and less to the area under regulation.[183] In other words: global administrative law approaches tell us more about the authors of norms and their conception of norms than about the regulated field. However, the normalization of transnational, increasingly detailed administration through non-state actors is an important element in the acculturation of private ordering[184] and has, to some degree, proven a template for the regulation of networked spaces.

It is especially the connection between global administrative law and global governance that is interesting for the purposes of the theoretical examination of concepts pursued presently.[185] Some have argued with some hyperbole that global administrative law is a new "approach to the new nomos of the earth in the global era."[186] Global

[178] Armin von Bogdandy, "Prinzipielles zur Pluralität normativer Ordnungen. Zu den Anforderungen an die Ausübung öffentlicher Gewalt," Normative Orders Working Paper 1/2013, 6.

[179] Ibid.

[180] Ibid., 39.

[181] Benedict Kingsbury, Nico Krisch, and Richard Stewart, "The Emergence of Global Administrative Law," Law and Contemporary Problems 2 (2005), 15. See further Nico Krisch, "The Pluralism of Global Administrative Law," EJIL 17 (2006), 247, and Benedict Kingsbury, "The Concept of 'Law' in Global Administrative Law," EJIL 20 (2009), 23.

[182] Sabino Cassese, "Administrative Law without the State? The Challenge of Global Regulation," New York University Journal of International Law and Policy 37 (2005), 663-693 (689).

[183] Gunther Teubner, *Verfassungsfragmente. Gesellschaftlicher Konstitutionalismus in der Globalisierung* (Frankfurt am Main: Suhrkamp, 2012), 85.

[184] See Matthias Goldmann, *Internationale öffentliche Gewalt. Handlungsformen internationaler Institutionen im Zeitalter der Globalisierung* (Heidelberg: Springer, 2015).

[185] Daniel C. Esty, "Good Governance at the Supranational Scale: Globalizing Administrative Law," Yale Law Journal 115 (2006), 1490.

[186] Ming-Sung Kuo, "Inter-public legality or post-public legitimacy? Global governance and the curious case of global administrative law as a new paradigm of law," International Journal of Constitutional Law 10 (2012), 4, 1050–75. On the inter-publicness dimension of international law, by contrast, which is nevertheless tied to administrative approaches: see Benedict Kingsbury, "International Law as Inter-Public Law," in Henry R. Richardson and Melissa S. Williams (eds.), *Moral Universalism und Pluralism* (New York: NYU Press, 2009), 167–204. In contrast, Ming-Sung Kuo ("Inter-public legality or post-public legitimacy? Global governance and the curious case of global

administrative law can function as a meta-constitution[187] in that it provides for global concepts of legality and it furthers, via the global administration of common interest goods, the legitimacy of global governance approaches, including internet governance approaches.

5.2.11 Normative Ordering and Undernormativity

A normative order of the internet provides justification for its norms within a space of reasons accessible to all.

Rainer Forst has long been engaged in questions of justice and global order.[188] Based on the conviction that transnational orders are orders of justice, he saw the need for "holistic, radical change,"[189] based on a critical theory of transnational justice.[190] Such a theory provides—at a minimum—a practice of justification of distribution of justice and, ultimately, the realization of a just society.[191] Its goal is the enabling of democratic self-determination in a justified fundamental structure.[192]

Forst conceptualizes a just society as having a justificatory superstructure, as positioned within an order of justification made up of a complex of different institutions, norms, and justification practices. Importantly, everyone has a *Recht auf Rechtfertigung*, a right to justification of the order in which they exist.[193] No one should be subjected to norms and institutions which cannot be justified toward them, based on reasons which they can question. Practices of justice are thus based on justifications, which are based on justification practices.[194] These are framed and ordered with an order of justification and narrativized. Such an order of justification is connected to the reasons for exercising power. The stories told about the exercise of this power are framed in justification narratives,[195] which, together with the normative orders they explain and justify, develop out of specific historical, religious, and cultural, economic, social, and political constellations and experiences, but can be contested and changed.[196]

administrative law as a new paradigm of law," International Journal of Constitutional Law 10 (2012), 4, 1050–75) calls global administrative law the "new paradigm of law centering on inter-public legality" in that it grounds publicness in the "distinct publics of regulatory regimes" and resolves "inter-regime conflicts into the question of balancing the legalities of individual regulatory regimes".

[187] In the sense of Carl Schmitt's notion of the "nomos of the earth": Carl Schmitt, *Der Nomos der Erde im Völkerrecht des Jus Publicum Europaeum*, 2nd edn. (Berlin: Duncker&Humblot, 1950/1974).

[188] See for a dense description of his and Klaus Günther's approach to normative orders: Rainer Forst und Klaus Günther, "Die Herausbildung normativer Ordnungen. Zur Idee eines interdisziplinären Forschungsprogramms," in Rainer Forst und Klaus Günther (eds.), *Die Herausbildung normativer Ordnungen. Interdisziplinäre Perspektiven* (Frankfurt/New York: Campus, 2011), 11–30 (16).

[189] Rainer Forst, *Das Recht auf Rechtfertigung. Elemente einer konstruktivistischen Theorie der Gerechtigkeit* (Frankfurt am Main: Suhrkamp, 2007), 341.

[190] Ibid., 357 et seq.

[191] Ibid., 369.

[192] Ibid., 380.

[193] Rainer Forst, *Kritik der Rechtfertigungsverhältnisse. Perspektiven einer kritischen Theorie der Politik* (Berlin: Suhrkamp, 2011), 107.

[194] Ibid., 109.

[195] Rainer Forst, *Normativität und Macht. Zur Analyse sozialer Rechtfertigungsordnungen* (Berlin: Suhrkamp, 2015), 85.

[196] Ibid., 86.

In this view, every normative order is an order of justification, namely of social rules, norms, and institutions, which are the foundation for the distribution of goods and the legitimacy of rule. The normative order as order of justification is *premised upon* justifications and produces them.[197] Each order is embedded in (a) justification narrative(s) which is/are developed over time, modified, and contested. As embodied rationality these narratives of justification are resources of order-sense (*Ressourcen der Ordnungssinngebung).*[198]

Forst develops this approach into a comprehensive "theory of fundamental transnational justice"[199] and ties transnational justice closely to democratization. Forcing privileged actors to justify their behavior and thus give up the prerogative of (at least) not explaining one's reasons (*L'État c'est moi; Mein Wille ist Gesetz*) is an act of democratization. In this view, "practical democracy is always democratization: a process of extending and equalizing the power of justification."[200]

Forst approaches normative orders as comprehensive conceptions, but they cannot (be expected to) explain all normative phenomena. Christoph Möllers cautions that we should not fall prey to a modernist overreliance on the powers of order to formalize, stabilize, and justify norms.[201] Normative orders in practice are gradual in nature. In some fields norms are more densely present, other fields of the same order are only loosely regulated, sometimes only with "formalism internal to the order."[202]

In assessing the norms present in the normative order of the internet, Christoph Möllers'[203] new theory of norms—the *Possibility of Norms*—is useful. He criticizes the way that too much of modern political theory is focused on unity and societal coherence. This endangers democratic orders by factually excluding deviance. In this view, an order characterized by undernormativity (he mentions digitalization as an example) is not *less* democratic but *more* democratic[204] as it allows for more decision-making freedom. Indeed, with Harcourt,[205] the predictive powers of institutionalized data-driven algorithmic processes can be seen very critically. In this view, any democratic normative order has to allow for deviance and to ensure that algorithms play only a minor role in regulating behavior.

For Möllers, algorithms exclude normativity: "a society whose behavior is programmed has no space for norms."[206] This applies, of course, only in cases where algorithms close the deliberative space and function as anti-deviance devices, either explicitly or through nudging.[207] Not every algorithm does. Möllers suggests the inclusion of chance mechanisms as variance enablers to ensure contingency as a precondition for normative practices.[208] This connects

[197] Ibid., 87.
[198] Ibid.
[199] Ibid., 229.
[200] Ibid., 233.
[201] Christoph Möllers, *Die Möglichkeit der Normen* (Berlin: Suhrkamp, 2016), 442.
[202] Ibid., 382.
[203] Ibid., 137–9.
[204] Ibid., 452.
[205] Bernard E. Harcourt, *Against Prediction. Profiling, Policing, and Punishing in an Actuarial Age* (Chicago: University of Chicago Press, 2007) (charting the rise of the "actuarial paradigm," identifying the efficiency argument as "illusory," critiquing the hidden social costs, including distorting effects on society's conceptions of punishments, and describing randomization as a virtue).
[206] Christoph Möllers, *Die Möglichkeit der Normen* (Berlin: Suhrkamp, 2016), 455.
[207] Richard H. Thaler and Cass R. Sustein, *Nudge. Improving Decisions about Health, Wealth, and Happiness* (New Haven: Yale University Press, 2008).
[208] Christoph Möllers, *Die Möglichkeit der Normen* (Berlin: Suhrkamp, 2016), 455.

Möllers to Luhmann's position on contingency.[209] Teubner, too, is critical of normative instruments that exclude interpretation: the binary logic of information and communication technology supplants, through self-executing technical standards, the decisional space reserved for law: "As far as the internet code reaches, this excludes interpretation in the [coded] programmes."[210]

This study submits that such an understanding of programs is too formalistic. They are normative in nature even if they are made up of code and encoded algorithmic decision-making. Each algorithmic decision can be traced back to a normative decision taken on the basis of certain normative standards. Only looking at the last "link" in the normative chain of commands (or the last step(s) in an algorithmic decision-making tree) and declaring that normativity is excluded because an algorithm applies operations automatically does not do justice to the complex nature of governance by[211] and of[212] algorithms.

5.3 Online Order Theories

5.3.1 Internet Constitutionalization

Societal constitutionalization processes on the internet contribute to the development of the normative order of the internet. Especially in the absence of a "constitutional moment," internet constitutionalization theory has epistemic value by identifying key tenets of online order.

Constitutionalization is the last element in the progressive solidification of regimes.[213] Unlike general approaches to regime consolidation or constitutionalization, such as Teubner's and an early Fischer-Lescano's, online order theories devoted to "internet constitutionalization" identify specific structural elements of an (or *the*) "internet's constitution." By this reference they usually do not mean that such elements should be contained in a constitutional document, akin to a traditional constitution. This would be challenging in light of the internet's character as a technical facility allowing information interchange and not a constitutionable entity even *sensu lato*, unlike, as will be submitted, its *normative order*.

Rather, internet constitutionalists identify certain fundamental tenets or structural elements of the internet's order as "constitutional" (as in: essential for the distribution of power and the control thereof). The process of progressively ensuring a semblance of rule-of-law protection online, based on these tenets, is then what internet constitutionalists

[209] Niklas Luhmann, *Kontingenz und Recht* (Frankfurt: Suhrkamp, 2013). For more legal approaches to contingency, see Isabelle Ley, "Opposition institutionalisieren—Alternativität und Reversibilität als Elemente eines völkerrechtlichen Legitimationskonzepts," Der Staat 53 (2014) 2, 227–62.

[210] Gunther Teubner, "Globale Zivilverfassungen: Alternativen zur staatszentrierten Verfassungstheorie," ZaöRV 63 (2003), 1–28, 24.

[211] See Tarleton Gillespie, "The Relevance of Algorithms," in Tarleton Gillespie et al. (eds.), *Media Technologies* (Cambridge, MA: MIT Press, 2014), 167–94; Natascha Just and Michael Latzer, "Governance by Algorithms: Reality Construction by Algorithmic Selection on the Internet," Media, Culture & Society, 39 (2017) 2, 238–58; and Francesca Musiani, "Governance by Algorithms," Internet Policy Review 2 (2013) 3, http://policy-review.info/articles/analysis/governance-algorithms.

[212] Florian Saurwein, Natascha Just, and Michael Latzer, "Governance of Algorithms: Options and Limitations," Digital Policy, Regulation and Governance 17 (2015) 6, 35–49.

[213] On regime constitutionalization generally, see 5.2.8.

would understand as "constitutionalization." They base this approach, as does for instance Ingolf Pernice, on an open interpretation of *constitutions* as "layered order[s]," which contain "elements as a legal foundation for societal direction on the political levels of community, *Land*, state, EU and the international level" with processes of self-regulation by society being accompanied by international legal ordering. In sum, a global constitutional law emerges.[214] States are important, but not to the detriment of others: in another contribution, Pernice sees the internet's constitution as the "order of internet governance, in which many actors are active in different, but corresponding forums—with states being one actor among others."[215]

Like transnational constitutionalization approaches generally, internet constitutionalization is a "German discipline,"[216] as Andrea Bianchi puts it, based on the assumption, identified by Martti Koskenniemi, of "German lawyers" that international problems "take place within a 'legal system' that can be articulated through the vocabularies of public law and the constitution."[217] This assumption holds water: "typical" German approaches are focused on "positive law and [are] idealistic"[218] and, by combining global governance approaches and an orientation toward fundamental norms in international law, they have made important contributions to the idea of the objectivity of the international legal order.[219] This study builds on these approaches by introducing the idea of the normative order of the internet, which provides for the infra- and suprastructure of the articulable legal system.

Internet constitutionalists usually start by identifying the necessity of an order or *Ordnungsrahmen* for the internet to distribute responsibility between private and public actors.[220] It is not essential for *internet constitutionalization* to take place to formally endorse transferal of public authority to non-states actors, but rather to develop and apply rules for the application and implementation of legal standards, themselves established in global

214 Ingolf Pernice, "Die Verfassung der Internetgesellschaft: Zur Rolle von Staat und Verfassung im Zuge der digitalen Revolution," in Alexander Blankenagel (ed.), *Den Verfassungsstaat nachdenken. Eine Geburtstagsgabe* (Berlin: Duncker & Humblot, 2014) 171–208, HIIG Discussion Paper Series No. 2017-03 (2017a), https://ssrn.com/abstract=2964926, 19: "So wird Verfassung eine gestufte Ordnung, in ihren Elementen als rechtliche Grundordnung der gesellschaftlichen Steuerung bezogen jeweils auf die politische Handlungsebene Kommune, Land, Staat und Europäische Union, bis hin zur globalen Ebene, wo Prozesse der gesellschaftlichen Selbstregulierung neben völkerrechtliche Ordnungsbemühungen treten und schrittweise Konturen eines globalen Verfassungsrechts erkennbar machen" (translation by the author).

215 Ingolf Pernice, "Vom Völkerrecht des Netzes zur Verfassung des Internets: Privacy und Digitale Sicherheit im Zeichen eines schrittweisen Paradigmenwechsels (International Law of the Net and the Constitution of the Internet: Privacy and Cybersecurity in the Light of a Progressive Change of Paradigm)," HIIG Discussion Paper Series No. 2017-02, https://ssrn.com/abstract=2959257, 22: "Verfassung des Internets soll vielmehr die Ordnung der Internetgovernance heißen, in der eine Vielzahl von Akteuren in einer Vielzahl unterschiedlicher, aber durchaus korrespondierender Foren tätig sind und Staaten nur ein Akteur unter anderen sind" (translation by the author).

216 Andrea Bianchi, *International Law Theories. An Inquiry into Different Ways of Thinking* (Oxford: OUP, 2016), 44.

217 Martti Koskenniemi, "Between Coordination and Constitution: International Law as a German Discipline," in Kari Palonen and Hubertus Buchstein (eds.), *Redescriptions. Yearbook of Political Thought, Conceptual History and Feminist Theory*, vol. 15 (Zurich/Berlin: Lit Verlag, 2011), 45–69 (64).

218 Stefan Kadelbach, "Völkerrecht als Verfassungsordnung? Zur Völkerrechtswissenschaft in Deutschland," ZaöRV 67 (2007), 599–621 (607).

219 Stefan Kadelbach and Thomas Kleinlein, "Überstaatliches Verfassungsrecht," AVR 44 (2006), 235.

220 Ingolf Pernice, "Vom Völkerrecht des Netzes zur Verfassung des Internets: Privacy und Digitale Sicherheit im Zeichen eines schrittweisen Paradigmenwechsels (International Law of the Net and the Constitution of the Internet: Privacy and Cybersecurity in the Light of a Progressive Change of Paradigm)," HIIG Discussion Paper Series No. 2017-02, https://ssrn.com/abstract=2959257, 23.

multistakeholder settings—all this in recognition of fundamental guarantees of democratic participation, rule of law, and fundamental rights.[221] Democratic constitutions of states function as the "foundation and departure point," but they must not "close themselves off to the influence and normative power of emerging orders."[222]

Key tenets of the sum of norms fulfilling functions similar to those of constitutional character within states—the internet's constitution—are thus *first*, the protection of human and fundamental rights, especially privacy, data protection, protection of property, and free access. *Second*, the constitution, according to internet constitutionalists, needs to be democratically legitimated by, for instance, developing mechanisms to aggregate and articulate opinions for instance through forums, such as the IGF.[223] *Third*, any constitution needs to reflect the responsibility of states (and, as applicable, non-state actors) for those elements of the infrastructure of the internet which are essential for cybersecurity: only a "secure infrastructure [. . .] can ensure that the internet become operational as an instrument for democratic decision-making structures globally."[224] Others have identified fundamental rights protection and power limitations in the internet ecosystem as central, in particular protection against private actors performing public functions.[225]

While internet constitutionalism is an attractive topic at the intersection of the burgeoning global governance and global constitutionalist approaches, the process is strong on rhetoric and weak on concrete standards.[226] It is true that the online order needs to be based on common commitments to ensure fundamental rights—but this is already the case, if one recalls the WSIS documents, where all states committed to an information society based on international law, including the UN Charter, human rights, as contained in the UDHR, and oriented toward development. It is also true that any online order needs to ensure that the responsibilities for safeguarding common interests, such as ensuring internet integrity, are differentiated according to the actors' roles.

Private entities need to be obliged to protect fundamental rights within the limits of the *Ruggie Framework* under the overall control of states who, following international human rights law, have to respect, protect, and ensure these rights to anyone within their control or jurisdiction.[227] In this reading internet constitutionalization is not particularly innovative in conceptual terms but is rather an application of Teubner's "regime constitutionalization" approach to the internet, identified as a special regime, coupled with insights from international public authority and global constitutional theory.

An important contribution of internet constitutionalization lies in the recognition that key normative challenges on the internet are public order challenges (or, if one subscribes to the use of the word in the trans-state context, "constitutional" challenges). Gunther

[221] Ibid., 25.
[222] Ibid., 26.
[223] Ibid., 27 et seq.
[224] Ibid., 29.
[225] Claudia Padovani and Mauro Santaniello, "Digital Constitutionalism: Fundamental Rights and Power Limitation in the Internet Eco-System," *The International Communication Gazette* (2018), 1–7, http://journals.sagepub.com/doi/pdf/10.1177/1748048518757114.
[226] Ibid.,5.
[227] Andreas Fischer-Lescano, "Struggles for a Global Internet Constitution: Protecting Global Communication Structures Against Surveillance Measures," Global Constitutionalism 5 (2016) 2, 145–72 (identifying protection of the Internet system, horizontal application of fundamental rights, democracy and public control as functions of the *Internetverfassung*).

Teubner, for instance, identifies the "lack of transparency in Google's governance structures" as pointing to "*constitutional questions* of democracy and of public control" (emphasis added).[228] Individual states can do little, by themselves, to answer these questions—they are international in character and need to be answered within the normative systems, and in discursive cooperation with the involved normative actors. Or, as Fischer-Lescano writes, "principles of democracy and of public control need to be anchored and, if necessary, legally enforced within the polycentric patterns of order themselves."[229]

In any case, the "constitutional moment"[230] seems to have passed. Commonly understood as a specific time when a shift can occur toward constitutionalization, or constitutional reform, because of extra-constitutional dynamics (e.g. revolutions[231]), such a moment was identified a number of times in the last two decades. In 1997, David G. Post had suggested that the internet was approaching a "critical moment for its governance scheme" and a "constitutional moment" for cyberspace.[232] Similarly, Susan Crawford described the reforms to ICANN in 2008 as that entity's "constitutional moment."[233] Others have linked the emergence of the internet freedom principle to the "constitutionalization" of internet governance.[234]

Most of the more recent internet constitutionalization literature was a scholarly backlash against the normative instability after the Snowden revelations. This explains the noticeable reliance on privacy as a key fundamental right (and not freedom of expression, usually considered the *enabling* right on the internet[235]), on anonymity[236] and pseudonymity, and on encryption-related rights: defined as a "right to digital self-defense"[237] and even a "fundamental right."[238]

It is indeed in this intersection of the related theories of regime constitutionalization, global governance, and international public authority that the normative solution to the online order problem, as presented here, lies, but, as is argued in the next chapter, the answer is more complex (but perhaps less elegant) than calling for a constitution.[239]

[228] Gunther Teubner, "The Project of Constitutional Sociology: Irritating Nation State Constitutionalism," Transnational Legal Theory (2013) 4, 44 (45).

[229] Andreas Fischer-Lescano, "Struggles for a Global Internet Constitution: Protecting Global Communication Structures Against Surveillance Measures," Global Constitutionalism 5 (2016) 2, 145–72 (167) (notes omitted).

[230] Bruce Ackerman is credited with creating the concept. See Bruce Ackerman, *We the People: Foundations* (Cambridge: Harvard University Press, 1991).

[231] For an empirical analysis of constitutional moments, see Daniel Taylor Young, "How Do You Measure a Constitutional Moment? Using Algorithmic Topic Modeling To Evaluate Bruce Ackermans' Theory of Constitutional Change," Yale Law Journal 122 (2013), 1990–2054.

[232] David G. Post, "Cyberspaces' Constitutional Moment," The American Lawyer, November 1998, http://www.temple.edu/lawschool/dpost/DNSGovernance.htm.

[233] Susan Crawford, "ICANNs' Constitutional Moment," *Publius*, May 20, 2008, http://publius.cc/icanns_constitutional_moment.

[234] Anne-Claire Jamart, "Internet Freedom and the Constitutionalization of Internet Governance," in Roxana Radu, Jean-Marie Chenou, Rolf H. Weber (eds.), *The Evolution of Global Internet Governance. Principles and Policies in the Making* (Zurich: Schulthess, 2014), 57–78.

[235] Human Rights Council, Resolution 32/13, The promotion, protection and enjoyment of human rights on the Internet, UN Doc. A/HRC/RES/32/13 of 18 July 2016.

[236] Report of UN Special Rapporteur for the Right to Freedom of Expression, David Kaye, UN Doc. A/HRC/29/32 of 22 May 2015, passim and para. 5: "Encryption and anonymity, separately or together, create a zone of privacy to protect opinion and belief."

[237] Andreas Fischer-Lescano, "Der Kampf um die Internetverfassung, Rechtsfragen des Schutzes globaler Kommunikationsstrukturen vor Überwachungsmaßnahmen," JZ 69 (2014) 20, 965–74 (974).

[238] Julia Gerhards, *(Grund-)Recht auf Verschlüsselung?* (Frankfurt am Main: Nomos, 2010).

[239] See chapter 6 on the normative order of the internet.

5.3.2 Interoperability

Interoperability means the ability of technology to transfer data across different platforms and programmes, components and applications. A similar approach can be applied to the legal system to create legal interoperability. Generally, interoperability should be encouraged because advantages of "interop" outweigh manageable drawbacks, such as technological lock-ins, path dependencies and monopolization threats.

The internet is an open and distributed network of interconnected networks. Among its founding architectural principles, we find openness in the sense of an absence of centralized legal control or controlling infrastructure (apart from the Domain Name System and the root servers). Scholars have also identified its redundancy/robustness/reliability and its end-to-end nature (the internet is a network, sometimes described as "dumb,"[240] that simply transmits data packages).[241] Yet we also find interoperability as a foundational principle of the internet. However, interoperability is not peculiar to the internet, as the success story of the "interoperable" shipping container shows, which can be used worldwide on land, sea, and air.[242]

As defined by Urs Gasser, interoperability (or "interop") in the digital ecosystem is "the ability to transfer and render useful data and other information across systems, applications, or components." This allows for seamless use and application of technologies and makes the concept of interop to be "central, and yet often invisible, to many parts of a highly interconnected modern society." The invisibility of well-interlinked interoperability regimes explains why the importance of interop may be underestimated. As Gasser reminds us, already the mere fact "that someone can make a seamless international telephone call [. . .] is a tribute to interop." This also applies to sending and receiving "the same e-mail on a phone or in a browser, regardless of device manufacturer or ISP,"[243] and without having to worry about microdecisions regarding the speed and route of the data packets carrying the email's content or the many virtual "handshakes" necessary to effect transportation or the standards used.

Early approaches have identified the importance of the interoperability of essential (emergency) services[244] and of the role of governments and standard-setting bodies,

[240] Though this is doubtful, see already Andrew Odlyzko, "Smart and Stupid Networks: Why the Internet is Like Microsoft," AT&T Labs Research Paper, Revised version, October 6, 1998, http://www.dtc.umn.edu/~odlyzko/doc/stupid.networks.pdf, 1 (arguing that "[like] the PC, the Internet offers an irresistible bargain to a crucial constituency, namely developers, while managing to conceal the burden it places on users"). It is interesting to read his assessment in light of today's technology: "The Internet is growing explosively, and *is even threatening to take over transport of voice calls*" (emphasis added). This "threat" (at least for AT&T, the company the scholar was affiliated with) has materialized with VoIP.

[241] Malte Ziewitz and Ian Brown, "A Prehistory of Internet Governance," in Ian Brown (ed.), *Research Handbook on Governance of the Internet* (Cheltenham: Edward Elgar, 2013), 3–26 (14–17); cf. B. Carpenter, RFC 1958: Architectural Principles of the Internet (1996), http://www.ietf.org/rfc/rfc1958.txt.

[242] Marc Levinson, *The Box: How the Shipping Container Made the World Smaller and the World Economy Bigger* (Princeton: Princeton University Press, 2006).

[243] Urs Gasser, "Interoperability in the Digital Ecosystem," ITU GSR discussion paper, 2015, https://www.itu.int/en/ITUD/Conferences/GSR/Documents/GSR2015/Discussion_papers_and_Presentations/Discussionpaper_interoperability.pdf, v.

[244] Viktor Mayer-Schönberger, "Emergency Communications: The Quest for Interoperability in the United States and Europe," Kennedy School of Government Faculty Research Working Papers Series RWP02-024, March 2002.

like the IETF, in ensuring interop[245] and have concluded that an increased politicization of interoperability has taken place.[246] Developing a theory of interoperability is urgent, as the pervasive presence of the internet of things is largely premised upon (technical) interoperability. Objects rely on seamless connection to other objects without human operabilitization.[247]

Apart from technical interoperability, what interests here chiefly is *legal* interoperability for the internet. Legal interoperability is both complex and crucial because it has the "ability to either enable upward mobility in the global economy or to reinforce existing power structures, depending on the choices made."[248] It is thus a normative concept and the process of identifying the necessity for interoperability, and developing rules regarding interoperability, is political.[249]

Gasser identifies four layers of interoperability: at the institutional layer, interop allows different societal systems (regimes, orders) to function. Here, legal interop comes into play. At the technological layer, hardware and code must ensure interop. At the data layer, interconnected systems must be able to meaningfully interact through data transfer.[250] Finally, there is a "human" layer, one of language-based interoperability.[251]

Apart from the economic case for interoperability (as Weber points out, "monetary costs of non-interoperable laws in a highly networked world will increase"[252]), there is a strong normative case to be made for legal interop: fairness demands that similar fact patterns should be treated similarly. Interoperability theorists have argued that the goal of legal interoperability should be to "achieve interoperable rules that create a level playing field for the next generation of technologies and social exchange." Non-interoperability of legal systems and norms within systems harms non-dominant states, as major powers have expansionist tendencies with regard to application of (non-interoperable) laws.[253]

Among the benefits of ensuring interoperability we also find the continuance of the innovation-led development of the internet,[254] and the fostering of innovation by reducing

[245] Stacy A. Baird, "Government Role and the Interoperability Ecosystem," I/S: A Journal of Law and Policy 5 (2009), 2, 219–90.

[246] Laura DeNardis, *Opening Standards: The Global Politics of Interoperability* (Cambridge, MA: MIT Press, 2011).

[247] Urs Gasser, "Interoperability in the Digital Ecosystem," ITU GSR discussion paper, 2015, https://www.itu.int/en/ITUD/Conferences/GSR/Documents/GSR2015/Discussion_papers_and_Presentations/Discussionpaper_interoperability.pdf, 1.

[248] Ibid., 25.

[249] For a more detailed analysis, see John Palfrey and Urs Gasser, *Interop: The Promise and Perils of Highly Interconnected Systems* (New York, NY: Basic Books, 2012).

[250] Think of the attachment that just will not open: at the technological layer, interop (the transfer of the file) worked; on the data layer, however, something (e.g. reading the format) went wrong (see Urs Gasser, "Interoperability in the Digital Ecosystem," ITU GSR discussion paper, 2015, https://www.itu.int/en/ITUD/Conferences/GSR/Documents/GSR2015/Discussion_papers_and_Presentations/Discussionpaper_interoperability.pdf, 3).

[251] Ibid.

[252] Rolf H. Weber, "Legal Interoperability as a Tool for Combatting Fragmentation," Global Commission on Internet Governance Paper Series No. 4, December 2014, https://www.cigionline.org/sites/default/files/gcig_paper_no4.pdf, 5.

[253] Urs Gasser, "Interoperability in the Digital Ecosystem," ITU GSR discussion paper, 2015, https://www.itu.int/en/ITUD/Conferences/GSR/Documents/GSR2015/Discussion_papers_and_Presentations/Discussionpaper_interoperability.pdf, 12.

[254] Ibid., 9–11.

lock-in effects and lowering entry barriers. Among the disadvantages we can count increased privacy and security risks by interoperable sharing of information between platforms (especially through in-company portability across services) and increased homogeneity on the internet, which might threaten cultural diversity.

Governments have an important role to play, especially on the institutional layer of interoperability as "caretakers of a robust and stable legal environment."[255] The law has to allow interoperability: it needs to "establish, adjust, or maintain interop," but interoperability is also a feature of the legal system itself. This refers to the quality of a norm to be vertically and horizontally "translatable" into other jurisdictions and across national borders. Complete interoperability would lead to a coherent body of supranational world law, but complete homogeneity of laws is not a sensible aim:

> Jurisdictions compete productively against one another, and learn from each other, through the creation of heterogeneous legal and policy regimes. Governments need to aim for interoperability among legal systems at an optimal, rather than maximum, level, just as in other interop challenges.[256]

Structurally, legal interoperability can either be achieved through multistakeholder norm-development processes with governmental authorities in a coordination function,[257] or through a bottom-up approach without central coordination. Neither full harmonization of laws nor complete fragmentation and non-interoperability makes sense from a legal-economic and normative viewpoint. Weber, Palfrey, and Gasser agree: "An in-between level of legal interoperability can usually be considered as good policy."[258] Apart from self-regulatory approaches to interoperability by companies, states can employ different regulatory models aiming at interoperability: harmonization (unification of law), standardization, mutual recognition, reciprocity, and cooperation.

In order to give some guidance to the applicable normative systems and ensure coherence, the legal community has developed rules on conflicts of law.[259] While substantive rules matter most in managing legal interoperability, procedural aspects can also play a role. The venue selection allows parties to choose the preferred normative order; venue selection is limited by public interest exceptions that restrict this choice and give a prevailing force to a specific national law. The venue selection can lead to legal interoperability within a private group, in the sense that all group entities act on the basis of the same normative order.[260]

[255] Ibid., 24.

[256] Ibid., 33.

[257] Rolf H. Weber, "Legal Interoperability as a Tool for Combatting Fragmentation," Global Commission on Internet Governance Paper Series No. 4, December 2014, https://www.cigionline.org/sites/default/files/gcig_paper_no4.pdf, 5.

[258] Ibid., 6 and John Palfrey and Urs Gasser, *Interop: The Promise and Perils of Highly Interconnected Systems* (New York, NY: Basic Books, 2012), 184.

[259] Rolf H. Weber, "Legal Interoperability as a Tool for Combatting Fragmentation," Global Commission on Internet Governance Paper Series No. 4, December 2014, https://www.cigionline.org/sites/default/files/gcig_paper_no4.pdf, 6.

[260] Ibid., 10.

5.3.3 Jurisdictional Approaches

Jurisdiction theory or "internet and jurisdiction" (I&J) approaches usefully identify the pitfalls of extraterritorial application of national internet-related laws and try to minimize unintended normative consequences of national actions upon global operations through the development of transnational due process frameworks and jurisdictional principles for the internet.

Sovereign jurisdictions are still an essential means to categorize spaces, inter alia for the law of state responsibility (states remain responsible for certain cyber activities emanating from their sovereign territory) and for the no harm principle with a view to the internet's public core. As previously discussed, the transborder nature of internet activity presents a "significant challenge to traditional legal institutions in enforcing jurisdiction over online activities,"[261] but it does not fundamentally change the importance of cooperation and coordination in jurisdictionally difficult questions.

There is indeed a tension between national jurisdiction to prescribe and enforce, based on sovereignty and the cross-border flows of data and services on the internet. Recognizing that normative development has a time delay, scholars within the I&J (internet & jurisdiction) network attempt to develop a transnational due process framework for jurisdictional conflicts on the internet by selecting, collating, and analyzing jurisdiction-related cases globally as an evidentiary basis for policy-making.[262] The I&J approach is based on the conviction that "[m]aintaining a global internet by default, which fulfills the ambitions of the Universal Declaration of Human Rights" requires "transnational legal cooperation."[263] Three core issues of particular transnational impact have been identified: first, the conditions and criteria under which domain name seizures (and thus DNS-level action) by states can be justified in light of their global impact;[264] second, how especially internet intermediaries can develop standards for content restriction and moderation that combine the respect for most norms of 190+ legal systems and for international human rights (and give priority to the latter in cases of conflicts);[265] and third, what limit national court judgments have to force companies to divulge (user) data located in a different country.[266]

Jurisdictional scholars are especially critical of the "extraterritorial extension of national jurisdiction," which they see as—problematically—"becoming the realpolitik of internet

[261] Andrew Murray, "Uses and Abuses of Cyberspace: Coming to Grips with the Present Dangers," in Antonio Cassese (ed.), *Realizing Utopia. The Future of International Law* (Oxford: OUP, 2012), 497–506 (502).

[262] Internet & Jurisdiction Observatory, https://www.internetjurisdiction.net/work/observatory.

[263] Bertrand de La Chapelle and Paul Fehlinger, "Jurisdiction on the Internet: From Legal Arms Race to Transnational Cooperation," CIGI Paper Series No. 28, April 2016, https://www.cigionline.org/sites/default/files/gcig_no28_web.pdf (also published as Internet and Jurisdiction Paper No. 1, https://www.internetjurisdiction.net/uploads/pdfs/Papers/IJ-Paper-Jurisdiction-on-the-Internet.pdf), 3.

[264] Internet & Jurisdiction, "Domains & Jurisdictions Policy Options, Cross-Border Domain Suspension," November 2017, Input Document for Workstream I of the 2nd Global Internet & Jurisdiction Conference, https://www.Internetjurisdiction.net/uploads/pdfs/Papers/Domains-Jurisdiction-Policy-Options-Document.pdf.

[265] Internet & Jurisdiction, "Domains & Jurisdictions Policy Options, Cross-Border Content Restrictions," November 2017, Input Document for Workstream II of the 2nd Global Internet & Jurisdiction Conference, https://www.internetjurisdiction.net/uploads/pdfs/Papers/IJ-Paper-Jurisdiction-on-the-Internet.pdf.

[266] Internet & Jurisdiction, "Domains & Jurisdictions Policy Options, Cross-Border Access to User Data," November 2017, Input Document for Workstream III of the 2nd Global Internet & Jurisdiction Conference, https://www.internetjurisdiction.net/uploads/pdfs/Papers/Data-Jurisdiction-Policy-Options-Document.pdf.

regulation,"[267] coupled with legislation including clauses with extraterritorial reach. Consider the GDPR: while previously the CJEU had to establish an extraterritorial application through its jurisprudence,[268] the GDPR is now formally endowed with a transnational reach.[269] The inward-looking dimension of resovereignization is the imposition, on foreign companies, of national laws, which may be in conflict with international law. "Data localization" and forced geo-targeting to re-erect a semblance of national border walls on the internet are part of this trend.

Within jurisdictional approaches, traditional means of inter-state cooperation in exchanging data, such as Mutual Legal Assistance Treaties (MLATs), are considered as ill equipped to handle jurisdictional challenges of extraterritoriality and sovereignty. This is due to the lack of the necessary speed of MLAT procedures for data-related queries, the "dual incrimination" problem (that MLATs only apply when the fact pattern lends itself to be qualified as a crime in both jurisdictions), and the lack of scalability (MLATs may work for single cases, but not among 190+ states with thousands of potential jurisdictionally intricate cases).[270]

Jurisdictional approaches aim at developing a transnational due process framework that ensures procedural interoperability. This is possible by reference to human rights as substantive strata of jurisdictional approaches, a basic commitment that then allows more intensive discussion as to the concrete standards in transborder disputes. A framework would also allow for "interoperability among heterogeneous actors [such as states on the one and intermediaries on the other hand] by providing shared vernacular and mechanisms for their interactions"[271]—just like TCP/IP functions as an interoperability enabler between heterogeneous networks.

The norms developed within these transnational due process frameworks would be "a new form of transnational soft law" and would have to guarantee procedural interoperability and due process.[272]

5.3.4 Governance by Microdecisions

Microdecisions are taken both in technical and content-related settings. Be it the implementation of the right to be delisted in daily content management or the up- or downranking of content based on algorithm-dominated recommender systems, the opaque nature of the procedures of microdecisionary systems and their lack of scientific interrogability (no developing

[267] Bertrand de La Chapelle and Paul Fehlinger, "Jurisdiction on the Internet: From Legal Arms Race to Transnational Cooperation," CIGI Paper Series No. 28, April 2016, https://www.cigionline.org/sites/default/files/gcig_no28_web.pdf (also published as Internet and Jurisdiction Paper No.1, https://www.internetjurisdiction.net/uploads/pdfs/Papers/IJ-Paper-Jurisdiction-on-the-Internet.pdf), 4.

[268] Consider that the CJEU found that entities outside the EU can fall under EU data protection law because of the activities of a separate operation in an EU Member State. See CJEU, C-230/14, *Weltimmo v. NAIH* and CJEU, C-131/12, *Google Spain SL, Google Inc. v. AEPD, Mario Costeja Gonzalez.*

[269] Just consider the new Article 3, para. 2 GDPR, pursuant to which non-EU established businesses are subject to the GDPR where and when they process personal data of data subjects in the EU in connection with (i) the offering of goods or services or (ii) monitoring the behavior of individuals in the EU.

[270] Bertrand de la Chapelle and Paul Fehlinger, "Jurisdiction on the Internet: From Legal Arms Race to Transnational Cooperation," CIGI Paper Series No. 28, April 2016, https://www.cigionline.org/sites/default/files/gcig_no28_web.pdf, 19.

[271] Ibid., 11.

[272] Ibid., 12.

jurisprudence, no reasoning, no explanation) serve as a reminder that algorithmic decision-making is highly problematic and needs to be comprehensively checked with a view to human rights compliance.

There is currently no global and uniform mechanism to solve disputes between users or between users, platforms, or third parties: "Each platform and online operator has its own system and method for handling these disputes," Jacques de Werra notes.[273] In solving these disputes there is, however, one commonality: the decisions are taken on a massive scale and are algorithmically predetermined.

While not as self-identifying as adherents of an independent school of thought, a number of scholars have focused on the role of these microdecisions in internet regulation.[274] Microdecisions are taken by usually private actors, i.e. internet intermediaries, on a huge scale and on a daily basis, often determined (or at least largely predetermined) by algorithms. They are often handed down without the possibility of redress provided in traditional grievance mechanisms and with no possibility for involved parties to review the logic of the algorithm behind the decision or demand an explanation.[275]

Further, the microdecisions taken by intermediaries are usually not collected in a disaggregated form and cannot be reviewed, by scholars or the public, as to the decision-making parameters. Quantitative indicators may be provided, but they are often incomplete or misleading.[276] It is impossible, on this basis, to develop either a comprehensive critique of the substantive decisions taken in microdecision processes (only very few cases are discussed and reviewed in public[277]) or to identify "jurisprudential" trends.

Google, in implementing the obligations under the CJEU's *Google Spain* judgment (ensuring a limited right to be delisted from a search engine's results when the information meets certain criteria of e.g. irrelevance[278]), had to develop its internal system of microdecisions, including a weighing of different human rights and thus a form of privatized human rights microjustice system largely outside of traditional avenues of recourse and redress. For this phenomenon, Jacques de Werra has coined the notion of "massive online micro

[273] Jacques de Werra, "ADR in Cyberspace: The Need to Adopt Global Alternative Dispute Resolution Mechanisms for Addressing the Challenges of Massive Online Micro-Justice," Swiss Review of International & European Law (2016), 289–306.

[274] Not to be confused with the term "microdecisions" as used by economists: day-to-day decisions taken by people. In an insurance agency, for instance, the decisions about how claims are settled, in a hospital, the decision how patients are billed (cf. Thomas H. Davenport, "Microdecisions for Macro Impact," March 4, 2009, Harvard Business Review, https://hbr.org/2009/03/microdecisions-for-macro-impac).

[275] But recall that Article 13 (2) (f) GDPR forces controllers to provide data subjects, in cases where personal data is collected from them, with certain information about the existence of automated decision-making and in serious cases with "meaningful information about the logic involved, as well as the significance and the envisaged consequences of such processing." This will apply to microdecisional dispute resolution models used by intermediaries. On algorithmic decision-making generally, see 2.4.4.

[276] See the critical assessment by Ranking Digital Right on the openness and transparency of intermediaries generally, and their content moderation decisions in particular. These decisions are microdecisions: Ranking Digital Rights, 2017 Corporate Accountability Index, https://rankingdigitalrights.org/index2017 (concluding, inter alia, that "company disclosure is inadequate across the board [and m]ost of the world's internet users lack the information they need to make informed choices").

[277] See, e.g., the controversy regarding the deletion and then reinstatement by Facebook of the iconic Vietnam war picture by Nick Ut of nine-year-old Kim Phúc running away from a napalm attack (see just Sam Levin, Julia Carrie Wong, and Luke Harding, "Facebook Backs Down from 'Napalm Girl' Censorship and Reinstates Photo," *The Guardian*, September 9, 2016, https://www.theguardian.com/technology/2016/sep/09/facebook-reinstates-napalm-girl-photo).

[278] CJEU, C-131/12, *Google Spain and Google*, judgment of May 13, 2014.

justice."[279] His critical premise is sound: as "balancing rights and interests is complex and delicate, it would seem reasonable to consider that this mission should ultimately be entrusted to an independent judicial or quasi-judicial body that shall decide quickly and in a uniform manner."[280] However, the de-indexing requests submitted to Google are not decided by such a body, but are rather decided within microdecision processes.

De-indexing is a very good example of both the advantages (for companies) and disadvantages (for the public) of microdecisionary systems: many small individual cases are submitted, organized algorithmically, and decided without hearing, evidence (beyond the context provided in the submission), or interaction between Google and the authors of the request. While the cases are simple by themselves, as de Werra readily admits, in aggregate they "raise potentially important and complex legal issues (in terms of balancing of conflicting rights), for which justice must be rendered."[281] These complex legal issues can only be comprehensively treated when qualitative transparency is ensured.[282]

One model of alternative dispute resolution (ADR), which deals successfully with internet-related disputes, is the Uniform Domain Name Dispute Resolution Policy (UDPR),[283] adopted by ICANN in 1999. The UDRP is a key element for many scholars looking for regime-internal juridification or constitutionalization trends with regard to the internet or the emergence of a "lex digitalis," including Teubner, Vesting, Fischer-Lescano, and extensively Viellechner, who have pointed to the "jurisprudence" resulting from UDRP procedures. Over recent years, the number of cases by year averaged 2,500.[284]

The UDRP provides a legal framework to resolve disputes between domain name registrants and third parties over abusive registration and use of generic Top Level Domains (e.g., .biz, .com, .info, .mobi, .name, .net, .org) and certain country code TLDs that have subscribed voluntarily to the UDRP.[285] Under the UDRP, the parties are required to submit to mandatory administrative proceedings, conducted by a dispute resolution service provider, when a third party claims that a domain is identical or confusingly similar to a trademark or service mark in which the complainant has rights; and the third party has no rights or legitimate interests in respect of the domain name; and the domain name has been registered and is being used in bad faith.[286]

UDPR proceedings handle much lower numbers than microdecision procedures and the panels do consider evidence (even though the decision-making processes are quick). What makes them interesting to global constitutionalists and regime theorists, however, is that the proceedings are, as de Werra puts it, "legally delocalized and essentially independent from any legal system because the substantive elements, on which the UDRP is based and

[279] Jacques de Werra, "ADR in Cyberspace: The Need to Adopt Global Alternative Dispute Resolution Mechanisms for Addressing the Challenges of Massive Online Micro-Justice," Swiss Review of International & European Law (2016), 289–306.

[280] Ibid., 294.

[281] Ibid., 294 (notes omitted).

[282] Ibid., 296.

[283] Uniform Domain Name Dispute Resolution Policy, August 26, 1999, https://www.icann.org/resources/pages/policy-2012-02-25-en.

[284] WIPO UDRP Domain Name Decisions (gTLD), Generic Top Level Domains (gTLDs), Numbers up to 2018, http://www.wipo.int/amc/en/domains/decisionsx/index.html.

[285] WIPO, WIPO Guide to the Uniform Domain Name Dispute Resolution Policy (UDRP) (2018), http://www.wipo.int/amc/en/domains/guide/index.html#a1.

[286] Ibid.

decisions are rendered, are independent from any national or regional regulation."[287] This shows that an internet-related alternative dispute resolution mechanism can be successful and respect rights related to redress of grievances on a global scale, using accepted procedures and being as transparent as possible about the substantive standards used.[288]

For de-indexation, an ADR procedure along the lines of the UDRP seems feasible, with some variations (including that applicants can decide whether to use the system or rather national courts).[289] For content moderation decisions, however, an ADR system avoiding microdecisions can only be conceived for exceptional cases as an external redress mechanism of the second or third recourse level, in addition to existing national judicial institutions. This demand becomes more pressing as microdecision systems persevere that are not even controlled by the lenient standards crystallizing under the Ruggie Principles.

A slightly different notion of microdecisions is one employed by Florian Sprenger, who focuses on technical microdecisions essential for internet-based communication flows. Content-related microdecisions within companies, such as Google, are taken "by machines for humans on data." Technical microdecisions, by contrast, are taken "by machines for machines on data"[290]—for humans (to communicate), one might add in times before the singularity. Indeed, the technical implementation of the transfer protocols used on the internet foresees that each "bit packet" (one of the smaller communicable units for online communication) on its way to the receiver is submitted to uncountable microdecisions—on the best path to the receiver, the speed of traffic, the priority between packages. These microdecisions are loci of power, with the internet protocol architecture being the power's modus.[291] Following Alexander Golloway, we can thus reconfirm the normative power of internet protocols,[292] which localize "control" in protocols at the moments of microdecisions after technical decentralization has attempted to distribute it.[293]

The protocols on which these microdecisions are based are, as this study has discussed, developed by different actors and are thus part of the normative frame of the internet.[294] Microdecisions in this sense are taken in the very brief moments of interruption at each node of the internet, when artificial intelligence decides, based on protocols, as to the direction, speed, and priority of the bit packet. The distributed nature of microdecisions ensures that power is not monopolized.[295] In that, microdecisions are subsidiarity-oriented.

The key problem with technical but to a much larger degree with content-related microdecisions is the lack of knowledge about and remedies against them.[296] As the Draft

[287] Jacques de Werra, "ADR in Cyberspace: The Need to Adopt Global Alternative Dispute Resolution Mechanisms for Addressing the Challenges of Massive Online Micro-Justice," Swiss Review of International & European Law (2016), 289–306 (298).

[288] DeWerra is slightly more enthusiastic, describing the process as the "most accomplished example of an affordable efficient global online alternative dispute resolution system for intellectual property disputes, and perhaps for all categories of Internet-related disputes" (ibid., 300).

[289] Ibid., 303.

[290] Florian Sprenger, *Politik der Mikroentscheidungen. Snowden, Netzneutralität und die Architekturen des Internets* (Lüneburg: Meson, 2016), 115.

[291] Ibid.

[292] See 2.2.4.3.

[293] Alexander Golloway, *Protocol: How Control Exists after Decentralization* (Cambridge, MA: MIT Press, 2004), 8.

[294] See 2.2.4.4.

[295] Florian Sprenger, *Politik der Mikroentscheidungen. Snowden, Netzneutralität und die Architekturen des Internets* (Lüneburg: Meson, 2016), 114.

[296] Cf. Ellen P. Goodman et al., "Open Letter to Google from 80 Internet Scholars," May 13, 2015, https://medium.com/@ellgood/open-letter-to-google-from-80-internet-scholars-release-rtbf-compliance-data-cbfc6d59f1bd (expressing, inter alia, the wish to see published "[a]ggregate data about how Google is responding

Recommendation on roles and responsibilities of internet intermediaries of the Council of Europe Committee of Ministers confirms, states shall not allow microdecisions to fall outside the protective ambit of human rights, here Article 13 of the ECHR. As the Recommendation puts it, states shall "guarantee an effective remedy for all violations of human rights and fundamental freedoms by internet intermediaries […] and ensure that intermediaries provide access to prompt, transparent and effective reviews of user or affected party grievances and alleged terms of service violations and provide for effective remedies."[297]

Intermediaries, too, are obliged—under the Ruggie Framework—to ensure that they make available effective remedies and dispute resolution systems to provide prompt and direct redress of grievances. Acknowledging that size matters ("the complaint mechanisms and their procedural implementation may vary with the size, impact and role of the internet intermediary"), all remedies must allow for an impartial and independent review and include "inquiry, explanation, reply, correction, apology, reinstatement, deletion, reconnection and compensation."[298] Microdecisional systems without adequate dispute resolution systems attached regularly fail these criteria and put intermediaries on the wrong side of their corporate responsibility regarding human rights obligations.

5.3.5 Governance by Infrastructure

Infrastructure theory is based on the "turn to infrastructure" of internet scholarship, which recognizes infrastructure as places of political interventions, and loci of power, through which various externalities are advanced. Governance by infrastructure emerges parallel to governance of infrastructure and must be carefully scrutinized.

In his *lex informatica*, Joel Reidenberg described how, in his take, rules are formed through technology.[299] Legal form follows technological function, law follows code. Twenty years on, the "turn to infrastructure" in internet governance is premised upon the perception of technical architecture "as one of the strongest, if not the strongest structuring element of internet governance."[300] First coined by Laura DeNardis, the "turn to infrastructure in

to the >250,000 requests to delist links […]. We should know if the anecdotal evidence of Google's process is representative […]. We all believe that implementation of the ruling should be much more transparent for at least two reasons: (1) the public should be able to find out how digital platforms exercise their tremendous power over readily accessible information; and (2) implementation of the ruling will […] generally inform global efforts to accommodate privacy rights with other interests in data flows."

297 The Recommendation also sketches the form these remedies may take: "These may include various forms, such as restoration of content, apology, rectification and damages. Judicial review must remain available, when internal and alternative dispute settlement mechanisms prove insufficient or where the affected parties opt for judicial redress or appeal" (Council of Europe, Recommendation CM/Rec(2018)2 of the Committee of Ministers to member states on the roles and responsibilities of internet intermediaries (2018), 1.5.2).

298 Ibid., 2.5.1.

299 Joel Reidenberg, "Lex Informatica: The Formulation of Internet Policy Rules Through Technology," Texas Law Review 76 (1998), 3.

300 Francesca Musiani, "Network Architecture as Internet Governance," Internet Policy Review 2 (2013) 4, https://policyreview.info/node/208/pdf, 6.

internet governance"[301] focuses the governance debate from governance *of* infrastructure to the challenges associated with governance *by* infrastructure.[302]

The infrastructures of internet governance have become important "sites of economic and political power and, as such, they are being co-opted for [non-technical] purposes"[303] and used as "proxies to regain (or gain) control or manipulate the flow of money, information, and the marketplace of ideas in the digital sphere."[304] Infrastructuralists point to the progressive recognition of infrastructure as a "means to advance various externalities" with battles on policy priorities escalating "in consort with the rising recognition of the role of infrastructure in mediating political and economic conflicts."[305]

The three key infrastructure-related aspects of internet governance are: the control over critical internet resources, the Domain Name System, and the protocols; network-layer security and interconnections technology; and the infrastructures of information intermediation.[306] The specificity of a protocol does not change the fact that protocols can be "sites of mediation over political and economic values debates."[307] A case in point would be the protocol-based mediation, by authentication and encryption standards, between competing values (privacy vs. security).

Governance by infrastructure in the 'information intermediation' prong also means that companies are actively shaping public policy issues by establishing policies and moderation rules regarding privacy and freedom of expression and by developing rules and processes to deal with, inter alia, enforcement of intellectual property rights and reactions to state requests for censorship. Policy decisions by companies are far-reaching. As DeNardis writes, "decisions of search engines address issues such as privacy in online advertising, censorship requests from governments, and reputational issues related to rankings and ratings."[308] All actors in the internet governance ecosystem are aware of the normative power of the factual control of companies over infrastructural resources.[309]

The internet's turn to infrastructure relies on the identification of network architecture *as* internet governance: by making design choices regarding the network, programmers affect its politics, including the balances between rights (and actors as rights enforcers).[310] Niva Elkin-Koren understands architecture as being a dynamic parameter in a process of

[301] Laura DeNardis, "Hidden Levers of Internet Control," Information, Communication & Society 15 (2012) 5, 720–38.

[302] See for infrastructure-oriented approaches in the corporeal world: Keller Easterling, *Extrastatecraft: The Power of Infrastructure Space* (London: Verso, 2014) (arguing rather similarly, namely that infrastructure sets invisible rules that govern how we lead our lives in today's cityscapes, that is: offline spaces).

[303] Laura DeNardis and Francesca Musiani, "Governance by Infrastructure," in Francesca Musiani, Derrick L. Cogburn, Laura DeNardis, and Nanette S. Levinson (eds.), *The Turn to Infrastructure in Internet Governance* (New York: Palgrave Macmillan US, 2016), 3–21 (3).

[304] Ibid., 4.

[305] Ibid., 19.

[306] Drawn from Laura DeNardis, "Hidden Levers of Internet Control," Information, Communication & Society 15 (2012) 5, 720–38 and Laura DeNardis, "Internet Points of Control as Global Governance," CIGI Internet Governance Paper No. 2 (2013), https://www.cigionline.org/sites/default/files/no2_3.pdf, 12.

[307] Laura DeNardis, "Hidden Levers of Internet Control," Information, Communication & Society 15 (2012) 5, 720–38 (723).

[308] Ibid., 725.

[309] See e.g. Astrid Mager, "Internet Governance as Joint Effort: (Re)Ordering Search Engines at the Intersection of Global and Local Cultures," New Media & Society (2018), 1–21 (on the basis of 18 qualitative interviews with key experts involved in search engine governance from the societal domains of policy, law, civil society, and the IT sector).

[310] Francesca Musiani, "Network Architecture as Internet Governance," Internet Policy Review 2 (2013) 4, https://policyreview.info/node/208/pdf, 4.

reciprocal influences of law and technology design. Yet in order to "make technology visible," as Elkin-Koren demands, the concept of law must be reassessed. According to Elkin-Koren the law does not just act responsively and bend itself to accept new technologies, rather it shapes them and affects their design.[311]

At the same time infrastructure is used as an element "of technological disruption and circumvention of critical infrastructure."[312] Human rights are impacted by infrastructure-related attacks.[313] At least after the transfer of oversight function from the US government to the "global multistakeholder community," reforming the oversight over the root zone file is no longer a symbolic internet governance reform demand.[314] Further, cybersecurity is a key focus of infrastructural turn theorists. This approach is already reflected in the GGE 2015 report, which emphasizes the importance of territorial sovereignty over internet resources but includes the obligation to use internet infrastructure lying within one's territory responsibly.[315]

Internet "kill-switches" are the most "extreme form" of internet control via infrastructure. Internet shutdowns have been described as the "intentional disruption of internet or electronic communications, rendering them inaccessible or effectively unusable, for a specific population or within a location, often to exert control over the flow of information."[316] Though the end-to-end nature, implying a lack of centralized control, is a key feature of the internet and usually ensures both its resilience and resistance to interventions, it is possible in some countries (or parts of a country) to "switch off" the internet by a number of feasible technological steps, especially when internet connectivity to the "outside" world is concentrated at a few entry points/ports under the control of a limited number of companies that are liable to be controlled by authorities.[317]

The cases of Egypt in 2011 and Libya before the NATO intervention, Iraq, Sudan, and Syria in 2012 and 2014, and parts of China in 2014 illustrate this use of infrastructure to further political agendas, even though switching off the internet is illegal in light of the international protection of communication (freedom of expression, freedom of opinion, and freedom of information) in almost all cases. Attempts by states to legitimize interferences

[311] Niva Elkin-Koren, "Making Technology Visible: Liability of Internet Service Providers for Peer-to-Peer Traffic," New York University Journal of Legislation and Public Policy, 9 (2016), 15–76.

[312] Laura DeNardis and Francesca Musiani, "Governance by Infrastructure," in Francesca Musiani, Derrick L. Cogburn, Laura DeNardis, and Nanette S. Levinson (eds.), *The Turn to Infrastructure in Internet Governance* (New York: Palgrave Macmillan US, 2016), 3–21 (14).

[313] Derrick L. Cogburn, "The Multiple Logics of Post-Snowden Restructuring of Internet Governance," in Francesca Musiani, Derrick L. Cogburn, Laura DeNardis, and Nanette S. Levinson (eds.), *The Turn to Infrastructure in Internet Governance* (New York: Palgrave Macmillan US, 2016), 25–44.

[314] Kenneth Merrill, "Domains of Control: Governance of and by the Domain Name System," in Francesca Musiani, Derrick L. Cogburn, Laura DeNardis, and Nanette S. Levinson (eds.), *The Turn to Infrastructure in Internet Governance* (New York: Palgrave Macmillan US, 2016), 89–106 and Francesca Musiani, "Alternative Technologies as Alternative Institutions: The Case of the Domain Name System," in Francesca Musiani, Derrick L. Cogburn, Laura DeNardis, and Nanette S. Levinson (eds.), *The Turn to Infrastructure in Internet Governance* (New York: Palgrave Macmillan US, 2016), 73–86.

[315] United Nations, Developments in the Field of Information and Telecommunications in the Context of International Security, Report of the Secretary General, A/70/174 of July 22, 2015, http://www.un.org/ga/search/view_doc.asp?symbol=A/70/174, para. 13 (c) ("States should not knowingly allow their territory to be used for internationally wrongful acts using ICTs"). But see ibid., para. 28 (e) ("States *must not* use proxies to commit internationally wrongful acts using ICTs, and should seek to ensure that their territory is not used by non-State actors to commit such acts") (emphasis added).

[316] Access Now, Keep it on: What is an Internet Shutdown? (2018), https://www.accessnow.org/keepiton.

[317] Patricia Vargas-Leon, "Tracking Internet Shutdown Practices: Democracies and Hybrid Regimes," in Francesca Musiani, Derrick L. Cogburn, Laura DeNardis, and Nanette S. Levinson (eds.), *The Turn to Infrastructure in Internet Governance* (New York: Palgrave Macmillan US, 2016), 167–88.

with communicative rights by arguing for a national security exception (e.g. Article 19 (3) lit a (1) ICCPR) will usually fail on the grounds of proportionality).[318] Exceptions may be, under special circumstances, calls for war or incitement to genocide through the internet that can only be effectively suppressed in a specific region or a specific time by a limited and proporationate shutdown.[319] As the Human Rights Committee, in *Mukong vs. Cameroon*, confirmed, promotion of human rights and democracy can never be suppressed by references to national security and unity.[320]

The number of partial shutdowns has increased greatly with sixty-one documented shutdowns in 2017 in states ranging from India and Pakistan to Belarus and Vietnam.[321] In 2018, too, internet shutdowns in parts of Bali, Cameroon, Chad, India, Togo, Venezuela, and other states were used as tools by governments to silence activists, oppositional politicians, or grassroots movements.[322] Even in a democratic state such as India, the government routinely uses partial shutdowns as a tool to police potential disruptions. Between January 2012 and April 2018, 172 partial shutdowns were recorded, with ninety-two being "preventive" in nature, i.e. imposed in anticipation of protests, and eighty being ordered in order to contain ongoing unrest.[323] Internet shutdowns as tools of states to manage information and communication exchanges and to use infrastructure control to reach certain, often illegitimate, policy objectives has become pervasive. Apart from the violations of human rights a shutdown causes, the periods of non-connectivity have a serious economic impact on the affected areas.[324]

Technically, any attempt to "shut down" the internet means trying to interrupt the transmission of data packets.[325] A state wishing to do so needs to control a number of elements on both the network interface and the application layer of the internet. On the network interface layer, a state attempting to shut down the "national" internet needs to stop national ISPs from providing their service, force local Internet Exchange Points to stop national network-to-international internet interconnections, or physically disrupt internet cables ("cutting" the connection in the most direct sense of the word). On the application layer of the internet, states may try to remove the access of their state's DNS to the root servers to disallow host name-to-IP address translation, thus rendering internet address queries

[318] See Matthias C. Kettemann, "Nationale Sicherheit und Informationsfreiheit. Zur Völkerrechtsmäßigkeit von Internetabschaltungen," in Kirsten Schmalenbach (ed.), *Aktuelle Herausforderungen des Völkerrechts. Beiträge zum 36. Österreichischen Völkerrechtstag 2011* (Frankfurt am Main:: Peter Lang, 2012), 41–61 (52).

[319] Matthias C. Kettemann, "Grotius goes Google: Der Einfluss der Internet Governance auf das Völkergewohnheitsrecht," in Christoph Vedder (ed.), *Richterliche Praxis und politische Realität. Tagungsband 37. Österreichischer Völkerrechtstag 2012* (Vienna: Verlag Österreich, 2013), 89–104 (arguing that a (partial) shutdown might be legitimate when the internet is being used as a tool such as radio in the ICTR's Radio Télévision des Mille Collines case and it is technically impossible to effect a more proportionate stop to incitement to genocide).

[320] Human Rights Committee, *Mukung v. Cameroon*, Comm. No. 458/1991, UN Doc. CCPR/C/51/D/458/1991 of 10 August 1994, para. 9.7.

[321] Access Now, "Internet Shutdowns in Context," Insights from the Shutdown Tracker Optimization Project, September 11, 2017, https://www.accessnow.org/keepiton.

[322] Internet Society, Internet Shutdowns (2018), https://www.internetsociety.org/tag/internet-shutdowns.

[323] Internet Shutdown Tracker India, Nature of Shutdown, https://www.internetshutdowns.in.

[324] Deloitte/Facebook, "The Economic Impact of Disruptions to Internet Connectivity," October 2016, https://globalnetworkinitiative.org/sites/default/files/The-Economic-Impact-of-Disruptions-to-Internet-Connectivity-Deloitte.pdf; Brooking Institution, "Internet Shutdowns Cost Countries $2.4 Billion Last Year," October 2016, https://www.brookings.edu/wp-content/uploads/2016/10/intenet-shutdowns-v-3.pdf.

[325] Patricia Vargas-Leon, "Tracking Internet Shutdown Practices: Democracies and Hybrid Regimes," in Francesca Musiani, Derrick L. Cogburn, Laura DeNardis, and Nanette S. Levinson (eds.), *The Turn to Infrastructure in Internet Governance* (New York: Palgrave Macmillan US, 2016), 169.

unsolvable for the national DNS. Finally, states can target the Border Gateway Protocol that ensures trans-ISP connections on the global internet.[326]

As previously mentioned, companies exercise substantial normative-factual power in an infrastructuralist reading of governance, in particular through their quasi-judicial powers on a large scale. These powers have sometimes accrued organically but have also been designated as such by courts. They include weighing human rights (as in *Google Spain*) or exercising moderation-related duties as providers of online platform services, toughened by *Delfi*[327] and the ECtHR's subsequent jurisprudence (*MTE and Index.hu ZRT v. Hungary* (2016)[328] and *Pihl v. Sweden* (2017)[329]). Intermediaries implement their duties and obligations "via [the] infrastructure"[330] they control. As they also run much of the physical infrastructure, such as online data storage facilities (server farms), they are directly responsible, similar to states, under the Ruggie Principles, toward the global community.

Just as interoperability is even more important in the internet of things than in the internet of people (devices cannot communicate without clear and precise conditions set by interoperability regimes; people can and often do[331]), governance by infrastructure will become an essential governing approach in the internet of things. As the internet of things is based on smart devices interconnecting seamlessly, the technological "backbone" on which this interoperability/interconnectedness rests becomes a key site of intervention and conflict. This is why politicized infrastructures need to be framed both as objects of protection to ensure the common interest in the integrity of the internet and as potential sources of danger for the international community, if misused.

The added value of infrastructure approaches is the identification of the gradual "siphon[ing] away [of control over the internet] from formerly more transparent processes," which is progressively "wielded by [...] hidden processes" of infrastructure management.[332] Co-option of infrastructure for the purposes of pursuing narrow policy goals can only be countered by ensuring that the processes of managing internet infrastructure are open and transparent. Using the law and changing norms to "bring about desired economic effects" now has an alternative: the use of architecture and internet infrastructure. Thus, legal interventions in architecture and infrastructure of the internet have become "another tool that actors can use to further their interests."[333]

Infrastructure-focused approaches are normatively important by underlining the controlling function of the corporeal dimensions of the internet, of the internet's physicality

326 Ibid., 170.

327 ECtHR, *Delfi AS v. Estonia* (June 16, 2015), application no. 64569/09.

328 ECtHR, *MTE and Index.hu ZRT v. Hungary* (February 2, 2016), application no. 22947/13.

329 ECtHR (3rd section), *Pihl v. Sweden* (February 7, 2017), application no. 74742/14.

330 Laura DeNardis and Francesca Musiani, "Governance by Infrastructure," in Francesca Musiani, Derrick L. Cogburn, Laura DeNardis, and Nanette S. Levinson (eds.), *The Turn to Infrastructure in Internet Governance* (New York: Palgrave Macmillan US, 2016), 3–21 (17).

331 Though human communication is fraught with difficulties of "interoperability" between the participants in the communicative process. Speech theory and linguistics teach us about misunderstandings that can happen e.g. by violations of felicity conditions in speech acts (cf. J. L. Austin, *How To Do Things With Words* (Cambridge, MA: Harvard University Press, 1962/1975)) or by differences in the interpretation of signifiers in communication (cf. John J. Gumperz, "Interethnic Communication," in Nikolas Coupland and Adam Jaworski (eds.), *Sociolinguistics* (London: Palgrave, 1997), 395–407).

332 Nanette S. Levinson and Derrick L. Cogburn, "The Next 'Turn' in Internet Infrastructure Governance," in Francesca Musiani, Derrick L. Cogburn, Laura DeNardis, and Nanette S. Levinson (eds.), The Turn to Infrastructure in Internet Governance (New York: Palgrave Macmillan US, 2016), 219–23 (219).

333 Barbara van Schewick, *Internet Architecture and Innovation* (Cambridge, MA: MIT Press, 2010), 389.

which is factually under control of private actors and, as applicable, of states exercising their sovereignty. Within the normative order of the internet rules need to be established to ensure both the protection of internet infrastructure as an essential element to internet integrity and the protection from misuses (or state/corporate capture) of internet infrastructure.

5.3.6 Reconceptualizing Governance

The online order theories presented above have focused on aspects of internet governance, such as jurisdiction and infrastructure, and have conceived of their approach as a tool to increase regulatory legitimacy, solve jurisdiction conflicts, and make the internet governance regime more answerable to non-state actors. There were, however, no comprehensive approaches attempting to change the basic set-up of the internet governance system.

One such approach, the new Global Cyberspace Framework, was developed by Rolf H. Weber.[334] It is based on and confirms the "specific nature of cyberspace," relies on the integration of all relevant actors by realizing "an appropriate multi-layer regime," and incorporates substantive principles.[335] The framework relies on structured rule-making processes on multiple layers: "multi-layer governance." For these, normative multilayer governance principles need to be developed.[336]

The "guiding principles" include formal/procedural and substantive principles. The formal/procedural principles ensure dynamism and flexibility, giving normative weight to institutions/actors most "apt to deal with the respective issue," user-centrality, and community-relatedness. The framework's substantive principles remain vague, including international legal principles developed in the "offline" world and newly adapted principles for the internet. Participation of all relevant actors in their respective roles is a key factor in legitimizing the framework. It must be comprehensively realized and procedurally protected.[337]

Weber argues that his framework must also comply with "basic socio-legal values,"[338] including an acknowledgment of cultural diversity, recognition of cyberspace openness, and acceptance of neutrality and interoperability. The framework will only be realizable, Weber writes, if the degree of "organization" of actors is high enough. Weber suggests that his Global Cyberspace Framework be embedded "into internationalized policy structures, and a procedural regime, which relies on the multi-layer/polycentric governance model and on multistakeholder participation, which takes proper account of the functional dimensions of a normative order."[339] To succeed, existing policy structures need to be internationalized. For Weber, the "most central issue" of his framework consists in the "need for reaching a consensus on the applicability of some guiding principles."[340] Such a consensus, however, remains elusive, as the promulgation of many declarations of principles illustrates.[341]

[334] Rolf H. Weber, *Realizing a New Global Cyberspace Framework. Normative Foundations and Guiding Principles.* (Zurich: Schulthess and Springer, 2014).
[335] Ibid., 154.
[336] Ibid., 109.
[337] Ibid., 117–20, 129.
[338] Ibid., 136.
[339] Ibid.
[340] Ibid., 156.
[341] See 3.4.9.

5.4 A Theory of the Normative Order of the Internet

5.4.1 Making Normative Change Visible

Not every illegal act points to a failure of the past norm entrepreneur, the lawmaker. Not every political change indicates a revolution. Not every anomaly in science points to a paradigm change, in Thomas S. Kuhn's sense. But, as he writes, "if they are more than the usual mysteries of normal science, then the transition to crisis has started."[342] There are quite a few "mysteries" with regard to the legitimacy and applicability of norms on the internet, some of which have been discussed in the previous chapters, some of which will be debated in the following ones.

It can therefore be said with more than a modicum of plausibility that something like Kuhn's transition to crisis is the current state of internet regulation. Applying his thinking on scientific revolutions to structural approaches to normative ordering, a new paradigm of regulation is at hand. This study calls this paradigm "the normative order of the internet." In Kuhn's telling, in these times, the rules of "normal research" are less rigid, as the previous paradigm (through which a certain scientific field is seen) becomes less strict. This study understands Kuhn to mean that this includes a great receptivity of the scientific (and regulatory) field to new methodological approaches and new theories.

It is characteristic (for Kuhn) for this moment in time (transition to crisis) that given data is used in a new (scientific) system differently. Similarly, this study argues that it is characteristic of the present state of the internet that what Kuhn terms "data," and what is presently understood to include norms and practices related to the internet, is "used" differently: that is norms and practices are assessed, under the normative orders approach, in a broader context, encompassing national law, international law, and regulatory arrangements of a different character.

In his chapter on the *Invisibility of Revolutions,* Kuhn complains that post-revolutionary academic writings (written after the paradigm change) tend to rewrite history by presenting scientific progress in a linear fashion: adding facts, notions, a law, a theory like bricks when constructing a building—all in light of the paradigm. Such historization is highly selective regarding the discourses considered authoritative for the framing of historical progress, as recounted or reconstructed.[343] Linearity and selective historization may render revolutions invisible.[344] This study, by contrast, strives to make the normative "revolution" regarding online rule (or at least the evolution toward a more stratified normative order) visible. Such an endeavor can only succeed if the process of visibilization rests upon a firm theoretical foundation.

[342] Thomas S. Kuhn, *The Structure of Scientific Revolutions* (Chicago: University of Chicago Press, 1962/1970) (in German: Die Struktur wissenschaftlicher Revolutionen, 2nd edn. (Frankfurt am Main: Suhrkamp, 1976)), 96.

[343] Gérard Leclerc, "Histoire de la vérité et généalogie de l'autorité," Cahiers internationaux de sociologie, 111 (2001) 2, 205–31 (para. 32: "L'histoire de l'autorité n'est à proprement parler ni nominaliste, ni idéaliste; non plus qu'elle n'est nihiliste ou métaphysique. Elle est une analyse historique et sociologique des discours collectifs (culturels) en tant qu'ils sont légitimes, fondés sur des bases institutionnelles, et gouvernés par le télos de la vérité, c'est-à-dire en tant qu'ils sont des croyances vécues sur le mode de la conviction, du savoir, de la recherche, bref différents modes de prétention à la possession de la vérité."

[344] Thomas S. Kuhn, *Die Struktur wissenschaftlicher Revolutionen*, 2nd edn. (Frankfurt am Main: Suhrkamp, 1976)), 147–51.

In the following, key tenets of the approach employed here to construct and evaluate the normative order of the internet will be presented. These are the foundations for a theory of the normative order of the internet and are thus coherent with a view to the common purposive denominator (they offer perspectives on (aspects of) the normative order of the internet).

5.4.2 Theoretical Imports

This study has looked into phenomena of normative ordering, especially the processes leading to the emergence of norms and their relationship with national legal systems. The following theoretical insights can be imported into a theory of the normative order of the internet.

Theoretical Scripts. With this as a background foil, the following imports can be made from the more general and online order-oriented theories and approaches discussed in the previous two sections. Looking back at the more general theories discussed above,[345] we can confirm that legal theory has developed different "scripts" to explain phenomena related to information society (Castells), "computer culture" (Vesting), and digitization more broadly.

Fluidity of the Normative. An import insight to be garnered from previously discussed theories is that the legal system is not that different, conceptually, from the internet. Like the internet, the legal system at its most basic level deals in binary operators (lawful/unlawful), is multilayered, and operates under conditions of uncertainty and contingency. Another theoretical import is that the networked society is ruled by "liquid" forms of law: law that is less static than non-internet-related law and that allows for regime-internal self-reflection and self-optimization processes. Also here, similarities to information technology become apparent. Self-optimization (including outlier detection and "dimensionality reduction" to reduce complexity[346]) and machine learning are essential technologies for complex algorithms in big data-driven systems.[347]

This liquid law is made up of different kinds of norms, including legal and non-binding ones, but also normative "arrangements" of a different character. They are also "liquid" in the sense that one may flow into the other. An anonymity-related standard, adopted in an IETF RFC process by rough consensus, might flow into respective regulation on the national and European levels. The Council of Europe recommendation on roles and responsibilities of internet intermediaries may influence national law. The EU GDPR, with its right to explanation regarding certain uses of algorithms, influences normatively relevant and codified internal practices and terms of service of companies worldwide.

Dehierarchization and Fragmentation. An important theoretical insight for understanding the normative challenges of regulating the internet is that "network culture" and digitization have impacted the normative hierarchy in legal orders. They have in particular contributed to the normative dynamics that resulted in the emergence of a substantial body of private norms by companies and standards by standard-setting bodies that have destabilized traditional hierarchical relations between norms based on an imagined *Geschlossenheit*

[345] See 5.2.
[346] Ethem Alpaydin, *Machine-Learning* (Cambridge, MA: MIT Press, 2016), 72.
[347] Ibid., 73.

(unity/solidity) of the (national) legal system, allowing "foreign" norms only under strict procedural rules.

Private norms, standards, and informal transnational normative arrangements impact to a much larger degree the social reality of a substantial part of individuals and objects active on the internet and the way they interact. This normativity of the factual overlays the facticity of the normative, i.e. the influence that traditional norms within the *Stufenbau* have on activities related to the internet. By this "vote of the practice," norms grow in importance (and their legitimacy demands with them) that are neither firmly anchored within the *Stufenbau* nor traditionally legitimated.

***Weltrecht* and Hybridity.** This intersects with theoretical approaches regarding the idea of *Weltrecht*, a body of norms encompassing all norms and, in the form of *Internetweltrecht*, all norms applicable to the *internet* or rather, more broadly still, all phenomena of digitality which, with Felix Stalder, can be understood as the "set of relations that today is realized on the basis of the infrastructure of digital networks in the production, use and transformation of material and immaterial goods as well as in the constitution and coordination of personal and collective action."[348] A transition to this idea of *Internetweltrecht* helps divorce normative ordering from national boundaries. Naturally, it is a construct, a philosophical support structure, that (1) helps understand how existing normative hierarchies within cognizably segmented legal systems (e.g. Austria, Germany, EU) can become diffuse and (2) how interactions between norms from different segmented systems can interact.

The concept of *Weltrecht* is thus a big normative equalizer by stripping away national denominators. It allows for the collection of *single unsystematized norms,* which can then be reconfigured in their concrete interaction without the insurmountable conflict-of-laws problems that theoretizing all possible normative interactions between a line of code, a soft law principle, an internet standard, a national constitutional law, an EU regulation, a Council of Europe recommendation, a clause in an international treaty etc. might enter into.

This ties in conceptually to the challenge of legal hybridity and its normative "management." The normative orders approach re-establishes normative unity in light of norm conflicts in hybrid legal spaces. Just as internet-related *Weltrecht* approaches are one way of showing that norms from different regimes, of varying normative pull, authored by different actors, exist and interact, and that designing abstract interaction protocols is difficult, the concept of legal hybridity directs the analytical view toward the exercise, in international administrations, of international public authority by non-traditionally legitimated regimes.

Transnational Politicization. A further import into a theory of the normative order of the internet is the normative deepening of regimes by their politicization in the form of self-constitutionalization. Fragmentation and decentralized norm production have dynamized normative processes leading to the development of self-constitutionalizing sub-legal orders, civil sectors or regimes, including and especially with regard to the internet. These regimes are transnational in character—such as the content management regimes at the intersection of international internet intermediaries' terms of service (though nationally different legal regimes on the ground need to be respected)—and need to be politicized internally (i.e. rendered normatively more detailed and more receptible to legitimacy demands).

[348] Felix Stalder, *Kultur der Digitalität* (Frankfurt am Main: Suhrkamp, 2016), 18 (translation by the author).

Transnational theory provides us with normative concepts of how to integrate different regimes, including the horizontal application of human rights. Even though the online order as *lex digitalis* has diversified to include non-highly coherent communities, its normative mixture of national legal orders, international regimes, and transnational regulatory arrangements makes it a characteristic regime in which actors/institutions exercise transnational legal authority to varying degrees.

Pragmatic Ordering. This study has also shown that theories focused on online order have developed important insights into the emergence of rule-based order on the internet.[349] Progressively, societal "constitutionalization" processes have supported the identification of key principles of online order by providing for the societal dynamics that have allowed key principles to exercise normative pull on other norms which then coalesce normatively around these principles, similar to how a magnet attracts metal (scraps).

This bottom-up approach that considers norms in their entirety and multifaceted nature (and the narratives that give an order meaning) is informed by pragmatism. In a departure from seemingly artificial academic constructs, such as a new Global Cyberspace Framework, the normative orders approach accepts the messy and fuzzy normative character of the internet and its governance, while nonetheless developing a normative frame through which the development and application of rules for the internet can be explained and criticized.

Interoperability. Transferring properties of internet architecture to the internet governance system, the (legal) interoperability approach is of special importance for the concept of normative order. Interop(erability) is the non-innate and non-trivial ability of technology to transfer data across different platforms and programs, components, and applications of a legal system to interact with other norms without undue friction or legal "transaction costs." In light of the internet's multilayer-multiplayer architecture and polycentric rule-making processes, the interoperability of norms is highly important, especially because problem-specific normative solutions might conflict: a conflict-of-laws law for the internet must be able to work at different levels of complexity and granularity.

This includes jurisdiction-oriented approaches, which try to minimize unintended normative consequences of national actions upon global operations through the development of transnational due process frameworks and jurisdictional principles for the internet.

Decisionary and Physical Infrastructure. A final import of online order theories for a theory of the normative order of the internet must be the role of the decisionary and physical infrastructure. With regard to decisions, a workable theory must find an approach to the microdecisions taken in both technical and content-related settings. Traditionally conceived of as lacking any interrogability, their prevalence online highlights the necessity of a human rights-sensitive and technology-neutral approach to normatively framing algorithmic decision-making with a view to human rights compliance.

The internet cannot work without its infrastructure. The loci of infrastructure (domain name systems, servers, Internet Exchange Points) have become targets of attack and instruments of normative power. Any theory of a normative order of the internet must integrate this "turn to infrastructure" of internet scholarship and recognize the externalities

[349] See 5.3.

advanced through existing infrastructure. Governance *by* infrastructure emerges parallel to governance *of* infrastructure and must be carefully scrutinized.

5.5 Envisaging the Normative Turn

For Pierre Bourdieu, codification needs to be accompanied by a theory on the effects of codification.[350] Codification enables "l'instauration d'une normativité explicite, celle de la grammaire ou du droit."[351] Codification produces objectification and formalization, rationalization and normalization—and thus coherence control. It changes the nature of things: "un changement de statut ontologique."[352] The normative order established by law, however, is not transhistorical but contingent: lawyers, who see this temporal and social contingency of law, are "gardiens de l'hypocrisie collective"[353] though even in hypocrisy they are amassing social and epistemic capital and then exercising substantial power. We can avoid this trap if we do not engage in formal codification. The normative order of the internet is not an exercise in changing the ontological status of the artifact "internet". Rather, it is a necessary construct of an approach toward ordering the interaction of normatively relevant players and the interfacing of normative layers.

Varying Bourdieu, this study posits that conceiving of and finding online order is necessary as an essential presupposition for societal interactions. Indeed, Boris Groys describes human life as a "prolonged dialogue with the world." This dialog is based on certain philosophical presuppositions defining its medium and form, and today "we practice our dialogue with the world primarily via the internet." Wanting to ask the world a question, "we act as internet users." Under the internet's current regime, intermediaries (Groys focuses on Google) define the rules under which we can ask this question. Today, says Groys, "Google plays the role that was traditionally fulfilled by philosophy and religion. [It is] the first known philosophical machine that regulates our dialogue with the world [...]."[354] By giving specific context to words searched for, Google "presupposes and codifies the radical dissolution of language into sets of individual words." Thus, Google dissolves all discourses by turning them into the word clouds that function as collections of words beyond grammar."[355]

The current state of the internet seems similar, if we supplant "words" with "norms" and "grammar" with "order." This is the argument presented here: we are faced with online norms without order; and we need order to stabilize normative expectations and to make sense of the implementation of the finality of sociopolitical processes collected within the rubrum of internet governance.

350 Soraya Nour, "Bourdieus juridisches Feld: Die juridische Dimension der sozialen Emanzipation," in Sonja Buckel, Ralph Christensen, and Andreas Fischer-Lescano (eds.), *Neue Theorien des Rechts*, 2nd edn. (Stuttgart: Lucius&Lucius, 2009), 179–99 (191).

351 Pierre Bourdieu, "Habitus, code et codification," Actes de la Recherche en Sciences Sociales (1986), 40–4 (42).

352 Ibid.

353 Pierre Bourdieu, "Les juristes, gardiens de l'hypocrisie collective," in F. Chazel und J. Commaille (eds.), *Normes juridiques et régulation sociale* (Paris: LGDJ, 1991), 95–9.

354 Boris Groys, "Google: Words beyond Grammar, 100 Notes—100 Thoughts," No. 46, *dOCUMENTA (13)* (Ostfildern: Hatje Cantz, 2012), 4–6.

355 Ibid., 7.

Just as theory orders the world, ordering itself—based on theory—is a way to make the world. Citing Nelson Goodman, Andrea Bianchi notes that "[t]heories are ways of world-making."[356] Goodman, in his own *Ways of Worldmaking*, describes composition and decomposition via labels, weighting according to relevance/irrelevance or other categories, ordering, deletion, and supplementation and deformation (corrections or distortions) as "ways" to make the world. Deletion and supplementation are especially interesting here. Goodman sees the scientist as

> rejecting or purifying most of the entities and events of the world of ordinary things while generating quantities of filling for curves suggested by sparse data, and erecting elaborate structures on the basis of meagre observations [thus striving] to build a world conforming to his chosen concepts and obeying his universal laws.[357]

We see that Goodman is critical of ordering and seems to suggest that scientists develop order for their own sake rather than for the sake of the "ordered." This is a pitfall this study seeks to avoid. However, we can agree that the subsequent normative order of the internet is an exercise in systematization and systematic deletion.[358] It must also be admitted that the normative order approach is a "chosen concept," but the choice was explained and the reasons discussed. This study tries to show how the norms within the order relate to the order as a whole and thus "obey" the universal laws posited. However, this study makes the case that epistemological reasons for the adoption of a normative orders approach to regulating digitality dominate. Varying Goodman, obeying universal laws makes sense, when data and norms point to their effectivity and legitimacy.

This normative order of the internet, as will be presented here on the next pages, is a meta-law of order for the internet. Such a meta-law can only be understood in light of the theoretical approaches described in the last chapter. They function like so many different lenses when targeted at digitality. These lenses all fit (each on its own, but most also together) within the "glasses" of *a theory* of a normative order of the internet. Some theories help sharpen the focus (or explain) how "regimes" auto-constitutionalize; some theories help explain how normative change happens. After this chapter's discussion, they are provided with enough substance that they can be used to put into focus so many key aspects of the normative order of the internet for it to become the object of the subsequent chapter.

This study has persistently, and again in the last paragraph, used the term "normative order of the internet" or "online order" and has thus accrued a substantial conceptual debt. It will be paid in full in the following chapter 6, where the order resulting from the internet's normative turn, whose foundations have been conceptually laid in the last chapters, will be presented.

[356] Andrea Bianchi, *International Law Theories. An Inquiry into Different Ways of Thinking* (Oxford: OUP, 2016), 16.

[357] Nelson Goodman, *Ways of Worldmaking* (Indianapolis, IN: Hackett, 1978), 7 et seq. (15).

[358] Ibid., 15: "Replacement of a so-called analog by a so-called digital system through the articulation of separate steps involves deletion; for example, to use a digital thermometer with readings in tenths of degrees is to recognize no temperature as lying between 90 and 90.1 degrees."

6
The Normative Order of the Internet

6.1 The Normative Turn

6.1.1 A New Regulatory Order for the Internet

In a recent analysis of cybersecurity norms, two authors identified a "huge void in international regulation" after the "failure" of the negotiations in the UN's Group of Governmental Experts. If correct, this would be troublesome, especially in light of "recent cyber-attacks with global reach."[1] But there is no normative void,[2] even less a "huge" one. The regulatory frame regarding the internet as a whole and cybersecurity in particular, as this chapter shows, is flexible, elastic, and scalable: we call it the *normative order of the internet*. This order will now be presented, contextualized, and tested in light of the legitimacy demands placed upon it by the international community and the normative demands set for it by its role as the body of norms governing the development and use of the internet.

In the evolution of the internet's regime, as has been hypothesized and will be shown in this chapter, a normative turn has taken place: the normative order's internal rules of norm-production produce the technological and societal forces that, through learning normativity, develop norms autonomously within the order. It is thus—and this is a key hypothesis—not technicity that forms the norm, but the normative order and its norms, which allow for the development of (and set the limits to) technicity.

Such an order must necessarily be characterized by elasticity in that its rules are markedly less tightly woven with regard to regulatory areas such as internet standards than, for instance, cybersecurity or cybercrime. The norms within the normative order are not only primarily *Regimeverfassung* or *Regimerecht* norms, but rather stem from a broad variety of legal and quasi-legal sources, including national law, international law, and transnational regulatory arrangements, such as standards and soft law. As a legal order it operates through the form of law and analogously to it. Its actors—states, legal persons, natural persons—fulfill diverse functions as norm entrepreneurs, norm appliers, and norm enforcers. Though not without autonomous elements, the normative order of the internet is interlinked through legitimation relationships with national and international legal orders.

The order's justification narratives control new norms by assessing their technical consistency and legal-cultural consonancy with the order's purpose. The order thus offers a

[1] Theodore Christakis and Karine Bannelier, "Reinventing Multilateral Cybersecurity Negotiation after the Failure of the UN GGE and Wannacry: The OECD Solution," EJIL Talk, February 28, 2018, https://www.ejiltalk.org/reinventting-multilateral-cybersecurity-negotiation-after-the-failure-of-the-un-gge-and-wannacry-the-oecd-solution.

[2] Similarly, Emilie Legris and Dimitri Walas, "Regulation of Cyberspace by International Law," ESIL Reflection 7 (2018) 1, http://www.esil-sedi.eu/node/2060.

The Normative Order of the Internet. Matthias C. Kettemann, Oxford University Press (2020). © Matthias C. Kettemann.
DOI: 10.1093/oso/9780198865995.001.0001

frame to assess the legitimacy of digitality-related norms, to explain their emergence and predict their success in terms of "community" adoption and implementation. The normative order of the internet is thus both an empirical-conceptual and normative construct: an epistemological concept of online order(ing) that provides for legitimacy (and justification) narratives and establishes an elastic normative space, with principles and processes for solving public policy conflicts connected to safeguarding the internet's integrity. Its central added value is to relate the disparate norms of different legal systems, and of different character, to one another in a holistic approach and to develop shared normative vocabularies for the internet and a common finality framed by common narratives of justification.

The normative order of the internet, as developed and defended in this chapter, is neither conceived of as being constructed on a blank normative slate nor does it purport to bring absolute stability of normative expectations, a key element of any legal (or quasi-legal) order. Rather, it builds upon and strongly draws from the existing regulatory structures that have previously been instrumental, if in an unstructured, ad hoc manner, in anchoring the inchoate field of internet regulation and governance. Again: the normative order of the internet, as envisaged by this study, encompasses conceptually all regulatory layers and all regulatory players. It is, however, no normative panacea. Serious conflicts pitting different actors online and clashes between legal orders and among the norms of single orders will persist. The concept introduced here is a frame through which to understand better the internet and the normative dynamics present on it and to help relate applicable norms from different legal systems to each other through a coherence-enhancing ordered framework of processes and principles and justification narratives.

It is not suggested that the normative order of the internet constitutes a new "reign" of or over the internet, even if some authors believe that such a "reign" might be necessary. In his book *Pax Technica*, Philip N. Howard describes the past twenty-five years as an "internet interregnum,"[3] with different actors demanding (states) or exercising (companies) regulatory (quasi-)authority to varying degrees.[4] But just as the internet has never been "without (any) rule," only without a traditionally legitimated and constructed legal frame and without an overarching comprehensive theory of online order, more recent historical scholarship sees even the historical *interregnum* period more positively.[5] Thus the historical *interregnum* was only a time *inter* a specific kind of *regnum*, but not the absence of a *regnum* per se.[6] The argument formulated here with regard to the internet is remarkably similar. There is and always has been some order, some *regnum* on the internet. Yet there have been few attempts to reconceptualize this *regnum* as an ordered system of norms, especially as it suffered from the lack of a centralized enforcing and legitimating institution.

The normative order of the internet, as conceived in this study, still does not exhibit a centralized enforcement institution. Arguably, this role has been systematized and diffused. It is, as will be made clear in this chapter, the order itself, with its principles and norms, which can be stabilized sufficiently to "stand on its own" and exert compliance pull. Just as

[3] Philip N. Howard, *Pax Technica. How the Internet of Things May Set Us Free or Lock Us Up* (New Haven/London: Yale University Press, 2015), 66.

[4] With a view to the internet of things as a new physical layer of networked devices, he develops a new public policy for a responsible internet, see ibid., 148 et seq.

[5] Marianne Kirk, *"Die kaiserlose, die schreckliche Zeit"—Das Interregnum im Wandel der Geschichtsschreibung* (Frankfurt am Main: Peter Lang, 2002).

[6] Peter H. Wilson, *The Holy Roman Empire. A Thousand Years of Europe's History* (London: Penguin, 2016), 37.

the non-interregna times usually saw a more solidified form of the exercise of power, the normative order of the internet can function as an explanatory model for creating more predictable and thus stable normative relations between players and decreasing legal and jurisdictional conflicts.

The argumentative structure in which the presentation and contextualization of the normative order of the internet takes place in this chapter is shaped as follows: after identifying the emergence of a normative turn on the internet (6.1), the chapter then discusses the "nomos of the internet" (6.2) as a concept configuring the normative order of the internet. Subsequently, the normativity of the order (6.3) and its legal status, including its norms and normative processes (6.4), are presented. Section 6.5 addresses the principles of the normative order, before the order's legitimacy and legitimation (6.6), including narratives of justification within the order (6.7), are analyzed. This chapter ends with a section on the facticity of the normative order of the internet (6.8) and conclusions (6.9.) leading toward the study's last thematic chapter 7.

6.1.2 Stopping the Singularity

The normative order of the internet, as it is constituted and presented, is a flexible, holistic, and dynamic order. Its presentation follows, varying Immanuel Kant, the gradual development of reason:[7] its evolution is a story of "reason developing from notions."[8] This is the approach followed by this study as well: by parsing normativity on the internet, this study develops its order. The approach is not focused on historicizing the normative evolution of internet regulation, but rather analyzing the evolution, status quo, and trajectory of the normative order of the internet. Therefore, the normative order of the internet is presented normatively as well as empirically.

Establishing a normative order of the internet is essential for reducing risks inherent in technological progress. Two important German thinkers of the mid-twentieth century have independently identified these dangers. Published before the advent of the internet, they nevertheless offer insights into the dangers of the technological condition (and the technological *conditioning* of society and its laws). *Current* and *future man*, as Günther Anders described them, meaning people today and people tomorrow, are characterized through a discrepancy between growing technological capacities and the failure of imagination to provide an *imaginarium* for technology's catastrophic consequences.[9] He thus feared technological advancements without a concomitant ethical base, without normative bounds.

Similarly, Hans Jonas argued that the "new territory of collective practice, which we enter through high technology, is a no man's land for ethical theory."[10] The regulatory polestar ("Kompaß") must be the "vorausgedachte Gefahr selbst," the "preimagined danger itself." From it develops, following Jonas, the "new obligations of new power" through a "heuristic

[7] Immanuel Kant, *Lose Blätter zu den Fortschritten der Metaphysik* (AA XX.), (edited by Gerhard Lehmann) (Berlin: Berlin-Brandenburgische Akademie der Wissenschaften, 1971), 330.

[8] Ibid., 343: "Geschichte der sich aus Begriffen entwickelnden Vernunft" (translation by the author).

[9] Günther Anders, *Die Antiquiertheit des Menschen Bd. I: Über die Seele im Zeitalter der zweiten industriellen Revolution* (Frankfurt am Main: Beck, 2009).

[10] Hans Jonas, *Das Prinzip Verantwortung. Versuch einer Ethik für die technologische Zivilisation* (Frankfurt am Main: Suhrkamp, 2003), 7–8 ("Das Neuland kollektiver Praxis, das wir mit der Hochtechnologie betreten haben, ist für die ethische Theorie noch ein Niemandsland").

of fear."[11] This is a precautionary approach to technology regulation *avant la lettre*, coupled with a clear identification of the commensurate growth in power and obligations of internet actors, today's "new powers."

The normative order of the internet serves to curtail Jonas' "new power," it provides a map stratifying ethical concerns for his "no-man's-land for ethical theory," to which we may add, for our purposes, legal theory and practice, and it complexifies the "heuristic of fear" by disaggregating the premises of the heuristic: put otherwise, the normative orders approach to the internet puts an end to what Jonas feared without specifically referring to it: the *legal singularity*. This is modeled upon the *technological singularity*, a concept introduced by I. J. Good and John von Neumann and popularized by Vernor Vinge[12] and Rey Kurzweil,[13] as the moment when "machine intelligence will surpass human intelligence." This leads to the "Singularity—technological change so rapid and profound it represents a rupture in the fabric of human history."[14]

For the purpose of this study, at the moment when non-traditional, transnational normative arrangements become so powerful that they create their own processes, legitimacy narratives, and normative logics—and in effect supplant traditional, democratically legitimated national and international processes, narratives, and normative logics—such a *legal singularity* would occur. It has not and, given residual and strong legal self-defense mechanisms of democratic states and the solidity of the case for the emergence of a normative order of the internet, it will not. A theoretical example would be the case of courts around the world refraining from ensuring citizens' rights against terms of service agreements by powerful internet companies. Rather, the inverse seems to be true.[15]

In any case, some authors have cautioned that this view of the coming of the singularity is faulty because of the "complexity break":[16] as machine intelligence approaches human intelligence, progress becomes slower. Something similar is happening on the internet. Cases are increasingly becoming more complex and the relations between actors have become more multilayered and diverse: this is complexity at work which slows down the fragmentation into different orders and the multiplication of normative sub-regimes which may, in aggregate, have led to the legal singularity.

In any case, the normative order of the internet, as it is presented here, serves to stop any legal singularity-based fears. The normative order is a comprehensive approach to limiting the dangers of a legal singularity and normalizing discussion on the state of the rule of law and the laws of ruling on the internet. The normative order fills the "void of

[11] Ibid.

[12] Vernor Vinge, "The Coming Technological Singularity: How to Survive in the Post-Human Era," in G. A. Landis (ed.), *Vision-21: Interdisciplinary Science and Engineering in the Era of Cyberspace* (Washington, DC: NASA, 1993), 11–22.

[13] Ray Kurzweil, *The Singularity is Near* (New York: Penguin, 2005), 135–6.

[14] Ray Kurzweil, "The Law of Accelerating Returns," Kurzweil Accelerating Intelligence (Blog), March 7, 2001, http://www.kurzweilai.net/the-law-of-accelerating-returns.

[15] Just see recently, Landgericht Berlin, Az 16 O 341/15, February 12, 2018 (declaring illegal a number of substantial clauses in Facebook's terms of service (AGBs)).

[16] But see Paul G. Allen, "The Singularity Isn't Near," MIT Technology Review, October 12, 2011, https://www.technologyreview.com/s/425733/paul-allen-the-singularity-isnt-near ("Rather than the ever-accelerating advancement predicted by Kurzweil, we believe that progress toward this understanding is fundamentally slowed by the complexity brake. Our ability to achieve this understanding, via either the AI or the neuroscience approaches, is itself a human cognitive act, arising from the unpredictable nature of human ingenuity and discovery").

ungovernability" on the internet caused by dissonances of power and law[17] in what one researcher called the "algorithmic state of exception."[18] In contrast to Giorgio Agamben, who—following Foucault—had declared these "states of exception"[19] (here: putting people outside the law) for the new normal, the normative order is comprehensively constructed.

Algorithms do not cause states of exception in which the law does not apply and fundamental rights are not protected. They can be governed, as this study shows throughout, and are part, as normative artifacts, of the online order. For that, algorithms just as all other moving parts of the normative infrastructure on the internet need to be addressed (that is: regulated). This is premised upon their addressability. In this view, we can argue that much of the perceived crisis of the regulatory power of law on the internet has been limited by "a crisis of addressability."[20] If this is the case, as seems plausible, then the approach of the normative order of the internet is chiefly to systematize the processes and principles for "addressing" actions online.

Consider early attempts to introduce street numbers in towns, such as in Vienna in 1770–1772, which were met with strong opposition from the better-off, who saw this as an illegitimate attempt to tag their palaces (we would call it "democratically') just as the small houses some doors down.[21] This systematized the houses and made them easier to find for postal workers. Similarly, the normative order of the internet, by making norms (and actors) addressable and thus comparable, is presented here as an important step toward ensuring that dangers emanating from the internet are normatively met and the integrity of the internet is thus ensured. The regulatory focus of the normative order must thus be holistic.

However, the introduction of a house-by-house numbering system in eighteenth-century Vienna contains another lesson. The measure was promoted publicly as a measure to fight crime: "[an initiative which aimed] blos allein zu besserer Ausfindigmachung derer verdächtig liederlich und gefährlich Leuten," used only for the "beybehaltung der ruhe, und Sicherheit" and to keep citizens safe.[22] However, the government's actual impetus behind the introduction was the possibility to increase tax revenue and to ensure a more effective recruitment system for the army by counting all young men and identifying their residences.[23] Rather than enhancing (human) security, the goal was ensuring financial stability and gathering military resources. With this small example we see already that exercises in ordering are not intrinsically positive. Rather, it is the actual and not the publicly stated goal of the exercise of ordering that is essential for measuring its legitimacy.

[17] Evan Light and Jonathan A. Obar, "Surveillance Reform: Revealing Surveillance Harms and Engaging Reform Tactics," in Ben Wagner, Matthias C. Kettemann, and Kilian Vieth (eds.), *Research Handbook on Information Technologies and Human Rights* (Cheltenham: Edward Elgar, 2019), 195–222.

[18] Dan McQuillan, "Algorithmic States of Exception," European Journal of Cultural Studies 18 (2015), 564–76.

[19] Giorgio Agamben, *Ausnahmezustand* (Homo sacer, part II, vol. 1) (Frankfurt am Main: Suhrkamp, 2004).

[20] Benjamin H. Bratton, *The Stack. On Software and Sovereignty* (Cambridge, MA/London: MIT Press, 2015), 26.

[21] First, red numbers were painted on houses big and small, starting from the center of Vienna, working outwards. As houses were demolished and new ones built, this led to disorder, which was remedied by a streetwise numbering system in 1862 and the introduction of postal codes in 1966. See, instructively, Anton Tantner, *Ordnung der Häuser, Beschreibung der Seelen: Hausnummerierung und Seelenkonskription in der Habsburgermonarchie (Wiener Schriften zur Geschichte der Neuzeit)* (Vienna: Studienverlag, 2007), 44.

[22] As cited in ibid., 35.

[23] Ibid.

6.1.3 Regulatory Remit

The regulatory remit of the normative order of the internet is challenging. Almost all societal interactions today have some connection "to the internet." Therefore, the normative order "of the internet" could be perceived as a concept so broad that its epistemic usefulness is limited. Fixing the normative order's focus on artifacts and devices is also problematic, as the importance of devices changes and new ones appear. They are merely instantiations of progress, prone to evolve and merely mediate human–machine interaction. The normative order is thus conceived as independent of any one concrete mediating technology.

Fixating on an artificial online/offline dichotomy also seems problematic. Be it smart devices,[24] (killer) robots,[25] the regulation of metadata,[26] or cloud computing,[27] trying to distinguish between legal questions of "internet-based" and unconnected use no longer serves to describe global social realities. Each of these fields, almost chosen at random among many social reifications of progress, has serious "offline" implications. Smart fridges can be programmed to refuse further food outtake, once a certain number of calories is judged to have been consumed by the owner, thus functioning as a public health instrument (with its use possibly positively incentivized, through nudging the user toward the regime-optimal decision, by reduced premiums on health insurance subsidized by states). Further, robots may be used for nefarious purposes, especially as weapons, to inflict kinetic *offline* damage.

Two conclusions can be drawn from this. First, the dichotomy between online and offline regulation—as a general rule—is epistemically irrelevant in today's connected world (with connected here meaning the connection between our lived world-realities and internet-enabled life-actions).

However, as Indra Spiecker has shown, this can be different for specific categories of norms or interferences with rights or public goods, such as interferences with data. As we take up multiple roles on the internet, traditional law, often wedded to concepts such as protection of the offline consumer and editorial responsibility in pre-internet times, falls short. Under the conditions of modern information society, consumers can be producers, readers can be editors. The function of law of assigning responsibility (and liability) is much more difficult under conditions of anonymity, a multiplicity of roles, and geographical uncertainty.[28] Online interferences with data (*Informationseingriffe*) are special because of the legal uncertainty, anonymity of users and data providers, limited legal protection, lack of limits regarding the time dimension, and methodology and space of collecting data. Interferences with information/data are different from interferences with other protected goods because they are not experienced physically, do not materialize readily, or do not (always) force behavioral changes.[29] A functional normative order of the internet needs to take into account the different results that normative interventions in regulatory processes and fields may have.

[24] Samuel Greengard, *The Internet of Things* (Cambridge, MA/London: MIT Press, 2015).
[25] John Jordan, *Robots* (Cambridge, MA/London: MIT Press, 2016).
[26] Jeffrey Pomerantz, *Metadata* (Cambridge, MA/London: MIT Press, 2015).
[27] Nayan B. Ruparelia, *Cloud Computing* (Cambridge, MA/London: MIT Press, 2016).
[28] Cf. Indra Spiecker gen. Döhmann, "Online- und Offline-Nutzung von Daten: Einige Überlegungen zum Umgang mit Informationen im Internetzeitalter," in Michael Bartsch und Robert G. Briner (eds.), *DGRI-Jahrbuch* (Cologne: Verlag Dr. Otto Schmidt), 39–53 (39).
[29] Ibid., 42.

In order to overcome the online/offline dichotomy, Mireille Hildebrandt developed the notion of "onli*fe*,"[30] arguing that the "current life world can no longer be described by dichotomizing online and offline." Therefore onli*fe* "singles out the fact that our 'real' life is neither on- nor offline but partakes in a new kind of world [. . .]."[31]

The second conclusion is that the normative order of the, using Hildebrandt's new coinage, onli*fe* world seems too artificial to make intuitive sense. Different normative orders exist with regard to different social fields, the internal differentiation of world society allows for many diverging, converging, overlapping, and conflicting normative orders. There is, however, substantial added value in identifying the normative forces shaping the use and development of the internet and framing them within a normative order of the internet. This is this chapter's goal.

But first, let us discuss the regulatory focus of the normative order of the internet. A normative order of the internet can therefore definitely not be a normative order of *only* the internet. If the limits of the order are thus difficult to fathom, does this mean that the whole approach followed in this study is flawed? Decidedly not. As smart fridges, robots, metadata, and clouds show, one can differentiate between norms related to the order of the internet and norms related to unconnected regulatory fields.

What is essential, for the purpose of this study, is that there must be a (1) *material (non-trivial) connection* between the regulatory question or the norm and the internet as a network of networks (2) *in the normative sense*. As an example, let us return to fridges: conducting online research for a new fridge meets the first criterion (use of the internet) but, as the use is merely a means to an end, this does not meet the second. The use of the internet is trivial (within the context of this study). If potential buyers, however, encounter a site on which the data protection practices and the protocols used by an online-enabled "smart fridge" are discussed, perhaps even its protection from being hacked and conscripted into botnets,[32] they engage with norms belonging to the normative order of the internet as conceived of here. Regulatory, security-related questions regarding the internet of things, including smart fridges, are part of the normative order of the internet. There is a *non-trivial* connection that is also *normative*.

Buying a robot is another example. The contract to buy a robot is based in civil law and civil law questions of contractual obligations (such as paying schedule and risk transferral upon receipt) do not engage the normative order of the internet as presently understood. However, robots work on the basis of artificial intelligence, which is only implementable through machine learning by algorithms based on big data sets. All these aspects of robot construction and programming, including norms and guidelines for behavioral standards of robots, are (1) materially connected to the internet in a (2) normative sense. The norms regulating these aspects are thus norms of the normative order of the internet.

The internet, in this context, is notably not only the network of networks, but rather a notion that encompasses both the infrastructure necessary to use the network of networks and also *digitality* in a broader sense. With Stalder, digitality can be understood as referring to "relations based on the infrastructure of digital networks in the production, use and

[30] Mireille Hildebrandt, *Smart Technologies and the End(s) of Law* (Cheltenham: Edward Elgar, 2015), 42.

[31] Ibid.

[32] As happens with regularity, just see Eric Limer, "How Hackers Wrecked the Internet Using DVRs and Webcams," *Popular Mechanics*, October 21, 2016, https://www.popularmechanics.com/technology/infrastructure/a23504/mirai-botnet-internet-of-things-ddos-attack.

transformation of material and immaterial goods and constitution and coordination of individuals and collective action."[33] The normative order of the internet could therefore also be called the normative order of digitality, but "internet," read as encompassing digitality for the purposes of this study, is more broadly accepted and thus more intuitive.

6.2 The Nomos of the Internet

Importantly, the normative order of the internet is not conceived of as a replacement of any other order or legal systems. Rather, it complements them by structuring, contextualizing, legitimizing existing norms and offering a frame and a space for their critique and contestation. In normatively challenging times, with states reconfiguring their sovereignty over the internet and its physical artifacts, with private actors pushing toward self-regulation through private law and its enforcement, and with a growing body of transnational regulatory arrangements of different normative density and breadth, the normative order of the internet can be used as a theoretical structure, a model of, with, and for norms that explains, justifies, and predicts normatively relevant behavior with a material connection to the internet.

The normative order of the internet is an innovative way of normatively perceiving and regulating social interactions with regard to the internet. Norms relevant for the order online are perceived according to meta-norms to be presented and legitimized in the following section and, through this perception, included within the order norms.[34] This brings us to the *nomos of the internet*. The concept, as used here, denotes a meta-order of the complex normative space of the internet.

This *nomos of the internet* constitutes the normative order of the internet. Norms partaking in the normative order of the internet are norms of the internet's nomos. This nomos, as presently understood, is neither purely a *taxis* nor a *kosmos:* neither a purely artificial normative order nor a *necessary* natural order.[35] The nomos of the internet, as configured in, and constituting, its normative order, combines elements of ordering ex material necessity and of principle-based ordering. It further appears as an argumentative suprastructure (or meta-narrative) that frames the development of the normative order of the internet. While there is no single decision or new norm that is determinative of the beginning of the "turn" to nomos, the solidification of the normative approach to the internet, through principles and processes, allows us to determine that such a turn is upon us.

By positing that the nomos of the internet configures the normative order of the internet, this study makes the case that the nomos of the internet is more than the sum of norms it is constituted of, a legal *Lebenswelt* of sorts. This approach was first taken by Robert M. Cover, who, in a 1983 article, introduced the notion of a nomos having a connected narrative. "We inhabit a nomos," he writes, "a normative universe. We constantly create and maintain a world of right and wrong, of lawful and unlawful, of valid and void." But rules form only a

[33] Felix Stalder, *Kultur der Digitalität* (Frankfurt am Main: Suhrkamp, 2016), 18.

[34] This is no different from modern philosophy and modern art, which does not strive to make the objectively "there" viewable, but rather denies the existence of the objective view and relies on, and glorifies, subjective impression.

[35] See for this usage: Thalin Zarmanian, "Ordnung und Ortung/Order and localisation," in Stephen Legg (ed.), *Spatiality, Sovereignty and Carl Schmitt* (Abingdon: Routledge, 2011), 291–297 (295).

small part of the "normative universe that ought to claim our attention." Apart from the set of legal institutions and prescriptions collectively called *nomos*, exists a *narrative* to "locate it and to give it meaning": "[f]or every constitution there is an epic, for each Decalogue a scripture."[36]

These normative poetics become important when we take Cover seriously. He writes that "each prescription is insistent in its demand to be located in discourse—to be supplied with history and destiny, beginning and end, explanation and purpose [and] every narrative is insistent in its demand for its prescriptive point, its moral."[37] With regard to the normative order of the internet this can be read as affirming, from a different perspective, a point made earlier in this study, namely that norms in order to be legitimate need to be consonant with the normative order of the internet and that a narrative's "moral" is conceptually close to the "regulatory purpose" of the online order (or one of its purposes), thus the legitimating "story" or "stories" of the normative order of the internet.

Conceiving of the normative order of the internet, as configured by the nomos, is of epistemic value in a different way as well: as Cover writes, the nomos is a concept requiring no formal authority, no state. The "creation of legal meaning," Cover calls the process "jurisgenesis," is a process distinct from the formalized process of creating laws. Legal meaning is created by applying laws in context "through an essentially cultural medium."[38] This is of course a conception of normativity premised upon a cultural approach. But even without adopting Cover's approach *pro toto*, the insight is important that we can (and have to) distinguish between normative processes leading to norms and their application.

Using Cover's concept of *jurisgenesis* as a conceptual lens allows us to recognize, for example, that within the nomos any norms/actor interaction that has an observable result, and be it the assurance of a right or the confirmation of a prescription, can be normatively relevant (thus creating "legal meaning"). It is the intrasocietal processes of applying norms, contesting them, and changing them that Cover refers to when he speaks about this act of creating legal meaning, which is part of the nomos. These theoretical approaches to the normative order are relevant for the assessment of the normative order's legitimacy from the perspective of the participant, the normative actor. They matter therefore for the present chapter. To illustrate the multifaceted nature of an act of jurisgenesis, we can employ a Platonion distinction: depending on the perspective of the normative actor, any legal decision taken by them can be one of *epistēmē* (knowledgful, conscious legal value-creating), one of *doxa* (based on common understanding without deeper reflection but with a sense of membership in a normative community), or one of *technē* (when the decision is automatic and represents unreflected practice).

This study will return to the role of narratives as instruments to gauge the legitimacy of the normative order of the internet below.[39] What readers should take with them at this stage is the dual nature of the nomos of the internet. The "richness of the nomos," as Cover calls it, marks the normative order in which the nomos is located and which it helps to constitute. The nomos of the internet with its "varied and complex materials" helps establish "paradigms for dedication, acquiescence, contradiction, and resistance."[40]

[36] Robert M. Cover, "The Supreme Court, 1982 Term—Foreword. Nomos and Narrative," Harvard Law Review 97 (1983) 4, 1–68 (4) (notes omitted).

[37] Ibid., 5.

[38] Ibid., 30.

[39] See 6.6.

[40] Cover (1983), 9–10.

6.3 Normativity of the Order

6.3.1 Explicit and Implicit Normativity

Normativity in the law of computer culture, in the digital condition, has a performative dimension: it performs a break with traditional concepts of normative hierarchy. There is no stringent separation of, and evaluation of, legal sources based on their origin.[41] Rather than the origin of norms or the identity of the norm-creators, two dimensions of normativity stratify the norms of the online order. With Vesting this study understands modern law as a "network of constituted, explicit legal norms [Rechtsnormen] on the one hand and an instituted, partially implicit normativity on the other hand." This understanding makes clear why the normative texts (the norms) cannot be separated from the "cultural texts" (which need not be written texts), influencing the conditions of implicit normativity. Vesting specifically refers to declarations of rights that—as documents with constitutional qualities—share an especially strong connection to the period, place, and practices of and at their adoption, but the point is equally valid with regard to norms generally.[42]

6.3.2 Constitutionalization

We have addressed constitutionalization of the internet before.[43] Societal constitutionalization processes with the normative order of the internet lead to stabilization of central principles of the normative order. The normative order of the internet is progressively stabilized through these normative developments. The trend of orders to become denser in terms of norms and more detailed with regard to the rights and obligations provided, but also to understand themselves as regulating on an important level a social substratum of society, are elements of constitutionalization.

Within the normative order of the internet, elements of *Eigenkonstitutionalisierung* and of *Fremdkonstitutionalisierung*, of auto- and hetero-constitutionalization, can be observed. The key difference is that auto-constitutionalization is premised upon the existence of meta-rules, allowing for a system's self-reflection, while hetero-constitutionalization allows for important legitimacy transfers from national constitutions and the implicit recognition of them as normatively relevant.[44]

The hetero-constitutionalization of the normative order of the internet encompasses all processes by which national legal orders and the regime of international law influence the development of the principles and processes—thus: the norms—of the internet's normative order. The international legal rules relevant for the normative order of the internet have already been discussed earlier.[45] The relationship of national legal orders to the normative order of the internet will be at the center of the next chapter.[46] At this stage, it shall suffice to say that normatively relevant interactions between international and national legal orders

[41] Thomas Vesting, *Die Medien des Rechts: Computernetzwerke* (Weilerswist: Velbrück Wissenschaft, 2015), 112.
[42] Thomas Vesting, *Rechtstheorie*, 2nd edn. (Munich: Beck, 2015), 11 (translation by the author).
[43] See 5.2.6 and 5.2.8.
[44] See 5.3.1.
[45] See 3.2 and 3.3.
[46] See chapter 7.

and the normative order of the internet are evidence of, first, the recognition of the normative order of the internet, and second, of the normative necessity to stratify this order. While certain implicit practices influence the constituted normativity of the normative order of the internet, national legal orders and the international law-based order are important sources of principles and processes determining the normativity of the normative order of the internet.

The techniques of managing interactions between the normative order and national legal orders (especially its recognition as a source of a normative *tertium*—beyond national or international law) are based on the online order's responsivity which allows, as Viellechner writes in a study of transnational normativity, "the interweaving of national legal orders, international regimes and transnational regulatory arrangements through a newly conceived collision law as horizontal constitutional law."[47] This "horizontal constitutional law" is an example of hetero-constitutionalization. It is based on the application in a transnational context of (national) fundamental and (international) human rights.[48] Such an application can be considered a "constitutionalizing" "Grund und Grenze" (foundation and limit) of transnational regulatory arrangements.[49] Through the increasingly detailed process of safeguarding human rights in transnational orders, and particularly with regard to digitality, national constitutions and the international legal order provide a legitimacy framework for transnational normative arrangements and accept them, under certain conditions, as law.[50]

This acceptance is, in a formal view, the central hetero-constitutional act, and will figure prominently in the analysis in the next chapter, as will more recent developments calling its centrality into question. These trends include a reduction of the significance of the gatekeeper function of national (constitutional) law when it comes to non-traditional norms. Progressively, as the next chapter will show, norms that belong neither to national nor to international legal orders are applied in national courts. They may not be formally accepted as law but are normatively relevant. As this study will show, they are best understood with a view to the evolution of a normative *tertium* that is neither part of the first (national) or second (international) category of laws. The *tertium* norms, such as internet standards and governance principles, are applicable (if their legal structure enables this) because of reasons other than (only) a national *Rechtsanwendungsbefehl*.[51]

This study has addressed auto-constitutionalization (self-constitutionalization) above,[52] so the presentation of this regime-internal normative solidification can be succinct here. Unlike hetero-constitutionalization processes, the autonomous regime-internal "thickening" of the norms and normative processes can take place independently of other regimes and traditional forces of constitutionalization, such as nation-state norms. The normative frame, in which autonomous normative processes take place, is defined by the normative order (in casu: of the internet) and, taking up the constituted/instituted normativity approach, by instituted practices that solidify into norms.

[47] Lars Viellechner, *Transnationalisierung des Rechts* (Weilerswist: Velbrück, 2013), 265 (translation by the author).

[48] Ibid., 293.

[49] Ibid., 217–18.

[50] Ibid., 287. See, on the conditions, below 6.4.

[51] A type of "order," contained in a law, decided by a democratically legitimated legislative body, for a non-national norm to be applied like national law. See 7.5.

[52] See 5.2.5.

Auto-constitutional tendencies are natural effects of regime-internal demands for increasingly detailed regulation, coupled with a growing disconnection from the principles and normative processes of non-regime norms. As the ILC's *Fragmentation Report* put it, this is merely an "adequate response to the complexification of global society."[53] The challenge of auto-constitutionalization lies less in the development of norms, but rather in the necessity to ensure the simultaneous evolution of a law of conflicts that allows regulation of one regime to interact with norms of other regimes horizontally, and vertically with national and international legal norms stratified in traditional normative hierarchies.

Transnational regulatory arrangements, such as the normative order of the internet, exist largely independently of traditional normative hierarchies.[54] Alternatively, we therefore have to identify, within these self-constitutionalizing orders, foundations for regime stabilization, self-affirmation, and plurality management.[55]

6.3.3 Localization

The normative order of the internet is not relegated to a particular social sphere, such as the public or the private sphere, or a particular system of law, such as public law or private law. As has been hypothesized and shown, it includes international and national legal norm, and the broad category of tertium norms—that is transnational regulatory arrangements, code, and standards. Its norms are (usually) part of either international or national legal systems and do not cease to be so when qualified as norms within the normative order of the internet. The order, as discussed earlier, encompasses norms that evidence a *material (non-trivial)* and *normative connection* between the regulatory question(s) or norm(s) and the internet as a network of networks.

The normative order of the internet is localizable only as a specific form of the internet's hypertext, namely not the successful links (taking those who click on one to another website or localized piece of internet content, such as media files)[56] but rather the lesser-known *StretchText*, a technological feature that has been largely ignored. With *StretchText*, gaps between information online are clickable and they then reveal additional layers of information. Content providers can thus establish a hierarchy of information encouraging readers to click on gaps to "show more," when more information is required.[57] Similarly, the normative order of the internet is an order that, given its layered nature, contains multiple levels of complexity. Prima facie only principles may be observable, especially internet governance-related principles, and among them chiefly human rights-oriented norms. However, once "users" (normative actors) "click on the gap" (apply the norms), new layers of normative complexity unfold that allow for a more nuanced regulation.

[53] Ibid.

[54] Gunther Teubner, "Globale Bukowina. Zur Emergenz eines transnationalen Rechtspluralismus," Rechtshistorisches Journal 15 (1996) 255 ff.

[55] See 6.4.

[56] Theodor H. Nelson, "Brief Words on the Hypertext," January 23, 1967, https://archive.org/details/SelectedPapers1977/mode/2up.

[57] George P. Landow, *Hypertext 3.0: Critical Theory and New Media in an Era of Globalization*, 3rd edn. (Baltimore: Johns Hopkins University Press, 2006), 95.

6.4 Legality of the Order

6.4.1 The Normative Order of the Internet as a Legal Order

No one would doubt that Germany's liberal and democratic basic social order, the *freiheitlich-demokratische Grundordnung*, is based on law, in particular constitutional law. The "normative order" of Germany is a proudly and profoundly *legal* order. Yet within the German legal system, there exist norms of very different character, from non-binding norms to DIN (*Deutsche Industrienorm; German Industrial Norm)* standards that exercise normative pull through epistemic authority,[58] from laws to fundamental rights guarantees enshrined in the Fundamental Law (Grundgesetz). The existence of non-binding norms within a normative system does not detract from the latter's qualification as a *legal* system or order.

National legal systems consist primarily of formally binding norms within a Kelsenian *Stufenbau*[59] and only comparatively few non-binding norms. This is particularly true for countries with strong protection of the rule of law, as the principle of legality prescribes that any state action needs to be based on law. This discourages normative innovation but safeguards fundamental rights, which is a valid trade-off given the conflicting interests involved. In the normative order of the internet the inverse is observable. There are, depending on how one approaches the definition of the order, many different normative instruments present: from national laws and international regulations to transnational regulatory arrangements, the majority of which, especially in the third category, are not formally binding norms (they do, however, exercise a normative pull toward adherence, as will be described below[60]).

When introducing the concept of "normative order," this study has referred to the approach by Forst and Günther, who see norms less in terms of legality grounded in *formality* and more in terms of *functionality*. Norms, to them, are "practical reasons to act [containing] the claim of being binding upon the addressee."[61] These claims are narrativized and contextualized, habituated in practices, and contained in customs (implicit, instituted normativity) and conventions *as social contracts* (implicit again) or conventions *as treaties* (explicit constituted normativity). The claims of being binding are thus *not legal* in that they are premised upon a legal procedure to ensure compliance, but nevertheless exercise, through their claim to be binding, a certain compliance pull (if they meet the legitimacy criteria discussed below, including consonance with the order's normative goal[62]).

But norms in the context of this study are *legal* in the sense that they shape and frame the *legal* space (*Rechts*raum), contribute to ensuring *legal* peace (*Rechts*frieden), provide for a *law* of collision (Kollisions*recht*) between applicable regimes and are treated by and large *as legal* norms or at least *legality* heuristics which ease decisionary burdens.

[58] Though some are referred to in laws and thus are part, by reference, of the legal system.

[59] Hans Kelsen, *Reine Rechtslehre* (1934), 21, (edited by Matthias Jestaedt) *Reine Rechtslehre*. Studienausgabe der 1. Auflage 1934, (Tübingen: Mohr Siebeck, 2008), 33.

[60] See 6.6.

[61] Rainer Forst und Klaus Günther, "Die Herausbildung normativer Ordnungen. Zur Idee eines interdisziplinären Forschungsprogramms," in Rainer Forst und Klaus Günther (eds.), *Die Herausbildung normativer Ordnungen. Interdisziplinäre Perspektiven* (Frankfurt/New York: Campus, 2011), 11–30 (16).

[62] See 6.6.

Taken together, the norms constituting the normative order of the internet (those *normatively* relevant for the internet and digitality in a *materially* relevant way) form a multilayered legal order. This does not mean that they are centrally *ordered* or *hierarchically* layered. A normative order is, this has been discussed above but merits to be reiterated here,[63] a "complex of norms and values with which the fundamental structure of a society (or the structure of international, supranational, or transnational relationships) is legitimated, in particular the exercise of political authority and the distribution of basic goods."[64] These are key *legal* functions. At the same time, the normative order of the internet is more than a purely legal order as it relies on norms and processes that cannot easily be conceptualized in the language, logic, and legitimacy structures of traditional legal systems.

The order extends to regulating and legitimating (or providing the normative tools for contestation of) the exercise of private or public authority and the distribution of basic goods in relation to the use and development of the internet by multiple actors, including internet access and access to internet content. It enshrines a *rule of norms*, the set of norms and normative expectations that shape the use and development of the internet, which lead to a *rule of law*.

The measure of *legality* of the normative order cannot be the "political constitution" (of states), against which it would fall short (but so does the international *legal* order). Rather the normative yardstick must be the normative order of the internet's *Eigenverfassung*,[65] as instituted by practices, and auto- and hetero-constituted. Norms from the third category (e.g. informal transnational regulatory arrangements and internet standards) may not be *legal norms* in traditional national or international legal approaches (they are the *tertium*), but they can be considered to have some or most of the qualities of legal norms (*Rechtsnormqualität*), if they meet internal, regime-specific transnationalized and objective human rights-based checks and balances as to their production, content, and application.[66]

This is why internet standards, contained for example in IETF's Request for Comments series,[67] are both legitimate as instruments of normative ordering and have *Rechtsnormqualität*. They may not *be Rechtsnormen*, but this is of little import, as they have both the procedural pedigree and normative content that gives them the potential to be norms.[68] This calls to mind Möllers' approach to norms as "positively marked possibilities," pointing to a "possible situation" or a "possible event" to be realized.[69]

[63] See 1.2.3.

[64] Rainer Forst und Klaus Günther, "Die Herausbildung normativer Ordnungen. Zur Idee eines interdisziplinären Forschungsprogramms," in Rainer Forst und Klaus Günther (eds.), *Die Herausbildung normativer Ordnungen. Interdisziplinäre Perspektiven* (Frankfurt/New York: Campus, 2011), 11–30 (15): "Unter 'normativer Ordnung' verstehen wir den Komplex von Normen und Werten, mit denen die Grundstruktur einer Gesellschaft (beziehungsweise die Struktur inter- bzw. supra- oder transnationaler Verhältnisse) legitimiert wird, namentlich die Ausübung politischer Autorität und die Verteilung von elementaren Lebens- und Grundgütern" (translation by the author).

[65] Teubner, Gunther, "Globale Zivilverfassungen: Alternativen zur staatszentrierten Verfassungstheorie," ZaÖRV 63 (2003), 1–28 (22).

[66] Vesting, *Die Medien des Rechts: Computernetzwerke* (2015),144.

[67] See 2.4.2.

[68] On the importance of processes, see Thomas Vesting, "Instituierte und konstituierte Normativität. Prozeduralisierung und multi-normative Systeme," in Tatjana Sheplyakova (ed.), *Prozeduralisierung des Rechts* (Tübingen: Mohr, 2018), 101–122.

[69] Christoph Möllers, *Die Möglichkeit der Normen* (Berlin: Suhrkamp, 2016), 13–14: "Normen sind [...] als positiv markierte Möglichkeiten zu verstehen. Normen verweisen auf einen möglichen Zustand oder ein mögliches Ereignis. [...] Die positive Markierung einer Möglichkeit zeigt an, dass diese sich verwirklichen soll" (translation by the author).

6.4.2 Norms of the Order

To which norms does the above apply? What are the norms of the normative order of the internet? As defined above, for a norm to be part of the normative order of the internet, there must be a (1) *material* (non-trivial) and a (2) *normative* (not merely factual) connection between the norm and the internet as a network of networks.

Civil law provisions regarding payment in a contract for internet access with an Internet Service Provider are norms that are connected to the internet, but in a trivial way. However, norms within that contract that would allow the Internet Service Provider to reduce connection speeds for downloading certain online content are non-trivial and normatively relevant for regulating digitality. Courts can decide whether payment is due on a contract by looking at the contract and past civil jurisprudence. When assessing norms related to net neutrality and preferential treatment of specific content, however, they have to enter the normative force field conceptualized in the normative order of the internet to understand holistically the genesis and importance of these norms both materially and normatively connected to the internet.

Just as it is virtually impossible (and also of little epistemic value) to enumerate all applicable norms within a national legal order, stratifying all norms of the normative order will not be attempted here. But some order is necessary for the norms of the order.

Norms within the normative order, which are both materially and normatively connected to regulating digitality, can be distinguished according to their normative character as formally *binding* or *non-binding* (materially, this bears repetition: they have effects independent of their formal genesis). Möllers calls non-binding norms "non-norms"[70] or, more convincingly, *cognitive norms.* A different, more often used term that avoids shouldering the metaphysical burden of the concept of *cognition* would be *soft law. Soft law* norms can be prescriptive, they are just not formally binding. They have normative implications and are, indeed, often a preferred tool of normation in normative arenas where multiple actors dominate or where timely regulation is important. Soft law norms have strong orientative value independent of any formal obligations, especially because already in the act of their adoption lies a certain *recognition* of their content by the normative actor.[71]

On the basis of their origin, we can distinguish between norms of national law, of international law, and other sources, be they private companies or internet standard-setter. These norms of the *normative tertium* will become particularly important in the next chapter, as their integration into national and international regulatory frameworks is of special interest to this study (and where it will be shown that a normative *tertium datur).* The normative tertium consists of the norms of transnational regulatory arrangements impacting the internet, from internet standards to terms of service of internet companies, from informal agreements between Internet Exchange Points to guidance on non-discriminatory use of algorithms in selecting advertisements shown to social network users or rules on the use of artificial intelligence in cloud server storage optimization. Their normative remit is vast. While they become visible primarily in cases of normative conflicts, their existence needs to be acknowledged.

[70] Which seems strange because the norms need not be binding to become norms, especially as he defines them as positively marked possibilities: as pointing to an achievable, changeable status post quod. See ibid., 139.

[71] Ibid.

To name but one example: certain coding practices, such as privacy by design, are explicitly normative and thus form part of the normative order's normativity, while others engaging questions of formal logic—that is the *techné* of using algorithms—may not. They are merely factual tools of coding, instantiated in lines of code without *material* normativity.

We can also differentiate norms within the normative order of the internet by their respective "legislator." Possible actors within the normative order of the internet include—as by the Working Group on Internet Governance (WGIG)—"Governments, the private sector and civil society."[72] Governments can also act via international or regional organizations. Companies can develop norms individually (e.g. terms of service) or collectively (e.g. industry standards). Civil society groups can become norm entrepreneurs by themselves or as a collective. Further, any configuration between the actors is possible. Indeed, reliance on multiple actors call for their inclusion in all stages of the normative process. "[I]n their respective roles," they develop and apply, as per the accepted definition of the WGIG, "shared principles, norms, rules, decision-making procedures, and programmes that shape the evolution and use of the internet."[73] For the purposes of the normative order, all these normative instruments can be understood as norms *sensu latiore*. The norms of the normative order of the internet have substantially enriched the legal vocabulary leading to, what Habermas terms, an evolution of the composition of the legal medium (*Rechtsmedium*)[74] and, following Vesting, of the media of law (*Die Medien des Rechts*[75]).

National Laws. National laws regulate the frame of internet use by anyone under a state's jurisdiction and control even though, as previously demonstrated,[76] the classic state-oriented law paradigms of *norm completeness* (all relevant social interactions are regulated by national norms) and *closed legitimacy loops* (all existing norms have been democratically legitimated and can provide for further normative developments imbued with the same legitimacy) are challenged by globalization and deterritorialization through the use of ICTs. Importantly, however, states and their legal systems do not fade away: "the virtual space does not mean [. . .] the end of the sovereign constitutional state."[77] States continue to fulfill (ideally) a constitutional and international law-based duty in protecting their citizens and their societies, including societal values, such as openness, concepts, such as publicness, and systems of public opinion, such as threats emanating from new technologies and from social change that these technological advances engender.

[72] Report of the Working Group on Internet Governance (2005), http://www.wgig.org/docs/WGIGREPORT.pdf.

[73] Ibid.

[74] Jürgen Habermas, "Im Sog der Technokratie, in Jürgen Habermas, *Im Sog der Technokratie: kleine politische Schriften XII* (Frankfurt: Suhrkamp, 2013), 7: "Heute zeigen sich auch auf internationaler Ebene Anzeichen für eine Rationalisierung der staatlichen Herrschaftsausübung, welche einer Veränderung in der Komposition des Rechtsmediums entspricht."

[75] The titular notion of Vesting's tetralogy is "Die Medien des Rechts." See Thomas Vesting, *Die Medien des Rechts: Sprache* (Weilerswist: Velbrück Wissenschaft, 2011); Thomas Vesting, *Die Medien des Rechts: Schrift* (Weilerswist: Velbrück Wissenschaft, 2011); Thomas Vesting, *Die Medien des Rechts: Buchdruck* (Weilerswist: Velbrück Wissenschaft, 2013); and Vesting, *Die Medien des Rechts: Computernetzwerke* (2015). See, in particular, Vesting, , *Die Medien des Rechts: Computernetzwerke* (2015), passim and 83–4. For an English version of the tetralogy, see Thomas Vesting, *Legal Theory and the Media of Law* (Cheltenham: Edward Elgar, 2018).

[76] See, 2.4.2.

[77] Stephan Hobe, "Cyberspace—der virtuelle Raum," in Josef Isensee, Paul Kirchhof, et al. (eds.), *Handbuch des Staatsrechts, Band XI: Internationale Bezüge*, 3rd edn. (2013), § 231, no. 44 ("Der virtuelle Raum bedeutet [. . .] nicht das Ende des souveränen Verfassungsstaates") (translation by the author).

Looking closely at national norms, it is highly difficult to emerge with a clear picture. It is only with more distance that the mosaic of rules ("Regelungsmosaik"[78]) to ensure rights and freedoms becomes visible. National norms that are materially connected in a normatively relevant way to the internet can be considered to form part of the normative order of the internet. Given the number of national legal systems, it does not make sense to undertake exercises of enumeration. What is notable, however, is that with most technology, periods of lax regulation turn into phases of more intensive regulatory activity leading to substantially more granular norms. This, in turn, can lead to both material and jurisdictional conflicts, especially as states have reemerged as territorial data controllers and have acted, through data localizations laws, against forces of deterritorialization through the use of ICTs.[79]

International Law. Reiterating a point made earlier: For a norm to be part of the normative order of the internet, there must be a (1) *material* (non-trivial) and (2) *normative* (not merely factual) connection between the norm and the internet as a network of networks. This study earlier (and passim) showed the applicability of international law to the internet.[80] Painting with broad brushes, international law protects the security, stability, robustness, resilience, and functionality of the internet, thus: its integrity as a matter of common interest.[81]

The applicability of international law to the internet, as a matter of principle, has not been seriously questioned in some time.[82] This WSIS consensus[83] lasted and allowed the UN's GGE to confirm, in its 2015 report,[84] that international law, the UN Charter, and international legal principles apply to the internet.[85] As the international community aspires to regulate the internet in a peaceful manner "for the common good of mankind,"[86] the report continues, "[t]he adherence by States to international law, in particular their Charter obligations, is an essential framework for their actions in their use of ICTs and to promote an open, secure, stable, accessible and peaceful ICT environment."[87]

What are the norms of international law that form part of the normative order of the internet? Since international law as a whole applies to the internet, one could argue that all international legal rules can be considered part of its normative order. However, this would ignore the dual materiality and normativity condition set for the relation of a norm's content and the internet. Rather, looking at the definition of the GGE cited in the paragraph above we can see that any norm regulating actors in their use of ICTs and in their policies toward safeguarding internet integrity are part of the normative order of the internet's "international law" branch.

78 Wolfgang Hoffmann-Riem, "Freiheitsschutz in den globalen Kommunikationsinfrastrukturen," JZ 69 (2014) 2, 53–63 (63).

79 Lars Viellechner, *Transnationalisierung des Rechts* (Weilerswist: Velbrück, 2013), 99. On ICANN's domain regime, see ibid., 127 et seq.

80 See 3.2.

81 See 2.3.

82 The last larger project with this goal seems to have been Jack L. Goldsmith and Tim Wu, *Who Controls The Internet? Illusions of a Borderless World* (Cambridge: CUP, 2006), xii.

83 World Summit on the Information Society (WSIS), Declaration of Principles, WSIS-03/GENEVA/ DOC/4-E, 12 December 2003, para. 1.

84 United Nations, Developments in the Field of Information and Telecommunications in the Context of International Security, Report of the Secretary General, A/70/174 of July 22, 2015, http://www.un.org/ga/search/view_doc.asp?symbol=A/70/174 ("GGE report (2015)").

85 Ibid., para. 26.

86 Ibid., para. 28 (c).

87 Ibid., para. 25.

This study has explained earlier[88] which rules of international law are especially relevant for the internet. It is, broadly speaking, the norms discussed there—ius cogens norms, treaty-based norms, customary rules, general principles, soft law—that also form part of the normative order of the internet. It is important to note that international legal norms do not only influence state behavior even though their primary regulatory objects (and subjects) are states.[89] International law-based rules within the normative order of the internet impact the behavior of all three actor groups:[90]

- *individuals* are empowered by normative commitments to ensuring that they can exercise their human rights online; conversely, they are obliged not to violate international rules prohibiting, for example, online calls to genocide or the propagation of qualified hate speech;
- *states* are allocated duties (e.g. regarding the internet's stability) and given certain rights based on a technology-sensitive reading of sovereignty; they are also obliged, within the "protect" dimension of their human rights obligations to adopt a legal framework which requires business entities to exercise "human rights due diligence";[91]
- *private sector companies* engaged in internet-related business models should respect the internationally recognized human rights for users and affected parties, independently of a state's ability or willingness to fulfill its own obligations,[92] by, for instance, employing safeguards relative to the public service value they provide with the intensity of the precautions the company should implement relative to the potential impact and damage and the importance of their service for the exercise of human rights.[93]

Other Normative Arrangements: The Normative Tertium. The internet is a space full of norms. Some form part of the normative order of the internet, others are developed and applied decentrally and unsystematically or fade away, when left unapplied. Norms that originate neither from states nor within the international legal order are of special interest in this study. It is their role as instantiations of a normative *tertium* (next to national and international law) that requires their assessment in terms of legality and legitimacy, especially since their normative role is substantial. With regard to actual internet use, it is these norms of the normative tertium that are most often encountered. Admittedly, being able to go online is premised largely upon "invisible" (functioning) national and international rules (which remain both essential and important), but the lived "normative experience" is structured overwhelmingly by normative arrangements that are neither specifically national nor international, but rather multifaceted and transnational.

The normative tertium includes technical "rules of the road," published in RFCs and developed bottom-up on mailing lists of engineers. It includes the large normative field of

[88] See 3.3.
[89] Cf. Ian Hurd, *How to Do Things with International Law* (Princeton: Princeton University Press, 2017).
[90] See 3.2.
[91] Committee on Economic, Social and Cultural Rights, General Comment No. 24 on State obligations under the International Covenant on Economic, Social and Cultural Rights in the context of business activities, UN Doc. E/C.12/GC/24 of 10 August 2017, para. 16.
[92] Council of Europe, Recommendation CM/Rec(2018)2 of the Committee of Ministers to member states on the roles and responsibilities of internet intermediaries, adopted by the Committee of Ministers on 7 March 2018, PP 6.
[93] Ibid., para. 2.1.2.

norms set by companies that structure the usage and experience in privately owned online communication spaces, including terms of service, user standards, and behavioral guidelines. True, these norms are situated in, bordered by, and normatively shaped by national and international rules. Courts may declare inapplicable certain terms of service.[94] International law may influence the formulation of hate speech-related community guidelines of a social network. Yet this does not change the fundamental role of norms of the tertium. Without their systematization bringing any added epistemic value, they perform, in their aggregate, an important internal "constitutionalization" function by stabilizing expectations.[95]

When stabilized expectations are particularly strong, internet governance principles emerge. They are part of the normative tertium and vary, in their normative character, between internet-specific restatements of principles of international law, soft law, and expressions of desired policy by the norm entrepreneur.

6.4.3 Normative Processes

Process as Product. The normative order of the internet encompasses not only substantive norms (and provides for their systematization) and rules regarding their interaction, but also norm-generative processes. This is important because within the normative order of the internet, as Finnemore and Hollis have argued, "in important ways, *the process is the product* when it comes to cybernorms."[96] Though the authors focus on cybernorms, their conclusion ties in with the process-orientation regarding internet (governance) norms more generally.

In the *NetMundial Principles* contained in the *NetMundial Multistakeholder Statement* (2014),[97] for example, internet governance process principles are given a special place. They clarify how internet governance should be practiced: through democratic processes involving all actors and ensuring the meaningful and accountable participation of all, through processes that are open, participative, and consensus-driven, transparent and accountable, inclusive, and equitable. Institutions and processes connected with the internet should be inclusive and open to all.

The internet governance process is, this study submits, only part of the normative product in the sense of Finnemore and Hollis. Yet processes matter also in an actor-oriented reading of the online order. Consider how Teubner differentiates between three constitutional orders: nation states, transnational regimes, and indigenous groups. The constitutional orders of nation states are embedded in national legal systems. The constitutions of transnational regimes are focused on a "functionally differentiated sector of world society and thus

[94] Cf., among many recent cases, Landgericht Berlin, Az 16 O 341/15, February 12, 2018 (declaring illegal some clauses in Facebook's terms of service (AGBs), including one for the Facebook mobile app, that activated by default location-based services and allowed chat partners to see one's location without previous explicit agreement by the user).

[95] See chapter 7.

[96] Martha Finnemore and Duncan B. Hollis, "Constructing Norms for Global Cybersecurity," AJIL 110 (2016), 425–79 (477) (emphasis added).

[97] NetMundial Multistakeholder Statement, Global Multistakeholder Meeting on the Future of Internet Governance, April 23–24, 2014, São Paulo, Brazil, http://netmundial.br/wp-content/uploads/2014/04/NETmundial-Multistakeholder-Document.pdf.

constitute a 'self-contained regime,' reflecting the internal rationality [Eigenrationalität] of the societal sector connected to the regime."[98] However, Teubner cautions that these *Regimeverfassungen*—being self-contained—are without a firm grounding in the political processes of society as a whole. In this light, the normative order of the internet is definitely not a *Regimeverfassung*. The normative order of the internet does not regulate any differentiated sector of society and thus cannot constitute a self-contained regime. Rather, it is connected to political processes oriented toward the "Gemeinwohl," the common good.[99] (But it can be contended that Teubner's definition of a *Regimeverfassung* is unnecessarily strict.)

Teubner's third category of normative orders, indigenous normative orders, are "much stronger embedded in the society as a whole than the law of nation states." They appear mainly in societies or parts of society without a functionally differentiated legal system and their norms are closely linked with "religious, political and economic systems of interaction and those focused on traditional knowledge."[100]

The normative order of the internet can hardly be considered an indigenous normative order, even if the early Barlowian discourse on internet freedom, anarchy and internet exceptionalism would seem to lend itself to precisely this argument as would notions of "digital natives;" and so would the reference to interactions between traditional knowledge (programming skills, codes, and practices later enshrined in RFCs) and the political ecosystem. But many aspects of the internet are regulated by functionally differentiated legal *systems*. What is missing is the overarching normative order to connect the legal systems and provide for principles to manage the interfaces between the orders: the normative order of the internet. This order must be able to develop through regime-internal change. This is only possible if the processes of norm production are also loci of normative learning.

Processes as Loci of Normative Learning. One such approch is "global experimentalist governance," developed by de Búrca, Keohane, and Sabel. This approach includes initial actor reflection, articulation of a framework understanding with open-ended goals, implementation of these goals, feedback provided from local contexts, and periodic re-evaluations of the goals and practices.[101]

Such a "learning"-oriented normative system is in constant flux and highly responsive to factual and political developments, while respecting subsidiarity. As the normative order of the internet cannot be based on such a model in light of its uncertain outcomes and the unresolved problem of avoiding special interest-capture, such a "learning and adapting" approach to norm development can be useful in closely monitored suborders. Unlike Ostrom's governing the commons model,[102] the experimental governance model does not preclude a center as information pooler and peer evaluation organizer.[103]

The scholars behind global experimentalist governance admit themselves that their "institutionalized process of participatory and multilevel collective problem solving, in which the problems (and the means of addressing them) are framed in an open-ended way and

[98] Gunther Teubner, *Verfassungsfragmente. Gesellschaftlicher Konstitutionalismus in der Globalisierung* (Frankfurt: Suhrkamp, 2012), 255 (translation by the author).

[99] Ibid.

[100] Ibid., 256.

[101] Gráinne De Búrca, Robert O. Keohane, and Charles Sabel, "Global Experimentalist Governance," British Journal of Political Science 44 (2014) 3, 477–86 (479).

[102] Elinor Ostrom, *Governing the Commons* (New York: CUP, 1990).

[103] Gráinne De Búrca, Robert O. Keohane, and Charles Sabel, "Global Experimentalist Governance," British Journal of Political Science 44 (2014) 3, 477–86 (478).

subjected to periodic revision by various forms of peer review in the light of locally generated knowledge," is an ideal-type in the Weberian sense and that actual implementations may not come close to the dynamic problem-solving approach.[104] The cognitive dimension of the process is echoed in other novel governance approaches and points to a perceived lack of reflexivity and reform potential based on "learning experiences" within traditional legal systems. In this vein, for instance, Calliess and Zumbansen, in their *Rough Consensus and Running Code* approach to transnational law, seek "to acknowledge [...] learning experiences in order to productively integrate them into an enriched concept of [...] governance."[105]

Already the Global Cyberspace Framework approach[106] attempts to substitute messy approaches to the normative order of the internet with a model of a multilayer regime composed of polycentric rule-making processes. Distributed internet governance approaches go one step further and are characteristic of a distributed proceduralization. They rely on highly dynamic normative ad hoc coalitions to issue problem-specific normative solutions. Their most interesting character trait is the attempted transfer of properties of internet architecture to the internet governance system.

Distributed processes are based on models of non-centralized deliberation, decision-making, and implementation of normative solutions.[107] The approach suggests a distributed model of normativity online, based on multi-institutionality that is seen as the final evolutionary step in a gradually changing process of norm development including centralized regulation, the multistakeholder appproach, and devolved national governance approaches. Distributed development of internet (governance) norms is based on flexible, decentralized "collaborative arrangements for actors and institutions to coordinate collective action."[108]

Based on open governance theory, distributed governance approaches promote inclusion of all actors and in particular citizen engagement. In a simulacrum of data packet transfers on the internet, distributed governance employs a "routing" function to ensure interoperability of normative responses by collecting and collating them. Distributed approaches are also considered to allow for granularity (through localization of finding solutions) and scale (through globalization of their implementation).[109]

Distributed governance so conceived is based on identifying and mapping the issues raised, formulating responses, and implementing or enforcing them. Thereafter, a review or evaluation period is set.[110] To allow normative processes to follow along these steps, "distributionists" favor the creation of roadmaps to guide actors within the so conceived internet governance ecosystem in their identification of the nature of the problem, its severity, the optimal geographical sphere and the appropriate actors to address the issue, and any preexisting framework equipped to deal with the issue.[111]

[104] Ibid., note 3.

[105] Gralf-Peter Calliess and Peer Zumbansen, *Rough Consensus and Running Code. A Theory of Transnational Private Law* (Oxford/Portland, OR: Hart, 2012), 247.

[106] See 5.3.6.

[107] Cf. Stefaan G. Verhulst, Beth S. Noveck, Jillian Raines, and Antony Declercq, "Innovations in Global Governance: Toward a Distributed Internet Governance Ecosystem," GCIG Paper Series No. 5, December 2014, http://www.thegovlab.org/static/files/publications/gcig_paper_no5.pdf.

[108] Ibid., 7.

[109] Ibid., 11–12.

[110] Ibid., 16 et seq.

[111] Ibid., 19.

A similar distributed approach was also suggested by the Panel on Global Internet Cooperation and Governance Mechanisms ("Ilves" panel),[112] which developed a "collaborative, decentralized internet governance ecosystem" based on "distributed governance groups," a four-step "internet governance process," and "enablers." The approach as presented is based on the conviction that three fundamental design properties of internet architecture—distributed, participatory, layered—should be transferred to the internet governance ecoystem.[113] A diversity of structures and governance systems should include all actors, with the ecosystem comprising local, regional, national, and global layers of governance, with the subsidiarity principle in mind.[114]

The key building blocks of the distributed internet governance ecosystem are the "distributed governance groups."[115] These are "loosely coupled, collaborative, and mutually-dependent groups or organizations and/or individual experts that come together through a set of mutual commitments to address a specific issue." They are created ad hoc with a specific issue in mind and solve the issue "with an outcome consisting of a policy recommendation/model, a standard, a specification, and/or a best practice"—and then they may "fade away."

The Ilves report sees several advantages in having short-lived normative actors, including: a shift of control away from top-down systems of singular authorities; rapidly coalescing experts acting "at internet speed" on solutions; localization; facilitation of informed dialog; and its function as a de-marginalization tool.[116] The latter is especially a reflection of the substantive basis for the distributed governance groups' decision-making: they should base themselves, according to the Ilves report, on the "NetMundial Principles," including human rights and shared values, the protection of intermediaries, assurances for internet architecture principles such as the unified and unfragmented internet space, its security, stability, and resilience, its open standards, and its open and distributed architecture.[117]

Under the Ilves report, the "internet governance process" includes four steps: issue identification, solution mapping, solution formulation, and solution implementation, with the implementation being primarily voluntary—unlike the enforced implementation foreseen in the previous approach. However, some solutions may be formalized through "social conventions, regulations, directives, treaties [or] contracts."[118]

Finally, the report relies on "enablers": "enabling information, communication, and empowerment mechanisms," including forums and dialogs, facilitating broad engagement; expert communities; and empowering capacity development and toolkits collection processes. Though the reconceptualization of governance as distributed governance seems prima facie attractive, the socio-legal preconditions allowing for such an approach have not yet materialized. The distributed governance theorists, however, make a good point in

[112] ICANN/World Economic Forum, Report by the Panel on Global Internet Cooperation and Governance Mechanisms, Towards a Collaborative, Decentralized Internet Governance Ecosystem (2014), https://www.icann.org/en/system/files/files/collaborative-decentralized-ig-ecosystem-21may14-en.pdf.

[113] This is an interesting normative echo of the governance by architecture/infrastructure approach, discussed at 5.3.5.

[114] ICANN/World Economic Forum, Report by the Panel on Global Internet Cooperation and Governance Mechanisms, Towards a Collaborative, Decentralized Internet Governance Ecosystem (2014), https://www.icann.org/en/system/files/files/collaborative-decentralized-ig-ecosystem-21may14-en.pdf, 5.

[115] Ibid., 8.

[116] Ibid., 10.

[117] Ibid., 6.

[118] Ibid., 10.

showing what kind of preplanned processes could legitimately take the place of the current inchoate institutionality of internet governance processes.

Differentiated Processes. Recall Finnemore and Hollis, who continue their process-orientation by arguing that an "approach that negotiates only content and ignores norm construction and evolution processes will have limited effects."[119] This, of course, does not mean turning the process into a subject of fundamental rights protection, which would be Teubner's solution. He elevates cultural processes to subjects of fundamental rights with "traditional knowledge itself" as the subject of fundamental rights in an institutional reading.[120] Nevertheless, in global legal approaches, fundamental rights need to be "de-individualized"[121] and processes repositioned as important normative vectors of development and thus protected by fundamental rights.

This further implies that the concept of the normative order of the internet, as employed here, must focus as much on establishing robust processes of norm production, including norm revision, as it must on the norms these processes generate. In brief: the normative order of the internet materializes as a profoundly process-oriented order. This process-orientation takes into account that norms of the online order are less static than traditional legal norms, both in their application and their evolution: online norms "will evolve over time through repeated interactions among those involved in the norms' construction and use."[122]

It can be observed that many normative processes within the third category of normative order norms—the transnational, soft law arrangements—are running along the lines of distributed governance approaches without explicit commitments to the Ilves report. Many normative processes within the normative order's transnational dimension include issue identification by informal networks and actors, the mapping of normative solutions by decentralized, distributed bodies, and the formulation and implementation of solutions (with the latter happening only sporadically), if these normative solutions are not, as the Ilves report suggested, formalized through "social conventions, regulations, directives, treaties [or] contracts."[123]

These processes are not very innovative, given comparable governance challenges in other regimes, such as climate change. However, there is one approach, conceptualized for transnational private law, which fits particularly well both as an epistemic model and normative proceduralization of the order: *rough consensus, running code*. This is backgrounded by the diagnosis, with Gralf-Peter Calliess and Peter Zumbansen, of "nothing less than a fundamental contestation and erosion of boundaries between state and non-state actors, official and unofficial law, public and private ordering"[124] happening on the internet.

For Calliess and Zumbansen, the special advantages of this fluid approach to normativity on the internet lie in the capacity to distinguish between norm-creation processes, understood as "contextualized learning processes ('rough consensus')" and the emergence

[119] Martha Finnemore and Duncan B. Hollis, "Constructing Norms for Global Cybersecurity," AJIL 110 (2016), 425–79 (477).

[120] Gunther Teubner, *Verfassungsfragmente. Gesellschaftlicher Konstitutionalismus in der Globalisierung* (Frankfurt: Suhrkamp, 2012), 255 (253).

[121] Ibid.

[122] Ibid.

[123] Ibid., 10.

[124] Gralf-Peter Calliess and Peer Zumbansen, *Rough Consensus and Running Code. A Theory of Transnational Private Law* (Oxford/Portland, OR: Hart, 2012), 246.

of normative bodies ("running code").[125] Applying this within the normative order of the internet, we can proceduralize questions of legality and negate the "validity of juxtaposing 'soft law' regimes with 'rule-of-law' regimes," which only serve "to immunize the latter against all methodological contestations."[126] We have already established that the normative order of the internet, at its core, is a legal order and that any clear delimitation of binding norms and non-binding norms is epistemically impossible and normatively unhelpful. Just as there are soft law elements in traditional rule-of-law regimes, particularly national legal systems, the normative order of the internet encompasses norms of different character and binding quality.

We note, finally, that an approach based on fluid notions of normativity, such as the one described here, can deliver a responsive and reflexive order. Norms emerge when there is rough consensus and they are integrated into the larger system of codes of the normative order, which they thus change, but without being immune to change themselves, just like running code.

The first two categories of norms within the normative order of the internet are thus established within traditional processes of international and national lawmaking, albeit with progressive dynamizations in light of the internet's normative challenges. The key normative challenge of the order now is the adequate incorporation of the "new host of norms into existing bodies of law,"[127] i.e. the development of a framework for the integration of transnational norms of the normative order of the internet into national legal systems (the subject of chapter 7). As principles form an important part of these norms, they will be addressed now.

6.5 Principles of the Order

6.5.1 Notions of Principles

Robert Alexy, who adapted and refined Ronald Dworkin's theory of principles, argued that norms can either be rules (*Regeln*) or principles (*Prinzipien*).[128] Their difference is a structural-formal one: rules "encode" definitive commands (*Rechtsfolgen*), while principles only do so *prima facie*. They are optimization commands.[129] This becomes evident especially when norms collide. When rule-norms collide, only one of them can be applied, thus requiring either an exception to be read into one of the rules or one to be declared inapplicable. When principle-norms collide, both remain applicable *prima facie* and must be weighed in light of the fact patterns to concretize them into a rule.[130]

Just as the optimization potential of the logical structure of principles as optimization commands has been raised,[131] the notion of principles in Alexy's theory of principles has

[125] Ibid.
[126] Ibid., 259–60.
[127] Ibid.
[128] Robert Alexy, *Theorie der Grundrechte* (Frankfurt am Main: Suhrkamp, 1986), 88–90.
[129] Alexander Heinold, *Die Prinzipientheorie bei Ronald Dworkin und Robert Alexy* (Berlin: Duncker & Humblot, 2011), 197.
[130] Robert Alexy, *Theorie der Grundrechte* (Frankfurt am Main: Suhrkamp, 1986), 77–86.
[131] Juan Alonso, "The Logical Structure of Principles in Alexys' Theory. A Critical Analysis," Revus - Journal for Constitutional Theory and Philosophy of Law 28 (2016), 53–61.

been criticized as overly demanding in that it differs substantially from the notion of general principles of law or legal principles.[132] This study's notion of principles leans strongly toward the latter, evidenced by previous analyses. This study has, for instance, previously analyzed which fundamental *principles* of international law are relevant for the normative order of the internet.[133] Following the reasoning of the Group of Governmental Experts in its 2015 report, among the key principles of international law we find sovereign equality, the settlement of international disputes by peaceful means, the prohibition of the threat or use of force against the territorial integrity or political independence of any state, the respect for human rights and fundamental freedoms, and the non-intervention in the internal affairs of other states.[134]

This study has also shown that within internet governance arrangements the notion of "principles" has a specific meaning, namely the collections of norms, standards, technical preference, and commitments that actors committed to in various "declarations of principles." A substantial number of these documents were adopted, starting from 2011 during a period of normative development described as the "internet principle hype."[135] As discussed, these "collections of principles" allowed actors to publicize their normative expectations and assert their normative preferences. The normative common ground between the diverging declarations of principles constitutes the principles of the normative order of the internet that (most) actors can agree on.

The "internet principles" thus vary widely in their thematic orientation. This contrasts with a more focused approach of some scholars identifying common principles across legal orders. Armin von Bogdandy, for example, has identified three normative (meta-)principles across national (German constitutional) law, European law, and international law.[136] These are the principles of the rule of law, of human rights protection, and of democracy. Though they have different legal foundations in the three orders, they can act as a common frame for the legal and political processes regarding the management of legal pluralism and, in particular, the relations between national, international, and European law. Following the international public authority theory, von Bogdandy identifies as the key meta-principle the inclusion of citizens in the exercise of that authority. This seems like a sensible procedural principle which legitimizes other principles, including substantial ones. With regard to the normative order of the internet, procedural and substantial principles can be identified. The key principles of the normative order of the internet function both as *principles* and *rules*. They can be applied directly and indirectly, and they influence the development of other norms within the system.

In a sense they are also optimization commands insofar (varying Alexy) as they influence (optimize) the normative development of the order of the internet. Reading other norms of the normative order of the internet as optimizable in light of commonly agreed principles lends them substantial power. Internet principles influence the development and application of all norms belonging to the normative order of the internet. These are, as can be

[132] Ralf Poscher, "Theorie eines Phantoms—Die erfolglose Suche der Prinzipientheorie nach ihrem Gegenstand," RW 4 (2010), 349–72 (350).

[133] See, on principles of international law, 3.3.4.

[134] GGE report (2015), 26.

[135] See, on the internet principle hype, 3.4.8.

[136] Armin von Bogdandy, "Prinzipien von Staat, supranationalen und internationalen Organisationen," § 232 (275–304), in Josef Isensee, Paul Kirchhof, et al. (eds.), *Handbuch des Staatsrechts, Band XI: Internationale Bezüge*, 3rd edn. (2013).

recalled, norms that evidence a (1) *material* (non-trivial) and a (2) *normative* (not merely factual) connection to the internet as a network of networks. Since the norms of the normative order of the internet, as will be shown in the next chapter, form part of national legal systems as a normative tertium, the principles that influence their evolution and application are important.

6.5.2 Substantial Principles

The most broadly accepted compilation of non-trivial principles related to the internet are the NetMundial Principles,[137] which are the outcome document of a long process of negotiations that included representatives from all actor groups.[138] The following are the key substantial principles that actor representatives reached agreement on:

- protection of human rights online just as offline, in accordance with international human rights legal obligations, based on the UDHR and the UN human rights conventions. Important rights include freedom of expression, including the right to seek, receive, and impart information and ideas through any media and regardless of frontiers; freedom of association, including the right to peaceful assembly and association online through social networks and platforms; the right to privacy, including a right not to be subjected to arbitrary or unlawful surveillance, collection, treatment, and use of personal data, and a right not to be subjected to mass surveillance unless lawful, necessary, and proportionate; rights of persons with disabilities, including full access to online resources through appropriate design and development; freedom of information and access to information; and the right to development, with the internet playing a vital role in helping to achieve the full realization of internationally agreed sustainable development goals;
- protection of intermediary liability with limitations only provided in a proportionate way with a view to, inter alia, the importance of economic growth and the free flow of information;
- cultural and linguistic diversity;
- unfragmented space: the internet needs to be kept and protected as a "globally coherent, interconnected, stable, unfragmented, scalable and accessible network-of-networks, based on a common set of unique identifiers, that allows data packets/information to flow freely end-to-end regardless of the lawful content";[139]
- security, stability, resilience, reliability, and trustworthiness of the internet premised upon strong cooperation between actors;
- enabling environment for permissionless innovation, which presupposes investment in ICT infrastructure.

[137] Based on the NetMundial Multistakeholder Statement, Global Multistakeholder Meeting on the Future of Internet Governance, April 23–24, 2014, São Paulo, Brazil, http://netmundial.br/netmundial-multistakeholder-statement.

[138] It should be noted that the author of this study was nominated by the global academic community as one of the members of the preparatory committee for the NetMundial Multistakeholder Meeting and took part in a number of preparatory sessions.

[139] NetMundial Multistakeholder Statement, Global Multistakeholder Meeting on the Future of Internet Governance, April 23–24, 2014, São Paulo, Brazil, http://netmundial.br/wp-content/uploads/2014/04/NetMundial-Multistakeholder-Document.pdf.

Some of these principles are drawn strongly from existing international (and national) law and conversely influence these normative orders, such as the principle of human rights protection online. Other principles, such as the protection of intermediaries, can influence the normative approaches by states to the regulation of internet companies through laws regulating their rights and obligations, such as the German Network Enforcement Law. Commitments to cultural and linguistic diversity on the internet are political exhortations rather than clear legal principles, though diversity as a value is not foreign to international or national legal systems.

The last three substantial principles all relate to characteristics of the internet space: it should remain unfragmented, based on common identifiers, with free information flows and permissionless innovation—a secure, stable, resilient, and reliable network of networks. This principle evidences the normatively non-distinct nature of "internet principles." The exhortation to keep the internet unfragmented is to be read in light of the dangers of governmental/legal, technical, and commercial internet fragmentation. The countervailing forces to fragmentation that have led to the development of the internet "regime" (the normative order of the internet) are informed by the principle of an unfragmented space. This is normatively relevant but is neither a norm as principle nor a norm as a rule, rather it is a *norm as policy*. These substantive principles procedurally frame and substantively inform the normative development of the normative order of the internet.

6.5.3 Procedural Principles

The NetMundial principles contain a number of procedural principles as well. As noted earlier (and as will be discussed in more detail below in light of its implications for legitimacy), the participation of actors in norm-setting processes is essential for the success of normative processes as measured by the legitimacy and effectivity of the normative output. Therefore, substantive and procedural standards regarding the normative order of the internet are interconnected and mutually reinforcing. One example is the substantive principle committing actors to the security, stability, resilience, reliability, and trustworthiness of the internet, which is described as premised upon "a strong cooperation between stakeholders," nationally, regionally, and globally.[140] Demanding such cooperation (at least) implies that procedural structures are in place that allow for such cooperation to be realized.

Further, in demanding open standards to be promoted as a matter of principle, and "informed by individual and collective expertise and decisions made by rough consensus, that allow for a global, interoperable, resilient, stable, decentralized, secure, and interconnected network, available to all,"[141] the cooperation structures foreseen by substantive principles are refined: expertise collection and its processing through rough consensus procedures. We thus see that a principle of the normative order of the internet clearly posits the importance

[140] Ibid.

[141] Ibid. Cf. on the importance of common efforts the Council conclusions on malicious cyber activities, April 10, 2018: Council of the European Union, Doc. 7517/18, http://data.consilium.europa.eu/doc/document/ST-7584-2018-INIT/en/pdf, 3.

of open standards developed in collaborative decision-making processes, allowing for collective stewardship of the processes, their evolution, and the resources managed. The principle encourages voluntary collaboration with "technical experts to resolve technical issues in the appropriate venue in a manner consistent with this open, collaborative approach."

The NetMundial Statement contains key internet governance "process principles." Processes related to the production of norms within the normative order of the internet more broadly need to be:

- multistakeholder-based and democratic, ensuring the meaningful and accountable participation of all actors;
- as open, participative, consensus-driven as possible (to allow for the full and balanced participation of all actors from around the globe);
- transparent (with easy-to-understand decisions and a thorough documentation of decision-making processes);
- accountable (ensuring independent checks and balances);
- inclusive and equitable (with all processes being as bottom-up as possible to enable the involvement of as many actors as possible);
- distributed (throughout the decentralized, multistakeholder-based ecosystem of norms);
- collaborative (based on encouraging cooperative approaches) and enabling meaningful participation (including capacity-building for newer or underrepresented groups); and
- agile (with both processes and standards being technology-neutral).

Most of the process-oriented principles regarding internet governance are important for the establishment of processes that lead to more legitimate outcomes and thus ensure the participation of all actors in the exercise of authority through the actors of the normative order of the internet. These include, in particular, transparency and accountability of normative processes and the integration of all relevant actors. The principle of agility and the integration of all relevant actors is an important element of procedural normativity.

In designing normative processes within the normative order of the internet, the procedural principles need to be implemented. Existing processes that meet many or most of these requirements are considered legitimate. One example is the procedure used by the IETF to discuss and adopt new technical internet standards, the Request for Comments (RFCs). The procedure is based on the inclusion of all relevant actors in their respective roles, open, participative, transparent (with all documents available online and discussions taking place chiefly through publicly accessible mailing lists), as inclusive as it can be given entrenched power disequilibria in global society, distributed and decentralized with the IETF providing only the factual frame for the normative debate, very collaborative, providing for capacity-building for newer or underrepresented groups, comparatively agile with standard improvement possible at a later stage,[142] and roughly consensus-based.[143]

[142] Cf. Gralf-Peter Calliess and Peer Zumbansen, *Rough Consensus and Running Code. A Theory of Transnational Private Law* (Oxford/Portland, OR: Hart, 2012), 135.

[143] Cf. RFC 2418: S. Bradner (ed.), RFC 2418, Working Group Guidelines, September 1998, http://tools.ietf.org/html/rfc2418#section-3.3, 3.3.

6.5.4 Normative Descriptors of the Order

Apart from substantive and procedural principles, there are also further characteristics or normative descriptors of the normative order of the internet, which do not amount to accepted "principles," but exert influence on the interpretation of online order norms and on their evolution. They are not principles or norms but rather characteristics or descriptive elements of the normative order of the internet, but nevertheless have normative relevance.

Layered Nature. The normative order of the internet is a layered order encompassing different levels of regulation. These layers are partly tied to (geo)political institutions, such as states and regional organizations. But, as Benjamin H. Stratton argues in a study of software and sovereignty, "planetary-scale computation" can only be made "accountable as a designable platform" by the "decentering of some conventional ideas about political geographic norms." The overlapping and intersecting layers have created a "thickened vertical jurisdictional complexity." It is for this "layered complexity" that the normative order of the internet establishes a model explaining and justifying normative developments.[144]

The normative order of the internet is an order for what Stratton terms the "*Stack*."[145] Arguing that computation takes different forms at different scales, he sees "energy and mineral sourcing and grids; subterranean cloud infrastructure; urban software and public service privatization; massive universal addressing systems [and various interfaces]" as part of a "vast […] software and hardware *Stack*," an "accidental megastructure." Within this megastructure, normatively relevant conflicts occur, which range from trivial to fundamental:

> the [NSA] versus Unit 6139 [Chinese People's Liberation Army's advanced persistent threat unit], NSA versus Anonymous, Anonymous versus Syrian Electronic Army [hackers supporting the Assad regime in Syria], NSA versus Syrian Electronic Army versus ISIL versus FSB [Federal Security Service of the Russian Federation] versus North Korea versus Samsung versus Apple versus European Parliament, and so and on.[146]

Though the conflicts alluded to here center around cybersecurity with only a small nod toward more mundane legal conflicts between companies (Samsung vs. Apple) and between them and regional organizations (Apple vs. European Parliament) and their legal systems, they serve to illustrate the necessity of a coherent normative approach explaining and justifying the management of normativity with regard to the internet.

Real-Time Law. Though the nomos of the internet has both a normative genealogy, explained in chapter 2, and normativity, its predictive power has certain limits. In a call for a new "experimental culture within the law and within legal theory,"[147] Vesting argues that *computer culture* (his description of what Castell termed *network society*, or Stalder *digitality*) has influenced private contract practices in that technological uncertainties require "vague frameworks […] for contractual arrangements," which are then progressively substantialized by instituted practices.[148]

[144] Benjamin H. Bratton, *The Stack. On Software and Sovereignty* (Cambridge, MA/London: MIT Press, 2015), 5.
[145] Ibid.
[146] Ibid., 9.
[147] Thomas Vesting, "Instituierte und konstituierte Normativität. Prozeduralisierung und multi-normative Systeme," in Tatjana Sheplyakova (ed.), *Prozeduralisierung des Rechts* (Tübingen: Mohr, 2018), 101–122 (translation by the author).
[148] Ibid. (translation by the author).

Similarly, within the normative order of the internet norms of different character and formality may apply to the same set of facts. Matthew Jennejohn has called this form of governance "braided" with a blend of formal agreements and informal contracts: "formal contracts 'braid' with informal social norms."[149] Vesting has shown that this dynamic normative approach can be made to react to societal developments, especially when technological advancements are concerned. He identifies braided governance as a model that unites constituted and instituted orders,[150] enabling the emergence of a legally binding frame that allows for technical innovations in a way that is fair to all participants.[151]

While traditional regulatory approaches provide norms ex ante, the normative order of the internet can be considered, in parts, a model of "just-in-time" regulation. Since circumstances change quickly, ex ante regulation may be out of date fast. Therefore, just-in-time regulation, which is reactive to changes in social reality, is characteristic of the normative order of the internet. As Vesting writes, the growing "reflexivity of law for new dynamic hybridizations cannot be ensured through regulation [...] ex ante, but rather happens in 'real time' [...] or ex post through monitoring and stabilization of coordination patterns [....]."[152] In order to be adaptable, norms and the normative order as a whole have to show some elasticity.[153]

6.6 Legitimacy of the Order

6.6.1 Conditions of Legitimacy

This study has hypothesized that the normative order of the internet is a legitimate order. Internationally, the integration of all actors in norm-setting processes proceduralizes legitimacy. Nationally, as will be discussed in the next chapter, existing procedures to legitimize non-legal norms can be applied mutatis mutandis with the same result. Returning to the international level, we can find that a substantial part of the norms making up the normative order of the internet are norms of international law. Therefore, Louis Henkin's finding that "almost all nations observe almost all principles of international law and almost all of their obligations almost all of the time"[154] is relevant for assessing the conditions of legitimacy of the normative order of the internet. Indeed, legitimacy is closely tied to rule-confirming behavior. Without a sense of obligation (which might be grounded in the epistemic superiority of a normative approach), rule-conforming behavior remains sporadic and erratic.

[149] Matthew Jennejohn, "The Private Order of Innovation Networks," Stanford Law Review 68 (2016), 281–366 (284).

[150] Cf. section 6.3.1.

[151] Vesting, "Instituierte und konstituierte Normativität. Prozeduralisierung und multi-normative Systeme," in Tatjana Sheplyakova (ed)(ed.), *Prozeduralisierung des Rechts* (Tübingen: Mohr, 2018), 101–122.

[152] Ibid. (translation by the author).

[153] This concept has applications in ICT management as well. Pooling virtual machines so that they can be activated ("instantiated") when needed, allows for the scaling of resources (Nayan B. Ruparelia, *Cloud Computing* (Cambridge, MA/London: MIT Press, 2016), 6).

[154] Louis Henkin, *How Nations Behave*, 2nd edn. (New York: Columbia University Press, 1979), 47 (emphasis omitted). For empirical studies confirming Henkin's dictum, see Harold Hongju Koh, "Why Do Nations Obey International Law?," Yale Law Journal 106 (1996–1997), 2599–659, note 2.

This sense of obligation is tied to the perceived legitimacy of a norm.[155] Thomas M. Franck defined legitimacy as a property of a rule or institution (or, it could be added, an order) "which itself exerts a pull towards compliance on those addressed normatively because those addressed believe that the rule or institution has come into being and operates in accordance with generally accepted principles of right process."[156] *Right process* is one way of formulating demands regarding the processes related to the genesis of norms. Franck argued further that a single norm's legitimacy (and thus compliance pull) depends on its determinacy (ascertainable normative content), symbolic validation through an authority figure/institution and coherence with, and adherence to, a broader system of rules.[157] A variation of these criteria will be useful to assess the legitimacy of online order norms.

The level of normativity of a normative order varies. The normativity of a norm—and of a normative order—is one of its properties. It is related to, and dependent on, its legitimacy.[158] It is impossible to make a general claim regarding the legitimacy of norms of the normative order of the internet. Depending on their character (international legal norms, national legal norms, norms forming part of the transnational regulatory arrangements), they are already situated within established legitimacy structures that do not need to be fundamentally revisited for the internet. Just consider: when applying international law's well-established non-intervention principle to online settings, there is no obvious need for providing a theory of the principle's (customary law rule's) legitimacy. Similarly, national laws providing for certain obligations for intermediaries, such as the German *Netzwerkdurchsetzungsgesetz*, may be flawed, but their legitimacy as laws is not prima facie in question. Only in cases of substantial violation of core principles of the normative order of the internet (such as minimum consultation levels with all relevant actors) will the legitimacy of norms of national or international law have to be revisited for the purposes of their position within the normative order of the internet.

This is not so for order-specific norms, such as internet governance principles, and for the order itself. Their legitimacy needs to be demonstrated. As explained previously, this study understands norms belonging to the normative order of the internet as being those having a (1) *material* (non-trivial) and a (2) *normative* (not merely factual) connection to the internet as a network of networks. Based on Franck's criteria for the legitimacy of norms, these norms need to be *formally* and *materially legitimated*. Formal legitimation is achieved through symbolic validation through norm emergence in a multistakeholder process.

For a norm to be *materially legitimated*, it needs to

- be *determinate* enough for its purpose (thus allowing for non-binding instruments),
- *cohere* with the core principles of the normative order of the internet,
- be *consonant* with the order's values as expressed in its principles, and
- *adhere* systematically to the normative order as a whole.

155 Thomas M. Franck, *The Power of Legitimacy Among Nations* (Oxford: OUP, 1990). For a more recent interpretation, see Thomas M. Franck, "The Power of Legitimacy and the Legitimacy of Power: International Law in an Age of Power Disequilibrium," AJIL 100 (2006), 88.

156 Thomas M. Franck, *The Power of Legitimacy Among Nations* (Oxford: OUP, 1990), 24.

157 Cf. Thomas M. Franck, "Fairness in the International Legal and Institutional System," Recueil des Cours de l'Academie de Droit International 240 (1993), Vol. III, 26.

158 Cf. Peter Koller, *Theorie des Rechts. Eine Einführung*, 2nd edn. (Vienna: Böhlau, 1997).

Thus, formally, legitimacy within the normative order of the internet is proceduralized (this is the input and throughput dimension of legitimacy). The norms emerging from these processes are often epistemically good normative solutions. This is the output dimension of legitimacy. This study will now address the role of integrating all relevant actors as a procedural approach to legitimacy (6.6.2) and then address the legitimacy of the order itself (6.6.3).

6.6.2 Proceduralizing Legitimacy

Norms that emerge through processes in which all actors that have stakes in the outcome of the process are involved are thus symbolically validated. Traditionally, global normative processes, such as the adoption of treaties, were state focused. Yet this primacy of states has been challenged by the emergence of heterogeneous actors.[159] However, reverting to a normative individualism[160] and centering legitimacy-enhancing processes on the individual ignores the important role states still have in international relations: As "states are officially held to be the legal representatives of citizens on the international plane (however fictitious this might be for some states)," Anne Peters argues, they are still "– as a group—the most powerful global actors, and are (in most areas of the world) important repositories of political, social, and cultural identity." Therefore, both international law and the normative order of the internet with its processes of legitimacy need to remain, "in order to preserve a sufficient level of legitimacy," linked to states.[161]

This link to states is dual in nature. H. H. Koh, in true New Haven fashion, argues that its origins lie in the transnational legal process that leads to "domestic obedience" through internalization of international norms[162] or, in the present case, normative order norms. Importantly, he finds that "[p]articipation in transnational legal process creates a normative and constitutive dynamic."[163] This participation implies the legitimacy of the outcome.

Though individuals are the ultimate unit of law and society and their protection the end of law and society, they, the non-state actors that represent them, and the private sector companies that count them as their customers cannot be the primary legitimacy-conferral agents to the exclusion of states. Rather, as Peters underlines, the "involvement of non-state actors in law-making and -enforcement can be an important additional source for the legitimacy of global governance" and of the legitimacy of the normative order of the internet and its norms.

With regard to the normative order of the internet, legitimacy is proceduralized through a reliance on multiple actors, normatively acting in their respective roles. This is an approximation of an ideal discourse setting as envisaged by Habermas. Within the normative order

[159] Derrick L. Cogburn, "Enabling Effective Multistakeholder Participation in Global Internet Governance Through Accessible Cyberinfrastructure," in Andrew Chadwick and Philip N. Howard (eds.), *Routledge Handbook of Internet Politics* (London: Routledge, 2009), 401–13.

[160] Which is not without conceptual pitfalls. See, on the precariousness of "individualizing," Dale Shin, "The Precarious Subject of Late Capitalism: Rereading Adorno on the 'Liquidation' of Individuality," in Zubin Meer (ed.), *Individualism: The Cultural Logic of Modernity* (Lanham, MD: Lexington, 2011), 203–18.

[161] Anne Peters, "Membership in the Global Constitutional Community," EJIL Talk, July 20, 2010, http://www.ejiltalk.org/membership-in-the-global-constitutional-community.

[162] Harold Hongju Koh,, "Why Do Nations Obey International Law?" Yale Law Journal 106 (1996–1997), 2599–659 (2659).

[163] Ibid.

of the internet, just as within any social order, both laws and institutions are less than perfect. The procedures they install may lead to normatively suboptimal results that may not be considered legitimate.[164] Therefore Habermas substituted a formal criterion in order to ensure legitimacy of results: perfect discourse situations in which every participant knows everything and has the same power.[165] The normative outcomes of these discourses would then be legitimate. As ideal discourse situations do not exist, different approximations have emerged.[166] With regard to the normative order of the internet, this approximation relies on the integration of various actors, based on inclusive normation processes in which all three actor groups of internet governance take part (states, the private sector, and civil society). Each of these actor groups, and the norms they produce, is legitimated differently.

Governments, as representatives of the states, draw their legitimacy from their traditional role as sovereign members of the international community through the exercise of jurisdiction over their territory. In Weberian terms they represent *traditional authority*,[167] and, as a legitimate global public authority has not yet emerged, they are also by default *rationally* legitimate. International organizations as participants in processes involving relevant actors are legitimated through their membership (states) and progressively seek to enhance their legitimacy by developing accountability mechanisms.

Private sector companies are also legitimate international actors. They are responsible, varying the Ruggie Principles, for the formative forces emanating from their spheres of influence. Their participation in normative processes is value-rationally justified. Companies, following Milton Friedman's argument that capitalism and freedom are intertwined and mutually reinforcing,[168] are important to counterweigh power allocation with political actors,[169] especially on the internet. Yet states need to ensure that ICT companies do not act irresponsibly due to a lack of regulation,[170] while at the same time avoiding the pitfalls of overregulation.[171]

Civil society represents individuals. Their justification is therefore instrumental-rational in Weberian terms. Civil society organizations collect and articulate the view of individuals as an efficient filter and focus in normative processes. Through processes of differentiation and specialization, civil society organizations have also gained legitimacy through their character as repositories of specialized (expert) knowledge on the basis of which they can intervene authoritatively in normative processes.[172]

164 Jürgen Habermas, *Faktizität und Geltung* (Frankfurt am Main: Suhrkamp, 1992), 138.

165 Cf. Jürgen Habermas, *Erläuterungen zur Diskursethik* (Frankfurt: Suhrkamp, 2001).

166 Michael A. Froomkin, "Habermas@discourse.net: Toward a Critical Theory of Cyberspace," Harvard Law Review 116 (2003), 749–873.

167 Max Weber, *The Theory of Social and Economic Organization*, (edited by Talcott Parsons) (New York: Free Press, 1964), 382.

168 Milton Friedman, *Kapitalismus und Arbeit* (Munich/Zurich: Piper, 2002), 30, 33.

169 Cf. Ibid., 38, 39.

170 But see Robert Nozick, *Anarchy, State, and Utopia* (New York: Basic Books, 1974). His proposal for a minimal state has, however, encountered substantial criticism, just see Jonathan Wolff, *Robert Nozick: Property, Justice and the Minimal State* (Oxford: Polity Press, 1991) and Barbara Fried, "Wilt Chamberlain Revisited: 'Nozick's Justice in Transfer' and the Problem of Market-Based Distribution," Philosophy and Public Affairs 24 (1995), 226–45.

171 Fundamentally: See Friedrich A. v. Hayek, *Die Verfassung der Freiheit*, 3rd edn. (Tübingen: Mohr Siebeck, 1991). But see Reinhard Zintl, *Individualistische Theorien und die Ordnung der Gesellschaft. Untersuchungen zur politischen Theorie von James M. Buchanan und Friedrich A. v. Hayek* (Berlin: Duncker&Humblot, 1983).

172 Cf. Matthias C. Kettemann, "Das Völkerrecht zwischen Rechtsordnung und Machtordnung: eine Abgrenzung," in Matthias C. Kettemann (ed.), *Grenzen im Völkerrecht* (Vienna: Jan Sramek Verlag, 2013), 111 et seq.

Participation by all relevant actors proceduralizes legitimacy and symbolically validates the norms, independent of the norm's epistemic legitimacy because of its regulatory focus.[173] The inclusion of all relevant actors in normative processes is not only the closest approximation to an ideal discourse but also the procedural translation of democratic legitimacy in transnational constellations. Understanding the integration of all actors who have stakes in the outcome of normative processes as a proceduralization of democracy is premised upon an appreciation of the importance of democratic legitimacy in transnational constellations.

Democracy is a controversial term in international law.[174] While commitments abound,[175] there is no single globally accepted model.[176] In terms of international law, democracy can now be considered a teleological principle[177] that is framed by the human rights to democratic governance and particularly periodic, secret, fair, and free elections. These rights can be inferred from the right to self-determination in common Article 1 of the Civil and Social Covenant, Article 25 of the Civil Covenant, Article 21 of the UDHR, and subsequent practice[178] as well as consistent regional codifications (Article 10 (2) of the ECHR, Articles 13, 15, and 16 of the American Convention on Human Rights (ACHR and Articles 10 and 11 of the African Convention on Human and People's Rights (AfrCHPR)).[179] Realizing these rights within states is difficult enough as the number of non-democratic regimes globally show. Ensuring democratic participation and thus increasing the legitimacy of normative outcomes in transnational settings can only be achieved by applying democratic principles—especially regarding participation, in casu through representatives, in normative processes within the normative order of the internet.

The process of including all relevant actors proceduralizes legitimacy in the normative order by institutionalizing qua procedure the democratic rights of actors with regard to decisions on the distribution of rights and obligations in the internet's order. Each actor has a specific role to play. In online settings, this is usually understood as the "practice of forms of participatory democracy that allow for all those who have a stake and who have the inclination to participate on equal footing in the deliberation of issues and the design of policy."[180] Enabling participation, legally and practically, is essential to ensure that all actors can participate in normative processes. There is no duty to participate ("inclination") and some normative processes will be influenced more strongly by one actor than another. The

[173] Cf. further contributions in Adrian Haddock, Alan Millar, and Duncan Pritchard (eds.), *Epistemic Value* (Oxford: OUP, 2009).

[174] Sidney Hook, "Democracy as a Way of Life," in John N. Andrews and Carl A. Marsden (eds.), *Tomorrow in the Making* (New York: Whittlesey House, 1939), 31–46.

[175] Wendy Brown, "We Are All Democrats Now," The Kettering Review 29 (2011), 44–52.

[176] In the 1996 UN *Agenda for Democratization* we read that "it is not for the United Nations to offer a model of democratization or democracy or to promote democracy in a specific case" (UN, Agenda for Democratization, A/51/761 of 20 December 1996, para. 10).

[177] Niels Petersen, *Demokratie als teleologisches Prinzip: Zur Legitimität von Staatsgewalt im Völkerrecht* (Frankfurt am Main: Springer, 2009).

[178] See, for an overview of normative commitments to democracy by international organizations: OHCHR, Compilation of documents or texts adopted and used by various intergovernmental, international, regional and sub-regional organizations aimed at promoting democracy, https://www.ohchr.org/EN/Issues/RuleOfLaw/CompilationDemocracy/Pages/DemocracyCompil.aspx.

[179] Thomas Franck, "The Emerging Right to Democratic Governance," 86 AJIL 1992, 46–91.

[180] Internet Governance Forum (IGF) 2014, Best Practice Forum on Developing Meaningful Multistakeholder Mechanisms, https://www.intgovforum.org/cms/documents/best-practice-forums/developing-meaningful-multistakeholder-participation-mechnisms/410-bpf-2014-outcome-document-developing-meaningful-multistakeholder-mechanisms/file.

process remains open, however, and participation must be possible. In order to ensure effectivity, enforcement/implementation can be assigned to a single actor. Yet implementers are accountable to the decision-making actors.[181]

Including all relevant actors in norm-making is lived practice in almost all relevant normative processes organically situated within the normative order of the internet, with the exception of exercises in norm entrepreneurship by some sovereignty-oriented states, such as the International Code of Conduct for Information Security developed by, inter alia, China and Russia.[182] Its lack of success in the face of propagation attempts shows the risks (from the perspective of norm entrepreneurs) of ignoring the legitimacy-enhancing function of including all relevant actors (and, in the case of the Code of Conduct, of drafting a sovereignty-oriented document that is materially at odds with tenets of the normative order of the internet).

Normative processes that include all relevant actors are in sum the most effective for legitimacy-conferring proceduralization of the interests or stakes of actors in the outcome of a normative process. By harnessing the legitimacy-conferring function of states, the power over communicative processes wielded by private sector companies (and their concomitant influence on user behavior) and the function of civil society actors as forces of aggregation and articulation of individual preferences through a fair and open process, this inclusive approach to norm-making ensures input and throughput legitimacy. This is coupled with regulatory results that profit from expert knowledge, thus increasing their epistemic legitimacy (output dimension of legitimacy).[183] Regulatory results of norm-making processes that include all relevant actors are also usually effective, which only increases their legitimacy, in turn making them more effective.

Normative processes that include all relevant actors as proceduralizations of legitimacy are not unique to the normative order of the internet.[184] Examples from environmental and international development law as well as international criminal law[185] show that whenever non-state actors fulfill key functions in "administering" a legal field, their input is sought out to enhance norm-conforming behavior by all actors after normation.

The optimal design of inclusive norm-making structures is difficult to establish. Existing problems include power differences and information disparities between actors and the monopolization of processes by advantaged actors, such as big countries, economically powerful internet companies, or experts with specialized knowledge. Bad actors, including those who only purport to belong to a different actor, such as non-governmental organizations that are actually governmental in terms of funding, staffing, and input into normative processes, need to be identified and sidelined.[186]

181 Ibid.

182 Ministry of Foreign Affairs of the People's Republic of China, International Code of Conduct for Information Security (February 2014), submission to NetMundial, http://content.netmundial.br/contribution/international-code-of-conduct-for-information-security/67.

183 See, on proceduralizing legitimacy transnationally, Michael Zürn, Martin Binder, Matthias Ecker-Ehrhardt, and Katrin Radtke, "Politische Ordnungsbildung wider Willen," Zeitschrift für Internationale Beziehungen 14 (2007) 1, 129–64 (154ff, 157).

184 Wolfgang Benedek, "The Relevance of Multi-Stakeholder Approach and Multi-Track Diplomacy for Human Rights Diplomacy," in Michael O'Flaherty et al. (ed.), *Human Rights Diplomacy: Contemporary Perspectives* (London: Stroud, 2011), 251–61 (253).

185 Dorothea Baur, *NGOs as Legitimate Partners of Corporations. A Political Conceptualization* (Heidelberg: Springer, 2012).

186 Internet Governance Forum (IGF) 2014, Best Practice Forum on Developing Meaningful Multistakeholder Mechanisms, http://www.intgovforum.org/cms/documents/best-practice-forums/developing-meaningful-

Concrete realizations of normative strategies to include all relevant actors have been discussed previously.[187] Ideally, these processes are institutionalized as forms of participatory and multilevel collective problem solving that ensure that both the problems and the procedures to overcome them are flexible and can be periodically revised.[188] Locally and regionally—respecting the subsidiarity principle[189]—"governance groups" that include all relevant actors have been shown to lead to legitimate and effective regulation.[190] Empirically, the representativity and leadership of the discussion process have emerged as key factors to reach normatively successful outcomes.[191]

6.6.3 Legitimation of the Order

Having shown why and how legitimacy is proceduralized in the normative order of the internet, this study now turns to the legitimation of the normative order of the internet itself. This study has already discussed one avenue of legitimacy-conferral, the hetero-constitutive process by which normative orders outside of states are legitimized by integration into existing, legitimate orders.[192] But other avenues of internal legitimation exist: first, the order enshrines the proceduralization of legitimacy through its commitment to including all relevant actors. Second, as discussed previously at length in chapter 3,[193] the normative order of the internet is *necessary* to ensure the common interest in the protection of the functionality of the internet and the protection of states and non-state actors from the dangers emanating from use and misuse of the internet, as such also legitimate. States alone cannot by themselves regulate the internet. International law provides a regulatory frame but is not detailed enough to regulate emerging online threats.

The normative order of the internet develops and legitimizes norms necessary to secure the internet as a critical infrastructural resource and as equally critical for other essential infrastructures. National legal systems cannot by themselves cope with the challenges of international data flows. A normative system is necessary to establish norms, entrench values in online ordering processes, and, inter alia, set limits to the power of non-state actors and the privatization of internet management functions.[194] As Möllers rightly analyzes, the

multistakeholder-participation-mechanisms. See further Moisés Naím, "What is a GONGO? How Government-Sponsored Groups Masquerade as Civil Society," Foreign Policy, October 13, 2009, http://foreignpolicy.com/2009/10/13/what-is-a-gongo.

[187] See 3.4.3.

[188] Gráinne De Búrca, Robert O. Keohane, and Charles Sabel, "Global Experimentalist Governance," British Journal of Political Science 44 (2014) 3, 477–86 (478).

[189] ICANN/World Economic Forum, Report by the Panel on Global Internet Cooperation and Governance Mechanisms, Towards a Collaborative, Decentralized Internet Governance Ecosystem (2014), https://www.icann.org/en/system/files/files/collaborative-decentralized-ig-ecosystem-21may14-en.pdf, 5.

[190] Ryan Budish, Sarah Myers West, and Urs Gasser, "Designing Successful Governance Groups: Lessons for Leaders from Real-World Examples," Berkman Center Research Publication No. 2015-11, August 2015, http://papers.ssrn.com/sol3/papers.cfm?abstract_id=2638006.

[191] Ryan Budish, Sarah Myers West, and Urs Gasser, "Multistakeholder as Governance Groups: Observations from Case Studies," Berkman Center Research Publication No. 2015-1, January 14, 2015, http://papers.ssrn.com/sol3/papers.cfm?abstract_id=2549270.

[192] See 6.6.1.

[193] See in particular, 3.2.1.

[194] For a similar argument related to the necessity of international law, see Matthias C. Kettemann, "Das Völkerrecht zwischen Rechtsordnung und Machtordnung: eine Abgrenzung," in Matthias C. Kettemann (ed.), *Grenzen im Völkerrecht* (Vienna: Jan Sramek Verlag, 2013), 247–73 (250).

legitimacy (justification) of normative orders can be differentiated according to the temporality of the act: original, actualizing, or prospective.[195] The normative order of the internet has emerged decentrally in an unplanned fashion and therefore only actualizing and prospective legitimacy seems to matter. Positing that the order is legitimate has consequences because with such an argument comes the order's "right to rule, understood to mean both that institutional agents [e.g. governance groups] are morally justified in making rules and attempting to secure compliance with them and that people [here: actors] subject to those rules have moral, content-independent reasons to follow them and/or to not interfere with others' compliance with them."[196] In the case of the normative order of the internet, the content of most norms is an added epistemic reason for their legitimacy and exercises additional, independent compliance pull.

Allen Buchanan and Robert O. Keohane, in an international relations-based reading of legitimacy, argue that institutions (but this applies to orders as well) are morally justified, if they do not "contribute to grave injustice ('minimal moral acceptability'), no obvious alternative […] would perform better (comparative benefit) and [they respect their] own guidelines and procedures (institutional integrity)."[197] The normative order of the internet, rather than contributing to injustice, is oriented toward ensuring the protection of and from the internet and has a clear development- and human rights-orientation. Alternatives, such as a state-led system or an international organization, have not yet emerged and do not seem imminent. The last element—institutional integrity—is more controversial and can be discussed under the notion of accountability.

Accountability in the context of the internet means that the formal and informal institutions that are relevant in internet governance and internet policy processes must justify themselves to the international community organized in normative structures that include all relevant actors in their respective roles.[198] Through accountability the democratic participation of all actors can be assessed. Decisions of these formations must be made in accordance with generally accepted principles of human rights, the rule of law, and democracy.[199] These principles are crucial for assessing the legitimacy of all acts of international public authority.[200] Even if no international public authority is exercised, but rather only (formless or only weakly proceduralized) influence over the "space of the reasons" (*Raum der Gründe*)[201] of other actors, the principles still remain normatively relevant.

195 Cf. Möllers (2016), 332.

196 Allen Buchanan and Robert O. Keohane, "The Legitimacy of Global Governance Institutions," Ethics and International Affairs 20 (2006) 4, 405–37 (411).

197 Ibid., 419 et seq.

198 Cf. Matthias C. Kettemann, "Menschenrechte im Multistakeholder-Zeitalter: Mehr Demokratie für das Internet," 1 ZFMR (2016), 24–36 .

199 Gerd Winter, "Transnationale informelle Regulierung: Gestalt, Effekte und Rechtstaatlichkeit," in Gralf-Peter Calliess (ed.), *Transnationales Recht* (Tübingen: Mohr Siebeck, 2014), 95–112 (108) (seeing the role of law as an instrument responsible for reigning in the subcutaneous power present in societal structures).

200 Armin von Bogdandy, "General Principles of International Public Authority: Sketching a Research Field," German Law Journal 9 (2008) 11, 1910–38 ; Armin von Bogdandy, "Prinzipien von Staat, supranationalen und internationalen Organisationen," § 232 (275–304), in Josef Isensee, Paul Kirchhof, et al. (eds.), *Handbuch des Staatsrechts, Band XI: Internationale Bezüge*, 3rd edn. (2013) (also published as Armin von Bogdandy, "Prinzipielles zur Pluralität normativer Ordnungen. Zu den Anforderungen an die Ausübung öffentlicher Gewalt," Normative Orders Working Paper 1/2013).

201 Rainer Forst und Klaus Günther, "Die Herausbildung normativer Ordnungen. Zur Idee eines interdisziplinären Forschungsprogramms," in Rainer Forst und Klaus Günther (eds.), *Die Herausbildung normativer Ordnungen. Interdisziplinäre Perspektiven* (Frankfurt/New York: Campus, 2011), 11–30 (16).

This claim—that all actors, including individuals, have a right to demand accountability from normative actors of internet governance, without a state mediating this right—can be interpreted as a *right to justification*. This right exists independently of, and concurrently to, the existing obligation of states to secure for anyone within their territory or under their jurisdiction all applicable rights, including through participation in international normative processes. This alone is a strong argument against exceptionalism and unilateralism and for participation in the normative machinery of international law and the conferral of some national authority to international or supranational organizations, as these processes actually increase sovereignty (through participation and influence on outcomes) rather than diminish it. Keeping with this approach is Rainer Forst's postulation of the right of everyone not to be subjected to norms or social conditions that cannot be adequately justified toward them.[202] Of course, the justification of policies is a matter of power.[203] ICANN, for example, is a powerful actor in the normative order of the internet and has historically been able to effectively defend itself against criticism. This is also due to ICANN's resources, including its communicative power:

> Whoever has greater and stronger economic resources or means of violence, who with the help of modern information technologies can successfully disseminate normative reasons or successfully immunize against criticism, determine the political agenda and successfully influence the political process with their own topics and reasons [...] has greater opportunities to enforce its normative order over others and to immunize against criticism, dissidence, and resistance, at least for extended periods of time.[204]

Enforced norms may be effective, but they are not necessarily legitimate (if they are not enforced and thus not effective, they could also be illegitimate; they can become legitimate if they are shown to be epistemically sound and if actors internalize them without resisting norm propagation efforts). But, fundamentally, legitimacy of the normative order is dependent in part on mechanisms that ensure that no online actors can use their economic resources or ownership of ICTs or control thereof (through a social network site or search engine, for example) to disseminate normative reasons (to shape justification narratives) to the exclusion of others. Following this approach, for example, both the normative practices and the terms of service of powerful providers of online communicative spaces, such as social networks, need to be viewed critically and tested as to their legitimacy.

In a study on the accountability of international organizations, the International Law Association has developed principles of accountability, the application of which can enhance citizens' "democratic participation" in non-traditional international organizations as well as private or hybrid forms of regulation and information. These include principles such as good governance (transparency, access to information, participatory decision-making process, traceable financial management), good faith, constitutionality and

[202] Rainer Forst, *Das Recht auf Rechtfertigung. Element einer konstruktivistischen Theorie der Gerechtigkeit* (Frankfurt am Main: Suhrkamp, 2007).

[203] Rainer Forst und Klaus Günther, "Die Herausbildung normativer Ordnungen. Zur Idee eines interdisziplinären Forschungsprogramms," in Rainer Forst und Klaus Günther (eds.), *Die Herausbildung normativer Ordnungen. Interdisziplinäre Perspektiven* (Frankfurt/New York: Campus, 2011), 11–30 (16).

[204] Günther, Klaus, "Normativer Rechtspluralismus—Eine Kritik," Normative Orders Working Paper 03/2014, http://publikationen.ub.uni-frankfurt.de/files/34664/Guenther_Normativer+Rechtspluralismus.pdf, 8 (translation by the author).

institutional balance, control, justification, procedural regularity, objectivity and impartiality, and due diligence.[205] Proceduralization, and with that we return to the arguments presented in the previous section, can ensure that informal regulation and non-formally legitimated formations nevertheless produce norms that can be considered democratically legitimized.[206]

6.7 Narratives of Justification

As Robert M. Cover argued, prescriptions (norms) need to be "located in discourse" (contextualized discursively) and "supplied with history and destiny, beginning and end, explanation and purpose"[207] (conceptualized functionally). For each *nomos*, a *narrative* exists which locates the nomos and "give[s] it meaning."[208] Narratives can perform an important function in legitimizing a normative order. The constitution, Cover argues, is a center "about which many communities teach, learn and tell stories."[209]

Within the normative order of the internet, the "constitution" at the center of narrativization are the principles and processes of the order. We cannot meaningfully analyze the impact of, for instance, changes in the terms of service of a social network to the detriment of privacy protection without understanding the way these are perceived by users. We cannot assess the likelihood of success of a treaty dealing with liberalization of intellectual property rights without understanding how these issues are perceived by the affected communities and may be (mis)used to channel normative discontent. Submission to, or objections against, changes in norms (thus elements of their legitimacy) are only intelligible if one understands the narratives underlying the normative practices on these sites. These processes do not end. For all practical purposes, normative orders are constantly evolving. Norms are narrativized and renarrativized: "Each stage of legal codification," as Steven Fraade argues, "produces the next stage of legal commentary [but] also necessitates the reframing of received laws in new (or renewed) narratives of historical, ideological, and teleological signification."[210] Fraade adapts Cover's notion of nomos *and* narrative by arguing that the dynamic interrelation of law and the narrativized history and destiny of the law are more condensed. Rather than nomos *and* narrative, he perceives nomos to exist *as* narrative.[211]

This provides the link to the legitimation of the normative order of the internet. The order (nomos) is narratively (practically) legitimated. Actors in the order can demand justification for the order's structure. With regard to global orders regulating the distribution and management of rights or goods, this demand is framed as one of transnational (distributive) justice. The demand for justification of the order vis-a-vis any actor is an antidote to

[205] International Law Association, Accountability of International Organisations (1996–2004), http://www.ila-hq.org/en/committees/index.cfm/cid/9, 1–2 (with substantial discussions on the importance of principles).

[206] Instructive in structuring participation rights to link decision-making processes to social decision-making processes: Andreas Fisahn, *Demokratie und Öffentlichkeitsbeteiligung* (Tübingen: Mohr Siebeck, 2002), 216f.

[207] Cover (1983), 5.

[208] Ibid.

[209] Ibid., 95ff, 121.

[210] Steven D. Fraade, "Nomos and Narrative Before Nomos and Narrative," Yale Journal of Law & the Humanities 17 (2005) 1, 81–96 (95).

[211] Ibid.

the entrenchment of (global) power asymmetries often reflected in the design of normative orders.

To remedy these asymmetries, Rainer Forst has introduced the *right to justification* (Recht auf Rechtfertigung), which institutionalizes a "duty to provide a better argument."[212] This duty is incumbent upon those individuals/institutions wielding powers in any social setting and provides for the establishment of procedures, which ensure that no order-internal power relationships remain unchallengeable. Through public pressure and institutionalized participation rights those wielding power and profiting from asymmetric power relationships are forced to provide justificatory reasons (or admit the lack thereof with illegitimacy as a consequence).[213]

In the Habermasian tradition Forst considers essential the breadth and effectivity of participation possibilities regarding "discussions and decisions on transnational global internal politics [Weltinnenpolitik]" and the "measure to which reciprocally shareable reasons are guaranteed in these procedures."[214] This approach anchors legitimacy in a process: the process of justification, which is narrativized. This proceduralization of legitimacy through processes in which norm emergence is tied to the provision of justificatory reasons for these norms must take place on a global scale, when issues of global (distributive) justice are concerned. The distribution of rights regarding the internet is undoubtedly an issue of global justice: a "context of social relations in which different actors have countervailing claims that need assessment in light of principles of justice,"[215] especially in light of global interdependence of economy and ecology, of treaties and institutions.

According to Forst everyone has a fundamental right to justification, amounting to a qualified "power of veto" against norms and practices which cannot be justified reciprocally towards all.[216] In a context of global transnational justice everyone has a right to the resources necessary to establish a democratic order in their state and to see that their state is becoming "a participant of the global economic and political system, with the same rights as others."[217] Similarly, everyone has a right to take part in the normative order of the internet as a stakeholder. As a condition for its legitimacy, the normative order must be set up in a way that ensures to all the possibility to take part in its evolution, through, for example, grants for participation in normatively relevant meetings of bodies within the order. Similarly, national legislation must be adapted to ensure that the state can function as an actor representing its citizens in the administration of questions of global distributive justice in the context of the internet.

Just as states have committed, in the GGE 2015 report, to confidence-building measures to strengthen international peace and security,[218] states are obliged (drawing from their duty to ensure the right to democratic governance and political participation) to support structures favoring participation. Since establishing national computer emergency response/cybersecurity incident response teams can be considered a duty under the precaution limb of the due diligence principle,[219] states should organize (as many do) national

[212] Rainer Forst, *Das Recht auf Rechtfertigung. Elemente einer konstruktivistischen Theorie der Gerechtigkeit* (Frankfurt am Main: Suhrkamp, 2007), 355–6.
[213] Ibid.
[214] Ibid., 356 (translation by the author).
[215] Ibid., 361 (translation by the author).
[216] Ibid., 370 (translation by the author).
[217] Ibid., 377 (translation by the author).
[218] GGE report (2015), 16.
[219] Ibid., para. 17.

multistakeholder-based opinion-aggregation forums, such as national Internet Governance Forums, as clearing houses for participation of their national actors in the normative order of the internet.

6.8 Facticity of the Order

6.8.1 Facticity and Ordering

The normative order of the internet is coded through law. It is a legal order, but a legal order *sui generis* in that it differs markedly from traditional centralized legal orders with their respective monopolistic exercise of authority and relatively simple constitutional justification narratives. In an insightful analysis of digital culture, Felix Stalder identified three characteristics of the "culture of digitality": *referentiality* (use of existing cultural material for one's own production), *communality* (collective frame of reference to stabilize meaning and generate options), and *algorithmicity* (use of algorithms to reduce and form information flows, so they become meaningful to humans)."[220]

These defining forms of digital culture can be repurposed as lenses through which to see the normative order of the internet, with each lens putting into focus specific "traits" of the normative order. The normative order of the internet contains referential, communal, and algorithmic elements. It is *referential* in that it is based on existing norms, which it systematizes; it is *communal* as it is relies on legitimacy-enhancing norm-making processes that encompass all actors and provide them with a collective frame of reference; finally, it is *algorithmic* in that algorithms are important regulatory artifacts within the normative order and, as part of machine learning programs, need to be measured against overarching values just as norms.[221]

The normative order of the internet is also an inferable order. This is in keeping with the dynamics of machine learning in the networked society. Machine learning means that the task of programmers is replaced with learning programs and algorithms that are coded so they can learn directly from data. As Ethem Alpaydin explains, the role of the programmer has changed substantially: "[once], it used to be the programmer who defined what the computer had to do, by coding an algorithm in a programming language." The agency is evolving: "[now] we do not write programs but collect data. The data contains instances of what is to be done, and the learning algorithm modifies a learner program automatically in such a way so as to match the requirements specified in the data."[222]

This is an interesting approach: if, having established a "learning algorithm" (the existence of regime-internal processes of normative reflection and self-learning within the normative order that allow for dynamic change), this study has succeeded in "collecting" (i.e. describing and successfully stratifying) the norms of the online order (and showing both their legitimacy *in abstracto* and the legitimacy of the order as a whole), and these norms

220 Felix Stalder, *Kultur der Digitalität* (Frankfurt am Main: Suhrkamp, 2016), 13.

221 World Wide Web Foundation, Algorithmic Accountability, Applying the Concept to Different Country Contexts, July 2017, http://webfoundation.org/docs/2017/07/Algorithms_Report_WF.pdf, 7.

222 Ethem Alpaydin, *Machine Learning* (Cambridge, MA: MIT Press, 2016), ix.

(as data in the simile here employed) can help the learning algorithm adapt the learner program (the normative order of the internet).

This is an intriguing proposition, especially given the large amounts of data/norms which meet the two criteria for inclusion in the normative order. The resources for machine learning (data) and for the self-controlled development of the normative order of the internet (norms) are constantly accruing. While companies moved first from singular data storage systems to decentralized solutions, now individuals store their data in various places, especially cloud-based services.[223] Data, like norms in this study's understanding, have become decentralized. It is no longer the company server/the national legal systems that alone contain all necessary data/norms. Yet they are still (usually) easily accessible and can be used by machines to detect patterns, something they are very good at, especially in large data sets: "the inference of a hidden model," namely the underlying factors of human behavior and their interaction, "from the observed data […] is at the core of machine learning."[224] (This is why machine learning has also energized the field of artificial intelligence[225]). Similarly, the "hidden model" of the normative order of the internet can be inferred from the norms related to it. Thus, the processes and principles of the normative order of the internet crystallize as *meta-law of the internet*.

It is important to note that the normative order of the internet, as any normative order, is by nature *gradual* and *open*, not determinate and closed.[226] Normative orders function in praxis through processes of normative thickening and widening. Neither the notion of "norms" nor that of "order" can be read to include or exclude ex ante norms from any single normative order: it is only with the help of a meta-law of order, what Möllers calls "order-internal formalisms,"[227] that orders of norms and normative orders are constituted. They emerge slowly but are also imbued with a certain continuity. Breaking a norm does not invalidate the order, just as crimes do not challenge legal systems if they remain exceptional and are treated as norm violations. Rather, an order reaches a breaking point only when deviance is no longer recognized as such or reacted to by the relevant "order community." Only when a violation of a norm is no longer perceived as such has the norm ceased to exist in the normative sense. This applies, mutatis mutandis, to the order as a whole.

The conception of "dynamic ordering" (*dynamische Ordnungsbildung*) is based on the realization that the internet challenges the legal order, a point this study has reiterated. The challenges include a dynamization of actors and instruments and the norms that have become hybridized and are structurally coupled to other social systems. This challenges theory (ideas), but it also challenges law (norms). In this sense the concept of a normative order of the internet can have substantial influence, given the destabilizing effect of "computer culture" in today's information society. Dynamization, hybridization, renarrativization are all reasons why the law must provide society with more *Erwartungssicherheit*, a better sense of what to expect, more security and reliability in terms of expectations, namely the realization of legal interests.

223 Ibid., 143.
224 Ibid., xi.
225 See the special section on Artificial Intelligence, *Science* 349 (July 15, 2015) 6245.
226 Cf. Möllers (2016), 382.
227 Ibid., 383.

6.8.2 Facticity and Imperfectness

Rather than an "attack on law as a normative instance,"[228] information and communication technologies challenge the law to develop further *as* a normative instance. Though law is important for regulating the internet, as variously mentioned in the foregoing chapters, "law" is not the only category of norms relevant for the normative order of the internet. Instead, a convincing theory of the normative order of the internet needs to be holistic in its approach to norms. It would be easy for purposes of systematization to argue that only norms that "make sense" within the normative order, that fit structurally, cohere in terms of purposiveness of the order, and have the same regulatory ethos, are "part" of the online order. But such an approach would amount to normative "à la carte-ism." Non-conforming norms are still "part" of the normative order, but they can be criticized because of these non-conforming traits from within the order.

The dynamics of ordering online settings may disappoint those favoring establishing formally binding norms on the internet. Recall the GGE 2015 report, which includes norms, rules, and principles for the responsible behavior of states, including the duty for states not to knowingly allow their territory to be used for internationally wrongful acts and the duty of states not to conduct or knowingly support ICT activity contrary to their obligations under international law.[229] These principles (and the applicability of international law on the internet more broadly) were endorsed by the leaders of the G20 (Group of 20) and referred to affirmatively by the UN General Assembly.[230] However, the cyberattack against the Ukrainian power grid happened only months after the submission of the GGE report, in December 2015, and the influence operations on social media regarding the US 2016 election shortly after that.[231]

This is evidence that the process of developing norms accepted by all actors on the internet is slow and incomplete. However, the norms for state behavior are still important commitments, which, as "multilateralization of norms" more generally, help raise the "reputational costs of bad behaviour."[232] In order to raise them, however, norm-non-conforming behavior needs to be identified and "called out" by, for instance, national criminal proceedings against individuals involved in Chinese cyberespionage against the US in 2015–2016[233] and Russian individuals targeting the US election system in information operations in 2016–2017.[234]

A holistic approach to the normative order considers norms during their whole life cycle. In political science terminology: they emerge as exercises of norm entrepreneurship, they are progressively implemented until a tipping point is reached, after which norms start to

[228] So Peter Mankowski, *Rechtskultur* (Tübingen: Mohr Siebeck, 2016), 129 (translation by the author).

[229] GGE report (2015), para. 13 (c), (f), and (g).

[230] Joseph S. Nye, Jr., "Normative Constraints on Cyber Arms," in Fen Osler Hampson and Michael Sulmeyer (eds.), *Getting Beyond Norms. New Approaches to International Cyber Security Challenges*, CIGI (Centre for International Governance Innovation) Special Report (2017), https://www.cigionline.org/sites/default/files/documents/Getting%20Beyond%20Norms.pdf, 19–22 .

[231] Ibid., 20.

[232] Ibid.

[233] Gary Brown and Christopher D. Yung, "Evaluating the US-China Cybersecurity Agreement," *The Diplomat*, January19,2017,https://thediplomat.com/2017/01/evaluating-the-us-china-cybersecurity-agreement-part-1-the-us-approach-to-cyberspace.

[234] Scott Shane, "The Fake Americans Russia Created to Influence the Election," *New York Times*, September 7, 2017, https://www.nytimes.com/2017/09/07/us/politics/russia-facebook-twitter-election.html.

cascade (and are applied broadly) and, in a final step, are decentrally internalized through prohibitive (reputational or economic) costs for non-compliance.

With regard to the internet, Nye sees the world as "largely at the first stage" (norm production), perhaps entering the second (progressive pre-tipping/cascading implementation).[235] This is undercomplex, as "norms" on the internet are in very different positions within their "life cycle." Some norms are far from being so "successful" as to cascade toward compliance (even if one does not look at the question of intrinsically motivated norm adherence). Other norms, such as technical neutrality of the Internet Exchange Points, are broadly accepted.

But a *norm*-centered (individualizing) approach to the normative order of the internet (instead of a *norms*-centered, systemic one) has its limits. In a critical review of norm-setting progress in the GGE, Eneken Tikk suggests giving up comprehensivity in normative approaches to the internet. She bases her suggestion on the experience of the 2017 process, which ended—unlike the normatively successful GGE process in 2015[236]—without a consensus document on new norms and good practices for states: "Given these near-dead ends, real issues might best be taken up bilaterally or multilaterally between countries and entities that have mutually agreed priorities and issues."[237] She suggests a "strategic pause in global talks" and then "bilateral consensus building" with an "à la carte" approach, enabling "willing countries to contribute according to their strategic ambitions, political priorities and available, realistic capabilities."[238]

A functional theory of the normative order of the internet, however, needs to be based on a more holistic approach. A la carte approaches, proceduralized through ad hoc governance groups that dissolve once a norm has been developed, may bridge short-term normative gaps, but are no equivalent—even and especially in aggregate—to a holistic normative order of the internet, which is able to explain and justify the normative development of the internet and can provide the normative frame for digitality. Just as international law is much more than the sum of legal developments traceable back to the self-interest of states (similar to the à la carte approach), the common-interest basis of the internet and the functional goal of information society, which the normative order of the internet is oriented toward (ensuring human rights, respecting international law, furthering human development), can be called upon as strong arguments for holistic ordering.

6.9 Conclusions

This chapter has established, as has been hypothesized, that a normative turn has taken place on the internet: the normative order's internal rules of norm-production produce the technological and societal forces that, through learning normativity, develop norms autonomously within the order. This chapter has thus shown that, by using the legal code, we can

[235] Nye (2017), 20–1.

[236] See 3.2.2.

[237] Eneken Tikk, "Norms à la Carte," in Fen Osler Hampson and Michael Sulmeyer (eds.), *Getting Beyond Norms. New Approaches to International Cyber Security Challenges*, CIGI (Centre for International Governance Innovation) Special Report (2017), https://www.cigionline.org/sites/default/files/documents/Getting%20 Beyond%Norms.pdf, 25.

[238] Ibid.

develop a normative order of the internet which does not ab initio depend on a state but includes states as normative actors and national law as a central source of norms. The order as envisaged here is largely autonomous, yet it is connected to other legal orders and has a global remit. The normative order of the internet is a legitimate order made up of norms which themselves are legitimated procedurally, through processes involving all relevant actors in their respective roles, and materially, through reference to the order's purposes. It is thus not technicity that forms the norm, but the normative order and its norms which allow for the development of (and sets the limits to) technicity.

This chapter has demonstrated that a (or rather: *the*) normative order of the internet has emerged and legitimately and effectively frames the development of norms that influence the use and development of the internet. It conceptually encompasses all regulatory layers and players, is flexible, holistic, and dynamic. Its goal is to reduce the risks inherent in technological progress. The order does not seek to regulate all fact patters with a connection to the internet but only those that evidence a (1) *material (non-trivial) connection* between the regulatory question or the norm and the internet as a network of networks (2) *in the normative sense*. The contract to buy a smart fridge would thus not be a question of the normative order of the internet. The powers of a smart fridge to communicate within the internet of things and the home appliances company's strategies to minimize the danger of the smart fridge being hacked and drafted into a botnet with spam coming out of the user's kitchen, however, are very much a topic normatively relevant for the online order.

Having reconstructed the normative turn, that is, the turn toward the nomos, this chapter then showed how the normative order of the internet undergoes processes of auto- and hetero-constitutionalization. The normative order of the internet, as presented here, is a legal order. There is no Kelsenian *Stufenbau* on the internet, but the order is legal in the sense that it frames the legal space, seeks to ensure legal peace (*Rechtsfrieden*, rule of law) and, in addition, operates through the form of law and analogously to it. Its actors—states, legal persons, natural persons—fulfill diverse functions as norm entrepreneurs, norm appliers, and norm enforcers.

The order's narratives of justification control new norms by assessing their technical consistency and legal-cultural consonancy with the order's purpose. The norms themselves can come from different sources and be of varying degrees of normativity. They include national laws and international legal acts, but also—importantly—a legal tertium: rules that belong to neither category. These include standards, soft law commitments, internet principles, terms of service, and hate speech guidelines. In their aggregate, they form an essential part of the normative order of the internet and are among the norms that most directly frame the user's experience with the internet.

The normative order of the internet encompasses norm-generative processes and includes, through these, all relevant actors. This is one of the key principles of the normative order. Among the others we find the protection of human rights and intermediaries, the protection of the internet's unfragmented nature and its functionality, and the furtherance of cultural and linguistic diversity.

As hypothesized, the normative order of the internet is a legitimate order with its legitimacy proceduralized through normative processes that include all actors. Each field of norms—international law, national law, transnational normative arrangements—is legitimated either through traditional normative processes or by their integration into national legal orders. Each actor group is legitimated directly or indirectly and transfers this legitimacy potential to the normative outcome, which is often—additionally—epistemically legitimate. The normative order itself is legitimate as a necessary order to ensure protection of and from the internet. The process of justifying the order is narrativized. As any order participant has a right to justification against norms and practices generally reciprocally, the normative order of the internet is, as most social orders, an order of justification.

The normative order of the internet has autonomous elements and is capable of self-constitutionalizing through a model of learning normativity on the basis of meta-rules (principles). Yet the order is also connected to international and national legal orders and is integrated into national law through judicial and systematic integration, as will be seen in the following chapter.

7
The Normative Order of the Internet in National Legal Orders

7.1 The Protective Dimension of National Legal Orders

The protective function of law is challenged by the internet: internet-based communication makes the protection of fundamental rights difficult because tangible "parts" of the internet necessary to ensure communication are physically situated outside of the territorial state.[1] While the possibility to communicate is broadly protected through cooperative measures (transnational data flows), there is, as Cornils argues, "no discernable trend to internationalization or transnationalization of the protection of legal interests [Rechtsgüter] in [national] communication law." The protective function of law is still exercised in essence by states while the dangers are progressively outside of their territories or within their territories, but emanating from private actors. But the distinction between enabling communication (internationally) and regulating content/protecting human rights (nationally) may not be a symptom of system dysfunction but rather a reflection of state interests.[2] In this case, it must also be in the interest of the state to ensure the integration of the norms within the normative order of the internet through controlled, legitimizing processes.

As hypothesized, the normative order of the internet is substantially a legitimate normative order. Internationally (and transnationally), designing normative processes to encompass participation possibilities for all relevant actors in their respective roles proceduralize legitimacy. However, under national legal systems, legitimacy conferral to the norms of the normative order of the internet works differently.

It has therefore been hypothesized that integrating the normative order of the internet internally leads to legitimate normative results, as traditional methods of legitimacy conferral in national legal systems for norms below the level of law (and thus created outside traditional legitimacy-conferral mechanisms) serve this purpose. It should be understood that this only applies to a certain category of norms within the normative order of the internet, that is the transnational normative arrangements, standards, and code. Some norms from within the normative order of the internet are directly implemented through technical standards, such as those agreed upon by rough consensus in the framework of RFC procedures,[3] without formal integration by states of the norm into their legal system or a general commitment to accept certain norms as being part of the law of the land, as applies to most rules of international law.

[1] Matthias Cornils, "Entterritorialisierung im Kommunikationsrecht," VVDStRL 76 (2017), 391–442 (433). (translation by the author).
[2] Ibid., 434.
[3] See chapter 3.1.

The Normative Order of the Internet. Matthias C. Kettemann, Oxford University Press (2020). © Matthias C. Kettemann.
DOI: 10.1093/oso/9780198865995.001.0001

This last chapter will thus analyze and systematize the integration of the norms of the normative order of the internet in the German legal system as an exemplary national legal regime. The first section will address the character of normative integration of order norms as exercises in legitimation (7.2). After this exposition, the following sections discuss the constitutional (7.3) and judicial (7.4) integration of the norms of the normative order. The legitimacy-conferring function of integrating tertium norms nationally is highlighted in 7.5, which differentiates between different techniques of integration that all have a long pedigree. After discussing and dismissing critique of the integration of the normative order in national legal systems from a functional perspective (7.6), the chapter ends with conclusions (7.7).

7.2 Normative Integration as Legitimation

The normative order of the internet is an order of internet-related norms of different character, including national laws, international law, and transnational normative arrangements. The last chapters have shown this order to be legitimate and constitutionalized (and constitutionalizable) through internal dynamics (auto-constitutionalization) and external processes (hetero-constitutionalization).[4]

National norms and international legal norms that form part of the normative order of the internet are legitimate within their regime-specific modalities and logics. This solves what Vesting terms the "problem of the digital constitution"[5] by ensuring that societal values and goals remain protected and are channeled, in their performative energy, through norms, by the *pouvoir constituant*, to influence the behavior of those (same selves) in the *pouvoir constitué* of the digital. Transnationally, normative processes have been found to give birth to and seek the implementation of non-traditional norms, with processes showing evidence of internalization and incorporation of norms created in transnational processes in different legal systems.[6] Fundamental and human rights come into play within national law as background to the constitutional self-control of the order norms as "norms of collision for evaluating contrary logics of acting."[7]

The normative order of the internet is a legitimate order. Its norms can be legitimated procedurally and materially. It consists of national law, international law, and transnational norms or normative arrangements. As states continue to play a central role in global society as repositories of culture and affiliation and as centers of narratives of belonging, any norms that apply need to be made relevant for the norm-applying powers within states through integration into national legal orders. This applies to all norms that form part of the normative order of the internet by being materially connected to the internet in a normative sense.

However, some norms are less in need of legitimation through national legal systems than others. National norms automatically form part of national law without any additional normative acts. International norms, belonging to the normative order of the internet, are

[4] On constitutionalization, see 6.3.2.

[5] Thomas Vesting, *Die Medien des Rechts: Computernetzwerke* (Weilerswist: Velbrück Wissenschaft, 2015), 144.

[6] Felix Hanschmann, "Theorie transnationaler Rechtsprozesse," in Sonja Buckel, Ralph Christensen, and Andreas Fischer-Lescano (eds.), *Neue Theorien des Rechts*, 2nd edn. (Stuttgart: Lucius&Lucius, 2009), 375–99 (390).

[7] Cf. Vesting (2015), 144.

part of national law following constitutionally provided processes of adoption or integration of international law. It is only the "tertium," the third category of norms—transnational arrangements, soft law standards, private norms, technical standards—which are more difficult to conceptualize through a national legal frame.

As Stefan Kadelbach recalled almost 15 years ago in a review of international legal scholarship in Germany, the hitherto unsatisfying discussion on monism vs. dualism has been substantially enriched in more recent times:[8] the direct application/applicability of "objective" international law has been dynamized by discussions on the proper role of international legal norms and on how national legal systems should cope with non-traditional norms that do not submit to constitutionally envisaged "checks" by presupposing a *Rechtsanwendungsbefehl* (an "order," contained in a law, decided by a democratically legitimated legislative body, for a non-national norm to be applied like national law).

National constitutions have traditionally treated national law and international law as the two possible sides of a legal "coin." As this study has shown in the previous chapters, however, the normative order of the internet contains a large number of norms that belong organically neither to international law nor to national legal orders. These transnational normative arrangements are a *tertium*, non-national and non-international legal norms that form part of the normative order of the internet and are nevertheless, through processes which will now be described, procedurally and materially legitimated as norms. When this chapter refers to the integration of the normative order of the internet into national legal systems, it mainly understands this to mean the integration of tertium norms. International legal norms forming part of the order, on the one hand, are legitimated—from an international law perspective—either through their emergence in traditional norm-making processes or, when they are new softer norms, through normative processes involving all relevant actors. National legal norms, on the other hand, have a presumption of legitimacy as they flow from constitutionally enshrined lawmaking processes.

7.3 Constitutional Integration of the Normative Order of the Internet

7.3.1 Multinormativity as Reality

The economic, social, and legal processes discussed under the heading of "globalization" have necessitated a progressive opening of national legal orders.[9] The following rough periodicization of norm interaction can be suggested:

[8] Stefan Kadelbach, "Völkerrecht als Verfassungsordnung? Zur Völkerrechtswissenschaft in Deutschland," ZaöRV 67 (2007), 599–621 (607).

[9] The opening of legal orders for another is linked to legal pluralism (Klaus Günther, "Normativer Rechtspluralismus—Eine Kritik," Normative Orders Working Paper 03/2014, http://publikationen.ub.uni-frankfurt.de/files/34664/Guenther_Normativer+Rechtspluralismus.pd and Ralf Seinecke, *Das Recht des Rechtspluralismus* (Tübingen: Mohr Siebeck, 2015)), while the "logical" necessity for a functional normative order to be open is demonstrated already by Ilmar Tammelo, "Logical Openness of Legal Orders: A Modal Analysis of Law with Special Reference to the Logical Status of Non Liquet in International Law," American Journal of Comparative Law, 8 (1959) 2, 187–203.

(1) only "national" (or territorial) law applies within specified territories;[10]
(2) non-territorial (i.e. international) law only applies after a consent act;
(3) international law can be applied directly (in certain cases) without the intermediation of states;[11] and
(4) non-international law-based norms, including standards and soft law, are applicable within states and integrated into the national legal order.

These four periods overlap to a certain degree. The application of international law via a consent act (2) and the direct application of ius cogens and certain objective international legal norms (3) is the accepted status quo.[12] The advent of standards as legal tertium and their integration into national law, however, is a more recent trend.

As shown earlier,[13] if a national legal order acknowledges the normative relevance of the tertium norms, it accepts multi-normativity,[14] and thus the "coexistence of different modi of normativity within the same social space."[15] Questions of implementation of the tertium norms and of their legitimation ensue. The German Basic Law (Grundgesetz, GG) appears to navigate the challenges of multinormativity well, as it shows instances of permeability and openness.

7.3.2 Permeability

There is no single treaty enshrining "international control over the internet."[16] However, such a treaty is not necessary. The normative order of the internet as a comprehensive normative framework for the regulation and governance of the internet is not premised upon the existence of such a treaty delineating rights and obligations of states and non-state actors. International law already provides the foil against which the normative tensions between global, regional, and national normative approaches to internet regulating can be measured.

Cornils fears that interpreting duties of normative restraint into the (German) constitution is problematic given the lack of such a "conventional anchor."[17] But this runs counter

[10] With "nationality" and "national" law being constructs that have only developed slowly. See Klaus Günther, "Normativer Rechtspluralismus—Eine Kritik," Normative Orders Working Paper 03/2014, http://publikationen.ub.uni-frankfurt.de/files/34664/Guenther_Normativer+Rechtspluralismus.pd, 3–4.

[11] Cf. Theodor Meron, *Humanization of International Law* (Amsterdam: Brill, 2014). On disintermediation, see Matthias C. Kettemann, *The Future of Individuals in International Law. Lessons from International Internet Law* (Utrecht: Eleven Publishing, 2013) and, on the special role of internet governance law as a key normative field of disintermediation which ushers in "a new trend whereby individuals enjoy recognition at the international level," Mary Rundle and Malcolm Birding, "Filtering and the International System: A Question of Commitment," in Ronald Deibert, John Palfrey, Rafal Rohozinski, and Jonathan Zittrain (eds.), *Access Denied. The Practice and Policy of Global Internet Filtering* (Cambridge, Mass./London: The MIT Press, 2008), 73–101 (74).

[12] On objective international law, see Jochen von Bernstorff, "German Intellectual Historic Origins of International Legal Positivism," in Jörg Kammerhofer and Jean d'Aspremont (eds.), *International Legal Positivism in a Post-Modern World* (Cambridge: CUP, 2014), 50–80 (68).

[13] See, on administering hybrid normative spaces through multinormativity, 5.2.9.

[14] Michael Grünberger, "Transnationales Recht als responsiver Rechtspluralismus," Der Staat 55 (2016), 117–33.

[15] Thomas Duve, "Was ist 'Multinormativität'?—Einführende Bemerkungen," Rechtsgeschichte—Legal History 25 (2017), 88–101 (90).

[16] Oliver Dörr, "Die Anforderungen an ein zukunftsfähiges Infrastrukturrecht," VVDStRL 73 (2014), 323–67 (359).

[17] Matthias Cornils, "Entterritorialisierung im Kommunikationsrecht," VVDStRL 76 (2017), 391–442 (433).

to the open conception of German constitutional law. Let us recall, with Andrea Bianchi, that transnational constitutionalization is a "German discipline."[18] German lawyers, Martti Koskenniemi argues, see normative developments taking place "within a 'legal system' that can be articulated through the vocabularies of public law and the constitution."[19] Thus, the normative order of the internet is closely linked to public law approaches, based on existing positive law but including certain idealistic elements—a feature of (international) legal approaches that Stefan Kadelbach considers typical of German (language) international law scholarship.[20]

International law, national law, and transnational normative arrangements are the three constituent orders of the normative order of the internet.[21] As with all law, it is public national law (especially constitutional law) that then ensures the implementation of these norms. When it comes to the internet, norms from all three normative sources regulate the same social space. This phenomenon is called multinormativity.[22] Multinormativity, however, is also present within the three orders, as even national legal systems, which are traditionally conceived mononormatively, share the normative space with other social orders.[23] Just as the management of legal pluralism necessitates meta-rules,[24] multinormative spaces (and the internet can be justly characterized as one) need to rely on orders (within the normative order of the internet) that are open to one another and responsive.

Ideally, the orders adapt and become responsive[25] and allow norms and concepts to migrate and to flow into each other. For this to happen, the normative orders must be provided with a level of permeability. Following Franzius, this normative permeability is based on the principle of constitutional plurality.[26] Collisions between the norms and narratives of different orders applying themselves to similar fact patterns have contributed to the emergence of a framework of collision.[27] This framework of collision in private law is the law of conflicts of law.

In public law, collisions of constitutions are usually impossible by definition. Either the constitutional law of one state applies or that of the other. While this is true with regard to many aspects a constitution usually regulates (for example: non-dual citizens can only vote once in one country, keeping in mind the problem of contested territories and normative nationality), the "impossibility" of collisions is dealt a serious blow by, e.g., human

[18] Andrea Bianchi, *International Law Theories. An Inquiry into Different Ways of Thinking* (Oxford: OUP, 2016), 44.

[19] Martti Koskenniemi, "Between Coordination and Constitution: International Law as a German Discipline," in Kari Palonen and Hubertus Buchstein (eds.), *Redescriptions. Yearbook of Political Thought, Conceptual History and Feminist Theory*, vol. 15 (Zurich/Berlin: Lit Verlag, 2011), 45–69 (64).

[20] Stefan Kadelbach, "Völkerrecht als Verfassungsordnung? Zur Völkerrechtswissenschaft in Deutschland," ZaöRV 67 (2007), 599–621 (607): "In dieser Lehre vom objektiven Völkerrecht einer Staatengemeinschaft kommt etwas für die deutschsprachige Völkerrechtswissenschaft Typisches wieder zum Vorschein: Sie ist zugleich am positiven Recht orientiert und idealistisch und steht damit in deutlichem Gegensatz zu realistischen Positionen" (notes omitted).

[21] Gerald Spindler, "Transnationalisierung und Renationalisierung des Rechts im Internet," in Gralf-Peter Calliess (ed.), *Transnationales Recht* (Tübingen: Mohr Siebeck, 2014), 193–222.

[22] Cf. 5.2.9. See also Thomas Duve, "Was ist 'Multinormativität'?—Einführende Bemerkungen," Rechtsgeschichte—Legal History 25 (2017), 88–101 (90).

[23] Ibid., 98.

[24] Klaus Günther, "Normativer Rechtspluralismus—Eine Kritik," Normative Orders Working Paper 03/2014, http://publikationen.ub.uni-frankfurt.de/files/34664/Guenther_Normativer+Rechtspluralismus.pd, 3.

[25] Niklas Luhmann, *Rechtssoziologie*, 4th edn. (Wiesbaden: Verlag für Sozialwissenschaften, 2008), 340 et seq.

[26] Claudio Franzius, *Recht und Politik in der transnationalen Konstellation* (Franfurt am Main: Campus, 2014), 258.

[27] Lars Viellechner, *Transnationalisierung des Rechts* (Weilerswist: Velbrück, 2013), 117.

rights-related norms transcending one order that enter into conflict, when applied, with other norms from a different order. Responsivity includes elements of complementarity and subsidiarity,[28] and is the conceptual bridge toward a "law of collision as horizontal constitutional law."[29]

German constitutional law provides ample space for normative self-reflection.[30] This ability is tied to the existence of meta-rules of self-reflection and premised upon a regime's or order's ability to "self-reflect without destabilizing itself."[31]

7.3.3 Openness

The ability of a normative order to self-reflect does not equal obligations of normative reticence in applying national legal rules. For Cornils, in light of a missing "international legal point of reference," "the constitutional friendliness towards international law cannot contain a subclause of internet friendliness [Internetfreundlichkeit] as long as the Internet is not an international institution [Einrichtung] in the sense of the law."[32]

This is in reference to the openness (or "friendliness") of the German constitution toward international law. Article 25 of the Basic Law prescribes that "general rules of international law shall be an integral part of federal law" and "shall take precedence over the laws and directly create rights and duties for the inhabitants of the federal territory." There are thus two parts to the friendliness/openness principle: first, general rules of international law are an integral part of federal law; and, second, they take precedence over the laws and citizens enjoy rights and duties stemming from them without interposition (or an act of acceptance) by the state, unless an additional state is necessary because of the non-self-executing nature of the norm.[33]

The internet is a global interconnection of networks, an "internetwork," and not an institution. What should rather be compared to international law as a potential target to open public law toward is thus not "the internet" but rather the normative order of the internet. This order has been defined in this study as the

> complex of norms, values, and practices that relate to the use and development of the internet and with which the activities of, and relationships among, states, private companies, and civil society with regard to the use and development of the internet are legitimated, in particular the exercise of private or public authority and the distribution of basic goods, including internet access and access to internet content.[34]

[28] Ibid., 269.

[29] Ibid., 265.

[30] Ibid., 268–9. Niklas Luhmann, "Selbstreflexion des Rechtssystems," Rechtstheorie 10 (1979), 159 et seq. See also 5.2.8.

[31] Gunther Teubner and Helmut Willke, "Kontext und Autonomie," Zeitschrift für Rechtssoziologie 5 (1984), 4–35 (14).

[32] Matthias Cornils, "Entterritorialisierung im Kommunikationsrecht," VVDStRL 76 (2017), 391–442 (436) (translation by the author).

[33] See Hans Dieter Jarass, Art. 25, in Hans Dieter Jarass and Bodo Pieroth (eds.), *Kommentar zum Grundgesetz*, 14th edn. (Munich: C.H.Beck, 2016), para. 3.

[34] See chapter 1.2.3.

At the same time, the Federal Constitutional Court confirmed that the Basic Law did not foresee a submission of the German legal system under the international order and the sine qua non primacy of international law. Rather, the formulation in Article 25 should increase respect for "international organizations that secure peace and freedom and international law without giving up the ultimate responsibility [of the German public authorities] to ensure the protection of human dignity and respect for fundamental rights."[35] There is no constitutional duty, however, to implement, without restrictions, all international legal norms.[36]

This study, however, submits that the Basic Law is generally open to the norms from within the normative order of the Internet—as delineated for instance in the Federal Constitutional Court's *Bodenreform III* and *Völkerrechtsdurchbrechung* cases—applicable to general rules of international law.

The case for this is further strengthened by past practice of the German government regarding the evolution of non-traditional internet-related norms in processes involving all relevant actors. In 2014, the German government submitted to the Global Multistakeholder Meeting on the Future of Internet Governance, the NetMundial meeting, the "German Government Proposal on Global Internet Principles (2014)."[37] It included, as Principle 1, a commitment to a "global, open and free nature of the internet as a single commons" and described the internet as "a driving force for progress towards development in its various forms including economic growth, encouraging innovation and allowing for creativity."[38] Further principles contained in Germany's document include that people have the same rights offline as online, that "access to the internet should respect the principles of non-discrimination, transparency and openness," that the "rule of law must be the foundation for legislation and normative development online," that states "must ensure full compliance with their obligations under international law," and that the "security, stability, robustness and resilience of the internet as well as its ability to evolve should be a key objective of internet governance."[39]

Already Human Rights Council Resolution 20/8 (2012) recognized the globality and *openness* of the internet as a key driving force toward progress.[40] We similarly find openness as a key architectural principle of the internet's fundamental make-up and as a key principle of standard-setting. This technical openness of the internet is mirrored by the openness (or friendliness) of German constitutional law into which the normative order of the internet, as presented and normatively constructed in this study, finds entry and gives rights and imposes obligations, without intermediation by the state, to non-state actors.

[35] BVerfG, judgment of 26 October 2004, 2 BvR 955/00, 2 BvR 1038/01, BVerfGE 112, 1 – *Bodenreform III*, para. 94: "Das Grundgesetz (...) ordnet nicht die Unterwerfung der deutschen Rechtsordnung unter die Völkerrechtsordnung und den unbedingten Geltungsvorrang von Völkerrecht vor dem Verfassungsrecht an, sondern will den Respekt vor friedens- und freiheitswahrenden internationalen Organisationen und dem Völkerrecht erhöhen, ohne die letzte Verantwortung für die Achtung der Würde des Menschen und die Beachtung der Grundrechte durch die deutsche öffentliche Gewalt aus der Hand zu geben [...]" (translation by the author).

[36] BVerfG, order of 15 December 2015, 2 BvL 1/12, BVerfGE 141, 1 – *Völkerrechtsdurchbrechung*, paras. 64, 69.

[37] Germany, Federal Foreign Office, Commissioner for International Cyber Policy, German Government Proposal on Global Internet Principles (February 2014), submission to NetMundial, http://content.NetMundial.br/contribution/german-government-proposal-on-global-internet-principles/32.

[38] Ibid.

[39] Ibid.

[40] Human Rights Council, Resolution 20/8, The promotion, protection and enjoyment of human rights on the Internet, UN Doc. A/HRC/RES/20/8 of 16 July 2012, para. 2.

Article 25 of the Basic Law provides for a duty to interpret German law in a way that is friendly to international law. Substantial parts of the normative order of the internet are made up of international legal norms. It is therefore not a stretch to argue that internet-related norms of international law must be respected.[41] In that reading, the Network Enforcement Act needs to be carefully measured not only against German law but also international law.

7.4 Judicial Integration of the Normative Order of the Internet

7.4.1 Threats to Rights as the Normative Background

States have a sovereignty-based obligation to ensure all human rights to everyone within their jurisdiction or control. Under German constitutional law, the state is obliged to ensure to all actors fundamental and human rights protection.[42] This includes the necessary infrastructure to communicate. Infrastructure law must be formulated in such a way as to enable the infrastructure-based provision of goods of general interest to the population.[43] Just as roads are essential for the existence of the state, enabling communication is important for the social cohesion of state and society.[44] Dörr traces this duty back to the responsibility of states, based on the principle of the social state, to provide fundamental goods to everyone and the protective duties of states (*Schutzpflichten*) to enable the realization of human rights, which in a country with an advanced system of the rule of law, such as Germany, happens via legislation.[45]

Protecting human rights is one of the ends of the normative order of the internet.[46] The protection of human rights is challenged by phenomena connected with progressively stronger use of ICTs in society[47] and the role of the internet in mediating or enabling economic and political, private, and public activities. These include the use of algorithms in shaping individual[48] and public[49] communicative spaces, mass collection of

[41] Hans Dieter Jarass in Hans Dieter Jarass and Bodo Pieroth (eds.), *Kommentar zum Grundgesetz*, 14th edn. (Munich: C.H.Beck, 2016), Art. 25, para. 4a.

[42] Cf. Thilo Marauhn, "Sicherung grund- und menschenrechtlicher Standards gegenüber neuen Gefährdungen durch private und ausländische Akteure," VVDStRL 74 (2015), 373–400 (385).

[43] Oliver Dörr, "Die Anforderungen an ein zukunftsfähiges Infrastrukturrecht," VVDStRL 73 (2014), 323–67 (337).

[44] Ibid., 338.

[45] See Thilo Marauhn, "Sicherung grund- und menschenrechtlicher Standards gegenüber neuen Gefährdungen durch private und ausländische Akteure," VVDStRL 74 (2015), 373–400 (394).

[46] World Summit on the Information Society (WSIS), Tunis Commitment, WSIS-05/TUNIS/DOC/7-E, 18 November 2005, para. 2; Human Rights Council, Resolution 32/13, The promotion, protection and enjoyment of human rights on the Internet, UN Doc. A/HRC/RES/32/13 of 18 July 2016; NetMundial, Multistakeholder Statement, Global Multistakeholder Meeting on the Future of Internet Governance, April 23–24, 2014, São Paulo, Brazil, http://netmundial.br/wp-content/uploads/2014/04/NETmundial-Multistakeholder-Document.pdf. See also 6.5.2.

[47] Internet Usage Statistics, World Internet Users and 2018 Population Stats, December 31, 2017, http://www.Internetworldstats.com/stats.htm.

[48] Jan-Hinrik Schmidt, "Filterblasen und Algorithmenmacht. Wie sich Menschen im Internet informieren," in C. Gorr and M. C. Bauer (eds.), *Gehirne unter Spannung: Kognition, Emotion und Identität im digitalen Zeitalter* (Berlin/Heidelberg: Springer, 2018), 35–51.

[49] Jan-Hinrik Schmidt, Jannick Sørensen, Stephan Dreyer, and Uwe Hasebrink, *Algorithmische Empfehlungen. Funktionsweise, Bedeutung und Besonderheiten für öffentlich-rechtliche Rundfunkanstalten* (Hamburg: Verlag Hans-Bredow-Institut, 2018), Hans-Bredow-Institut Working Papers No. 45, https://www.hans-bredow-institut.de/uploads/media/default/cms/media/w188msk_45AlgorithmischeEmpfehlungen.pdf.

data,[50] the new roles of private actors, especially intermediaries,[51] and the transnationalization of communicative and contractual relations.[52] States can still regulate the internet, and ensure human rights protection effectively, as long as the underlying fact patterns remain "purely national."[53] Germany's Basic Law is "incorporated into the social-ethical principles of German society," so that rule of law and peaceful relations between individuals (Rechtsfrieden), both offline and online, are assured. Yet as soon as cases exhibit international dimensions, the reliance on the state's guarantee of citizens' fundamental rights is becomes more challenging—and may ultimately be factually impossible.[54]

7.4.2 Internet Access as a Precondition for Exercising Fundamental Rights

Ensuring internet access is an important human right that is intimately connected to the exercise of other human rights online.[55] In some states, the right to internet access is specifically prescribed or can be developed dogmatically.[56] In the case of *Yıldırım v. Turkey*, the ECtHR confirmed that a right to internet access is part of the right to information and communication, protected by national constitutions: "it can therefore be inferred from all the general guarantees protecting freedom of expression that a right to unhindered internet access should also be recognized."[57]

International and European law provide for the frame in which constitutional law guarantees the right to internet access. Responsible state organs should not wait passively for international law to crystallize into a conventional guarantee of internet access but should rather actively seek to integrate the right to access into national law. In doing so, the legislator, as per the Federal Constitutional Court, has a certain leeway.[58] The Basic Law protects primarily subject rights, but there exist objective-legal duties of the legislator to provide for the (normative and technical) infrastructure necessary to realize these rights. Ensuring the infrastructure necessary for the realization of human rights has been termed *Grundrechtsvoraussetzungschutz*: ensuring a status for all in which fundamental rights can be realized.[59]

[50] Critically, Council of Europe, Parliamentary Assembly, Report on Mass surveillance, Rapporteur Mr. Pieter Omtzigt, Doc. 13734 of 18 March 2015.

[51] Cf. Council of Europe, Recommendation CM/Rec(2018)2 of the Committee of Ministers to member states on the roles and responsibilities of internet intermediaries, adopted by the Committee of Ministers on 7 March 2018, preamble.

[52] Gerald Spindler, "Transnationalisierung und Renationalisierung des Rechts im Internet," in Gralf-Peter Calliess (ed.), *Transnationales Recht* (Tübingen: Mohr Siebeck, 2014), 219.

[53] Utz Schliesky, Christian Hoffmann, Anika D. Luch, Sönke E. Schulz, and Kim Corinna Borchers, *Schutzpflichten und Drittwirkung im Internet. Das Grundgesetz im digitalen Zeitalter* (Baden-Baden: Nomos, 2014), 146.

[54] Ibid., 147.

[55] ECtHR, *Yıldırım v. Turkey* (December 18, 2012), application no. 3111/10.

[56] This section draws on Matthias C. Kettemann, "Das Recht auf Internet zwischen Völkerrecht, Staatsrecht und Europarecht," Völkerrechtsblog, October 7, 2015, doi: 10.17176/20170920-161413, Matthias C. Kettemann, "Das Internetgrundrecht zwischen Völkerrecht, Staatsrecht und Europarecht (II)," Völkerrechtsblog, October 9, 2015, doi: 10.17176/20170920-161818, and Matthias C. Kettemann, "Das Internetgrundrecht zwischen Völkerrecht, Staatsrecht und Europarecht (III)," Völkerrechtsblog, October 12, 2015, doi: 10.17176/20170920-162122.

[57] ECtHR, *Yıldırım v. Turkey* (December 18, 2012), application no. 3111/10, para. 31.

[58] But see BVerfG, judgment of the First Senate of July 18, 2012, 1 BvL 10/10, *Asylbewerberleistungsgesetz*, para. 94.

[59] Cf. Wolfgang Weiß, *Privatisierung und Staatsaufgaben. Privatisierungsentscheidungen im Lichte einer grundrechtlichen Staatsaufgabenlehre unter dem Grundgesetz* (Tübingen: Mohr Siebeck, 2002), 147.

The *status negativus* of fundamental rights—the right to unhindered internet access as per the ECtHR's *Yıldırım* case—needs to be understood in conjunction with a state duty to implement rights.

In 2008, the Federal Constitutional Court ruled that the general right of personality pursuant to Article 2 (1) in conjunction with Article 1 (1) of the Basic Law encompasses a "fundamental right to the guarantee of the confidentiality and integrity of information technology systems." The Court first focused on the *status negativus*, confirming that "[t]he individual relies on the state respecting the expectations of the integrity and confidentiality of such systems which are justified with regard to the unhindered development of the personality."[60]

The state has to respect ("achten") fundamental rights, but it must do more. Since the (negative) right to informational self-determination does not provide for a normative defense in situations where "personality endangerments" emerge from reliance by the individual on the use of information technology systems by entrusting personal data to the system,[61] a further right needed to be established. This "fundamental right to the guarantee of the integrity and confidentiality of information technology systems" is to be applied, by contrast, "if the empowerment to encroach covers systems which alone or in their technical networking can contain personal data of the person concerned to such a degree and in such a diversity that access to the system facilitates insight into significant parts of the life of a person or indeed provides a revealing picture of the personality."[62] Forcing the state to ensure the integrity of these IT systems closes a protection loophole and ensures that new types of endangerment of human rights due to scientific and technical progress are met.

Already in 2013, the German Federal Court of Justice (BGH) confirmed that the internet is used on a daily basis by the majority of German citizens and that the internet is of "central importance" for daily life; non-access "significantly impacts the material foundation of living."[63] The facts underlying this case go back to 2008 and 2009. In the twelve years since Germany's highest civil court ruled internet access as significant for the way citizens live their lives, the importance of internet access has only increased.

In light of these judgments a right to access can therefore be developed dogmatically as an objective-legal fundamental rights implication, as an independent right to internet access within the right to the provision of a subsistence minimum by the state (Article 1 in conjunction with Article 20 (1) of the Basic Law) or, finally, as a "gateway" right to the exercise of other rights.[64]

[60] BVerfG, judgment of the First Senate of February 27, 2008, 1 BvR 370/07, para. 181.

[61] Ibid., para. 200.

[62] Ibid., para. 203.

[63] BGH, Judgment of January 24, 2013, III ZR 98/12, 22 ("Die Nutzbarkeit des Internets ist ein Wirtschaftsgut, dessen ständige Verfügbarkeit seit längerer Zeit, jedenfalls vor dem hier maßgeblichen Jahreswechsel 2008/2009, auch im privaten Bereich für die eigenwirtschaftliche Lebenshaltung typischerweise von zentraler Bedeutung ist und bei dem sich eine Funktionsstörung als solche auf die materiale Grundlage der Lebenshaltung signifikant auswirkt") (translation by the author).

[64] Wolfgang Hoffmann-Riem, "Freiheitsschutz in den globalen Kommunikationsinfrastrukturen," JZ 2 (2014), 53–63.

7.4.3 Access and Subsistence Minimum

In light of the central role of the internet as a locus of communication, ensuring access amounts to a duty of states as part of the right to be provided with a subsistence minimum. In its *Hartz IV* judgment, the Federal Constitutional Court confirmed each citizen a "direct constitutional benefit claim to a guarantee of a subsistence minimum." This minimum must cover "those means which are vital to maintain an existence that is in line with human dignity." The uniform fundamental rights guarantee related to the subsistence minimum encompasses "both the physical existence of the individual, that is food, clothing, household goods, housing, heating, hygiene and health and [ensures] the possibility to maintain inter-human relationships and a minimum of participation in social, cultural and political life, given that humans as persons of necessity exist in social relationships"[65] The minimum participation in social, cultural, and political life cannot be conceived of, under the conditions of modernity, without access to the internet. Humans become persons (social beings) by defining themselves in communicative processes with others. These processes now often take place on the internet.

The Court guarantees the subsistence minimum as a statutory claim ensured by a parliamentary statute, containing "a concrete benefit claim on the part of the citizen towards the competent benefit institution." Parliament needed to implement the subsistence minimum: "[the] obligation incumbent on the legislature to make the provisions material to the realisation of the fundamental right itself already emerges from the principles of the rule of law and of democracy."[66]

The Court also recognizes that needs change as society evolves, both in absolute and relative terms. What is necessary to ensure a dignified existence depends on the circumstances of the rights holder and "the respective economic and technical circumstances." Note the reference to the "technical circumstances," which must be read to include the evolution of internet technologies, especially when the Court goes on to explain that the principle of the social welfare (Article 20 (1) of the Basic Law) forces Parliament to assess social reality "in a manner that is appropriate to the present day and realistic with regard to the guarantee of the subsistence minimum that is in line with human dignity, which for instance is different in a technological information society than was previously the case."

What matters are the "actual circumstances" in today's internet age: the legislature has a narrower scope to determine what is necessary when concretizing the needs related to rightsholders' physical existence and a broader one "when it comes to the nature and scope of the possibility to participate in social life."[67] In a follow-up 2014 ruling, the Court reiterates that the requirements of the Basic Law to effectively ensure a dignified minimum existence need to be adapted to actual conditions and constantly scrutinized by the legislator.[68]

[65] BVerfG, judgment of the First Senate of February 09, 2010—1 BvL 1/09, *Hartz IV*, para 135 (notes omitted).
[66] Ibid., para. 137.
[67] Ibid., para. 138.
[68] BVerfG, order of the First Senate of July 23, 2014, 1 BvL 10/12, paras. 1–149.

7.4.4 Fundamental Right to Access as a Human Right to Access

In its 2012 judgment on the *Asylbewerberleistungsgesetz*, the Federal Constitutional Court extended the protective ambit of the *Hartz IV* decision while keeping its reasoning intact. Article 1 (1) of the Basic Law, read together with Article 20 (1) (the principle of the social welfare state), guarantees dignity through the instrument of a subsistence minimum. But the *fundamental* right to this subsistence minimum is a *human* right as per Article 1 (1) of the Basic Law.[69]

Using language identical to that of the *Hartz IV* decision, the Court confirmed the existence of a "direct constitutional benefit claim to the guarantee of a dignified minimum existence" for all. It guarantees "the entire minimum existence," encompassing physical existence (food, clothing, household items, housing, heating, hygiene, and health) but also guaranteeing "the possibility to maintain interpersonal relationships and a minimal degree of participation in social, cultural and political life, since a human as a person necessarily exists in social context."[70] Again, the Court confirmed that the scope of the benefit claim depends on societal and technological developments: "on the specific living conditions of the persons in need, and on the respective economic and technical circumstances."[71]

Ensuring that everyone within Germany can develop their personality in social contexts is essential for their development into citizens. Establishing communicative relations through participation in, and ownership of, communicative and socializing processes[72] is key to sociality.[73] Sociology informs us that we, as human beings, are constantly at work on ourselves: we are "Existenzbastler,"[74] and in today's internet age the important aspects of one's "existence" in technologically advanced societies (as an employee, as a person, as a rightsholder) are mediated through the internet and need to be protected as such by states. Conversely, users (and online media) engage in attempts to construct audiences (views, likes, upvotes) to enhance one's reputation.[75] The right to internet access is thus a key right not only of *information society*, but of *society* in times when the *conditio humana* is (de)constructed and (re)narrativized through media, and the media of law are changing.

We can therefore conclude that German law contains an *Internetgrundrecht*, a fundamental right to internet access, which imposes upon the state a number of different obligations. These include ensuring the infrastructure necessary for internet access, the individual's ability to access the internet through provision of minimum subsistence, and a legal framework that ensures to everyone secure communication online. This *Internetgrundrecht*, as normatively preconfigured in international law, ties in with the constitutional principle of friendliness to public law and respect for human and fundamental

[69] BVerfG, judgment of the First Senate of July 18, 2012, 1 BvL 10/10, *Asylbewerberleistungsgesetz*.

[70] Ibid., para. 64.

[71] Ibid., para. 66.

[72] Oliver Dimbath, "Vergemeinschaftende Vergesellschaftung und die Intention eines Dritten" in Gert Albert, Rainer Greshoff, and Rainer Schützeichel (eds.), *Dimensionen und Konzeptionen von Sozialität* (Berlin: Springer VS, 2010), 33–45.

[73] Bernhard Waldenfels, *Sozialität und Alterität—Modi sozialer Erfahrung* (Frankfurt am Main: Suhrkamp, 2015).

[74] Cf. Ronald Hitzler, "Der Goffmensch," in Anne Honer, Michael Meuser, and Michaela Pfadenhauer (eds.), *Fragile Sozialität. Inszenierungen, Sinnwelten, Existenzbastler* (Berlin: Springer VS, 2010), 17–34.

[75] Nora A. Draper and Joseph Turow, "Audience Constructions, Reputations, and Emerging Media Technologies: New Issues of Legal and Social Policy," in Roger Brownsword, Eloise Scotford, and Karen Yeung (eds.), *Oxford Handbook of Law, Regulation, and Technology* (Oxford: OUP, 2017), 1143–68.

rights and is further evidence of the integration of the normative order of the internet into the German legal system.

7.5 Systematic Integration of Tertium Norms

7.5.1 Automatic Application

The normative order of the internet is made up of international norms, national norms, and transnational normative arrangements.[76] Previously, this study has argued that for a norm to be part of the normative order of the internet it must be (1) materially (non-trivially) and (2) normatively (not merely factually) connected to the internet. International legal norms, such as the principle of custodial sovereignty regarding critical internet resources, e.g. Internet Exchange Points, are part of the normative order, and, as general rules of international law, part of Germany's legal order as per Art. 25 of the Basic Law. National laws forming part of the normative order of the internet are applicable per se and provide for rights and duties for citizens without further normative intervention.

7.5.2 Post-Consent Application

The origin of norms influences their impact and legitimacy. A national norm of one country is (usually) not applied in another country. Cases of extraterritorial application of norms are few[77] and often controversial.[78] International law, by contrast, is often universally conceived and thus most states have developed techniques of integrating international legal norms. Under Article 25 of the German Basic Law, general rules of international law are an "integral part of federal law" and shall "take precedence over the laws and directly create rights and duties for the inhabitants of the federal territory." The rules are different regarding treaties. These are concluded pursuant to Article 59 (1) of the Basic Law by the Federal President, but are not directly applicable if they regulate "political relations of the Federation or relate to subjects of federal legislation." In these cases, the Basic Law reserves a role for the Bundestag. These treaties "shall require the consent or participation, in the form of a federal law, of the bodies responsible in such a case for the enactment of federal law" (Article 59 (2) of the Basic Law).[79]

[76] See chapter 6.4.2.

[77] See for instance the approach of the General Data Protection Regulation, Regulation (EU) 2016/679 OJ L 119/1 of 4 May 2016. Pursuant to Article 3(2), the GDPR applies to controllers or processors of data not established in the EU in cases where "the processing activities are related to: (a) the offering of goods or services, irrespective of whether a payment of the data subject is required, to such data subjects in the Union; or (b) the monitoring of their behaviour as far as their behaviour takes place within the Union."

[78] Cf. the US Alien Tort Claims Act of 1789: Harold Berman, "The Alien Tort Claims Act and the Law of Nations," Emory International Law Review 9 (2005), 69. For a recent application of the Act, see Deutscher Bundestag (Wissenschaftlicher Dienst), Voraussetzungen für die Zuständigkeit US-amerikanischer Gerichte nach dem Alien Torts Claim Act Schadensersatzklagen der Herero und Nama, AZ WD 2-3000-021/17, March 2, 2017, https://www.bundestag.de/blob/502258/30c9d52ce0e5a6f0a97c3e99b05264f6/wd-2-021-17-pdf-data.pdf.

[79] Article 32 (3) GG provides that insofar as "the Länder have power to legislate, they may conclude treaties with foreign states with the consent of the Federal Government."

This consent or participation, taking the form of a federal law, nationalizes the international norm (that is not already part of nationally applicable law pursuant to Article 25) by reconfiguring it as part of national law: this is the *Rechtsanwendungsbefehl.* The assessment becomes more difficult when it comes to "objective international law": norms which are universal-idealistic in character but oriented toward positive law. Their role has changed substantially in recent years to the point that they have reinvigorated and added nuance to the debate between monist and dualist approaches to international law.[80] This is especially true for the growing body of international human rights law and its judicial interpretation and ius cogens rules.

The approach pursued here goes beyond the debates surrounding monist and dualist approaches to international law. Both are of little use as dogmatic constructions for solving questions of the normativity of transnational regulation: they serve "neither analytically nor normatively as theoretical constructions"[81] to conceptualize the legal order. Dualist approaches provide little help in establishing how to integrate transnational norms (as tertium) into national legal orders, given that they argue for the existence of a primum (national law) and secundum (international law) and leave the integration of the latter into the former to national law's rules on consent acts. Monism with an international law primacy might be the base of a liberal-cosmopolitan reading of international law but suffers from the same shortcomings as global-legalist approaches. Monism with a national law primacy is difficult to unite with conceptions of an international law-based global community of states.

This act of consent remains a central figure in the integration of international/transnational rules in national legislation. Premising the "legality" of norms on formal acts of consent, however, risks ignoring the influence of transnational regulation that is not part of traditional international law (which can be "nationalized" through formal acts of consent). In the 2004 *Görgülü* decision, the German Constitutional Court confirmed that the principle according to which German judges are bound by statute and law (pursuant to Article 20 (3) of the Basic Law) includes decisions of the ECtHR "as part of a methodologically justifiable interpretation of the law":[82] "Both a failure to consider a decision of the EC[t]HR and the 'enforcement' of such a decision in a schematic way, in violation of prior-ranking law, may therefore violate fundamental rights in conjunction with the principle of the rule of law."[83]

While decisions by international courts are not per se binding, their application becomes an obligation for states when the treaty underlying their function is integrated into federal law by a parliament consent act.[84] But what, this section will ask, if such a consent act is missing? This study has posited throughout that there are non-national and non-international legal norms that form part of the normative order of the internet and are

[80] Stefan Kadelbach, "Völkerrecht als Verfassungsordnung? Zur Völkerrechtswissenschaft in Deutschland," ZaöRV 67 (2007), 599–621 (607).

[81] Armin von Bogdandy, "Prinzipien von Staat, supranationalen und internationalen Organisationen," § 232 (275–304), in Josef Isensee, Paul Kirchhof, et al. (eds.), *Handbuch des Staatsrechts, Band XI: Internationale Bezüge*, 3rd edn. (2013) (also published as Armin von Bogdandy, "Prinzipielles zur Pluralität normativer Ordnungen. Zu den Anforderungen an die Ausübung öffentlicher Gewalt," Normative Orders Working Paper 1/2013), 12 (translation by the author).

[82] BVerfG, order of the Second Senate of October 14, 2004, 2 BvR 1481/04, para. 47.

[83] Ibid.

[84] See Christoph Gusy, "Wirkungen der Rechtsprechung des Europäischen Gerichtshofs für Menschenrechte in Deutschland," JA (2009), 406; and Matthias Ruffert, "Die Europäische Menschenrechtskonvention und innerstaatliches Recht," EuGRZ (2007), 245.

procedurally and materially legitimated as norms. They are a "tertium." Thus, this study posits, not only tertium datur,[85] but so does this normative tertium contain formally and materially legitimated norms that form part of national legal systems.

7.5.3 Deformalized Application

The example of cybersecurity can illustrate what norms are to be counted as transnational normative arrangements (tertium) and not as international legal norms, which are either (as general rules of international law) an "integral part of federal law" under Article 25 of the German Basic Law or incorporated into German law through a consent act by the legislative power.

Many of the norms of cybersecurity are part of the international legal duty of cooperation.[86] Recognizing this, the GGE report of 2015 recommended setting confidence-building measures to strengthen international peace and security, which would increase interstate cooperation, transparency, predictability, and stability, in particular by facilitating "cross-border cooperation to address critical infrastructure vulnerabilities."[87] Duties to cooperate can thus be internationally legally mandated obligations for states. Depending on their normative form, they can be part of the normative tertium. This is particularly applicable for norms developed in technical norm-setting processes, such as the RFC series, or soft law standards.

As illustrated by the April 10, 2018, Council conclusions on malicious cyber activities, however, international law and transnational soft norms are often interrelated. First, the EU confirms that it is committed to upholding that "existing international law is applicable to cyberspace and emphasizes that respect for international law, in particular the UN Charter, is essential to maintaining peace and stability."[88] Yet the EU also recognizes that the interconnected nature of cyberspace necessitates "joint efforts by governments, private sector, civil society, technical community, users and academia to address the challenges faced" and calls on actors to accept their "responsibilities to maintain an open, free, secure and stable cyberspace."[89] This norm can be termed a "tertium" norm within the normative order of the internet and can be reformulated as follows: *each actor should participate in norm-making processes in light of its specific responsibilities.* Clearly, this rule cannot be directly applied by national courts. A parliamentary consent act cannot be sought due to the lack of clarity as to the normative content. However, the norm has *relevance* for national legal systems due to

[85] This study thus varies the law of the excluded middle: tertium non datur. Formulated more fully as *principium exclusi tertii sive medii inter duo contradictoria*, the notion goes back to Aristotle (Met. III, 7, p. 1011 b 23): "alla mên oude metaxy antiphaseôs endechetai einai outhen" ("there is nothing between the contradictions"), as quoted in Friedrich Kirchner, *Wörterbuch der philosophischen Grundbegriffe* (Heidelberg: Georg Weiss Verlag, 1890/1907), s.v. *Principium exclusi tertii seu medii inter duo contradictoria* (online at http://www.textlog.de/2117.html).

[86] See Rüdiger Wolfrum, "Cooperation, International Law of," in Rüdiger Wolfrum (ed.), *Max Planck Encyclopedia of Public International Law* (MPEPIL) (Oxford: OUP, 2008) (December 2010), paras. 10–12, and 3.3.4.5.

[87] United Nations, Developments in the Field of Information and Telecommunications in the Context of International Security, Report of the Secretary General, A/70/174 of July 22, 2015, http://www.un.org/ga/search/view_doc.asp?symbol=A/70/174 ("GGE report (2015)"), para. 19.

[88] Council of the European Union, Council conclusions on malicious cyber activities, 10 April 2018, Doc. 7517/18, Annex, http://www.consilium.europa.eu//media/33721/malicious-cyber-activities-en.pdf.

[89] Ibid., 3.

its soft *normativity*. It can enter national legal systems as a soft law standard, a legal tertium beyond national and international law.

Similarly, fostering and ensuring cybersecurity are prerequisites for the full realization of all human rights,[90] and as such normative approaches supporting cybersecurity are international law-based and, through national Cybersecurity Declarations (and consent acts by parliaments), form part of the "primum" and "secundum" of law from a national perspective. By contrast, the May 2017 WannaCry Ransomware attack shows how vulnerabilities are caused by a number of factors, including software companies who fail to provide updates or no longer service vulnerabilities, affected companies that have slow patch cycles, secret services that stockpile vulnerabilities, and states that do not force essential service providers (like healthcare companies) to ensure that their systems are stable and secure.[91] The norm "software companies need to provide updates and service vulnerabilities" has at least some identifiable normative content. However, it is neither international law nor national law, but rather forms a specific transnational norm.

Directive (EU) 2016/1148, concerning measures for a high common level of security of network and information systems across the Union,[92] identifies the need for "closer international cooperation to improve security standards and information exchange, and to promote a common global approach to security issues" regarding network and information systems.[93] Most of these security standards are norms that are neither national nor international law-based though they are normatively relevant for the purposes of both orders. This is particularly relevant because these norms influence directly the activities of operations of essential services and digital service providers.

The Directive also provides that a "culture of risk management, involving risk assessment and the implementation of security measures appropriate to the risks faced, should be promoted and developed through appropriate regulatory requirements and voluntary industry practices."[94] Similarly, the Directive considers that states should "encourage compliance or conformity with specified standards so as to ensure a high level of security of network and information systems at Union level"[95] and, in Article 19 (1) of the Directive, requires member states to "encourage the use of European or internationally accepted standards and specifications relevant to the security of network and information systems." Article 16 (1) references the "state of the art" that states need to consider in passing measures to ensure that digital service providers develop a normative and organizational framework responsive to the risks posed to the security of network and information systems by their services, including (lit e.) "compliance with international standards."

Thus, in this one Directive alone references are made to "appropriate regulatory requirements," "voluntary industry practices," "European standards," "internationally accepted standards," "international standards," and "specifications." All of the norms underlying

90 Matthias C. Kettemann, "Ensuring Cybersecurity through International Law," Revista Española de Derecho internacional 69 (2) (2017), 281–89, 283.

91 CCDCOE, "WannaCry Campaign: Potential State Involvement Could Have Serious Consequences," May 16, 2017, https://ccdcoe.org/wannacry-campaign-potential-state-involvement-could-have-serious-consequences.html.

92 Directive (EU) 2016/1148 of the European Parliament and of the Council of 6 July 2016 concerning measures for a high common level of security of network and information systems across the Union, OJ L 194, 19 July 2016.

93 Ibid., recital 43.

94 Ibid., recital 44.

95 Ibid., recital 66.

these normative notions belong to the tertium as neither clearly national nor clearly international. Their position and role in national legal orders is difficult to pinpoint. Generalizing assessments of their relative position are impossible to make. Transnational norms are either (1) ignored by states; (2) translated into national law (or applied after formal consent); or (3) de facto applied and, through its application, integrated and legitimized without a clear *Rechtsanwendungsbefehl*. The first "avenue" consists of a failure of effective norm propagation;[96] the second "avenue" is the traditional normative track for non-national law; the third avenue is most challenging as a tool for norm integration. Reconstructing the application of tertium norms is the task of the following sections.

7.5.4 Transposition

One approach that German law takes to incorporate tertium norms is the transposition of European legislation into national laws. With regard to the normative order of the internet, a recent example is Directive (EU) 2016/1148 of the European Parliament and of the Council of 6 July 2016 concerning measures for a high common level of security of network and information systems across the Union,[97] which was transposed into German law by a 2016 law introducing changes to the Law on the Federal Office for the Security of Information Technology (Gesetz über das Bundesamt für Sicherheit in der Informationstechnik (BSI-Gesetz—BSIG)).[98]

The Directive's recitals reference transnational regulatory arrangements, such as "security standards":[99] "appropriate regulatory requirements and voluntary industry practices […] for a culture of risk management, involving risk assessments and the implementation of security measures appropriate to the risks faced."[100] Recital 66 recalls that standardizing security requirements is a "market-driven process." States should encourage actors to comply or conform with "specified standards" to ensure the "convergent application of security standards" leading to a "high level of security of network and information systems."[101] The European institutions may even "draft harmonised standards" in accordance with Regulation (EU) 1025/2012 on European standardization.[102]

Returning to the Directive, Article 16 (1) on security requirements and incident notification obligations of digital service providers includes references to the "state of the art," that is internationally accepted standards.[103] States are obliged to ensure that digital service providers take necessary technical and organization-related measures to manage risks.

[96] See chapter 6.8.

[97] Directive (EU) 2016/1148 of the European Parliament and of the Council of 6 July 2016 concerning measures for a high common level of security of network and information systems across the Union, OJ L 194, 19 July 2016, p. 1–30.

[98] Gesetz über das Bundesamt für Sicherheit in der Informationstechnik of 14 August 2009 (BGBl. I S. 2821) (last changed by Article 1 of the Law of 23 June (BGBl. I S. 1885)).

[99] Directive (EU) 2016/1148 of the European Parliament and of the Council of 6 July 2016 concerning measures for a high common level of security of network and information systems across the Union, OJ L 194, 19 July 2016, recital 43.

[100] Ibid., recital 44.

[101] Ibid., recital 66.

[102] Regulation (EU) 1025/2012 of the European Parliament and of the Council of 25 October 2012 on European standardisation, OJ L 316/12, 14 November 2012.

[103] The new § 8c of the BSI-Gesetz turns this into the obligation to ensure an adequate level "unter Berücksichtigung des Stands der Technik."

These measures must be "state of the art" and take into account, inter alia, "compliance with international regulations." This section was transposed into German law in the new § 8c of the BSIG,[104] which translates compliance as "Einhaltung" and international standards as "internationale Normen." This illustrates one problem with the German concept of *Normen* (norms): *Normen* can be standards and *Normen* can be norms.

Article 19 of the Regulation on standardization encourages the use of standards, namely "European or internationally accepted standards and specifications relevant to the security of network and information systems," but the Regulation, as a matter of principle, recognizes the existence of "technical specifications that are not national, European or international standards."[105] These technical specifications include standard-like normative instruments that have not been formally endorsed by standard-setting organizations nationally or internationally.

As a key regulatory instrument of the normative order of the internet, Directive (EU) 2016/1148 shows clearly how references to standards and standardized practices can enter into German law through transposition of supranational law. Similarly, direct application of European regulations, such as the Standardization Regulation, provides for the inclusion of non-standard "technical specifications" into the national normative order.

7.5.5 Referencing

While soft law can be applied without formal consultation of the legislature,[106] the inclusion of soft law standards (directly or by reference) in German legislation increases their rational and formal legitimacy. This process may occur in tandem with the transposition of EU law. However, even without EU foundations, German laws regulating national aspects of the normative order of the internet have included references to transnational normative arrangements, such as internet standards. A good example is the Act on the Federal Office for Information Security, the BSIG.[107]

Already § 2 (2) of the BSIG, on the concepts used in the law, defines "security of information technology" as compliance with "certain security standards for the availability, integrity, or confidentiality of information, by means of security precautions." How can these *certain* security standards develop if not through international standard-setting in inclusive processes involving all relevant actors? Furthermore, § 3 (1) (4) defines the tasks of the Federal Office for Information Security, including "developing criteria, procedures and tools to test and evaluate the security of information

[104] Through this law: Gesetz zur Umsetzung der Richtlinie (EU) 2016/1148 des Europäischen Parlaments und des Rates vom 6. Juli 2016 über Maßnahmen zur Gewährleistung eines hohen gemeinsamen Sicherheitsniveaus von Netz- und Informationssystemen in der Union (BGBl. I, Nr. 40 of June 29, 2017).

[105] Chapter VI of Regulation (EU) 1025/2012 of the European Parliament and of the Council of 25 October 2012 on European standardisation, OJ L 316/12, 14 November 2012.

[106] Stefan Oeter, "Vom Völkerrecht zum transnationalen Recht – 'transnational administrative networks' und die Bildung hybrider Akteursstrukturen," in Gralf-Peter Calliess (ed.), *Transnationales Recht. Stand und Perspektiven* (Tübingen: Mohr Siebeck, 2014), 388–402 (394–5).

[107] BSI Act of 14 August 2009 (Federal Law Gazette I, 2821), last amended by Article 1 of the Act of 23 June 2017 (Federal Law Gazette I, 1885).

technology systems or components and to test and evaluate compliance *with IT security standards*."[108]

Similarly, § 3 (1) (6) charges the Office with "testing information technology systems and components and confirming compliance *with IT security standards* defined in the Federal Office's technical guidelines" (emphasis added). Again, these standards are not standards derived (only) from German law and practice, but rather draw substantially from international normative developments of norms that this study has identified as belonging to the normative tertium within the normative order of the internet.

German law, in casu the BSIG, distinguishes between standards developed by the Federal Office (based—as non-fragmentation-producing, standard-setting endeavors usually are—on standards developed in international normative processes or identical to them) and their "enactment" as a formal part of Germany's public law. Under § 8 (1) of the BSIG, on the Federal Office's guideline powers, the Office is provided with the power to "develop minimum standards for ensuring the security of federal information technology." In a second step, these standards can then be developed as "general administrative regulations for all federal bodies": "[i]n consultation with the Council of Chief Information Officers of the federal ministries, the Federal Ministry of the Interior may issue the standards developed in full or in part as general administrative regulations for all federal bodies."

These *standards* as *regulations* can take a different form when other bodies are involved, especially "courts and [certain] constitutional bodies," such as the Bundestag, the Bundesrat, and the Federal President (see § 2 (3), second sentence). Then the regulations have the status of *recommendations*.

A further reference included in German legislation that invokes the international normative development of transnational norms is one to "state of the art," when information and communication technologies are concerned. As argued previously, the "state of the art" can only realistically be determined with reference to sources outside of Germany. These sources are the normatively relevant practices among, and connected standards produced by, the global internet community.

Moreover, § 8a (1) BSIG obliges operations of critical infrastructures "to take appropriate organisational and technical precautionary measures in order to avoid disruptions of the availability, integrity, authenticity and confidentiality of their information technology systems, components or processes that are decisive for the functionality of the critical infrastructures operated by them" and, in so doing, "the *state of the art* shall be observed" (emphasis added). Also, § 8c (2) on special requirements regarding providers of digital services prescribes that they "shall ensure a security level of the network and information systems corresponding to the existing risk, taking into account the *state of the art*."

The last sentence of this norm confirms the integration by law of the normative tertium: "In this context," that is the one of providers of digital services ensuring appropriate security, among the "aspects" to consider we find, at number five, "the compliance with international regulations." "International regulations" figures in the law's German original as "internationale Normen." As the previous section shows, this illustrates how *Normen* (norms) can be both standards and legal norms.

[108] Emphasis added.

7.6 Reterritorialization as a Challenge to the Normative Order of the Internet

The previous sections have proven the claim that Germany's legal system systematically "nationalizes" and legitimizes the norms of the normative order of the internet through processes of, inter alia, transposition and referencing. This approach is based on the conception that the norms of the normative order of the internet need to be integrated into national law to be effectively propagated. This duty to anchor the normative order of the internet in (a) national legal system(s), however, can be viewed critically in light of the deterritorialization of law,[109] which includes a "pluralistic symbiosis of private-autonomously created norms, international law and national law."[110] Applying this definition, the norms of the normative order of the internet seem like an exemplary deterritorialized order. However, even though territoriality is challenged in different legal arenas, tying legal relations to a territory remains a key element of the process of implementing a normative order. Does this mean that we need to withdraw *in toto* any claim to a transnational normative order, which conflicts with the claim for "just one territorial legal culture and order?"[111]

The case is more differentiated. Though deterritorialization (and globalization processes) substantially challenge the classic state-oriented law paradigm,[112] states as constituted in their territories (and, essentially, *by* their territories) do not fade away: "the sovereign constitutional state does not end with the emergence of virtual space".[113] "Virtual spaces" make the essential role of states in protecting their citizens from threats emanating from new technologies more difficult to fulfill, but do not fundamentally alter it. The biggest challenge is posed by the plurality of normativity ("Regelungsmosaik"[114]). Yet public law has reacted to these developments. Scholars have identified successful processes of functional and spatial adaption.[115] Public law recognizes progressively the emergence and existence of norms from transnational spaces, their relevance and legality within national legal orders, and the existence of "social spaces in which more than territorial law is applicable."[116]

There are also strong arguments that the territoriality of the legal order of a state needs to undergo a new calibration in light of the "federalization processes" states are faced with.[117] This federalization of national legal orders needs to be both responsive to legitimate norms from non-national sources and develop normative permeability with regard to these.[118] International law especially is necessary to qualify whether "unilateral regulatory demands of powerful actors" are legitimate—or not.[119] In German constitutional law,

[109] On the notion of deterritorialization, see Kirsten Schmalenbach, "Völker- und unionsrechtliche Anstöße zur Entterritorialisierung des Rechts," VVDStRL 76 (2017), 245–76 (249).
[110] Ibid., 251–2 (translation by the author).
[111] Matthias Cornils, "Entterritorialisierung im Kommunikationsrecht," VVDStRL 76 (2017), 391–442 (436–7).
[112] See, further, 2.4.2.
[113] Hobe, Stephan, "Cyberspace—der virtuelle Raum," in Josef Isensee, Paul Kirchhof, et al. (eds.), *Handbuch des Staatsrechts, Band XI: Internationale Bezüge*, 3rd edn. (2013), § 271, no. 44 ("Der virtuelle Raum bedeutet [. . .] nicht das Ende des souveränen Verfassungsstaates" (translation by the author).
[114] Wolfgang Hoffmann-Riem, "Freiheitsschutz in den globalen Kommunikationsinfrastrukturen," JZ 69 (2014) 2, 53–63 (63).
[115] Kirsten Schmalenbach, "Völker- und unionsrechtliche Anstöße zur Entterritorialisierung des Rechts," VVDStRL 76 (2017), 245–76 (271).
[116] Ibid., 271.
[117] Ibid., 271 (translation by the author).
[118] Ibid., 272 (translation by the author).
[119] Ibid. (translation by the author).

the international law friendliness of the Basic Law internalizes (and constitutionalizes) this qualification. As this study has argued, the normative order of the internet can be qualified as legitimate by applying international law and international legal theory.[120]

Though the notion of territoriality is changing, the more important development seems to be the differentiation of international law and the emergence of functional regimes, in which sectoral regulatory objects are more relevant as qualifiers for the application of law than territoriality. This ties in with the development of international legal regimes, outside of treaty regimes, "in more broadly 'cultural' ways," as the ILC's Fragmentation Report put it.[121] These sectoral, functional regimes include non-governmental participants and "represent non-governmental interests in a fashion that might influence their interpretation and operation." They operate through normatively loose administrative coordination (or none at all) and include a cognitive-motivation element for normative engagement, namely participation as a proxy for "mutual supportiveness" to the point where participants seek regime-optimal outcomes.[122]

Regimes are thus examples of functional normativity. Jürgen Bast referred to global governance and International Public Authority as examples of functional normative layers.[123] This study argues that the normative order of the internet as a whole can be considered such a functional regime, which thus transcends territoriality as the application nexus. It is the function of the normative order, conceptualized through international legal theory and constituted by national normative orders, that gives the normative orders its normative impetus. It is a functional and necessary order. This approaches what a commentator on Bast termed the innovative "constitution of spaces [...] in the sense of output legitimation of power."[124] Indeed, the normative order of the internet is constituted in and constitutes (through auto- and hetero-constitutionalization processes)[125] the normative space of internet regulation that, in a second step, permeates national legal orders.

Rather than acceding to the territorial argument—that the normative order of the internet is only valid through its implementation in national legal orders—the functional argument reiterates that the normative order of the internet is one of necessity. It is legitimated through its effectiveness, which increases its effectivity. As Jürgen Bast argues, we need to be aware of the "*historical* gains in rationality through territorial authority"[126] (emphasis added), but also take into account that under the conditions of today's political, social, cultural, and economic processes social processes can no longer be effectively steered through normative processes within nation states. Deterritorialization of these societal processes must coincide with a deterritorialization of normative processes. This is especially true for the internet.

Yet even in light of existing normative mechanisms within (German) national law to include the newly created norms, some authors argue that deterritorializing communicative

[120] See chapter 6.6.

[121] ILC, Fragmentation of International Law: Difficulties arising from the Diversification and Expansion of International Law, Report of the Study Group of the International Law Commission, 13 April 2006, A/CN.4/L.682, 252.

[122] Ibid.

[123] Jürgen Bast, "Völker- und unionsrechtliche Anstöße zur Entterritorialisierung des Rechts," VVDStRL 76 (2017), 277–315 (292).

[124] Heiko Sauer, Aussprache, VVDStRL 76 (2017), 317 (translation by the author).

[125] See chapter 6.2.

[126] Jürgen Bast, "Völker- und unionsrechtliche Anstöße zur Entterritorialisierung des Rechts," VVDStRL 76 (2017), 277–315 (309) (translation by the author) (notes omitted).

processes has actually led to a "reterritorialization of the law of communication."[127] This argument, put forward lately by Matthias Cornils, runs counter to much of what this study has argued. He posits, inter alia, that the "expertocratic design" of normative processes is suitable for "technical-operative" questions, but there were no indicia that "transnational rule-making in the field of the law of communication [Kommunikationsrecht]" can be extended beyond that.[128] However, he admits himself that this is changing in the field of youth protection law and the law of hate speech.[129]

Though some functional areas of the normative order of the internet, such as internet standard-setting, are very effectively developed by non-state regimes,[130] states continue to regulate "localizable" dimensions of internet-related activities.[131] As long as fact patterns remain national, the legal and constitutional framework, at least in Germany according to a study on the role of the Grundgesetz in the internet age, has adapted well:[132] rule of law and peaceful relations between individuals (*Rechtsfrieden*) are assured both offline and online. While some argued that geography (or more precisely territoriality) has "ended" in terms of international law,[133] others saw rather a new role for the concept.[134] But ensuring that transnational rules within the normative order, and the order as a whole, are implemented within the territory of one state is a task that falls ultimately to the state exercising sovereignty.

The Group of Governmental Experts in its 2015 report underlined the importance of sovereignty: "State sovereignty and international norms and principles that flow from sovereignty apply to the conduct by States of ICT-related activities and to their jurisdiction over ICT infrastructure within their territory."[135] States therefore continue to have (and must exercise) jurisdiction over those parts of the internet, physical and non-kinetic, that are located within their territory, and, in doing so, ensure that the normative purposes of the normative order of the internet are implemented.

Cornils argues that states have agreed to the establishment of the internet as a "transnational entity with transnational traffic control," with the "open and ubiquitous communication" which transnational infrastructure is inherently based on. This would imply that the transborder communication flows should not be subjected to territorial "special districts [Sonderbezirke] with their own laws."[136] The history of the internet's normative evolution,[137] however, suggests that states have not actually established the internet as such an

[127] Matthias Cornils, "Entterritorialisierung im Kommunikationsrecht," VVDStRL 76 (2017), 391–442 (437).

[128] Ibid., 428 (translation by the author).

[129] Ibid., 428.

[130] Gerd Winter, "Transnationale informelle Regulierung: Gestalt, Effekte und Rechtsstaatlichkeit," in Gralf-Peter Calliess (ed.), *Transnationales Recht. Stand und Perspektiven* (Tübingen: Mohr Siebeck, 2014), 95–112 (96).

[131] Matthias C. Kettemann, *Völkerrecht in Zeiten des Netzes: Perspektiven auf den effektiven Schutz von Grund- und Menschenrechten in der Informationsgesellschaft zwischen Völkerrecht, Europarecht und Staatsrecht* (Bonn: Friedrich-Ebert-Siftung, 2015), 53 et seq.

[132] Utz Schliesky, Christian Hoffmann, Anika D. Luch, Sönke E. Schulz, and Kim Corinna Borchers, *Schutzpflichten und Drittwirkung im Internet. Das Grundgesetz im digitalen Zeitalter* (Baden-Baden: Nomos, 2014), 146.

[133] See David Bethlehem, "The End of Geography: The Changing Nature of the International System and the Challenge to International Law," EJIL 25 (2014) 1, 9–24.

[134] David S. Koller and Carl Landauer: David S. Koller, "The End of Geography: The Changing Nature of the International System and the Challenge to International Law: A Reply to Daniel Bethlehem," EJIL 25 (2014) 1, 25–29 and Carl Landauer, "The Ever-Ending Geography of International Law: The Changing Nature of the International System and the Challenge to International Law: A Reply to Daniel Bethlehem," EJIL 25 (2014) 1, 31–34.

[135] GGE report (2015), para. 27.

[136] Matthias Cornils, "Entterritorialisierung im Kommunikationsrecht," VVDStRL 76 (2017), 391–442 (436) (notes omitted) (translation by the author).

[137] See chapter 3.4.4.

entity, but it has emerged in a bottom-up, decentralized, and mainly expert-led process over decades.

It was also, arguably, not *states* that influenced the emergence of the fundamental administrative infrastructure of the internet but rather *a state*, namely the USA. It was not until the mid-1990s that discussions on internationalizing and diversifying accountability over decisions regarding critical internet resources resulted in the commitment by the US government to transition IANA functional management to ICANN as a private sector entity.[138]

The cross-border data flows characteristic of the internet and the bordered nature of states (limiting organically their jurisdiction) are in conflict.[139] But Cornils seems to make the case that the "transport level and internet regulation [...] are not necessarily normatively firmly correlated," thus "allowing only a regulatory minimum on the level of application."[140] This approach of *two* "levels" of rules on the internet is not sufficiently detailed. As this study has shown above,[141] more nuanced approaches[142] to the internet argue for the existence of at least four "internet layers." These range from physical infrastructure and logical resources (including IP addresses) (and often a third transport layer) to an application(s) and content/transactions (data) layer, but often also include a specific legal layer (national law, international law). There are thus not only a transport layer and a regulatory layer.

Further, authors seeking to differentiate between the "universal" technological dimension and the "local"/"national," regulatory/legal dimension often focus on the case of China's model of censorship[143] to show that the choice of how content is regulated remains a purely national one. It is correct that attempts by sovereignty-oriented states, such as Russia, UAE, China, Saudi Arabia, Algeria, Sudan, and Egypt, to include greater state oversight over infrastructure and logical layer-related decisions have been largely unsuccessful,[144] while national regulatory internet management has been scaled up, by some states, to restrictive and authoritarian levels without clear condemnation by the international community.

China itself, in an earlier white paper, argues that an "authoritative and just international internet administration organization" should be installed under UN auspices with all countries being able to participate "in the administration of the fundamental international resources of the internet, and a multilateral and transparent allocation system should be established on the basis of the current management mode."[145] However, section III of the white paper references the importance of human rights ("Chinese citizens fully enjoy freedom of speech on the internet"[146]). While this is inaccurate in light of

[138] US DOC/NTIA, Management of Internet Names and Addresses, ICANN Statement of Policy ("White Paper"), June 10, 1998, http://www.icann.org/en/about/agreements/whitepaper. Cf. Mueller et al. (2007), 238–40.

[139] See chapter 4.3.4.

[140] Matthias Cornils, "Entterritorialisierung im Kommunikationsrecht," VVDStRL 76 (2017), 391–442 (438) (translation by the author).

[141] See chapter 4.3.1.

[142] These include Laura DeNardis, "One Internet: An Evidentiary Basis for Policy Making on Internet Universality and Fragmentation," CIGI/Chatham House, Global Commission on Internet Governance Paper Series No. 38 (2016), 4; William J. Drake, Vinton G. Cerf, and Wolfgang Kleinwächter, "Internet Fragmentation: An Overview," World Economic Forum, Future of the Internet Initiative White Paper, January 2016, 14.

[143] Matthias Cornils, "Entterritorialisierung im Kommunikationsrecht," VVDStRL 76 (2017), 391–442 (434).

[144] Russia, UAE, China, Saudi Arabia, Algeria, Sudan, and Egypt, Proposal for the Work of the Conference [WCIT-12], ITU Doc. DT-X of 5 December 2012, WCIT12/27(Rev.1)-E, §§ 3A.2 and 3A.3, http://files.wcitleaks.org/public/Merged%20UAE%20081212.pdf.

[145] People's Republic of China, State Council, The Internet in China, June 8, 2010, http://www.china.org.cn/government/whitepaper/node_7093508.htm, sect. I.

[146] Ibid., chapter 3.

international human rights standards,[147] it shows that national regulation, even in illiberal states (in terms of internet rule), refers to international standards. In addition, the Chinese member of the UN Group of Independent Experts did not object to the commitment, in the GGE report of 2015, to international law as being applicable to ICTs and on the internet as a whole.

This brings us to the argument that only a "minimum" of rules can be developed regarding the non-transport dimension of the internet in light of the challenges of territoriality. This is inaccurate. As the GGE report of 2015 concluded, "international law [is] an essential framework for [state] actions in their use of ICTs."[148] Six principles are particularly relevant: state sovereignty; sovereign equality; settlement of international disputes by peaceful means; non-intervention in the internal affairs of other States; prohibition of the threat or use of force; and respect for human rights and fundamental freedoms.[149]

As previously shown,[150] rather than being inapplicable to the normative challenges of the internet, due to the bordered nature of some regulatory questions, international law (especially through its human rights regime) protects individuals on the internet (and from dangers emanating from the internet). This study has shown the power of general principles of international law which, in aggregate, provide substantial protection for the internet's integrity and, conversely, protect states (and individuals) from attacks through cyberspace. Applicable principles (and largely customary norms) include the non-use of (the threat of) force, peaceful settlement of international disputes, non-intervention in domestic affairs, the duty of cooperation, the principle of sovereign equality, the no harm principle, the principle of good faith, and the principle of prevention and due diligence.

When Cornils argues that content regulation just as the control over physical internet infrastructure remains "in essence a domain of states and conglomerates of states,"[151] he fails to add that this regulation can only be exercised within the limits imposed upon states by international legal norms within the normative order of the internet. States that exercise control over critical internet resources, especially infrastructure, are bound by customary international duties based on the recognition that the protection of and from the internet lies in the common interest.[152] This has been discussed in this study under the notion of custodial sovereignty.[153] States that exercise authority over critical internet resources, such as infrastructural resources, act as custodians of the global interest in the internet's integrity which the resource located in their territory, such as an important Internet Exchange Point or a root server, contributes to. So as to ensure that states exercise this custodial duty in a way that meets their international obligations, other states have certain monitoring rights and assistance duties.[154]

[147] Cf. Rebecca MacKinnon, *Consent of the Networked. The Worldwide Struggle for Internet Freedom* (New York: Basic Books, 2012), 133–9 (recounting Yahoo's complicity in human rights violations in China).
[148] GGE report (2015), para. 25.
[149] Ibid., para. 26.
[150] See chapter 3.5.
[151] Matthias Cornils, "Entterritorialisierung im Kommunikationsrecht," VVDStRL 76 (2017), 391–442 (431).
[152] See chapter 2.3.
[153] See chapter 2.3.5.
[154] Cf. Wolfgang Benedek, Koen De Feyter, Matthias C. Kettemann, and Christina Voigtde, "Introduction," in Wolfgang Benedek et al. (eds.), *The Common Interest in International Law* (Antwerp: Intersentia, 2014), 1–8.

7.7 Conclusions

Having shown earlier in this study that a normative turn has taken place on the internet and that the normative order of the internet thus constituted is legitimated in international norm-making arenas by the inclusion of all relevant actors in normative processes, this chapter takes on the more challenging task of establishing how the normative order of the internet is integrated in national legal orders. This is a key argumentative step because the legitimacy of the normative order as such and of its norms is dependent not only on self-constitutionalization processes but on the acceptance by overarching regimes, international law, and national legal systems, which is symbolically validated through system interaction.

The integration of the tertium norms from the normative order of the internet into national legal orders can be assimilated to an external "constitutionalization" of the normative order of the internet through national law. (National) law, as Karl-Heinz Ladeur writes, integrates the norms which were privately produced in a self-organized manner: "it makes their content more binding and their applicability last longer; the self-binding nature of the norm is enriched by a *Fremdbindung*."[155]

In terms of international law, the process of norm production that is characterized by the inclusion of all relevant actors serves as a powerful proxy for intrinsic legitimation. This is shown to be different for national legal systems which are more wedded to the traditional notion of legitimacy of norms through their emergence in constitutionally framed normative processes. But national legal systems are imbued with an important protection function toward its citizens and, as member of the international legal community, the global public.

The chapter proves the hypothesis that through integration by national legal systems, in this case the German one, the norms of the normative order of the internet are legitimated. This particularly concerns, as has been shown, one category of the three that make up the normative order of the internet: the transnational normative arrangements and standards which amount to a "tertium" alongside international legal rules and national norms.

The chapter has identified three major arenas of integration of "tertium" norms from within the normative order of the internet. First, constitutional integration, which is premised upon the recognition by the state's constitution, the Basic Law in this case, of multinormative influences, characterized then by a certain permeability of the constituted order and an openness toward norms emanating from the normative order of the internet. Second, normative order norms, especially tertium norms, are integrated by the judicial system, which recognizes the importance of reacting dynamically to emerging threats. This means taking into account the non-binary and flexible normativity of transnational normative arrangements within the bounds of German law in deciding cases. As a case in point the study shows how internet access as a precondition for exercising fundamental rights is ensured by the judicial system.

The human rights standards applied in these settings have international legal foundations, but are also developed, and necessarily so, from a national perspective, through a process described as horizontal application (or horizontalization) of human rights (protection).[156] This development is an important aspect of the progressive crystallization of

[155] Karl-Heinz Ladeur, "Die objektiv-rechtliche Dimension der wirtschaftlichen Grundrechte – Relativierung oder Abstützung der subjektiven Freiheitsrechte," in Thomas Vesting and Ino Augsberg (eds.), *Karl-Heinz Ladeur. Das Recht der Netzwerkgesellschaft* (Tübingen: Mohr, 2013), 497–518 (514) (translation, italics by the author).

[156] Lars Viellechner, *Transnationalisierung des Rechts* (Weilerswist: Velbrück, 2013), 217.

transnational constitutional law[157] at the intersection of a plurality of normative orders. Or as Stefan Kadelbach put it, human rights travel through a progressive attachment not to state territories, "but to actors as well, so that they cross state borders with international organisations, transnational enterprises, or development agencies"[158] or, it may be added, while navigating on the internet.

Courts, especially, apply a horizontalized version of national human rights to tertium norms and thereby preempt the application of (internet) standards that violate tenets of national legal orders. As Gerd Winter argues, the normative approaches of private actors (and many tertium norms are the results of such normative projects) cannot create islands of exclusively private norms within sovereign states.[159] The legislative duty to protect the rights of all within a state's territory or under its control cannot be avoided by states. However, we can coclude that states should exercise caution in demanding the sine qua non application of their national constitutional human rights protection framework. If every state evaluates all emerging non-traditional norms in light of all human rights (especially ex ante), transnational cooperation becomes difficult.[160]

Third, and most tellingly, the chapter analyzes the systematic integration of "tertium" norms within German law. It is here that traditional normative processes of including non-legal (i.e. non-binding) norms are shown to develop into a meaningful instrument to legitimize these norms and with it the order. The study differentiates between automatic application of tertium norms and application after a form of "consent" by the state. Most interesting, however, are the deformalized processes of applying tertium norms. Finally, transposition and referencing, both well-entrenched legislative techniques, are presented and examples of their application to, and thereby legitimation of, tertium norms are provided.

In a concluding section, the study shows how reterritorialization of the normative order of the internet seems to run counter to the international and non-bounded character of the internet. Yet, a functional perspective on "nationalization" trends of especially tertium norms will lead to the conclusion that additional legitimacy-conferral mechanisms (including habituation to these norms when they are integrated into national legal processes) add an important national layer to the international legitimation approaches previously described.

[157] Stefan Kadelbach and Thomas Kleinlein, "Überstaatliches Verfassungsrecht," AVR (2006), 235. For a more function-oriented analysis, see Anne Peters, "Compensatory Constitutionalism: The Function and Potential of Fundamental International Norms and Structures," Leiden Journal of International Law (2006), 579.

[158] Stefan Kadelbach, "The Territoriality and Migration of Fundamental Rights," in Günther Handl, Joachim Zekoll, and Peer Zumbansen (eds.), *Beyond Territoriality. Transnational Legal Authority in an Age of Globalization* (Leiden/Boston: Martinus Nijhoff, 2012), 295–326 (323).

[159] Gerd Winter, "Transnationale informelle Regulierung: Gestalt, Effekte und Rechtsstaatlichkeit," in Gralf-Peter Calliess (ed.), *Transnationales Recht. Stand und Perspektiven* (Tübingen: Mohr Siebeck, 2014), 95–112 (111–12).

[160] Ibid., 111.

8
Conclusions

The internet has evolved into a central medium for societal interaction, individually and communally, locally and globally. Our communicative practices have changed substantially. This has impacted the development and application of rules for the internet. Online just as offline, law is society's most important medium to ensure order, rule, and justice. Understanding the genesis, content, and legitimation of legal and non-legal rules on the internet, and the constitution of *the* rule of the internet, thus becomes essential. The supposition that the complexity of the internet's relational space can only be met with an equally sophisticated multilayered model of a regulatory order makes intuitive sense. But the normative order of the internet—posited as such for the first time in this study—is part of an epistemic exercise of complexity *reduction*. By explaining the genesis, ontology, and legitimation of the normative order of the internet, this study decomplexifies and demystifies rules and rule on the internet and has developed a unique theory of online regulation. The study shows, importantly, that there is *a* rule on the internet and that international rules (or norms), national laws, and transnational regulatory arrangements are all essential parts of this theory of online rule and regulation..

The study is neither motivated by utopian ideals of the internet as a liberating medium, nor is it characterized by technocratic pessimism. Information and communication technologies are not imbued with ethereal qualities. Rather, they are the objects of regulation, to which norms of different origin are applied. Similarly, code and algorithms, Internet Exchange Points, and clouds are not actants in the sense of Bruno Latour. Though code and algorithms produce normative effects and Internet Exchange Points, cloud services providers and communication platforms exercise (some degree of) control and power over vast amounts of data running through or stored on their infrastructure, they are constrained by regulation and subjected to norms forming part of the normative order of the internet.

The overall question that motivates this research is related to a concept this study established for the first time: the *normative order of the internet*. What is the genealogy, ontology, legitimacy, finality, and impact of the normative order of the internet? Put differently: how did it evolve, what is it made up of, how is it legitimized, what is its regulatory goal, and how is it (and its constituent norms) implemented and legitimated within and through the international legal order and in national legal orders?

The leading hypothesis of this study is that actors on the internet fulfill diverse functions as norm entrepreneurs, norm appliers, and norm enforcers. States, individuals, and private sector companies create and execute, contest and confirm norms. The norms' genealogy, legitimacy, and enforceability vary greatly: from normative practices to non-binding standards by standard-setting bodies, from laws and national constitutions to ius cogens norms. It is only through a careful analysis of the facticity and normativity of the rules applied on the internet in these interactions that a model of a comprehensive and nuanced normative order of the internet can be distilled. Importantly, this order—though conceived holistically

The Normative Order of the Internet. Matthias C. Kettemann, Oxford University Press (2020). © Matthias C. Kettemann.
DOI: 10.1093/oso/9780198865995.001.0001

with a unifying function—is hybrid in nature and is made up of international legal norms, national law, and transnational regulatory arrangements.

This normative order of the internet integrates norms that are materially and normatively connected to the use and development of the internet at three different levels (national, regional, international), of two types (privately and publicly authored), and of substantially different character (from ius cogens to technical standards). It is shown to be a legal order that operates through the form of law and analogously to it. Its actors—states, legal persons, natural persons—fulfill diverse functions as norm entrepreneurs, norm appliers, and norm enforcers. As this study has demonstrated, the order's justification narratives control new norms by assessing their technical consistency and legal-cultural consonancy with the order's purpose. Though not without autonomous elements, the normative order of the internet is interlinked through legitimation relationships with national and international legal orders.

The normative order of the internet is decidedly not a hierarchical system of explicit norms in the Kelsenian tradition. There is no *Grundnorm*. It is rather a complex of norms, values, and practices that relate to the use and development of the internet. Through the order, the activities and interaction of different actors—including states, private companies, and civil society, as they relate to, or are mediated by, the internet—are regulated, and the exercise of private or public authority and the distribution of basic goods, including internet access and access to internet content, are normatively framed. The normative order of the internet is thus the set of norms, normative expectations, and legitimation narratives that shape the use and development of the internet. This being in essence a study grounded in law, the epistemic spotlight remained on the normativity of the order, though the importance of narratives in establishing justification (orders) is expressly noted.

This internet has indeed developed into a vital medium of communication through which individuals exercise their human rights, especially through the enabling right of freedom of expression, including the right to seek, receive, and impart information and ideas of all kinds, through any media of one's choice, regardless of frontiers. "The internet," however, is not an ethereal subject of utopian normative projects and projections; it is merely a hardware-based data-transfer capability, running software based on protocols that ensure interconnectivity. Both the internet's public core and the servers necessary for it to function are indispensable for critical infrastructure (power grids, for example) to work and are, in themselves, critical (information) infrastructure. Therefore, safeguarding the internet's integrity (its security, stability, robustness, resilience, and functionality) in the common interest has evolved into an international legal obligation of states, individually and as members of the global community. This obligation is meant to mitigate substantial societal risks incurred by states, their citizens, and the private sector by misues of the internet and attacks against the integrity of the internet.

As this study has demonstrated, the normative actors on the internet have influenced the composition of the medium of law, as it applies to online settings, and have moved it toward a more flexible geometry of normativity. Non-binding norms and principles, standards, and code have developed into a "tertium," a third category of norms apart from international and national norms. Emerging in the contested space between technical necessity and socio-legal values, they evidence a variable normative density and transcend legal binarity (lawful/unlawful) in their content. Yet this non-legal normativity needs to be (and actually is) reoriented through a value-based normative approach that nevertheless embraces standard-setting procedures, including internal norm (re)production mechanisms of technical standard-setters. Thus refuting the internal logics of technicity as controlling (in) normative debates, the study confirms that code *is* law in that it is normative, but not law in the sense that it supplants legal norms or is hierarchically superior or practically controlling. Code does not just appear, it is written in processes that can be regulated, by coders who can be subjected to norms, employed by companies with values and targets to be debated in public forums, with aims and functions that can be measured against the finalities of the normative order of the internet. Protocols therefore "have politics" and norms need to be consistently applied to their development and implementation. This finding applies to algorithms and algorithmic decision-making, including selection and recommendations logics that have clear implications for rights and freedoms, by, for example, influencing design and content of the informational basis for discourse essential to any democratic society in algorithmified media markets.

In a substance-oriented analysis of international legal rules applicable to the internet, arguments for the development of a *new* system of "international law for the internet" are shown to be without foundation. International law fully applies to the internet. Sovereignty over territory and all layers/artifacts of the internet within them is exercised by nation states increasingly effectively, sometimes overzealously, but based on constitutional obligations to secure rights of citizens and international law. Though there are no general international conventions pertaining to the management and use of the internet, its technical foundations are protected indirectly through the enabling dimension of human rights treaties. There are no customary rules that directly protect the integrity of the internet, but important general principles of international law that offer indirect protection of and from the internet, some of which have crystallized into binding custom or have even reached ius cogens status and can now, as is shown, be applied to the internet. One example is the inclusion of cyberattacks as prohibited forms of the use of force and as a prohibited form of intervention, if the level of "force" is not quite reached, in the non-intervention principle

Apart from international law, the second foundational order of the internet is the normatively less stringent but nevertheless influential internet governance regime. The norms developed within the normative processes of internet governance are part of the category of transnational regulatory arrangements, which form—as was hypothesized—an element of the normative order of the internet. Internet governance is a normatively valuable addition to international law as a system of stewardship of internet resources and the sociopolitical processes related to their steering. It normatively frames, in a non-binary (legal/illegal) logic, with varying, flexible normativity, the "softer" and "broader" topics of internet regulation, such as accountability in contrast to traditional (international) legal approaches focusing on, say, international cooperation to fight cybercrime. Yet the study critically engages internet governance processes and shows them to suffer from normative indeterminateness. The constant commitment to the integration of all actors in normative processes ("multistakeholderism') also suffers from substantial conceptual deficits, as references to the importance of the concept cloud meaningful discussion on the realization of the goals pursued by such an integrative normative approach. Process is important, but (the normative) product, too. Yet the inclusion of multiple actors that have (to varying degrees) legally protected, or at least legally relevant, interests in the outcome of an international normative process is not per se new in international law, as examples from civil society participation in treaty-making in environmental law and international criminal law demonstrate.

Before developing the notion of the normative order of the internet further, the study then addresses dimensions of disorder on the internet. Acknowledging that every (legal) order has chaotic tendencies, the lack of formal institutions (such as in national law), or decentralized control through states (such as the rules of international law), makes the internet especially prone to normative disorder. Three phenomena are identified: (1) normative froth is present when a number of different norms are applicable to similar situations without clear indications that one norm is preferred. During the "internet principle hype" many actors developed similar norms without recourse to another or any sensitivity to the liquidification of commitments by their variation. In that, an exercise in norm-making can have anti-normative effects, just as attempts to introduce a new standard to supplant existing ones may result in just *another* standard. (2) Normative frictions are more serious norm conflicts that go beyond non-hierarchical coexistence of duplicative or slightly varied norms. Examples include diverging national judgments on factually similar issues or when states introduce regulation that is not responsive to similar challenges in neighboring jurisdictions. (3) Normative fractures evidence a larger problem of rule on the internet and include substantial conflicts (of norms, practices, or even trust) that can lead to disorder. Fractures have appeared, for instance, in the normative treatment of cyberwar, with some states arguing for and others against inclusion of cyberattacks into the logic of the UN Charta's Chapter VII. This has even led to the breakdown of an important UN-led exercise in developing shared understandings of the meaning of international law on the internet. Further fractures, as this study shows, have appeared with regard to normative approaches between human rights-oriented states, such as Sweden and Switzerland, and sovereignty-oriented states, such as Russia and China, that seek, and regulate for, more governmental control of the internet, nationalize telecommunications providers, provide for data localization laws, and apply strong penalties to online dissent (or filter dissenting speech).

Serious counterarguments against the validity of the normative order of the internet, as a unifying concept, can be drawn from the technical, commercial, and governmental fragmentation of the internet. Technical fragmentation impedes the full interoperability of the underlying internet infrastructure. Commercial fragmentation is caused by business practices constraining or preventing internet universality. Political-legal, or governmental, fragmentation includes policies, laws, and judgments that inhibit the free flow of information regardless of frontiers.

Proving the hypothesis correct, the study identifies countervailing technical forces (the internet invariants), which are the foundation of a technical defragmentation pull that the law—through the normative turn—realizes through norms. Interoperability theory and jurisdiction-based conflict-of-laws approaches are also shown to work toward a unified normative order of the internet.

In order to situate the normative order of the internet within theoretical approaches to establish (online) order, the objectification and formalization, rationalization and normalization (and thus coherence-controlling) functions of ordering are theoretically established. The rich body of theories on order(ing) is parsed with a view to their relevance to the normative order of the internet. Systems theory, in particular, proves relevant with its description of binary coding as a property of the legal system. This theoretical import is meaningfully coupled with theories of dehierarchization, which transcend the presupposition of the existence of basic norms in legal systems and focus on norms as products of the "network society" (and sectors of society) constituting it.

No single theory of the normative order of the internet has yet emerged, but as, in Kuhn's terminology, the paradigm shift toward a normative order of the internet seems imminent, key theoretical imports are made that help delineate and substantiate that order. These imports include notions of the fluidity of the normative, the concept of meta-law influencing the evolution of order, the dehierarchization of norms and normative systems, the tendencies of normative orders to fragment, the transnational politicization of commons-management, and the role of governing by control over infrastructure.

Having laid the necessary theoretical foundations, the study—in a key step—then posits the emergence of a *normative order of the internet*. This approach has considerable explanatory and predictive potential as to the evolution of norms impacting the use and development of the internet. At this point the study answers some of the key elements of the questions formulated at the beginning and, as has been hypothesized, establishes that a normative turn has taken place on the internet: the normative order's internal rules of norm-production produce the technological and societal forces that, through "learning normativity," develop norms autonomously within the order, but controlled by the principles of the order. These norms are contested—as they emerge—in light of their internal coherence, their consonance with other order norms, and their consistency with the order's finality. However, normativity that learns from its environment can no longer be described using traditional categories of, and criteria for, subjectivity. Thus a theory of normativity ("of the law") that goes back to Kant needs to be fundamentally rethought: with norm-based self-organization as the principle of life that enables the transcendental constitution of normativity.

The study shows that a normative order of the internet has emerged that self-constitutionalizes, builds its own "nomos," and stabilizes this nomos through narratives it produces. The order does not ab initio depend on a state but includes states as normative actors and national law as a central source of both norms and the legitimation of transnational normative arrangements. Importantly, the study shows how a normative order has emerged on the internet that conceptually encompasses normative activities by all actors on all regulatory levels (national and international juro-political spheres and private spaces). The order is selective in that it does not seek to regulate all fact patterns with a connection to the internet, but only those that evidence a (1) *material (non-trivial) connection* between the regulatory question and the internet as a network of networks (2) *in the normative sense*.

The normative order of the internet encompasses norm-generative processes and includes, through its processes, normatively relevant action by all actors. These actors develop normative expectations, which are debated, contested, and realized on the basis of shared principles within the order. The study shows which substantial and procedural principles are applicable, including commitments to ensuring human rights, keeping the internet as an unfragmented space, and ensuring the security, stability, reliability, and trustworthiness of the internet, premised upon a strong cooperation between actors. Such cooperation is proceduralized within the order as well.

As hypothesized, the normative order of the internet is a legitimate order, with its legitimacy proceduralized through normative processes that include all actors. As shown, the order is also legitimate in a utilitarian reading because it is a *necessary* order. States cannot by themselves regulate the internet; international legal norms, or public law, are not enough. International law provides a regulatory frame but is not detailed enough to regulate emerging online threats and technological challenges. Transnational arrangements alone cannot solve questions of distribution of basic goods and rights and legitimize—by themselves—the exercise of international public authority. Taken together, however, the order's norms secure the internet as a critical infrastructural resource and as equally critical for other essential infrastructures.

Each field of norms within the order is legitimized through either traditional normative processes (international law, national law) or by its integration into national legal orders (transnational normative arrangements). Each actor group in the norm-making processes is legitimized directly or indirectly and transfers this legitimacy potential to the normative outcome, which is often—additionally—epistemically legitimate. The normative order itself is legitimate (additionally) as a necessary order to ensure protection of and from the internet. The process of justifying the order is narrativized. As any order participant has a right to justification against norms and practices generally reciprocally, the normative order of the internet is an order of justification.

In the concluding chapter, the study delves more deeply into the relationship of national legal orders and the normative order of the internet, especially in light of processes of legitimation of the "tertium" norms, the category that includes standards and other transnational normative arrangements. Internationally, the norm creation process, which allows for the integration of all actors, legitimizes the normative outcome. This is not a particularly new approach for international law, but its link to the normative order of the internet has not yet been clearly made. Tertium norms have been progressively recognized within national legal orders through processes of formal and non-formal application, transposition, and referencing.

The normative order of the internet thus established, parsed, and legitimized is both an empirical-conceptual and a normative construct: it provides legitimacy (and justification) narratives and functions as an elastic normative space, with principles and processes for solving public policy conflicts connected to safeguarding the internet's integrity and protecting states and societies, natural and legal persons, from dangers related to internet use and misuse. It importantly includes the normative tertium and is thus a unifying theory. These transnational norms and normative arrangements transcend binary normative solutions and can counteract diffusions of regulatory responsibility in transnational settings.

Establishing the normative order of the internet was a conservative exercise in that the study showed how to secure not the internet, which is merely a technological facility, but the interests of all actors, individually and collectively, in the use and development of the internet insofar as this invokes the exercise of private or public authority and the distribution of basic goods and rights.

We can conclude: if the project of establishing a normative order of the internet undertaken in this study has succeeded, it is at this point of the study evident that law (as a system with the *function* of protecting shared values, legitimizing the exercise of authority and the distribution of basic goods and rights) does not follow technicity (as a quasi-normative *form*). This is both an empirical and a normative argument. Rather, only a holistic and systematic approach to normative ordering on the internet, as has been pursued in this study, can lead to a theory of a just rule on (and of) the internet.

This rule must protect rights and values online (the internet's nomos), legitimize the exercise of private and public authority (through stabilizing the nomos normatively and through narratives), and ensure the fair distribution of basic goods and rights as they relate to the internet, including internet access and access to internet content.

Bibliography

Books and Articles

Abbate, Janet, *Inventing the Internet* (Cambridge: MIT Press, 2009)

Ablon, Lillian, Martin C. Libicki, and Andrea A. Golay, "Markets for Cybercrime Tools and Stolen Data. Hackers' Bazaar," RAND National Security Research Division (March 2014), http://www.rand.org/pubs/research_reports/RR610.html

Access Now, "Internet Shutdowns in Context," Insights from the Shutdown Tracker Optimization Project, September 11, 2017, https://www.accessnow.org/keepiton

Ackerman, Bruce, *We the People: Foundations* (Cambridge: Harvard University Press, 1991)

Afisha Daily, "Альтернативный интернет из России: что это такое и чем он нам грозит," November 30, 2017, https://daily.afisha.ru/technology/7543-alternativnyy-internet-iz-rossii-chto-eto-takoe-i-chem-on-nam-grozit

Agamben, Giorgio, *Ausnahmezustand* (Homo sacer, part II, vol. 1) (Frankfurt am Main: Suhrkamp, 2004)

Alexander, Adam, "Digital Surveillance 'Worse Than Orwell,' Says New UN Privacy Chief," *The Guardian*, August 24, 2015, http://www.theguardian.com/world/2015/aug/24/we-need-geneva-convention-for-the-internet-says-new-un-privacy-chief

Alexy, Robert, *Theorie der Grundrechte* (Frankfurt am Main: Suhrkamp, 1986)

Allen, Paul G., "The Singularity Isn't Near," MIT Technology Review, October 12, 2011, https://www.tech nologyreview.com/s/425733/paul-allen-the-singularity-isnt-near

Allott, Philip, "The Idealist's Dilemma: Re-Imagining International Society," EJIL: Talk!, June 9, 2014, https://www.ejiltalk.org/the-idealists-dilemma-re-imagining-international-society

Alonso, Juan, "The Logical Structure of Principles in Alexy's Theory. A Critical Analysis," Revus - Journal for Constitutional Theory and Philosophy of Law 28 (2016), 53–61

Alpaydin, Ethem, *Machine Learning* (Cambridge, MA: MIT Press, 2016)

Anders, Günther, *Die Antiquiertheit des Menschen Bd. I: Über die Seele im Zeitalter der zweiten industriellen Revolution* (Frankfurt am Main: Beck, 2009)

Angwin, Julia, "Make Algorithms Accountable," *New York Times*, August 1, 2016, https://www.nytimes.com/2016/08/01/opinion/make-algorithms-accountable.html

Arangio-Ruiz, Gaetano, "The Normative Role of the General Assembly of the United Nations and the Declaration of Principles of Friendly Relations," Recueil des Cours de l'Academie de Droit International 137 (1972), 419–742

Auerbach, Karl, "Deconstructing Internet Governance" (2004), http://www.cavebear.com/archive/rw/deconstructing-internet-governance-ITU-Feb26-27-2004.htm

Aust, Helmut Philipp, "Opinion of the Expert Witness Testimony," June 5, 2014, 1st Investigation Committee of the 18th German Bundestag, https://www.bundestag.de/blob/282870/fc52462f2ffd-254849bce19d 25f72fa2/mat_a_sv-4-1_aust-pdf-data.pdf

Austin, J. L., *How To Do Things With Words* (Cambridge, MA: Harvard University Press, 1962/1975)

Baak, Jeonghyun and Carolina Rossini, "Issue Comparison of Major Declarations on Internet Freedom" (2013), https://bestbits.net/wp-uploads/2013/10/ChartConceptNote_MB_CR.pdf

Bäckstrand, Karin, "Multi-Stakeholder Partnerships for Sustainable Development: Rethinking Legitimacy, Accountability and Effectiveness," *European Environment* 16 (2006) 5, 290–306

Baird, Stacy A., "Government Role and the Interoperability Ecosystem," I/S: A Journal of Law and Policy 5 (2009), 2, 219–90

Bannelier, Karine and Theodore Christakis, "Cyber-Attacks—Prevention-Reactions: The Role of States and Private Actors," Les Cahiers de la Revue Défense Nationale, Paris (2017), https://papers.ssrn.com/sol3/papers.cfm?abstract_id=2941988

Barlow, John Perry, "A Declaration of the Independence of Cyberspace," Davos, February 8, 1996, https://projects.eff.org/~barlow/Declaration-Final.html

Bast, Jürgen, "Völker- und unionsrechtliche Anstöße zur Entterritorialisierung des Rechts," VVDStRL 76 (2017), 277–315

Baur, Dorothea, *NGOs as Legitimate Partners of Corporations. A Political Conceptualization* (Heidelberg: Springer, 2012)

BBC, "Scorpions Censored," August 12, 2008, https://www.bbc.co.uk/6music/news/20081208_scorpians.shtml

Becker, Claus, *Von Namen und Nummern. Kollisionen unverträglicher Rechtsmassen im Internet* (Baden-Baden: Nomos 2005)

Behr, Ines von, Anais Reding, Charlie Edwards, and Luke Gribbon, "Radicalisation in the Digital Era. The Use of the Internet in 15 Cases of Terrorism and Extremism," RAND Europe (2013), https://www.rand.org/content/dam/rand/pubs/research_reports/RR400/RR453/RAND_RR453.pdf

Benedek, Wolfgang, "Human Security and Prevention of Terrorism," in Wolfgang Benedek and A. Yotopoulos-Marangopoulos (eds.), *Anti-terrorist Measures and Human Rights* (Leiden: Brill, 2004), 171–83

Benedek, Wolfgang and Matthias C. Kettemann, "Menschliche Sicherheit und Menschenrechte," in Claudia Ulbert and Sascha Werthes (eds.), *Menschliche Sicherheit. Globale Herausforderungen und regionale Perspektiven* (Vienna/Baden-Baden: Nomos, 2008), 94–109

Benedek, Wolfgang, Veronika Bauer, and Matthias C. Kettemann (eds.), *Internet Governance and the Information Society: Global Perspectives and European Dimensions* (Utrecht: Eleven International Publishing, 2008)

Benedek, Wolfgang, "The Human Security Approach to Terrorism and Organized Crime in Post-Conflict Situations," in Wolfgang Benedek, Christopher Daase, Vojin Dimitrijevic, and Petrus van Duyne (eds.), *Transnational Terrorism, Organized Crime and Peace Building* (London: Palgrave, 2010), 3–16

Benedek, Wolfgang, "Mainstreaming Human Security in United Nations and European Union Peace and Crisis Management Operations: Policies and Practice," in Wolfgang Benedek, Matthias C. Kettemann and Markus Möstl (eds.), *Mainstreaming Human Security in Peace Operations and Crisis Management. Policies, Problems, Potential* (Routledge: London, 2010), 13–31

Benedek, Wolfgang, "Multi-Stakeholderism in the Development of International Law," in Ulrich Fastenrath, Rudolf Geiger, Daniel-Erasmus Khan, Andreas Paulus, Sabine von Schorlemer, and Christoph Vedder (eds.), *From Bilateralism to Community Interest. Essays in Honour of Bruno Simma* (Oxford: OUP, 2011), 201–10

Benedek, Wolfgang, "The Relevance of Multi-Stakeholder Approach and Multi-Track Diplomacy for Human Rights Diplomacy," in Michael O'Flaherty et al. (ed.), *Human Rights Diplomacy: Contemporary Perspectives* (London: Stroud, 2011), 251–61

Benedek, Wolfgang and Matthias C. Kettemann, *Freedom of Expression on the Internet* (Strasbourg: Council of Europe, 2014)

Benedek, Wolfgang, Koen De Feyter, Matthias C. Kettemann, and Christina Voigt, "Introduction," in Wolfgang Benedek et al. (eds.), *The Common Interest in International Law* (Antwerp: Intersentia, 2014), 10

Benedek, Wolfgang, Koen De Feyter, Matthias C. Kettemann, and Christina Voigt (eds.), *The Common Interest in International Law* (Antwerp: Intersentia, 2014)

Benkler, Yochai, "From Consumers to Users: Shifting the Deeper Structures of Regulation Towards Sustainable Commons and User Access," Federal Communications Law Journal 52 (2000), 561

Bentley, Jerry, "Globalizing History and Historicizing Globalization," Globalizations 1 (2004) 1, 68–81

Berman, Harold, "The Alien Tort Claims Act and the Law of Nations," Emory International Law Review 9 (2005), 69

Berman, Paul Schiff, "Global Legal Pluralism," Southern California Law Review 80 (2007), 1155

Berman, Paul Schiff, *Global Legal Pluralism: A Jurisprudence of Law Beyond Borders* (Cambridge: CUP, 2012)

Berners-Lee, Tim, "Information Management: A Proposal' (1989/1990), http://www.w3.org/History/1989/proposal.html

Bernstorff, Jochen von, "The Structural Limitations of Network Governance: ICANN as a Case in Point," in Christian Jörges, Inger-Johanne Sand, and Gunther Teubner (eds.), *Transnational Governance and Constitutionalism* (Oxford: Hart, 2004), 257–81

Bernstorff, Jochen von, "German Intellectual Historic Origins of International Legal Positivism," in Jörg Kammerhofer and Jean d'Asprement (eds.), *International Legal Positivism in a Post-Modern World* (Cambridge: CUP, 2014), 50–80

Besson, Samantha, "Sovereignty," in Rüdiger Wolfrum (ed.), *Max Planck Encyclopedia of Public International Law (MPEPIL)* (Oxford: OUP, 2008)

Besson, Samantha and John Tasioulas, *The Philosophy of International Law* (Oxford: OUP, 2010)

Bethlehem, David, "The End of Geography: The Changing Nature of the International System and the Challenge to International Law," EJIL 25 (2014) 1, 9–24

Beyerlin, Ulrich, "Sustainable Development," in Rüdiger Wolfrum (ed.), *Max Planck Encyclopedia of Public International Law (MPEPIL)* (Oxford: OUP, 2008) (2009) [online]

Bianchi, Andrea, *International Law Theories. An Inquiry into Different Ways of Thinking* (Oxford: OUP, 2016)

Bickert, Hans Günther and Norbert Nail, *Marburger Karzer-Buch: Kleine Kulturgeschichte des* Universitätsgefängnisses (Marburg: Jonas Verlag, 2013)

Biddle, Sam, "How to Destroy the Internet," *Gizmodo*, May 23, 2012, http://gizmodo.com/5912383/how-to-destroy-the-internet

Bienfait, Agathe, "Die 'Verantwortungsgesellschaft' als 'Konfliktgesellschaft': Max Webers Beitrag jenseits von Fatalismus und Moralismus," in Ludger Heidbrink and Alfred Hirsch (eds.), *Verantwortung in der Zivilgesellschaft. Zur Konjunktur eines widersprüchlichen Prinzips* (Frankfurt/New York: Campus, 2006), 165–87

Boston Consulting Group, "The Internet Economy in the G-20: The $4.2 Trillion Growth Opportunity' (March 2012), https://www.bcgperspectives.com/content/articles/media_entertainment_strategic_planning_4_2_trillion_ opportunity_internet_economy_g20

Boström Magnus and Kristina Tamm Hallström, "Global Multi-Stakeholder Standard Setters: How Fragile Are They?," Journal of Global Ethics 9 (2013) 1, 93–110

Bourdieu, Pierre, *Habitus, code et codification, Actes de la Recherche en Sciences Sociales* (1986), 40–4

Bourdieu, Pierre, "Les juristes, gardiens de l'hypocrisie collective," in F. Chazel und J. Commaille (eds.), *Normes juridiques et régulation sociale* (Paris: LGDJ1991), 95–9

Boutros-Ghali, Boutros, "An Agenda for Peace. Preventive Diplomacy, Peacemaking and Peace-Keeping. Report of the Secretary-General Pursuant to the Statement Adopted by the Summit Meeting of the Security Council on 31 January 1992," in Adam Roberts and Benedict Kingsbury (eds.), *United Nations, Divided World. The UN's Role in International Relations* (Oxford: OUP, 1993), 468–98

Bowcott, Owen, "Twitter Joke Trial: Paul Chambers Wins High Court Appeal Against Conviction," *The Guardian*, July 27, 2012, www.guardian.co.uk/law/2012/jul/27/twitter-joke-trial-high-court

Box, Sarah, "Openness and Fragmentation: Toward Measuring the Economic Effects," GCIG Papers Series No. 36 (2016), https://www.cigionline.org/sites/default/files/gcig_no.36_web.pdf

Braman, Sandra, *Change of State: Information, Policy, and Power* (Cambridge: MIT Press, 2009)

Bratton, Benjamin H., *The Stack. On Software and Sovereignty* (Cambridge, MA/London: MIT Press, 2015)

Brooking Institution, "Internet Shutdowns Cost Countries $2.4 Billion Last Year," October 2016, https://www.brookings.edu/wp-content/uploads/2016/10/intenet-shutdowns-v-3.pdf

Brousseau, Eric, Meryem Marzouki, and Cécile Méadel (eds.), *Governance, Regulation, and Powers on the Internet* (Cambridge: CUP, 2012)

Brown, Gary and Christopher D. Yung, "Evaluating the US-China Cybersecurity Agreement," *The Diplomat*, January 19, 2017, https://thediplomat.com/2017/01/evaluating-the-us-china-cybersecurity-agreement-part-1-the-us-approach-to-cyberspace.

Brown, Ian and Christopher T. Marsden, *Regulating Code. Good Governance and Better Regulation in the Information Age* (Cambridge: MIT Press, 2013).

Brown, Wendy, "We Are All Democrats Now," The Kettering Review (2011) 29, 44–52

Brownsword, Roger, Eloise Scotford, and Karen Yeung (eds.), *Oxford Handbook of Law, Regulation, and Technology* (Oxford: OUP, 2017)

Brunnée, Jutta, "Sic utere tuo ut alienum non laedas," in Rüdiger Wolfrum (ed.), *Max Planck Encyclopedia of Public International Law (MPEPIL)* (Oxford: OUP, 2008) (2010)

Buchanan, Allen and Robert O. Keohane, "The Legitimacy of Global Governance Institutions," Ethics and International Affairs 20 (2006) 4, 405–37

Budish, Ryan, Sarah Myers West, and Urs Gasser, "Designing Successful Governance Groups: Lessons for Leaders from Real-World Examples," Berkman Center Research Publication No. 2015-11, August 2015, http://papers.ssrn.com/ sol3/papers.cfm?abstract_id=2638006

Budish, Ryan, Sarah Myers West, and Urs Gasser, "Multistakeholder as Governance Groups: Observations from Case Studies," Berkman Center Research Publication No. 2015-1, January 14, 2015, http://papers.ssrn.com/sol3/papers. cfm?abstract_id=2549270

Bygrave, Lee A. and Jon Bing (eds.), *Internet Governance: Infrastructure and Institutions* (Oxford: OUP, 2009)

Bygrave, Lee A., *Data Privacy Law: An International Perspective* (Oxford: OUP, 2014)

Bygrave, Lee A., *Internet Governance by Contract* (Oxford: OUP, 2015)

Calliess, Gralf-Peter, "Systemtheorie," in Sonja Buckel, Ralph Christensen, and Andreas Fischer-Lescano (eds.), *Neue Theorien des Rechts*, 2nd edn. (Stuttgart: Lucius&Lucius, 2009), 53–71

Calliess, Gralf-Peter and Peer Zumbansen, *Rough Consensus and Running Code. A Theory of Transnational Private Law* (Oxford/Portland, OR: Hart, 2012)

Cameron, Lindsey and Vincent Chetail, *Privatizing War. Private Military and Security Companies under Public International Law* (Cambridge: CUP, 2013)

Cassese, Sabino, "Administrative Law without the State? The Challenge of Global Regulation," New York University Journal of International Law and Policy 37 (2005), 663-693

Cassese, Antonio (ed.), *Realizing Utopia. The Future of International Law* (Oxford: OUP, 2012)

Castells, Manuel, *The Information Society: Economy, Society and Culture; Vol. 1: The Rise of the Network Society*, 2nd edn. (Oxford: Blackwell, 1996/2000)

Castells, Manuel, *The Information Society: Economy, Society and Culture; Vol. 2: The Power of Identity* (Oxford: Blackwell, 1997)

Castells, Manuel, *The Information Society: Economy, Society and Culture*; *Vol. 3: End of Millennium*, 2nd edn. (Oxford: Blackwell, 1998/2000)

Castoriadis, Cornelius, "Pouvoir, politique, autonomie," Revue de Métaphysique et de Morale (1988) 1, reprinted in Cornelius Castoriadis, *Le Monde Morcelé* (Paris: Le Seuil, 1990)

Cavell, Stanley, "This New Yet Unapproachable America. Lectures after Emerson after Wittgenstein," *Carpenter Lectures, II. Finding as Founding* (Chicago: University of Chicago Press, 1989/2013)

CCDCOE, "WannaCry Campaign: Potential State Involvement Could Have Serious Consequences," May 16, 2017, https://ccdcoe.org/wannacry-campaign-potential-state-involvement-could-have-serious-consequences.html

Center for Democracy and Technology (CDT), "What Does 'Governance' Mean? What are 'Critical Internet Resources'?" November 2007, https://www.cdt.org/files/pdfs/20071114Internet%20gov.pdf

Cerf, Vint, Patrick Ryan, and Max Senges, "Internet Governance is our Shared Responsibility," I/S: A Journal of Law and Policy for the Information Society 10 (2014) 1

Cerf, Vinton G. et al., "ICANN's Role in the Internet Governance Ecosystem," Report of the ICANN Strategy Panel, February 20, 2014, http://www.icann.org/en/about/planning/strategic-engagement/governance-ecosystem/ report-20feb14-en.pdf

Chadwick, Andrew and Philip N. Howard (eds.), *Routledge Handbook of Internet Politics* (London: Routledge, 2009)

Chander, Anupam and Uyen P. Le, "Breaking the Web: Data Localization vs. the Global Internet," UC Davis Legal Studies Research Paper Series No. 378 (April 2014)

Chango, Mawaki, "Accountability in Private Global Governance: ICANN and Civil Society," in Jan Aart Scholte (ed.), *Building Global Democracy? Civil Society and Accountable Global Governance* (Cambridge: CUP, 2011), 267–88

Charney, Jonathan I., "Universal International Law," AJIL 87 (1993) 4, 529–51

Chayes, Abram and Antonia H. Chayes, *The New Sovereignty: Compliance with International Regulatory Agreements* (Cambridge, MA: Harvard University Press, 1995)

Chertoff, Michael and Paul Rosenzweig, "A Primer on Globally Harmonizing Internet Jurisdiction and Regulations," GCIG Paper Series No. 10 (2015), http://www.ourinternet.org/publication/a-primer-on-globally-armonizinginternet-jurisdiction-and-regulations

Chinkin, Christine M., "The Challenge of Soft Law: Development and Change in International Law," International and Comparative Law Quarterly 38 (1989) 4, 850–66

Christakis, Theodore and Karine Bannelier, "Reinventing Multilateral Cybersecurity Negotiation after the Failure of the UN GGE and Wannacry: The OECD Solution," EJIL Talk, February 28, 2018, https://www.ejiltalk.org/reinvent ting-multilateral-cybersecurity-negotiation-after-the-failure-of-the-un-gge-and-wannacry-the-oecd-solution

Clark, David D., "A Cloudy Crystal Ball, Visions of the Future," plenary presentation, 24th meeting of the Internet Engineering Task Force, Cambridge, MA, July 13–17, 1992, http:/ietf20.isoc.org/videos/future_ietf_92.pdf

Clemente, Dave, "Cyber Security and Global Interdependence: What Is Critical?," Chatham House Programme Report (2013), http://www.chathamhouse.org/publications/papers/view/189645

Cogburn, Derrick L., "Enabling Effective Multistakeholder Participation in Global Internet Governance Through Accessible Cyberinfrastructure," in Andrew Chadwick and Philip N. Howard (eds.), *Routledge Handbook of Internet Politics* (London: Routledge, 2009), 401–13

Cogburn, Derrick L., "The Multiple Logics of Post-Snowden Restructuring of Internet Governance," in Francesca Musiani, Derrick L. Cogburn, Laura DeNardis, and Nanette S. Levinson (eds.), *The Turn to Infrastructure in Internet Governance* (New York: Palgrave Macmillan US, 2016), 25–44

Clough, Jonathan, *Principles of Cybercrime* (Cambridge: CUP, 2010)

Collin, Peter, *Privat-staatliche Regelungsstrukturen im Frühen Industrie- und Sozialstaat* (Berlin/Boston: De Gruyter, 2016)

Conklin, Jeffrey, "Hypertext: An Introduction and Survey," Computer 20 (1987), 17–41, www.ics.uci.edu/~andre/informatics223s2009/conklin.pdf

Corbett, Philip B., "The Latest Style," *New York Times*, October 29, 2013, http://afterdeadline.blogs.nytimes.com/ 2013/10/29/the-latest-style/?_php=true&_type=blogs&_r=0

Cornils, Matthias, "Entterritorialisierung im Kommunikationsrecht," VVDStRL 76 (2017), 391–442

Corrias, Luigi, "Guises of Sovereignty: 'Rogue States' and Democratic States in the International Legal Order," in Wolfgang Wagner, Werner Wouter, and Michal Onderco (eds.), *Deviance in International Relations* (London: Palgrave Macmillan, 2014), 38–57

Cover, Robert M., "The Supreme Court, 1982 Term—Foreword. Nomos and Narrative," Harvard Law Review 97 (1983) 4, 1–68

Cowie, James, "Egypt Leaves the Internet," January 28, 2011, http://www.renesys.com/blog/2011/01/egypt-leaves-the-internet.shtml

Coy, Wolfgang, *Computer als Medien: drei Aufsätze*, vol. 93–94 (Bremen: University of Bremen, Fachbereich Mathematik/Informatik) (1994)

Cragg, Wesley (ed.), *Business and Human Rights* (Cheltenham: Edward Elgar, 2012)

Crawford, Susan, "ICANN's Constitutional Moment," Publius, May 20, 2008, http://publius.cc/icanns_constitutional_moment

Cuceranu, Dragos, *Aspects of Regulating Freedom of Expression on the Internet* (Antwerp: Intersentia, 2012)

d'Aspremont, Jean, "Bindingness," in Jean d'Aspremont and Sahib Singh (eds.), *Concepts for International Law. Contributions to Disciplinary Thought* (Cheltenham: Edward Elgar, 2018), 67–82

Dalberg, "Impact of the Internet in Africa: Establishing Conditions for Success and Catalysing Inclusive Growth in Ghana, Kenya, Nigeria and Senegal" (April 2013), http://www.impactoftheinternet.com

Dahm, Georg, Jost Delbrück, and Rüdiger Wolfrum, *Völkerrecht*, Vol. I/3 (Berlin: De Gruyter, 2002), 41, 43.

Das, Dilip K., "Globalisation: Past and Present," Economic Affairs 30 (2010) 1, 66–70

Davenport, Thomas H., "Microdecisions for Macro Impact," March 4, 2009, Harvard Business Review, https://hbr.org/2009/03/microdecisions-for-macro-impact

De Búrca, Gráinne, Robert O. Keohane, and Charles Sabel, "Global Experimentalist Governance," British Journal of Political Science 44 (2014) 3, 477–86

de la Chappelle, Bertrand, "The Internet Governance Forum: How a United Nations Summit Produced a New Governance Paradigm for the Internet Age," in OSCE/The Representative on Freedom of the Media, *Governing the Internet. Freedom and Regulation in the OSCE Region* (Vienna: OSCE RFoM, 2007)

de la Chapelle, Bertrand and Paul Fehlinger, "Jurisdiction on the Internet: From Legal Arms Race to Transnational Cooperation," CIGI Paper Series No. 28, April 2016, https://www.cigionline.org/sites/default/files/ gcig_no28_web.pdf (=Internet and Jurisdiction Paper No.1, https://www.internetjurisdiction.net/uploads/pdfs/ Papers/IJ-Paper-Jurisdiction-on-the-Internet.pdf)

de Werra, Jacques, "ADR in Cyberspace: The Need to Adopt Global Alternative Dispute Resolution Mechanisms for Addressing the Challenges of Massive Online Micro-Justice," Swiss Review of International & European Law (2016), 289–306

Debiel, Tobias, *UN-Friedensoperationen in Afrika. Weltinnenpolitik und die Realität von Bürgerkriegen* (Bonn: J.H.W. Dietz Nachf., 2003)

Deibert, Ronald, John Palfrey, Rafal Rohozinski, and Jonathan Zittrain (eds.), *Access Denied: The Practice and Policy of Global Internet Filtering* (Cambridge: MIT Press, 2008)

Deibert, Ronald, John Palfrey, Rafal Rohozinski, and Jonathan Zittrain (eds.), *Access Controlled: The Shaping of Power, Rights, and Rule in Cyberspace* (Cambridge: MIT Press, 2010)

Deibert, Ronald, John Palfrey, Rafal Rohozinski, and Jonathan Zittrain (eds.), *Access Contested: Security, Identity, and Resistance in Asian Cyberspace* (Cambridge: MIT Press, 2011)

Delbrück, Jost, "The International Obligation to Cooperate: An Empty Shell or a Hard Law Principle of International Law? – A Critical Look at a Much Debated Paradigm of Modern International Law," in Holger P. Hestermeyer (et al.) (eds.), *Coexistence, Cooperation and Solidarity, Liber Amicorum Rüdiger Wolfrum* (2 vols.) (Amsterdam: Brill, 2011), vol. 1, 1–16

DeNardis, Laura, *Protocol Politics: The Globalization of Internet Governance* (Cambridge, MA: MIT Press, 2009)

DeNardis, Laura, *Opening Standards: The Global Politics of Interoperability* (Cambridge, MA: MIT Press, 2011)

DeNardis, Laura, "Hidden Levers of Internet Control," *Information, Communication & Society 15* (2012) 5, 720–738

DeNardis, Laura, "Internet Points of Control as Global Governance," CIGI Internet Governance Paper No. 2 (2013), https://www.cigionline.org/sites/default/files/no2_3.pdf

DeNardis, Laura, *The Global War for Internet Governance,* 2nd edn. (New Haven: Yale University Press, 2014)

DeNardis, Laura and Francesca Musiani, "Governance by Infrastructure," in Francesca Musiani, Derrick L. Cogburn, Laura DeNardis, and Nanette S. Levinson (eds.), *The Turn to Infrastructure in Internet Governance* (New York: Palgrave Macmillan US, 2016), 3–21

DeNardis, Laura, "One Internet: An Evidentiary Basis for Policy Making on Internet Universality and Fragmentation," CIGI/Chatham House, Global Commission on Internet Governance Paper Series No. 38 (2016)

Descombes, Vincent, *Die Rätsel der Identität* (Berlin: Passagen, 2013)

Diakopoulos, Nicholas, "Algorithmic Accountability," Digital Journalism 3 (2015) 3, 398–415

Dickenson, Donna, "The Common Good," in Roger Brownsword, Eloise Scotford, and Karen Yeung (eds.), *Oxford Handbook of Law, Regulation, and Technology* (Oxford: OUP, 2017), 135–52

Dietz, Thomas, *Global Order Beyond Law. How Information and Communication Technologies Facilitate Relational Contracting in International Trade* (London: Bloomsbury, 2014)

Dimbath, Oliver, "Vergemeinschaftende Vergesellschaftung und die Intention eines Dritten," in Gert Albert, Rainer Greshoff, and Rainer Schützeichel, (eds.), *Dimensionen und Konzeptionen von Sozialität* (Berlin: Springer VS, 2010), 33–45

Dimitrov, Radoslav S., "Hostage to Norms: States, Institutions and Global Forest Politics," Global Environmental Politics 5 *(2005), 4*

Doria, Avri, "The IETF as a model for the IGF," http://www.intgovforum.org/contributions/IETF-as-model.pdf

Dörr, Oliver, "Use of Force, Prohibition of," in Rüdiger Wolfrum (ed.), *Max Planck Encyclopedia of Public International Law (MPEPIL)* (Oxford: OUP, 2008) (2011) [online]

Dörr, Oliver, "Die Anforderungen an ein zukunftsfähiges Infrastrukturrecht," VVDStRL 73 (2014), 323–67

Drake, William and Ernest Wilson III, *Governing Global Electronic Networks: International Perspectives on Policy and Power* (Cambridge: MIT Press, 2008)

Drake, William, *Reforming Internet Governance: Perspectives from the Working Group on Internet Governance* (New York: UN Publications, 2008)

Drake, William J., Vinton G. Cerf, and Wolfgang Kleinwächter, "Internet Fragmentation: An Overview," World Economic Forum, Future of the Internet Initiative White Paper, January 2016

Duff, Alistair, *Information Society Studies* (London: Routledge, 2000)

Dutton, William H. and Malcolm Peltu, "The New Politics of the Internet: Multi-Stakeholder Policy-Making and the Internet Technocracy," in Andrew Chadwick and Philip N. Howard (eds.), *Routledge Handbook of Internet Politics* (London: Routledge, 2009), 384–99

Dutton, William H., *The Oxford Handbook of Internet* Studies (Oxford: OUP, 2013)

Duve, Thomas, "Was ist 'Multinormativität'?—Einführende Bemerkungen," Rechtsgeschichte—Legal History 25 (2017), 88–101

Easterling, Keller, *Extrastatecraft: The Power of Infrastructure Space* (London: Verso, 2014)

Economist, "When Did Globalization Start?," September 23, 2013, https://www.economist.com/blogs/freeexchange/2013/09/economic-history-1

Efrony, Dan and Yuval Shany, "A Rule Book on the Shelf? Tallinn Manual 2.0 on Cyber Operations and Subsequent State Practice," Hebrew University of Jerusalem Legal Research Paper No. 18-22, https://papers.ssrn.com/sol3/papers.cfm?abstract_id=3 172743

Elkin-Koren, Niva, "Making Technology Visible: Liability of Internet Service Providers for Peer-to-Peer Traffic," New York University Journal of Legislation and Public Policy 9 (2016), 15–76

Elliott, Lorraine, Climate Diplomacy, Andrew F. Cooper, Jorge Heine, and Ramesh Tahkur (eds.), *The Oxford Handbook on Modern Diplomacy* (Oxford: OUP, 2013), 840–55

Elmer, Greg, "Exclusionary Rules? The Politics of Protocols," in Andrew Chadwick and Philip N. Howard (eds.), *Routledge Handbook of Internet Politics* (London: Routledge, 2009), 376–82

Epstein, Dmitry, "The Making of Institutions of Information Governance: The Case of the Internet Governance Forum," Journal of Information Technology 28 (2013), 2

Esty, Daniel C., "Good Governance at the Supranational Scale: Globalizing Administrative Law," Yale Law Journal 115 (2006), 1490

Etro, Federico, "The Economic Impact of Cloud Computing on Business Creation, Employment and Output in Europe. An application of the Endogenous Market Structures Approach to a GPT innovation," Review of Business and Economics 2 (2009), 180–208

Fältström, Patrik, "Market-Driven Challenges to Open Internet Standards," GCIG Papers Series No. 33 (2016), http://www.cigionline.org/publications/marketdriven-challenges-open-internet-standard

Farivar, Cyrus, "Twitter Must Identify Racist, Anti-Semitic Posters, French Court Says," *CNN*, http://edition.cnn.com/2013/01/24/tech/social-media/twitter-racist-posts-france/index.html

Fassbender, Bardo, "Zwischen Staatsräson und Gemeinschaftsbindung. Zur Gemeinwohlorientierung des Völkerrechts der Gegenwart," in Herfried Münkler and Karsten Fischer (eds.), *Gemeinwohl und Gemeinsinn im Recht: Konkretisierung und Realisierung öffentlicher Interessen* (Berlin: Akademie Verlag, 2002), 231–74

Fehl, Caroline, "Navigating Norm Complexity.A Shared Research Agenda for Diverse Constructivist Perspectives," August 2018, PRIF Working Paper No. 41 (Frankfurt: HSFK, 2018)

Fell, Jan, "Chinese Internet Law: What the West Doesn't See. Yes, China's Internet Policy Quashes Dissent—But it Also Fosters Innovation," *The Diplomat*, October 18, 2017, https://thediplomat.com/2017/10/chinese-internet-law-what-the-west-doesnt-see

Fidler, David P., "Internet Governance and International Law: The Controversy Concerning Revision of the International Telecommunication Regulations," ASIL Insights 17 (2013) 6, https://www.asil.org/insights/volume/17/issue/6/internet-governance-and-international-law-controversy-concerning-revision

Finnemore, Martha and Duncan B. Hollis, "Constructing Norms for Global Cybersecurity," AJIL 110 (2016), 425–79

Fisahn, Andreas, *Demokratie und Öffentlichkeitsbeteiligung* (Tübingen: Mohr Siebeck, 2002)

Fischer-Lescano, Andreas and Gunther Teubner, "Prozedurale Rechtstheorie: Wiethölter," in Sonja Buckel, Ralph Christensen, and Andreas Fischer-Lescano (eds.), *Neue Theorien des Rechts*, 2nd edn. (Stuttgart: Lucius&Lucius, 2009), 75–89

Fischer-Lescano, Andreas and Gunther Teubner, *Regime-Kollisionen. Zur Fragmentierung des globalen Rechts* (Frankfurt am Main: Suhrkamp, 2006)

Fischer-Lescano, Andreas, *Rechtskraft* (Berlin: August Verlag, 2013)

Fischer-Lescano, Andreas, "Der Kampf um die Internetverfassung. Rechtsfragen des Schutzes globaler Kommunikationsstrukturen vor Überwachungsmaßnahmen," JZ 69 (2014), 20, 965–74

Fischer-Lescano, Andreas, "Struggles for a Global Internet Constitution: Protecting Global Communication Structures Against Surveillance Measures," Global Constitutionalism 5 (2016) 2, 145–72

Fisher, Tim, "What is Fragmentation and Defragmentation," *Lifewire*, April 6, 2017, https://www.lifewire.com/ what-is-fragmentation-defragmentation-2625884

Fleischer, Peter, "Reflecting on the Right to be Forgotten," December 9, 2016, https://blog.google/topics/google-europe/reflecting-right-be-forgotten

Flyverbom, Mikkel, *The Power of Networks: Organizing the Global Politics of the Internet* (London: Edward Elgar, 2011)

Forst, Rainer, *Das Recht auf Rechtfertigung. Elemente einer konstruktivistischen Theorie der Gerechtigkeit* (Frankfurt am Main: Suhrkamp, 2007)

Forst, Rainer und Klaus Günther, "Die Herausbildung normativer Ordnungen. Zur Idee eines interdisziplinären Forschungsprogramms," in Rainer Forst und Klaus Günther (eds.), *Die Herausbildung normativer Ordnungen. Interdisziplinäre Perspektiven* (Frankfurt/New York: Campus, 2011), 11–30

Forst, Rainer, *Normativität und Macht. Zur Analyse sozialer Rechtfertigungsordnungen* (Frankfurt am Main: Suhrkamp, 2015)

Fraade, Steven D., "Nomos and Narrative Before Nomos and Narrative," Yale Journal of Law & the Humanities 17 (2005) 1, 81–96

Franck, Thomas M., *The Power of Legitimacy Among Nations* (Oxford: OUP, 1990)

Franck, Thomas M., "The Emerging Right to Democratic Governance," 86 AJIL (1992), 46–91

Franck, Thomas M., "Fairness in the International Legal and Institutional System," Recueil des Cours de l'Academie de Droit International 240 (1993), 26

Franck, Thomas M., "The Power of Legitimacy and the Legitimacy of Power: International Law in an Age of Power Disequilibrium," AJIL 100 (2006), 88

Franklin, M.I., *Digital Dilemmas: Power, Resistance, and the Internet* (Oxford: Oxford University Press, 2013)

Frankopan, Peter, *The Silk Roads: A New History of the World* (London: Bloomsbury, 2016)

Franzius, Claudio, *Recht und Politik in der transnationalen Konstellation* (Franfurt am Main: Campus, 2014)

Fraser, Nancy, "Transnationalizing the Public Sphere: On the Legitimacy and Efficacy of Public Opinion in a Post-Westphalian World," Theory, Culture & Society 24 (2007) 4, 7–30

Frau, Robert (ed.), *Drohnen und das Recht. Völker- und verfassungsrechtliche Fragen automatisierter und autonomer Kriegführung* (Tübingen: Mohr, 2014)

Fried, Barbara, "Wilt Chamberlain Revisited: 'Nozick's Justice in Transfer' and the Problem of Market-Based Distribution," Philosophy and Public Affairs 24 (1995), 226–45

Friedmann, Wolfgang, *The Changing Structure of International Law* (New York: Columbia University Press, 1974)

Friedman, Milton, *Kapitalismus und Arbeit* (Munich/Zurich: Piper, 2002)

Froomkin, Michael A., "Habermas@discourse.net: Toward a Critical Theory of Cyberspace," Harvard Law Review 116 (2003), 749–873

Froomkin, Michael, "Almost Free: An Analysis of ICANN's 'Affirmation of Commitments,'" Journal of Telecommunications and High Technology Law 9 (2011), 187–233

Fuchs, Christian, "Baidu, Weibo and Renren: The Global Political Economy of Social Media in China," Asian Journal of Communication 26 (2016) 1, 14–41

Galloway, Alexander, *Protocol: How Control Exists after Decentralization* (Cambridge: MIT Press, 2004)

Gasser, Urs, "Interoperability in the Digital Ecosystem," ITU GSR discussion paper, 2015, https://www.itu.int/en/ITUD/Conferences/GSR/Documents/GSR2015/Discussion_papers_and_Presentations/Discussionpaper_interoperability.pdf.

Gerhards, Julia, *(Grund-)Recht auf Verschlüsselung?* (Frankfurt am Main: Nomos, 2010)

Gerstenberg, Oliver, "Privatrecht, Demokratie und die lange Dauer der bürgerlichen Gesellschaft," Rechtshistorisches Journal 16 (1997), 152

Giles, Keir, "Countering Russian Information Operations in the Age of Social Media," *Council on Foreign Relations*, November 21, 2017, https://www.cfr.org/report/countering-russian-information-operations-age-social-media

Gillespie, Tarleton, "The Relevance of Algorithms," in Tarleton Gillespie et al. (eds.), *Media Technologies* (Cambridge, MA: MIT Press, 2014), 167–94

Global Commission on Internet Governance, "Statement: Toward a Social Compact for Digital Privacy and Security," Wednesday, April 15, 2015, https://www.ourinternet.org/publication/toward-a-social-compact-for-digital-privacy-and-security

Goldmann, Matthias, "Principles in International Law as Rational Reconstructions. A Taxonomy," November 13, 2013, https://ssrn.com/abstract=2442027

Goldmann, Matthias, *Internationale öffentliche Gewalt. Handlungsformen internationalen Institutionen im Zeitalter der Globalisierung* (Heidelberg: Springer, 2015)

Goldsmith, Jack L., "Regulation of the Internet: Three Persistent Fallacies," Chicago-Kent Law Review 73 (1998), 1119

Goldsmith, Jack L. and Eric A. Posner, *The Limits of International Law* (New York: OUP, 2005), 188–9

Goldsmith, Jack and Tim Wu, *Who Controls the Internet? Illusions of a Borderless World* (Oxford: OUP, 2006)

Golloway, Alexander, *Protocol: How Control Exists after Decentralization* (Cambridge, MA: MIT Press, 2004)

Goodman, Nelson, *Ways of Worldmaking* (Indianapolis, IN: Hackett, 1978)

Goodman, Ellen P. et al., "Open Letter to Google from 80 Internet Scholars," May 13, 2015, https://medium.com/@ellgood/open-letter-to-google-from-80-internet-scholars-release-rtbf-compliance-data-cbfc6d59f1bd

Graham, Mark, "Geography/Internet: Ethereal Alternate Dimensions of Cyberspace or Grounded Augmented Realities?" The Geographical Journal 179 (2013) 2, 177–82

Greengard, Samuel, *The Internet of Things* (Cambridge, MA/London: MIT Press, 2015)

Greenspan, Gideon, "Avoiding the Pointless Blockchain Project," *MultiChain* (2015), http://www.multi chain.com/blog/2015/11/avoiding-pointless-blockchain-project

Greenstein, Shane and Victor Stango (eds.), *Standards and Public Policy* (Cambridge: CUP, 2007)

Griffin, Andrew, "How Facebook Is Manipulating You to Vote," *The Independent*, http://www.independent.co.uk/life-style/gadgets-and-tech/news/uk-elections-2016-how-facebook-is-manipulating-you-to-vote-a7015 196.html

Groys, Boris, "Google: Words beyond Grammar, 100 Notes—100 Thoughts," No. 46, *dOCUMENTA (13)* (Ostfildern: Hatje Cantz, 2012)

Grünberger, Michael, "Transnationales Recht als responsiver Rechtspluralismus," Der Staat 55 (2016), 117–33

Guggenberger, Nikolaus, "Das Netzwerkdurchsetzungsgesetz—schön gedacht, schlecht gemacht," ZRP (2017), 98

Guggenberger, Nikolaus, "Das Netzwerkdurchsetzungsgesetz in der Anwendung," NJW (2017), 2577

Gumperz, John J., "Interethnic Communication," in Nikolas Coupland and Adam Jaworski (eds.), *Sociolinguistics* (London: Palgrave, 1997), 395–407

Günther, Klaus, "Normativer Rechtspluralismus—Eine Kritik," Normative Orders Working Paper 03/2014, http://publikationen.ub.uni-frankfurt.de/files/34664/Guenther_Normativer+Rechtspluralismus.pdf

Gusy, Christoph, "Wirkungen der Rechtsprechung des Europäischen Gerichtshofs für Menschenrechte in Deutschland," JA (2009), 406

Habermas, Jürgen, *Between Facts and Norms. Contributions to a Discourse Theory of Law and Democracy* (translated by William Rehg) (Cambridge, MA: MIT Press, 1996/1998)

Habermas, Jürgen, *Faktizität und Geltung. Beiträge zur Diskurstheorie des Rechts und des demokratischen Rechtsstaats* (Frankfurt: Suhrkamp, 1992/1998)

Habermas, Jürgen, *Erläuterungen zur Diskursethik* (Frankfurt: Suhrkamp, 2001)

Habermas, Jürgen, "Hat die Konstitutionalisierung des Völkerrechts noch eine Chance?" in Jürgen Habermas (ed.), *Der gespaltene Westen. Kleine politische Schriften X* (Frankfurt: Suhrkamp, 2004)

Habermas, Jürgen, "Im Sog der Technokratie," in Jürgen Habermas (ed.), *Im Sog der Technokratie: kleine politische Schriften XII* (Frankfurt: Suhrkamp, 2013), 7

Haddock, Adrian, Alan Millar, and Duncan Pritchard (eds.), *Epistemic Value* (Oxford: OUP, 2009)

Handl, Günther, "Extra-territoriality and Transnational Legal Authority," in Günther Handl, Joachim Zekoll, and Peer Zumbansen (eds.), *Beyond Territoriality. Transnational Legal Authority in an Age of Globalization* (Leiden/Boston: Martinus Nijhoff, 2012), 3–12

Hanschmann, Felix, "Theorie transnationaler Rechtsprozesse," in Sonja Buckel, Ralph Christensen, and Andreas Fischer-Lescano (eds.), *Neue Theorien des Rechts*, 2nd edn. (Stuttgart: Lucius&Lucius, 2009), 375–99

Harcourt, Bernard E., "Against Prediction: Sentencing, Policing and Punishing in an Actuarial Age," University of Chicago Law School Public Law and Legal Theory Working Papers No. 94 (2005)

Hargittai, Eszter and Yuli Patrick Hsieh, "Digital Inequality," in William H. Dutton (ed.), *The Oxford Handbook of Internet Studies* (Oxford: OUP, 2013), 129–50

Hassan, Robert, *The Information Society* (Cambridge: Polity, 2008)

Hayek, Friedrich A. v., *Die Verfassung der Freiheit*, 3rd edn. (Tübingen: Mohr Siebeck, 1991)

Heinold, Alexander, *Die Prinzipientheorie bei Ronald Dworkin und Robert Alexy* (Berlin: Duncker & Humblot, 2011)

Heintschel von Heinegg, Wolff, "Legal Implications of Territorial Sovereignty in Cyberspace," in Christian Czosseck, Rain Ottis, and Katharina Ziolkowski (eds.), *Proceedings of the 4th International Conference on Cyber Conflict* (Tallinn: NATO CCD COE Publications, 2012), 7–14

Henkin, Louis, *How Nations Behave*, 2nd edn. (New York: Columbia University Press, 1979)

Hildebrandt, Mireille, *Smart Technologies and the End(s) of Law* (Cheltenham: Edward Elgar, 2015)

Clinton, Hillary, "Remarks on Internet Freedom", Speech, Newseum, Washington, D.C., January 21, 2010, https://www.ft.com/content/f0c3bf8c-06bd-11df-b426-00144feabdc0

Hitzler, Ronald, "Der Goffmensch," in Anne Honer, Michael Meuser, and Michaela Pfadenhauer (eds.), *Fragile Sozialität. Inszenierungen, Sinnwelten, Existenzbastler* (Berlin: Springer VS, 2010), 17–34

Hobe, Stephan, "Cyberspace—der virtuelle Raum," in Josef Isensee, Paul Kirchhof, et al. (eds.), *Handbuch des Staatsrechts, Band XI: Internationale Bezüge*, 3rd edn. (Heidelberg: C.F. Müller, 2013)

Hoffman, Paul (ed.), "The Tao of IETF: A Novice's Guide to the Internet Engineering Task Force," (2012), https:// www.ietf.org/tao.html

Hoffmann-Riem, Wolfgang, "Freiheitsschutz in den globalen Kommunikationsinfrastrukturen," JZ 69 (2014) 2, 53–63

Hoffmann, Jeanette, "Multistakeholderism in Internet Governance: Putting a Fiction into Practice," Journal of Cyber Policy 1 (2016) 1, 29–49

Hoofnagle, Chris Jay, "Behavioural Advertising: The Offer You Cannot Refuse," Harvard Law & Policy Review 6 (2012), 273–96

Hook, Sidney, "Democracy as a Way of Life," in John N. Andrews and Carl A. Marsden (eds.), *Tomorrow in the Making* (New York: Whittlesey House, 1939), 31–46

Hooton, Christopher, "Refreshing Our Understanding of the Internet Economy," Internet Association (2017), https://internetassociation.org/reports/refreshing-understanding-internet-economy-ia-report

Howard, Philip N., *Pax Technica. How the Internet of Things May Set Us Free or Lock Us Up* (New Haven/London: Yale University Press, 2015)

Huang, Zhixiong and Kubo Mačák, "Towards the International Rule of Law in Cyberspace: Contrasting Chinese and Western Approaches," Chinese Journal of International Law 16 (2017), 271, https://ssrn.com/abstract=2979896

Hughes, Thomas, "UN: Don't Overlook Access to Information in Goal on Governance," *The Guardian*, February 11, 2014, http://www.theguardian.com/global-development-professionals-network/2014/feb/11/un-information-sdg-account ability-development

Independent International Commission on Kosovo, *The Kosovo Report: Conflict, International Response, Lessons Learned* (Oxford: OUP, 2000)

Internet & Jurisdiction, "Domains & Jurisdictions Policy Options, Cross-Border Domain Suspension," November 2017, Input Document for Workstream I of the 2nd Global Internet & Jurisdiction Conference, https://www.Internetjurisdiction.net/uploads/pdfs/Papers/Domains-Jurisdiction-Policy-Options-Document.pdf

Internet & Jurisdiction, "Domains & Jurisdictions Policy Options, Cross-Border Content Restrictions," November 2017, Input Document for Workstream II of the 2nd Global Internet & Jurisdiction Conference, https://www.internetjurisdiction.net/uploads/pdfs/Papers/IJ-Paper-Jurisdiction-on-the-Internet.pdf

Internet & Jurisdiction, "Domains & Jurisdictions Policy Options, Cross-Border Access to User Data," November 2017, Input Document for Workstream III of the 2nd Global Internet & Jurisdiction Conference, https://www.internetjurisdiction.net/uploads/pdfs/Papers/Data-Jurisdiction-Policy-Options-Document.pdf

International Digital Economy Alliance, "The Trillion Dollar Question: How Trade Agreements Can Maximise the Economic Potential of Data in the Networked Economy and Support the Internet as the World's Trading Platform," (2013), http://www.internet-economy.org

Jamart, Anne-Claire, "Internet Freedom and the Constitutionalization of Internet Governance," in Roxana Radu, Jean-Marie Chenou, and Rolf H. Weber (eds.), *The Evolution of Global Internet Governance. Principles and Policies in the Making* (Zurich: Schulthess, 2014), 57–78.

Jarass, Hans Dieter and Bodo Pieroth (eds.), *Kommentar zum Grundgesetz*, 14th edn. (Munich: C.H.Beck, 2016)

Jellinek, Georg, *Die rechtliche Natur der Staatsverträge. Ein Beitrag zur Juristischen Construction des Völkerrechts* (Vienna: Alfred Hölder, 1880)

Jennejohn, Matthew, "The Private Order of Innovation Networks," Stanford Law Review 68 (2016) 281–366

Johnson, David R. and David G. Post, "Law and Borders," Stanford Law Review 48 (1996), 1367

Jonas, Hans, *Das Prinzip Verantwortung. Versuch einer Ethik für die technologische Zivilisation* (Frankfurt am Main: Suhrkamp, 2003)

Jordan, John, *Robots* (Cambridge, MA/London: MIT Press, 2016)

Jørgensen, Rikke F. (ed.), *Human Rights in the Global Information Society* (Cambridge: MIT Press, 2006)

Jørgensen, Rikke F., *Framing the Net. The Internet and Human Rights* (Cheltenham Edward Elgar, 2013)

Joyce, Daniel, "Internet Freedom and Human Rights," EJIL 26 (2015) 2, 493–514

Just, Natascha and Michael Latzer, "Governance by Algorithms: Reality Construction by Algorithmic Selection on the Internet," Media, Culture & Society 39 (2017) 2, 238–58

Kadelbach, Stefan and Thomas Kleinlein, "Überstaatliches Verfassungsrecht," AVR 44 (2006), 235

Kadelbach, Stefan, "Völkerrecht als Verfassungsordnung? Zur Völkerrechtswissenschaft in Deutschland," ZaöRV 67 (2007), 599–621

Kadelbach, Stefan und Klaus Günther, "Recht ohne Staat?," in Stefan Kadelbach und Klaus Günther (eds.), *Recht ohne Staat? Zur Normativität nichtstaatlicher Normsetzung* (Frankfurt/New York: Campus, 2011)

Kadelbach, Stefan, "The Territoriality and Migration of Fundamental Rights," in Günther Handl, Joachim Zekoll, and Peer Zumbansen (eds.), *Beyond Territoriality. Transnational Legal Authority in an Age of Globalization* (Leiden/Boston: Martinus Nijhoff, 2012), 295–326

Kalscheuer, Fiete and Christian Hornung, "Das Netzwerkdurchsetzungsgesetz—Ein verfassungswidriger Schnellschuss," NVwZ (2017), 1721- 1725

Kammerhofer, Jörg and Jean d'Aspremont (eds.), *International Legal Positivism in a Post-Modern World* (Cambridge: CUP, 2014)

Kant, Immanuel, *Lose Blätter zu den Fortschritten der Metaphysik* (AA XX.) (edited by Gerhard Lehmann), Berlin: Berlin-Brandenburgische Akademie der Wissenschaften, 1971)

Kaplan, James and Kayvaun Rowshankish, "Addressing the Impact of Data Location Regulation in Financial Services," GCIG Paper Series No. 14 (2015), http://www.ourinternet.org/publication/addressing-the-impact-ofdata-location-regulation-in-financial-services

Katzenbach, Christian, *Die Regeln digitaler Kommunikation: Governance zwischen Norm, Diskurs und Technik* (Berlin: Springer VS, 2017)

Keller, Helen "Friendly Relations Declaration," in Rüdiger Wolfrum (ed.), *Max Planck Encyclopedia of Public International Law* (MPEPIL) (Oxford: OUP, 2008) (June 2009) [online]

Kelsen, Hans, *Reine Rechtslehre* (1934) (edited by Matthias Jestaedt) (ed.), *Reine Rechtslehre.* Studienausgabe der 1. Auflage 1934) (Tübingen: Mohr Siebeck, 2008)

Kenderdine, Tristan, "Coordinating China's Satellite Constellations. A New Era in the Space Race Begins," Asia & the Pacific Policy Society, APPS Policy Forum, July 20, 2017, https://www.policyforum.net/coordinating-chinas-satellite-constellations

Kennedy, Duncan, "Form and Substance in Private Law Adjudication," Harvard Law Review 89 (1976), 1685–778

Kettemann, Matthias C., "How to Implement Controversial Court Decisions: International Constitutional Lessons from Brown v. Board of Education for the Austrian Cases on Topographical Signs in Carinthia," International Constitutional Law Online Journal (ICL Online) 4 (2010), 590–623

Kettemann, Matthias C., "Nationale Sicherheit und Informationsfreiheit. Zur Völkerrechtmäßigkeit von Internetabschaltungen," in Kirsten Schmalenbach (ed.), *Aktuelle Herausforderungen des Völkerrechts. Beiträge zum 36. Österreichischen Völkerrechtstag 2011* (Frankfurt am Main: Peter Lang, 2012), 41–61

Kettemann, Matthias C., "Das Internet als internationales Schutzgut: Entwicklungsperspektiven des Internetvölkerrechts anlässlich des Arabischen Frühlings," ZaöRV 72 (2012), 469–82

Kettemann, Matthias C., "Grotius goes Google: Der Einfluss der Internet Governance auf das Völkergewohnheitsrecht," in Christoph Vedder (ed.), *Völkerrecht 2012. Richterliche Praxis und politische Realität. Tagungsband 37. Österreichischer Völkerrechtstag 2012* (Vienna: Peter Lang Verlag, 2013)

Kettemann, Matthias C., "Internet Governance," in Dietmar Jahnel, Peter Mader, and Elisabeth Staudegger (eds.), *IT-Recht*, 3rd edn. (Vienna: Verlag Österreich, 2013), 48-62

Kettemann, Matthias C., "Das Völkerrecht zwischen Rechtsordnung und Machtordnung: eine Abgrenzung," in Matthias C. Kettemann (ed.), *Grenzen im Völkerrecht* (Vienna: Jan Sramek Verlag, 2013), 247–73

Kettemann, Matthias C., *The Future of Individuals in International Law. Lessons from International Internet Law* (Utrecht: Eleven International Publishing, 2013)

Kettemann, Matthias C., "The Common Interest in the Protection of the Internet: An International Legal Perspective," in Wolfgang Benedek et al. (eds.), *The Common Interest in International Law* (Antwerp: Intersentia, 2014), 167–84

Kettemann, Matthias C., "Das Internetgrundrecht zwischen Völkerrecht, Staatsrecht und Europarecht (II)," Völkerrechtsblog, October 9, 2015, doi: 10.17176/20170920-161818

Kettemann, Matthias C., "Das Internetgrundrecht zwischen Völkerrecht, Staatsrecht und Europarecht (III)," Völkerrechtsblog, October 12, 2015, doi: 10.17176/20170920-162122

Kettemann, Matthias C., "Das Recht auf Internet zwischen Völkerrecht, Staatsrecht und Europarecht," Völkerrechtsblog, October 7, 2015, doi: 10.17176/20170920-161413

Kettemann, Matthias C., *Völkerrecht in Zeiten des Netzes: Perspektiven auf den effektiven Schutz von Grund- und Menschenrechten in der Informationsgesellschaft zwischen Völkerrecht, Europarecht und Staatsrecht* (Bonn: Friedrich-Ebert-Siftung, 2015), http://library.fes.de/pdf-files/akademie/12068.pdf

Kettemann, Matthias C., "Menschenrechte im Multistakeholder-Zeitalter: Mehr Demokratie für das Internet," ZFMR 1 (2016), 24–36

Kettemann, Matthias C., "Ensuring Cybersecurity through International Law," Revista Española de Derecho internacional (2017), 281–90

Kettemann, Matthias C., "Hassrede und Katzenbilder: Wie können im globalen Netz nationale Gesetze respektiert werden?," in Lorena Jaume-Palasí, Julia Pohle, and Matthias Spielkamp, *Digitalpolitik. Eine Einführung* (Berlin: Wikimedia, 2017)

Kettemann, Matthias C., "Report of the General Rapporteur," Council of Europe and OSCE Conference on Internet freedom "The Role and Responsibilities of Internet Intermediaries," October 13, 2017, Vienna, https://rm.coe.int/osce-coe-internet-conference-2017-report/1680785d71

Kingsbury, Benedict, Nico Krisch, and Richard Stewart, "The Emergence of Global Administrative Law," Law and Contemporary Problems 2 (2005), 15

Kingsbury, Benedict, "International Law as Inter-Public Law," in Henry R. Richardson and Melissa S. Williams (eds.), *Moral Universalims und Pluralism* (New York: NYU Press, 2009), 167–204

Kingsbury, Benedict, "The Concept of 'Law' in Global Administrative Law," EJIL 20 (2009), 23

Kingsbury, Benedict and Megan Donaldson, "From Bilateralism to Publicness in International Law," in Ulrich Fastenrath et al. (eds.), *From Bilateralism to Community Interests: Essays in Honour of Judge Bruno Simma* (Oxford: OUP, 2011), 79–89

Kirchner, Friedrich, *Wörterbuch der philosophischen Grundbegriffe* (Heidelberg: Georg Weiss Verlag, 1890/1907)

Kirk, Marianne, *"Die kaiserlose, die schreckliche Zeit'— Das Interregnum im Wandel der Geschichtsschreibung* (Frankfurt am Main: Peter Lang, 2002)

Klabbers, Jan, Anne Peters, and Geir Ulfstein, *The Constitutionalization of International Law* (Oxford: OUP, 2009)

Klarman, Michael J., *Brown v. Board of Education and the Civil Rights Movement* (Oxford: OUP, 2007)

Klarman, Michael J., *From the Closet to the Altar: Courts, Backlash and the Struggle for Same-Sex Marriage* (Oxford: OUP, 2012)

Kleinlein, Thomas, *Konstitutionalisierung im Völkerrecht. Konstruktion und Elemente einer idealistischen Völkerrechtslehre* (Heidelberg: Springer, 2012)

Kleinwächter, Wolfgang, "Internet Governance Outlook 2018: Preparing for Cyberwar or Promoting Cyber Détente?," *CircleID*, January 6, 2018

Kleinwächter, Wolfgang, "Internet Principle Hype: How Softlaw is Used to Regulate the Internet," dotnxt, http://news.dot-nxt.com/2011/07/27/internet-principle-hype-anon

Kleinwächter, Wolfgang, "Multi-Stakeholder Internet Governance: The Role of Governments," in Wolfgang Benedek, Veronika Bauer, and Matthias C. Kettemann (eds.), *Internet Governance and the Information Society. Global Perspectives and European Dimensions* (Utrecht: Eleven, 2008), 9–29

Kleinwächter, Wolfgang, "Towards an Improvement of the IGF. Eight Proposals for an Enhanced Role of the IGF," March 14, 2011, http://www.unctad.info/upload/CSTD-IGF/Contributions/M1/Wolfgang_Kleinwachter.pdf

Koh, Harold Hongju, "Why Do Nations Obey International Law?" Yale Law Journal 106 (1997), 2599–659

Koivurova, Timo, "Due Diligence," in Rüdiger Wolfrum (ed.), *Max Planck Encyclopedia of Public International Law (MPEPIL)* (Oxford: OUP, 2008) (2010) [online]

Koller, David S., "The End of Geography: The Changing Nature of the International System and the Challenge to International Law: A Reply to Daniel Bethlehem," EJIL 25 (2014) 1, 25–9

Koller, Peter, *Theorie des Rechts. Eine Einführung*, 2nd edn. (Vienna: Böhlau, 1997)

Koskenniemi, Martti, "Hierarchy in International Law: A Sketch," EJIL 8 (1997), 571–2

Koskenniemi, Martti, "Between Coordination and Constitution: International Law as a German Discipline," in Kari Palonen and Hubertus Buchstein (eds.), *Redescriptions. Yearbook of Political Thought, Conceptual History and Feminist Theory*, vol. 15 (Zurich/Berlin: Lit Verlag, 2011), 45–69

Kotzur, Markus, "Good Faith (Bona fide)," in Rüdiger Wolfrum (ed.), *Max Planck Encyclopedia of Public International Law (MPEPIL)* (Oxford: OUP, 2008) (2009) [online]

Kovacs, Anja, "A Third Way? Proposal for a Decentralised, Multistakeholder Global Internet Governance Involving All Stakeholders," (2011) http://internetdemocracy.in

Krikorian, Gaëlle and Amy Kapczynski (eds.), *Access to Knowledge in the Age of Intellectual Property* (Cambridge: MIT Press, 2010)

Krisch, Nico, "International Law in Times of Hegemony: Unequal Power and the Shaping of the International Legal Order," EJIL (2005), 369–408

Krisch, Nico, "The Pluralism of Global Administrative Law," EJIL 17 (2006), 247

Krisch, Nico, *Beyond Constitutionalism. The Pluralist Structure of Postnational Law* (Oxford: OUP, 2012)

Kroll, Joshua A., *Accountable Algorithms*, Dissertation, Princeton University (2015), https://www.jkroll.com/papers/dissertation.pdf

Kronenberger, Matthias, "Theorien der radikalen Fragmentierung," in Sonja Buckel, Ralph Christensen, and Andreas Fischer-Lescano (eds.), *Neue Theorien des Rechts*, 2nd edn. (Stuttgart: Lucius&Lucius, 2009), 229–52

Kuhn, Thomas S., *The Structure of Scientific Revolutions* (Chicago: University of Chicago Press, 1962/1970)

Kuhn, Thomas S., *Die Struktur wissenschaftlicher Revolutionen*, 2nd edn. (Frankfurt am Main: Suhrkamp, 1976)

Kulesza, Joanna, *International Internet Law* (London: Routledge, 2012)

Kuner, Christopher, "Data Nationalism and its Discontents," Emory Law Journal 64 (2015), 2089–98, http://law.emory.edu/elj/_documents/volumes/64/online/kuner.pdf

Kunig, Philip, "Prohibition of Intervention," in Rüdiger Wolfrum (ed.), *Max Planck Encyclopedia of Public International Law (MPEPIL)* (Oxford: OUP, 2008) (2008) [online]

Kuo, Ming-Sung, "Inter-Public Legality or Post-Public Legitimacy? Global Governance and the Curious Case of Global Administrative Law as a New Paradigm of Law," International Journal of Constitutional Law 10 (2012), 4, 1050–75

Kurbalija, Jovan, *An Introduction to Internet Governance*, 7th edn. (Geneva: DiploFoundation, 2016).

Kurzweil, Ray, "The Law of Accelerating Returns,' Kurzweil Accelerating Intelligence (Blog), March 7, 2001, http://www.kurzweilai.net/the-law-of-accelerating-returns

Kurzweil, Ray, *The Singularity is Near* (New York: Penguin, 2005)

Ladeur, Karl-Heinz, "Computerkultur und Evolution der Methodendiskussion in der Rechtswissenschaft," ARSP 74 (1988), 218

Ladeur, Karl-Heinz, *Der Staat gegen die Gesellschaft* (Tübingen: Mohr, 2006)

Ladeur, Karl-Heinz, "Die objektiv-rechtliche Dimension der wirtschaftlichen Grundrechte – Relativierung oder Abstützung der subjektiven Freiheitsrechte," in Thomas Vesting and Ino Augsberg (eds.), *Karl-Heinz Ladeur. Das Recht der Netzwerkgesellschaft* (Tübingen: Mohr, 2013), 497–518

Ladeur, Karl-Heinz, *Cyber Courts: Private Rechtsprechung in den neuen Medien*, Kursbuch 177 (Hamburg: Murmann, 2014)

Ladeur, Karl-Heinz, *Die Textualität des Rechts. Zur poststrukturalistischen Kritik des Rechts* (Weilerswist: Velbrück, 2016)

Laidlaw, Emily, *Regulating Speech in Cyberspace. Gatekeepers, Human Rights and Corporate Responsibility* (Cambridge: CUP, 2015)

Land, Molly K., "Toward an International Law of the Internet," Harvard International Law Journal 54 (2013), 393–458

Landauer, Carl, "The Ever-Ending Geography of International Law: The Changing Nature of the International System and the Challenge to International Law: A Reply to Daniel Bethlehem," EJIL 25 (2014) 1, 31–4

Landow, George P., *Hypertext 3.0: Critical Theory and New Media in an Era of Globalization*, 3rd edn. (Baltimore: Johns Hopkins University Press, 2006)

Lauterpacht, Hersch, *The Function of Law in the International Community* (Oxford: Clarendon Press, 1933)

Leclerc, Gérard, "Histoire de la vérité et généalogie de l'autorité," Cahiers internationaux de sociologie 111 (2001) 2, 205–31

Legris, Emilie and Dimitri Walas, "Regulation of Cyberspace by International Law," ESIL Reflection 7 (2018), 1, http://www.esil-sedi.eu/node/2060

Leiner, Barry M., Vinton G. Cerf, David D. Clark, Robert E. Kahn, Leonard Kleinrock, Daniel C. Lynch, Jon Postel, Larry G. Roberts, and Stephen Wolff, "Brief History of the Internet," Internet Society (2012), http://www.internetsociety.org/brief-history-internet

Lessig, Lawrence, "The Code Is the Law," The Industry Standard, August 9, 1999, http://www.lessig.org/content/standard/0,1902,4165,00.html

Lessig, Lawrence, *Code: Version 2.0* (New York: Basic Books, 2007)

Levin, Sam, Julia Carrie Wong, and Luke Harding, "Facebook Backs Down from 'Napalm Girl' Censorship and Reinstates Photo," *The Guardian*, September 9, 2016, https://www.theguardian.com/technology/2016/sep/09/facebook-reinstates-napalm-girl-photo

Levinson, Marc, *The Box: How the Shipping Container Made the World Smaller and the World Economy Bigger* (Princeton: Princeton University Press, 2006)

Levinson, Nanette S. and Derrick L. Cogburn, "The Next "Turn' in Internet Infrastructure Governance," in Francesca Musiani, Derrick L. Cogburn, Laura DeNardis, and Nanette S. Levinson (eds.), *The Turn to Infrastructure in Internet Governance* (New York: Palgrave Macmillan US, 2016), 219–23

Ley, Isabelle, "Opposition institutionalisieren – Alternativität und Reversibilität als Elemente eines völkerrechtlichen Legitimationskonzepts," Der Staat 53 (2014) 2, 227–62

Light, Evan and Jonathan A. Obar, "Surveillance Reform: Revealing Surveillance Harms and Engaging Reform Tactics," in Ben Wagner, Matthias C. Kettemann, and Kilian Vieth (eds.), *Research Handbook on Information Technologies and Human Rights* (Cheltenham: Edward Elgar, 2019), 195–222

Limer, Eric, "How Hackers Wrecked the Internet Using DVRs and Webcams," *Popular Mechanics*, October 21, 2016, https://www.popularmechanics.com/technology/ infrastructure/a23504/ mirai-botnet-internet-of-things-ddos-attack

Long, Norton E., "Power and Administration," Public Administration Review 9 (1949) 4, 257–64

Long, Tony, "It's Just the "internet" Now," August 16, 2004, http://www.wired.com/culture/lifestyle/news/2004/ 08/64596

Lucas, Jim, "What Are Centrifugal & Centripetal Forces?," Live Science, October 15, 2015, https://www.livescience.com/52488-centrifugal-centripetal-forces.html

Luhmann, Niklas, "Selbstreflexion des Rechtssystems," Rechtstheorie 10 (1979), 159

Luhmann, Niklas, "Die Codierung des Rechtssystems," Rechtstheorie 17 (1986), 171

Luhmann, Niklas, *Das Recht der Gesellschaft* (Frankfurt am Main: Suhrkamp, 1993)

Luhmann, Niklas, *Rechtssoziologie*, 4th edn. (Wiesbaden: Verlag für Sozialwissenschaften, 2008)

Luhmann, Niklas, *Kontingenz und Recht* (Frankfurt: Suhrkamp, 2013)

Lum, Kristian, William Isaac, "To Predict and Serve?" Significance 13 (2016) 5, 14–19, http://onlinelibrary.wiley.com/doi/10.1111/j.1740-9713.2016.00960.x/full

Lutz-Bachmann, Matthias, "The Concept of the Normativity of Law: 'Ius gentium' in the Writings of Francisco Suárez and Thomas Aquinas," in Thilo Marauhn and Heinhard Steiger (eds.), *Universality and Continuity in International Law* (The Hague: Eleven, 2011), 235–47

Macak, Kubo, "From Cyber Norms to Cyber Rules: Re-engaging States as Law-makers," Leiden Journal of International Law 30 (2017) 4, 877–99

MacKinnon, Rebecca, *Consent of the Networked: The Worldwide Struggle for Internet Freedom* (New York: Basic Books, 2012)

MacLean, Don, *Internet Governance: A Grand Collaboration* (New York: UN Publications, 2005)

Macleod, Alistair M., "Human Rights and International Trade: Normative Underpinnings," in Wesley Cragg (ed.), *Business and Human Rights* (Cheltenham: Edward Elgar, 2012), 179–96.

Mager, Astrid, "Internet Governance as Joint Effort: (Re)Ordering Search Engines at the Intersection of Global and Local Cultures," New Media & Society (2018), 1–21

Malcolm, Jeremy, *Multi-Stakeholder Governance and the Internet Governance Forum* (Perth: Terminus Press, 2008)

Malloy, Michael and Pavel Arievich, "Russia's Data Localization Requirement Will Take Effect September 1," Data Protection, Privacy and Security Alert (US), July 8, 2015, https://www.dlapiper.com/en/us/insights/public cations/ 2015/07/russia-data-localization-requirement

Mandel, Gregory N., "Legal Evolution in Response to Technological Change," in Roger Brownsword, Eloise Scotford, and Karen Yeung (eds.), *Oxford Handbook of Law, Regulation, and Technology* (Oxford: OUP, 2017), 225–45

Mankowski, Peter, *Rechtskultur* (Tübingen: Mohr Siebeck, 2016)

Mansell, Robin, *Imagining the Internet. Communication, Innovation, and Governance* (Oxford: OUP, 2012)

Manyika, James, McKinsey Global Institute Research, "Digital Economy: Trends, Opportunities and Challenges' (2016), https://www.ntia.doc.gov/files/ntia/publications/james_manyika_digital_economy_deba_may_16_v4.pdf

Marauhn, Thilo, "Sicherung grund- und menschenrechtlicher Standards gegenüber neuen Gefährdungen durch private und ausländische Akteure," VVDStRL 74 (2015), 373–400

Mares Radu (ed.), *The UN Guiding Principles on Business and Human Rights. Foundations and Implementation* (Leiden: Nijhoff, 2011)

Markoff, Michele G., Deputy Coordinator for Cyber Issues, US State Department, "Explanation of Position at the Conclusion of the 2016-2017 UN Group of Governmental Experts (GGE) on Developments in the Field of Information and Telecommunications in the Context of International Security," June 23, 2017, https://www.state.gov/s/cyberissues/releasesandremarks/272175.htm

Marsden, Christopher T., *Net Neutrality: Towards a Co-Regulatory Solution* (London: Bloomsbury, 2010)

Marsden, Christopher T., *Internet Co-Regulation* (Cambridge: CUP, 2011)

Marshall, Monty and Benjamin Cole, "Global Report 2009: Conflict, Governance, and State Fragility," (2009), http://www.humansecuritygateway.com/documents/CSP_GlobalReport2009_ConflictGovernanceState Fragility.pdf

Martin, Katherine Connor, "Should You Capitalize the Word Internet?," Oxford Dictionaries Blog, April 5, 2016, https://blog.oxforddictionaries.com/2016/04/05/should-you-capitalize-internet

Mathiason, John, *Internet Governance: The New Frontier of Global Institutions* (London: Routledge, 2008)

Maupin, Julie, "Mapping the Global Legal Landscape of Blockchain and Other Distributed Ledger Technologies," CIGI Paper No. 149, October 13, 2017, https://www.cigionline.org/publications/mapping-global-legal-landscape-blockchain-and-other-distributed-ledger-technologies

May, Christopher, *The Information Society: A Skeptical View* (Cambridge: Polity, 2002)

Mayer-Schönberger, Viktor, "Emergency Communications: The Quest for Interoperability in the United States and Europe," Kennedy School of Government Faculty Research Working Papers Series RWP02–024, March 2002

Mayer, Franz C., "Europe and the Internet," EJIL (2000), 149

Mayer, Franz C., "Das Internet, das Völkerrecht und die Internationalisierung des Rechts," ZfRSoz (2002), 93

McKinsey Global Institute, "Internet Matters: The Net's Sweeping Impact on Growth, Jobs and Prosperity," (May 2011), http://www.mckinsey.com/insights/high_tech_telecoms_internet/internet_matters

McLuhan, Marshall, *The Gutenberg Galaxy* (Toronto: University of Toronto Press, 1962)

McQuillan, Dan, "Algorithmic States of Exception," European Journal of Cultural Studies 18 (2015), 564–76

Meron, Theodor, *Humanization of International Law* (Amsterdam: Brill, 2014)

Merrill, Kenneth, "Domains of Control: Governance of and by the Domain Name System," in Francesca Musiani, Derrick L. Cogburn, Laura DeNardis, and Nanette S. Levinson (eds.), *The Turn to Infrastructure in Internet Governance* (New York: Palgrave Macmillan US, 2016), 89–106

Mihr, Anja, "Cyber Justice: Cyber Governance through Human Rights and Rule of Law in the Internet," US-China Law Review 13 (2016), 314

Milanovic, Marko, "Human Rights Treaties and Foreign Surveillance: Privacy in the Digital Age," Harvard International Law Journal 56 (2015) 1, 81–146

Minnerop, Petra, *Paria-Staaten im Völkerrecht* (Heidelberg: Springer, 2004)

Moe, Terry, "The Positive Theory of Public Bureaucracy," in Dennis C. Mueller (ed.), *Perspectives on Public Choice: A Handbook* (Cambridge: CUP, 1996)

Möllers, Christoph, *Die Möglichkeit der Normen* (Berlin: Suhrkamp, 2016)

Moore, Robert, *Cybercrime: Investigating High-Technology Computer Crime* (Oxford: Elsevier, 2011)

Morozov, Evgeny, *To Save Everything, Click Here. Technology, Solutionism and the Urge to Fix Problems That Don't Exist* (London: Allen Lane, 2013)

Mosco, Vincent, *The Digital Sublime: Myth, Power, and Cyberspace* (Cambridge, MA: MIT Press, 2005)

Mueller, Milton, *Ruling the Root: Internet Governance and the Taming of Cyberspace* (Cambridge: MIT Press, 2002)

Mueller, Milton, John Mathiason, and Hans Klein, "The Internet and Global Governance: Principles and Norms for a New Regime," Global Governance 13 (2007), 237–54

Mueller, Milton, *Networks and States: The Global Politics of Internet Governance* (Cambridge: MIT Press, 2010)

Mueller, Milton, "The Need to Abolish Stakeholder 'Roles,'" Submission to NetMundial (2014), http://content.netmundial.br/contribution/the-need-to-abolish-stakeholder-roles/80

Mueller, Milton, *Will the Internet Fragment? Sovereignty, Globalization and Cyberspace* (Malden, MA: Polity Press, 2017)

Murray, Andrew, "Uses and Abuses of Cyberspace: Coming to Grips with the Present Dangers," in Antonio Cassese (ed.), *Realizing Utopia. The Future of International Law* (Oxford: OUP, 2012), 497–506

Musiani, Francesca, "Alternative Technologies as Alternative Institutions: The Case of the Domain Name System," in Francesca Musiani, Derrick L. Cogburn, Laura DeNardis, and Nanette S. Levinson (eds.), *The Turn to Infrastructure in Internet Governance* (New York: Palgrave Macmillan US, 2016), 73–86

Musiani, Francesca, "Governance by Algorithms," Internet Policy Review 2 (2013) 3, http://policyreview.info/ articles/analysis/governance-algorithms

Musiani, Francesca, "Network Architecture as Internet Governance," Internet Policy Review 2 (2013) 4, https://policyreview.info/node/208/pdf

Naím, Moisés, "What Is a GONGO? How Government-Sponsored Groups Masquerade as Civil Society," Foreign Policy, October 13, 2009, http://foreignpolicy.com/2009/10/13/what-is-a-gongo

Naso, Publius Ovidius (Ovid), *Metamorphoses* (translated by Anthony S. Kline) (London: Borders, 2004)

Negro, Gianluigi, "Chinese Internet Governance—Some Domestic and Foreign Issues," in Roxana Radu, Jean-Marie Chenou, and Rolf H. Weber (eds.), *The Evolution of Global Internet Governance. Principles and Policies in the Making* (Zurich: Schulthess, 2014), 141–56

Nelson, Theodor H., "Brief Words on the Hypertext," January 23, 1967, https://archive.org/details/SelectedPapers1977/mode/2up

NetAffair (Mariann Unterluggauer), "Background," March 2014, http://www.netaffair.at/background.html

Noam, Eli, "Russia Orders Alternate Root Internet System," *Net Policy News*, December 15, 2017, http:// netpolicynews.com/index.php/component/content/article/89-r/941-russia-orders-alternate-internet-system

Nolte, Georg, "Hate-Speech, Fake-News, das 'Netzwerkdurchsetzungsgesetz' und Vielfaltsicherung durch Suchmaschinen," ZUM (2017), 552

Nora A. Draper and Joseph Turow, "Audience Constructions, Reputations, and Emerging Media Technologies: New Issues of Legal and Social Policy," in Roger Brownsword, Eloise Scotford, and Karen Yeung (eds.), *Oxford Handbook of Law, Regulation, and Technology* (Oxford: OUP, 2017), 1143–68

Northrup, David, "Globalization and the Great Convergence: Rethinking World History in the Long Term," Journal of World History 16 (2005) 3, 249–67

Nour, Soraya, "Bourdieus juridisches Feld: Die juridische Dimension der sozialen Emanzipation," in Sonja Buckel, Ralph Christensen, and Andreas Fischer-Lescano (eds.), *Neue Theorien des Rechts*, 2nd edn. (Stuttgart: Lucius&Lucius, 2009), 179–99

Nozick, Robert, *Anarchy, State, and Utopia* (New York: Basic Books, 1974).

Nussbaum, Arthur, *A Concise History of the Law of Nations* (New York: Macmillan, 1947)

Nye Jr., Joseph S., "Normative Constraints on Cyber Arms," in Fen Osler Hampson and Michael Sulmeyer (eds.), *Getting Beyond Norms. New Approaches to International Cyber Security Challenges*, CIGI (Centre for International Governance Innovation) Special Report (2017), https://www.cigionline.org/sites/default/files/documents/Getting%20Beyond%20Norms.pdf, 19–22

Oberleitner, Gerd, "Human Security: Idea, Policy and Law," in Mary Martin and Taylor Owen (eds.), *Routledge Handbook on Human Security* (London: Routledge, 2013), 219–30

Odlyzko, Andrew, "Smart and Stupid Networks: Why the Internet is Like Microsoft," AT&T Labs Research Paper, Revised version, October 6, 1998, http://www.dtc.umn.edu/~odlyz ko/doc/stupid.networks.pdf

Oeter, Stefan, "Vom Völkerrecht zum transnationalen Recht – 'transnational administrative networks' und die Bildung hybrider Akteursstrukturen," in Gralf-Peter Calliess (ed.), *Transnationales Recht. Stand und Perspektiven* (Tübingen: Mohr Siebeck, 2014), 388–402

Orakhelashvili, Alexander, "State Jurisdiction in International Law: Complexities of a Basic Concept," in Alexander Orakhelashvili (ed.), *Research Handbook on Jurisdiction and Immunities in International Law* (Cheltenham: Edward Elgar, 2015), 10

Ostrom, Elinor, *Governing the Commons* (New York: CUP, 1990)

Oxford English Dictionary, s.v. "Internet" (2018), https://en.oxforddictionaries.com/definition/internet

Oxford Living Dictionaries, s.v. "2.0," https://en.oxforddictionaries.com/definition/2.0

Padovani, Claudia and Mauro Santaniello, "Digital Constitutionalism: Fundamental Rights and Power Limitation in the Internet Eco-System," *The International Communication Gazette* (2018), 1–7

Palfrey, John, "The End of the Experiment: How ICANN's Foray into Global Internet Democracy Failed," Harvard Journal of Law & Technology 17 (2004) 2, 409–73

Palfrey, John and Urs Gasser, *Born Digital: Understanding the First Generation of Digital Natives* (New York: Basic Books, 2008), http://borndigitalbook.com

Palfrey, John and Urs Gasser, *Interop: The Promise and Perils of Highly Interconnected Systems* (New York: Basic Books, 2012)

Paré, Daniel J., *Internet Governance in Transition: Who Is the Master of This Domain?* (London: Rowman & Littlefield, 2003)

Pariser, Eli, *The Filter Bubble: How the New Personalized Web Is Changing What We Read and How We Think* (New York: Penguin, 2012)

Parziale, Lydia, David T. Britt, Chuck Davis, Jason Forrester, Wie Liu, Carolyn Matthews, and Nicolas Rosselot, *TCP/IP Tutorial and Technical Overview*, 8th edn. (IBM: IBM Redbooks, 2006)

Pavan, Elena, *Frames and Connections in the Governance of Global Communications* (New York: Lexington Books, 2012)

Pekkanen, Saadia M., "China's Ambitions Fly High: 'One Belt, One Road' To Extend Into Space," *Forbes.com*, May 26, 2017, https://www.forbes.com/sites/saadiampekkanen/2017/05/26/chinas-ambitions-fly-high-one-belt-one-road-to-extend-into-space/#48bfb10d4c0c

Pellet, Alain, "Peaceful Settlement of International Disputes," in Rüdiger Wolfrum (ed.), *Max Planck Encyclopedia of Public International Law (MPEPIL)* (Oxford: OUP, 2008) (2010) [online]

People's Republic of China, State Council, "The Internet in China," June 8, 2010, http://www. china.org.cn/government/whitepaper/node_7093508.htm

Pernice, Ingolf, "Die Verfassung der Internetgesellschaft: Zur Rolle von Staat und Verfassung im Zuge der digitalen Revolution," in Alexander Blankenagel (ed.), *Den Verfassungsstaat nachdenken. Eine Geburtstagsgabe* (Berlin: Duncker & Humblot, 2014) 171–208

Pernice, Ingolf, "Vom Völkerrecht des Netzes zur Verfassung des Internets: Privacy und Digitale Sicherheit im Zeichen eines schrittweisen Paradigmenwechsels (International Law of the Net and the Constitution of the Internet: Privacy and Cybersecurity in the Light of a Progressive Change of Paradigm)," HIIG Discussion Paper Series No. 2017-02, https://ssrn.com/abstract=2959257

Perreau-Suassine, Amanda, "Immanuel Kant on International Law," in Samantha Besson and John Tasioulas (eds.), *The Philosophy of International Law* (Oxford: OUP, 2010), 53–75

Peters, Anne, "Compensatory Constitutionalism: The Function and Potential of Fundamental International Norms and Structures," Leiden Journal of International Law (2006), 579

Peters, Anne, "Membership in the Global Constitutional Community," EJIL Talk, July 20, 2010, http://www.ejiltalk.org/membership-in-the-global-constitutional-community

Peters, Anne, "Realizing Utopia as A Scholarly Endeavour," EJIL 24 (2013), 533–52

Peters, Anne, *Jenseits der Menschenrechte. Die Rechtsstellung des Individuums im Völkerrecht* (Tübingen: Mohr Siebeck, 2014)

Peters, Anne, "The Refinement of International Law: From Fragmentation to Regime Interaction and Politicization," ICON 15 (2017) 3, 671–704 (702)

Petersen, Niels, *Demokratie als teleologisches Prinzip: Zur Legitimität von Staatsgewalt im Völkerrecht* (Frankfurt am Main: Springer, 2009)

Pettit, Philipp, "The Globalized Republican Ideal," Global Justice 9 (2016) 1, 48–68

Peukert, Alexander, "Gewährleistung der Meinungs- und Informationsfreiheit in sozialen Netzwerken. Vorschlag der Ergänzung des NetzDG um sog. Put-Back-Verfahren," MMR (2018), 572

Piketty, Thomas, *Le capital au XXI siècle* (Paris: Éditions du Seuil, 2013)

Pleuger, Gunter, "Die normativen Wirkungen multilateralen Verhaltens," in Andreas Fahrmeier (ed.), *Rechtfertigungsnarrative. Zur Begründung normativer Ordnungen durch Erzählen* (Frankfurt/New York: Campus 2013), 89–99

PoKempner, Dinah, "The Internet is Not the Enemy. As Rights Move Online, Human Rights Standards Move with Them' (2017), Human Rights Watch, World Report 2017, https://www.hrw.org/world-report/2017/country-chapters/the-internet-is-not-the-enemy

Polański, Przemysław Paul, *Customary Law of the Internet: in the Search for a Supranational Cyberspace Law* (The Hague: T.M.C. Asser, 2007)

Pomerantz, Jeffrey, *Metadata* (Cambridge, MA/London: MIT Press, 2015)

Poscher, Ralf, "Theorie eines Phantoms—Die erfolglose Suche der Prinzipientheorie nach ihrem Gegenstand," RW 4 (2010), 349–72 (350)

Pöschl, Magdalena, "Sicherung grund- und menschenrechtlicher Standards gegenüber neuen Gefährdungen durch private und ausländische Akteure," VVDStRL 74 (2015), 405–52

Post, David G., "Cyberspace's Constitutional Moment," The American Lawyer, November 1998, http://www.temple.edu/lawschool/dpost/DNSGovernance.htm

Powell, Alison, "Arguments-by-technology: How Technical Activism Contributes to Internet Governance," in Ian Brown (ed.), *Research Handbook on Governance of the Internet* (Cheltenham: Edward Elgar, 2013), 198–217

Prensky, Marc, "Digital Natives, Digital Immigrants," *On The Horizon* 9 (October 2001)

Proulx, Vincent-Joel, "Babysitting Terrorists: Should States Be Strictly Liable for Failing to Prevent Transborder Attacks?," 23 Berkeley Journal of International Law 615, 629 (2005)

Przychodniak, Marcin, "China's Internet Policy," Polish Institute of International Affairs (PISM) Bulletin 75 (August 4, 2017) 1015, http://www.pism.pl/publications/bulletin/no-75-1015

Radu, Roxana, Jean-Marie Chenou, and Rolf H. Weber (eds.), *The Evolution of Global Internet Governance. Principles and Policies in the Making* (Zurich: Schulthess, 2014)

Randel, Judith, "Why Access to Information Needs to Be Central to the Debate on Poverty," *The Guardian*, February 18, 2013, http://www.theguardian.com/global-development-professionals-network/2013/jan/18/mdgs-poverty-eradication-information-access

Rayfuse, Rosemary, "Public International Law and the Regulation of Emerging Technologies," in Roger Brownsword, Eloise Scotford, and Karen Yeung (eds.), *Oxford Handbook of Law, Regulation, and Technology* (Oxford: OUP, 2017), 500–21

Raymond, Mark and Laura DeNardis, "Multi-stakeholderism: Anatomy of an Inchoate Global Institution," Centre for International Governance Innovation Paper Series No. 41, September 2016, https://www.cigionline.org/si tes/default/files/gcig_no.41web.pdf

Raymond, Mark and Gordon Smith, "Reimaging the Internet: The Need for a High-level Strategic Vision for Internet Governance, 2015–2020," CIGI Internet Governance Paper Series No. 1 (2013), http://www.cigionline.org/ sites/default/files/no1_4.pdf.

Reed, David, Jennifer Haroon, and Patrick Ryan, "Technologies and Policies to Connect the Next 5 Billion," Berkeley Technology Law Journal 29 (2015) 2, 1205–52

Reidenberg, Joel, "Lex Informatica: The Formulation of Internet Policy Rules Through Technology," Texas Law Review 76 (1998), 3

Reilly, Michael, "Prediction Models Gone Wild: Why Election Forecasts and Polls Were So wrong," November 9, 2016, https://www.technologyreview.com/s/602829/prediction-models-gone-wild-why-election-forecasts-and-polls-were-so-wrong

Rioux, Michèle, "Competing Institutional Trajectories for Global Regulation – Internet in a Fragmented World," in Roxana Radu, Jean-Marie Chenou, and Rolf H. Weber (eds.), *The Evolution of Global Internet Governance. Principles and Policies in the Making* (Zurich: Schulthess, 2014), 37–56

Ruffert, Matthias, "Die Europäische Menschenrechtskonvention und innerstaatliches Recht," EuGRZ (2007), 245

Rundle, Mary and Malcolm Birding, "Filtering and the International System: A Question of Commitment," in Ronald Deibert, John Palfrey, Rafal Rohozinski, and Jonathan Zittrain (eds.), *Access Denied. The Practice and Policy of Global Internet Filtering* (Cambridge, Mass./London: The MIT Press, 2008), 73–101

Ruparelia, Nayan B., *Cloud Computing* (Cambridge, MA/London: MIT Press, 2016)

Ryan, Patrick S., "The ITU and the Internet's Titanic Moment," Stanford Technology Law Review 8 (2012)

Saleh, Nivien, *Third World Citizens and the Information Technology Revolution* (London: Palgrave Macmillan, 2010)

Sands, Philippe and Jacqueline Peel, *Principles of International Environmental Law*, 3rd edition (Cambridge: CUP, 2012)

Sartor, Giovanni, "Human Rights and Information Technologies," in Roger Brownsword, Eloise Scotford, and Karen Yeung (eds.), *Oxford Handbook of Law, Regulation, and Technology* (Oxford: OUP, 2017), 424–50

Saurwein, Florian, Natascha Just, and Michael Latzer, "Governance of Algorithms: Options and Limitations," Digital Policy, Regulation and Governance 17 (2015) 6, 35–49.

Schiff, Benjamin N., *Building the International Criminal Court* (Cambridge: CUP, 2008)

Schliesky, Utz, Christian Hoffmann, Anika D. Luch, Sönke E. Schulz, and Kim Corinna Borchers, *Schutzpflichten und Drittwirkung im Internet. Das Grundgesetz im digitalen Zeitalter* (Baden-Baden: Nomos, 2014)

Schmahl, Stefanie, "Zwischenstaatliche Kompetenzabgrenzung im Cyberspace," Archiv des Völkerrechts 47 (2009) 3, 284–327

Schmalenbach, Kirsten, "Völker- und unionsrechtliche Anstöße zur Entterritorialisierung des Rechts," VVDStRL 76 (2017), 245–76

Schmidt, Jan-Hinrik, Jannick Sørensen, Stephan Dreyer, and Uwe Hasebrink, *Algorithmische Empfehlungen. Funktionsweise, Bedeutung und Besonderheiten für öffentlich-rechtliche Rundfunkanstalten* (Hamburg: Verlag Hans-Bredow-Institut, 2018), Hans-Bredow-Institut Working Papers No. 45, https://www.hans-bredow-institut.de/uploads/media/default/cms/ media/w188msk_45AlgorithmischeEmpfehlungen.pdf

Schmidt, Jan-Hinrik, "Filterblasen und Algorithmenmacht. Wie sich Menschen im Internet informieren," in C. Gorr and M. C. Bauer (eds.), *Gehirne unter Spannung: Kognition, Emotion und Identität im digitalen Zeitalter* (Berlin/Heidelberg: Springer, 2018), 35–51

Schmitt, Carl, *Der Nomos der Erde im Völkerrecht des Jus Publicum Europaeum*, 2nd edn. (Berlin: Duncker&Humblot, 1950/1974)

Schmitt, Michael N., "Computer Network Attack and the Use of Force in International Law: Thoughts on a Normative Framework," Columbia Journal of Transnational Law 37 (1999) 3, 885–913

Schmitt, Michael N. (ed.), *Tallinn Manual on the International Law Applicable to Cyber Warfare* (Cambridge: CUP, 2013)

Schmitt, Michael N. and Liis Vihul, "The Nature of International Law Cyber Norms," Tallinn Paper No. 5 (NATO CCD COE), 2014

Schmitt, Michael N. (ed.), *Tallinn Manual 2.0 on the International Law Applicable to Cyber Operations* (Cambridge: CUP, 2017)

Scholtz, Werner, "Collective (Environmental) Security: The Yeast for the Refinement of International Law," in Ole Kristian Fauchald, David Hunter, and Wang Xi (eds.), *Yearbook of International Environmental Law*, Vol. 19 (Oxford: OUP, 2008), 135–62

Scholtz, Werner, "Custodial Sovereignty: Reconciling Sovereignty and Global Environmental Challenges amongst the Vestiges of Colonialism," Netherlands International Law Review 3 (2008), 323–41

Schulte, Heinz, RFCs und Internetstandards im Überblick (Kissing: Interest-Verlag, 2004)

Schulz, Wolfgang, "Regulating Intermediaries to Protect Privacy Online—the Case of the German NetzDG," HIIG Discussion Paper Series 2018-01, https://www.hiig.de/publication/regulating-intermediaries-to-protect-privacy-online-the-case-of-the-german-netzdg

Schulze, Sven Hendrik, *Cyber-"War"—Testfall der Staatenverantwortlichkeit* (Tübingen: Mohr Siebeck, 2015)

Segal, Adam, "Chinese Cyber Diplomacy in a New Era of Uncertainty," Hoover Institution, Aegis Paper Series No. 1703, June 2, 2017, https://www.hoover.org/research/chinese-cyber-diplomacy-new-era-uncertainty

Segal, Adam, "The Development of Cyber Norms at the United Nations Ends in Deadlock. Now What?" *Council on Foreign Relations*, June 29, 2017, https://www.cfr.org/blog/development-cyber-norms-united-nations-ends-deadlock-now-what

Segura-Serrano, Antonio, "Internet Regulation and the Role of International Law," in *Max Planck Yearbook of United Nations Law*, Vol. 10 (The Hague: Brill, 2006), 191–272

Seinecke, Ralf, *Das Recht des Rechtspluralismus* (Tübingen: Mohr Siebeck, 2015)

Sen, Amartya, *Development as Freedom* (Oxford: OUP, 1999)

Senn, Myriam, *Non-State Regulatory Regimes. Understanding Institutional Transformation* (Heidelberg: Springer, 2011)

Shane, Scott, "The Fake Americans Russia Created to Influence the Election," *New York Times*, September 7, 2017, https://www.nytimes.com/2017/09/07/us/politics/russia-facebook-twitter-election.html

Shaw, Malcolm N., *International Law*, 6th edn. (Oxford: OUP, 2008)

Shaw, Malcolm N., *International Law*, 8th edn. (Oxford: OUP, 2017)

Shin, Dale, "The Precarious Subject of Late Capitalism: Rereading Adorno on the 'Liquidation' of Individuality," in Zubin Meer (ed.), *Individualism: The Cultural Logic of Modernity* (Lanham, MD: Lexington, 2011), 203–18.

Simma, Bruno, "Universality of International Law from the Practice of a Practitioner," EJIL 20 (2009) 2, 265–97

Simondon, Gilbert, "About Technical Mentality," Revue philosophique de la France et de l'étranger 131 (2006), 343

Sklerov, Matthew J., "Solving the Dilemma of State Responses to Cyberattacks: A Justification for the use of Active Defenses Against States Who Neglect Their Duty to Prevent," Military Law Review 201 (2009), 1–85

Smith, Adam, *An Inquiry into the Nature and Causes of the Wealth of Nations* (London: Strahan and Cadell, 1775)

Sorell, Tom and John Guelke, "Liberal Democratic Regulation and Technological Advance," in Roger Brownsword, Eloise Scotford, and Karen Yeung (eds.), *Oxford Handbook of Law, Regulation, and Technology* (Oxford: OUP, 2017), 90–112

Spiecker gen. Döhmann, Indra, "Kontexte der Demokratie: Parteien—Medien—Sozialstrukturen," VVDStRL 77 (2018), 9–56

Spiecker gen. Döhmann, Indra, "Online- und Offline-Nutzung von Daten: Einige Überlegungen zum Umgang mit Informationen im Internetzeitalter," in Michael Bartsch und Robert G. Briner (eds.), *DGRI-Jahrbuch* (Cologne: Verlag Dr. Otto Schmidt), 39–53

Spindler, Gerald, "Transnationalisierung und Renationalisierung des Rechts im Internet," in Gralf-Peter Calliess (ed.), *Transnationales Recht* (Tübingen: Mohr Siebeck, 2014)

Sprenger, Florian, *Politik der Mikroentscheidungen. Snowden, Netzneutralität und die Architekturen des Internets* (Lüneburg: Meson, 2016)

Stalder, Felix, *Kultur der Digitalität* (Frankfurt am Main: Suhrkamp, 2016)

Stein, Torsten and Thilo Marauhn, "Völkerrechtliche Aspekte von Informationsoperationen," Zeitschrift für ausländisches öffentliches Recht und Völkerrecht 60 (2000), 6

Stellman, Andrew and Jennifer Greene, *Applied Software Project Management* (Boston, MA: O'Reilly, 2005)

Stevens, Tim, "BRICS Vision for International Information Security' (2015), http://thesigers.com/analysis/ 2015/7/3/brics-set-out-vision-for-international-information-security

Stirling, Andres, "Precaution in the Governance of Technology," in Roger Brownsword, Eloise Scotford, and Karen Yeung (eds.), *Oxford Handbook of Law, Regulation, and Technology* (Oxford: OUP, 2017), 645–69

Stolleis, Michael, "Vormodernes und postmodernes Recht?" Quaderni Fiorentini 37 (2008), 543–51

Struett, Michael J., *The Politics of Constructing the International Criminal Court: NGOs, Discourse, and Agency* (Basingstoke: Palgrave Macmillan, 2008), 83–107

Sukumar, Arun M., "The UN GGE Failed. Is International Law in Cyberspace Doomed As Well?" Lawfare, July 4, 2017, https://lawfareblog.com/un-gge-failed-international-law-cyberspace-doomed-well

Sunstein, Cass R., *Laws of Fear. Beyond the Precautionary Principle* (Cambridge: CUP, 2005)

Svantesson, Dan Jerker B., *Solving the Internet Jurisdiction Puzzle* (Oxford: OUP, 2017)

Tadjbakhsh, Shahrbanou and Anuradha M. Chenoy, *Human Security. Concepts and Implications* (London: Routledge, 2007), 98–122

Tadjbakhsh, Shahrbanou, "In Defense of the Broad View of Human Security," in Mary Martin and Taylor Owen (eds.), *Routledge Handbook on Human Security* (London: Routledge, 2013), 43–56

Tammelo, Ilmar, "Logical Openness of Legal Orders: A Modal Analysis of Law with Special Reference to the Logical Status of Non Liquet in International Law," American Journal of Comparative Law 8 (1959) 2, 187–203

Tantner, Anton, *Ordnung der Häuser, Beschreibung der Seelen: Hausnummerierung und Seelenkonskription in der Habsburgermonarchie (Wiener Schriften zur Geschichte der Neuzeit)* (Vienna: Studienverlag, 2007)

Teubner, Gunther and Helmut Willke, "Kontext und Autonomie," Zeitschrift für Rechtssoziologie 5 (1984), 4–35

Teubner, Gunther, *Recht als autopoietisches System* (Suhrkamp: Frankfurt am Main, 1989)

Teubner, Gunther, "Globale Bukowina. Zur Emergenz eines transnationalen Rechtspluralismus," Rechtshistorisches Journal 15 (1996), 255

Teubner, Gunther, "Globale Zivilverfassungen: Alternativen zur staatszentrierten Verfassungstheorie," ZaÖRV 63 (2003), 1–28

Teubner, Gunther, *Verfassungsfragmente. Gesellschaftlicher Konstitutionalismus in der Globalisierung* (Frankfurt: Suhrkamp, 2012)

Teubner, Gunther, "The Project of Constitutional Sociology: Irritating Nation State Constitutionalism," Transnational Legal Theory (2013) 4, 44

Thaler, Richard H. and Cass R. Sustein, *Nudge. Improving Decisions about Health, Wealth, and Happiness* (New Haven: Yale University Press, 2008)The Guardian, "AI Programs Exhibit Racial and Gender Biases, Research Reveals," *The Guardian*, April 13, 2017, https://www.theguardian.com/technology/2017/apr/13/ai-programs-exhibit-racist-and-sexist-biases-research-reveals

The Guardian, "The Great British Brexit Robbery: How Our Democracy Was Hijacked," *The Guardian*, May 7, 2017, https://www.theguardian.com/technology/2017/may/07/the-great-british-brexit-robbery-hijacked-democracy

Thierer, Adam and Clyde Wayne Crews Jr. (eds.), *Who Rules the Net? Internet Governance and Jurisdiction* (Washington: Cato Institute, 2003)

Thürer, Daniel and Thomas Burri, "Self-Determination," in Rüdiger Wolfrum (ed.), *Max Planck Encyclopedia of Public International Law (MPEPIL)* (Oxford: OUP, 2008) (2008) [online]

Tigerstrom, Barbara, *Human Security and International Law—Problems and Prospects* (Oxford: Hart, 2007)

Tikk, Eneken and Mika Kerttunen, "The Alleged Demise of the UN GGE: An Autopsy and Eulogy," Cyber Policy Institute (2017), http://cpi.ee/wp-content/uploads/2017/12/2017-Tikk-Kerttunen-Demise-of-the-UN-GGE-2017-12-17-ET.pdf

Tikk, Eneken, "Norms à la Carte," in Fen Osler Hampson and Michael Sulmeyer (eds.), *Getting Beyond Norms. New Approaches to International Cyber Security Challenges*, CIGI (Centre for International Governance Innovation) Special Report (2017), https://www.cigionline.org/sites/default/files/documents/Getting%20Beyond%Norms.pdf

Treisman, Loren, "Power to the People: How Open Data is Improving Health Service Delivery," *The Guardian*, December 2, 2013, http://www.theguardian.com/global-development-professionals-network/2013/dec/02/open-data-healthcare-accountability-africa

Treves, Tullio, "Customary International Law," in Rüdiger Wolfrum (ed.), *Max Planck Encyclopedia of Public International Law (MPEPIL)* (Oxford: OUP, 2008)

Uerpmann-Wittzack, Robert, "Internetvölkerrecht," Archiv des Völkerrechts 47 (2009) 3, 261–83

Uerpmann-Wittzack, Robert, "Principles of International Internet Law," German Law Journal 11 (2010), 1245–63

Unwin, Tim, *ICT4D: Information and Communication Technologies for Development* (Cambridge: CUP, 2009)

Unwin, Tim, "The Internet and Development: A Critical Perspective," in William H. Dutton (ed.), *The Oxford Handbook of Internet Studies* (Oxford: OUP, 2013), 531–54

Vajic, Nina and Panayotis Voyatzis, "The Internet and Freedom of Expression: A 'Brave New World' and the European Court of Human Rights' Evolving Case Law," in Josep Casadevall et al. (eds.), *Freedom of Expression. Essays in Honour of Nicolas Bratza* (Osterwijk: Wolf, 2012), 391–420

Väljataga, Ann, "Back to Square One? The Fifth UN GGE Fails to Submit a Conclusive Report at the UN General Assembly," NATO CCDCOE Incyder database, https://ccdcoe.org/incyder-articles/back-to-square-one-the-fifth-un-gge-fails-to-submit-a-conclusive-report-at-the-un-general-assembly

van Aaken, Anne, "To Do Away with International Law? Some Limits to 'The Limits of International Law,'" EJIL (2006), 289–308 van Gelder, Stéphane, "The Rise of Cyrillic Domain Names," *CircleID*, June 3, 2013, http://www.circleid.com/posts/ 20130603_the_rise_of_cyrillic_domain_names

van Schewick, Barbara, *Internet Architecture and Innovation* (Cambridge, MA: MIT Press, 2010)

Vargas-Leon, Patricia, "Tracking Internet Shutdown Practices: Democracies and Hybrid Regimes," in Francesca Musiani, Derrick L. Cogburn, Laura DeNardis, and Nanette S. Levinson (eds.), *The Turn to Infrastructure in Internet Governance* (New York: Palgrave Macmillan US, 2016), 167–88

Vec, Miloš, *Recht und Normierung in der Industriellen Revolution: neue Strukturen der Normsetzung in Völkerrecht, staatlicher Gesetzgebung und gesellschaftlicher Selbstnormierung* (Frankfurt am Main: Klostermann, 2006)

Verdross, Alfred and Bruno Simma, *Universelles Völkerrecht. Theorie und Praxis* (reprint of the 3rd edn.) (Berlin: Duncker & Humblot, 1984/2010)

Verhulst, Stefaan G., Beth S. Noveck, Jillian Raines, and Antony Declercq, "Innovations in Global Governance: Toward a Distributed Internet Governance Ecosystem," GCIG Paper Series No. 5, December 2014, http://www.thegovlab.org/static/files/publications/gcig_paper_no5.pdf

Vesting, Thomas, *Die Medien des Rechts: Schrift* (Weilerswist: Velbrück Wissenschaft, 2011)

Vesting, Thomas, *Die Medien des Rechts: Sprache* (Weilerswist: Velbrück Wissenschaft, 2011)

Vesting, Thomas, *Die Medien des Rechts: Buchdruck* (Weilerswist: Velbrück Wissenschaft, 2013)

Vesting, Thomas, *Rechtstheorie*, 2nd edn. (Munich: Beck, 2015)

Vesting, Thomas, *Die Medien des Rechts: Computernetzwerke* (Weilerswist: Velbrück Wissenschaft, 2015)

Vesting, Thomas, *Legal Theory and the Media of Law* (Cheltenham: Edward Elgar, 2018)

Vesting, Thomas, "Instituierte und konstituierte Normativität. Prozeduralisierung und multinormative Systeme," in Tatjana Sheplyakova (ed.), *Prozeduralisierung des Rechts* (Tübingen: Mohr, 2018), 101–122

Viellechner, Lars, *Transnationalisierung des Rechts* (Weilerswist: Velbrück, 2013)

Villafiorita, Adolfo, *Introduction to Software Project Management* (Boca Raton, FL: CRC Press, 2016)

Vinge, Vernor, "The Coming Technological Singularity: How to Survive in the Post-Human Era," in G. A. Landis (ed.), *Vision-21: Interdisciplinary Science and Engineering in the Era of Cyberspace* (Washington, DC: NASA, 1993)

von Bogdandy, Armin, Philipp Dann, and Matthias Goldmann, "Völkerrecht als öffentliches Recht: Konturen eines rechtlichen Rahmens für Global Governance," Der Staat 49 (2010), 23

von Bogdandy, Armin, "Prinzipielles zur Pluralität normativer Ordnungen. Zu den Anforderungen an die Ausübung öffentlicher Gewalt," Normative Orders Working Paper 1/2013

von Bogdandy, Armin, "Prinzipien von Staat, supranationalen und internationalen Organisationen," § 232 (275–304), in Josef Isensee, Paul Kirchhof, et al. (eds.), *Handbuch des Staatsrechts, Band XI: Internationale Bezüge*, 3rd edn. (2013)

von Bogdandy, Armin and Ingo Venzke, *In wessen Namen?—Internationale Gerichte in Zeiten globalen Regierens* (Frankfurt am Main: Suhrkamp, 2014)

von Schorlemer, Sabine, "Telecommunications, International Regulation," in Rüdiger Wolfrum (ed.), *Max Planck Encyclopedia of Public International Law (MPEPIL)* (Oxford: OUP, 2008) (March 2009) [online]

Waldenfels, Bernhard, *Sozialität und Alterität—Modi sozialer Erfahrung* (Frankfurt am Main: Suhrkamp, 2015)

Wall, David S., *Cybercrime* (Cambridge: CUP, 2007)

Wall, David S., "Crime, Security, and Information Communication Technologies: The Changing Cybersecurity Threat Landscape and Its Implications for Regulation and Policing," in Roger Brownsword, Eloise Scotford, and Karen Yeung (eds.), *Oxford Handbook of Law, Regulation, and Technology* (Oxford: OUP, 2017), 1075–96

Walter, Christian, "Cyber Security als Herausforderung für das Völkerrecht," JZ 14 (2015), 685–93

Weber, Max, *The Theory of Social and Economic Organization*, (edited by Talcott Parsons) (New York: Free Press, 1964), 382

Weber, Rolf H., *Shaping Internet Governance: Regulatory Challenges* (Vienna/New York: Springer, 2009)

Weber, Rolf H., "New Sovereignty Concepts in the Age of Internet?" Journal of Internet Law 14 (2010), 12–20

Weber, Rolf H., "Overcoming the Hard Law/Soft Law Dichotomy in Times of (Financial) Crises," Journal of Governance and Regulation 1 (2012), 8–14

Weber, Rolf H., "Legal Interoperability as a Tool for Combatting Fragmentation," Global Commission on Internet Governance Paper Series No. 4 (2014), https://www.cigionline.org/sites/default /files/gcig_paper_no4.pdf, 5

Weber, Rolf H., *Realizing a New Global Cyberspace Framework. Normative Foundations and Guiding Principles* (Zurich: Schulthess and Springer, 2014)

Weber, Rolf H., *Principles for Governing the Internet. a Comparative Analysis* (Paris: UNESCO, 2015), http://unesdoc.unesco.org/images/0023/002344/234435e.pdf

Webster, Frank, *Theories of the Information Society*, 3rd edn. (London: Routledge, 2006)

Weiler, Joseph H. H., "The Geology of International Law—Governance, Democracy, and Legitimacy," ZAÖRV 64 (2004), 547–62

Weiß, Wolfgang, *Privatisierung und Staatsaufgaben. Privatisierungsentscheidungen im Lichte einer grundrechtlichen Staatsaufgabenlehre unter dem Grundgesetz* (Tübingen: Mohr Siebeck, 2002)

Weitzenboeck, Emily M., "Hybrid Net: The Regulatory Framework of ICANN and the DNS," International Journal of Law and Information Technology 22 (2014) 1, 49–73

Werbach, Kevin, "The Centripetal Network: How the Internet Holds Itself Together, and the Forces Tearing It Apart," University of California, Davis Law Review (2008) 42, 343–412

Whitt, Richard S., "A Deference to Protocol: Fashioning a Three-Dimensional Public Policy Framework for the Internet Age," Cardozo Arts & Entertainment Law Journal 31 (2013), 689–768

Wiethölter, Rudolf, "Begriffs- und Interessenjurisprudenz—falsche Fronten im IPR und Wirtschaftsverfassungsrecht. Bemerkungen zur selbstgerechten Kollisionsnorm," in Alexander Lüderitz and Jochen Schröder (eds.), *Internationales Privatrecht und Rechtsvergleichung im Ausgang des 20. Jahrhunderts. Bewahrung oder Wende? Festschrift für Gerhard Kegel* (Frankfurt am Main: Suhrkamp, 1977), 213

Wiethölter, Rudolf, "Recht-Fertigungen eines Gesellschaftsrechts," in Christian Joerges and Gunther Teubner (eds.), *Rechtsverfassungsrecht. Recht-Fertigung zwischen Privatrechtsdogmatik und Gesellschaftstheorie* (Baden-Baden: Nomos, 2003)

William Waters, Timothy, "The Momentous Gravity of the State of Things Now Obtaining: Annoying Westphalian Objections to the Idea of Global Governance," Indiana Journal of Global Studies 16 (2009), 25–58

Wilson, Peter H., *The Holy Roman Empire. A Thousand Years of Europe's History* (London: Penguin, 2016)

Winter, Gerd, "Transnationale informelle Regulierung: Gestalt, Effekte und Rechtsstaatlichkeit," in Gralf-Peter Calliess (ed.), *Transnationales Recht. Stand und Perspektiven* (Tübingen: Mohr Siebeck, 2014), 95–112

Wolff, Jonathan, *Robert Nozick: Property, Justice and the Minimal State* (Oxford: Polity Press, 1991)

Wolfrum, Rüdiger, "Cooperation, International Law of," in Rüdiger Wolfrum (ed.), *Max Planck Encyclopedia of Public International Law* (MPEPIL) (Oxford: OUP, 2008) (December 2010) [online]

Wolfrum, Rüdiger, "General International Law (Principles, Rules and Standards)," in Rüdiger Wolfrum (ed.), *Max Planck Encyclopedia of Public International Law* (MPEPIL) (Oxford: OUP, 2008) (December 2010) [online]

Woltag, Johann-Christoph, "Internet," in Rüdiger Wolfrum (ed.), *Max Planck Encyclopedia of Public International Law* (MPEPIL) (Oxford: OUP, 2008) (September 2010) [online]

Wood, Michael, "Use of Force, Prohibition of Threat," in Rüdiger Wolfrum (ed.), *Max Planck Encyclopedia of Public International Law* (MPEPIL) (Oxford: OUP, 2008) (2013) [online]

Wu, Tim, *The Master Switch: The Rise and Fall of Information Empires* (New York: Vintage, 2011)

Wüst, Karl and Arthur Gervais, "Do You Need a Blockchain?," International Association for Cryptologic Research, Working Paper 375 (2017), https://eprint.iacr.org/2017/375.pdf

Xinhua, "President Xi Stresses Int'l Cooperation in Cyberspace Governance," November 17, 2016, http://www.wuz henwic.org/2016-11/17/c_61495.htm.

Young, Daniel Taylor, "How Do You Measure a Constitutional Moment? Using Algorithmic Topic Modeling To Evaluate Bruce Ackerman's Theory of Constitutional Change," Yale Law Journal 122 (2013), 1990–2054

Zagzebski, Linda, *On Epistemology* (Belmont, CA: Wadsworth, 2009)

Zander, Joakim, *The Application of the Precautionary Principle in Practice. Comparative Dimensions* (Cambridge: CUP, 2010)

Zarmanian, Thalin, "Ordnung und Ortung/Order and localisation," in Stephen Legg (ed.), *Spatiality, Sovereignty and Carl Schmitt* (Abingdon: Routledge, 2011), 291–297 (295)

Zhanga, Yong-Xiang, Qing-Chen Chaoa, Qiu-Hong Zheng, Lei Huang, "The withdrawal of the U.S. from the Paris Agreement and its impact on global climate change governance," Advances in Climate Change Research 8 (2017) 4, 213–19

Zhen-Wei Qiang, Christine, Carlo M. Rossotto, and Kaoru Kimura, "Economic Impacts of Broadband," in World Bank, *Information and Communications for Development 2009: Extending Reach and Increasing Impact* (2009), http://siteresources.worldbank.org/EXTIC4D/Resources/IC4D_Broadband_35_50.pdf, 25-50

Ziewitz, Malte and Ian Brown, "A Prehistory of Internet Governance," in Ian Brown (ed.), *Research Handbook on Governance of the Internet* (Cheltenham: Edward Elgar, 2013), 3–26

Zimmermann, Andreas, "International Law and 'Cyber Space'," ESIL Reflections 3 (2014) 1, http://www.esil-sedi.eu/node/481, 4

Zintl, Reinhard, *Individualistische Theorien und die Ordnung der Gesellschaft. Untersuchungen zur politischen Theorie von James M. Buchanan und Friedrich A. v. Hayek* (Berlin: Duncker & Humblot, 1983)

Ziolkowski, Katharina, "Confidence Building Measures for Cyberspace," in Katharina Ziolkowski (ed.), *Peacetime Regime for State Activities in Cyberspace. International Law, International Relations and Diplomacy* (Tallinn: NATO CCD COE Publications, 2013), 533–64

Ziolkowski, Katharina, "General Principles of International Law as Applicable in Cyberspace," in Katharina Ziolkowski (ed.), *Peacetime Regime for State Activities in Cyberspace. International Law, International Relations and Diplomacy* (Tallinn: NATO CCD COE Publications, 2013), 135–84

Ziolkowski, Katharina (ed.), *Peacetime Regime for State Activities in Cyberspace, International Law, International Relations and Diplomacy* (Tallinn: NATO CCD COE Publications, 2013), http://ccd-coe.org/427.html

Zittrain, Jonathan, "No, Barack Obama Isn't Handing Control of the Internet over to China," *The New Republic*, March 24, 2014

Zürn, Michael, Martin Binder, Matthias Ecker-Ehrhardt, and Katrin Radtke, "Politische Ordnungsbildung wider Willen," Zeitschrift für Internationale Beziehungen 14 (2007) 1, 129–64

Index

Note: *For the benefit of digital users, indexed terms that span two pages (e.g., 52–53) may, on occasion, appear on only one of those pages.*
Tables are indicated by *t* following the page number

1970 Friendly Relations Declaration, 82, 89, 92–94
1975 Helsinki Final Act, 91
2000 United Nations Millennium Declaration, 92–93
2001 Draft Articles on the Prevention of Transboundary Harm from Hazardous Activities, 95–97, 100
2005 World Summit Outcome Document, 82

adherence, 13
Algeria, 69, 156–57, 301
algorithm, 55, 58, 208–9, 218, 273–74
alternative dispute resolution, 198, 219–20
anarchy, 4, 60, 252
anonymity, 67, 74–75, 212, 228, 238
application programming interface, 171–72
arbitration, 92, 95–96, 116–17
ARPAnet, 20–21
Australia, 114, 151–52
Austria, 2, 149–50, 229
autonomous systems, 33
availability, 129, 154, 296–97

balance, 101, 147, 154, 270–71
Barlow, John Perry, 46
Berners-Lee, Tim, 21
binary addresses, 29
blackout, 26
Border Gateway Protocols, 33
borders, 23
Brazil, 38, 120–22, 143, 157
Brexit, 84
browser, 23

censorship, 52, 171, 222
Charter of Fundamental Rights (CFR), 75
Charter of Internet Rights and Principles, 121–22, 139*t*, 141, 142*t*
child protection, 87
China, 6–7, 38, 65–69, 78, 86–87, 118, 121–22, 138–43, 139*t*, 142*t*, 156–58, 161, 176–78, 223–24, 267, 301–2, 308
citizens, 47–48, 56, 59–60, 62–63, 84–85, 157, 164, 165–66, 176, 236–37, 248, 257, 264, 270–72, 283–84, 286–88, 290–91, 298, 301–2, 303, 306–7
Clark, David, 46
climate change, 34–35
cloud-based services, 23
cloud computing, 39
code, xix, 8, 14–15, 17, 29, 45–46, 47–53, 55, 57–58, 60, 78, 86, 108, 118, 120–22, 137*t*, 138–39, 139*t*, 140–41, 142*t*, 150, 185–90, 191, 198, 208–9, 214, 219, 221–22, 229, 244, 248, 252–53, 255–56, 267, 276–77, 279, 305, 306–7
Code of Conduct on illegal online hate speech, 150
Committee on Economic, Social and Cultural Rights, 150–51
common concerns of humanity, 33–34
common interest, 4–5, 10–11
compliance pull, 179–80, 234–35, 245
computer, 25
confidence-building, 92, 100, 102, 156, 272–73, 293
confidence, 27
conflict studies, 16
consensus, 16–17, 30–33, 45–46, 59, 64–66, 88–89, 99, 108, 111, 123, 126, 147, 153–56, 176–77, 206, 226, 228, 251–53, 255–56, 259–60, 276, 279
constitutional law, 34–35
constitutionalization, 18, 64, 73–74, 127, 195, 199–200, 209–26, 230, 242–44, 250–51, 277, 280, 282–83, 299, 303
consumer protection, 87
contingency, 97, 100, 185–86, 208–9, 228, 231
Convention Concerning the Protection of the World Cultural and Natural Heritage, 34
Convention on the Law of the Non-Navigational Uses of International Watercourses, 98
corporate social responsibility, 56, 62–63, 105
Council of Europe, viii, 76, 118, 132, 137*t*, 138–39, 139*t*, 141, 143–46, 151, 163, 220–21, 228–29
Council of Europe Commissioner for Human Rights, 76, 163
Council of Europe Declaration on Internet Governance Principles, 145
Court of Justice of the European Union (CJEU), 74
Cover, Robert M, 12
creativity, 77–78, 126, 147, 162–63, 178, 285
crime, vii, 5–6, 75, 105, 111, 217, 237
Crimea, 94
critical infrastructure, 14, 23, 26–27, 37, 42, 56, 87, 90–92, 93, 96–97, 99, 100, 102, 223, 293
critical internet resources, xxvii, 11, 23, 27–33, 44, 56–57, 61, 70, 111, 118–19, 123, 134–35, 146, 153, 222, 291, 301–2

critical positivism, 16
cultural heritage, 34–35
cyberattacks, 6–7, 88, 275
cybercrime, 42–43, 44, 62, 96–97, 98, 107, 111, 123, 128, 233, 307
cybernorms, 18, 47–48, 251
cybersecurity, vii–viii, 14, 42, 73–74, 87, 90, 99, 100–2, 106, 118–19, 123, 161, 211, 223, 233, 261, 272–73, 293, 294
cyberspace, 4–5, 9–10, 16–17, 35, 45–46, 48–50, 59, 63, 66–70, 83–84, 121–22, 129, 137*t*, 139*t*, 142*t*, 157–58, 161–62, 212, 224–26, 250, 253, 293–94, 302
cyberterrorism, 42–43
cyberwar, 5–6, 160–61, 178, 308

dark web, 142*t*, 171
data centers, 24–25, 27–29, 56
data flows, 23, 76, 86, 159, 173–74, 196, 268–69, 279, 301
data packets, 24–25
data transfer, 23, 56, 74, 214, 306
DE-CIX, 45
Declaration of the Independence of Cyberspace, 59
dehierarchization, 189–91, 228–29, 308–9
democratic governance, 35
democratization, 39
deterritoralization, 47–48
development law, 34–35, 39–40,
Digital Agenda, 39
digital divide, 41
digital enclosures, 172
Digital Single Market, 172–73
digitalization, 167–68, 179, 208
diversity, 39
Domain Name System (DNS), 21, 51, 52–53, 108–9, 116, 156–57
domain reserve, 84
dualism, 19, 195, 281
Dynamic Coalitions, 113–14

economic growth, 39
ecosystem, 31–32
effectiveness, 8–9, 59–60, 124, 159, 299
Egypt, 69, 156–57, 178, 223–24, 301
election, 54
Electronic Frontier Foundation, 45–46
encryption technology, 74–75, 164
enforcement, 46
entrepreneurship, 15, 101, 267, 275–76
environment, xx, 6–7, 21–23, 27, 42, 65, 95–98, 101, 126, 135–40, 147, 151, 155–56, 161, 163–64, 186, 215, 249, 258, 309
epistemology, 183–85, 198
espionage, 60–61, 75, 93, 162–63
European Commission, 51, 68, 97, 125–26, 137*t*, 138–39, 139*t*, 142*t*, 143
European Court of Human Rights (ECtHR), xxvii, 21–22, 72
European Organization for Nuclear Research (CERN), 21
European Parliament, 27
European Union (EU), 26

Facebook, 53–54, 172
facticity, 33–34, 147–48, 229, 235, 273–74, 275–76, 305–6
filter bubble, 54
fluidity, 60, 93, 188, 228, 309
Forst, Rainer, 11, 12–13
fragmentation, 15, 21, 81–83, 104–5, 131–32, 142*t*, 166–81, 191–93, 215, 228–29, 236, 244, 259, 297–99, 308
France, 87, 149–50, 151–52
Franck, Thomas M., 33–34
functionality, 6, 24–29, 28*t*, 35–43, 56, 60–64, 78–79, 88–93, 123, 131, 168, 175–76, 187, 245–49, 268, 277, 297, 306

gender divide, 41
General Data Protection Regulation (GDPR), 54–55
general principles of international law, 6–7
  duty of cooperation, 82, 90–92, 128, 293, 302
  no harm principle, 43, 95–98, 128, 216, 302
  non-intervention in domestic affairs, 82, 89–90, 128, 302
  non-use of (the threat of) force, 82, 87–89, 128, 302, 307
  peaceful settlement of international disputes, 82, 92–93, 128, 302
  precautionary principle, 43–44, 82–83
  principle of equal rights, 82, 93–94, 128
  principle of good faith, 82, 95, 117, 128, 302
  principle of good neighborliness, 82–83, 95–97, 128
  principle of prevention, 82–83, 97–101, 128, 302
  principle of sustainable development, 82–83, 100, 101–2, 128
  self-determination of peoples, 82, 93–94, 128
  sic utere tuo principle, 43
  sovereign equality of states, 82
geo-blocking, 142*t*, 172–73
geography, 68, 300
geo-targeting, 172–73, 216–17
Germany, 6–7, 45, 75, 76, 83–84, 149–50, 159, 162–63, 178, 194, 205–6, 229, 245, 281, 286, 290, 297, 300
Global Commission on Internet Governance, 161
Global Commission on the Stability of Cyberspace, 129
global constitutionalism, 16
Global Multistakeholder Meeting on the Future of Internet Governance, 126, 285
globalization, 8, 47–48, 59–63, 122, 125–26, 143, 160, 165–68, 179, 194–97, 248, 253, 281, 298
Goethe, Johann Wolfgang von, 196–97
good governance, 112, 126, 133, 135, 270–71
Google, 53, 74, 151–52, 173–74, 211–12, 218–20, 225, 231
Gross Domestic Product, 38
Group of Governmental Experts, xxvii, 6–7, 43, 65, 77, 160, 174, 233, 256–57, 300
Grundnorm, 189–90, 306
Günther, Klaus, 11, 13

Habermas, Jürgen, 19, 47–48, 63–64, 203, 248, 264–65
hardware, 23, 31–32
Henkin, Louis, 155
heterarchy, 189–91
hetero-constitutionalization, 200, 242–43, 277, 280, 299
 interdependence, 95, 112, 133, 272
 singularity, 189–90, 220, 235–37
hierarchy, 103, 131, 189–92, 228–29, 242, 244
human development, 24–27, 36, 37–41, 49–50, 65–66, 71, 135–36, 144*t*, 144, 276
human dignity, 33–35, 132–33, 285, 289
human rights, vii–ix, xxvii, 6–11, 17, 21–25, 27, 32–41, 49–54, 56–58, 60–65, 70–78, 83–87, 98–99, 106, 111–12, 118–23, 124–27, 132–33, 135–38, 137*t*, 139*t*, 141–48, 142*t*, 144*t*, 145*t*, 149–55, 156–63, 173–79, 188–93, 197–99, 202–6, 211, 216–21, 223–25, 230, 243–46, 250, 254–59, 266–76, 277, 279–80, 285–92, 294, 301–4, 306–9
 due process, 54, 144*t*, 154, 216–17, 230
 freedom from discrimination, 54
 freedom of artistic expression, 36
 freedom of assembly and association online, 36
 freedom of cultural expression, 36
 freedom of expression, vii–viii, 8–9, 10–11, 20–25, 36–39, 54, 56–58, 70–76, 111–12, 120–22, 126–27, 137*t*, 139*t*, 141, 142*t*, 143–44, 144*t*, 145*t*, 149–51, 164, 173, 212, 222–24, 258, 287, 306
 freedom of information, 5, 36, 223–24, 258
 freedom of opinion, 36, 70–72, 85–86, 120, 223–24
 freedom of the press and the media, 36
 freedom of science, 36
 human security, 37, 237
 intellectual property, xxix, 9–10, 27, 69, 87, 140–41, 154, 271
 privacy, 5, 8–10, 137*t*, 139*t*, 141, 142*t*, 143–44, 144*t*, 153–54, 161–64, 178, 211–12, 215, 222, 248, 258, 271
 right of access to digital knowledge, 36
 right to be forgotten, 14, 74, 151–52, 173–74
 right to (digital) education, 36
 right to an effective remedy, 54
 right to an explanation, 54–55, 228
 right to internet access, 9–10, 25, 36, 71, 127, 287–91
 right to privacy, 72–76, 127, 141, 161–64, 258
Human Rights Council, 10–11n77, 39, 58, 70–74, 106, 137*t*, 139*t*, 143, 285
humanitarian intervention, 45
hybridity, 182, 229
hyperlink, 23
hypertext, xxviii, 7, 31–33, 183–84, 244
 HyperText Markup Language, xxviii, 32–33
 HyperText Transfer Protocol, 31–32

inclusivity, 124
India, xxvii, 38, 87, 121–22, 157, 224
Industrial Revolution, 167
information and communication technologies (ICTs), x, 2–6, 20, 85, 101–4, 115, 156–59, 160–65, 193, 196–203, 248–49, 270–75, 286–87, 297–302, 305
 impact, vii–xix, 5–6, 10, 38–41, 49–54, 59–72, 84–86, 98, 115, 141, 145*t*, 147–54, 161–62, 173–79, 216–29, 250, 271, 291, 305
information dissemination system, 72
information society, xxix, 4–8, 20–22, 36, 44–50, 56, 62–70, 76–79, 109–12, 121–27, 132–35, 137–42*t*, 148–55, 162–65, 177, 188–89, 211, 228, 238, 274–76, 289, 290
informationalization, 6–14, 18–19, 23–28, 25–28*t*, 33–43, 48, 56–58, 60–71, 79–111, 124–29, 140–47, 156–66, 169, 169*t*, 171–79, 182–83, 211–13, 221–26, 229–31, 237–40, 258–61, 286–93, 300–2, 305–9
infrastructuralization, 18, 182–83
infrastructure, 5–9, 14, 18–19, 23–25, 25*t*, 111, 124–29, 140–47, 156–69, 169*t*, 171–79, 182–83, 211–13, 221–26, 229–31, 237–40, 254–61, 286–93, 300–2, 305–9
innovation, 40–41, 77–78, 101–2, 113–14, 125–26, 135–47, 154, 175, 214–15, 245, 258–59, 285
Institute of Electrical and Electronic Engineers (IEEE), 32–33
integrity, vii–viii, 6, 8–9, 12–13, 28–45, 51–58, 62–79, 81, 99, 101, 102–3, 127–29, 140–44, 145*t*, 147–57, 161–64, 168–78, 212–26, 234–37, 249–57, 269, 288–302, 306–10
intelligence services, 76, 163
interconnectedness, 31–32, 76, 163
intercontinental cables, 24–25, 27
interdisciplinarity, ix, 7–9, 17
Interior Gateway Protocols, 33
International Code of Conduct for Information Security, 78, 86, 121–22, 137*t*, 139*t*, 142*t*, 267
international community, 33–34, 43–46, 80–81, 89
International Court of Justice (ICJ), 4–5, 67, 68–69, 76–77, 79–82, 83–84, 87–88, 89, 90, 92–93, 94, 95, 96, 97, 101, 128
International Covenant on Civil and Political Rights, 10, 70, 71–72, 75
International Covenant on Economic, Social and Cultural Rights, 93–94
international crimes, 34–35
international criminal law, 34–35, 114, 202, 267, 307
international law, 9–10, 33–35, 45–46, 50–51, 61–69, 76–79–, 81–85, 117, 127–30, 155–56, 192, 249–50, 280–81, 282, 286, 291–93, 307–8
 erga omnes duties, 34–35, 43–44
 ius cogens, 14, 34–35, 79, 87–88, 102–3, 127, 128, 182, 250, 282, 292, 305–6, 307
 peremptory norm of international law, 82–84, 87–88, 92–93
 self-defense, 66, 88–89, 92, 161, 164, 178, 212, 236
International Organization for Standardization, 108
international organizations, 2, 3, 16–17, 36, 59, 63, 64–65, 84–85, 91, 105–6, 111, 121–22, 133–34, 135, 137, 138–39, 140, 141–43, 144–45, 197, 205, 265, 270–71, 285

international peace, 33–34, 42, 43, 65, 83, 90–91, 92–93, 100, 163–64, 272–73, 293
internet intermediaries, viii, 17, 25–26, 39, 68, 149–52, 167–68, 197, 218, 220–21, 228, 229
  terms of service, 47–49, 148–50, 151–52, 160, 171–72, 189–90, 198, 220–21, 228, 229, 236, 247, 248, 250–51, 270, 271, 277
internet protocols, 20–21, 29–30, 51–52, 220
  Transfer Control Protocol/Internet Protocol (TCP/IP), 20–21, 23, 31–32, 217, 220
  Internet Protocol version 4 (IPv4), 29, 142*t*, 169, 171
  Internet Protocol version 6 (IPv6), 29, 142*t*, 169, 171
  Protocol Wars, 21
International Strategy for Cyberspace, 97, 137*t*, 139*t*, 142*t*
International Telecommunication Regulations, 69, 122, 176–77
International Telecommunication Union, 41, 63–64, 69, 109, 122, 156–57, 176–77
internationalization, 118, 122, 156, 204, 205–6, 279
internet
  definition of, 22–23
  evolution, xix, 7, 8, 14–15, 20, 31–32, 49, 68, 111, 119, 128, 153, 155–56, 233, 248, 289
internet age, 20, 74, 290, 300
Internet Architecture Board, 51
Internet Assigned Numbers Authority (IANA), 29–31, 44, 45, 69, 94, 107, 108–9, 110, 112, 117–18, 123, 125–26, 143, 301
Internet Corporation for Assigned Names and Numbers (ICANN), 29–31, 33, 64–65, 103, 105–7, 108–9, 110, 112, 113, 116–18, 122, 125–26, 132–33, 143, 194, 197–98, 212, 219, 270, 301
internet economy, 38–39, 42–43
Internet Engineering Task Force (IETF), 32, 45–46, 50, 59, 153–54, 193, 213–14, 228, 246, 260
Internet Exchange Points (IXPs), ix–x, 14, 24–25, 27, 33, 45, 56, 57, 64–65, 68, 102, 169, 224–25, 230–31, 247, 291, 305
internet governance
  actors, 14, 29, 50–51, 103, 105–7, 113–15, 118–20
  non-state actors, 5, 11, 57, 113–14, 119, 121–22, 124, 129, 132, 136, 147–48, 206, 210–11, 226, 255, 264, 268–69, 285
Internet Governance Forum, 106, 112, 113–16, 123, 124, 125–26, 211, 272–73
internet invariants, xix–xx, 15, 18, 132, 175–77, 179, 308
internet of things, 5–6, 29, 168, 169, 171, 187, 188, 190, 213–14, 225, 239, 277
internet principles, 47–48, 60, 257–58, 259, 277
  hype, 120–21, 177, 257, 308
  Internet Rights and Principles Coalition, viii, 114, 121–22, 141
Internet Service Providers (ISPs), 26, 29, 31, 33, 72, 111, 120, 123, 172, 224–25
Internet Society, 32
interoperability, 8, 18, 31–32, 78, 141, 142*t*, 144*t*, 145*t*, 154, 171–72, 175, 176–77, 179–80, 182–83, 213–15, 217, 225, 226, 230, 308
ius necessarium, 61–68

Jellinek, Georg, 63
jurisdiction, 43, 67–68, 85–86, 160, 173–74, 216–17
jurisdictional conflicts, 8–9, 234–35, 249
jurisgenesis, 13, 241
justice, 16, 18, 33–34, 53–54, 83, 92, 207–8, 209, 218–19, 271–72, 305

numerical addresses, 28–29

open network, 141, 145*t*
Open System Interconnect (OSI), 21
openness, 39, 111, 121–22, 141, 154, 213, 248, 282, 284, 285, 303
Organization for Economic Cooperation and Development (OECD), 39
Organization for Security and Cooperation in Europe (OSCE), 121–22
oversecurization, 27

Pakistan, 66, 161, 224
Paris Agreement, 62, 84, 116
permeability, 188, 199–200, 203–4, 209, 282–84
physical data, 27–28
politicization, 3, 21, 46, 116–18, 128, 194–95, 213–14, 229, 309
positivism, 16, 186
Postel, Jon, 48, 108
pouvoir constituant, 148, 193, 280
pouvoir constitué, 148, 193, 280
poverty, x, 38, 39–22
power, ix–x, 5, 8, 10–11, 12–13, 16, 35, 37, 41, 49–50, 56, 59, 62, 75, 83–61, 84–85, 102–3, 137, 148, 153, 154, 175, 180, 182, 188, 195–84, 196, 202–3, 204–5, 207–8, 214, 225, 230–182, 234–37, 260, 261, 264–65, 275, 277, 280, 288, 293, 297, 302, 303, 305, 306
proceduralization, 104–5, 253, 255, 266, 268, 270–71, 272
programming language, 32
progress, 46–47
protocol politics, 8
public core of the internet, 57
Public Technical Identifiers, 30

radicalization, 43
reciprocity, 16, 200, 215
Regional Internet Registries, 29–30
regulated self-regulation, 10, 16–17
Requests for Comments (RFC), 10, 59
resilience, 6, 26, 27, 35–36, 56, 62–63, 64, 125–26, 141, 145*t*, 147, 223, 249, 254, 258, 259, 285, 306

reterritorialization, 159–60, 298–302, 304
Rio Declaration of 1992, 95–96
risk management, 77, 294, 295
robustness, 6, 26, 27, 35–36, 56, 62–63, 64, 106, 113, 135, 141, 145*t*, 213, 249, 285, 306
root zone file, 29, 30–31, 69, 103–61, 110, 112, 223
router, 25, 33, 171
routing system, 28
Ruggie Framework, 151, 211, 221
Russia, 63–64, 66, 69, 75, 78, 86, 89, 114, 121–64, 137*t*, 139, 139*t*, 140, 142*t*, 143, 156–57, 158, 161, 162–63, 166, 178, 179, 300, 308

Saudi Arabia, 69, 156–57, 178, 301
scalability, 154, 217
science, 8, 17, 36, 46, 59, 91–62, 121–22, 175, 201, 227, 275–76
search engine, 23, 270–71
Security Council, 158, 161, 178, 204–5
security, vii–ix, 5–1, 6–7, 14, 24, 26–27, 35–38, 41–43, 50, 51–52, 64, 65, 69, 73–74, 75, 76, 78, 82, 83, 86, 87, 90, 91, 92–63, 99–60, 100–2, 106, 111, 113, 115, 116, 134–35, 214–15, 259, 261–40, 267, 285, 293, 294, 295, 296–97, 306, 309
securization, 37
self-constitutionalization, 15, 18, 243
self-regulation, 16–17, 46, 47, 48, 59, 149, 150, 198, 209–10, 240
Shaw, Malcolm N., 4
small and medium enterprises, 39
social and economic progress, 33–34
social contract, 161
social media, 14, 23, 25*t*, 28*t*, 53, 58, 89–90, 154, 275
social mores, 5–6, 67, 131
social networks, 6, 22–23, 43, 64–65, 173, 258, 270–71
soft law, vii, 5, 14, 19, 62–59, 78, 124, 155–56, 178, 180, 182, 217, 229, 233, 247, 250, 251, 255–56, 277, 280–81, 282, 293–80, 296
software, 17, 23, 31–22, 56, 171, 172, 261–35, 294, 306
software engineering, 32
South Africa, 121–22, 157
sovereignty, 23, 43
  custodial sovereignty, 44, 45, 291, 302
  territorial sovereignty, 16–17, 60–61, 67, 83–84, 85–60, 102, 160–61, 174, 223, 250
stability, 6–7, 26, 27, 35–36, 37, 42, 52–53, 56, 60–61, 62–63, 64, 65, 79, 87, 90–91, 113, 116–60, 118–19, 122, 125–26, 129, 134–33, 135–31, 140, 141, 143–44, 237, 249, 250, 254, 258, 259, 285, 293–80, 306, 309
standardization, 7, 9–10, 32, 103–4, 114, 158–59, 165, 191, 215, 295, 296–80
state failure, 37
state fragility, 37
state responsibility, 77, 95
Statute of the International Court of Justice, 68–69
subsidiarity, 87, 125, 156–59, 199, 202, 205, 220, 252, 254, 268, 283–84
Sudan, 10, 156–57, 178, 223–24, 301
supranational organizations, 84–85, 270
surveillance, 6–7, 51–52, 70, 73–75, 76, 111, 125–26, 137*t*, 139*t*, 141, 142*t*, 143, 155, 161–63, 164, 178–79, 258
sustainable development, 34–35, 37–38, 40–41, 65, 77, 82–83, 100, 101–59, 112, 122, 128, 133, 145*t*, 146, 258
Sweden, 38, 143, 225, 308
systems theory, 16

Tallinn Manual, 70, 88, 89–90, 98–99, 127
taxation, 87
technical community, 59, 106, 108, 145*t*, 293–94
technical standards, xix, 5, 14, 31–33, 58, 105, 117, 128–29, 134, 142*t*, 143–44, 153–54, 208–9, 279, 280–81, 306
technological development, 3, 45–46
technological solutionism, 8, 49–50, 190
telegraphs
  regulation of, 1
terrorism, 42–43, 75, 94, 98, 105, 140, 162–63
tertium norms, 14, 15, 60, 128, 247, 250, 257–58, 277, 281, 291, 293, 303–4
Teubner, Gunther, 18, 184, 185, 186, 191, 192–93, 203, 206, 208–9, 211–12, 219, 251–52, 255
top-level domains, 29
  country code, 29
  generic, 29
transboundary harm, 95–60, 97–61, 100
Transfer Control Protocol/Internet Protocol (TCP/IP), 20–21
transnational regulatory arrangements, x, 2, 5, 7–2, 19, 45–46, 128–29, 196, 199, 200–183, 230, 233, 240, 243, 244–34, 247, 263, 295, 305–6, 307
transnationalism, 16, 18, 182, 198–84, 199
transparency, 52, 55, 58, 92, 100, 111, 118, 124, 126, 135, 137*t*, 138–39, 139*t*, 142*t*, 144*t*, 161, 211–12, 219, 260, 270–71, 285, 293
transposition, xx, 15, 295, 296, 298, 304, 310
treaty law, 6
trust, 27

UN 2030 Agenda for Sustainable Development, 40–41
Uniform Resource Locators, 151–52
United Kingdom, 152, 154, 178–79
United Nations, 33–34, 41, 65, 71, 87–88, 96, 113, 161–62
United Nations Educational, Scientific and Cultural Organization (UNESCO), 34
United States of America, 45, 61, 108–9, 117, 121–22, 223
universality, 4, 31–32, 57–58, 133, 135, 141–32, 145*t*, 156–59, 168–35, 171–37, 173, 174, 179, 193, 198, 308

virtual reality, 23
Voice over IP, 31–32

web architecture, 32–33
website, 23
whistleblowers, 76, 178
Wi-Fi, 32–33
Wikipedia, 154–55
World Bank, 38
World Conference on International Telecommunications, 64, 122
World Economic Forum, 6, 122
World Intellectual Property Organization, 69
World Wide Web (WWW), 1, 7
World Summit on the Information Society, 7
  Geneva Declaration of Principles, 110–11, 133
  Tunis Commitment, 6
  Tunis Agenda for the Information Society, 44
Working Group on Internet Governance (WGIG), 104, 111–12, 113, 121–22, 248

zero-rating, 172
Zimmermann, Andreas, 66–67

www.ingramcontent.com/pod-product-compliance
Lightning Source LLC
LaVergne TN
LVHW062206200926
848484LV00006B/1328
* 9 7 8 0 1 9 8 8 6 5 9 9 5 *